Changing Interpretations of America's Past

VOLUME 1

Second Edition

The Pre-Colonial Period Through the Civil War

Jim R. McClellan
Northern Virginia Community College

Dushkin/McGraw-Hill

A Division of The McGraw-Hill Companies

Book Team

Vice President and Publisher *Jeffrey L. Hahn*
List Manager *Theodore Knight*
Developmental Editor *Ava Suntoke*
Production Manager *Brenda S. Filley*
Director of Technology *Jonathan Stowe*
Designer *Charles Vitelli*
Typesetting Supervisor *Juliana Arbo*
Permissions Editor *Rose Gleich*
Proofreading Editors *Elizabeth Stevens, Diane Barker*
Copier Coordinator *Larry Killian*

Dushkin/McGraw-Hill

A Division of The McGraw-Hill Companies

Cover © 2000 PhotoDisc, Inc.
Cover Design *Thomas Goddard*

The credit section for this book begins on page 404 and is considered an extension of the copyright page.

Library of Congress Catalog Card Number 99-74550

ISBN 0-07-228506-0

Printed in the United States of America

12345678FGRFGR543210

http://www.mhhe.com

Preface

Two cars collide at an intersection surrounded by pedestrians. The sounds of the crash turn every head instantly. Shattering glass and pieces of metal fly off in every direction. Horns blare. A hubcap rolls across the road and comes to rest against the curb. A moment later, the whole incident is a part of history. Twenty witnesses see the accident, and it would seem an easy matter to piece together the story of what happened. Yet the twenty witnesses give twenty different accounts of what they think happened.

The truth about the past, whether of a minor matter or a matter of earth-shaking importance, is not easy to discover; yet the search for the truth is the goal of academic pursuit.

It is certain that the accident in question will in some way affect those directly involved. It may affect them enough to alter the course of the rest of their lives or only inconvenience them for a few days. If the public takes note at all, it may be in the form of a few words buried deep inside the next day's newspaper.

But it is also possible that the incident could affect the course of history. Seemingly insignificant events often do. Perhaps the accident delays a senator on the way to a crucial vote and the result is a change in the direction of government. Or, maybe the crash leads to the development of some automobile safety feature that subsequently saves the lives of thousands. Or maybe the accident takes the life of someone society finds irreplaceable.

The general public may be instantly aware that the accident has produced a turning point in history. Just as likely, years may pass before the importance of the event is recognized. Or, perhaps, its significance will never be fully understood. Succeeding generations will search for the truth. They will try to discover what happened, but the truth will most likely remain, like other forms of beauty, in the eyes of the beholder.

This work of two volumes attempts to present moments from the American past that in some way altered the course of history. It views these moments first through the eyes of those who lived them and then through the views of succeeding generations observing the moment from ever more distant vantage points over the passage of time. Each generation rewrites history. It has no choice but to do so. It finds itself at a place along the continuum of time different from that of its predecessors and must understand how it got there. It searches the records of the past to explain its present. Consequently, though what has passed cannot be changed, interpretations of what has passed are forever changing.

Each chapter in the book approaches its examination of a moment in history in a similar manner. Following an introduction to the event is a section entitled *First Impressions*. Here the event is described in the words of those who participated in it or through the commentary of contemporary observers. From the writings and speeches of participants, journalists, political leaders, scholars, and others, as well as from an examination of primary documents, a firsthand view of the event may be secured within the context of its times.

The next section is called *Second Thoughts.* It presents the ongoing effort to make sense of the past from a new vantage point. Some of the scholars represented in this section look at the past with the biases of their time; others seek to challenge those biases by drawing on the lessons of the past. All seek to make sense in their own time of the events that have led to their present.

The third section of each chapter is entitled *Questioning the Past.* A chapter might be conceived of as a seminar. Around the conference table sit scholars of the past and students of the present. After the topic is introduced with the words of those who lived it, scholars of succeeding generations offer their interpretations of the historical moment under review. Students of the present then continue the search for the meaning of the moment.

The moments chosen for inclusion in this book were selected because they in some way affected a large segment of the American people. Their impact may have been political, social, cultural, economic, diplomatic, psychological, or even a combination of these. No claim is made that the events studied in the chapters that follow constitute a complete listing of all the moments that have shaped the direction of American history. Indeed, every single moment finds the American people acting and reacting in ways that shape their course through history.

 New to this edition are Web sites that offer valuable resources to bring history to life. Look for them through the chapters. An annotated list of Web site addresses appears on page xxi.

The second edition has also benefited from the reviews of several scholars, whose suggestions merit the mention of their names here:

Lex Adler Sonoma State University
Martha Bonte Clinton Community College
Lillian Taiz California State University, Los Angeles

This work has also been enriched by the editing skills of Ava Suntoke of Dushkin/McGraw-Hill and by research assistance from Sylvia J. Rortvedt, librarian at the Alexandria Campus of Northern Virginia Community College, who was always quick to locate documents I could not. My wife, Catherine Lee Burwell, fortunately shares my interest in history and offered crucial support and encouragement to carry me through the necessary task of revision of the book.

Two chapters were added to Volume I for the second edition, one on the institution of slavery and another tracing the development of petroleum as an ever more important energy source.

The final chapter—the one that would have pulled all history together into a unified and simple truth, revealed that the fundamental laws of physics, math, law, economics, nature, and cosmetology are integrated and obvious, and decoded the mysteries of life and VCR programming—was regrettably lost in the auto accident.

Jim R. McClellan

Contents in Brief

To my parents
John A. and Earline McClellan
whose lives were long and yet too brief

About the Author

A native of Texas, Jim McClellan has served since 1975 on the faculty of Northern Virginia Community College, one of the nation's two largest community colleges. A professor of history, he teaches a wide variety of courses, most frequently American History and Native American History. He has also joined with colleagues to lead a number of seminars abroad, including field expeditions to the Maya lands of Mexico and Central America.

Dr. McClellan's previous publications and writing activities include articles on politics, book reviews, and a variety of scholarly pieces. *Historical Moments* was developed in his classroom in a continuing effort to challenge his students to think critically about historical events.

In 1997, the University of Texas at Arlington presented Professor McClellan with its Distinguished Alumni Award, the highest honor the university bestows on its graduates. He was also the recipient of the 1993–1994 Outstanding Distance Educator Award, presented by the College of the Air Tele-Consortium, for his history lectures broadcast over television in the Northern Virginia area.

Professor McClellan's many outside interests include the outdoors, travel, and community service. He is Commissioner of Human Rights and former chairman of the Alexandria Human Rights Commission. He currently serves as president of the Virginia Association of Human Rights Commissioners and has been a director of a school for adults with special needs and a child care center. He paddles his kayak on the Potomac daily, enjoys playing football and basketball, and fondly remembers dunking a basketball during halftime in front of 15,000 spectators at a Bulls game—from an exceptionally tall unicycle. In 1998, he won two silver and one bronze medals for sprint kayaking at the World Masters Games.

Contents

3 *The Requirement*   28

4 *Jamestown*   36

5 *Samoset and Squanto*   46

6 *Fort Mystic*   53

7 *Slavery*   65

8 *An Act of Toleration* 85

9 *Bacon's Rebellion* 94

14 *The Declaration of Independence*   147

15 *The Constitution*   162

16 *The Alien and Sedition Acts*   **177**

17 *The Monroe Doctrine*   **189**

18 *Uniting the States* 202

19 *Nat Turner* 214

20 *Prudence Crandall*   228

21 *The Cherokee Removal*   241

22 *The Texas Question*   258

23 *War with Mexico*   273

24 *The Seneca Falls Convention*   286

25 *Oil*   300

26 *Harper's Ferry*   318

27 *Civil War*   334

28 *The Emancipation Proclamation*   351

29 *Pickett's Charge*   362

Web Sites

The following World Wide Web sites have been carefully researched and selected to support the text. At the appropriate location in each chapter, you will find the title of the Web site. The Web addresses, (URLs) with a brief descriptive note about each site, are listed below. We have made every effort to provide sites that will remain current, but Web sites sometimes change. We regret that any discrepancies are beyond our control.

Chapter 1 Mysterious Mounds

1.1 The Mounds and the Constant Fire: The Old Sacred Things
http://www.powersource.com/cherokee/mounds.html

Hear the firsthand account of the myth of the Cherokee and learn about the building of the mounds and sacred fires.

1.2 Cahokia Mounds State Historic Site
http://medicine.wustl.edu/~mckinney/cahokia/cahokia.html

Visit this site to learn about recent excavations and upcoming events. Click on the "Site Tour and Map" and guide yourself through the monument with a detailed description of each mound.

1.3 Ancient Architects of the Mississippi
http://www.cr.nps.gov/aad/feature/feature.htm

Learn about one of the most highly organized civilizations of the world. The importance of the Mississippi River as well as the lives and labor of the ancient farmers in the Delta are highlighted in this site.

Chapter 2 Columbus

2.1 The Columbus Navigation Home Page
http://www1.minn.net/~keithp/

This interesting site reveals the truth about the navigation techniques used by Columbus on his four voyages to America. In addition, links to the ship, crew, and landfall in America are provided.

2.2 Christopher Columbus and Early European Exploration
http://www.nypl.org/research/chss/grd/resguides/columbus.html

This useful Web site provides many primary and secondary source references concerning Columbus's life and voyages.

2.3 Christopher Columbus Internet Resources
http://home.ici.net/~panther/francis/columbus.html

A unique perspective on Columbus is presented here. You can learn about his deep religious persuasions, read excerpts from his journal, and get to know him as he was known by his contemporaries.

Chapter 3 The Requirement

3.1 The Internet Modern History Sourcebook: Colonial Latin America
http://www.fordham.edu/halsall/mod/modsbook08.html

Visit this informative page for an encompassing view of life in colonial Latin America, European conquest and exploitation, and the creation of a new culture.

3.2 The History of the Inca Empire
http://www.sscf.ucsb.edu/~ogburn/inca/history.htm

From the beginnings of this grand empire in the 1200s to its conquest in the 1500s, you can learn about the growth of the dynasty and many Inca rulers. Click on "Conquest" for a complete overview of Attahuallpa's fall from power.

3.3 Diplomacy and War in Spanish Relations with the New World
http://www.uwinnipeg.ca/campus/uwsa/diplomac.htm

Themes explored in this thesis include fundamental questions about why the Spaniards engaged in an American war as well as the means by which they were able to conquer the Indian civilizations.

Chapter 4 Jamestown

4.1 Jamestown Rediscovery

http://www.apva.org

The Association for the Preservation of Virginia Antiques is involved in an archaeological project uncovering the remains of 1607 Jamestown. Select "Visiting Jamestown" to take a tour of the "Olde Towne" or view the artifacts by clicking on "Our Exhibits."

4.2 John Rolfe Tries a Tobacco Crop

http://www.tobacco.org/History/
Jamestown.html#aa4

A useful timeline and an excellent biography of John Rolfe and his tobacco experiment are provided in this Web site.

4.3 Virtual Jamestown

http://jefferson.village.virginia.edu/
vcdh/jamestown/

This site is a digital research-teaching-learning project to explore the legacies of the Jamestown settlement and "the Virginia experiment."

Chapter 5 Samoset and Squanto

5.1 The Plimoth Plantation

http://www.plimoth.org/Museum/
museum.htm

This home page of the Plymouth Plantation will lead you through the village house by house (click on "1627 Pilgrim Village"). Discover how the Wampanoag warriors lived and see a reproduction of the Mayflower.

5.2 Plymouth: Its History and People

http://pilgrims.net/plymouth/history/

An excellent resource for the history of the early settlement in Plymouth, this Web site includes a short biography of some of the founding settlers.

5.3 Wampanoag History

http://www.dickshovel.com/Compacts.
html

Visit this Web page for an extensive history of the First Nations, and follow the links to a thorough article about the Wampanoag Indians of southeastern Massachusetts.

Chapter 6 Fort Mystic

6.1 Pequot History

http://www.dickshovel.com/peq.html

Pequot history and culture are covered in extensive detail in this Web site. Learn about their rivalry with the Narragansett and their initial contacts with Europeans.

6.2 The Taking of the Fort at Mystic

http://www.flash.net/~pthomp1/
mason.htm

Written by Major John Mason in 1638, this essay is his narrative of the expedition to the Pequot fort and the subsequent Puritan attack.

6.3 The Pequot War: A Television Documentary

http://ourworld.compuserve.com/
homepages/cclemmons/

This site outlines the making of a television documentary and provides an interesting narrative and a brief introduction to the subject.

Chapter 7 Slavery

7.1 The Avalon Project: Statutes of the United States Concerning Slavery

http://www.yale.edu/lawweb/avalon/
statutes/slavery/slmenu.htm

This informative Web site contains many firsthand documents concerning slavery in colonial America.

7.2 Excerpts from Slave Narratives

http://vi.uh.edu/pages/mintz/primary.
htm

Visit this interesting and well-organized Web site to learn about the living conditions, religion, family life, resistance, and emancipation as documented by slaves in the eighteenth and nineteenth centuries.

7.3 Africans in America

http://www.pbs.org/wgbh/aia/part1/
index.html

Read about people and events in the history of slavery, and explore the viewpoints of current historians in this comprehensive and thorough Web site from PBS.

Chapter 8 An Act of Toleration

8.1 The Catholic Encyclopedia

http://www.csn.net/advent/cathen/
09755b.htm

An excellent, detailed history of the Calverts and religion in the colonial period is presented in this well-organized and extensive Web page.

8.2 Religion and the Founding of the American Republic

http://lcweb.loc.gov/exhibits/religion/
rel01.html

A beautiful collection of artwork and engravings accompany this outline of religion from European persecution to the Puritans and the Commonwealths. Check out Parts I and II for a description of the various religious groups present in America in the seventeenth century.

8.3 The History of St. Margaret's Church 1692–1792

http://www.st-margarets.org/history.htm

This Web site takes you through the history of the establishment of St. Margaret's Church in colonial Maryland, with an excellent, detailed description of the religion in this state.

8.4 Citizen Legislators and Toleration

http://www.mdarchives.state.md.us/msa/
stagser/s1259/123/html/mdayremarks.html

These informative remarks made by the Maryland State Archivist Dr. Edward Papenfuse are in celebration of the 365th anniversary of the founding of Maryland. They provide an interesting look back at Maryland's Act of Toleration from a modern perspective.

Chapter 9 Bacon's Rebellion

9.1 ALHN Military Resources

http://www.rootsquest.com/~amhisnet/
mil/.mil.html

The American Local History Network has compiled a vast array of information about American wars from the colonial period onward. Click on "Bacon's Rebellion" and the related sites to read his declaration and find out how Robert Beverly, a contemporary of Bacon, described the events of the uprising.

9.2 The American Nation Online: The American Society in the Making

http://longman.awl.com/garraty/
primarysources_2.htm

Discover for yourself what Nathaniel Bacon said in the full-length, readable selection, The Declaration.

9.3 Virginia Records Time Line

http://lcweb2.loc.gov/ammem/mtjhtml/
mtjvatm7.html

Read about the events occurring in Virginia before and after Bacon's Rebellion, view a portrait of Nathaniel Bacon, and click on "The Beginning, Progress, and Conclusion of Bacon's Rebellion" for more details. This compilation of manuscripts allows you to view original documents and read texts as they appeared in late seventeenth-century papers.

Chapter 10 The Zenger Trial

10.1 Links to Sites concerning the John Peter Zenger Trial

http://www.law.umkc.edu/faculty/
projects/ftrials/Zengerlinks.htm

This site contains links to an overview of the trial, jury participation in the case, and Zenger's acquittal.

10.2 Considering Zenger

http://old.law.columbia.edu/my_pubs/
zenger.html

The author if this detailed, informative Web site deals with politics and the legal profession in provincial New York, and presents the Zenger trial, using primary sources.

10.3 CNN Interactive: Speaking Freely

http://cnn.com/US/9703/cda.scotus/
case.history/free.speech/

CNN provides an interesting article about the Zenger trial and its relation to free speech in the twentieth century. Voice your opinion or follow the links to other free speech–related sites.

Chapter 11 Eleven Days that Never Were

11.1 Gregorian Calendar

http://ghs1.greenheart.com/billh/
gregory.html

View this all-encompassing Web site about calendars for a history of the evolution of the Gregorian calendar. Also included are links to early Roman and Julius calendar pages.

11.2 The Calendar Act

http://www.urbanlegends.com/legal/
calendar_act.html

The author presents, with commentary, the act of the British government regulating the commencement of the year 1751.

11.3 The Gregorian Calendar

http://www.cinderella.co.za/glosg.txt

The author provides an insightful look into the history of the 1751 calendar change, as well as an algorithm to calculate leap years.

Chapter 12 Eliza Lucas

12.1 Seventeenth and Eighteenth-Century Women

http://www.cocc.edu/cagatucci/classes/
ws101/wstml/wstml2.htm

Click on "Eliza Lucas Pinckney" for a look at her life and accomplishments and read an informative letter she wrote to her brother, Thomas Lucas.

12.1 The Cooper River Bridges

http://www.insiders.com/charleston-sc/
daytrips2.htm

Tour Eliza Lucas's neighborhood and read about Snee Farm, the colonial plantation home of Charles Pinckney. To help you further understand the colonial South, this site provides a description of several plantations, churches, and gardens around Charleston.

12.2 Women in the Workplace

http://www.thehistorynet.com/
WomensHistory/articles/19962_text.htm

Visit this site for an inspiring look at American women's involvement in business from the colonial era to the mid-twentieth century.

Chapter 13 The American Revolution

13.1 Core Knowledge of United States History

http://quaboag.k12.ma.us/amrev.html

Of the many Web sites documenting the events of the American Revolution, this site has an excellent, well-organized detailed set of links about everything from events behind the Revolution, battles, turning points and deciding factors in the war, to founding documents and debates.

13.2 Birth of a Nation

http://tqjunior.advanced.org/3803/

Explore people, places, and events associated with the American Revolution. Click on "Timeline" for an hour-by-hour playback of the Battle of Concord.

13.3 The Road to Independence

http://douglass.speech.nwu.edu/ooah/ooah3.htm

A description of the acts that demanded direct taxation is provided in this history of the revolution.

13.4 Samuel Adams, The Rights of Colonists

http://history.hanover.edu/texts/adamss.html

Get an inside look at one of the nation's founding fathers by reading firsthand his *Rights of Colonists*. In addition to this primary source, a preface by Benjamin Franklin and editor's notes are provided.

13.5 The Declaration of Arms

http://earlyamerica.com/earlyamerica/milestones/decofarms/index.html

Learn about the causes of the revolution and read a complete text of the *Declaration of Arms,* exactly as it appears in the *Gentleman's Magazine,* London, August 1755.

Chapter 14 Declaration of Independence

14.1 History of the Declaration of Independence

http://www.nara.gov/exhall/charters/declaration/dechist.html

The National Archives and Records Administration has compiled a Web site that relates the unique circumstances under which the Declaration was drafted. Click on "Declaration Exhibit" to view a transcript of this document.

14.2 Declaring Independence

http://lcweb.loc.gov/exhibits/declara/declara1.html

This Library of Congress Web site takes you through the drafting of the Declaration of Independence and lets you view LOC Exhibit items such as fragments of the earliest-known drafts.

14.3 The Unfulfilled Promise of the Declaration of Independence

http://www.tbwt.com/views/rd/rd_06-30-99.asp

Explores one person's view of the faults of the Declaration of Independence: the exclusion of African Americans and Native Indians.

14.4 "We Hold These Truths to Be Self-Evident"

http://www.usia.gov/topical/rights/hrpamp/wehold.htm

Human rights and the principles of freedom are topics explored in this extensive Web site. The views of Lincoln and Douglas provide additional insight into the debate over slavery.

Chapter 15 The Constitution

15.1 To Form a More Perfect Union

http://memory.loc.gov/ammem/bdsds/bdexhome.html

Visit this site to learn about the workings of the Continental Congress, including their discussion about slavery and their attempts to appease the Indians of the South.

15.2 Learning Page of the Library of Congress

http://lcweb2.loc.gov/ammem/ndlpedu/bdsd/bdsdfile.html

This extensive Web page is filled with fascinating exhibits and interesting links from the colonial period to the Age of Revolution and beyond. Click on "The Washington Papers" to browse through the largest collection of original Washington documents in the world or "The Temple of Liberty" to learn of the building of the Capitol.

15.3 The American Constitution

http://www.yale.edu/lawweb/avalon/constpap.htm

This site provides a documentary record of the Constitution. Explore the roots of the Constitution or read the ratification documents drafted by individual states.

15.4 What the Anti-Federalist Can Teach Us

http://www.ashbrook.org/publicat/onprin/v5n1/knott.html

Visit this interesting Web site for an in-depth analysis of the views of Federalists and Anti-Federalists.

15.5 Today in History, Oct 27, 1787

http://lcweb2.loc.gov/ammem/today/oct27.html

Put yourself in the Constitutional debate; read Alexander Hamilton's articles in the *Federalist Papers,* the correspondence between Washington and Hamilton, and learn about the role the *Federalist* played in ratifying the Constitution in New York.

Chapter 16 Alien and Sedition Acts

16.1 State Interposition

http://www.snowcrest.net/siskfarm/interpos.html

Visit this site to learn about the Alien and Sedition Acts and the arguments supporting state nullification of Federal laws. The site is filled with quotes from the original sources.

16.2 Thomas Jefferson on Politics and Government

`http://etext.lib.virginia.edu/`
`jefferson/quotations/jeff0900.htm`

This informative site is a compilation of quotes by Thomas Jefferson about a variety of topics, such as constitutional authority and limitations and restrictions on power.

16.3 *United States* vs. *Cooper*: A Violation of the Sedition Law

`http://www.nara.gov/education/cc/`
`cooper.html`

Explore the "List of Documents" to learn about the case filed against Thomas Cooper, his plea, and the verdict.

Chapter 17 The Monroe Doctrine

17.1 The American Presidency: James Monroe

`http://gi.grolier.com/presidents/ea/`
`bios/05pmonr.html`

This informative Web site spans the life and career of James Monroe, with excellent links to many aspects of politics in the nineteenth century.

17.2 James Monroe (1758–1831)

`http://odur.let.rug.nl/~usaP/jm5/`
`jm5.htm`

Read the words of James Monroe in this extensive list of Monroe primary sources. Included are his inaugural addresses as well as his State of the Nation speeches from 1817 to 1824.

17.3 Primary Source: James Monroe

`http://campus.northpark.edu/history/`
`Classes/Sources/Monroe.html`

Visit this Web site to learn about Monroe's foreign policy objectives as he outlined them in this 1823 speech to a joint session of Congress.

17.4 Monroe Doctrine

`http://www.optonline.com/comptons/ceo/`
`03230_A.html`

Learn about the impact of the Monroe Doctrine in recent history as well as the changes that have been made in the policy since its inception.

Chapter 18 Uniting the States

18.1 The Erie Canal: A Brief History

`http://www.canals.state.ny.us/history/`
`index.html`

Visit the Web site to discover the early history of the canal, ideas about its creation, and the building of this famous engineering marvel.

18.2 America's First Trains

`http://mikes.railhistory.railfan.net/`
`r013.html`

Learn about the dangers of building railroads and the introduction of steam power as you browse through this interesting Web site.

18.3 U.S. History II: Railroad Links

`http://bweb.bradford.edu/Steele/`
`his206/Railroad.html`

This site has interesting links to America's early railroads. Click on "History of the First Locomotives in America" to read from a large selection of essays that include original documents and the testimony of living witnesses.

18.4 Transportation Developments in the Early Republic

`http://www.connerprairie.org/`
`travel.html`

This Web site provides an overview of early American transportation. Topics include the national politics leading to the need for better transportation and modes and costs of transportation.

Chapter 19 Nat Turner

19.1 Southampton Slave Revolt

`http://www.historybuff.com/library/`
`refslave.html`

A detailed playback of Nat Turner's revolt is presented here along with letters to the governor of Virginia as well as to several newspapers.

19.2 The Confessions of Nat Turner

`http://odur.let.rug.nl/~usa/D/`
`1826-1850/slavery/confes02.htm`

This Web site contains the narrative of Nat Turner, given voluntarily when he was visited by Thomas Gray on the evening he was committed to prison.

19.3 Chronology on the History of Slavery

`http://innercity.org/holt/`
`chron_1830_end.html`

Follow this history timeline to the 1831 Nat Turner Slave Rebellion and beyond to familiarize yourself with the events leading up to Turner's revolt. Explore the links to learn about major slave revolts and escapes.

Chapter 20 Prudence Crandall

20.1 Women's Stories

`http://writetools.com/women/`
`06_25-07_01.html`

Learn about the "Equal Opportunity Scapegoat" Prudence Crandall, and read about her as the state heroine of Connecticut.

20.2 Debate over School for Colored Girls

`http://www.sp.uconn.edu/~hi231is1/`
`Crandall.html`

Read the informative entries of the Reverend Samuel May's journal concerning the debates at Canterbury town meetings.

Chapter 21 The Cherokee Removal

21.1 North Georgia's Cherokee Indians

`http://ngeorgia.com/history/`
`cherokee.html`

This comprehensive Web site provides the reader with a detailed history of the Cherokee Indians. Click on "Cherokee in North Georgia" to learn about the history, culture, removal forts, Trail of Tears, and other aspects of the lives of the Cherokee.

21.2 History of the Cherokee

`http://pages.tca.net/martikw/`

This is a detailed Web site that provides the reader with Cherokee legends, maps, geneologies, and other useful links.

21.3 Agreement with the Cherokee, 1835

`http://www.library.okstate.edu/kappler/`
`che1041.htm`

Visit this Web site for a look at the articles of a treaty between the United States and a delegation of the Cherokee Tribe on March 14, 1835.

21.4 The Cherokee Trail of Tears

`http;//rosecity.net/tears/trail/`
`tearsnht.html`

This Web site provides a brief history of the Cherokee and quotes from survivors of the Trail of Tears. Click on "The Trail Today" and follow the related links to the Trail of Tears Timeline.

Chapter 22 The Texas Question

22.1 Lone Star Junction

`http://www.lsjunction.com`

This Web site has a list of "People, Places, Documents, and Events" in Texas history. Learn about the Texas Declaration of Independence, the battle of the Alamo, and many prominent people in Texas history.

22.2 President John Tyler

`http://historyoftheworld.com/pres/`
`jtyler.htm`

Visit the Web site for interesting links about the tenth president of the United States, Read his White House biography and his inaugural address.

22.3 Texas History and Culture

`http://pw2.netcom/~wandaron/`
`txhist.html`

This Web site contains links to all aspects of Texas history. Click on the links to learn more about "Mexican Texas," "The War for Independence," and "Texas as a Republic."

Chapter 23 War with Mexico

23.1 The U.S.–Mexican War

`http://www.dmwv.org/mexwar/`
`mexwar1.htm`

This interesting Web site contains excellent documentation of the American war with Mexico. Read about the history, view images and documents from the war, and follow the links to other relevant pages.

23.2 PBS Online: The U.S.–Mexican War

`http://www.pbs.org/kera/usmexicanwar/`

This PBS site provides the reader with a broad overview of the war. Click on "Dialogues" to read more about President Polk's intentions during the war, or go to "Timeline" for a detailed chronology of events,.

23.3 California History: Mexican Period

`http://www.ccnet.com/~laplaza/`
`calhist3.htm`

Visit this Web site to learn about California history from 1821 to its conquest by the United States.

Chapter 24 The Seneca Falls Convention

24.1 The Seneca Falls Conference: The Beginning of Women's Rights

`http://www.ipl.org/inksub/Vol1No6/`
`higraph/womenhistory.html`

This informative Web site contains excellent links to the women of the Seneca Falls conference, as well as to the Declaration of Sentiments and the Women's Rights National Historic Park.

24.2 "All Men and Women are Created Equal"

`http://www.thehistorynet.com/`
`AmericanHistory/articles/1999/`
`04992_text.htm`

Visit this Web site to read about the inspirational story of the early women pioneers of Seneca Falls.

24.3 150th Anniversary of Seneca Falls Convention

`http://www.abanet.org/irr/cedaw.html`

Read about the events celebrating women's rights in 1998 and click on "Living the Legacy" for a history of the movement.

Chapter 25 Oil

25.1 Oil History

`http://www.oilhistory.com/contents/`
`contents.html`

This informative Web site, created by a local western Pennsylvania petroleum geologist, offers a wealth of information about oil history, the life of Edwin Drake, oil gathering, and drilling techniques.

29.3 Gettysburg Revisited

`http://home.sprynet.com/~carlreed/`

Read information and opinions about the famous battle. Click on "Resources" to read a detailed account of the first, second, and third day of the battle of Gettysburg.

29.4 Civil War Resources on the Internet

`http://www.libraries.rutgers.edu/`
`rulib/socsci/hist/civwar-2.html`

This Web site has links to all aspects of the Civil War.

Chapter 30 A Surprise Ally

30.1 National Civil War Association

`http://www.ncwa.org`

Read about the Union forces and New York's volunteer infantries, and follow some interesting historical links to learn about the people who fought in the Civil War.

30.2 New York State and the Civil War

`http://www.snymor.edu/pages/library/`
`local_history/sites/`

Read about the Empire State's role in the Civil War and find out about New York soldiers in battles in the state as well as elsewhere.

30.3 The Diplomats and Diplomacy of the American Civil War

`http;//www.iol.ie/~kiersey/civwar.html`

This is an interesting modern-day perspective about the understanding of foreign affairs and diplomacy by the North and the South.

Chapter 31 The Assassination

31.1 Abraham Lincoln: Sixteenth President

`http://www.whitehouse.gov/WH/glimpse/`
`presidents/html/al16.html`

Read a short White House biography about the famous president, his inaugural addresses, or click on "Mary Todd Lincoln" for a biography of his wife.

31.2 The History Place Presents Abraham Lincoln

`http://www.historyplace.com/lincoln`

This is an excellent detailed timeline of President Lincoln's life, and includes his family history as well as his years as president. View portraits of Lincoln, read letters to his wife, and see pictures of his box at Ford's Theater.

31.3 Abraham Lincoln's Assassination

`http://members.aol.com/RVSNorton/`
`Lincoln.html`

Visit this Web site for an informative and detailed description of Lincoln's assassination. Many aspects, such as an eyewitness account of Booth's capture, the 1865 conspiracy trial, and several photographs, are presented.

Chapter 1

Mysterious Mounds

The Great Mound at Cahokia Is Completed
ca. 1250

Six miles east of the modern city of St. Louis stands a monument to a civilization long vanished. It is a massive mound of earth molded by human labor into the shape of a truncated pyramid. It contains 22 million cubic feet of earth and its base covers an area of 16 acres. It rises in a series of terraces to a height of 100 feet above the surrounding land.

This great mound of Cahokia was completed around the year 1250, after some 350 years of intermittent construction. At the time of the European arrival in the New World, and for many years thereafter, it was the most massive product of human labor north of the Rio Grande. Within the immediate vicinity of this mound were 100 more of smaller size. To the west, on the left bank of the Mississippi River, was another cluster of earthen mounds. And across the river in what is now the center of downtown St. Louis there stood until the middle of the nineteenth century a grouping of 27 mounds, the largest of which was an oval-shaped platform, 30 feet in height and measuring 319 feet by 159 feet in length and breadth. Such mound clusters are not unique. In fact, they are to be found across a wide area of North America. Thousands, perhaps tens of thousands, still emboss the landscape of the eastern half of the United States. They are a legacy of a people who inhabited the land in pre-Columbian times.

❧ *First Impressions*

"Where They Cried"

The civilization of the mound builders was already well past its peak before the Europeans arrived in the New World in the late fifteenth century. Even for the Native Americans who occupied the interior of North America at that time, the mound builders of antiquity were a matter of legends. Anthropologist James Mooney, during the nineteenth century, recorded one of the ancient Cherokee legend about the mounds. European explorers and scholars of the sixteenth and seventeenth centuries ventured into the lands of the mound builders and found the mounds still in use.

Source 1   Cherokee legend

1.1 The Mounds and the Constant Fire: The Old Sacred Things

Long ago a powerful unknown tribe invaded the country from the southeast, killing people and destroying settlements wherever they went. No leader could stand against them, and in a little while they had wasted all the lower settlements and advanced into the mountains. The warriors of the old town of Nikwasi, on the head of the Little Tennessee, gathered their wives and children into the townhouse and kept scouts constantly on the lookout for the presence of danger. One morning just before daybreak the spies saw the enemy approaching and at once gave the alarm. The Nikwasi men seized their arms and rushed out to meet the attack, but after a long, hard fight they found themselves overpowered and began to retreat, when suddenly a stranger stood among them and shouted to the chief to call off his men and he himself would drive back the enemy. From the dress and language of the stranger the Nikwasi people thought him a chief who had come with reinforcements from the Overhill settlements in Tennessee. They fell back along the trail, and as they came near the townhouse they saw a great company of warriors coming out from the side of the mound as through an open doorway. Then they knew that their friends were the Nunne'hi, the Immortals, although no one had ever heard before that they lived under Nikwasi mound.

The Nunne'hi poured out by the hundreds, armed and painted for the fight, and the most curious thing about it all was that they became invisible as soon as they were fairly outside of the settlement, so that although the enemy saw the glancing arrow or the rushing tomahawk, and felt the stroke, he could not see who sent it. Before such invisible foes the invaders soon had to retreat. . . . As they retreated they tried to shield themselves behind rocks and trees, but the Nunne'hi arrows went around the rocks and killed them from the other side, and they could find no hiding place. All along the ridge they fell, until when they reached the head of Tuckasegee not more then a half a dozen were left alive, and in despair they sat down and cried out for mercy. Ever since then the Cherokee have called the place Dayulsun'yi, "Where they cried." Then the Nunne'hi chief told them they had deserved their punishment for attacking a peaceful tribe, and he spared their lives and told them to go home and take the news to their people. This was the Indian custom, always to spare a few to carry back the news of defeat. They went home toward the north and the Nunne'hi went back to the mound.

And they are still there.

Source 2   Garcilaso de la Vega, *La Florida,* 1605

The Indians try to place their villages on elevated sites; but inasmuch as in Florida there are not many sites of this kind where they can conveniently build, they erect elevations themselves in the following manner: They select the spot and carry there a quantity of earth, which they form into a kind of platform two or three **pikes** in height, the summit of which is large enough to give room for twelve, fifteen, or twenty houses, to lodge the **cacique** and his attendants. At the foot of this elevation they mark out a square place, according to the size of the village, around which the leading men have their houses. . . . To ascend the elevation they have a straight passageway from bottom to top, 15 or 20 feet wide. Here steps are made by massive beams, and others are planted firmly in the ground to serve as walls. On all other sides of the platform the sides are cut steep.

The Mounds Become a Mystery

The great mound of Cahokia once towered over a city of great size and importance. By the middle of the thirteenth century it was home to between 10,000 and 30,000 people—comparable in population to London at that time. Even in ruins it was astonishing to behold. With its 100 massive earthen mounds, sculpted to the shape of truncated pyramids, platforms, and cones, it was a puzzling place whose features raised more questions than they answered. Modern archaeology has supplied some of the missing pieces of the puzzle. Excavations indicate that atop the fourth and highest terrace there once stood a public building. It was constructed of wood, rose perhaps 50 feet high, and encompassed 4,800 square feet of floor space. This structure and the grounds of the fourth terrace were enclosed by a wall. A stairway led from the enclosure to the lower terraces and ultimately onto a large public plaza at ground level. Around and on the plaza were 16 additional mounds, and the whole of this complex, encompassing 300 acres of land, was surrounded by a wooden wall 15 feet high.

1.2 Cahokia
Mounds State
Historic Site

Beyond this palisaded city core was a community spanning six square miles. Mounds were scattered throughout. Some served as elevated platforms upon which homes and public buildings were constructed. Others were places of burial. Four were circular in shape and appear to have served as mechanisms for astronomical observation and calendric reckoning. Thatched houses, plazas, and marketplaces were also part of the city. Dugout canoes loaded and unloaded cargoes of foodstuffs, copper, shells, ceramics, and other goods at a landing on Cahokia Creek, a stream that once flowed near the great mound. Cahokia Creek connected the city to the Mississippi River and through it to much of North America, making it in all probability the dominant commercial center of the interior of North America. The Mississippi and its great tributaries, like the Nile of ancient Egypt, served as the connecting highway for commerce. All along this network of waterways were cities, towns, and villages built around clusters of mounds. These communities have been labeled the Mississippian Culture by archaeologists. This culture was not unique in its construction of mounds. Other peoples—known today as the Hopewell, Adena, and Poverty Point Cultures—began building such structures not only centuries before Columbus, but even centuries before the Mississippians. Thousands of their mounds are still scattered across North America from the eastern slopes of the Rockies to just east of the Appalachians. Many are designed like the mounds at Cahokia. Some, however, are fashioned into the shapes of geometric figures or creatures—birds, panthers, serpents, fanciful beasts of assorted kinds—whose outlines are distinguishable only when seen from above.

The mystery of the mounds is compounded by the fact that those who built them left no written record. All that is known of these people is what may be learned from those remains that have stood the test of time—statuettes and stone etchings, stone and metal trinkets buried with the dead, and, of course, the earthen mounds themselves. It is hard to draw an accurate picture of a people from such scanty information.

As one example, imagine that several thousand years into the future archeologists going through the remains of twentieth-century American civilization might find scattered across the country foundations of small buildings. In front of these foundations would be large golden arches made of indestructible plastic. These, the archaeologists might deduce, were roadside temples. In the trash heaps adjacent to these temples they find clear plastic discs bearing the image of a character with a round nose, its face painted with cosmetics, and head shaved clean except for a ring of hair above the ears. This plastic disc, four inches in diameter, had an X-shaped cut in its center, presumably so the people could run a string through the hole and wear the image of their principal deity around their necks. These assumptions made, the archaeologists might then conclude that the capital of our arch-building civilization had been St. Louis, where the giant stainless steel Gateway Arch, 630 feet tall, stands as a testimonial to twentieth-century America's preoccupation with arches.

To define the Mississippian and other ancient cultures as mound builders because of their apparent preoccupation with earthen mounds may do ancient Americans a similar disservice. Nevertheless, much supposition has been devoted to the mysteries of the mound builders. That the mounds are the work of different peoples at different times is widely accepted. Just who built them, and what became of the builders, has been the source of considerable speculation throughout American history.

Source 3   Writings of Thomas Jefferson, 1781

I know of no such thing existing [in Virginia] as an Indian monument: . . . unless indeed it be the Barrows [mounds], of which many are to be found all over the country. These are of different sizes, some are constructed of earth, and some of loose stones. That they were repositories of the dead, has been obvious to all: but on what particular occasion constructed, was matter of doubt. Some have thought they covered the bones of those who had fallen in battles fought on the spot of internment. Some ascribed them to the custom, said to prevail among the Indians, of collecting, at certain periods, the bones of all their dead. . . . Others have supposed them the general sepulchres for towns. . . . There being one of these in my neighbourhood, I wished to satisfy myself whether any, and which of these opinions were just.

For this purpose I determined to open and examine it thoroughly. It was situated on the low grounds of the Rivanna, about two miles above its principal fork, and opposite to some hills, on which had been an Indian town. It was of a spheroidical form, of about 40 feet diameter at the base, and had been of about twelve feet altitude. . . .

I first dug superficially in several parts of it, and came to collections of human bones . . . lying in the utmost confusion. . . . The bones nearest the surface were the least decayed. No holes were discovered in any of them, as if made with bullets, arrows, or other weapons. I conjectured that in this barrow might have been a thousand skeletons. Every one will readily seize the circumstances above related, which militate against the opinion, that it covered the bones only of those fallen in battle; and against the tradition also, which would make it the common sepulchre of a town. . . . Appearances certainly indicate that it has derived both origin and growth from the accustomary collection of bones, and deposition of them together; that the first collection had been deposited on the common surface of the earth, a few stones put over it, and then a covering of earth, that the second had been laid on this, . . . and was then also covered with earth; and so on. . . .

But on whatever occasion they may have been made, they are of considerable notoriety among the Indians: for a party passing, about thirty years ago, through the part of the country where the barrow is, went through the woods directly to it, without any instructions or enquiry, and having staid about it some time, with expressions which were construed to be those of sorrow, they returned to the high road, which they had left about half a dozen miles to pay this visit, and pursued their journey.

📖 *Second Thoughts*

"A Knowledge of Art and Labor Foreign to the Red Man"

1.3 Ancient Architects of the Mississippi

Late eighteenth- and nineteenth-century scholars found it difficult to accept that the architects of the mounds had been the aboriginal peoples of America. Instead they theorized about lost civilizations, Danes, Romans, Greeks, Israelites, Phoenicians, Malays, and even the lost continent of Atlantis, under siege by the "savages" of America, building elaborate defensive earthworks. Only at the beginning of the twentieth century did scholars begin to credit the mounds to the Native Americans themselves.

Source 4   Benjamin Smith Barton, "Observations on Some Parts of Natural History: An Account of Several Remarkable Vestiges of an Ancient Date, which Have Been Discovered in Different Parts of North America," 1787

The artificial mounts of eminences, which are scattered over the Western parts of North America, deserve our attention. Some of these eminences are of an amazing magnitude, particularly one near the mouth of a small river, called Grave Creek, which discharges itself into the Ohio, one hundred and six miles below the junction of the Alleghaney and Monaungahela.

This stupendous eminence appears to be composed of huge quantities of earth, which have probably been procured from adjacent grounds. . . . No traces of either walls, or of a ditch, are, at present, observable near this remarkable monument of the industry of a former age; yet it is not improbable that both have once existed there: they may have been entirely defaced by the accidents of a very few years; whereas the eminence, from its huge bulk, might have resisted those accidents for many centuries.

Notwithstanding all the inquiries which have been made, the oldest Indians are incapable of giving any account of this curious antiquity: they, indeed, seem to regard it with a species of veneration; but then it is to be remembered, that many of the productions of nature, such as the falls or rapids of a river, a mountain, a tree, or a reptile of uncommon size, nay, even the productions of art, such as a watch, a compass, and many others, are regarded with a similar superstition.

No wonder, then, that an appearance so singular, as this eminence, of which I have endeavoured to convey an imperfect idea, should excite in the rude minds of the savages some degree of admiration; yet it is probable they are even ignorant whether it is a production of nature or of art. Large eminences have also been discovered in the neighborhood of . . . the river Mississippi: they are of different forms and sizes, some of them being nearly square, others oblong, some octagonal, and others again almost spherical.

In some parts of the country in which these eminences are to be seen, they are called by the inhabitants, Indian Graves, from a supposition that they are the repositories of immense numbers of the deceased heroes, &c., of the savages.

It is indeed true, that a custom of burying their dead in small tumuli or barrows did formerly, and, perhaps, does still prevail among the American tribes—great numbers of these barrows are scattered over different parts of the continent. I have seen a few of them. . . . They are, in general, nearly of a spheroidical form, of about fifteen or twenty feet in diameter at the base, and from six to ten or more feet altitude. One of them has been curiously examined by a gentleman of distinction, and of profound philosophical, as well as of political knowledge: he (Thomas Jefferson) found it to be the repository of collections of human bones, both of the adult, and of the infant, lying in utmost confusion, and in such great numbers, that he conjectured it might contain a thousand skeletons.

But although the state in which many of these bones were found . . . render it highly probable that the barrow which Mr. Jefferson examined had been constructed many years, perhaps a century before, and although in its form it somewhat resembled some of the eminences which I have mentioned, yet, to me, it does not seem at all probable that they also are repositories of the bones of Indians; on the contrary, I think it almost certain that they have been constructed for some other purpose. . . .

It is, I think, made more than probable that if the ancestors of any of the savage tribes which, at present, inhabit the continent of North America, had ever been in the custom of entombing their dead in large eminences, that custom would have been transmitted to their posterity, or, at least, there would still be preserved some tradition of such a custom. . . .

These eminences are sometimes found in the neighbourhood of, and enclosed by walls and ditches, a species of workmanship with which none of the American nations, hitherto discovered, are acquainted.

Source 5   Letter of Samuel P. Hildreth, M.D., of Marietta, Ohio, July 19, 1819

Of what language, or of what nation were this mighty race, that once inhabited the territory watered by the Ohio, remains yet a mystery, too great for the most learned to unravel. But from what we see of their works, they must have had some acquaintance with the arts and sciences. They have left us perfect specimens of circles, squares, octagons, and parallel lines, on a grand and noble scale.

Source 6   Caleb Atwater, *Description of the Antiquities Discovered in the State of Ohio and Other Western States,* 1820

It is time to consider the . . . most highly interesting class of Antiquities, which comprehends those belonging to that people who erected our ancient forts and tumuli; those military works, whose walls and ditches cost so much labour in their structure, those numerous and sometimes lofty mounds, which owe their origin to a people far more civilized than our Indians, but far less than Europeans. These works are interesting . . . especially when we consider the immense extent of the country which they cover; the great labour which they cost their authors; the acquaintance with the useful arts; which that people had, when compared to our present race of Indians; the grandeur of many of the works themselves; the total absence of all historical records, or even traditionary accounts respecting them. . . . They were once forts, cemeteries, temples, altars, camps, towns, villages, race grounds, and other places of amusement, habitations of chieftains, videttes, watch towers, monuments, &c.

    The skeletons found in our mounds never belonged to a people like our Indians. The latter are a tall, rather slender, strait limbed people; the former were short and thick. They were rarely over five feet high, and few indeed were six. Their foreheads were low, cheek bones rather high; their faces were very short and broad; their eyes were very large; and, they had broad chins. I have examined more than fifty skulls found in tumuli, several of which I have before me. . . . The limbs of our fossils are short and very thick, and resemble the Germans, more than any Europeans with whom I am acquainted.

Source 7   William Cullen Bryant, "The Prairies," 1832

> As o'er the verdant waste I guide my steed,
> Among the high rank grass that sweeps his sides
> The hollow beating of his footsteps seems
> A sacrilegious sound. I think of those
> Upon whose rests he tramples. Are they here—
> The dead of other days?—and did the dust
> Of these fair solitudes once stir with life
> And burn with passion? Let the mighty mounds
> That overlook the river or that rise
> In the dim forest crowded with old oaks,
> Answer. A race that long has passed away,
> Built them;—a disciplined and populous race
> Heaped with long toil the earth while yet the Greek
> Was hewing the **Pentelicus** to forms
> Of symmetry, and rearing on its rock
> The glittering Parthenon. These ample fields
> Nourished their harvests, here their herds were fed,
> When haply by the stalls the bison lowed,
> And bowed his maned shoulder to the yoke.
> All day this desert murmured with their toils,
> Till twilight blushed, and lovers walked and wooed
> In a forgotten language, and old tunes,
> From instruments of unremembered form,
> Gave the soft winds a voice. The red man came—

The roaming hunter tribes, warlike and fierce
And the mound-builders vanished from the earth.
The solitude of centuries untold
Has settled where they dwelt. The prairie-wolf
Hunts in their meadows, and his fresh-dug den
Yawns by my path. The gopher mines the ground,
Where stood the swarming cities. All is gone;
All—save the piles of earth that hold their bones,
The platforms where they worshipped unknown gods,
The barriers which they builded from the soil
To keep the foe at bay—till o'er the walls
The wild beleaguerers broke, and one by one,
The strongholds of the plain were forced and heaped
With corpses. The brown vultures of the wood
Flocked to those vast uncovered sepulchres,
And sat unscared and silent at their feast.

Source 8   Account of Josiah Priest, 1833

Ancient millions of mankind had their seats of empire in America. Many of the mounds are completely occupied with human skeletons, and millions of them must have been interred in these vast cemeteries, that can be traced from the Rocky Mountains, on the west, to the Alleghenies on the east, and into the province of Texas . . . on the south: revolutions like those known in the old world, may have taken place here, and armies, equal to those of Cyrus, of Alexander the Great, or of Tamerlane the powerful, might have flourished their trumpets, and marched to battle, over these extensive plains.

Source 9   George Bancroft, *History of the Colonization of the United States*, 1842

[T]he country east of the Mississippi has no monuments. The numerous mounds which have been discovered in the alluvial valleys of the west, have by some been regarded as the works of an earlier and more cultivated race of men, whose cities have been laid waste, whose language and institutions have been destroyed or driven away; but the study of the structure of the earth strips this imposing theory of its marvels. Where imagination fashions relics of artificial walls, geology sees but crumbs of decaying sandstone, clinging like the remains of mortar to blocks of greenstone that rested on it; it discovers in parallel intrenchments a trough, that subsiding waters have ploughed through the centre of a ridge; it explains the tessellated pavement to be but a layer of pebbles aptly joined by water; and, on examining the mounds, and finding them composed of different strata of earth, arranged horizontally to their very edge, it ascribes their creation to the Power that shaped the globe into vales and hillocks. When the waters had gently deposited their alluvial burden on the bosom of the earth, it is not strange that, of the fantastic forms shaped by the eddies, some should resemble the ruins of a fortress; that the channel of a torrent should seem even like walls that connected a town with its harbor; that natural cones should be esteemed monuments of inexplicable toil. . . . When Nature has taken to herself her share in the construction of the symmetrical hillocks, nothing will remain to warrant the inference of a high civilization, that has left its abode or died away—of an earlier acquaintance with the arts of the Old World.

Source 10 John D. Baldwin, "Ancient America," in *Notes on American Archaeology*, 1872

It can be seen, without long study of their works as we know them, that the Mound-Builders had a certain degree of civilization which raised them far above the condition of savages. To make such works possible under any circumstances, there must be settled life, with its accumulations and intelligently organized industry. Fixed habits of useful work, directed by intelligence, are what barbarous tribes lack most of all. A profound change in this respect is indispensable to the beginning of civilization in such tribes.

No savage tribe found here by Europeans could have undertaken such constructions as those of the Mound-Builders. The wild Indians found in North America lived rudely in tribes. They had only such organization as was required by their nomadic habits, and their methods of fighting and hunting. These barbarous Indians gave no sign of being capable of the systematic application to useful industry which promotes intelligence, elevates the condition of life, accumulates wealth, and undertakes great works. This condition of industry, of which the worn and decayed works of the Mound-Builders are unmistakable monuments, means civilization. . . .

Some inquirers, not always without hesitation, suggest that the Indians inhabiting the United States two hundred years ago were degenerate descendents of the Mound-Builders. The history of the world shows that civilized communities may lose their enlightenment, and sink to a condition of barbarism; but the degraded descendents of a civilized people usually retain traditional recollections of their ancestors, or some traces of the lost civilization, perceptible in their customs and their legendary lore. The barbarism of the wild Indians of North America had nothing of this kind. It was original barbarism. . . .

There is no trace or probability of any direct relationship whatever between the Mound-Builders and the barbarous Indians found in the country. The wild Indians of this continent had never known such a condition as that of the Mound-Builders. They had nothing in common with it. In Africa, Asia, and elsewhere among the more uncultivated families of the human race, there is not as much really original barbarism as some anthropologists are inclined to assume; but there can be no serious doubt that the wild Indians of North America were original barbarians, born of a stock which had never, at any time, been either civilized or closely associated with the influences of civilization.

Source 11 Account of scientist J. W. Foster, 1873

The evidences of the former existence of a prehistoric race known as the Mound-builders, who at one time occupied the principal affluents of the Mississippi, the Gulf coast, and the region of the Great Lakes, are too conclusive to admit of doubt. These evidences consist of **tumuli** symmetrically raised and often enclosed in mathematical figures, such as the square, the octagon, and circle, with long lines of **circumvallation**; of pits in the solid rock, and rubbish heaps formed in the prosecution of their mining operations; and of a variety of utensils wrought in stone or copper, or molded in clay, which evinces a knowledge of art and methodical labor foreign to the red man. . . .

The Indian possesses a conformation of skull which clearly separates him from the pre-historic Mound Builder, and such a conformation must give rise to different mental traits. His brain, as compared with the European . . . differs widely in the proportions of the different parts. The anterior lobe is small, the middle lobe is large, and the central convolutions on the anterior lobe and upper surface, are small. The brain-case is boxlike, with the corners rounded off. . . .

His character, since first known to the white man has been signalized by treachery and cruelty. He repels all efforts to raise him from his degraded position: and whilst he has not the moral nature to adopt the virtues of civilization, his brutal instincts lead him to welcome its vices. He was never known voluntarily to engage in an enterprise requiring methodical labor; . . . he imposes the drudgery of life upon his squaw; he takes no heed for the future.

To suppose that such a race threw up the strong lines of circumvallation and the symmetrical mounds which crown so many of our river terraces is as preposterous as to suppose that they built the pyramids of Egypt.

Source 12 Archaeologist Cyrus Thomas, "Report on the Mound Explorations of the Bureau of Ethnology," 1894

It is . . . contended that the magnitude of some of the earthworks indicates a much higher culture and a more systematic government and centralized power than have been found in Indian history. That there must have been sufficient intelligence to plan the works is evident; that there must have been some means of bringing into harmony the views of the people and of combining their forces is also apparent. But the fact that at the discovery of the country several of the tribes were accustomed to build villages, surround them with palisades and moats, and in some cases to erect just such mounds as we now find, shows, beyond contradiction, that they had the necessary intelligence to plan such works and the means of combining forces to build them. . . .

It is strange that most writers who claim for these remains such high antiquity contend at the same time for a much more advanced culture than that attained by the Indians. It is true that when we stand at the base of the great Cahokia mound and study its vast proportions, we can scarcely bring ourselves to believe it was built without some other means of collecting and conveying material than that possessed by the Indians. But what other means could a lost race have had? The Indians had wooden spades, baskets, skins of animals, wooden and clay vessels, and textile fabrics; they also had stone implements. . . . It is also more than likely that all the people of a tribe, both men and women, aided in the work, and that the large works were built by additions made during successive generations. But the best evidence that they could build such structures is the fact that they did build them, that in truth they made every form of ancient works known to exist in the bounds of our country, even to the large canals of which there are yet traces.

Source 13 J. W. Powell, "Report of the Director," Bureau of Ethnology, 1894

[I]t was [until recently] the prevailing opinion among archeologists that the mounds and other aboriginal earthworks of the eastern half of the United States are vestiges of a people more ancient and more advanced than the tribes of Indians that occupied the continent at the time of the discovery by Columbus. . . .

It is difficult to exaggerate the prevalence of this romantic fallacy, or the force with which the hypothetic "lost races" had taken possession of the imaginations of men. For more than a century the ghosts of a vanished nation have **ambuscaded** in the vast solitudes of the continent, and the forest-covered mounds have been usually regarded as the mysterious sepulchers of its kings and nobles. It was an alluring conjecture that a powerful people, superior to the Indians, once occupied the valley of the Ohio and the Appalachian ranges, their empire stretching from Hudson Bay to the Gulf, with its flanks on the western prairies and the eastern ocean; a people with a confederate government, a chief ruler, a great central capital, a highly developed religion, with homes and husbandry and advanced textile, **fictile**, and **ductile** arts, with a language, perhaps with letters, all swept away before an invasion of copper-hued Huns from some unknown region of the earth, prior to the landing of Columbus. . . .

But the assumption that the mounds . . . were the work of a lost and nameless race . . . has been losing ground before recent evidence accumulated by archeologists. The spade and the pick, in the hands of patient and sagacious investigators, have every year brought to light facts tending more and more strongly to prove that the mounds, which have excited so much curiosity and become the subject of so many hypotheses, were constructed by the historic Indians of our land and their lineal ancestors.

Source 14 Archaeologist Robert Silverberg, *Mound Builders of Ancient America,* 1968

The dream of a lost prehistoric race in the American heartland was profoundly satisfying; and if the vanished ones had been giants, or white men, or Israelites, or Danes, or Toltecs, or giant white Jewish Toltec Vikings, so much the better. The people of the United States were then engaged in an undeclared war against the Indians who blocked their path to expansion, transporting, imprisoning, or simply massacring them; and as this century-long campaign of genocide proceeded, it may have been expedient to conjure up a previous race whom the Indians had displaced in the same way. Conscience might ache a bit over the uprooting of the Indians, but not if it could be shown that the Indians, far from being long-established settlers in the land, were themselves mere intruders who had wantonly shattered the glorious Mound Builder civilization of old. What had been a simple war of conquest against the Indians now could be construed as a war of vengeance on behalf of that great and martyred ancient culture.

Source 15   George E. Stuart, "Who Were the Mound Builders?" *National Geographic,* 1972

Generations have seen and puzzled over the continent's man-made earthen lumps. The first settlers east of the Mississippi Valley came upon thousands, many flanked by geometric earthworks of astonishing precision. Some formed shapes of humans or animals; others were flat-topped.

And their discovery led to wild speculation. Accounts of the 18th and 19th centuries, reflecting the attitudes of their times, simply could not credit the mounds to those "forest primitives," the eastern Indians. Gradually conjecture crystallized into a myth of "Mound Builders," a highly civilized race that supposedly flourished before the Indians came.

Who were the Mound Builders? Survivors of a sunken Atlantis, some said. Egyptians and Phoenicians wandering far from home, ventured others.

The real story is just as intriguing, and it does concern sophisticated people. Not a mythical super race, but American Indians—ancestors of the Creeks, Cherokees, Natchez, and others who first greeted the white men.

Source 16   Heather Pringle, *Science,* September 19, 1997

Millennia before the arrival of Europeans, early Native Americans went on a construction binge, dotting the eastern side of the continent with thousands of vast earthen mounds. With shapes ranging from massive cones and quadrangular platforms to gigantic serpents, the mounds were clearly legacies from many different cultures, serving purposes that ranged from ceremonial centers to channel houses. A new finding in Louisiana has now extended the tradition of mound building back in time by nearly 2000 years—and opened a new perspective on the cultures of ancient North America.

Most archaeologists believed that the first large earthworks were built 3500 years ago at Poverty Point, Louisiana, by a people who had prospered from trading. But. . . . a multidisciplinary team headed by archaeologist Joe Saunders of Northeast Louisiana University . . . reports dating construction of an elaborate earthern enclosure in northeastern Louisiana to a 400 year period beginning 5400 years ago. . . . That makes Watson Brake, as it is now called, the oldest extant mound complex in the Americas.

The existence of this extensive public architecture, consisting of eleven mounds and connecting ridges that enclose nearly 9 hectares, is hard to reconcile with archaeologists' traditional picture of the small, mobile bands of hunter-gatherers that inhabited the eastern United States 5400 years ago. . . . To construct an earthern enclosure 280 meters in diameter according to a pre-conceived plan, however, the builders had to have sophisticated leadership skills. They must also have had a wealth of food to sustain the hard labor of raising mounds as tall as a two-story house.

Source 17   Colin G. Calloway, *First Peoples,* 1999

The Mississippian town of Cahokia was a thriving urban market center. Founded around A.D. 700 close to the confluence of the Missouri, Mississippi, and Illinois

Rivers and occupied for about seven hundred years, Cahokia had a population of between 10,000 and 30,000 at its height, about the population of medieval London. Cahokia was the largest settlement north of the Rio Grande before the end of the eighteenth century, when it was surpassed by New York and Philadelphia. Trade routes linked Cahokia to distant regions of the continent bringing shells from the Atlantic coast, copper from Lake Superior, obsidian from the Rocky Mountains, and mica from the southern Appalachians. By the fourteenth century, Cahokia was in decline. Most likely, the growing population had exhausted the resources needed to support it in a period of climatic change; archaeological evidence suggests there may have been increasing pressure from enemies. Whatever the causes, the once-thriving metropolis lay abandoned half a century before Columbus. The remains of Cahokia's spectacular mounds can still be seen after five hundred years of erosion . . . and offer impressive testimony to a civilization that developed before Europe entered its middle ages, flourished longer than the United States has existed as a nation, and declined before Europeans set foot in America.

✍ Questioning the Past

1. What theories might a student of today offer to explain why people of long ago would build the massive mounds that mark the landscape of the eastern United States? Speculate as well about what functions—political, cultural, social, economic, and religious—might be served by the various forms of mounds: truncated pyramids, conical burial mounds, effigy mounds. What techniques, if any, might be used to test these theories?

2. Imagine ways in which future archeologists, sifting through the remains of twentieth-century American civilization, might misinterpret the artifacts and structures of our time.

3. Why would the Americans of the nineteenth century resist the idea that the mounds were the work of Native Americans?

Chapter 2

Columbus

Columbus Arrives in America *October 12, 1492*

To say that Columbus discovered America is to overlook the fact that he was greeted on the beach by a welcoming committee. America before 1492 was not an empty land. The peoples Columbus incorrectly thought to be Indians lived in the New World as hundreds of distinct nations. Each had its own governance system, its own customs and costumes, its own religion, and often its own language. Some of these peoples lived simply as hunters and gatherers. Others built cities of stone and wood as great and as beautiful as anything in Europe or Asia or Africa. In fact, several great civilizations had come and gone in the Americas long before the Europeans even learned of the existence of the New World. The **Arawaks** who assembled to observe the momentous landing of Columbus wore golden earrings, and not much else. Even if they had been decked out in fineries, it was not certain that the Spaniards would have noticed much beyond the earrings anyway. Gold, silver, and precious stones taken from the New World and its people helped to lay the foundation upon which would rest the subsequent European economic and political domination of the world. Political values prevalent among many of the native nations—liberty, equality, democracy—provided both challenge and example to an Old World ruled by monarchy and aristocracy. Columbus may have been moved by greed; he may have been driven by a vision. He may have been one of history's greatest geniuses; he may have been history's luckiest incompetent. But his action changed the world profoundly. It is possible to count on the fingers of one hand the number of individuals in the entire recorded history of the planet whose actions have had equal or greater impact.

❧ *First Impressions*

"No One Would Believe It Who Has Not Seen It"

Before 1492, two worlds had unknowingly inhabited the same planet. Each of these worlds—one centered on the landmass of Asia, Europe, and Africa, the other comprising the Americas—had been making steady advances for untold generations. When Columbus breached the wall of water that separated these worlds, two streams of civilization began to merge. Columbus's writings describe this historical moment.

Source 1 Diary of Columbus

Thursday, 11 October, 1492

He steered west-southwest. They took much water aboard, more than they had taken in the whole voyage. They saw petrels and a green bulrush near the ship. The men of the caravel *Pinta* saw a cane and a stick, and took on board another small stick that appeared to have been worked with iron, and a piece of cane, and other vegetation originating on land, and a small plank. The men of the caravel *Nina* also saw other signs of land and a small stick loaded with barnacles. With these signs everyone breathed more easily and cheered up. On this day, up to sunset, they made 27 leagues.

After sunset he steered on his former course to the west. They made about twelve miles each hour and, until two hours after midnight, made about 90 miles, which is twenty-two leagues and a half. And because the caravel *Pinta* was a better sailer and went ahead of the Admiral it found land and made the signals that the Admiral had ordered. A sailor named Rodrigo de Triana saw this land first, although the Admiral, at the tenth hour of the night, while he was on the sterncastle, saw a light, although it was something so faint that he did not wish to affirm that it was land. But he called Pero Gutierrez . . . and told him that there seemed to be a light, and for him to look: and thus he did and saw it. He also told Rodrigo Sanchez de Segovia . . . who saw nothing because he was not in a place where he could see it. After the Admiral said it, it was seen once or twice; and it was like a small wax candle that rose and lifted up, which to few seemed to be an indication of land. . . . At two hours after midnight the land appeared, from which they were about two leagues distant. They hauled down all the sails . . . , passing time until daylight Friday, when they reached an islet . . . which was called Guanahani in the language of the Indians. Soon they saw naked people; and the Admiral went ashore in the armed launch, and Martin Alonso Pinzon and his brother Vicente Anes, who was captain of the *Nina*. The Admiral brought out the royal banner and the captains two flags with the green cross, which the Admiral carried on all the ships as a standard. . . . Thus put ashore they saw very green trees and many ponds and fruits of various kinds. The Admiral called to the two captains and to the others who had jumped ashore . . . and he said that they should be witnesses that, in the presence of all, he would take, as in fact he did take, possession of the said island for the king and for the queen his lords, making the declarations that were required. . . . Soon many people of the island gathered there. What follows are the very words of the Admiral in his book about his first voyage to, and discovery of, these Indies. I, he says, in order that they would be friendly to us—because I recognized that they were people who would be better . . . converted to our Holy Faith by love than by force—to some of them I gave red caps, and glass beads which they put on their chests, and many other things of small value, in which they took so much pleasure and became so much our friends that it was a marvel. Later they came swimming to the ships' launches where we were and brought us parrots and cotton thread in balls and javelins and many other things, and they traded them to us for other things which we gave them, such as small glass beads and bells. In sum, they took everything and gave of what they had very willingly. . . . They are very well formed, with handsome bodies and good faces. . . . They wear their hair down over their

2.1 The Columbus Navigation Home Page

eyebrows except for a little in the back which they wear long and never cut. Some of them paint themselves with black, and they are of the color of the Canarians, neither black nor white; and some of them paint themselves with white, and some of them with red, and some of them with whatever they find. And some of them paint their faces, and some of them the whole body, and some of them only the eyes, and some of them only the nose. . . . All of them alike are of good-sized stature and carry themselves well. . . . They should be good and intelligent servants, for I see that they say very quickly everything that is said to them; and I believe that they would become Christians very easily, for it seemed to me that they had no religion. Our Lord pleasing, at the time of my departure I will take six of them from here to Your Highnesses in order that they may learn to speak. No animal of any kind did I see on this island except parrots. All are the Admiral's words.

Source 2   Columbus to His Spanish Patrons

February 15, 1493

Sir:

Since I know that you will be pleased at the great victory with which Our Lord has crowned my voyage, I write this to you, from which you will learn how in thirty-three days I passed from the Canary Islands to the Indies, with the fleet which the most illustrious King and Queen, our Sovereigns, gave to me. There I found many islands, filled with innumerable people, and I have taken possession of them all for their Highnesses, done by proclamation and with the royal banner unfurled, and no opposition was offered to me.

To the first island which I found I gave the name "San Salvador," in remembrance of the Divine Majesty, Who had marvelously bestowed all this; the Indians call it "Guanahani." To the second, I gave the name the island of "Santa Maria de Concepcion," and to the third, "Fernandina," to the fourth, "Isabella," to the fifth island, "Juana," and so each received from me a new name.

When I came to Juana, I followed its coast westward, and I found it to be so extensive that I thought it must be the mainland, the province of **Cathay**. . . . I sent two men inland to learn if there were a king or great cities. They travelled three days' journey, finding an infinity of small hamlets and people without number, but nothing of importance. For this reason, they returned.

I understood sufficiently from other Indians, whom I had already taken, that this land was an island, and I therefore followed its coast eastward for one hundred and seven leagues to the point where it ended. From that point, I saw another island, distant about eighteen leagues from the first, to the east, and to it I at once gave the name "Espanola." . . . This island and all the others are very fertile to a limitless degree, and this island is extremely so. In it there are many harbours on the coast of the sea, beyond comparison with others that I know in Christendom, and many rivers, good and large, which is marvelous. Its lands are high; there are in it many sierras and very lofty mountains. . . . All are most beautiful, of a thousand shapes; all are accessible and are filled with trees of a thousand kinds and tall, so that they seem to touch the sky. I am told that they never lose their foliage, and this I can believe, for I saw them as green and lovely as they are in Spain in May, and some of them were flowering, some bearing fruit. . . . The nightingale was singing and other birds of a thousand kinds, in the month of November, there where I went. . . . In this island, there are many spices and great mines of gold and other metals.

The people of this island which I have found and of which I have information, all go naked, men and women, as their mothers bore them, although some of the women cover a single place with the leaf of a plant or with a net of cotton which they make for the purpose. They have no iron or steel or weapons, nor are they fitted to use them. This is not because they are not well built and of handsome stature, but because they are very marvelously timorous. . . . It is true that . . . they are so guileless and so generous with all that they possess, that no one would believe it who has not seen it. They refuse nothing that they possess, if it be asked of them; on the contrary, they invite any one to share it and display as much love as if they would give their hearts.

In conclusion, to speak only of what has been accomplished on this voyage, which was so hasty, their Highnesses can see that I will give them as much gold as they may need, if their Highnesses will render me very slight assistance; presently, I will give them spices and cotton, as much as their Highnesses shall command; and **mastic**, as much as they shall order to be shipped . . . ; and aloe, as much as they shall order to be shipped; and slaves, as many as they shall order, . . . and I shall find a thousand other things of value. . . .

This is an account of the facts, thus abridged.

Done in the caravel, off the Canary Islands, on the fifteenth day of February, in the year one thousand four hundred and ninety-three.

At your orders.

The Admiral

The Meeting of Two Worlds

It must have been a bewildering sight for the Arawak people—men of an appearance unlike any they had ever seen, landing on the beach of the Caribbean isle they called Guanahani, performing strange rituals and unfurling banners that bore unfamiliar symbols. Still, the Arawaks responded to these newcomers as was their custom: they greeted Columbus and his party with genuine goodwill and hospitality. Though Columbus described these natives as extraordinarily loving and generous, within a generation of the Spanish arrival the peaceful Arawaks had lost their independence, been declared the subjects of a distant king, seen their own religion banned, suffered the destruction of their villages as the newcomers searched for treasure, and had been impressed as a slave labor force to work the mines and plantations of the Spaniards.

In the first 20 years of the European presence among the Arawaks, the population of this native nation fell from a quarter of a million to a mere 14,000. This catastrophic decline was primarily the consequence of diseases of the Old World unwittingly introduced into the environment of the New. But the magnitude of the death toll was no doubt amplified by the physiological and psychological effects of the Spanish conquest and subsequent exploitation of the Arawaks. The contact between the Spanish and the Arawaks, as consequential as it may have been for both, had an even greater impact on the subsequent course of history. It signaled the beginning of a new era for the two worlds represented by these two nations.

📖 *Second Thoughts*

"The Dawn of Modern Times"

> For five centuries scholars have recognized the significance of the arrival of Columbus in the New World. But, as the sources that follow indicate, they have not always agreed on what made his arrival significant.

Source 3   Account of Peter Martyr, Royal Chronicler of Spain, October.1, 1493

2.2 Christopher Columbus and Early European Exploration

A certain Columbus has sailed to the **Western Antipodes**, even, as he believes, to the very shores of India. He has discovered many islands beyond the Eastern ocean adjoining the Indies, which are believed to be those of which mention has been made among **cosmographers**. I do not wholly deny this, although the magnitude of the globe seems to suggest otherwise, for there are not wanting those who think it but a small journey from the end of Spain to the shores of India; however this may be, they declare that a great thing has been accomplished. Concerning the things of which he speaks, he brought proof; greater things still are promised to be discovered. It is enough for us that the hidden half of the globe is brought to light and that day by day the Portuguese go farther and farther beyond the **equinoctial** circle itself. Regions hitherto unknown, as if they were all so many thoroughfares, will soon be explored.

Source 4   Bartolomé de Las Casas, bishop of Chiapas, ca. 1561

[H]e introduced and commenced to establish such beginnings, and sowed such seeds from which originated and grew such deadly and pestilential herbs producing from themselves such deep roots, that it has been enough to destroy and devastate all these Indies, without human power being enough to prevent or overcome such supreme and irreparable injuries.

I do not doubt that if the Admiral had believed that such pernicious harm would follow as did follow, and had known as much of the simple conclusions of natural and divine right as he knew of cosmography and other human sciences, that he would never have dared to introduce nor begin a thing which must occasion such calamitous injuries.

Source 5   William Robertson, *The History of the Discovery and Settlement of North America,* 1788

The first care of Columbus was to inform the King and Queen, who were then at Barcelona, of his arrival and success. Ferdinand and Isabella, no less astonished than delighted with this unexpected event, desired Columbus, in terms the most respectful and flattering, to repair immediately to court, that from his own mouth they might receive a full detail of his extraordinary services and discoveries. During his journey to Barcelona, the people crowded from the adjacent country, following him everywhere with admiration and applause. His entrance into the city was conducted, by order of Ferdinand and Isabella, with pomp suitable to the great event, which added such distinguishing lustre to their reign. The people whom he had brought along with him from the countries which he had discovered, marched first, and by their singular complexion, the wild peculiarity of their features, and uncouth finery, appeared like men of another species. Next to them were carried the ornaments of gold, fashioned by the rude art of the natives, the grains of gold found in the mountains, and the dust of the same metal found in the rivers. After these appeared the various commodities of the new discovered countries, together with their curious productions. Columbus himself closed the procession, and attracted the eyes of all the spectators, who gazed with admiration on the extraordinary man, whose superior sagacity and fortitude had conducted their countrymen, by a route concealed from past ages, to the knowledge of the new world. Ferdinand and Isabella received him clad in their royal robes, and seated upon a throne, under a magnificent canopy. When he approached, they stood up, and raising him as he kneeled to kiss their hands, commanded him to take his seat upon a chair prepared for him, and to give a circumstantial account of his voyage. . . . When he had finished his narration, the king and queen kneeling down, offered up solemn thanks to Almighty God for the discovery of those new regions, from which they expected so many advantages to flow in upon the kingdoms subject to their government.

Source 6 Richard Hildreth, *The History of the United States of America,* 1853

When Columbus undertook his first voyage across the Atlantic, the passage to India by the Cape of Good Hope was as yet unknown. The fabulous wealth of the regions of the East, especially as set forth by Venetian Marco Polo, fired the imagination of that great navigator, sustained his hopes, and prompted his persevering efforts. . . . With scientific heroism, relying on the theory of the earth's rotundity, while the prevailing under-estimate as to its size diminished to his ardent mind the dangers of an untried voyage—first of men, he dared to hope to reach Asia by a western passage. He thought he had done so; . . . and he zealously persisted, and died in the belief, that those new lands were a part of Cathay, or Farther India.

Source 7 Woodrow Wilson, *A History of the American People,* 1902

The success of Columbus solved the mystery of the Atlantic, but it did little to instruct Europe, or even to guide her fancy, concerning the real nature of the lands he had found. No one dreamed that they were the coasts of a new world. Who could believe the globe big enough to have held through all the ages a whole continent of which Christendom had never heard, nor even so much as had poetic vision,—unless, perchance, this were the fabled Atlantis? Slowly, very slowly, exploration brought the facts to light; but even then, men were loath to receive the truth.

Source 8   John Fiske, *The Discovery of America,* 1902

The grandeur of the achievement was quite beyond the ken of the generation that witnessed it. For we have since come to learn that in 1492 the contact between the eastern and western halves of our planet was first really begun, and the two streams of human life which had flowed on for countless ages apart were thenceforth to mingle together. The first voyage of Columbus was a unique event in the history of mankind. Nothing like it was ever done before, and nothing like it can ever be done again. No worlds are left for a future Columbus to conquer. The era of which this great Italian mariner was the most illustrious representative has closed forever.

2.3 Christopher
Columbus
Internet
Resources

Source 9   Henry Bamford Parkes, *The American Experience,* 1959

In a symbolic sense Columbus can appropriately be regarded as the first American. Here was a man of obscure birth, without influential family connections or financial resources, who had the audacity to plan an enterprise without precedent in history. He was a skillful seaman, and his project was supported by the best geographical learning of his time; yet it was not primarily by his ability or his knowledge of navigation that he earned his immortality, but by the quality of his will. To discover America required the courage to sail westward across the ocean for as long as might be necessary, not knowing where one was going or whether one would ever return. Other men had believed that there might be land on the other side of the Atlantic; but nobody else had dared to put the hypothesis to a conclusive test. This kind of enterprise and audacity, and this energy and confidence of the will, were to be the primary characteristics of the settlers and builders of America as well as of its first discoverer.

Source 10   Samuel Eliot Morison, *The Oxford History of the American People,* 1971

America was discovered accidentally by a great seaman who was looking for something else; when discovered it was not wanted; and most of the exploration for the next fifty years was done in the hope of getting through or around it. America was named for a man who discovered no part of the New World. History is like that, very chancy.

Source 11   Alfred W. Crosby Jr., *The Columbian Exchange,* 1972

Tradition has limited historians in their search for the true significance of the renewed contact between the Old and New Worlds. Even the economic historian may occasionally miss what any ecologist or geographer would find glaringly obvious after a cursory reading of the basic original sources of the sixteenth century: the most important changes brought on by the Columbian voyages were biological in nature. . . .

    The connection between the Old and New Worlds, which for more than ten millennia had been no more than a tenuous thing of Viking voyages, drifting fishermen, and shadowy contacts via Polynesia, became on the twelfth day of October 1492 a bond as significant as the Bering land bridge had once been.

The two worlds, which God had cast asunder, were reunited, and the two worlds, which were so different, began on that day to become alike. That trend toward biological homogeneity is one of the most important aspects of the history of life on this planet since the retreat of the continental glaciers. . . .

The long-range biological effects of the Columbian exchange are not encouraging. If one values all forms of life and not just one's own species—then one must be concerned with the genetic pool, the total potential of all living things to produce descendants of various shapes, colors, internal structures, defenses against both multicellular and unicellular enemies, maximum fertility, and, to speak generally—maximum ability to produce offspring with maximum adaptive possibilities. The genetic pool is usually expanded when continents join. As plants and creatures move into virgin territory, the adaptations to new environments of those who survive the increased competition produce new types and even new species. Paleontologists and comparative zoologists call the event "explosive evolution," meaning it often takes a few million years. This is normally what would be happening after the joining of the Old and New Worlds after 1492—but for man.

Not for half a billion years, at least, and probably for long before that, has an extreme or permanent physical change affected the whole earth. The single exception to this generality may be European man and his technologies, agricultural and industrial. He has spread all over the globe, and non-European peoples have adopted his techniques in all but the smallest islets. . . .

The Columbian exchange has included man, and he has changed the Old and the New Worlds sometimes inadvertently, sometimes intentionally, often brutally. It is possible that he and the plants and animals he brings with him have caused the extinction of more species of life forms in the last four hundred years than the usual processes of evolution might kill off in a million. Man kills faster than the pace of evolution: there has been no million years since Columbus for evolution to devise a replacement for the passenger pigeon. No one can remember what the pre-Columbian flora of the Antilles was like, and the trumpeter swan and the buffalo and a hundred other species have been reduced to such small numbers that a mere twitch of a change in ecology or man's wishes can eliminate them. The flora and fauna of the Old and especially of the New World have been reduced and specialized by man. Specialization almost always narrows the possibilities for future changes: for the sake of present convenience, we loot the future.

The Columbian exchange has left us with not a richer but a more impoverished genetic pool. We, all of the life on this planet, are the less for Columbus, and the impoverishment will increase.

Source 12 Howard Zinn, *A People's History of the United States,* 1980

Thus began the history, five hundred years ago, of the European invasion of the Indian settlements of the Americas. . . . When we read the history books given to children in the United States, it all starts with heroic adventure—there is no bloodshed—and Columbus Day is a celebration.

To emphasize the heroism of Columbus and his successors as navigators and discoverers, and to deemphasize their genocide, is not a technical necessity but an ideological choice. It serves—unwittingly—to justify what was done.

My point is not that we must, in telling history, accuse, judge, condemn Columbus in absentia. It is too late for that; it would be a useless scholarly exercise in morality. But the easy acceptance of atrocities as a deplorable but necessary price to pay for progress (Hiroshima and Vietnam, to save Western civilization; **Kronshtadt** and Hungary, to save socialism; nuclear proliferation, to save us all)—that is still with us. One reason these atrocities are still with us is that we have learned to bury them in a mass of other facts, as radioactive wastes are buried in containers in the earth. . . .

The treatment of heroes (Columbus) and their victims (the Arawaks)—the quiet acceptance of conquest and murder in the name of progress—is only one aspect of a certain approach to history, in which the past is told from the point of view of governments, conquerors, diplomats, leaders. . . . The history of any country, presented as the history of a family, conceals fierce conflicts of interest (sometimes exploding, most often repressed) between conquerors and conquered, masters and slaves, capitalists and workers, dominators and dominated in race and sex. And in such a world of conflict, a world of victims and executioners, it is the job of thinking people, as **Albert Camus** suggested, not to be on the side of the executioners.

Thus, in that inevitable taking of sides which comes from selection and emphasis in history, I prefer to try to tell the story of the discovery of America from the viewpoint of the Arawaks, of the Constitution from the standpoint of the slaves, of Andrew Jackson as seen by the Cherokees, . . . of the rise of industrialism as seen by the young women in the Lowell textile mills, . . . the Gilded Age as seen by southern farmers, . . . the New Deal as seen by blacks in Harlem, . . . the postwar American empire as seen by peons in Latin America. . . .

What Columbus did to the Arawaks of the Bahamas, Cortes did to the Aztecs of Mexico, Pizarro to the Incas of Peru, and the English settlers of Virginia and Massachusetts to the Powhatans and the Pequots. . . . Was all this bloodshed and deceit—from Columbus to Cortes, Pizarro, the Puritans—a necessity for the human race to progress from savagery to civilization? . . .

If there *are* necessary sacrifices to be made for human progress, is it not essential to hold to the principle that those to be sacrificed must make the decision themselves? We can all decide to give up something of ours, but do we have the right to throw into the pyre the children of others, or even our own children, for a progress which is not nearly as clear or present as sickness or health, life or death?

Source 13 Stuart B. Schwartz, *The Iberian Mediterranean and the Atlantic Traditions in the Formation of Columbus as a Colonizer,* 1986

From the outset Columbus perceived the Indians not only as prospective subjects but as a labor force. . . . Despite popular attempts to make Columbus an early abolitionist, he was in truth the first slave trader in the Americas, and the Catholic monarchs at first did not interfere with the Admiral's plans to sell Indians in the slave market of Seville.

Source 14 J. M. Roberts, *The Pelican History of the World,* 1987

In the name of the "West Indies" the map commemorates his continuing belief that he had accomplished the discovery of islands off Asia by his astonishing leap in the dark, so different from the cautious, though brave, progress of the Portuguese towards the East round Africa. Unlike them, but unwittingly, he had in fact discovered an entire continent, though even on the much better-equipped second voyage which he made in 1493 he explored only its islands. . . . Soon, though Columbus to his dying day refused to admit it . . . , it began to be realized that this might not be Asia after all. In 1494 the historic name "New World" was first applied to his discoveries. Not until 1724, though, was it to be realized that Asia and America really were not joined together in the region of the Bering Straits.

Source 15 Kirkpatrick Sale, *The Conquest of Paradise,* 1990

Surprising as it may seem from the present perspective, the man we know as Christopher Columbus died in relative obscurity, his passing not even recorded at the time on the subcontinent whose history he so decisively changed. But the true importance of his Discovery became clearer with every passing decade as the New World yielded up its considerable treasure to the Old, and as the historical significance became appreciated in scholarly, and then in popular, opinion. . . .

Only now can we see how completely the Discovery and its legacy over the last five centuries have altered the cultures of the globe and the life-processes upon which they depend:

• It enabled the society of the European subcontinent to expand beyond its borders in a fashion unprecedented in the history of the world, and to come today to dominate virtually every other society it touches, Westernizing the great bulk of humanity, imposing its institutions and ideas, its language and culture, its technologies and economy, around the earth.

• It enabled Europe to accumulate wealth and power previously unimaginable, the means by which it created and developed the most successful synergy of systems ever known, a mixture of humanism and secularism, rationalism and science, materialism and capitalism, nationalism and militarism—in short the very structures of what we know as modern civilization.

• It enabled the vast redistribution of life-forms, purposely and accidentally, that has changed the biota of the earth more thoroughly than at any time since the end of the Permian Period, in effect rejoining the continents of the earth that were separated so many geological eons ago and thereby causing the extinction, alteration, and even creation of species at a speed and on a scale never before experienced.

• And most significant, it enabled humanity to achieve, and sanctify, the transformation of nature with unprecedented proficiency and thoroughness, to multiply, thrive, and dominate the earth as no single species ever has, modifying systems of soils and water and air, altering stable atmospheric and climatic balances, and now threatening, it is not too much to say, the existence of the earth as we have known it and the greater proportion of its species, including the human.

Source 16 Paolo Emilio Taviani, *Columbus, the Great Adventure,* 1991

The Columbian discovery was of greater magnitude than any other discovery or invention in human history. Europeans realized that in the sixteenth century. In the centuries since then, the importance of Columbus's discovery has continued to swell, both because of the prodigious development of the New World and because of the numerous other discoveries that have stemmed from it. It was after Columbus's voyages that the task of integrating the American continents into Greco-Roman-Christian—European—culture was carried out. Notwithstanding errors, egoism, and unheard-of violence, the discovery was an essential, in many ways, determining, factor in ushering in the modern age. It was brought about first and above all by the Spanish and then by the Portuguese, French, English, Italians, Irish—to some extent by all the peoples of Europe. But this recognition cannot diminish the value of the inception of that task, which was Columbus's discovery.

Nevertheless, nearly every year the argument against the value of Columbus's undertaking and his claim to priority breaks out anew in the European and American Press. Who reached America first? Couldn't someone have found the Atlantic route before Columbus? Didn't the Norsemen reach Greenland and Canada? It is an argument completely without justification from a scientific point of view. . . . It is not a question of who the first European was to set foot on some beach on the American mainland, but who was the person who brought the new continent to the awareness of the old continents, who thrust it suddenly and overwhelmingly into the development of civilization, effecting a decisive turning point in human history.

Source 17 Edwin M. Yoder, *Washington Post,* November 24, 1991

Presumably the surrogate Nuremburg trial now being conducted on every hand concerning the crimes of Columbus will render some verdict by October of 1992. Is he to be symbolically hanged for ecocide, genocide, the enslavement of native peoples, or all three at once?

If you think this an unserious question, consider . . . that the forthcoming New Year's Day Tournament of Roses parade in Pasadena caused an uproar by appointing a Columbus descendant grand marshal. . . .

In the earliest heroic version of the explorer's place in history, almost certainly derived from Washington Irving's fanciful 1828 "biography," we were invited to view him as a dreamy young Genoan who spent hours staring out to sea and asking himself why departing ships had a strange way of sinking gradually from sight at the horizon. It didn't look flat to him! One day he realized— eureka!—that Earth had to be round and ventured forth to challenge the delusions of a scornful and superstitious age.

It is a charming story, a brilliant fable of pertinacity, and it is also, as we now know, historical nonsense. The spherity of Earth was never seriously questioned in his time or any other. Indeed, it was because Columbus underestimated the actual size of Earth that he imagined he could reach Japan by sailing west. His geometry was unequal to that of the great Egyptians and Greeks of antiquity. . . .

The harder you try to see history through the eyes of those who lived through it, the harder it is to patronize it. . . . Consider, for instance, the much-discussed issue of Columbus's treatment of the native peoples. It isn't true that the "Indians" were seen as prey for wanton exploitation, like so many game animals. They were exploited; and tragically slaughtered by communicable "European" diseases to which they lacked immunity. . . . Had the Indians' fate been deliberately willed by Columbus and the Spanish monarchs who commissioned his expeditions, it would indeed be a shocking crime. But it was not willed. On the contrary, the "Indians" were viewed chiefly, instead, as prospects for Christian conversion—not as beasts of prey but as people with souls. . . .

What was this, you may ask, but condescension of another sort? Condescension it was, perhaps, but the historical view of Columbus requires us to notice that in his time European Christendom felt itself under siege from the Ottoman invasions on the East and South. We ought to sense the anxiety they felt, since we too have just come through a siege of our own. . . .

The metaphysical certainties that allowed Columbus to view "Indians" (and Jews, who were expelled from Spain in 1492 if they refused to convert to Christianity) as candidates for forced conversion may be repugnant to us in our state of enlightenment. . . . But we have our own certainties.

Source 18 Boris Biancheri, Italian ambassador to the United States, *Washington Post,* October 4, 1992

"Good Guy Columbus"

One cannot ignore the bloody conquest, nor the cruelties and injustices that followed Columbus, but one should also allow the events of 1492 to be considered from a different perspective. It was the dawn of modern times. . . . After 1492, the geographical, political, economic, cultural, religious and philosophical frames of reference were radically different from those that had set the stage of the Middle Ages.

The revisionist approach is understandable. . . . And, certainly, one cannot completely detach colonial exploitation from the Columbus adventure. But to view such an event from only that perspective would be unbalanced. . . . Clearly, Columbus was no saint; some of the long-term effects of his expedition have been devastating. But neither is it just to condemn him for environmental consequences and epidemics of which he could not possibly have been aware.

The Columbus voyage was first and foremost a great moment of integration between world societies and civilizations.

Source 19 Peter H. Gibbon, "Apologize for Columbus?" *Washington Post,* October 12, 1998

For the past two years I have been visiting classrooms all over America, talking to students about heroes. Why today should they admire an explorer whose discovery was a blunder, who thought he had reached China, when he was in fact in Cuba?

Why admire a man who was searching for gold and tolerant of slavery? In Mexico and Peru, Indians call this a day of darkness. They blame the Spanish conquistadors who followed Columbus to the Americas for destroying their culture. In an age of contrition, when world leaders apologize for their nations' sins, should we apologize for Christopher Columbus? In 1998, how can students face reality yet admire the man who first sailed from Europe to the New World?

Students should know that Columbus did not discover America by himself. Thousands of sailors before him had inched down the African coast and out into the Atlantic. He was enlightened by mapmakers in Florence and Lisbon. The printing press made available the books he read in monasteries. New instruments, the astrolabe and the compass, helped him find his way. Improved ships kept him afloat. And his motives were complex. Columbus was seeking adventure, glory, and wealth. At the same time, he believed he was doing God's work. With his Bible, he could convert the citizens of China and Japan. Columbus was from far from perfect. He demanded 10 percent of the profits for himself and titles of nobility he could pass on to his children. Brilliant as a navigator, he failed as a colonizer. Most regretfully, he came to see the Caribbean Indians not as fellow humans but as workers to be exploited, as sources of gold. While smallpox and swine fever inadvertently introduced by the sailors killed far more Caribbean Indians than did Spanish bullets, Columbus' acceptance of slavery also contributed to the destruction of a people. Further, there were Spaniards who, unlike Columbus, transcended their time and abjured slavery. Bartolome de Las Casas, settled in Hispaniola and became a landowner. He treated the Indians kindly but still profited from their labor. In 1512 he became a Dominican priest. Two years later, in a famous sermon, he announced that he was returning his serfs to the governor of Hispaniola.

Thus commenced his 40-year campaign against the cruelty of Spanish colonizers. Las Casas traveled to Spain and harangued the government. In his books and articles, he demanded that the Spaniards return Indian land and end forced labor. By the end of his life, he also proclaimed a revolutionary idea: the equality of all human races.

Columbus was not a humanitarian. Still, while others talked about sailing west to new lands, he did it. Through a combination of intuition, faith, scholarship and reason, he believed he could sail to the Indies. Rebuffed by the king of Portugal, he traveled to Spain where he pleaded his case for six years. Spain was skeptical. He turned toward France. At the last minute, Ferdinand and Isabella, fearing France might acquire colonies before Spain, financed three ships.

It took courage to sail into the unknown. It required faith to keep going when his crew lost hope and wanted to turn back. Above all, it took extraordinary navigational skills to keep three clumsy ships on course. In the fifteenth century, ships could languish for days, be blown off course, sink without a trace.

Columbus had a mastery of winds and currents. He could predict hurricanes and navigate at night.

Today, with all continents traveled, all mountains climbed, all oceans mapped, it is easy to underestimate the boldness and bravery of an explorer. Accustomed to motorized ships, we take for granted the skill of a sailor. In comfortable times, we forget the misery Columbus endured in his years at sea: the moldy hardtack, rancid wine, rats, lice and dysentery; the arthritis that slowly crippled and killed him.

Columbus discovered land where no European knew it existed. His voyage opened a century of exploration and led to the creation of the American colonies. It also produced a beneficial exchange easily overlooked: From the New World came corn and potatoes that fended off hunger for millions of people in Africa and Europe. . . .

In the 19th century classroom, history was patriotic, heroes were perfect. Today we want to educate our students in the complexity of history without extinguishing their idealism.

We must admit that Columbus lacked the sense of justice and charity that made Las Casas a moral hero, but we need not apologize for a brave explorer whose voyage transformed the world. We can recognize Columbus as a visionary, a sailor of uncomparable skill and a hero of exploration.

⚺ Questioning the Past

1. Paolo Emilio Taviani stated that the "Columbian discovery was of greater magnitude than any other discovery or invention in human history." Offer arguments in support of this assertion. Offer arguments in refutation of it. Which set of arguments is more persuasive?

2. What were the positive and the negative repercussions of the voyages of Columbus to America?

3. What evidence could be used to prove that Columbus is one of the great heroes of history? What evidence can be offered to show that Columbus is one of history's worst villains? How should Columbus be remembered?

Chapter 3

The Requirement

Gonzalo Fernandez de Oviedo Makes the First Attempt to Read the Requerimiento *June 14, 1514*

Pedrarias de Avila was not known as a patient man. Arbitrary, tough, suspicious, fiery, intimidating—these were words appropriate for Pedrarias. In July of 1513, Pedrarias had been appointed by the king of Spain to be the governor of Darien, a rich region encompassing the present state of Panama. Yet for the better part of a year he waited in Seville for permission to launch his expedition to America. What delayed his departure was nothing more than a question: By what right and under what conditions could the Spanish conquer and exploit the lands and treasures belonging to the peoples of the New World? The best legal, religious, and philosophical minds in Spain were in conference developing an answer at the San Pablo monastery at Valladolid, Spain. The outcome was a remarkable document called "El Requerimiento." Henceforth, all Spanish adventurers would be required to read this document to the indigenous peoples of America before making claims on the Indians or their property.

❧ *First Impressions*

"In Order that They May Be Saved"

The Spanish were the first of the European nations to confront justifying their New World conquests, but in time the Portuguese, Dutch, French, Swedes, and English would have to face it, too. They wanted to spread the faith of Christianity, as well as gain wealth and power from their ventures in America. But what they wanted often belonged to someone else.

Source 1   *El Requerimiento*, drafted primarily by lawyer Palacios Rubios, 1514

I, (Name of Spanish official), servant of the most high and powerful kings of Castile and Leon, the conquerors of barbarous nations, their messenger and captain, notify to you, and declare in as ample form as I am capable, that God our Lord, who is one and eternal, created the heaven and the earth, and one man and one woman, of whom you and we, and all the men who have been or shall be in the world are descended. But as it has come to pass through the generations during more than five thousand years, that they have been dispersed into different parts of the world, and are divided into various kingdoms and provinces, because one country was not able to contain them, nor could they have found in one the means of subsistence and preservation: therefore God our Lord gave the charge of all those people to one man named St. Peter, whom he constituted the lord and head of all the human race, that all men, in whatever place they are born, or in whatever faith or place they are educated, might yield obedience unto him. He hath subjected the whole world to his jurisdiction, and commanded him to establish his residence in Rome, as the most proper place for the government of the world. He likewise promised and gave him power to establish his authority in every other part of the world, and to judge and govern all Christians, Moors, Jews, Gentiles, and all other people of whatever sect or faith they may be. To him is given the name of *Pope*, which signifies admirable, great father and guardian, because he is the father and governor of all men. Those who lived in the time of this holy father obeyed and acknowledged him as their Lord and King, and the superior of the universe. The same has been observed with respect to them who, since his time, have been chosen to the pontificate. Thus it now continues, and will continue to the end of the world.

One of those Pontiffs, as lord of the world, hath made a grant of these islands, and of the Tierra Firme of the ocean sea, to the Catholic Kings of Castile, Don Ferdinand and Donna Isabella, of glorious memory, and their successors, our sovereigns, with all they contain, as is more fully expressed in certain deeds passed upon that occasion, which you may see if you desire it. Thus His Majesty is King and lord of these islands, and of the continent, in virtue of this donation; and, as King and lord aforesaid, most of the islands to which this title hath been notified, have recognised His Majesty, and now yield obedience and subjection to him as their lord, voluntarily and without resistance; and instantly, as soon as they received information, they obeyed the religious men sent by the King to preach to them, and to instruct them in our holy faith; and all these, of their own free will, without any recompense or gratuity, became Christians, and continue to be so; and His Majesty having received them graciously under his protection, has commanded that they should be treated in the same manner as his other subjects and vassals. You are bound and obliged to act in the same manner. Therefore I now entreat and require you to consider attentively what I have declared to you; and that you may more perfectly comprehend it, that you take such time as is reasonable in order that you may acknowledge the Church as the superior and guide of the universe, and likewise the holy father called the Pope, in his own right, and his Majesty, by his appointment, as King and sovereign lord of these Islands, and of the Tierra Firme; and that you consent that the aforesaid holy fathers shall declare and preach to you the doctrines above mentioned. If you do this, you act well, and perform that to which you are bound and obliged; and His Majesty, and I in his name, will receive you with love and kindness, and relieve you, your wives and children, free and exempt from servitude, and in the enjoyment of all you possess, in the same manner as the inhabitants of the islands. Besides this, His Majesty will bestow upon you many privileges, exemptions, and rewards. But if you will not comply, or maliciously delay to obey my injunction, then, with the help of God, I will enter your country by force, I will carry on war against you with the utmost violence, I will subject you to the yoke of obedience to the church and king, I will take your wives and children, and will make them slaves, and sell or dispose of them according to His Majesty's pleasure; I will seize your goods, and do you all the mischief in my power, as rebellious subjects, who will not acknowledge or submit to their lawful sovereign. And I protest that all the bloodshed and calamities which shall follow are to be imputed to you, and not to His Majesty, or to me, or the gentlemen who serve under me; and as I have now made this declaration and requisition unto you, I require the notary here present to grant me a certificate of this, subscribed in proper form.

"These Indians Will Not Listen"

Finally, on April 12, 1514, Pedrarias set sail. He carried with him a force of 1,500 conquistadors and a small container, which encased a copy of the Requerimiento. Pedrarias wasted no time once he arrived in the New World. He immediately dispatched a scholar named Gonzalo Fernandez de Oviedo with 300 soldiers to read the Requerimiento to the Native Americans who lived adjacent to the bay of Santa Martha, in what is now Colombia. The Indians of the area had become aware of the Spanish from previous intrusions upon their hospitality and had no interest in greeting Oviedo's party when it came ashore. Consequently, on June 14, 1514, when Oviedo stepped from his launch onto the beach and unfolded the document, he found himself without an audience. Oviedo and his military escort marched deeper inland. The Indians along their path vanished from sight ahead of them. Never were the Spaniards close enough to even see the natives, much less read them the Requeriemiento. Meanwhile, Governor Pedrarias was growing increasingly agitated over the delay. He came ashore himself with an additional 1,000 soldiers and met up with Oviedo in a just-deserted Indian village. The governor confronted Oviedo about the delay. Oviedo, likewise frustrated, handed the Requerimiento back to the governor with this advice: "My Lords, it appears to me that these Indians will not listen to the theology of this requirement, and that you have no one who can make them understand it: would Your Honor be pleased to keep it until we have some one of these Indians in a cage, in order that he may learn it at his leisure and my Lord Bishop may explain it to him." The governor took the advice in the manner Oviedo intended: he and all around him broke into laughter. It was a concession to the absurdity of the Requerimiento.

Source 2   Treatise of Dominican Friar Matias de Paz, professor of theology at the University of Salamanca, 1512

"Concerning the Rule of the King of Spain over the Indies"

1. **Whether Our Most Christian King may govern these Indians despotically or tyrannically.**

Answer: It is not just for Christian Princes to make war on infidels because of a desire to dominate or for their wealth, but only to spread the faith. Therefore, if the inhabitants of those lands never before Christianized wish to listen to and receive the faith, Christian Princes may not invade their territory. . . .

2. Whether the King may exercise over them political dominion.

Answer: If an invitation to accept Christianity has not been made, the infidels may justly defend themselves even though the King, moved by Christian zeal and supported by papal authority, has waged just war. Such infidels may not be held as slaves unless they pertinaciously deny obedience to the prince or refuse to accept Christianity.

Source 3 Account of lawyer and conquistador Martin Fernandez de Enciso, 1513

Moses sent Joshua to require the inhabitants of Jericho, the first city in the promised land of Canaan, to abandon their city because it belonged to the people of Israel inasmuch as God had given it to them; and when the people of Jericho did not give up their land Joshua surrounded them and killed them all. . . . And afterwards Joshua conquered all the land of Canaan by force of arms, and many were killed and those who were captured were given as slaves and served the people of Israel. And all this was done by the will of God because they were **idolaters**.

[Therefore,] the king might very justly send men to require those idolatrous Indians to hand over their land to him, for it was given him by the pope. If the Indians would not do this, he might justly wage war against them, kill them and enslave those captured in war, precisely as Joshua treated the inhabitants of the land of Canaan.

3.1 The Internet Modern History Sourcebook: Colonial Latin America

Source 4 Description of scholar Gonzalo Fernandez de Oviedo, ca. 1514

It appears that . . . [the Indians] had been suddenly pounced upon and bound before they had learnt or understood anything about Pope or Church, or any one of the many things said in the Requirement; and that after being put in chains some one read the Requisition without knowing their language and without any interpreter, without either reader or Indians understanding what was read. And after this had been explained to them by some one understanding their language, they had no chance to reply, being immediately carried away prisoners, the Spaniards not failing to use the stick on those who did not go fast enough.

Source 5 Account of Atahuallpa, ruler of the Inca, 1532

I will be no man's tributary. I am greater than any prince upon earth. Your emperor may be a great prince; I do not doubt it, when I see that he has sent his subjects so far across the waters; and I am willing to hold him as a brother. As for this Pope of whom you speak, he must be crazy to talk of giving away countries which do not belong to him. For my faith, I will not change it. Your own God, as you say, was put to death by the very men whom he created. But mine, my God still lives in the heavens, and looks down on his children.

3.2 History of the Inca Empire

Source 6   Account of scholar Juan Ginas de Sepulveda, 1547

Compare . . . those blessings enjoyed by Spaniards of prudence, genius, magnanimity, temperance, and religion with those of the little men (hombrecillos) in whom you will scarcely find even vestiges of humanity, who not only possess no science but who also lack letters and preserve no monument of their history except certain vague and obscure reminiscences of some things on certain paintings. Neither do they have written laws, but barbaric institutions and customs. They do not even have private property.

How can we doubt that these people—so uncivilized, so barbaric, contaminated with so many impieties and obscenities—have been justly conquered by such an excellent, pious, and most just king as was Ferdinand the Catholic and is now Emperor Charles, and by such a most humane nation and excellent in every kind of virtue?

Source 7   Bishop Bartolomé de Las Casas, *Coleccion de Tratados,* 1552–1553

The aim which Christ and the Pope seek and ought to seek in the Indies—and which the Christian Kings of Castile should likewise strive for—is that the natives of these regions shall hear the faith preached in order that they may be saved. And the means to effect this end are not to rob, to scandalize, to capture or destroy them, or to lay waste their lands, for this would cause the infidels to abominate our faith.

📖 *Second Thoughts*
"Folly of Human Nature"

Historians and scholars from the late eighteenth century to present times have viewed the Requerimiento with apology, scorn, and comicality. The sources following trace the evolution of critical thinking on the document's justification of conquest.

Source 8   William Robertson, *The History of the Discovery and Settlement of America,* 1788

In order to give their title to those countries some appearance of validity, several of the most eminent divines and lawyers in Spain were employed to prescribe the mode in which they should take possession of them. There is not in the history of mankind anything more singular or extravagant than the form which they devised for this purpose. . . .

As the inhabitants of the continent could not at once yield assent to doctrines too refined for their uncultured understandings, and explained to them by interpreters imperfectly acquainted with their language; as they did not conceive how a foreign priest, of whom they had never heard, could have any right to dispose of their country, or how an unknown prince should claim jurisdiction over them as his subjects; they fiercely opposed the new invaders of their territories.

Source 9   William H. Prescott, *History of the Conquest of Mexico,* 1843

But, to judge the action fairly, we must transport ourselves to the age when it happened. The difficulty that meets us at the outset is, to find a justification of the right of conquest, at all. But it should be remembered, that religious infidelity, at this period, and till much later, was regarded—no matter whether founded on ignorance or education, whether hereditary or acquired, heretical or Pagan— as a sin to be punished with **fire and faggot** in this world, and eternal suffering in the next. This doctrine, monstrous as it is, was the creed of the Romish, in other words, of the Christian Church—the basis of the Inquisition, and of those other species of religious persecution, which have stained the annals, at some time or other, of nearly every nation in Christendom. Under this code, the territory of the heathen, wherever found, was regarded as a sort of religious waif, which, in default of a legal proprietor, was claimed and taken possession of by the Holy See, and as such was freely given away by the head of the Church, to any temporal potentate whom he pleased, that would assume the burden of conquest. Thus, Alexander the Sixth generously granted a large portion of the Western hemisphere to the Spanish, and of the Eastern to the Portuguese. These lofty pretensions of the successor of the humble fisherman of Galilee, far from being nominal, were acknowledged and appealed to as conclusive in controversies between nations.

   With the right of conquest, thus conferred, came, also, the obligation, on which it may be said to have been founded, to retrieve the nations sitting in darkness from eternal perdition. This obligation was acknowledged by the best and the bravest, the gownsman in his closet, the missionary, and the warrior in the crusade. However much of it may have been debased by temporal motives and mixed up with worldly considerations of ambition and avarice, it was still active in the mind of the Christian conqueror. . . . The concession of the Pope, then, founded on, and enforcing, the imperative duty of conversion, was the assumed basis—and, in the apprehension of the age, a sound one—of the right of conquest. . . .

   The ground on which Protestant nations asserted a natural right to the fruits of their discoveries in the New World is very different. They consider that the earth was intended for cultivation; and that Providence never designed that hordes of wandering savages should hold a territory far more than necessary for their own maintenance, to the exclusion of civilized man.

Source 10   Sir Arthur Helps, *The Spanish Conquest in America,* 1900

I must confess that the comicality of the document has often cheered me in the midst of tedious research. . . . The logic, the history, even the grammatical construction, are all, as it seems to me, alike in error. Stupendous assumptions are the staple of the document; and the very terms "Church," "privileges," "vassalage," "exemptions," are such as require a knowledge of Christianity and of the peculiar civilization of Europe for any one to understand. Then, when it is

3.3 Diplomacy
and War
in Spanish
Relations with
the New World

imagined how little these difficulties would be smoothed by translation, we may fancy what ideas the reading of the document . . . conveyed to a number of Indians sitting in a circle, and listening to European voices for the first time. . . . If our own age did not abound in things as remote from all commonsense as this Requisition (Requerimiento), we should wonder how such a folly could ever have been put forward, or even acquiesced in, by persons of such intelligence as those who surrounded the Spanish court.

Source 11 Lewis Hanke, *The Spanish Struggle for Justice in the Conquest of America,* 1949

A complete list of the events that occurred when the Requirement formalities ordered by King Ferdinand were carried out in America . . . might tax the reader's patience and credulity, for the Requirement was read to trees and empty huts when no Indians were to be found. Captains muttered its theological phrases into their beards on the edge of sleeping Indian settlements, or even a league away before starting the formal attack, and at times some leather-lunged Spanish notary hurled its sonorous phrases after the Indians as they fled into the mountains. Once it was read in camp before the soldiers to the beat of the drum. Ship captains would sometimes have the document read from the deck as they approached an island, and at night would send out enslaving expeditions, whose leaders would shout the traditional Castilian war cry "Santiago!" rather than read the Requirement before they attacked the nearby villages. . . .

Ever since this Requirement was made part of the baggage that every conquistador was expected to carry with him to America various and divergent interpretations have been placed upon it. Foreign critics naturally seized upon it to illustrate what they considered the hypocrisy of sixteenth-century Spaniards. The eighteenth century rationalist philosophers saw in the Requirement another piece of evidence of the all-pervading folly of human nature.

Modern historians have usually treated it in a derisive or ironical spirit, have condemned it for one reason or another, and have substantially agreed with Lewis Bertrand and Sir Charles Petrie, who state that " . . . the invaders brandished bulls and theological texts, a whole rubbish heap of documents, by way of justifying their invasions. . . ."

Apologists or semiapologists, however, are to be found even today. Constantino Bayle, the Spanish Jesuit who has been vigorously combatting the black legend, declares: "What was wrong with the Requirement was that it was intended for men, but read to half-beasts."

Source 12 Gerhard von Glahn, *Law among Nations,* 1986

Discovery is the oldest and, historically, the most important method of acquiring title to territory. Up to the eighteenth century, discovery alone sufficed to establish a legal title, but since then such discovery has had to be followed by an effective occupation in order to be recognized as the basis of a title to territory. The history of Spanish exploration abounds with the landing of explorers in new territories and the establishment of claims to title by a proclamation of annexation, coupled with the performance of such symbolic acts as the burying of inscribed lead or brass tablets.

The doctrine of the sufficiency of mere discovery to establish a valid title was asserted as late as 1823 by Chief Justice John Marshall in *Johnson and Graham's Lessee v. M'Intosh* (Supreme Court of the United States, 1823, 8 Wheaton 543), but the learned judge did qualify his dictum by adding that the "title might be consummated by possession."

✒ Questioning the Past

1. Why did the Spaniards feel a need to develop and use a document such as the Requerimiento?

2. In the context of the sixteenth century, why would the Spanish Crown have believed the Requerimiento gave justification to its actions?

3. Present the arguments that might support the claim of one people to a right, or even a duty, to rule another. Argue, as well, the case for a claim to control land and territory based on the right of discovery, or on a right derived from conquest, or a right based on a religious or humanitarian rationale. Present the arguments in opposition to such claims. Which arguments seem the more valid? Why?

Jamestown

Jamestown Reaches a Turning Point *July 30, 1619*

It was not easy for the English to establish a foothold on the North American continent. Between 1578 and 1583, Sir Humphrey Gilbert made two unsuccessful voyages with groups of colonists, losing his life during the second return trip to England. Two years later, 100 men landed on Roanoke Island off the Carolina coast, but after only a season, they sailed back to England. New colonists were dropped off on Roanoke Island in 1587, and four years passed before a supply ship called on the English outpost at Roanoke again. By that time the settlers had vanished, leaving just one clue: someone had carved CROATAN on a post. What this message meant is a mystery even today. In 1606, King James I issued charters to two groups of English merchants—one in London and the other at Plymouth—granting them permission to colonize areas of North America. A Plymouth Company party that attempted to settle at the mouth of the Kennebec River in what is now Maine gave up within a year. The London Company outfitted three ships for a voyage to America, which arrived at an island in the James River, some 60 miles inland from the mouth of the Chesapeake Bay, on May 14, 1607. Their voyage had been difficult, but worse hardships lay before these colonists than those behind them. Of the 105 who landed, only 38 survived the first winter. They were reinforced by 200 more colonists who arrived in 1608, and by an additional 400 a year later. But their foothold at the edge of the forest was still tenuous. After the winter of 1609–10, which they called the "starving time," their numbers had fallen to 60.

✎ *First Impressions*

"The Most Happy People in the World"

4.1 Jamestown
Rediscovery

Miraculously, the Jamestown colony clung to life. Tobacco gave it a reason to live, and Native Americans and the London Company gave it the means. By 1617 new settlements had spread beyond Jamestown, swelling the English population of Virginia to over 1,000. In two years the number of immigrants had doubled, and other events of that time gave still more evidence that this New World colony would achieve permanence.

Source 1   John Pory, secretary of estate, to Sir Dudley Carleton

Virginia, September 30, 1619

At my first coming hither the solitary uncouthness of this place, compared with those partes of Christendome or Turky where I had bene: and likewise my being sequestred from all occurrents and passages which are so rife there, did not a little vexe me. And yet in these five moneths of my continuance here, there have come at one time or another eleven saile of ships into this river; being fraighted more with ignorance, then with any other marchandize. At length being hardned to this custome of abstinence from curiosity, I am resolved wholly to minde my busines here, and nexte after my penne, to have some good book always in store, being in solitude the best and choicest company. Besides, among these Christall rivers and oderiferous woods I doe escape muche expense, envye, contempte, vanity, and vexation of minds.

Source 2   Notes of John Rolfe, Jamestown resident, 1619

The 25. of June came in the *Triall* with Corne and Cattell all in safety, which tooke from us cleerly all feare of famine; then our governour and councell caused Burgesses to be chosen in all places, and met at a generall Assembly, where all matters were debated thought expedient for the good of the Colony, and Captaine Ward was sent to . . . new England, to fish in May, and returned the latter end of May, but to small purpose, for they wanted Salt: the *George* also was sent to New-found-land . . . , there she bought fish . . . and made a good voyage in seven weekes. About the last of August came in a dutch man of warre that sold us twenty Negars, and Iapazous King of Patawomeck, came to James towne, to desire two ships to come trade in his River, for a more plentifull yeere of Corne had not been in a long time. . . . Now you are to understand, that because there have beene many complaints against the Governors, Captaines, and Officers in Virginia, for buying and selling men and boies, that the very report thereof brought great scandall to the generall action. The Councell in England did send many good and worthy instructions for the amending those abuses which good law I pray God it be well observed, and then we may truly say in Virginia, we are the most happy people in the world.

4.2 John Rolfe
Tries a Tobacco
Crop

Source 3   Captain John Smith's report of 1619, *Generall Historie of Virginia,* 1624

There went this yeere by the Companies records, 11. ships and 1216. persons to be thus disposed on: Tenants for the Governors land fourscore, besides fifty sent the former spring; for the Companies land a hundred and thirty, for the College a hundred, for the **Glebe land** fifty, young women to make wives ninety, servants for publike service fifty, and fifty more whose labours were to bring up thirty of the infidels children, the rest were sent to private Plantations.

A State of Temporary Slavery

On July 30, 1619, the governor of Virginia and delegates from all 10 settlements opened the New World's first European legislative assembly in Jamestown. The rules and regulations they drafted for colonial government were the first signs that the settlers would increasingly rely on themselves rather than their mother country for solutions to their problems. Foremost among the problems the Virginia Assembly faced was a shortage of labor. Accordingly, the members outlawed idleness and created a system of servitude. Those who chose to emigrate to America would contract to serve upon arrival as temporary slaves to finance their passages. Ultimately, half to three-fourths of the Europeans who would come to the colonies south of New England did so under the terms set down by the assembly. These terms were later adapted for transporting women to the New World to become wives of the colonists. But for Africans, these rules of temporary servitude would evolve into the rules of perpetual servitude.

Source 4   **Proceedings of the Virginia Assembly, 1619**

First, Sir George Yeardley, Knight, Governor and Captaine general of Virginia, having sent his sumons all over the Country, as well to invite those of the Counsell of Estate that were absent as also for the election of **Burgesses**, [the Burgesses] were chosen and appeared. . . .

4.3 Virtual
Jamestowne

The most convenient place we could finde to sitt in was the Quire of the Churche Where Sir George Yeardley, the Governor, being sett downe in his accustomed place, those of the Counsell of Estate sate next him on both hands excepte onely the Secretary, then appointed Speaker, who sate right before him, John Twine, clerke of the General assembly, being placed nexte the Speaker, and Thomas Pierse, the Sargeant, standing at the barre, to be ready for any service the Assembly shoulde comaund him. But forasmuch as men's affairs doe little prosper where God's service is neglected, all the Burgesses tooke their places in the Quire till a prayer was said. . . . Prayer being ended, to the intente that as we had begun at God Almighty, so we must proceed with awful and due respecte towards the Lieutenant, our most gratious and dread Soveraigne, all the Burgesses were intreatted to retyre themselves into the body of the Churche, which being done, before they were fully admitted, they were called in order and by name, and so every man (none staggering at it) tooke the oathe of Supremacy, and entred the Assembly. . . .

Monday, Aug. 2nd.

Here begin the lawes drawn out of the Instructions given by his Majesties Counsell of Virginia in England. . . .

By this present General Assembly be it enacted that no injury or oppression be wrought by the English against the Indians whereby the present peace might be disturbed and antient quarrells might be revived. . . .

Against Idlenes, Gaming, drunkenes and excesse in apparell the Assembly hath enacted as followth:

First, in detestation of Idlenes be it enacted, that if any man be founde to be an Idler . . . it shalbe lawful for that Incorporation or Plantation to which he belongeth to appoint him a Mr to serve for wages, till he shewe apparant signes of amendment.

Against gaming at dice and Cardes be it ordained by this present assembly that the winner or winners shall lose all his or their winninges and both winners and loosers shall forfaite ten shillings a man, one ten shillings whereof to go to the discoverer, and the rest to charitable and pious uses. . . .

Against drunkenness be it also decreed that if any private person be found culpable thereof, for the first time he is to be reprooved privately by the Minister, the second time publiquely, the third time to lye in boltes 12 howers in the House of the Provost Marshall and to paye his fee, and if he still continue in that vice, to undergo suche severe punishment as the Governor and Counsell of Estate shall think fitt to be inflicted on him. . . .

Against excess in apparell that every man be cessed in the Church for all publique contributions, if he be unmarried according to his owne apparell, if he be married, according to his owne and his wives, or either of their apparell. . . .

As touching the busines of planting corne this present Assembly doth ordain that year by year all and every householder and householders have in store for every servant he or she shall keep, and also for his or their owne persons, whether they have any Servants or no, one spare barrell of corne, to be delivered out yearly, either upon sale or exchange as need shall require. For the neglecte of which duty he shalbe subjecte to the censure of the Governor and Counsell of Estate. . . .

Be it further ordained by this General Assembly, and we doe by these presents enacte, that all contractes made in England between the owners of the lande and their Tenants and Servants which they shall send hither, may be caused to be duly performed. . . .

Be it established also by this present Assembly that no crafty or advantagious means be suffered to be put in practise for the inticing awaye the Tenants or Servants of any particular plantation from the place where they are seatted. And that it shalbe the duty of the Governor and the Counsell of Estate most severely to punish both the seducers and the seduced, and to returne these latter into their former places. . . .

Wednesday, August 4, 1619

This daye (by reason of extreme heat, both paste and likely to ensue and by that meanes of the alteration of the healthes of diverse of the general Assembly) the Governour, who himself also was not well, resolved should be the last of this first session; so in the morning the Speaker redd over all the laws and orders that had formerly passed the house. . . . This being done, the third sorte of lawes . . . were . . . thoroughly discussed, which, together with the former, did nowe passe the laste and finall consente of the General Assembly.

A thirde sorte of lawes, such as may issue out of every man's private conceipte.

It shalbe free for every man to trade with the Indians, servants onely excepted, upon paine of whipping.

That no man doe sell or give any of the greatter howes to the Indians, or any English dog of quality, as a mastive, greyhound, bloodhound, lande or water spaniel, or any other dog or bitche whatsoever, of the Englishe race, upon pain of forfaiting 5s sterling to the publique uses. . . .

That no man do sell or give any Indians any piece shott or **poulder**, or any other armes, offensive or defensive upon paine of being held a Traytour to the Colony, and of being hanged as soon as the facte is proved. . . .

That no man living in this Colony, but shall between this and the first of January nexte ensueing come or sende to the Secretary of Estate to enter his own and all his servants' names, and for what terme or upon what conditions they are to serve. . . . Also, whatsoever Misters or people doe come over to this plantation that within one month of their arrivall they shall likewise resorte to the Secretary of Estate and shall certifie him upon what termes or conditions they come hither, to the ende that he may record their grauntes and comissions, and for how long and upon what conditions their servants (in case they have any) are to serve them. . . .

The Ministers and Churchwardens shall seeke to presente all ungodly disorders, the comitters wherofe if, upon goode admonitions and milde reprooff, they will not forbeare the said skandalous offenses, as suspicions of whordomes, dishonest company keeping with woemen and suche like, they are to be presented and punished accordingly. . . .

For the reformation of swearing, every freeman after thrise admonition shall give 5s . . . to the use of the church where he dwelleth; and every servant after the like admonition, except his Mr discharge the fine, shalbe subject to whipping. . . .

All persons whatsoever upon the Sabaoth daye shall frequente divine service and sermons both forenoon and afternoon, and all suche as beare armes shall bring their pieces swordes, poulder and shotte. . . .

No maid or woman servant, either now resident in the Colonie or hereafter to come, shall contract herselfe in marriage without either the consent of her parents, or of her Mr or **Mris**, or of the magistrate and minister of the place both together. And whatsoever minister shall marry or contracte any suche persones without some of the foresaid consentes shalbe subject to the severe censure of the Governor and Counsell of Estate.

Be it enacted by this present assembly that whatsoever servant hath heretofore or shall hereafter contracte himself in England, either by Indenture or otherwise, to serve any Master here in Virginia, and shall afterward, against his said former contracte depart from his Mr without leave, or, being once imbarked shall abandon the ship he is appointed to come in, and so, being lefte behinde, shall putt himselfe into the service of any ather man that will bring him hither, that then at the same servant's arrival here, he shall first serve out his time with that Mr that brought him hither and afterward also shall serve out his time with his former Mr according to his covenant. . . .

Here ende the lawes.

[T]he General Assembly doth humbly beseech the . . . Treasurer, Counsell and Company, that albeit it belongeth to them onely to allow or to abrogate any laws which we shall make here, and that it is their right so to doe, yet that it would please them not to take it in ill parte if these lawes which we have now brought to light, do passe currant and be of force till suche time as we knowe their farther pleasure out of Englande: for otherwise this people would in shorte time growe so insolent, as they would shake off all government, and there would be no living among them. . . .

In sume Sir George Yeardley, the Governour prorogued the said General Assembly till the firste of Marche . . . and in the mean season dissolved the same.

John Pory, Secretary and Speaker

Source 5   Remarks of Sir Edwin Sandys, *Records of the Virginia Company*

November 3, 1619. Lastly he wished that a fitt hundreth might be sent of woemen, Maids young and uncorrupt to make wifes to the Inhabitants and by that meanes to make the men there more setled and less moveable. . . . These woemen if they marry to the public ffarmors, to be transported at the charges of the Companie; if otherwise, then those that takes them to wife to pay the said Company their charges of transportation, and it was never fitter time to send them then nowe. Corne being here at home soe cheape and plentifull, and great promises there for the Harvest ensuing. He also shewed . . . the Inhabitants having had great joy by the Charters of Graunts and Liberties lately sent. . . .

November 19, 1619. And because he understood that the people thither transported, though seated there in their persons for some fewe yeares, are not setled in their mindes to make it their place of rest and continuance, but having gotten some wealth there, to return to England: ffor the remedying of that mischiefe, and establishing of a perpetuitie to the Plantation, he advised and made it his Third Proposition, to send them over One hundreth young Maides to become wifes; that wifes, children and familie might make them less moveable and settle them, together with their Posteritie in that soile.

Source 6   *Records of the Virginia Company,* November 21, 1621

The Third Roll was for sendinge of Mayd to Virginia to be made Wyves, which the Planters there did verie much desire by the want of whome have sprange the greatest hinderances of the encrease of the Plantacon, in that most of them esteeminge Virginia not as a place of Habitacon but onely of a short sojourninge have applyed themselves and their labors wholly to the raisinge of present proffitt and utterly neglected not only staple Comodities but even the verie necessities of mans life, in reguard whereof and to prevent so great an inconvenience hereafter whereby the Planters minds may be the faster tyed to Virginia by the bonds of Wyves and Children, care hath bin taken to provide them younge handsome and honestly educated mayds whereof 60 are already sent to Virginia being such as were specially recomended unto the Companie for their good bringinge up by their parents or friends of good worth: Which mayds are to be disposed in marriage to the most honest and industrious Planters who are to defraye and satisfie to the Adventurers the charges of their passages and provisions at such rate as they and the Adventurers Agents there shall agree and in case they faile through mortality it is ordered that a proportionable addicon shalbe made upon the rest.

📖 *Second Thoughts*

When the Ethiopian and Caucasian Races Met in Equal Numbers, Who Could Foretell the Issue?

The Virginia Assembly's laws regarding immigrant Englishmen were later adapted to cover both women and Africans. The influence of their decisions on the histories of these two groups of Americans has occupied historians and other scholars ever since.

Source 7   William Robertson, *The History of the Discovery and Settlement of America,* 1788

[A]nd by two events, which happened nearly at the same time, both population and industry were greatly promoted. As few women had hitherto ventured to encounter the hardships which were unavoidable in an unknown and uncultivated country, most of the colonists, constrained to live single, considered themselves as no more than sojourners in a land to which they were not attached. . . . . In order to induce them to settle there, the company took advantage of the apparent tranquility in the country, to send out a considerable number of young women of humble birth indeed, but of exceptional character, and encouraged the planters, by premiums and immunities, to marry them. These new companions were received with such fondness, and many of them so comfortably established, as invited others to follow their example; and by degrees, thoughtless adventurers, assuming the sentiments of virtuous citizens and of provident fathers of families, became solicitous about the prosperity of a country which they now considered as their own. As the colonists began to form more extensive plans of industry, they were unexpectedly furnished with means of executing them with greater facility. A Dutch ship from the coast of Guinea, having sailed up James River, sold a part of her cargo of Negroes to the planters; and as that hardy race was found more capable of enduring fatigue under a sultry climate than Europeans, their number has been increased by continual importation; their aid now seems essential to the existence of the colony, and the greater part of field labour in Virginia is performed by servile hands.

Source 8   George Bancroft, *History of the United States of America,* 1888

The inauguration of legislative power in the Ancient Dominion preceded the introduction of negro slavery. . . . A perpetual interest attaches to this first elective body that ever assembled in the western world, representing the people of Virginia, and making laws for their government, more than a year before the Mayflower, with the pilgrims, left the harbor of Southampton, and while Virginia was still the only British colony on the continent of America. . . . The enactments of these earliest American law-givers were instantly put in force, without waiting for their ratification by the company in England. Former griefs were buried in oblivion, and they who had been dependent upon the will of a governor, having recovered the privileges of Englishmen, under a code of laws of their own, "fell to building houses and planting corn," and henceforward "regarded Virginia as their country." . . .

While Virginia, by the concession of a representative government, was constituted the asylum of liberty, it became the abode of hereditary bondsmen. . . . In the month of August, 1619, . . . a Dutch man-of-war entered James river and landed twenty negroes for sale. . . . Had no other form of servitude been known in Virginia than of men of the same race, every difficulty would have been promptly obviated. But the Ethiopian and Caucasian races were to meet together in nearly equal numbers beneath a temperate zone. Who could foretell the issue? The negro race, from its introduction, was regarded with disgust, and its union with the whites forbidden under ignominious penalties.

Source 9   John Fiske, *Old Virginia and Her Neighbors,* 1897

This gift of free government to England's first colony was the work of the London Company—or, as it was now in London much more often called, the Virginia Company. . . . That great corporation was soon to perish, but its boon to Virginia and to American liberty was to be abiding. . . . [T]he first introduction of negro slaves into Virginia . . . came just after the sitting of the first free legislature, and thus furnished posterity with a theme for moralizing. . . . The same year, 1619, which witnessed the introduction of slaves and a House of Burgesses, saw also the arrival of a shipload of young women—spinsters carefully selected and matronized—sent out by the Company in quest of husbands. In Virginia, as in most new colonies, women were greatly in the minority, and the wise Sir Edwin Sandys understood that without homes and family ties a civilized community must quickly retrograde into barbarism.

Source 10   Ernest R. Groves, *The American Woman,* 1944

If we ask, How did settlements prosper when they were made without women? we discover the indispensableness of woman's part. For example, when with the second supply ship two white women, Mrs. Forest and Anne Buras, her maid, were introduced to the Jamestown colony, we have the beginning of a stability that never could have come about if the colony had remained an exclusively male settlement. There had to be at the foundation of colonial success not only domestic life but also the contribution which was characteristically feminine. Men could make and write the history, but only as women played their part in establishing the civilization that grew up in the New World. In 1618 we find the company promoting the Virginia settlement shipping a hundred apprentices and servants and a hundred "maids young and uncorrupt to make wives to the inhabitants and by that means to make the men more settled and less moveable." This does not mean merely that women were needed to prevent the restlessness and discontent that were sure to undermine the settlements, but also that the work of women—their industrial as well as their domestic contribution—was required if the colony was to have any hope of permanency and prosperity. . . .

Experience soon demonstrated that lack of women in the Virginia colony led the men to the disposition to regard their staying as merely temporary, a hardship endured with the hope of soon gathering wealth and then returning to the mother country. . . .

The first installment of women brought to Virginia . . . appears to have been, with two exceptions, persons of "proper character." Although they were free not to marry if they so preferred, and in many cases were allowed to make their own choice as to their husbands, they soon became wives and the colony began to make substantial progress.

Source 11   Abbot E. Smith, *Colonists in Bondage,* 1947

It is a familiar story that mankind, when confronted in America with a vast and trackless wilderness awaiting exploitation, threw off its ancient shackles of caste and privilege and set forth upon the road to freedom. Among the social institutions found most useful in the course of this march were those of African slavery and white servitude. While the former boasted extensive precedents from the remotest antiquity, the latter was less familiar, and in fact was to a considerable degree the peculiar creation of the Americans themselves. The "custom of the country," by which the lives of white servants were governed in practically all matters, grew up gradually. At first it was no more than the common average of relationships between a thousand masters and servants; later it was more carefully defined, sometimes in written indentures, more generally in the decisions of colonial judges. Before long its more important particulars were embodied in acts passed by the colonial legislatures. The mass of this legislation became very large, while the number of judicial decisions based upon it was truly imposing, and we have finally a legal, social, and economic institution which is a monument to the peculiar necessities and native ingenuity of the early Americans. The proceedings of the "first legislative body in America" at Jamestown in 1619 excellently illustrate the beginnings of this development. Concerning servants this assembly first formulated into law certain instructions which the governors had received from England, and provided "that all contracts made in England betweene the owners of lande & their Tenants and Servantes which they shall send hither, may be caused to be duly performed, and that the offenders be punished as the Governr & Councell of Estate shall think just & convenient." Then they turned to another sort of laws "suche as might proceed out of every mans private conceipt," or, we may put it, such as colonial conditions had demonstrated to be necessary. Under this head they provided for the registration of servants' contracts and conditions, they forbade servants to trade with the Indians, prohibited women servants from marrying without the consent of their masters, and provided that for crimes such as swearing and Sabbath-breaking, for which freemen were fined, servants should be whipped. Finally, sitting rather as a high court than as a legislative body, they heard a petition of Captain William Powell against one of his servants for various misdoings, and sentenced the culprit to stand four days with his ears nailed to the pillory.

Source 12   John Hope Franklin, *From Slavery to Freedom,* 1974

The twenty Africans who were put ashore at Jamestown in 1619 . . . were not slaves in a legal sense. And at the time the Virginians seemed not to appreciate the far-reaching significance of the introduction of Africans into the fledgling colony. These newcomers, who happened to be black, were simply more indentured servants. They were listed as servants in the census counts of 1623 and

1624; and as late as 1651 some Negroes whose period of service had expired were being assigned land in much the same way that it was being assigned to whites who had completed their indenture. During its first half-century of existence Virginia had many Negro indentured servants; and the records reveal an increasing number of free Negroes.

But as time went on Virginia increasingly fell behind in satisfying the labor needs of the colony with Indians and indentured servants, and serious thought was given to the "perpetual servitude" of Negroes....

The actual statutory recognition of slavery in Virginia came in 1661.

Source 13 Eleanor Flexner, *Century of Struggle,* 1975

When the London merchants who were putting capital into the Virginia colony as a business venture began to realize that men alone would not build a stable community, but would remain a loose, constantly shifting aggregation of adventurers, they began to send out women. Ninety came on one ship alone in 1619....

Perhaps the knowledge that each would find a husband among the several hundred bachelors eagerly awaiting them made up for subsequent hardships, but they cannot have found life easy. Virginia was only a toehold in the wilderness, fighting an unceasing war against plague, encroaching vegetation, and the Indians, who bitterly resented the white influx.

Source 14 Carl Bridenbaugh, *Jamestown,* 1979

Human abasement did not begin at Jamestown in 1619 when the first blacks arrived; it commenced in 1607 with the landing of the first white colonists from the *Susan Constant,* the *Godspeed,* and the *Discovery.* For nearly two decades (1619–38) this outpost of empire served as a market for the sale of white Englishmen and Irishmen into servitude before it became a mart for black slaves.

✍ Questioning the Past

1. How did events in Virginia in 1619 help to shape the course of American history? What precedents were set and how do they affect, if at all, the America of today?

2. What clues about conditions in the Virginia colony may be gleaned from a reading of the laws enacted by the Virginia Assembly of 1619?

3. Some historians have asserted that in permitting the colonists in Virginia to convene an assembly and take part in governance, the British planted the seed that grew into American independence. Argue the merits of this assertion.

4. The immediate demand for labor in Virginia led the colony to develop a plan for indentured servitude that, though easing the short-term problem, evolved in ways probably never anticipated by those who devised the plan. Was it inevitable that indentured servitude for African Americans would evolve into perpetual servitude? Was there a risk that indentured servitude for European Americans could evolve into slavery? Was it conceivable that the practice of turning European women into American wives through indentured servitude reduced women in the New World to greater subordination than they had endured in the Old World? Should the assemblymen of 1619 have considered more thoroughly the possible consequences of their decisions? Why or why not?

Chapter 5

Samoset and Squanto

The Pilgrims Get a Surprise Visitor   *March 16, 1621*

After a stormy, 64-day voyage from England, the *Mayflower* dropped anchor off the tip of Cape Cod in November 1620. The ship's passengers explored the Cape and foraged for food, even stealing corn from the Native Americans, before concluding a month later that the Cape could not sustain them. They crossed Cape Cod Bay and began to build a settlement at Plymouth on December 16. Those 102 men, women, and children could hardly have foreseen that the winter would take the lives of half their number and cast doubt on the survival of the rest.

They had arrived in a season when planting seeds brought from England was impossible. They had little food, no shelter, and none of the skills necessary to survive in a land so foreign to their experience. But they were not alone in their new home, where Native Americans had lived for tens of thousands of years. There had been just enough prior contact between the peoples of the New World and the immigrants from the Old to make them wary of each other. The Native Americans cautiously watched the newcomers from the concealment of the forest, while the settlers sensed they were being spied on and lived in constant fear.

Imagine the shock of the Pilgrims when, after months of anxiety over the intentions of the "savages" surrounding them, they saw a native stride purposefully into their village and heard him deliver the one message they would never have expected. "Much welcome, Englishmen!" said their visitor, Samoset. His words were the turning point in the settlers' efforts to colonize New England, for Samoset introduced them to their Native American neighbors, including Squanto, yet another resident who spoke English.

❦ *First Impressions*

Welcome Englishmen!

In the following accounts, the colonists at Plymouth comment on the hardships of their journey to America and their first winter in the New World. They also describe their first encounter with Samoset and acknowledge the importance of Native Americans in the founding of a permanent colony at Plymouth.

Source 1 Notes of William Bradford, governor of Plymouth Colony, 1620

Being thus passed the vast ocean, and a sea of troubles before in their preparation, they had now no friends to wellcome them, nor inns to entertaine or
refresh their weatherbeaten bodies, no houses or much less towns to repaire too,
to seeke for succoure. . . . And for the season, it was winter, and they that know
the winters of the cuntrie know them to be sharp & violent, & subjecte to
cruell & fierce stormes, dangerous to travill to known places, much more to
serch an unknown coast. Besids, what could they see but a hidious & desolate
wildernes, full of wild beasts & wild men?

5.1 The
Plimoth
Plantation

Source 2 Notes of William Bradford, 1621

All this while the Indians came skulking about them, and would sometimes
show them selves aloofe of, but when any approached near them, they would
rune away. And once they stoale away their tools wher they had been at
worke, & were gone to diner. But about the 16. of March a certaine Indian
came bouldly amongst them, and spoke to them in broken English, which
they could well understand, but marvelled at it. At length they understood
by discourse with him, that he was not of these parts, but belonged to the
eastrene parts, wher some English-ships came to fhish, with whom he was
acquainted, & could name sundrie of them by their names, amongst whom
he had gott his language. He became profitable to them in acquainting them
with many things concerning the state of the cuntry in the east-parts wher
he lived. . . . His name was Samaset; he tould them also of another Indian
whos name was Squanto, a native of this place, who had been in England
& could speake better English then him selfe. Being, after some time of
entertainmente & gifts, dismist, a while after he came againe, & 5. more
with him, & they brought againe all the tooles that were stolen away before,
and made way for the coming of their great **Sachem**, called Massasoyt; who,
about 4. or 5. days after came with the cheefe of his friends & other attendance, with the aforesaid Squanto. With whom, after friendly entertainment,
& some gifts given him, they made a peace.

   After these things he returned to his place caled Sowams, some 40. mile
from this place, but Squanto continued with them, and was their interpreter,
and was a spetiall instrument sent of God for their good beyond their expecta-
tions. He directed them how to set their corne, wher to take fish, and how to
procure other comodities, and was also their pilott to bring them to unknowne
places for their profitt, and never left them till he dyed.

A Turning Point in the Struggle for Survival

In most of the first encounters between the peoples of the Americas and
the explorers and emigrants from the Old World, the natives greeted the

newcomers with warmth and hospitality. Yet even these friendly contacts often had deadly consequences that neither side could have foreseen. In fact, the Europeans unwittingly killed most of the peoples of the Americas before ever meeting them, by exposing them to Old World diseases that rippled outward at an alarming rate. Europeans, Asians, and Africans had interacted with one another for centuries, sharing their plagues so extensively that their immunities had been strengthened throughout the generations. Native Americans, isolated as they had been from the Old World, had neither immunity nor medicines to protect them. The Pilgrims were unaware that their countries' deadly diseases had swept across New England for a decade before their arrival, decimating the native population of **Massachusett**. The sole survivor of the original owners of the land, Squanto, willingly guided the colonists through their first few years in America, teaching them what crops to plant and how to care for them, before he too succumbed to the diseases brought to his country from across the sea.

Source 3   Puritan leader Edward Johnson, 1654

5.2 Plymouth: Its History and Its People

The Summer after the blazing Starre (Whose motion in the Heavens was from East to West, poynting out to the sons of men the progresse of the glorious Gospell of Christ, the glorious King of his Churches) even about the yeare 1618. a little before the removeall of that Church of Christ from Holland to Plimoth in New England, as the ancient Indians report, there befell a great mortality among them, the greatest that ever the memory of Father to Sonne tooke notice of, chiefly desolating those places, where the English afterward planted. The Country . . . was almost wholly deserted. . . . But by this meanes Christ (whose great and glorious workes the Earth throughout are altogether for the benefit of his Church and chosen) not only made roome for his people to plant; but also tamed the hard and cruell hearts of these barbarous Indians, insomuch that halfe a handfull of his people landing not long after in Plimoth-Plantation, found little resistance . . . and verily herein they quit themselves like men, or rather Christ for and by them, maintaining the place notwithstanding the multitude of difficulties they met withall at their first landing, being in doubtfull suspence what entertainment these Barbarians would give them. . . .

But hee, whose worke they went about, wrought so rare a Providence for them, which cannot but be admired of all that heare it. Thus it fell as they were discoursing in the . . . shelter, all of a sudden, an Indian came in among them, at whose speech they were all agast, he speaking the English Language, Much welcome Englishmen, their wonder was the greater, . . . and verily Christ had prepared him on purpose to give his people intertainment, the Indian having lived in England two year or thereabout, after which he returned home, and at this time had wandred into these parts in company of other Indians. All this, and the condition of the neere adjoyning Indians, hee soon discovered unto them, at which they were transported beyond themselves very much, what with joy and the mixture of their former feare and affection intervening with the other, surprised all their senses of a sudden, that long it was ere each party could take its proper place . . . they made use of the present opportunity, and by the instrumentall meanes of this Indian, became acquainted and reconciled with most of the Neighbouring Indians.

📖 *Second Thoughts*
With the Help of a Friendly Indian

If the Pilgrims saw Samoset and Squanto as part of the plan of an all-powerful God to help them, later views varied. Most historians have seen them as significant but not providential, while others have chosen not to see them at all.

Source 4   William Robertson, *The History of the Discovery and Settlement of North America,* 1788

No season could be more unfavorable to settlement than that in which the colony landed. . . . Above one half of them was cut off before the return of spring, by diseases, or by famine: the survivors, instead of having leisure to attend to the supply of their own wants, were compelled to take arms against the savages in their neighbourhood. Happily for the English, a pestilence which raged in America the year before they landed, had swept off so great a number of the natives that they were quickly repulsed and humbled.

Source 5   Richard Hildreth, *The History of the United States of America,* 1853

As they stood in some fear of the natives, who seemed carefully to avoid them, they adopted a military organization, and chose for their leader Miles Standish. . . .

During the winter little or nothing was seen of the natives, but in the early spring an Indian walked boldly into the village, and surprised the inhabitants by calling out, "Welcome Englishmen!" He was a sagamore, or petty chief from the eastward, by name Samoset, and had learned a little English of the fishermen who frequented that coast. He introduced another Indian, named Squanto, . . . who also spoke a little English, and, in conjunction with Samoset, acted as interpreter, guide, and pilot, to the settlers.

Source 6   John Fiske, *The Beginnings of New England,* 1902

That the Indians in the neighborhood had not taken advantage of the distress of the settlers in that first winter, and massacred every one of them, was due to a remarkable circumstance. Early in 1617 a frightful pestilence had swept over New England and slain, it is thought, more than half the Indian population between the **Penobscot** River and the **Narragansett** Bay. Many of the Indians were inclined to attribute this calamity to the murder of two or three white fishermen the year before. They had not got over the superstitious dread with which the first sight of white men had inspired them, and now they believed that the strangers held the demon of the plague at their disposal and had let him loose upon the red men in revenge for the murders they had committed. This wholesome delusion kept their tomahawks quiet for a while. When they saw the Englishmen establishing themselves at Plymouth, they at first held a powwow in the forest, at which the newcomers were cursed with all the elaborate ingenuity that the sorcery of the medicine-men could summon for so momentous an occasion; but it was deemed best to refrain from merely human methods of attack. It was not until the end of the first winter that any of them mustered courage to visit the palefaces. Then an Indian named Samoset, who . . . was inclined to be friendly, came one day into the village with words of welcome. He was so kindly treated that presently Massasoit, principal sachem of the **Wampanoags**, . . . came with a score of painted and feathered warriors and squatting on a green rug and cushions in the governor's log-house smoked a pipe of peace. . . . An offensive and defensive alliance was then and there made between King Massasoit and King James, and the treaty was faithfully kept for half a century.

5.3 First
Nations
Histories

Source 7   Andrew C. McLaughlin, *A History of the American Nation,* 1913

The land offered but a dreary prospect. . . . The first winter was full of terrible distress. In two or three months' time half their company were laid away in graves under the snow. . . . When the *Mayflower* sailed back to England, not one of the settlers returned. They planted corn, they built homes, they met together in town meeting, they worshiped God in their own simple fashion. . . . Where there was so much energy and devotion, success was sure to follow.

Source 8   James Truslow Adams, *The Epic of America,* 1931

But in 1620 the little band of English "Pilgrims," . . . settled themselves on the inhospitable shore of Plymouth, and with rugged devotion grafted another bud of the English nation on the continent. They were a simple and gentle folk, but their courage was no less and of a finer quality than that of the most swash-buckling of the "sea dogs." . . .

Sickness, incessant and unremitting labor, hunger, attacks from savage men and savage beasts, were among the "mosquito bites" that these first founders . . . had to face and endure. In the first winter at Plymouth, half the little company of a hundred died from sickness and hardship. At times there were but six or seven strong enough to hunt, cook, and care for the entire company.

Source 9   Henry Bamford Parkes, *The American Experience,* 1959

They chose Plymouth as the best site for a permanent settlement, and landed there on December 16, just as the most severe period of winter was beginning. The horrors of the next three months were almost beyond human endurance. They were already weakened by scurvy, lack of food, and the long confinement on shipboard. . . . Alone in an unknown wilderness, during a winter longer and colder than any of them had known before, with savages lurking in the woods outside, and famine and pestilence among themselves, they could rely only upon their own courage and their willingness to help each other.

They earned their place in history by the manner in which they came through the ordeal. . . .

Their first piece of good fortune was to find a friendly Indian willing to show them how to plant corn (kernels of which they had found in an abandoned Indian settlement) and catch fish. Without his assistance they would probably have died of starvation. These artisans and craftsmen were accustomed to urban life and had little knowledge of farming or of hunting and fishing; and the seeds they had brought from England, and which they planted when they were able, "came not to good, either by the badness of the seed, or the lateness of the season, or both, or some other defect." But with help from the Indians, they were able to support themselves through the summer of 1621.

Source 10 Amelia G. Bingham, *Mashpee, Land of the Wampanoags,* 1970

History records that the Pilgrims would have perished during the first bitter winter had it not been for the humanity of the Wampanoags and their readiness to accept the white man as a brother.

They taught the stranger how to keep warm in the wilderness, where to find game. They revealed to him the secrets of nature important to survival. Above all they shared with him their precious winter stocks of food.

Source 11 T. J. Brasser, *Handbook of North American Indians,* 1974

Though fur traders had frequented the New England coast continually and a few of them had actually been living there before 1620, no proper settlement took place until December of that year, when the Pilgrims established themselves in Massachusetts. They expected to find there "savage people, who are cruell, barbarous, and most trecherous."

They first landed on Cape Cod, where they plundered somebody's store of corn and opened some graves out of curiosity. This was not the best way to start, particularly since the local Nausets still were furious about the kidnapping of seven of their people by Capt. Thomas Hunt in 1614. Besides the seven Nausets, Hunt had also captured 20 **Pawtuxets**, whom he had sold as slaves in Malaga, Spain. One of these Indians was Squanto, who managed to escape to England. Capt. Thomas Dermer brought him back to New England in 1619, but, in the meantime, an epidemic—of European origin—had ravaged the coast and exterminated his Pawtuxet people. In 1620 the Pilgrims founded their settlement in the former Pawtuxet territory. Squanto introduced their leaders to Chief Massasoit, who welcomed the settlers.

Source 12 Robert F. Berkhofer, *Handbook of North American Indians,* 1987

To Puritan divines and laymen alike, the interaction of Native Americans with the New England saints represented something larger in significance than mere contact. Hospitality and kindness represented not native friendliness and goodness but the Lord's mercy to his chosen people. Gov. William Bradford of Plymouth Plantation wrote of Squanto, whose assistance to the Pilgrims enabled them to survive in the new environment, as "a Speciall instrument sent of God for their good beyond their expectation."

⚖ Questioning the Past

1. Assess the importance of Squanto and Samoset to the survival of the Plymouth Colony. Were their contributions essential or merely beneficial?

2. What were the attitudes of the Pilgrims toward the Native Americans who had befriended them? What actions toward the Native Americans or statements about them may be cited as revealing these attitudes? What might account for these attitudes?

3. What explanations might be offered for the decision of native peoples of Massachusetts to provide assistance to the people of the Plymouth Colony? If the Wampanoags had met the settlers as enemies rather than as friends, how might the future of English colonization in North America have been affected?

Chapter 6

Fort Mystic

The English Settlers Torch Fort Mystic

May 26, 1637

Four strong native nations coexisted in southern New England at the beginning of the seventeenth century: the Massachusett, the Wampanoag, the Narragansett, and the **Pequot**. Each had a territory it controlled as its own, and each was wary of the others. Until the arrival of visitors from the Old World, these four nations maintained an armed, but relatively stable, peace. The arrival of European explorers, fishermen, traders, and colonists, and the epidemics unleashed by their presence, upset that stability. An epidemic that swept southward along the Atlantic coast hit the Massachusett people hard and the Wampanoag even harder. Whole villages were left deserted. The decimation of their populations led these two nations to be more receptive to English settlers than they otherwise might have been. They permitted the English to settle among them, hoping the colonists would reinforce their numbers and restore equilibrium to the balance of power among the peoples of southern New England.

The Narragansetts, however, had been only slightly touched by the epidemic of 1617. They acknowledged the arrival of the Pilgrims not with gestures of friendship, but with a bundle of arrows wrapped in snakeskin. The Pilgrims presumed this to be a message of hostility and sent a bundle of bullets back in reply. Similarly, the Pequots were not disposed to view the English kindly. At first the newcomers had been few in number and more a matter of curiosity than concern. After all, the Pequots were strong and confident. No wave of epidemic had yet passed across their lands. Their warriors were respected for their skill and courage and their villages were fortified. The Pequots dominated the valley of the Connecticut and most of their neighbors acquiesced to their leadership. But with the passage of time, the English settlements had begun to proliferate. The handful of immigrants had grown to 5,000 by 1636, and what had been a novelty was quickly turning into a potential menace as the English outposts moved ever closer to Pequot lands. For each, the mere presence of the other posed a threat. To the English, the Pequots were an obstacle to expansion of settlement and trade. By dominating the Connecticut River valley, the Pequots controlled the natural pathway into the New England interior, and they seemed more inclined to direct the flow of furs and other commerce toward the Dutch, the commercial rivals of the English. To the Pequots, repeated English demands to accede to new settlements, embrace the newcomers' religion, and acknowledge the supremacy of English authority left them offended and defiant. Tensions grew and exploded into open warfare in 1637.

6.1 Pequot History

53

❧ *First Impressions*
"To See Them Thus Frying in the Fyer"

The war was brief, brutal, and conclusive, having but two main battles: the first at Fort Mystic and the second at the Sadqua Swamp near New Haven. Both produced wholesale massacres of the Pequot people. The ferocity of the massacre at Fort Mystic is described here by the soldiers involved. Unfortunately, there are no known contemporary accounts of the massacre by the Pequots or other native peoples of the time.

Source 1   Sermon of the Reverend Edward Johnson, 1637

Fellow soldiers, countrymen, and companions in this wilderness work, . . . you need not question your authority to execute those whom God, the righteous Judge of all the world, hath condemned for blaspheming His sacred majesty, and murdering his servants: every common soldier among you is now installed a magistrate; then show yourselves men of courage. . . . [T]he Lord hath prepared this honor for you, oh you courageous soldiers of His, to execute vengeance upon the heathen, and correction among the people, to bind their kings in chains, and nobles in fetters of iron, that they may execute upon them the judgements that are written: this honor shall be to all His saints. But some of you may suppose death's stroke may cut you short of this: let every faithful soldier of Christ Jesus know, that the cause why some of His endeared servants are taken away by death in a just war (as this assuredly is) is not because they should fall short of the honors accompanying such noble designs, but rather because earth's honors are too scant for them, therefore the everlasting crown must be set upon their heads forthwith. Then march on with a cheerful Christian courage in the strength of the Lord and the power of His might, who will forthwith enclose your enemies in your hands, make their multitudes fall under your warlike weapons, and your feet shall soon be set upon their proud necks.

Source 2   Notes of William Bradford, governor of Plymouth Colony

Anno Dom:1637.
     In the fore parte of this year, the Pequents fell openly upon the English at Conightecute, in the lower parts of the river, and slew sundry of them [as they were at work in the fields], both men & women, to the great terrour of the rest; and wente away in great prid & triumph. . . . They allso assalted a fort at the rivers mouth, though strong and well defended; and though they did not their prevaile, yet it struk them with much fear & astonishmente to see their bould attempts in the face of danger; which made them on all places to stand upon their gard, and to prepare for resistance, and to solissite their friends and confederats in the Bay of Massachusets to send them speedy aide, for they looked for more forcible assaults. . . .
     In the mean time, the Pequents, espetially in the winter before, sought to make peace with the Narigansets, and used very pernicious arguments to move

them therunto: as that the English were stranegers and begane to overspred their countrie, and would deprive them therof in time, if they were suffered to grow & increse; and if the Narigansets did assist the English to subdue them, they did but make way for their owne overthrow, for if they were rooted out, the English would soone take occasion to subjugate them; and if they would harken to them, they should not neede to fear the strength of the English; for they would not come to open battle with them, but fire their houses, kill their katle, and lye in ambush for them as they went abroad on their occasions; and all this they might easily doe without any or little danger to them selves. The which course being held, they well saw the English could not long subsiste, but they would either be starved with hunger, or be forced to forsake the countrie. . . . [T]he Narigansets were once wavering, and were halfe minded to have made peace with them, and joyned against the English. But againe when they considered, how much wrong they had received from the Pequents, and what an oppertunitie they now had by the help of the English to right them selves, revenge was so sweete unto them, as it prevailed above all the rest; so as they resolved to joyne with the English against them, & did.

From Connightecute, they sett out a partie of men, and an other partie mett them from the Bay, at the Narigansets, who were to joyne with them. The Narigansets were ernest to be gone before the English were well rested and refreshte . . . It should seeme their desire was to come upon the enemie sudenly, & undiscovered. . . .

So they went on, and so ordered their march, as the Indians brought them to a forte of the enemies (in which most of their cheefe men were) before day. They approached the same with great silence, and surrounded it with both English & Indeans, that they might not breake out; and so assaulted them with great courage, shooting amongst them, and entered the forte with all speed.

Source 3 Account of Captain John Underhill, second in command of Connecticut troops, May 26, 1637

6.2 The Taking of Fort Mystic

Having our swords in our right hand, our carbines or muskets in our left hand, we approached the fort, Master Hedge being shot through both arms, and more wounded. Though it be not commendable for a man to make mention of anything that might tend to his own honor, yet because I would have the providence of God observed, and His name magnified, as well for myself as others, I dare not omit, but let the world know, that deliverance was given to us that command, as well as to private soldiers. Captain Mason and myself entering into the wigwams, he was shot, and received many arrows against his head-piece. God preserved him from many wounds. Myself received a shot in the left hip, through a sufficient buff coat, that if I had not been supplied with such a garment, the arrow would have pierced me. Another I received between neck and shoulders, hanging in the linen of my head-piece. Others of our soldiers were shot, some through the shoulders, some in the face, some in the head, some in the legs, Captain Mason and myself losing each of us a man, and had nearly twenty wounded. Most courageously these Pequots behaved themselves. But seeing the fort was too hot for us, we devised a way how we might save ourselves and prejudice them. Captain Mason entering into a wigwam, brought out a firebrand, after he had wounded many in the house. Then he set fire on the west side, where he entered; myself set fire on the south end with a train of powder. The fires of both meeting in the center of the fort, blazed most terribly, and burnt all in the space of half an hour. Many courageous fellows were unwilling to come out, and fought most desperately through the palisadoes, so as they were scorched and burnt with the very flame, and were deprived of their arms—in regard to the fire burnt their very bowstrings—and so perished valiantly. Mercy did they deserve for their valor, could we have had opportunity to have bestowed it. Many were burnt in the fort, both men, women, and children. Others forced out, and came in troops . . . , twenty and thirty at a time, which our soldiers received and entertained with the point of the sword. Down fell men, women, and children. . . .

Great and doleful was the bloody sight to the view of young soldiers that never had been in war, to see so many souls lie gasping on the ground, so thick, in some places, that you could hardly pass along. It may be demanded, Why should you be so furious? Should not Christians have more mercy and compassion? But I would refer you to David's war. . . . Sometimes the Scripture declareth women and children must perish with their parents. Sometimes the case alters; but we will not dispute it now. We have sufficient light from the Word of God for our proceedings. . . .

So remarkable it appeared to us, as we could not but admire at the providence of God in it, that soldiers so unexpert in the use of their arms, should give so complete a volley, as though the finger of God had touched both match and flint. . . .

Our Indians came to us, and much rejoiced at our victories, and greatly admired the manner of Englishmen's fight, but cried mach it, mach it; that is, It is naught, it is naught, because it is too furious, and slays too many men.

Source 4   Notes of William Bradford, 1637

[A]nd those that first entered found sharp resistance from the enimie, who both shott at & grapled with them; others rane into their howses & brought out fire, and sett them on fire, which soon took in their matts, &, standing close togeather, with the wind, all was quickly on a flame, and thereby more were burnte to death then was otherwise slain; it burnte their bowstrings, and made them unservisable. Those that scaped the fire were slaine with the sword; some hewed to peeces, others rune throw with their rapiers, so as they were quickly dispatchte, and very few escaped. It was conceived they thus destroyed about 400 at this time. It was a fearfull sight to see them thus frying in the fyer, and the streams of blood quenching the same, and horrible was the stinck & sente ther of; but the victory seemed a sweete sacrifice, and they gave the prays therof to God, who had wrought so wonderfuly for them, thus to inclose their enimise in their hands, and give them so speedy a victory over so proud & insulting an enimie.

Source 5   Journal of John Winthrop, governor of Massachusetts Bay, 1637

Our English from Connecticut, with their Indians, and many of the Narragansetts, marched in the night to a fort of the Pequods at Mistick, and, besetting the same about break of the day, after two hours' fight, they took it, (by firing it) and slew therein two chief sachems, and one hundred and fifty fighting men, and about one hundred and fifty old men, women, and children, with the loss of only two English, whereof but one was killed by the enemy. Divers of the Indian friends were hurt by the English, because they had not some mark to distinguish them from the Pequods.

Source 6   John Winthrop to William Bradford, May 28, 1637

Worthy sr:

I received your loving letter, and am much provocked to express my affections towards you, but straitnes of time forbids me; for my desire is to acquainte you with the Lords great mercies towards us, in our prevailing against his & our enimies, that you may rejoyce and praise his name with us. . . .

Ther have been now slaine & taken, in all, aboute 700. The rest are dispersed, and the Indeans in all quarters so terrified as all their friends are affraid to receive them.

Yours assured,
Jo. Winthrop
The 28. of the 5. month, 1637.

Source 7   Notes of the Reverend Edward Johnson, 1637

The Lord in mercy toward his poore Churches having thus destroyed these bloudy barbarous Indians, he returned his people in safety . . . where they may take account of their prisoners: the Squawes and young youth they brought home with them, and finding the men to be deeply guilty of the crimes they undertooke the warre for, they brought away onely their heads as a token of their victory. By this means the Lord strook a trembling terror into all the Indians round about.

The Pequot War

The Pequot War was the first time that any of the native peoples who shared their lands in the New World with the pious newcomers had witnessed the full force of the European style of warfare, and they were left stunned by what they saw. Though Native Americans had warred among themselves for centuries before the English colonists settled in their midst, they recognized something fundamentally different in the style of warfare waged by the newcomers. Native Americans fought with ferocity but they fought mostly to demonstrate superiority. It was not necessary to annihilate the enemy to prove dominance. The Puritans waged war with a viciousness that shocked the so-called savages of America. By the manner in which they dealt with the Pequots,

6.3 The Pequot War: A Television Documentary

the Puritans opened the way for the expansion of English settlements across southern New England. And it was many years before any native people dared again to challenge them.

📖 *Second Thoughts*

"Where Today Are the Pequot?"

The massacre at Fort Mystic brought an end to the Pequot as a powerful nation. Tecumseh, a leader of the Shawnee Nation, observed in 1811, "Where today are the Pequot? Where are the Narragansett, the Mohican, the Pocanet, and other powerful tribes of our people? They have vanished before the avarice and oppression of the white man, as snow before the summer sun." The manner in which the Pequots were destroyed has provoked a great deal of comment over the years, as indicated by the selections that follow. As for the Pequots themselves, the nation has rebounded somewhat in vitality and numbers, as Pequot descendants have settled into a peaceful—and increasingly profitable—co-existence with the state of Connecticut.

Source 8   John Oldmixon, *The British Empire in America,* 1741

The Pequots were retir'd into two strong Forts, one on the River Mystick. . . . The English surpriz'd the . . . Fort in the Night, on Intelligence from an Indian Spy, that the Enemy was asleep. The Huts in the Fort being made of combustible Matter, the English soon set fire to them. Many of the Savages were burnt, and those that endeavoured to escape were killed by the English, being shot as they climb'd the Pallisades or sallied out at the Gates. Not above 7 or 8 of 4 or 500 Indians that were in the Fort, made their Escape. The English had but two kill'd. . . . The Narrangantsets stood all the while aloof, and with infinite Pleasure saw the Destruction of the Pequots, showing their barbarous Joy by dancing, howling, and insulting over their late dreaded Enemy. Wequash, the Indian Spy was struck with such Admiration at this Victory, that he turn'd Christian upon it, and in Time became a Preacher to his Countrymen, who insulted, and at last poisoned him. He died very religiously, committing his Soul to Christ, and his only child to the English, wishing it might know more of Jesus than its poor Father had done.

Source 9   Thomas Hutchinson, *The History of the Colony and Province of Massachusetts Bay,* 1765

The Indians, in alliance with the English, had taken eighteen captives, ten males and eight females, four of the males were disposed of, one to each of four sachems, the rest put to the sword. Four of the females were left at the fort, the other four carried to Connecticut, where the Indians challenged them as their prize; the English not agreeing to it they were sacrificed also to end the dispute. The policy, as well as the morality of this proceeding, may well be questioned. The Indians have ever shewn great barbarity toward their English captives, the English in too many instances have retaliated it. This has only enraged them the more. Besides, to destroy women and children, for the barbarity of their husbands and parents, cannot easily be justified.

Source 10 William Robertson, *The History of the Discovery and Settlement of America,* 1788

The Pequods were a formidable people, who could bring into the field a thousand warriors not inferior in courage to any in the New World. They foresaw, not only that the extermination of the Indian race must be the consequence of permitting the English to spread over the continent of America, but that, if measures were not speedily concerted to prevent it, the calamity would be unavoidable. With this view they applied to the Narragansets, requesting them to forget ancient animosities for a moment, and to co-operate with them in expelling a common enemy who threatened both with destruction. . . .

But the Narragansets and Pequods, like most of the contiguous tribes in America, were rivals, and there subsisted between them an hereditary and implacable enmity. Revenge is the darling passion of savages. . . . The Narragansets, instead of closing with the prudent proposal of their neighbors, . . . entered into an alliance with the English against them. The Pequods, more exasperated than discouraged by the impudence and treachery of their countrymen, took the field, and carried on the war in the usual mode of Americans. . . .

The troops of Connecticut . . . found it necessary to advance towards the enemy. They [the Pequot] were posted on a rising ground, in the middle of a swamp towards the head of the river Mystic, which they had surrounded with palisadoes, the best defence that their slender skill in the art of fortification had discovered. Though they knew that the English were in motion, yet, with the usual improvidence and security of savages, they took no measures either to observe their progress, or to guard against being surprised themselves. The enemy [English settlers], unperceived, reached the palisadoes [May 25]; and if a dog had not given the alarm by barking, the Indians must have been massacred without resistance. In a moment, however, they startled to arms, and raising the war cry, prepared to repel the assailants. But at that early period of their intercourse with the Europeans, the Americans were little acquainted with the use of gunpowder, and dreaded its effects extremely. While some of the English galled them with an incessant fire through the intervals between the palisadoes, others forced their way by the entries into the fort, filled only with branches of trees; and setting fire to the huts which were covered by reeds, the confusion and terror quickly became general. Many of the women and children perished in the flames; and the warriors, in endeavoring to escape, were either slain by the English, or, falling into the hands of their Indian allies, who surrounded the fort at a distance, were reserved for a more cruel fate. After the junction of the troops from Massachusetts, the English resolved to pursue their victory; and hunting the Indians from one place of retreat to another, some subsequent encounters were hardly less fatal to them than the action on the Mystik. In less than three months the tribe of Pequods were extirpated. . . .

In this first essay of their arms, the colonists of New England seem to have been conducted by skilful and enterprising officers, and displayed both courage and perseverance as soldiers. But they stained their laurels by the use which they made of victory. Instead of treating the Peqouds as an independent people, who made a gallant effort to defend the property, the rights, and the freedom of their nation, they retaliated upon them all the barbarities of American war. Some they massacred in cold-blood, others they gave up to be tortured by their Indian allies, a considerable number they sold as slaves in Bermudas, the rest were reduced to servitude among themselves.

But reprehensible as this conduct of the English must be deemed, their vigorous efforts in this decisive campaign filled all the surrounding tribes of Indians with such a high opinion of their valour as secured a long tranquility to all their settlements.

Source 11   George Bancroft, *History of the United States,* 1882

To the tribe on Mystic river their bows and arrows seemed formidable weapons; ignorant of European fortresses, they viewed their palisades with complacency; and, as the English boats sailed by, it was rumored that their enemies had vanished through fear. Hundreds of the Pequods spent much of the last night of their lives in rejoicing, at a time when the sentinels of the English were within hearing of their songs. . . .

The vigor and courage displayed by the settlers on the Connecticut, in this first Indian war in New England, secured a long period of peace. The infant was safe in its cradle, the laborer in the fields, the solitary traveller during the night-watches in the forest; the houses needed no bolts, the settlements no palisades. The constitution which, on the fourteenth of January, 1639, was adopted, was of unexampled liberality.

Source 12   John Fiske, *The Beginnings of New England,* 1889

The tribe which had lorded it so fiercely over the New England forests was all at once wiped out of existence. So terrible a vengeance the Indians had never heard of. If the name of Pequot had hitherto been a name of terror so now did the Englishmen win the inheritance of that deadly prestige. . . .

Such scenes of wholesale slaughter are not pleasant reading in this milder age. But our forefathers felt that the wars of Canaan afforded a sound precedent for such cases; and, indeed, if we remember what the soldiers of **Tilly and Wallenstein** were doing at this very time in Germany, we shall realize that the work of Mason and Underhill would not have been felt by anyone in that age to merit censure or stand in need of excuses. As a matter of practical policy the annihilation of the Pequots can be condemned only by those who read history so incorrectly as to suppose that savages, whose business is to torture and slay, can always be dealt with according to the methods in use between civilized peoples. A mighty nation, like the United States, is in honor bound to treat the redman with scrupulous justice and refrain from cruelty in punishing his delinquencies. But if the founders of Connecticut in confronting a danger which threatened their very existence, struck with savage fierceness, we can not blame them. The world is so made that it is only in that way that the higher races have been able to preserve themselves and carry on their progressive work.

The overthrow of the Pequots was a cardinal event in the planting of New England.

Source 13 Woodrow Wilson, *A History of the American People,* 1902

That very summer [1637] war came—war with the bold and dangerous Pequots, the masters of the Connecticut and the shores of the Sound; and nobody but Roger Williams could have held the Narragansett tribes off from joining them to destroy the settlements. A hostile union and concerted onset of all the tribes, effected then, as the Pequot plotted, might have meant annihilation. There were but five thousand Englishmen . . . scattered in the settlements, and such a rising put everything at stake. The Narragansetts occupied the lands which lay between Plymouth and the valley of the Connecticut. Mr. Williams had been much among them while he lived at Plymouth; had learned their language, and thoroughly won their liking. . . . They had given him lands very gladly when he came among them a fugitive; now they hearkened to him rather than to the fierce Pequot chiefs. . . .

The Pequots had grown very hot against the English crowding in. No Englishman's life was safe anywhere . . . because of them through the anxious winter of 1636–1637. . . . When summer came, therefore, the settlers set themselves ruthlessly to exterminate the tribe. A single bloody season of fire and the sword, and the work was done. . . . The terrible business cleared all the river valley and all the nearer regions by the Sound, and English settlers began to pour in again with a new heart.

Source 14 Charles Segal and David C. Stineback, *Puritans, Indians, and Manifest Destiny,* 1977

Ultimately, the problems that led to the outbreak of the Pequot War were generated within the Massachusetts Bay Colony itself and were stimulated by the Puritan desire to control all settlement in New England. In 1634, the authority of the Boston magistrates had been questioned by the Reverend Thomas Hooker and his followers—a challenge that matured in 1635, when the dissenters decided to colonize an area of Connecticut that was outside the Massachusetts Bay Company patent and comprised a portion of the territory yielded by the Pequots. But this location already had been claimed by the Dutch and by a group of Englishmen known as the Seabrook Company, who were controlled by Massachusetts Bay. . . .

Connecticut was now a powder keg. While the treaty between the Pequots and Massachusetts facilitated orderly settlement of Connecticut, it did not quell intertribal feuding or arrest the rivalry between Connecticut and the Bay Colony. The success of both Puritan colonies depended upon forcing the Pequots into a degree of subjugation. . . .

But if the Connecticut settlers were permitted to punish the Pequots, they might make them tributaries to Connecticut or fight them and claim the territory by right of conquest. Massachusetts could not permit this to happen.

Source 15 James Axtell, *The European and the Indian,* 1981

The first encounter with Indian warfare, during the Pequot War in Connecticut, was too brief for the English to learn very much and too successful for them to need to. In a conflict that lasted only a few months, the English troops and their Mohegan allies obliterated the Pequots with a final surprise attack and superior firepower. Since the Indians had not yet acquired guns from the Dutch and the French, the English found their fighting methods simply ludicrous. After Fort Mystic, the Pequot stronghold, had been fired and riddled with English bullets, killing most of its five hundred inhabitants, the male survivors charged the English battalia surrounding it with little success, so Capt. John Underhill sent the Mohegans against them "that we might see the nature of the Indian war." By English standards this was so ineffective that "they might fight seven years and not kill seven men . . . ," remarked Underhill. . . . "This fight," he concluded, "is more for pastime, than to conquer and subdue enemies."

    Its ineffectiveness, however, was not due to lack of European firearms. . . . When the Indians wanted to kill their opponents, especially the English, they had the means and the skill necessary.

Source 16 Gary B. Nash, *Red, White, and Black: The Peoples of Early
              America,* 1982

The Pequots understood . . . they were embroiled in a complicated set of disputes over land and trade. These were the real causes of the war. . . . At the center of the tensions was the English-Dutch rivalry and intertribal Indian hostilities. Since 1622 the Dutch in New Amsterdam had controlled the Indian trade of New England through their connections to both the Pequot and the Narragansett, the regions's two strongest tribes. After the arrival of the English and their rapid expansion in the early 1630s, the Dutch perceived that their trading empire was greatly threatened. Hence, they purchased land on the lower Connecticut River—an area on which several English groups had their eyes—and built a trading post there to defend their regional economic hegemony. Some of the Pequots' discontented client tribes, however, were already breaking away, signing separate trade agreements with and ceding to the English. Amidst such fragmentation, expansionist New England was ready, with the aid of its Narragansett allies, to drive the Dutch traders from southern New England and subdue the Pequots who occupied some of the area's most fertile soil. The Pequots first tried to placate the English; when this proved impossible, they chose to resist.

    In the war that ensued, the English found the Pequots more than a match until they were able to surround a secondary Pequot village on the Mystic River in May 1637. The English and their Narragansett allies attacked before dawn, infiltrated the town, and set fire to the Pequot wigwams inside before beating a fast retreat. . . . Retreating from the flame-engulfed village, the English regrouped and waited for fleeing survivors from the inferno. Most of the victims were noncombatants since the Pequot warriors were gathered at another village about five miles away. Before the day was over a large part of the Pequot tribe had been slaughtered, many by fire and others by gun. . . .

    For the Puritans the extermination of the Pequots was proof of their political and military ascendancy. Its additional function was to provide a response to anxiety and disunity that had become widely diffused throughout the colony. These fears were associated not only with the threat of the Pequots but also with the dissensions within Puritan society. It is well to remember that the war came on the heels of three years of intense internal discord centered around the challenges to the power of the magistrates by Roger Williams and Anne Hutchinson. These challenges, in turn, involved not only theological questions but economic restrictions, the distribution of political power, and competing land claims among English settlers in Massachusetts, Connecticut, and Rhode Island. Their colonies beset with controversy, the Puritan leaders talked morbidly about God's anger at seeing his chosen people subvert the **City on the Hill**. In this sense, the Puritan determination to destroy the Pequots and the level of violence manifested at Fort Mystic can be partially understood in terms of the self-doubt and guilt that Puritans could expiate only by exterminating so many of "Satan's agents." Dead Pequots were offered to God as atonement for Puritan failings.

Source 17 Yasuhide Kawashima, "Indian Servitude in the Northeast," 1988

Faced with a constant problem of scarcity of labor, English colonists in the Northeast made attempts from the very beginning to obtain Indian labor. . . .

The Whites tried to enslave Indians whenever they could. Principle was not so much at issue as convenience. The Puritans justified the enslavement of the prisoners taken in a just war. Following the Pequot War of 1637, for example, Massachusetts not only enslaved 48 captive women and children within the colony but also sold some fierce Pequots to the West Indies in exchange for more docile Blacks, who became the first Negro slaves in New England.

Source 18 "Mashantucket Pequot Tribal Nation History," 1998

The history of the Mashantucket Pequot Tribal Nation is one of dramatically changing fortunes. Native peoples have continuously occupied Mashantucket in Southestern Connecticut for over 10,000 years. By the early 17th century, just prior to European contact, the Pequots had approximately 8,000 members and inhabited 250 square miles. However, the Pequot War (1636–1638)—the first major conflict between colonists and an indigenous New England people—had a devastating impact on the Tribe.

When the Pequot War formally ended, many tribal members had been killed and others placed in slavery or under the control of other tribes. Those placed under the rule of the Mohegans eventually became known as the Mashantucket (Western) Pequots and were given land at Noank in 1651. In 1666, the land at Noank was taken from the Tribe, and it was given back property at Mashantucket.

In the enduring decades, the Pequots battled to keep their land, while at the same time losing reservation members to outside forces. By 1774, a Colonial census indicated that there were 151 tribal members in residence at Mashantucket. By the early 1800s, there were between 30 and 40 as members moved away from the reservation seeking work. Others joined the Brotherton movement, a Christian-Indian movement that attracted Natives from new England to a settlement in upstate New York and later, Wisconsin. As for the remaining land in Connecticut, by 1856 illegal land sales had reduced the 989-acre reservation to 213 acres.

In the early 1970s, tribal members began moving back to the Mashantucket reservation, hoping to restore their land base and community, develop economic self-sufficiency, and revitalize tribal culture. By the mid-1970s, tribal members had embarked on a series of economic ventures, in addition to instituting legal action to recover illegally seized land.

With the assistance of the Native American Rights Fund and the Indian Rights Association, the Tribe filed suit in 1976 against neighboring landowners to recover land that had been sold by the State of Connecticut in 1856. Seven years later the Pequots reached a settlement with the landowners, who agreed that the 1856 sale was illegal, and who joined the Tribe in seeking the state government's support.

The state responded, and the Connecticut Legislature unanimously passed legislation to petition the federal government to grant tribal recognition to the Mashantucket Pequots and settle the claim. With help from the Connecticut delegation, the Mashantucket Pequot Indian Land Claims Settlement Act was enacted by the U.S. Congress and signed by President Reagan on Oct. 18, 1983. It granted the Tribe federal recognition, enabling it to repurchase and place in trust the land covered in the Settlement Act. Currently, the reservation is 1,250 acres.

As the Mashantucket Pequot Tribal Nation sought to settle its land claims, it also actively engaged in a number of economic enterprises, including the sale of cord wood, maple syrup, and garden vegetables, a swine project and the opening of a hydroponic greenhouse. Once the land claims were settled, the Tribe purchased and operated a restaurant, and established a sand and gravel business. In 1986, the Tribe opened its bingo operation, followed, in 1992, by the establishment of the first phase of Foxwoods Resort Casino.

The ceremonial groundbreaking for the Mashantucket Pequot Museum and Research Center took place on Oct. 20, 1993, in a ceremony marking the 10th anniversary of federal recognition of the Mashantucket Pequot Tribal Nation. The new facility . . . is located on the Mashantucket Pequot Reservation, where many members of the Mashantucket Pequot tribal members continue to live. It is one of the oldest, continuously occupied Indian reservations in North America.

✍ Questioning the Past

1. What were the causes and the consequences of the Pequot War?

2. John Fiske asserted that "the annihilation of the Pequots can be condemned only by those who read history so incorrectly as to suppose that savages . . . can always be dealt with according to the methods in use between civilized peoples." Defend this statement and then offer the counterargument to it. Define "savage" and list characteristics that imply savagery. Compare this list to the various parties involved in the Pequot War.

3. Were wars such as that between the English colonists and the Pequot inevitable? Why or why not?

Chapter 7

Slavery

Slavery Extends Its Roots into the Law

December 1641

When the colonists from the Old World spread the seeds of their civilization across the soil of the New, they could not be sure what would take root, or even what form their transplanted culture would take when shaped by the forces of an environment unfamiliar to them. Some of their transplantations—the rigid class structure of the Old World and a nobility defined by blood lines—withered and died under the economic climate of North America. Others of their transplants—notably their notions of liberty and learning—flowered and bore fruit. Their effort to replant the familiar labor practices, however, produced a deadly vine, relatively mild in appearance as a sprout, but overwhelming as its roots bore deep into the foundations of politics and its tendrils wound their way into every part of the nation. Its foliage for a time blocked the nation's vision. Somehow, even though removed at great cost more than a century ago, its shadow still darkens the present.

🕶 *First Impressions*

"Lawful Captives Taken in Just Wars"

"So vast is the Territory of North America that it will require many Ages to settle it fully," Benjamin Franklin noted at the midpoint of the eighteenth century, "and, till it is fully settled, Labour will never be cheap here, where no Man continues long a Labourer for others, but gets a plantation of his own." Though Franklin certainly exaggerated when he implied that every colonist owned a plantation, it is equally certain that every colonist who did own one needed help to work it, and that finding help was not easy in the conditions prevailing in the colonies.

From the first moment the settlers from the Old World stepped foot on the shores of North America and gazed across the densely forested landscape from which they hoped to derive a living, and even a profit, it was clear that there was more work to be done than there were people willing to do it. Labor was always in short supply in the colonies, and those who were willing to work for wages instead of setting out in search of a plantation of their own, could demand and receive high wages. Moreover, they were prone to work only a short time, lured away by better opportunity.

65

Prospective employers wanted a supply of labor that would be inexpensive and long-serving. Indentured servitude was a solution. Akin to the Old World practice of apprenticeship, indentured servitude gave a master the services of an emigrant from abroad for a fixed period of time, usually four to seven years, in exchange for his paying the servant's passage to America and providing food, clothing, shelter, and drink for the period of service. Indentured servitude was a source of labor cheaper and more permanent than unbound labor, but still not profitable and secure enough to satisfy many employers. Over time, while emigrants from Britain and Europe continued to work in relatively short-term servitude, Africans and many Native Americans were reduced to subsistence level under a practice of involuntary and perpetual servitude, or slavery.

There is no way to know the name of the first slave. There is no way to know what thoughts were in the mind of the first master. Nor is it known when or where slavery first took its form. History did not record these things. There is no law that can be said to have established slavery. Slavery was a practice in the colonies before any law could be passed to permit or exclude it.

By the time the Massachusetts *Bodie of Liberties* was enacted in 1641—granting slavery its first clear recognition in the law—Africans and their offspring were to be found living in "perpetual servitude" throughout the English colonies. Virginia gave slavery legal status in 1661 and Maryland in 1664. With the passage of time, the institution of slavery became more and more deeply entrenched in the laws of the New World. By the eighteenth century, layers of incredibly restrictive laws covered the institution and held African Americans in bondage. The culmination of this ever-growing volume of law came in the decision of the Founding Fathers to provide recognition and protection of slavery in the Constitution, the highest law of the land. This placed slavery beyond the immediate reach of both Congress and the Court.

Source 1   Massachusetts *Body of Liberties,* 1641

7.1 The Avalon Project: Statutes of the United States concerning Slavery

There shall never be any bond slavery, **villinage** or captivity among us unless it be lawful captives taken in just wars, and such strangers as willingly sell themselves or are sold to us. And these shall have all the liberties and Christian usages which the law of God established in Israel concerning such do morally require. This exempts none from servitude who shall be judged thereto by authority.

Source 2   "An Act Concerning Negroes and Other Slaves," Maryland Assembly, 1664

Be it enacted by the Right Honorable the Lord Proprietor by the advice and consent of the upper and lower house of this present General Assembly, that all Negroes or other slaves already within the province, and all Negroes and other slaves to be hereafter imported into the province, shall serve *durante vita*. And all children born of any Negro or other slave shall be slaves, as their fathers were, for the term of their lives.

And forasmuch as divers freeborn English women, forgetful of their free condition and to the disgrace of our nation, do intermarry with Negro slaves, by which also divers suits may arise touching the issue of such women, and a great damage does befall the masters of such Negroes for prevention whereof, for deterring such freeborn women from such shameful matches. Be it further enacted, by the Authority advice and consent aforesaid, that whatsoever freeborn woman shall intermarry with any slave from and after the last day of this present Assembly, shall serve the master of such slave during the life of her husband, and that all the issue of such freeborn women so married shall be slaves as their fathers were. And be it further enacted that all the issues of English and other freeborn women that have already married Negroes shall serve the masters of their parents till they be thirty years of age and no longer.

Source 3   "An Act for Regulating Negro, Indian, and Mulatto Slaves within this Province of New Jersey," 1704

[W]hereas the baptizing of slaves is thought by some to be a sufficient reason to set them at liberty, which being a groundless opinion and prejudicial to the inhabitants of this province, be it . . . enacted by the authority aforesaid that the baptizing of any Negro, Indian or mulatto slave shall not be any reason or cause for setting them, or any of them, at liberty. . . .

And be it enacted by the authority aforesaid, that all the children that have been born or shall be born in the county of such Negro, Indian, or mulatto slaves as have been formerly or may hereafter be set at liberty, and all their posterity, shall be and are hereby forever after rendered incapable of purchasing or inheriting any lands and tenements within this province.

And be it further enacted by the authority aforesaid, that any person or persons within this province, who shall knowingly keep or entertain any Negro, Indian, or mulatto slave in his or their house, or otherwise, for above the space of two hours, without their master's or mistress' leave, or some other reasonable cause or occasion, shall forfeit the sum of one shelling for each hour to the master or mistress of such slave.

Source 4   "An Act for the Better Ordering and Governing of Negroes and Slaves," *Statutes at Large of South Carolina,* 1712

Whereas, the plantations and estates of this Province cannot be well and sufficiently managed and brought into use, without the labor and service of negroes and other slaves; and forasmuch as the said negroes and other slaves brought unto the people of this Province for that purpose, are of barbarous, wild, savage natures, and such as renders them wholly unqualified to be governed by the laws, customs, and practices of this Province; but that it is absolutely necessary, that such other constitutions, laws and orders, should in this Province be made and enacted, for the good regulating and ordering of them, as may restrain the disorders, rapines and inhumanity, to which they are naturally prone and inclined, and may also tend to the safety and security of the people of this Province and their estates; to which purpose,

    I. Be it therefore enacted. . . That all negroes, mulattoes, mustizoes or Indians, which at any time heretofore have been sold, or now are held or taken to be, or hereafter shall be bought and sold for slaves, are hereby declared slaves; and they, and their children, are hereby made and declared slaves. . . .

II. And for the better ordering and governing of negroes and all other slaves in this Province, Be it enacted . . . That no master, mistress, overseer, or other person whatsoever, that hath the care and charge of any negro or slave, shall give the negroes and other slaves leave, on Sundays, holidays, or any other time, to go out of their plantations, except such negro or other slave as usually wait upon them at home or abroad, or wearing a livery; and every other negro or slave that shall be taken hereafter out of his master's plantation, without a ticket, or leave in writing, from his master or mistress, or some other person by his or her appointment, or some white person in the company of such slave, to give an account of his business, shall be whipped. . . .

III. And be it further enacted . . . That every master, mistress or overseer of a family in this Province, shall cause all his negro houses to be searched diligently and effectually once every fourteen days, for fugitives or runaway slaves, guns, swords, clubs, and any other mischievous weapons. . . .

Source 5   **Excerpts from "An Act Reducing into One, the Several Acts concerning Slaves, Free Negroes, and Mulattoes,"** *Revised Code of the Laws of Virginia,* 1819

61. If any slave hereafter emancipated, shall remain within this Commonwealth more than twelve months after his or her right to freedom shall have accrued, he or she shall forfeit all such right, and may be apprehended and sold by the overseer of the poor of any county or corporation, in which he or she shall be found, for the benefit of the literary fund. . . .

64. It shall not be lawful for any free negro or mulatto, to migrate into this Commonwealth; and every free negro or mulatto, who shall come into this Commonwealth, contrary to this act, shall and may be apprehended and carried by any citizen before some justice of the peace of the county where he shall be taken; which justice is hereby authorised to examine, send, and remove every such free negro or mulatto out of this Commonwealth . . . and every free negro or mulatto so removed or exported, and thereafter returning to this Commonwealth, upon proof thereof made before any magistrate of this Commonwealth, shall receive, by order of such magistrate, thirty-nine lashes on his or her bare back well laid on; which punishment may, at the discretion of any magistrate, be repeated once in every week, so long as such free negro or mulatto shall remain within the Commonwealth.

An Experiment in Tyranny

7.2 Excerpts from Slave Narratives

Slavery was not restricted to the South. During the colonial period, it was found in every colony—North and South—and it was found everywhere within them. It worked farms large and small. It serviced the needs of merchants and mechanics. It served in the homes of the rich as well as the not-so-rich. It was a part of the economic and social structure of colonial life.

Most Americans during the colonial era seem to have been at least mildly troubled by the institution. The American Revolution, and the ideals for which it was waged, forced many Americans to confront their uneasiness. First Pennsylvania, in 1780, and then Massachusetts in 1783, moved to eradicate the institution of slavery within their borders. By 1790, Rhode Island, Connecticut, New York, and New Jersey had followed this lead. In 1787, the Continental Congress banned slavery in the Northwest Territory.

As the eighteenth century came to its close, many Americans accepted as inevitable the notion that slavery would die out within a few decades. The tobacco plantations of the Virginia and Maryland tidewater were in economic decline and slavery was becoming as much a burden as an asset to the planters.

But technology intervened: The invention of the cotton gin gave the South a new cash crop and breathed new life into the institution of slavery. With each succeeding decade following 1800, cotton became more important to the economy of the South, the nation as a whole, and the world at large. The prosperity of the South rested upon a foundation of slavery. The political and social structure of the South rested upon this foundation as well.

As long as slavery existed, there were voices denouncing it. These voices were muffled at first but grew louder and more determined over time. At first, the critics, a minority of society until the eve of the Civil War, saw the emancipation of slaves as a gradual operation followed by the exile, or "colonization," of freed African Americans to the Caribbean or West Africa. By 1830, a minority of this minority shook North and South with the radical suggestion that slavery should end immediately and result in the incorporation of the freed slaves within American society.

As criticism of slavery grew louder, the South grew more defensive. Where the generation of Jefferson viewed slavery as a wrong eventually to be remedied, the generation of Calhoun called it "a positive good," good for the master, good for the slave, good for society as a whole. "Nothing is more certainly written in the book of fate than that these people are to be free," Jefferson noted, "nor is it less certain that the two races, equally free, cannot live in the same government." John C. Calhoun two generations later declared "Slavery . . . the most safe and stable basis for free institutions."

Source 6 Letter from Thomas Jefferson to Representative John Holmes of Massachusetts concerning the Missouri Compromise, April 22, 1820

I thank you, dear Sir, for the copy you have been so kind to send me of the letter to your constituents on the Missouri question. It is a perfect justification to them. I had for a long time ceased to read newspapers, or pay any attention to public affairs, confident they were in good hands, and content to be a passenger in our **bark** to the shore from which I am not distant. But this momentous question, like a fire-bell in the night, awakened and filled me with terror. I considered it at once as the knell of the union. It is hushed, indeed, for the moment. But this is a reprieve only, not a final sentence. A geographical line, coinciding with a marked principle, moral and political, once conceived and held up to the angry passions of men, will never be obliterated; and every new irritation will mark it deeper and deeper. I can say, with conscious truth, that there is not a man on earth who would sacrifice more than I would to relieve us from this heavy reproach, in any *practicable* way. The cession of that kind of property, for so it is misnamed, is a **bagatelle** which would not cost me a second thought, if, in that way, a general emancipation and *expatriation* could be effected; and gradually, with due sacrifices, I think it might be. But as it is, we have the wolf by the ears, and we can neither hold him, nor safely let him go. Justice is on one scale, and self-preservation is on the other. . . .

I regret that I am now to die in the belief, that the useless sacrifice of themselves by the generation of 1776, to acquire self-government and happiness to their country, is to be thrown away by the unwise and unworthy passions of their sons, and that my only consolation is to be, that I live not to weep over it.

Source 7   David Walker, *Walker's Appeal*, 1829

Americans! notwithstanding you have and do continue to treat us more cruel than any heathen nation ever did a people it had subjected to the same condition that you have us. Now let us reason—I mean you of the United States, whom I believe God designs to save from destruction, if you will hear. . . . Remember Americans, that we must and shall be free and enlightened as you are, will you wait until we shall, under God, obtain our liberty by the crushing arm of power? Will it not be dreadful for you? I speak Americans for your good. We must and shall be free I say, in spite of you. You may do your best to keep us in wretchedness and misery, to enrich you and your children, but God will deliver us from you. And wo, wo, will be to you if we have to obtain our freedom by fighting. Throw away your fears and prejudices then, and enlighten us and treat us like men, and we will like you more than we now hate you, and tell us now no more about colonization, for America is as much our country, as it is yours.— Treat us like men, and there is no danger but we will all live in peace and happiness together. For we are not like you, hard-hearted, unmerciful, and unforgiving. What a happy country this will be, if the whites will listen. What nation under heaven, will be able to do any thing with us, unless God gives us up into its hand? But Americans, I declare to you, while you keep us and our children in bondage, we cannot be your friends. . . .

If any are anxious to ascertain who I am, know the world, that I am one of the oppressed, degraded and wretched sons of Africa, rendered so by the avaricious and unmerciful, among the whites—If any wish to plunge me into the wretched incapacity of a slave, or murder me for the truth, know ye, that I am in the hand of God, and at your disposal. I count my life not dear unto me, but I am ready to be offered at any moment. For what is the use of living, when in fact I am dead?

Source 8   Robert Young Hayne of South Carolina, Webster-Hayne
Debate, speech to the United States Senate, January 21, 1830

Mr. President, . . . I embrace the occasion presented by the remarks of the gentleman from Massachusetts to declare that we are ready to meet the question promptly and fearlessly. It is one from which we are not disposed to shrink in whatever form or under whatever circumstances it may be pressed upon us.

We are ready to take up the issue with the gentleman as to the influence of slavery on the prosperity and greatness of the United States or of particular States. Sir, when arraigned before the bar of public opinion on this charge of slavery we can stand up with conscious rectitude, plead not guilty, and put ourselves upon God and our country. Sir, we will not consent to look at slavery in the abstract. We will not stop to inquire whether the black man, as some philosophers have contended, is of an inferior race, nor whether his color and condition are effects of a curse inflected for the offences of his ancestors? We deal in no abstractions. We will not look back to inquire whether our fathers were guiltless in introducing slaves into this country? If an inquiry should ever be instituted in these matters, however, it will be found that the profits of the slave-trade were not confined to the South. Southern ships and Southern sailors were not the instruments of bringing slaves to the shores of America, nor did our merchants reap the profits of that "accursed traffic."

But, sir, we will pass over all this. If slavery, as it now exists in this country, be an evil, we of the present day found it ready made to our hands. Finding our lot cast among a people whom God had manifestly committed to our care we did not sit down to speculate on abstract questions of theoretical liberty. We met it as a practical question of obligation and duty. We resolved to make the best of the situation in which Providence had placed us, and to fulfill the high trusts which had devolved upon us as the owners of slaves in the only way in which such a trust could be fulfilled without spreading misery and ruin throughout the land.

We found that we had to deal with a people whose physical, moral, and intellectual habits and character totally disqualified them from the enjoyment of the blessings of freedom. We could not send them back to the shores from whence their fathers had been taken; their numbers forbade the thought, even if we did not know that their condition here is infinitely preferable to what it possibly could be among the barren sands and savage tribes of Africa; and it was wholly irreconcilable with our notions of humanity to tear asunder the tender ties which they had formed among us to gratify the feelings of a false philanthropy.

What a commentary on the wisdom, justice, and humanity of the Southern slave-owner is presented by the example of certain benevolent associations and charitable individuals elsewhere! Shedding weak tears over sufferings which had existence only in their own sickly imaginations, these "friends of humanity" set themselves systematically to work to seduce the slaves of the South from their masters. By means of missionaries and political tracts the scheme was in great measure successful. Thousands of these deluded victims of fanaticism were seduced into the enjoyment of freedom in our northern cities.

And what has been the consequences? Go to these cities now and ask the question. Visit the dark and narrow lanes and obscure recesses which have been assigned by common consent as the abodes of those outcasts of the world—the free people of color. Sir, there does not exist on the face of the whole earth a population so poor, so wretched, so vile, so loathsome, so utterly destitute of all the comforts, conveniences, and decencies of life as the unfortunate blacks of Philadelphia, New York, and Boston. Liberty has been the greatest of calamities, the greatest of curses.

Sir, I have had some opportunities to make comparison between the condition of the free negroes of the north and the slaves of the south, and the comparison has left not only an indelible impression of the superior advantages of the latter, but has gone far to reconcile me to slavery itself. Never have I felt so forcibly that touching description, "The foxes have holes, and the birds of the air have nests, but the Son of Man hath not where to lay his head," as when I have seen this unhappy race, naked and houseless, almost starving in the streets, and abandoned by all the world. Sir, I have seen, in the neighborhood of one of the most moral, religious, and refined cities of the north, a family of free blacks driven to the caves of the rocks, and there obtaining a precarious subsistence from charity and plunder.

Source 9   Daniel Webster of Massachusets, Webster-Hayne Debate,
speech to the United States Senate, January 26, 1830

I know full well that it is, and has been, the settled policy of some persons in the South, for years, to represent the people of the North as disposed to interfere with them in their own exclusive and peculiar concerns. This is a delicate and sensitive point in Southern feeling; and of late years it has always been touched, and generally with effect, whenever the object has been to unite the whole South against Northern men or Northern measures. This feeling, always carefully kept alive, and maintained at too intense a heat to admit discrimination or reflection, is a lever of great power in our political machine. It moves vast bodies, and gives to them one and the same direction. But it is without all adequate cause; and the suspicion which exists wholly groundless. There is not, and never has been, a disposition in the North to interfere with these interests of the South. Such interference has never been supposed to be within the power of the government; nor has it been in any way attempted. The slavery of the South has always been regarded a matter of domestic policy, left with the States themselves, and with which the Federal Government had nothing to do. Certainly, sir, I am and ever have been of that opinion. The gentleman, indeed, argues that slavery in the abstract is no evil. Most assuredly I need not say I differ with him, altogether and most widely, on that point. I regard domestic slavery as one of the greatest of evils, both moral and political. But though it be a malady, and whether it be curable, and if so, by what means; or, on the other hand, whether it be the *vulnus immedicabile* of the social system, I leave it to those whose right and duty it is to inquire and to decide. And this, I believe, sir, is, and uniformly has been, the sentiment of the North.

Source 10   Abolitionist Angelina E. Grimke of South Carolina, speech
delivered at the Women's Anti-Slavery Convention,
Pennsylvania, May 16, 1838

As a Southerner I feel it is my duty to stand up here tonight and bear testimony against slavery. I have seen it—I have seen it. I know it has horrors that can never be described. I was brought up under its wing; I witnessed for many years its demoralizing influences; and its destructiveness to human happiness.

It is admitted by some that the slave is not happy under the *worst* forms of slavery. But I have *never* seen a happy slave. I have seen him dance in his chains, it is true; but he is not happy. There is a wide difference between happiness and mirth. Man cannot enjoy the former while his manhood is destroyed, and that part of the being which is necessary to the making, and to the enjoyment, of happiness is completely blotted out. . . .

Many times I have wept in the land of my birth over the system of slavery.

Source 11 Horace Mann, "The Institution of Slavery," speech delivered in the House of Representatives, August 17, 1852

Let me inquire whether it be not demonstrable that the relation of slavery between man and man comprehends, perpetuates, multiplies, and aggravates all forms of crime which it is possible for a human being to commit.

Is the stealing, even of one shilling, a crime? Slavery steals all that a man can call his own; and is not the whole greater than a part? Is robbery, which is defined to be the taking of any part of a man's goods "from his person, or in his presence, against his will, by violence, or putting him in fear," a crime? Slavery answers the exact definition of the law books, for it is by violence and by putting in bodily fear that a master ravishes from a slave all his earnings and all his ability to earn, from birth till death. And again, I say, is not the whole greater than a part? Is the destruction of any man's house by fire a crime? How much greater the crime of preventing millions of men from having a house they can call their own?

Is concubinage a crime? In this Union all the adult portion of more than three millions of people are now forced to live in a state of concubinage. Is it a crime to abandon innocent females to the lusts of guilty men without the slightest protection of law? In this country a million and a half of females constantly are so abandoned; and the rearing of dark-skinned beauties for the harems of republican sultans is a systematized and legalized business.

Is it a crime to break asunder all the ties of human affection, to tear children from the arms of their parents and parents from each other? There is no conjugal or parental or filial affection among more than three millions of people in this land which is sacred from such violation.

Is it a crime to let murder and all other offences go unpunished? There is no form of crime which a white man may not commit against a slave with entire impunity, if he will take the precaution to let none but slaves witness it.

The darkening of the intellect, the shrouding of a soul in the gloom of ignorance, the forbidding of a spirit which God made in his own image to commune with its Maker; is more than a common crime; it is sacrilege; it is the sacrilege of sacrileges. It is a crime which no other nation on this earth, civilized, heathen, or barbarian, ever committed to the extent that it is committed here.

And yet this locking of the temple of knowledge against a whole race, this drawing of an impenetrable veil between the soul of man and his Maker, this rebellion against all that God has done to reveal himself to his offspring through the works of nature and the revelations of his providence, is enacted into laws, guarded by terrible penalties and administered by men who call themselves Christians as though Christ could have subscribed or executed such laws. . . .

I repeat, then, that the worst forms of all the crimes which a human being can commit—theft, robbery, murder, adultery, incest, sacrilege, and whatever else there is that inflicts wide-wasting ruin upon society, and brings the souls of men to perdition—the word "slavery" is the synonym of them all.

Analyze slavery and you will find its ingredients to consist of every crime. Define any crime and you will find it to be incorporated in slavery and aggravated by it.

Source 12   Orestes Augustus Brownson, Vermont theologian, "Oration on Liberal Studies," June 29, 1853

The prejudice against aristocracy arises from the very common error that if there is an aristocracy it must exist for itself, and that the people must be held to exist for the aristocracy, not the aristocracy for the people. I have as little sympathy as any of my democratic countrymen with the doctrine which teaches that the many are made to be "hewers of wood and drawers of water" to the few. I am a Christian, not a pagan, and I hold all men to be of one blood and to have the common rights of humanity, and one man has and can have no dominion over another except in consideration of services rendered. I say not with our Abolitionists that man can have no property in man, but I do say, after the Supreme Pontiff Alexander III, that all men by the law of nature are free. I do not deny the right of the Southern master to the services of his slave; but I do deny that he derives that right from the municipal law which recognizes and defends it. As between him and his slave the master's right is founded, and can be founded, only on the benefits he confers on the slave, and the measure of these benefits is the measure of the services he has the right to exact in return. The slave, no matter what his color or his race is a man, a human being, with all the natural rights of his master. He has the *jus dominii* of himself as fully as his master. I must go against common sense, and the spirit of Catholic teachings, to deny this. But the master has a claim upon him for the services he renders him. He protects and nurses him during his infancy, feeds and clothes him during life, and takes care of him in sickness and old age. This may not be, and probably is not, ordinarily as much as the services of the slave are worth to the master; but it is more than the labor of the slave, upon a general average, would be worth to himself if obliged to take the sole care of himself. Take the class of slaves, and suppose the masters take proper care of them and do not overwork them, which seldom happens, and there can be no doubt that the slave receives his maintenance, in the provision made for him in infancy, sickness, and old age, a reasonable compensation for his services, and more than the Northern laborer ever does or can receive for the same amount of labor, for the Northern laborer works nearly double the number of hours that the slave does, with far more intensity and with fewer recreations. Your negroes when properly treated are no doubt better off and better paid for their labor than they would be if emancipated, and therefore the masters have a right to their services and to retain them in their present condition. No doubt there are instances in which the relation is abused, but this is another consideration and to be disposed of on other principles, for the abuse of a thing does not deny the legitimacy of its use.

Society is to be regarded as a whole as a sort of living organism in which there are many parts, distinguishable but not separable one from another. All the parts are necessary, all should be knit together in a living union and move on in concert as a living and reasonable being. The head is not to be valued without the body; nor the body without the members; yet the body should have a head, and the head should be regarded as the more noble part. The aristocracy are not to be separated from the body of the nation, are not to be regarded as existing apart and for themselves alone, but as existing for the nation, for the service of the people, and the common good of the whole. Nobility is not a personal right, it is a trust—a trust from God for the common good of the nation.

Source 13 French philosopher Victor Cousin, *The True, the Beautiful, and the Good,* 1854

I ought to respect your body, inasmuch as it belongs to you, inasmuch as it is the necessary instrument of your person. I have neither the right to kill you, nor to wound you, unless I am attacked and threatened; then my violated liberty is armed with a new right, the right of self-defence and even constraint.

I owe respect to your goods, for they are the product of your labor; I owe respect to your labor, which is your liberty itself in exercise; and, if your goods come from an inheritance, I still owe respect to the free will that has transmitted them to you.

Respect for the rights of others is called justice; every violation of a right is an injustice.

Every injustice is an encroachment upon our person. . . .

The greatest of all injustices, because it comprises all others, is slavery. Slavery is the subjecting of all the faculties of one man to the profit of another man. The slave develops his intelligence a little only in the interest of another—it is not for the purpose of enlightening him, but to render him more useful, that some exercise of mind is allowed him. The slave has not the liberty of his movements; he is attached to the soil, is sold with it, or he is chained to the person of the master. The slave should have no affection, he has no family, no wife, no children—he has a female and little ones. His activity does not belong to him, for the product of his labor is another's. But, that nothing may be wanting to slavery, it is necessary to go further—in the slave must be destroyed the inborn sentiment of liberty; in him must be extinguished all idea of right; for, as long as this idea subsists, slavery is uncertain, and to an odious power may respond the terrible right of insurrection, that last resort of the oppressed against the abuse of force.

Justice, respect for the person in everything that constitutes the person, is the first duty of man toward his fellowman.

Source 14 Historian Richard Hildreth, *Despotism in America: An Inquiry into the Nature, Results, and Legal Basis of the Slave-Holding System in the United States,* 1854

The relation of master and slave, like most other kinds of despotism, has its origin in war. By the confession of its warmest defenders, slavery is at its best, but a substitute for homicide.

Savages take no prisoners; or those they do take, they first torture, and then devour. But when the arts of life have made some progress, and the value of labor begins to be understood, it is presently discovered that to eat prisoners is not the most profitable use to which they can be put. Accordingly their lives are spared; and they are compelled to labor for the benefit of their captors. Such is the origin of Slavery.

It was formerly a practice in America to sell as slaves such Indians as were captured during the frequent wars waged with the aboriginal inhabitants. But the great mass of those unfortunate persons held in servitude throughout the southern states, derive their origin from another source.

A Virginia planter deduces the legitimacy of his dominion by the following process. Your great-grandmother being captured by a certain African prince,—in a war, undertaken, doubtless, for the mere purpose of making prisoners,—was sold upon the coast of Guinea to a certain Yankee slave-trader; and being transported by him to James River, was there sold to a certain tobacco planter. In time, your great-grandmother died; but she left children to which as a part of her produce, the owner of the mother was justly entitled. From that owner, through diverse alienations and descents, the title has passed to me; and as you are descended from the woman above referred to, it is quite clear, how perfectly reasonable and just my empire is.

Whether in point of logic and morals, the above deduction is completely satisfactory, is not now the question. The nature of the master's claim is stated here, only as an assistance towards apprehension of the relations which grow out of it.

Slavery then is a continuation of the state of war. It is true that one of the combatants is subdued and bound; but the war is not terminated. If I do not put the captive to death, this apparent clemency does not arise from any good-will towards him, or any extinction on my part of hostile feelings and intentions. I spare his life merely because I expect to be able to put him to a use more advantageous to myself. And if the captive, on the other hand feigns submission, still he is only watching for an opportunity to escape my grasp, and if possible to inflict on me evils as great as those to which I have subjected him.

Source 15 James Henry Hammond of South Carolina, speech to the
United States Senate, March 4, 1858

In all social systems there must be a class to do the menial duties, to perform the drudgery of life. That is, a class requiring but a low order of intellect and but little skill. Its requisites are vigor, docility, fidelity. Such a class you must have, or you would not have that other class which leads progress, civilization, and refinement. It constitutes the very mud-sill of society and of political government; and you might as well attempt to build a house in the air, as to build either the one or the other, except on this mud-sill. Fortunately for the South, she found a race adapted to that purpose to her hand. A race inferior to her own, but eminently qualified in temper, in vigor, in docility, in capacity to stand the climate, to answer all her purposes. We use them for our purpose and we call them slaves. . . . I will not characterize that class at the North by that term; but you have it; it is there; it is everywhere; it is eternal.

The Senator from New York said yesterday that the whole world had abolished slavery. Aye, the *name,* but not the *thing;* all the powers of the earth cannot abolish that. . . . The difference between us is, that our slaves are hired for life and well compensated; there is no starvation, no begging, no want of employment among our people, and not too much employment either. Yours are hired by the day, not cared for, and scantily compensated, which may be proved in the most painful manner, at any hour in any street of your large towns. Why, you meet more beggars in one day, in any single street of the city of New York, than you would meet in a lifetime in the whole South. We do not think that whites should be slaves either by law or necessity. Our slaves are black, of another and inferior race. The *status* in which we have placed them is an elevation. They are elevated from the condition in which God first created them, by being made our slaves. None of that race on the whole face of the globe can be compared with the slaves of the South. They are happy, content, unaspiring, and utterly incapable, from intellectual weakness, ever to give us any trouble by their aspirations. Yours are white, of your own race; you are brothers of one blood. They are your equals in natural endowment of intellect, and they feel galled by their degradation.

Source 16 William Henry Seward, "On the Irrepressible Conflict," October 25, 1858

Our country is a theatre which exhibits in full operation two radically different political systems; the one resting on the basis of servile or slave labor, the other on the basis of voluntary labor of freemen.

The laborers who are enslaved are all negroes, or persons more or less purely of African derivation. But this is only accidental. The principle of the system is, that labor in every society, by whomsoever performed, is necessarily unintellectual, grovelling, and base; and that the laborer, equally for his own good and for the welfare of the State, ought to be enslaved. The white laboring man, whether native or foreigner, is not enslaved, only because he cannot as yet be reduced to bondage.

You need not be told that the slave is the older of the two and that once it was universal. . . . One of the chief elements of the value of human life is freedom in the pursuit of happiness. The slave system is not only intolerable, unjust, and inhuman towards the laborer, whom, only because he is a laborer, it loads down with chains and converts into merchandise; but is scarcely less severe upon the freeman, to whom, only because he is a laborer from necessity, it denies facilities for employment, and whom it expels from the community because it cannot enslave and convert him into merchandise also. It is necessarily improvident and ruinous, because, as a general truth, communities prosper and flourish, or droop and decline, in just the degree that they practise or neglect to practise the primary duties of justice and humanity. The fee-labor system conforms to the divine law of equality which is written in the hearts and consciences of men, and therefore is always and everywhere beneficent.

The slave system is one of constant danger, distrust, suspicion, and watchfulness. It debases those whose toil alone can produce wealth and resources for defence to the lowest degree of which human nature is capable, to guard against mutiny and insurrection, and thus wastes energies which otherwise might be employed in national development and aggrandizement.

The free-labor system educates all alike, and by opening all the fields of industrial employment and all the departments of authority to the unchecked and equal rivalry of all classes of men at once secures universal contentment and brings into the highest possible activity all the physical, moral, and social energies of the whole State. In States where the slave system prevails, the masters, directly or indirectly, secure all political power and constitute a ruling aristocracy. In States where the free-labor system prevails universal suffrage necessarily obtains and the State becomes, sooner or later, a republic or democracy. . . .

The two systems are at once perceived to be incongruous. But they are more than incongruous—they are incompatible. They never have permanently existed together in one country and they never can. It would be easy to demonstrate this impossibility from the irreconcilable contrast between their great principles and characteristics. But the experience of mankind has conclusively established it. . . .

In the United States slavery came into collision with free labor at the close of the last century, and fell before it in New England, New York, New Jersey, and Pennsylvania, but triumphed over it effectually, and excluded it for a period yet undetermined, from Virginia, the Carolinas, and Georgia. Indeed, so incompatible are the two systems that every new State which is organized within our ever-extending domain makes its first political act a choice of the one and the exclusion of the other, even at the cost of civil war if necessary. . . .

Hitherto the two systems have existed in different States, side by side within the American Union. This has happened because the Union is a confederation of States. But in another aspect the United States constitute only one nation. Increase of population, which is filling the States out to their very borders, together with a new and extended network of railroads and other avenues, and an internal commerce which daily becomes more intimate, is rapidly bringing the States into a higher and more perfect social unity or consolidation. Thus, these antagonistic systems are continually coming into closer contact and collision results.

Shall I tell you what this collision means? They who think that it is accidental, unnecessary, the work of interested or fanatical agitators, and therefore ephemeral, mistake the case altogether. It is an irrepressible conflict between opposing and enduring forces, and it means that the United States must and will, sooner or later, become either entirely a slave-holding nation or entirely a free-labor union.

Source 17   *New Orleans Picayune,* August 21, 1859

The law enacted last Winter by the Legislature of Louisiana, placing all free negroes under the most rigid surveillance, who may arrive in this state on shipboard or steamboats, goes into effect the 1st of September next.

All free persons of color, arriving in port from abroad, must immediately be lodged in jail, and remain there until the departure of the boat or vessel on which they came; masters of steamboats and ships must report to the Chief of Police all such persons belonging to their crews, or incur severe penalties.

It will be well for all masters of vessels and steamboats trading with this State, to bear in mind the provisions of this law, as it will save them from much trouble, and perhaps pecuniary loss. The evils attending the increase of a free negro population, and more particularly the intercourse of free persons of color from abroad with our slaves, caused the passage of this stringent law.

Source 18 Professor C. F. McCay, Columbia College, South Carolina, *Eighty Years' Progress of the United States,* 1860

Probably the greatest advantage we have ... is in the cheapness of our labor. ... We have the cheapest and most efficient labor in the world.

The African slave in the southern states is well fed with good and substantial food, that gives him strength, endurance, and health. He is well clad in winter, and well lodged, to protect him from the inclemencies of the season. He is cheerful, able to work, and he works faithfully. As the whole cost of this labor to the state is made up of the simplest necessities of life, the support of the young, and the old, and the feeble, it is evident that the south has the cheapest labor that is possible. It was the doctrine of Malthus, that in every country there is a constant tendency to reduce the wages of labor down to the mere support of the laborer. That limit, however approximated to elsewhere, has never been reached but in the south.

The slave is supplied with all he wants of meal, and with as much meat as is needed for his health and strength. This meal is prepared in many ways, and makes a most palatable bread. His master generally feeds on it in preference to flour. He has a garden, where he can raise potatoes, cabbage, collards, greens, turnips, beans, and such other vegetables as the taste and industry of the family may desire. He has clothing—cheap, it is true, but warm and substantial.

There is a separate dwelling for each family, and an unlimited supply of fuel for the winter. The old, who are unable to labor in the field, find some slight work about the house—the men in the garden, the women in the care of young children whose mothers are out on the usual plantation work. The sick are carefully attended to by regular physicians and good nursing.

All this is essential to the health and strength of the laborer, and to his efficiency on the plantation. The humanity and sympathy of the master, who has often been reared by some of his slaves, are sufficient to secure their comfort; but if there should be wanting, there is an inexorable law securing the necessary wants of the servant. With less meat, or with insufficient food, the slave is unfitted for regular work. With less clothing, he is liable to sickness and disease. Without attention and nursing in sickness, his life is endangered, and his services lost to his master. These demands, united with the influences of humanity and sympathy, secure him the necessities and some of the comforts of life.

Another element of the cheapness of this labor is that nothing is wasted in vicious indulgences. In other countries, a large part of the wages of labor is expended in strong drink; but the most stringent laws are everywhere passed against selling spirits to slaves. ...

Much time is lost in free countries in holidays and shows; in idleness and neglect of work; in seeking employment; in change from one place to another; but all this is saved in the south, for there are no idle hands about the plantation, and excepting the week between Christmas and New Year's day, when there is a general holiday, there is no lost time, except for sickness, in any part of the year.

The children are all put to work at eleven or twelve years of age, as soon as they are able to guide a plough or pick cotton in the fields. The women and men are both efficient workers, and the division of labor is so complete that the children of many mothers are watched over and cared for by one, and the cooking for many families attended to by a single cook.

This system of labor is thus the cheapest possible. The corn and the meat being, in most cases, raised on the plantation, and not burdened with the cost of transportation, are supplied at the cheapest prices; the work is all light and easy, so that women and boys, as well as men, can engage in it efficiently. Everything is arranged so that labor is secured at the lowest possible rate.

Some philanthropists, indeed, object to the system on this account: that the slave obtains no wages. But he has food and clothing, a house and fire, proper attention when sick, and support in old age. His children are taken care of, and every necessary want supplied. For an idle and improvident race like the negro, these are more than wages. They are more than his industry would secure. He would not earn as much for himself were he free, as he now receives from his master; and these earnings would be wasted in drink, or in excessive indulgences, or in dress, or in luxuries, leaving for himself and his family times of want and suffering, with nothing laid up for sickness and old age. Now he is industrious and temperate, and receives the necessities of life in return; then he would be lazy, and wasteful, and destitute. As industry and temperance are great virtues, and the necessities of life at all seasons and times, in sickness and heath, in youth and old age are a great boon to the laboring poor; and as want, and suffering, and neglect when sick or aged are great and real evils, philanthropy surely wastes its sympathy on the slave when it complains that he is denied his wages. . . .

On many plantations there are one or two hundred negroes, all descended from three or four families; while the children of the first master have been scattered from Maine to Texas. They have regularly improved since introduced from Africa, and are now improving, from year to year, in intelligence, in moral culture, in intellectual development, in appearance, in habits, in comfort; and they are as cheerful and faithful; as devoted to the interests of their master, as attached to him and his family, as if they were free hired servants, receiving regular wages. There is no mendicity, no need for poor houses, asylums, hospitals; for the master's house is the asylum of the slaves.

📖 *Second Thoughts*

"A Substitute for Homicide"

7.3 Africans
in America

The Puritans of New England found Biblical references to people taken as captives in war being compelled into the service of their captors, and they took this as divine approval for slavery. First, Native Americans, and then Africans and African Americans, were enslaved by the New Englanders on this basis. Colonists in the South found justification enough for slavery in the prevailing economic and social circumstances. By the time of the Civil War, one of every eight people living in the United States was a slave.

Slavery remained legal in the United States until the ratification of the Thirteenth Amendment, December 18, 1865. Historians have offered differing opinions about slavery and how it came to exist in America.

Source 19 John Fiske, *Old Virginia and Her Neighbors*, 1897

The economic circumstances which chiefly determined the complexion of society in South Carolina was the cultivation of rice and indigo. . . . Rice and indigo absorbed the principal attention of the colony, as tobacco absorbed the attention of Virginia. . . . Now the cultivation of rice and indigo are both very unhealthy occupations. The work in the swamps is deadly to white men. But after 1713 negroes were brought to South Carolina in such numbers that an athletic man could be had for 40 pounds or less. Every such negro could raise in a single year much more indigo or rice than would repay the cost of his purchase, so that it was actually more profitable to work him to death than to take care of him.

Source 20 Ulrich B. Phillips, *Life and Labor in the Old South*, 1929

Let us begin by discussing the weather, for that has been the chief agency in making the South distinctive. It fostered the cultivation of the staple crops, which promoted the plantation system, which brought the importation of negroes, which not only gave rise to chattel slavery but created a lasting race problem. These led to controversy and regional rivalry for power, which produced apprehensive reactions and culminated in a stroke for independence. Thus we have the house that Jack built, otherwise known for some years as the Confederate States of America.

Source 21 Charles and Mary Beard, *A Basic History of the United States*, 1944

As early as 1619 Negroes were brought to Virginia and soon slavery became an established institution under the law. Before many years it spread to all the colonies, and by 1770 about one-sixth of the entire population were Negro slaves.

In the North, however, climate, soil, and types of agriculture made slavery on a large scale unprofitable; and, comparatively speaking, the proportion of Negro slaves remained small. In the colony of New York, for example, where it was high, it amounted to about one-seventh of the population at the end of the colonial period. On the other hand the climate, soil, staple crops, and plantation system of the South favored the use of slave labor. White bond servants were often intractable, their terms of service made them impermanent laborers, and the most enterprising among them valiantly struggled to get land for themselves as soon as they became free. Negro slaves by contrast had to work for their masters as long as they lived and could be bought in great numbers as the slave traffic increased. Only by slavery, planters insisted, was it possible for them to expand the cultivation of the soil and make profits in large amounts. At all events, two-thirds of the inhabitants of South Carolina were slaves at the close of the colonial period, and along the Southern seaboard the labor of Negroes underlay the wealth and power of masters.

Source 22 Kenneth M. Stampp, *The Peculiar Institution*, 1956

What caused the growth of this institutional affliction which had so severe an impact upon the lives of so many Southerners? Some historians have traced the origin of southern slavery to a morbidic quality in the southern climate. Though admitting great climatic variations within the South and the normal mildness of the winter season, they have emphasized the weather's fiercer moods—the torrential rains, the searing droughts, above all, the humid heat of subtropical summers. Since Southerners were unable to control the weather, they had to come to terms with it. So it was the climate that determined the nature of their institutions and the structure of their society. . . .

If climate alone could not explain everything, then perhaps certain additional factors, such as soil, topography, and watercourses, contributed to a broader geographical determinism. Combine the hot summers and long growing seasons with the rich southern soils—the alluvial river bottoms, the sandy loams of the coastal plains, the silt loams of the black belt, and the red clay of the piedmont—and an agricultural economy was the logical result. Add the navigable rivers which facilitated the movement of bulky staples from considerable distances inland to coastal ports, and all the requirements for a commercial form of agriculture were at hand. Commercial agriculture induced a trend toward large landholdings which in turn created a demand for labor. Thus some have argued that Southerners, in permitting slavery to grow, had merely submitted to compelling natural forces.

Human institutions, however, have not been formed by forces as rigidly deterministic as this. To be sure, men must inevitably make certain adjustments to fixed environmental conditions. But, within limits, these adjustments may take a variety of forms. At different times and in different places roughly similar environmental conditions have produced vastly different human responses. Some human adaptations have been far more successful than others. For this reason one must examine the forms of southern institutions as closely as the facts of the southern environment.

It may be that unfree labor alone made possible the early rise of the plantation system, but this proves neither the necessity nor the inevitability of slavery. Actually, the southern plantation was older than slavery and survived its abolition. More important, there was nothing inevitable about the plantation. Without a continuing supply of bondsmen, southern agriculture, in its early development at least, would probably have depended more upon small-farm units and given less emphasis to the production of staple crops. Under these circumstances the South might have developed more slowly, but it would not have remained a wilderness. There was no crop cultivated by slaves that could not have been cultivated by other forms of labor, no area fit for human habitation that would have been passed by for want of slave labor. The slave-plantation system answered no "specific need" that could not have been answered in some other way.

Slavery, then, cannot be attributed to some deadly atmospheric miasma or some irresistible force in the South's economic evolution. The use of slaves in southern agriculture was a deliberate choice (among several alternatives) made by men who sought greater returns than they could obtain from their own labor alone, and who found other types of labor more expensive. "For what purpose does the master hold the servant?" asked an ante-bellum Southerner. "Is it not that by his labor he, the master, may accumulate wealth?" The rise of slavery in the South was inevitable only in the sense that every event in history seems inevitable after it has occurred.

Source 23 Eugene Genovese, *The Political Economy of Slavery,* 1967

I have rejected the currently fashionable interpretation of slavery as simply a system of extra-economic compulsion designed to sweat a surplus out of black labor. It supported a plantation community that must be understood as an integrated social system, and made this community the center of Southern life. It extruded a class of slaveholders with a special ideology and psychology and the political and economic power to impose their values on society as a whole. Slavery may have been immoral to the world at large, but to these men, notwithstanding their doubts and inner conflicts, it increasingly came to be seen as the very foundation of a proper social order and therefore as the essence of morality in human relationships.

Source 24 Dick Gregory, *No More Lies: The Myth and the Reality of American History,* 1971

American mythology states that originally black folks were treated the same as white indentured servants; that slavery did not appear until certain colonial statutes . . . and that the good colonial church folks would have practiced racial equality if they had been left alone to pursue their better instincts. Some very early legal statutes indicate that black folks were the victims of racial discrimination at the outset of colonization. In Virginia, between 1630 and 1646, statutes and resolutions appear: (1) accusing a white man of defiling his body and dishonoring himself because he had intercourse with a black woman; (2) prohibiting black men and no one else from carrying guns; and (3) wording the text in such a way as to indicate that the black man was in the same category as an object and not as a human being.

Source 25 John Hope Franklin, *From Slavery to Freedom,* 1974

Virginians began to see what neighboring islands in the Caribbean had already recognized, that is, that Negroes could not easily escape without being identified; that they could be disciplined, even punished, with impunity since they were not Christians; and that the supply was apparently inexhaustible. Black labor was precisely what Virginia needed in order to speed up the clearing of the forests and the cultivation of larger and better tobacco crops. All that was required was the legislative approval of a practice in which many Virginians were already engaged. Indeed, by 1640, some Africans in Virginia had become bondmen for life. The distinction between black and white servants was becoming well established. In that year, when three runaway servants, two white and one black, were recaptured, the court ordered the white servants to serve their master one additional year. Meanwhile, the Negro was ordered "to serve his said master or his assigns for the time of his natural life here or elsewhere." Thus, within the first generation of Virginia's existence, African servitude was well on the way to becoming African slavery.

Source 26 David Brion Davis, *The Problem of Slavery in Western Culture,* 1988

For three and a half centuries the principal maritime powers competed with one another in the lucrative slave trade, and carried nearly ten million Africans to the New World. Historians have long been inclined to regard this vast movement of population as an unfortunate but relatively minor incident in American history. Interest in national and sectional history has often obscured the significance of Negro slavery in the overall development of the Americas. But if the institution was of little economic importance in Massachusetts or Nova Scotia, it nevertheless extended from Rio de la Plata to the Saint Lawrence, and was the basic system of labor in the colonies most valued by Europe. In the most profitable colonies Negro slaves were employed in mines and in clearing virgin land, or on the great plantations which provided Europe with sugar, rice, tobacco, cotton, and indigo. The northern colonies that were unsuited for the production of staple crops became dependent, early in their history, on supplying the slave colonies with goods and provisions of various kinds. As a stimulus to shipbuilding, insurance, investment, and banking, the slave trade expanded employment in a diversity of occupations and encouraged the growth of seaports on both sides of the Atlantic. Africa became a prized market for iron, textiles, firearms, rum, and brandy. Investments in the triangular trade brought dazzling rewards, since profits could be made in exporting consumer goods to Africa, in selling slaves to planters, and especially in transporting sugar and other staples to Europe. By the 1760's a large number of the wealthy merchants in Britain and France were connected in some way with the West Indian trade; and capital accumulated from investment in slaves and their produce helped to finance the building of canals, factories, and railroads. Even after the United States had achieved independence and a more diversified economy, her principal export was slave-grown cotton, which was the chief raw material for the industrial revolution.

Without exaggerating the economic significance of Negro slavery, we may safely conclude that it played a major role in the early development of the New World and in the growth of commercial capitalism. Given the lack of an alternative labor supply, it is difficult to see how European nations could have settled America and exploited its resources without the aid of African slaves.

Questioning the Past

1. For what reasons did slavery take root in the American colonies?

2. Present the arguments offered by proponents of slavery in support of the institution. Assess the merits of these arguments. Present the arguments offered by the opponents of human bondage. Assess the merits of these arguments.

3. Present the arguments in support of the view that slavery was both an inevitable and essential part of the successful founding of the English colonies in the New World. Present the arguments in opposition to the notion of the inevitability and necessity of slavery in the New World. Which argument is the stronger?

4. James Henry Hammond argues that all societies are built on a "mud-sill" class. Is this true? Does every society have an aristocracy and a class of slaves, whether those names are applied to them or not?

5. Did racism create and perpetuate slavery? Can slavery be plausibly explained by any other motivation?

Chapter 8

An Act of Toleration

The Maryland Assembly Passes a Toleration Act   *April 21, 1649*

By the middle of the sixteenth century, Europe had suffered several generations of conflict between Catholics and Protestants. Religious differences had turned neighbor against neighbor and nation against nation; warfare over such differences was common. To be a Protestant in a Catholic country or a Catholic in a Protestant country was to invite persecution. It was therefore something of an anomaly to find in one small corner of the British Empire—a kingdom whose armies had often fought forces loyal to the Church of Rome—a place of sanctuary for Catholics. This was the small colony called Maryland, which King Charles I had carved from Virginia, from the **right bank** of the Potomac River to the Atlantic coast, and given to his friend and confidant, George Calvert, Lord Baltimore. Calvert, a former Privy Council member and secretary of state under Charles, had converted to Catholicism in 1624 and hoped that Maryland might become a place of refuge for England's persecuted Catholics. He also hoped his proprietorship would bring him wealth. He died while preparing to colonize the area, leaving the task to his son Cecil Calvert.

Funded by the Calverts, the *Ark* and the *Dove* set sail from England and made landfall in southern Maryland in 1634, where the colonists purchased land already under cultivation from native peoples. The settlement was an economic success from its beginnings, producing income for the Calvert family throughout the colonial period. Their annual fee to the Crown for proprietorship was two Indian arrows and a fifth of all the gold and silver found—a small price to pay, since arrows were plentiful in Maryland and gold and silver were not.

Religious politics thus occupied the Calverts far more than economics did. Most of the *Ark* and *Dove* passengers were Anglicans, as were most of the English settlers in surrounding colonies. Concerned for the Catholic minority, Calvert advised them to conduct their worship as privately as possible, and dispatched his brother Leonard to serve as governor of Maryland, directing him not to interfere with Protestant religious practices. Both sets of instructions were followed, but other factors increased religious tension in the colony. Maryland had accepted a community of Puritans from Virginia; the Protestant ranks in England were divided by Puritans who wanted to "purify" the Anglican Church of its Catholic influences and were intolerant of views other than their own; and a Puritan faction in Parliament led by Oliver Cromwell had overthrown the English monarchy, beheaded Charles I, and plunged the nation into civil war. In this volatile atmosphere, Lord Baltimore appointed a Protestant, William

Stone, as governor, and granted the majority a greater voice in colonial affairs. Lord Baltimore took one more step; he presented his colony with an extraordinary document.

❧ *First Impressions*
A Law of Maryland concerning Religion

8.1 The
Catholic
Encyclopedia

Lord Baltimore, hoping to protect the ruling Catholic minority from colonial tensions and those in the Empire, directed his new governor and the legislature, composed of Catholics and Protestants, to approve an act that became a milestone in American history—the Maryland Toleration Act of 1649.

Source 1   The Toleration Act of 1649

For as much as in a well-governed and Christian Commonwealth, Matters concerning Religion and the Honour of God ought to be in the first place taken into serious consideration, and endeavored to be settled. Be it therefore Ordained and Enacted by the Right Honourable Cecilius Lord Baron of Baltemore, absolute Lord and Proprietary of this Province, with the Advise and Consent of the Upper and Lower House of this General Assembly, That whatsoever person or persons within this Province and the Islands thereunto belonging, shall from henceforth blaspheme GOD, that is curse him; or shall deny our Saviour JESUS CHRIST to be the Son of God; or shall deny the Holy Trinity, Son, & Holy Ghost; or the Godhead of any of the Three Persons of the Trinity, or the Unity of the Godhead, or shall use or utter any reproachful speeches, words, or language, concerning the Holy Trinity, or any of the said three Persons thereof, shall be punished with death, and confiscation or forfeiture of all his or her Lands and Goods to the Lord Proprietor and his Heirs.

And be it also Enacted by the Authority, with the advise and assent of the aforesaid, That whatsoever person or persons shall from henceforth use or utter any reproachful words or speeches concerning the blessed Virgin MARY, the Mother of our Saviour, or the holy Apostles or Evangelists, or any of them, shall in such case for the first Offense forfeit to the said Lord Proprietary and his Heirs, Lords and Proprietors of this Province, the sum of Five pounds Sterling, or the value thereof levied on the goods and chattels of every such person so offending. . . . And that every such offender and offenders for every second offence shall forfeit Ten Pounds Sterling . . . and that every person or persons before mentioned, offending herein a third time, shall for such third offence, forfeit all his lands and goods, and be forever banisht and expelled out of this Province.

And be it also further Enacted by the same Authority, advise, and assent, That whatsoever person or persons shall from henceforth upon any occasion of offence, or otherwise in a reproachful manner or way, declare, call, or denominate, any person or persons whatsoever, inhabiting, residing, trafficking, trading, or commercing within this Province . . . an Heretick, Schismatick, Idolater, Puritan, Presbyterian, Independent, Popish Priest, Jesuit, Jesuited Papist, Lutheran,

Calvinist, Anabaptist, **Brownist, Barrowist, Antinomian, Roundhead,** Separatist, or any other name or term in a reproachful manner relating to the matter of Religion, shall for every such offence forfeit and lose the sum of Ten shillings Sterling, . . . the one half thereof to be forfeited and paid unto the person & persons of whom such reproachful words are, or shall be spoken or uttered, and the other half thereof to the Lord Proprietary and his Heirs . . . : But if such person or persons who shall at any time utter or speak any such reproachful words or language, shall not have goods or chattels sufficient and overt within this Province to be taken to satisfy the penalty aforesaid, . . . that then the person or persons so offending shall be publickly whipt, and shall suffer imprisonment without Bail . . . until he, she, or they, respectively, shall satisfy the party offended or grieved by such reproachfull Language, by asking his or her respectively forgiveness publickly . . . before the Magistrate or Chief Officer or Officers of the Town or place where such offence shall be given.

And be it further likewise Enacted . . . that every person or persons . . . that shall at any time hereafter prophane the Sabbath, or Lord's Day, called Sunday, by frequent swearing, drunkenness, or by any uncivil or disorderly Recreation, or by working on that day when absolute necessity does not require, shall for every such offence forfeit two shillings six pence Sterling, . . . and for the third offence and for every time after shall also be publickly whipt.

And whereas the inforcing of the Conscience in matter of Religion hath frequently fallen out to be of dangerous consequence in those Commonwealths where it hath been practiced, and for the more quiet and peaceable Government of this Province, and the better to preserve mutual love & unity amongst the Inhabitants here, Be it also . . . Ordained and Enacted . . . that no person or persons whatsoever within this Province . . . professing to believe in Jesus Christ, shall from henceforth be in any ways troubled, molested, or discountenanced, for, or in respect of his or her Religion nor the free exercise thereof within this Province . . . nor in any way compell'd to the belief or exercise of any other Religion, against his or her consent. . . . And that all and every person and persons that shall presume contrary to this Act and the true intent & meaning thereof . . . willfully to wrong, disturb, or trouble, or molest any person or persons whatsoever within this Province, professing to believe in Jesus Christ, for or in respect of his or her Religion . . . that such person or persons so offending shall be compelled to pay treble damages to the party so wronged or molested, and for every such offence shall also forfeit Twenty shillings Sterling . . . half thereof for the use of the Lord Proprietary and his Heirs . . . and the other half thereof for the use of the Party so wronged or molested as aforesaid.

8.2 Religion and the Founding of the American Republic

📖 *Second Thoughts*

An Act of Tolerance or Intolerance?

While a great many colonists came to America to enjoy religious freedom, few, if any, came to the New World for the purpose of practicing religious toleration. It is the nature of those who believe strongly in the absolute truth of their own particular convictions to view those who disagree with them as being in error. Why should they tolerate falsehood?

The recognition of a need to tolerate those of different religious beliefs, as well as those without religious beliefs, was an ideal not readily embraced by the rulers of the English colonies, nor has it ever come easily to the rulers of the American states. Maryland, not unlike the other states that form the American Union, has struggled with the notion of religious toleration throughout its history.

Source 2   **Proceedings of a Maryland Assembly of Protestants commissioned by Parliament, October 1654**

"An Act Concerning Religion"

It is enacted and declared in the name of his Highness the Lord Protector, with the consent and by the authority of the present General Assembly, that none who profess and exercise the Popish religion, commonly known by the name of the Roman Catholic religion, can be protected in this Province. . . .

Such as profess faith in God by Jesus Christ shall not be restrained from, but shall be protected in the profession of the faith and exercise of their religion, so as they abuse not this liberty to the injury of others, or the public peace on their part. Provided that this liberty be not extended to popery or prelacy, nor to such as under the profession of Christ hold forth and practice licentiousness.

Source 3   **Oliver Cromwell's nullification of "An Act concerning Religion," January 1655**

We . . . at the request of Lord Baltimore, and of divers other persons of quality here . . . , do for preventing of disturbances or tumults there, will and require you and all others deriving any authority from you, to forbear disturbing the Lord Baltimore, or his officers or people in Maryland; and to permit all things to remain as they were before any disturbance or alteration made by you, or by any other upon pretense of authority from you.

Source 4   **Maryland Proclamation, March 29, 1698**

By His Excellency
The Captain General & c.
Maryland, ss.

8.3 The History
of St. Margaret's
Church

Whereas, I have lately received information from Charles County and other parts of this His Majesty's Province, how several Popish Priests and zealous Papists make it their constant business (under pretense of visiting the sick during this time of common calamity and sickness) to seduce, delude, and persuade divers of His Majesty's good Protestant subjects to the Romish faith. . . . And forasmuch as it hath been likewise represented unto me how that Protestant Servants living with Popish **Recusants** are restrained from going to Church: for prevention of all such mischiefs and growing evils for the future I have thought fit to issue this my Proclamation strictly prohibiting and forewarning all Priests and Papists whatsoever to cease and forbear their notorious and open violation of His Majesty's known laws, under pain of prosecution and suffering such penalties as by the said laws are prescribed.

Source 5   Proceedings of the Maryland Assembly, 1701

An Act for the Service of Almighty God, and Establishment of Religion in this Province, according to the Church of England.

Forasmuch as in a well grounded Christian Commonwealth, matters concerning Religion and the honour of God, ought in the first place to be Endeavored, and taken into Consideration, as that which is not only most acceptable to God, but the best way and means to Obtain His Mercy and Blessing upon a People or Country; Be it therefore enacted By the King's most Excellent Majesty, by & with the Advice and Consent of this present General Assembly, and the authority of the same, that . . . the Book of Common Prayer, and Administration of the Sacraments, with other Rites and Ceremonies of the Church, according to the use of the Church of England, the Psalter and Psalms of David, and Morning and Evening Prayer therein contained, be Solemnly Read, and by all and every Minister or Reader in every Church, or Other Place of Public Worship, within this Province. . . . Be it Enacted by the Authority aforesaid . . . that a Tax or assessment of 40 pounds of tobacco per Poll, be yearly and every year Successively levied upon every Taxable person, within each respective parish within this Province . . . which said assessment . . . shal always be paid and allowed to the Minister of each respective Parish.

Source 6   John Oldmixon, *The British Empire in America,* 1741

The Lord Baltimore was at a vast Expence to bring this Province to its present Perfection; and allowing for his Partiality to the Roman Catholicks, which, in a great measure, helpt to lose him the Government of it, he behaved himself with so much Justice and Moderation, while he kept the Power in his own Hands, that the Inhabitants lived easily and happily under him. They flourished and encreased in Number and Riches. He procured an Act of Assembly, for Liberty of Conscience to all Persons who profess Christianity, tho' of different Persuasions. By which means Protestant Dissenters, as well as Papists, were tempted to settle there; and that Liberty having never been infringed in any manner, is a severe Reflection on those pretended Protestants in other Colonies, where Dissenters have been oppress'd; while here, under a Popish Proprietary, they enjoy'd all the Rights, Liberties and Privileges of Englishmen, as far as the Laws permitted them.

Source 7   Report of the Maryland Assembly Committee, December 21, 1818

That with respect to the justice of the case submitted to their consideration, your committee thinks there can be no question: in society, mankind have civil and political duties to perform, but with regard to religion, that it is a question which rests, or ought to rest, between man and his Creator alone; there is no law that can reach the heart—no human tribunal that has a right to take cognizance of this matter. . . .

It is in the interest and it ought to be the wish of every religious sect among us to see all political distinction forever abolished. Under the Constitution of the United States, the most perfect freedom is allowed in this respect, and it is surely inconsistent, it is surely strange, that a Jew who may hold a seat in Congress, who may even be raised to the highest and most honorable station in the universe, the chief magistrate of a free people, cannot hold any office of profit or trust under the Constitution of Maryland.

Source 8   Act proposed in the Maryland Assembly, January 1819

[Although this act was voted down by 50 to 24, a similar law was enacted in 1826.]

Whereas, . . . religious tests for civil employment, though intended as a barrier against the depraved, frequently operate as a restraint upon the conscientious; and as the Constitution of the United States requires no religious qualification for civil office, therefore,

Sec. 1. Be it enacted, By the General Assembly of Maryland, that no religious test, declaration or subscription of opinion as to religion, shall be required from any person of the sect called Jews, as a qualification to hold or exercise any office or employment of profit or trust in this state.

Source 9   John Leeds Bozman, *The History of Maryland,* 1837

The act of assembly may be said, indeed, to have been a political measure of a Roman Catholic nobleman. . . . But, without the slightest endeavour to detract from the personal merit of Cecilius, Lord Baltimore, it may be safely maintained, that this measure of general religious toleration, now adopted by his lordship, flowed rather from a prudent policy than any personal disposition to a general religious toleration. The Catholics throughout England and Ireland were evidently now endeavouring to make their peace with the Puritans, who held the reins of power. . . . The lord proprietary had adopted, almost at the first commencement of the population of his province, the measure of admitting persons of every sect, without discrimination, to become inhabitants of his province; and it was not, therefore, now possible for him to avoid its necessary consequences. The government of Virginia was now also ferreting out from their hiding places all the Puritans, who lurked within that ancient dominion. Maryland, unfortunately for his lordship, became an asylum for most of them. The inhabitants of this province now formed a heterodox mixture of almost every Christian sect. To keep peace among them a general toleration was obviously the only prudential measure to be adopted.

Source 10   Amendments to the Maryland Constitution, 1851

Art. 33. That it is the duty of every man to worship God in a manner as he thinks most acceptable to him, all persons are equally entitled to protection in their religious liberty; wherefore, no person ought, by any law, to be molested in his person or estate, on account of his religious persuasion or profession, or for his religious practice. . . .

Art. 34. That no other test or qualification ought to be required, on admission to any office of trust or profit, than such oath of office as may be prescribed by this constitution, or by the laws of the State, and a declaration of belief in the Christian religion; and if the party shall profess to be a Jew, the declaration shall be of his belief in a future state of rewards and punishments.

Source 11 Section of the Maryland bill of rights, adopted 1867

That no religious test ought to be required as a qualification for any office of profit or trust in this State, other than a declaration of belief in the existence of God.

Source 12 George Bancroft, *History of the United States of America,* 1882

The design of the law of Maryland was undoubtedly to protect freedom of conscience; and, some years after it had been confirmed, the apologist of Lord Baltimore could assert that his government, in conformity with his strict and repeated injunctions, had never given disturbance to any person in Maryland for matter of religion; that the colonists enjoyed freedom of conscience, not less freedom of person and estate. The disfranchised friends of prelacy from Massachusetts, and the exiled Puritans from Virginia, were welcomed to equal liberty of conscience and political rights by the Roman Catholic propriety of Maryland; and the usage of the province from its foundation was confirmed by its statutes. The attractive influence of this liberality for the province appeared immediately: a body of Puritans . . . in Virginia, whom [Anglican governor] Sir William Berkeley had ordered to leave that province for their nonconformity, negotiated successfully with the propriety for lands in Maryland; and, before the end of the year 1649, the greater part of the congregation planted themselves on the banks of the Severn. To their place of refuge, now known as Annapolis, they gave the name of Providence.

Source 13 Woodrow Wilson, *A History of the American People,* 1902

There were others besides the Puritans who felt uneasy at home in England. . . . It happened that Roman Catholics felt almost as uneasy. . . . It was for them that Maryland was founded by Cecilius Calvert, Lord Baltimore. . . .

The colonists whom Cecilius Calvert sent out to Maryland late in the autumn of 1633 were by no means all Romanists, but probably quite half of them were. . . . Protestants and Catholics, however, consorted very comfortably together on the voyage and after the landing. It was no part of Lord Baltimore's purpose to be a proselytizer and make converts of all whom he sent out, and he was too cool and prudent a man to wish to set up a colony to which none but Roman Catholics should be admitted. He knew very well how all England would soon be talking and protesting about such a colony as that, should he attempt it. He meant only to make a place so free that Roman Catholics might use full liberty of worship there no less than Protestants, for he knew that there was as yet no such place in America.

Source 14   Herbert L. Osgood, *The American Colonies in the Seventeenth Century,* 1904

No provision was made for the toleration of Quakers, Jews, or Unitarians, or in fact for any type of opinion other than that to which Catholics, Anglicans, Presbyterians, and Independents could subscribe. A toleration such as this, of certain definite forms of belief, provided their adherents kept the peace, does not differ in principle from the policy which had generally been pursued by European governments, and was far removed from absolute religious freedom. . . . It is clear that this statute originated from motives of political expediency, and that it was intended to meet specific conditions as they then existed in Maryland, with slight regard to freedom of thought as a universal principle.

Source 15   Findings of the Maryland Supreme Court, *Judefind* v. *State,* 1911

[Judefind was convicted of husking corn on Sunday.]

We have not the slightest hesitation in announcing that the law complained of is not in conflict with the Constitution of the United States or of Maryland. . . .

Nature, experience and observation suggests the propriety and necessity of one day of rest and the day generally adopted is Sunday. . . .

It is undoubtedly true that rest from secular employment on Sunday has a tendency to foster and encourage the Christian religion—of all sects and denominations that observe that day—as rest from work and ordinary occupations enables many to engage in public worship who probably were not otherwise to do so. . . . If the Christian religion is, incidentally or otherwise, benefited or fostered by having this day of rest, as it undoubtedly is, there is all the more reason for the enforcement of laws that help to preserve it. . . .

There are many most excellent citizens of this State who worship God on a day different than Sunday, and our Constitution guarantees them the right to do so. . . . The legislature of this State has not undertaken to prohibit work on the day observed by them, and hence they do not have in their religious work the advantage of having their Sabbath made a "day of rest" by human law; but the legislature has not in any way interfered with their religious liberty, or with their worship of God in such manner as they think most acceptable to Him.

Source 16   Charles M. Andrews, *The Colonial Period of American History,* 1936

On Baltimore's part the drafting of the act was no trimming of the sails to meet an on-coming storm, for the policy of toleration for all Trinitarians had prevailed in the colony from the beginning. The necessity of such public and statutory declaration must have been borne in upon him in order to meet the charge, which had been brought by those who sought the annulment of the charter, that Maryland was a hot-bed of popery. To be able to say that in Maryland no one professing to believe in Jesus Christ should henceforth be molested . . . was . . . certain to aid his cause in England. . . . The Act rejected all outside the Trinitarian fold and it is not pleasant to read the fate which it meted out to those who denied the divinity of Christ. This inhuman clause was no part of Baltimore's original text, for it was an amendment added by the Puritan-Protestant assembly in the colony. . . . The act did not guarantee full religious liberty, freedom of religious thought, or separation of church and state, for though there were men of the period who envisioned such an ideal, it was not part of the common human consciousness in the middle of the seventeenth century. The act went no further than to give, as a matter of expedience and necessity, formal expression to that toleration of one religious body by another.

Source 17 Supreme Court justice William O. Douglas, *The Right of the People,* 1962

8.4 Citizen Legislators and Toleration

In colonial days bitter religious conflicts raged here. Most of the American colonies carried anti-Catholic legislation on their books. Some also discriminated against Jews and atheists. Some colonies were founded to protect only one religious sect. Thus Massachusetts in the early days allowed people to be tried for sedition when they criticized what the majority called the true faith. The penalty was banishment. Maryland made the denial that Jesus was the Son of God a capital offense. Some of the colonies required public officials to satisfy a religious test in order to hold office. Moreover, a majority of the colonies had an established church. That one church was supported by taxation; and only its clergy could officiate at marriages and baptisms. The established church frequently represented a minority of the people. Yet all were taxed to support it.

Questioning the Past

1. Why did Maryland pass a Toleration Act in 1649?
2. Argue the position that the Maryland Toleration Act of 1649 was an example of religious toleration. Argue the position that it was actually an example of intolerance. Which is the stronger argument?
3. Why should a majority feel any obligation to tolerate in its own country religious beliefs that it finds offensive?
4. Why has the achievement of religious toleration proved a difficult and elusive goal in America?

Chapter 9

Bacon's Rebellion

Bacon Takes the Virginia Government Hostage

June 23, 1676

9.1 ALHN
Military
Resources

By 1676, Virginia was home to more than 40,000 colonists and tens of thousands of Native Americans of various tribes. The time when these native peoples had the power to destroy the colonies in their midst had passed. But the steady expansion of English settlements up the great tidal rivers of Virginia created constant tension. Sir William Berkeley, governor of Virginia, hoped to avoid a general war with the Indians. In March of 1676, he called a special session of the Virginia Assembly to devise a response to the crisis, which immediately was considered too passive by the planters and farmers of the vulnerable western frontier. The westerners launched an offensive against the Indians, and Nathaniel Bacon, a young planter and relative newcomer to the colony, was elected to lead the frontiersmen in battle. Governor Berkeley demanded that Bacon disband his unauthorized force. Bacon refused to comply and was declared a rebel. Nathaniel Bacon, however, had public opinion behind him, having become an instant folk hero.

Needing to bolster his position as the colony's leader, the governor dissolved the assembly. New elections were held and, though still a wanted fugitive, Bacon himself was elected to represent his county. He was captured while legislators were gathering in Jamestown and brought before the governor on June 9, 1676. Said Berkeley, "Now I behold the greatest rebell that ever was in Virginia! Sir, doe you continue to be a gentleman and may I take your word? If soe you are at liberty on your owne parrol." Bacon presented Berkeley with a written confession of guilt. The governor pardoned Bacon and promised to commission him an officer in the colony's war against the Indians. For several days, Bacon waited impatiently in Jamestown for the commission. It never came; Bacon returned home, raised an army, and marched on Jamestown.

At two o'clock on the afternoon of June 23, 1676, Nathaniel Bacon and a force of militiamen moved methodically into Jamestown. With a precision normally unattained by volunteer troops, they seized the strategic points of the city, took captive those who might have forcibly opposed them, and formed ranks around the Virginia Statehouse where the assembly was in session. It was a bold move whose motives and implications have been debated for more than three centuries.

❧ *First Impressions*
"A Commission I Will Have before I Goe!"

Bacon's Rebellion was nurtured from the seeds of discontent of most colonists in western Virginia. These frontier people felt both unprotected and unrepresented by what they viewed as the privileged aristocrats who ruled Virginia in the 1630s. As Bacon put it, "The poverty of the Country is such that all the power and sway is in the hands of the rich, who by extortious advantages, having the common people in their debt, have always curbed and oppressed them in all manner of wayes." But, on the other hand, as Governor Berkeley lamented, "How miserable that man is that Governes a People wher six parts of seaven at least are Poore, Endebted, Discontented, and Armed."

Source 1 Petition of frontier planters to Governor William Berkeley, 1676

To the Right Honorable Sir William Barkly Knight governor and Capt. Generall of Verginia: The Humble petition of the poore distressed subjects in the upper parts of the James River in Verginia Humbly Complain that the Indians hath already most barbarously and Inhumanly taken and Murdered severall of our bretheren . . . and wee . . . are in dayly dandger of loosing our lives by the Heathen in soe much that wee are all afraid of going about our demesticall affaires. Wherefore we Most Humbly request that your gratious Honor would be pleased to grant us a Committion and to make choice of Comitioned Officers to lead his party now redy to take arms in defence of our lives and estates.

Source 2 Account of Nathaniel Bacon, April 1676

Wee found the Indians in all places unwilling to assist us against the Common Enemy, they having received orders to the contrary from the Right Honourable the Governer, soe that wee were forced to goe quite out of our way . . . to get what assistance wee could . . . during which time our provisions were soe much wasted That when wee came to Action wee had not to half the company one dayes provision . . . yett being promised Releife from the Hockinnechy [Occaneechee] King Posseclay . . . wee entrd the iland hoping to find some small releif to the weary and faint; wee had made our Agreement that the Manakins and Annalectins, who joyned with the Susquahannocks and lived . . . in the[ir] fort should at a signe cutt of[f] the Susquahannocks being in number but 30 men besides woeman and children, this accordingly was effected, and the Prisoners by the King brought in with triumph, and severall of the Susquahannocks, by them put to death. . . . After these were destroid wee again complained to the King for want of provision and demanded the expected supply. But he having viewed the posture of our men [who were many of them leaving the Island at the very instant and returning home] began to alter his story, and desired us to stay six daies, and went from us gathering togither all his Indians, as also the . . . Manakins and Annalectons, mand all his Forts and lined the other side of the River thick with men so that wee could neither well attack them, nor depart the Island, without some danger. . . . Wee ordered our men to surround the fort with all expedition, and if they could to enter it, but tho the Indians had allready possest 3 Forts, and were in a condition to fight, soe that what wee could doe was to hinder the rest from entering the Fort which were very many still crowding in and to demand satisfaction of their King. . . .

In this Posture things stood when by a watchword from the other side of the River they killed one of our men which wee quickly repaid them firing at all their owne forts, holes and other places soe thick That the groans of men, woemen and children were soe loud that all their howling and singing could not hinder them from being heard. Immediately wee fell upon the men, woemen and children without, disarmed and destroid them all, and the King's Forts where all his Treasures his wife, children and ammunition were with a strong guard of men, woemen and children, wee stuck close to the Port holes fired and destroid them[.] A great number of men, woemen and children whose groans were heard but they all burnt except three or four men who happening to escape brok out and had a Welcome by a liberall volley of shott from our men who lay close upon them. . . . Next day our Fight continued till towards night during which time they made severall sculking attempts but our men were soe conveniently placed everywhere . . . that . . . few or none of them escaped but were shott. . . . [I]n short what wee did in that short time and poor condition wee were in was to destroy the King of the Susquahannocks and the King of Oconogee [Occaneechee] and the Manakin King with a 100 men. . . . The King's daughter wee took Prisonner with some others and could have brought more, but in the heat of the Fight wee regarded not the advantage of the Prisoners nor any plunder, but burn'd and destroid all. And what we reckon most materiall is That wee left all nations of Indians ingaged in a civill warre amongst themselves, so that with great ease wee hope to manadge this advantage to their utter Ruine and destruction.

Source 3   Statement of Governor William Berkeley, May 29, 1676

And NOW loving frends I wil State the Question betweene me as Governor and Mr. Bacon and Say that if any Ennimies should envade England any councelor Justice of the peace or other superior Officer might rayse what forces they could to protect his majesties subjects. But I say againe if after the Kings knowledge of this invasion any [of] the greatest **Peare of England** should rayse forces against the Kings prohibition this would be now and was ever in al Ages and nations accounted Treason . . . and for the Truth of this I appeale to al the lawes of England and the lawes and constitutions of al other nations in the World . . . I doe therefore againe declare that Bacon proceeding against al lawes of al nations modern and ancient is a Rebel to his Sacred majectie and the country. . . .

Now my friends I have liv'd amongst you fower and thirty years as uncorrupt and diligent as ever governor was: Bacon is a man of two years amongst you his person and qualities unknown to most of you and to al men . . . Yet . . . he lost more men then I did in three wars and by the Grace of God wil put myselfe to the same dangers and troubles againe when I have brought Bacon to acknowledge the lawes are above him and I doubt not by the assistance of god to have better success than Mr. Bacon has had. The reason of my hopes are that I wil take councel of wiser men than my selfe. But Mr. Bacon has none aboute him but the lowest of the people. . . .

Now after al this if Mr. Bacon can shew me presedent or examples where such actings in any nation what soever was approved of I wil mediate with the King and you for a pardon and excuse for him. But I can shew him an hundred examples where brave and greate men have ben put to death for gaining victories against the command of their superiors.

Source 4 William Berkeley to Secretary of State Coventry, June 3, 1676

This Rebellion is the more formidable because it has no ground and is not against any particular Person but the whole Assembly Sir I am so over weaned with riding into al parts of the Country to stop this violent Rebellion that I am not able to support my selfe at this Age six months longer and therefore on my Knees I beg his sacred majesty would send a more Vigorous Governor.

Source 5 Affidavit of Nathaniel Bacon, June 9, 1676

I Nathaniel Bacon, Jr. of Henrico County in Virginia doe hereby most Readily freely and most Willingly Acknowledge that I have been Guilty of diverse late unlawfull mutinous and Rebellious Practices Contrary to my duty to his most Sacred Majesties Governor and this Country by beating up of drums raiseing of men in Armes marching them into Severall parts of his most Sacred Majesties Colony not only without Order and Commission but Contrary to the Expresse Orders and Comands of the Right Honourable Sir William Berkeley Knight his Majesties Most Worthy Governor and Captain General of Virginia. . . . And I doe hereby upon my Knees most humbly begg of Almighty God and of his Majesties said Governor that . . . he will please to grant me his Gracious Pardon.

[To which Berkeley replied: "God forgive you, I forgive you."]

Source 6 Account of William Sherwood, "Virginia's Deploured Condition," 1676

Mr. Bacon goes home, harbouring private discontent, and studying revenge for his late confinement, sends to the factious, discontented people of New Kent, and those parts, . . . and getts the discontented rabble togeather, and with them resolved to putt himselfe, once more on the stage, and . . . he entred James Towne, with 400 foot, and 120 horse, sett guards at the state howse, kept the Governor, Councell and Burgesses prisoners, . . . and having drawne up all his souldiers to the very doore and windows of the state howse, he demanded a Commission to be a Generall of all the forces that should be raised dureing the Indian Warr. . . .

The Assembly acquainted him they had taken all possible care for carrying on the Indian . . . Mr. Bacon answered there would be noe Laws read there, that he would not admitt of any delays, that he came for a Commission, and would imediately have itt, thereupon sending his souldiers into the State howse, where the Governor Councell and Burgesses were sitting and thretning them with fyer and sword iff itt was not granted, his souldiers mounting their Guns ready to fyer.

Source 7   Demand of Nathaniel Bacon, June 23, 1676

I came for a commission against the heathen who dayly and inhumanely murder us and spill our brethrens blood, and noe care is taken to prevent it.

God damne my blood, I came for a commission, and a commission I will have before I goe!

Source 8   Account of Assemblyman Thomas Mathews, 1676

Mr. Bacon came up to our Chamber and Desired a Commission from us to go against the Indians; Our Speaker sat Silent, When one Mr. Blayton a Neighbour to Mr. Bacon and Elected with him a Member of the Assembly for the same County made Answer, "'twas not in our Province, or Power, nor of any other, save . . . Our Governour"; he press'd hard nigh half an hours Harangue on the Preserving our Lives from the Indians, Inspecting the Publick Revenues, th' exorbitant Taxes and redressing the Grievances and Calamities of that Deplorable Country.

Source 9   Account of William Sherwood, 1676

[F]or feer all would be in a flame, the Councell and Burgesses Joyned in a request to the Governor to grant Mr. Bacon such a Commission as he would have, the Governor declaired he would rather loose his life then consent . . . but for the preservation of that ruin, which was then threatened upon their second request, Order was given for such a Commission as Mr. Bacon would have himselfe, and according to his own dictates. . . .

[N]ow Mr. Bacon haveing a Commission, . . . hangs out his flagg of defiance Imprisoning severall loyall Gentlemen and his rabble used reproachfull words of the Governor. Mr. Bacon alsoe with his guard forcably entred amongst the Burgesses, and demanded that severall persons who had beene active in obeying the Governors comands, should be made incapable of beareing any public office. . . . [H]e also required order against Capt. Gardner [who was then his prisoner] for seventy pounds sterling for his sloope. . . . The Burgesses answered they were not Court of Judicature. . . . Att this he swore his useuall Oath (God dam his blood). . . . These thretnings and compulsions being upon them, the Assembly granted whatever he demanded, soe that itt was imagined he and his souldiers would martch out of Town, yett they continued drinking and domineereing. . . . Mr. Bacon after fower days stay, marched out of Towne.

Source 10   Address of Nathaniel Bacon to his troops, June 1676

Gentlemen and Fellow Soldiers, the news just now brought me, may not a little startle you as well as myselfe. But seeing it is not altogether unexpected, wee may the better beare it and provide for our remedies. The Governour is now in

Gloster County endeavouring to raise forces against us, having declared us Rebells and Traytors. . . . It is Revenge that hurries them on without regard for Peoples safety. [They] had rather wee should be Murder'd and our Ghosts sent to our slaughter'd Countrymen by their actings, then wee live to hinder them of their Interest with the Heathen. . . . Now then wee must be forced to turne our Swords to our own Defence, or expose ourselves to their Mercyes.

Source 11 Manifesto of Bacon, 1676

[I]f to plead the cause of the oppressed, . . . bee Treason God Almighty Judge and lett guilty dye, But since wee cannot in our hearts find one single spott of Rebellion or Treason or that wee have in any manner aimed at subverting the setled Government . . . let Truth be told and all the world know the real Foundations of pretended guilt, Wee appeale to the Country itselfe what and of what nature their Oppressions have bin . . . those whom wee call great men . . . , but let us trace these men in Authority and Favour to whose hands the dispensations of the countries wealth has been commited; let us observe the sudden Rise of their Estates . . . , And lett us see wither their extractions . . . have not bin vile, . . . let us consider their sudden advancement . . . , now let us compare these things togither and see what spounges have suckt up the Publique Treasure and wither it has not bin privately contrived away by unworthy Favourites and juggling Parasites whose tottering Fortunes have bin repaired and supported at the Publique chardg. . . .

Another main article of our Guilt is our open and manifest aversion of all, not onely the Foreign but the protected and Darling Indians, this wee are informed is Rebellion of a deep dye. . . .

Another main article of our Guilt is our Design not only to ruine and extirpate all Indians in Generall but all Manner of Trade and Commerce with them. . . . Since the Right honorable Governour hath bin pleased by his Commission to warrant this trade who dare oppose it. . . . Although Plantations be deserted, the Blood of our dear Brethren Spilt, . . . Murder upon Murder renewed upon us, who . . . dare think of the generall Subversion of all Mannor of Trade and Commerce with our enemies . . . who can or dare impeach any of (these) Traders at the Heades of the Rivers if contrary to the wholesome provision made by lawes . . . , who dare say That these Men at the Heads of the Rivers buy and sell our blood, and doe still . . . admit Indians painted and continue to Commerce. . . .

Another Article of our Guilt is To Assert all those neighbour Indians as well as others to be outlawed, wholly unqualifyed for the benefitt and Protection of the law. . . .

If it be said that the very foundation of all these disasters, the Grant of the Beaver trade to the Right Honourable Governour, was illegall and not granteable to any power here present as being a monopoly, were not this to deserve the name of Rebell and Traytor.

9.2 The American Nation Online: American Society in the Making

Civil War, Class War, or Greed?

In September, the governor retook Jamestown. Bacon and his supporters marched to confront the loyalists. Berkeley's troops showed little willingness to fight and the governor fled; Bacon burned Jamestown to the ground to prevent it from being retaken. Now in firm control of the greatest part of Virginia, Bacon turned to the task of establishing an administration for the colony and resumed efforts to mount an attack against the Indians. But the strain of campaigning in Virginia's swamps was too great, and Bacon died of fever on October 26, 1676. With his death, the rebellion fizzled. Berkeley was restored to power, and the surviving leaders of the revolt were executed.

Was this the first attempt at an American revolution? Did Bacon and his band of Virginia farmers begin a struggle that Patrick Henry, Thomas Jefferson, George Washington, and other Virginians of the later generation would help to finish? Or perhaps these rebels of 1676 were not in revolt against the British Empire, but engaged in a civil war, a confrontation between easterners and westerners, the planter class versus the poor farmers of the frontier. And then again, maybe shame is the fitting memorial for the Bacon mutineers, for were their motives based upon anything more noble than greed, their actions on anything more than a blind hatred of the natives whose land they coveted? No one in 1676 had a satisfactory answer to these questions. No one since has answered them convincingly, either.

📖 *Second Thoughts*

Torchbearer of the American Revolution?

9.3 Virginia
Records
Time Line

Exactly where Bacon was trying to lead Virginia, and what might have happened had he lived, no one can say with certainty. However, a historical marker on Chamberlayne Avenue in Richmond, Virginia, site of Bacon's plantation, describes him as heading "a rebellion that was the forerunner" of the American Revolution.

Source 12 Report of the Royal Commission, 1677

He was said to be about four or five and thirty years of age, . . . tall but slender, black-haired and of an ominous, pensive, melancholly Aspect, of a pestilent and prevalent Logical discourse tending toward atheisme. . . . He seduced the Vulgar and the most ignorant people . . . (two thirds of each county being of that Sort) Soe that their whole hearts and hopes were set now upon Bacon. Next he charges the Governour as negligent and wicked, treacherous and incapable, the Lawes and Taxes as unjust and oppressive. . . . Thus Bacon encouraged the Tumult and as the unquiet crowd follow and adhere to him, . . . he went and infected New Kent County ripe for Rebellion.

Source 13 Writings of historian Robert Beverly, 1705

The Occasion of this Rebellion is not easie to be discover'd: But 'tis certain there were many Things that concurr'd towards it. For it cannot be imagined, that upon the Instigation of Two or Three Traders only, who aim'd at a Monopoly of the *Indian* trade, as some pretend to say, the whole Country would have fallen into so much Distraction; in which People did not only hazard their Necks by Rebellion: But endeavor'd to ruine a Governour, whom they all entirely loved, and had unanimously chosen; a Gentleman who had devoted his whole Life and Estate to the Service of the Country; and against whom in Thirty Five Years Experience, there had never been one single Complaint. Neither can it be supposed, that upon so slight Grounds, they would make Choice of a Leader they hardly knew, to oppose a Gentlemen, that had been so long, and so deservedly the Darling of the People. So that in all Probability there was something else in the Wind, without which the Body of the Country had never been engaged in that Insurrection.

Four Things may be reckon'd to have been the main Ingredients towards this intestine Commotion, *viz.* First, the extream low Price of Tobacco, and the ill Usage of the Planters in the Exchange of Goods for it, which the Country, with all their earnest Endeavours, could not remedy. Secondly, The Splitting the Colony into Proprieties, contrary to the original Charters; and the extravagant Taxes they were forced to undergo, to relieve themselves from those Grants. Thirdly, The heavy Restraints and Burdens laid upon their Trade by Act of Parliament in *England.* Fourthly, The Disturbance given by the *Indians.*

Source 14 Poem of Ebenezer Cooke, ca. 1730

> . . . little Nat, presumptuous **Hector,**
> (Aspiring, like the Lord Protector)
> O'er the Atlantick Ocean came,
> And put the People in a Flame;
> Set folks together by the Ears,
> Who liv'd in Friendship many Years.
> And in a Snare drew headstrong Rabble,
> Who too much listen'd to his Babble.

Source 15 John Oldmixon, *The British Empire in America,* 1741

Col. Nathaniel Bacon, Jun. was a Gentleman who had been liberally bred in England, having studied some time at the Temple: He was young, bold, active, hansom and eloquent; his Merit advanced him to the Degree of a Counsellor, and his good qualities got him the Love and Respect of the People, who were at that time very much disaffected with the Government, and ready to take Fire; which Bacon perceiving, blew up the Coals of Dissention among them so much, that at last it burst out in a Flame. . . . The King, when he was inform'd of this Rebellion, was so far from hearkening to the Pretences of Bacon's Assembly, that he order'd a Squadron of Men of War to be fitted out, and a Regiment of Soldiers to embark aboard it for Virginia. . . . The Hopes of these Succours confirmed the Governor in his Severity, and all Terms of Accommodation were offer'd to no Purpose. Such was the dreadful Prospect of Affairs in Virginia, when, happily for the Peace of the Colony, Col. Bacon died. . . . He was privately buried, and the Place kept very secret, to prevent his Enemies insulting his Body, as would have been done, could the Corpse have been found; for strict Enquiry was made after it, with a Design to expose his Bones to public Infamy.

Source 16   Edmund Randolph, *History of Virginia,* 1813

Nathaniel Bacon . . . was a member of the king's council in Virginia and a perfect master of colonial politics and feelings. From his official station he could detect, if not create, the vulnerable parts in the conduct of the governor. A nefarious ambition prompted him to blazon them abroad; and by His eloquence and spirit of enterprise, he attracted the weak, the furious, the men of ruined fortunes, who would hazard any change, upon schemes possessing no other merit than that of being specious while untried. . . .

A legitimate government existed. . . . In a country like ours, where the will of the people justly predominates, let us not lend a sanction to any perversion of that will by approving a resort to arms until all which ought to be endured shall have been endured, and redress sought in every legal, constitutional, and reasonable shape.

Source 17   George Bancroft, *History of the United States,* 1855

The little army of Bacon had been exposed, by night, to the damp dews of the lowlands; and the evening air of the balmy autumn was laden with death. Bacon himself suddenly sickened; his vital energies vainly struggled with the uncertain disease, and on the first day of October he died. Seldom has a political leader been more honored by his friends. "Who is there now," said they, "to plead our cause? His eloquence could animate the coldest hearts; his pen and sword alike compelled the admiration of his foes, and it was but their own guilt that styled him a criminal. His name must bleed for a season; but when time shall bring to Virginia truth crowned with freedom, and safe against danger, posterity shall sound his praises."

The memory of those who have been wronged is always pursued by the ungenerous. England, ambitious of absolute colonial supremacy, could not render justice to the principles by which Bacon was swayed. No printing-press was allowed in Virginia. To speak ill of Berkeley or his friends, was punished by whipping or a fine; to speak or write, or publish any thing, in favor of the rebels or the rebellion, was made a misdemeanor; if thrice repeated, was evidence of treason. Is it strange that posterity was for more than a hundred years defrauded of the truth?

Source 18   Observation of historian Philip Bruce, 1893

Bacon is known to history as the Rebel, but the fuller information which we have now as to the motives of his conduct shows that he can with more justice be described as Bacon the Patriot. He headed a powerful popular movement in which the sovereignty of the people was for the first time relied upon on American soil by a great leader as the justification of his acts.

Source 19   Frederick Jackson Turner, *Frontier and Section,* 1893

From the beginning of the settlement of America, the frontier regions have exercised a steady influence toward democracy. In Virginia, to take an example, it can be traced as early as the period of Bacon's Rebellion, a hundred years before our Declaration of Independence. The small landholders, seeing that their powers were steadily passing into the hands of the wealthy planters who controlled Church and State and lands, rose in revolt.

Source 20   Thomas Jefferson Wertenbaker, *Virginia under the Stuarts,* 1914

Nathaniel Bacon is depicted as . . . melancholy, pensive, and taciturn. In conversation he was logical and convincing; in oratory magnetic and masterful. His successful expeditions against the Indians and the swift blows he directed against the loyal forces mark him as a military commander of no mean ability. . . . Bacon was regarded by a large part of the people as their leader in a struggle for justice and liberty. . . . Bacon was the torchbearer of the [American] Revolution.

. . . Yet this attack of an outraged people upon an arbitrary and corrupt government . . . gave birth in the breasts of brave men to the desire to resist by all means possible the oppression of the Stuart kings. It stirred the people to win, in their legislative halls, victories for the cause of liberty, as real as those which Bacon and his followers had failed to secure on the field of battle. . . .

Never again was an English governor to exercise the despotic power that had been Sir William Berkeley's. This was not due to the greater leniency of the British government, or to lack of ambition in the later governors. But the Rebellion and the events following it, had weakened the loyalty of the people and shown them the possibility of resisting the King's commands. . . . They were to become more and more impatient of the control of the Governors, more and more prone to defy the commands of the English government.

Source 21   Louis B. Wright, *The First Gentlemen of Virginia,* 1939

The governor who exerted the greatest influence was Sir William Berkeley, who ruled Virginia for nearly a quarter of a century, his various terms falling between the years 1642 and 1677. Since this was the most critical period in the crystallization of an aristocratic social order, the influence of a courtier having the gallantry and polish of Sir William cannot be doubted. One should remember that not until his last years did he become an unpopular tyrant, and even then, during the Bacon Rebellion, most of the conservative ruling class stood by him. . . . Though Berkeley's reputation has suffered as a result of his revenge on the Bacon rebels in his irascible old age, his earlier contribution to courtly manners and fashionable social life should not be forgotten.

Source 22   Wilcomb E. Washburn, *The Governor and the Rebel,* 1957

Throughout the nineteenth and twentieth centuries the rebellion of Nathaniel Bacon in Virginia in 1676 has been presented as a valiant but premature attempt to overthrow an oppressive royal government in order to establish a just and democratic society. Most accounts of the rebellion written in the last century and a half . . . have held to this view. In them Bacon is the torchbearer of revolutionary democracy, while the royal governor, Sir William Berkeley, plays the despotic villain. Yet how strange would this view have seemed to persons living in the seventeenth and eighteenth centuries! In both of those centuries accounts of the rebellion tended to defend Berkeley and to denounce Bacon. . . .

The key that unlocks the "meaning" of Bacon's Rebellion is to be found in the American Revolution. The "Spirit of 1776" lent an appearance of legitimacy and respectability to all revolts against British authority. Bacon's Rebellion, seen as a democratic movement, was one of its results. Within a few years of the Revolution the democratic interpretation of the earlier rebellion became orthodox. When the justice of the colonial leadership was accepted, however, Bacon's Rebellion was excluded from historical respectability. . . .

The one cause of Bacon's Rebellion that has been consistently overlooked . . . is the aggressiveness of the frontiersmen. The careful [Richard] Hildreth nearly stumbled onto this conception when he wrote, with unconscious humor, that "the Indian war, the immediate cause of all the late disturbances, seems to have subsided as soon as expeditions against the Indians were dropped." What has caused English and American historians to overlook the frontiersmen's aggressiveness? The reason lies in the white historian's unconscious immersion in his racial bias. According to the mythology of the white view of the world, the Indian is ever "primitive," "warlike," and "aggressive," while the "civilized" white man is constantly on guard against his attacks. But the aggressiveness of the frontiersmen has been overlooked. . . .

The record of the June Assembly proves that the real grievance against Governor Berkeley was not that he refused to defend the country from the Indians—a ridiculous charge against the conqueror of Opechancanough—but that he refused to authorize the slaughter and dispossession of the innocent as well as the "guilty."

The causes of Bacon's Rebellion are complex and profound. They cannot be explained in terms of Berkeley's "greed" and "oppression," Bacon's love of "liberty," the "savagery" of the Indians, or the "patriotism" of the frontiersmen. . . . Nor can the rebellion be explained in terms of the concealed identities and mysterious motives of a Gothic romance. Bacon does not change, with the hemispheres, from the spoiled son of a well-to-do English squire to a dedicated democratic frontier hero. Nor does Governor Berkeley, after being the "Darling of the People" for thirty-five years, suddenly reveal his true identity as their blackest oppressor.

Source 23 Virginius Dabney, *Virginia: The New Dominion,* 1971

Nathaniel Bacon, who led this rebellion, was no saint, despite the tablet at Gloucester Courthouse which thus describes him. He had his irreconcilable enemies and severe critics, and some of the criticism was justified. But he gave courageous leadership to Virginians who were outraged by atrocities and suffering under tyrannical rule. Thanks to Bacon, the Indian threat was effectively countered, and some of the worst injustices of Berkeley's regime were ameliorated. While Bacon's Laws were repealed a few months after his death, some of them were partially re-enacted. The revolt also had the salutary effect of warning the British Crown against future excesses. True, full-fledged revolution erupted a century later, so the warning seems not to have been fully taken to heart.

Source 24 Wilcomb E. Washburn, "Seventeenth-Century Indian Wars," 1976

While earlier views of the rebellion emphasized the political aspects of the conflict, the most recent interpretation has attempted to relate the clash of arms among the English to a basic difference of policy on how to deal with the Indians. . . .

Governor Berkeley . . . concluded that the possibility of a combination of Indians all the way from New England to Virginia was a real one. Should the tributary Indians be induced to defect, the very existence of the colony would be threatened. Hence, Berkeley worked diligently to carry on the Indian war against the professed enemies of the colony and to preserve the friendly tributary Indians as spies and auxiliaries. In this hope Berkeley was to be disappointed by the antics of a young planter, Nathaniel Bacon, Jr., who had recently come to the colony. Bacon insisted on raising a group of volunteers who, illegally and unjustifiedly, attacked many of the colony's tributary Indians and foreign tribes still friendly to the colony, thus raising the specter of a general combination, which the governor sought to avoid. Bacon killed not a single enemy Indian, only Indians denominated friends by the governor. The efforts of the governor to put down the unauthorized expeditions of Bacon and his plunder-seeking volunteers led to civil war. . . . The Indian war ceased as soon as the English stopped attacking the Indians.

⚹ Questioning the Past

1. List the causes cited by Bacon and his contemporaries for the rebellion that broke out in Virginia in 1676. List also the causes cited by observers who have since commented on the rebellion. Which cause, or causes, seem most convincing? Why was there a rebellion? What, if anything, might have been done to prevent bloodshed?

2. Present a defense of Governor Berkeley and his administration of the Virginia Colony. Present a criticism of Governor Berkeley. Was he a tyrant or a gifted and devoted public servant?

3. Was Nathaniel Bacon the torchbearer of the American Revolution or merely a racist demagogue? What evidence is there to support each of these positions regarding Bacon?

4. Looking back at the Virginia turmoil of 1676 from the vantage point of the present, what impact did Bacon's Rebellion have on the development of the American nation?

Chapter 10

The Zenger Trial

The Jury Returns a Verdict in the Seditious Libel Trial of John Peter Zenger *August 4, 1735*

In 1732 the English king appointed William Cosby governor of the colony of New York. A man destined to make enemies, Cosby was arrogant, arbitrary, avaricious, autocratic, and abusive of his authority, to exhaust only the first letter of the alphabet. His opponents had comparable lists for the other 25. Within months of his arrival in New York, the colony was divided between Cosby supporters and those of Lewis Morris, a powerful New York City figure whom Cosby had removed from the colony's supreme court.

The *New York Gazette,* long the colony's only newspaper, chose to support the governor and his policies. Cosby's opposition responded by creating the *New York Weekly Journal* in November 1733, published by John Peter Zenger. With articles critical of arbitrary political power in general and of Cosby in particular, along with satirical advertisements, the *Journal* carried on a vigorous campaign against the governor. Bent on silencing Zenger, Cosby made his first attempt in January 1734—a suit against Zenger for publishing "scandalous" songs—which failed when the jury refused to indict. Frustrated, Cosby next ordered four issues of the *Journal* "burnt by the hands of the Common Hangman" of New York. When this, too, failed to deter the *Journal's* criticism, he determined to move against Zenger himself.

❧ *First Impressions*

Factions and Tumults

William Cosby faced a dilemma. He could ignore Zenger or he could silence him. With either choice he risked inciting his opponents to new heights. But could he afford to tolerate libelous attacks that undermined his ability to govern? His own responsibilities and the law argued that he could not, and should not, permit his efforts to administer the colony to be subverted by a vocal opposition. To silence Zenger, the governor decided to rely on the English legal opinions stated in Sources 1 and 2 and the "libelous" material in Sources 3, 4, and 5.

Source 1   Sir John Holt, lord chief justice, King's Bench, 1704

To say that corrupt officers are appointed to administer affairs is certainly a reflection on the government. If people should not be called to account for possessing the people with an ill opinion of the government, no government can subsist, for it is necessary for all governments that the people should have a good opinion of it. And nothing can be worse to any government than to endeavor to procure animosities; as to the management of it, this has been always looked upon as a crime and no government can be safe without it be punished.

Source 2   Legal scholar William Hawkins, *A Treatise of the Pleas of the Crown,* 1721

Nor can there be any doubt but that a writing which defames a private person only is as much a libel as that which defames persons entrusted in a public capacity, in as much as it manifestly tends to create ill blood, and to cause a disturbance of the public peace; however, it is certain that it is a very high aggravation of a libel that it tends to scandalize the government, by reflecting on those who are entrusted with the administration of public affairs, which does not only endanger the public peace, as all other libels do, by stirring up the parties immediately concerned in it to acts of revenge, but also has a direct tendency to breed in the people a dislike of their governors, and to incline them to faction and sedition.

Source 3   The *New York Weekly Journal*

Numb. 2. Monday, November 12, 1733

There are two sorts of monarchies, an absolute and a limited one. In the first, the liberty of the press can never be maintained, it is inconsistent with it; for what absolute monarch would suffer any subject to **animadvert** on his actions when it is in his power to declare the crime and to nominate the punishment? This would make it very dangerous to exercise such a liberty. Besides the object against which the pens must be directed is their sovereign, the sole supreme magistrate; for there being no law in those monarchies but the will of the prince, . . . what the minister there acts being in obedience to the prince, he ought not to incur the hatred of the people. . . . Besides, in an absolute monarchy, the will of the prince being the law, a liberty of the press to complain of griev-ances would be complaining against the law and the constitution, . . . so that under an absolute monarchy, I say, such a liberty is inconsistent with the con-stitution, having no proper subject to politics . . . and if exercised would incur a certain penalty.

But in a limited monarchy, as England is, our laws are known, fixed, and established. They are the straight rule and sure guide to direct the king, the ministers, and . . . his subjects: And therefore an offense against the laws is such an offense against the constitution as ought to receive a proper adequate punishment; the several constituents of the government, the ministry, and all subordinate magistrates, having their certain, known, and limited sphere in which they move; one part may certainly err, misbehave, and become criminal, without involving the rest or any of them in the crime or punishment.

But some of these may be criminal, yet above punishment ... since most reigns have furnished us with too many instances of powerful and wicked ministers, some of whom by their power have absolutely escaped punishment. . . .

That *might overcomes right,* or which is the same thing, that might preserves and defends men from punishment, is a proverb established and confirmed by time and experience. . . . It is this therefore which makes the liberty of the press in a limited monarchy and in all its colonies . . . proper, convenient, and necessary. . . .

It is indeed urged that the liberty of the press ought to be restrained because not only the actions of evil ministers may be exposed, but the character of good ones traduced. . . . But when did calumnies and lies ever destroy the character of one good minister? Their benign influences are known, tasted, and felt by everybody: Or if their characters have been clouded for a time, yet they have generally shined forth in greater luster: Truth will always prevail over falsehood.

The facts exposed are not to be believed because said or published; but it draws people's attention, directs their view, and fixes the eye in a proper position that everyone may judge for himself whether the facts are true or not.

Source 4   The *New York Weekly Journal*

Numb. 13. Monday, January 28, 1734

THE PEOPLE of this city and province think, . . . as matters now stand, that their LIBERTIES and PROPERTIES are precarious, and that SLAVERY is like to be entailed on them and their posterity, if some past things be not amended.

Source 5   The *New York Weekly Journal*

Numb. 23. Monday, April 8th, 1734.

To the Editor:

I was at a public house some days since in company with some persons that came from New York: Most of them complained of the deadness of trade: Some of them laid it to the account of the repeal of the Tonnage Act . . . which has been almost the ruin of that town, by paying the Bermudians about 12,000 [pounds sterling] a year to export those commodities which might be carried in their own **bottoms**. They said the Bermudians were an industrious frugal people who bought no one thing in New York, but lodged the whole freight money in their own island, by which means, since the repeal of that Act, there has been taken from New York above 90,000 [pounds sterling]. . . . But this is not all; this money being carried away which would otherwise have circulated in this province and city, and have been paid to the baker, the brewer, the smith, the carpenter, the shipwright, the boatman, the farmer, the shopkeeper, etc., has deadened our trade in all its branches, and forced our industrious poor to seek other habitations; so that within these three years there has been above 300 persons have left New York; the houses stand empty, and there is as many houses as would make one whole street with bills upon their doors: And this has been as great a hurt as the carrying away the money. . . .

Another replies, it is the excessive high wages you tradesmen take prevents your being employed: Learn to be contented with less wages, we shall be able to build, and then no need to employ Bermudians. Very fine, replied the first, now the money is gone you bid us take less wages, when you have nothing to give us, and there is nothing to do.

Says another, I know nobody gets estates with us but the lawyers; we are almost come to the pass that an acre of land can't be conveyed under half an acre of parchment. The fees are not settled by our legislature, and everybody takes what they please; and we find it better to bear the disease than to apply for a remedy that's worse. . . .

One of our neighbors being in company, observing the strangers full of complaints, endeavored to persuade them to move into Jersey. To which it was replied, that would be leaping out of the frying pan-into the fire; for, says he, we both are under the same Governor. . . .

One that was then moving to Pennsylvania (to which place it is reported several considerable men are moving) expressed in terms very moving much concern for the circumstances of New York, seemed to think them very much owing to the influence that some men had in the administration; said he was now going from them, and was not to be hurt by any measures they would take; but could not help saving some concern for the welfare of his countrymen, and should be glad to hear that the Assembly would exert themselves as became them, by showing that they have the interest of their country more at heart than the gratification of . . . their members, or being at all affected by the smiles or frowns of a governor. . . .

You, says he, complain of the lawyers, but I think the law itself is at an end: We see men's deeds destroyed, judges arbitrarily displaced, new courts erected without consent of the legislature, by which it seems to me trials by juries are taken away when a governor pleases; men of known estates denied their votes contrary to the received practice, the best expositor of any law: Who is then in that province that call anything his own, or enjoy any liberty longer than those in the administration will condescend to let him do it?

One of our company replied; if these are illegal impositions, why don't your Assembly impeach the authors of them. *Impeach!* says a Gentleman (once an officer of the Customs) would you have the mob and **canaille** impeach gentlemen? American assemblies, that have only the power to make little paltry by-laws, pretend to the power of a British Parliament! . . .

Give me leave to tell you, Sir, you talk indecently of those that differ from you: There are many among them of equal if not superior knowledge to any of your party, and more of superior estates; and our assemblies are very far from deserving the name of *canaille* or dregs of the people. . . .

The Gentleman was going on upon the duty of an Assembly: But one of the company desired him to leave his politics to another time; which makes me unable to say more, but that I am,

Sir, etc.
No Courtier

The Zenger Trial

In November 1734 Cosby ordered the sheriff of New York to arrest Zenger for libels "tending to raise factions and tumults among the people . . . , inflaming their minds with contempt of His Majesty's government, and greatly disturbing the peace thereof." In the first two months of Zenger's imprisonment, Cosby delayed formal charges and ordered the chief justice to disbar two prominent attorneys from the Morris faction who were preparing his defense. The court then appointed a Cosby supporter, attorney John Chambers, to defend Zenger, whose trial began on August 4, 1735. Chambers's opening remarks were bland, and the judges seemed confident of convicting the publisher. But Chambers then startled the court by introducing as his cocounsel Philadelphia lawyer Andrew James Hamilton, considered the most skilled and eloquent attorney in the New World.

Source 6   Transcript of the trial of John Peter Zenger

10.1 Links to Sites concerning the John Peter Zenger Trial

Mr. Attorney. May it please Your Honors, and you, gentlemen of the jury; the information now before the Court, and to which the Defendant Zenger has pleaded not guilty, is an information for printing and publishing a false, scandalous, and seditious libel, in which his Excellency the Governor of this Province, who is the King's immediate representative here, is greatly and unjustly scandalized as a person that has no regard to law nor justice. . . . This . . . libeling is what has always been discouraged as a thing that tends to create differences among men, ill blood among the people, and oftentimes great bloodshed between the party libeling and the party libeled. There can be no doubt but that you gentlemen of the jury will have the same ill opinion of such practices as the judges have always shown on such occasions. . . .

Mr. Hamilton. May it please Your Honor: I am concerned in this cause on the part of Mr. Zenger the Defendant. . . . I cannot think it proper for me (without doing violence to my own principles) to deny the publication of a complaint which I think is the right of every free-born subject to make when the matters so published can be supported with truth; and therefore I'll save Mr. Attorney the trouble of examining his witnesses to that point; and I do (for my client) confess that he both printed and published the two newspapers set forth in the information, and I hope in so doing he has committed no crime.

Mr. Chief Justice. Well Mr. Attorney, will you proceed?

Mr. Attorney. Indeed sir, as Mr. Hamilton has confessed the printing and publishing these libels, I think the jury must find a verdict for the King; for supposing they were true, the law says that they are not the less libelous for that; nay indeed the law says their being true is an aggravation of the crime.

Mr. Hamilton. Not so neither, Mr. Attorney, there are two words to that bargain. I hope it is not our bare printing and publishing a paper that will make it a libel: You will have something more to do before you make my client a libeler; for the words themselves must be libelous, that is, false, scandalous, and seditious or else we are not guilty. . . .

I agree with Mr. Attorney that government is a sacred thing, but I differ very widely from him when he insinuates that the just complaints of a number of men who suffer under a bad administration is libeling that administration. . . .

Mr. Chief Justice. You cannot be admitted, Mr. Hamilton, to give the truth of a libel as evidence. A libel is not to be justified; for it is a nevertheless a libel that it is true.

Mr. Hamilton. I am sorry the Court has so soon resolved upon that piece of law; I expected first to have been heard to that point. . . .

Mr. Chief Justice. The law is clear, that you cannot justify a libel.

Mr. Hamilton. . . . [I]s it not against common sense that a man should be punished in the same degree for a true libel (if any such thing could be) as for a false one? I know it is said that truth makes a libel the more provoking, and therefore the offense is the greater, and consequently the judgment should be the heavier. Well, suppose it were so, and let us agree for once that truth is a greater sin than falsehood: Yet as the offenses are not equal, and as the punishments are arbitrary, that is, according as the judges in their discretion shall direct to be inflicted; . . . is it not absolutely necessary that they should know whether the libel is true or false, that they may by that means be able to proportion the punishment? For would it not be a sad case if the judges, for want of a due information, should chance to give as severe a judgment against a man for writing or publishing a lie as for writing or publishing a truth? And yet this, as monstrous and ridiculous as it may seem to be, is the natural consequence of Mr. Attorney's doctrine that truth makes a worse libel than falsehood. . . .

Mr. Chief Justice. Mr. Hamilton, the Court is of the opinion, you ought not to be permitted to prove the facts in the papers: These are the words of the book, "It is far from being a justification of a libel, that the contents thereof are true, or that the person upon whom it is made had a bad reputation, since the greater appearance there is of truth in any malicious invective, so much the more provoking it is."

Mr. Hamilton. These are Star Chamber cases, and I was in hopes that practice had been dead with the Court.

Mr. Chief Justice. Mr. Hamilton, the Court have delivered their opinion, and we expect you will use us with good manners; you are not permitted to argue against the opinion of the Court.

Mr. Hamilton. With submission, I have seen the practice in very great courts, and never heard it deemed unmannerly to—

Mr. Chief Justice. After the Court have declared their opinion, it is not good manners to insist upon a point in which you are overruled.

Mr. Hamilton. I will say no more at this time; the Court I see is against us in this point; and that I hope I may be allowed to say.

Mr. Chief Justice. Use the Court with good manners, and you shall be allowed all the liberty you can reasonably desire.

Mr. Hamilton. I thank Your Honor. Then, gentlemen of the jury, it is to you we must now appeal for witnesses to the truth of the facts we have offered and are denied the liberty to prove; and let it not seem strange. that I apply myself to you in this manner, I am warranted so to do both by law and reason. The law supposes you to be summoned out of the neighborhood where the fact is alleged to be committed; and the reason of your being taken out of the neighborhood is because you are supposed to have the best knowledge of the fact that is to be tried. And were you to find a verdict against my client, you must take upon you to say the papers referred to in the information, and which we acknowledge we printed and published, are false, scandalous, and seditious; but of this I can have no apprehension. You are citizens of New York; you are really what the law supposes you to be, honest and lawful men; and, according to my brief, the facts which we offer to prove were not committed in a corner; they are notoriously known to be true; and therefore in your justice lies our safety. And as we are denied the liberty of giving evidence to prove the truth of what we have published, I will beg leave to lay it down as a standing rule in such cases, that the suppression of evidence ought always to be taken for the strongest evidence; and I hope it will have that weight with you. . . .

For though I own it to be base and unworthy to scandalize any man, yet I think it is even more villainous to scandalize a person of public character, and I will go so far into Mr. Attorney's doctrine as to agree that if the faults, mistakes, nay even the vices of such a person be private and personal, and don't affect the peace of the public, or the liberty or property of our neighbor, it is unmanly and unmannerly to expose them either by word or writing. But when a ruler of a people brings his personal failings, but much more his vices, into his administration, and the people find themselves affected by them, either in their liberties or properties, that will alter the case mightily, and all the high things that are said in favor of rulers, and of dignities, and upon the side of power, will not be able to stop people's mouths when they feel oppressed. . . . It is true that in times past it was a crime to speak truth, and . . . many worthy and brave men suffered for so doing; and yet even . . . in those bad times, a great and good man durst say, what I hope will not be taken amiss of me to say in this place, to wit, "The practice of informations for libel is a sword in the hands of a wicked king and an arrant coward to cut down and destroy the innocent; the one cannot because of his high station, and the other dares not because of his want of courage, revenge himself in another manner."

Mr. Attorney. Pray Mr. Hamilton, have a care what you say, don't go too far neither, I don't like those liberties.

Mr. Hamilton. Sure, Mr. Attorney, you won't make any applications; all men agree that we are governed by the best of kings. . . .

But to proceed; I beg leave to insist that the right of complaining or remonstrating is natural; and the restraint upon this natural right is the law only, and those restraints can only extend to what is false: For it is truth alone which can excuse or justify any man for complaining of bad administration. . . .

It is agreed upon by all men that this is a reign of liberty, and while men keep within the bounds of truth, I hope they may with safety both speak and write their sentiments of the conduct of men in power. I mean of that part of their conduct only which affects the liberty or property of the people under their administration; were this to be denied, then the next step may make them slaves: For what notions can be entertained of slavery beyond that of suffering the greatest injuries and oppressions without the liberty of complaining; or if they do, to be destroyed, body and estate, for so doing? . . .

If a libel is understood in the large and unlimited sense urged by Mr. Attorney, there is scarce a writing known that may not be called a libel, or scarce a person safe from being called to an account as a libeler: For Moses, meek as he was, libeled Cain; and who is it that has not libeled the Devil? For according to Mr. Attorney, it is no justification to say one has a bad name. . . . How must a man speak or write, or what must he hear, read, or sing? Or when must he laugh, so as to be secure from being taken as a libeler? . . .

I hope to be pardoned, sir, for my zeal upon this occasion. . . . And you see I labor under the weight of many years, and am borne down with great infirmities of body; yet old and weak as I am, I should think it my duty . . . to go to the utmost part of the land where my service could be of any use in assisting to quench the flame of prosecutions upon informations set on foot by the government to deprive people of the right of remonstrating of the arbitrary attempts of men in power. Men who injure and oppress the people under their administration provoke them to cry out and complain; and then make that very complaint the foundation for new oppressions and prosecutions. . . .

But to conclude; the question before the Court and you gentlemen of the jury is not of small nor private concern, it is not the cause of a poor printer, nor of New York alone, which you are now trying: No! It may in its consequence affect every freeman that lives under a British government on the main of America. It is the best cause. It is the cause of liberty. . . . [E]very man who prefers freedom to a life of slavery will bless you and honor you as men who baffled the attempt of tyranny; and by an impartial and uncorrupt verdict, have laid a noble foundation for securing to ourselves, our posterity, and our neighbors, that to which nature and the laws of our country have given us a right—the liberty—both of exposing and opposing arbitrary power by speaking and writing truth.

Mr. Chief Justice. Gentlemen of the jury. The great pains Mr. Hamilton has taken to show how little regard juries are to pay to the opinion of the judges . . . is done no doubt with a design that you should take very little notice of what I might say upon this occasion. I shall therefore only observe to you that as the facts or words in the information are confessed: The only thing that can come in question before you is whether the words as set forth in the information make a libel.

Source 7 John Peter Zenger's description of the verdict

The jury withdrew and in a small time returned and being asked by the Clerk whether they were agreed of their verdict, and whether John Peter Zenger was guilty of printing and publishing the libels in the information mentioned? They answered by Thomas Hunt, their foreman, "Not Guilty," upon which there were three huzzas in the hall which was crowded with people and the next day I was discharged from my imprisonment.

Source 8 Attorney Andrew James Hamilton, 1735

Power may justly be compared to a great river, while kept within its due bounds, is both beautiful and useful: but when it overflows its banks, it is then too impetuous to be stemmed, it bears down all before it and brings destruction and desolation wherever it comes. If then this is the nature of power, let us at least do our duty, and like wise men (who value freedom) use our utmost care to support liberty, the only bulwark against lawless power, which in all ages has sacrificed to its wild lust and boundless ambition the blood of the best men that ever lived.

📖 *Second Thoughts*
"A Principal Pillar in a Free Government"

10.2 Considering Zenger

Many American historians have seen the Zenger trial as a landmark case, establishing truth as a defense and setting a precedent for the freedom of the press. Andrew James Hamilton is said to have conducted his defense according to the law of the future, which he thereby helped to create.

Source 9   Attorney "Anglo-Americanus," *Barbados Gazette,* July 1737

The right of remonstrating or publishing just complaints the barrister [Hamilton] thinks the right of all freemen: and so think I, provided such remonstrances are made in a lawful way. . . . I know the law books assert the right of complaining to the magistrates and courts of justice, to the Parliament, to the King himself; but the right of complaining to the neighbors is what has not occurred to me. After all, I would not be thought to derogate . . . from that noble privilege of a free people, the liberty of the press. I think it the bulwark of all other liberty, and the surest defense against tyranny and oppression. But still it is a two-edged weapon, capable of cutting both ways, and is not therefore to be trusted in the hands of every discontented fool or designing knave. Men of sense and address (who alone deserve public attention) will ever be able to convey proper ideas to the people, in a time of danger, without running counter to all order and decency. . . .

Now I would be very glad to know what the neighbors can do towards effecting the desired reformation that will be attended with so good success and so few ill consequences as a regular application to His Majesty would be. . . . I confess it surpasses my comprehension to conceive what the neighbors inspired with weekly revelations from the city journalist can do with their governor and Assembly. . . .

In a word; I shall agree with the barrister that the liberty of exposing and opposing arbitrary power is the right of a free people; and he ought at the same time to admit that the order of things and the peace of society require that extraordinary means should not be used for this purpose till the ordinary have failed.

Source 10   James Alexander's response to "Anglo-Americanus,"
Pennsylvania Gazette, November 10, 1737

THE FREEDOM OF SPEECH is a principal pillar in a free government: when this support is taken away the constitution is dissolved, and tyranny is erected on its ruins. Republics and limited monarchies derive their strength and vigor from a popular examination into the actions of the magistrates. This privilege in all ages has been and always will be abused. The best of princes could not escape the censure and envy of the times they lived in. But the evil is not so great as it may appear at first sight. A magistrate who sincerely aims at the good of the society will always have the inclinations of a great majority on his side; and impartial posterity will not fail to render him justice.

These abuses of the freedom of speech are the excrescences of liberty. They ought to be suppressed; but to whom dare we commit the care of doing it? An evil magistrate entrusted with a POWER to punish words is armed with a WEAPON the most destructive and terrible. Under pretense of pruning off the exuberant branches, he frequently destroys the tree.

Source 11 John Oldmixon, *The British Empire in America*, 1741

The information charges Zenger with printing and publishing a false, malicious, scandalous, and seditious Libel, called the *New-York Weekly Journal*. Thus the Attorney General inserted some Parcels of the Paper before-mentioned (in his argument to the Court). . . . It imply'd, that the Administration was so oppressive, that the People were leaving the Province to avoid it; that their Liberties and Properties are precarious, and Slavery is like to be intailed on them and their Posterity. . . . Now if all these things were true, could there be a greater Libel on Majesty itself, than to shew that a Man, guilty of such Oppression, had been kept in the Government so long as this Governor had been at New York? If all or any of these things were true, what Madness was it for him to expose, I will not say his own Dignity, but that of his Office, by staking it against a Croud of Witnesses, offering to prove he was unworthy of it by various Acts of Power?

I am sensible that this Attorney-General said no more than what the Judgments of the Courts . . . established for Law, That to speak evil of Dignities is never the less, nay, that it is the more criminal for being true; but . . . Common Sense is directly contrary in this to Common Law.

Source 12 Salma Hale, *History of the United States,* 1841

Zenger pleaded not guilty; and . . . on the day of the trial, Andrew Hamilton, an eloquent lawyer of Philadelphia, who had secretly been engaged appeared in court to speak in his defence. His friends anticipated that . . . all evidence offered to prove the truth of the publications would be rejected. . . . The evidence was offered and rejected; but the jury—after listening with delight to a bold and animated address from the eloquent advocate, in which he animadverted freely on the decision of the court, appealed to their own knowledge of the truth of the charges, and uttered, in fervid language, those cardinal principles of universal liberty and free discussion, which, though then heresies, are now acknowledged doctrines—gave a verdict of acquittal. Applause resounded through the hall. The court threatened to imprison the leader of the tumult; but from the same lips an applauding shout, longer and louder than before, again burst forth. Mr. Hamilton was conducted from the hall to a splendid entertainment. A salute of cannon was fired at his departure from the city.

Source 13 George Bancroft, *History of the United States of America,* 1856

A newspaper was established to defend the popular cause; and, in about a year after its establishment, its printer, John Peter Zenger, was imprisoned, on the charge of publishing false and seditious libels. . . . At the trial, the publishing was confessed; but the aged Andrew Hamilton . . . justified the publication by asserting its truth. . . .

A patriot of the revolution esteemed this trial to have been the morning star of the American revolution. But it was not one light alone that ushered in the dawn of our independence: the stars of a whole constellation sang together for joy.

Source 14 Carl Degler, *Out of Our Past,* 1970

The trial of John Peter Zenger in New York in 1735 is justly considered a landmark in the history of freedom. . . .

It is true that censorship of the press, particularly by the assemblies, and even trial for libel in which truth was not accepted as a defense, occurred after the Zenger case. But there were no more trials for seditious libel in New York for the rest of the colonial period. Moreover, the trial and its outcome produced repercussions in England. Radicals and Whigs, won over by the brilliant colonial innovation in behalf of a free press, began a campaign in support of American liberty which was to reach its full power at the time of the Revolution. . . .

The principle inherent in the Zenger decision was not quickly implemented in America. . . . It was not until 1798, during the Jeffersonians' powerful attacks upon the theory of the Sedition Act that the modern view of freedom of the press was worked out. Heretofore, all sides to the question, including the Jeffersonians themselves, had accepted the idea that a government had a right to suppress statements critical of its officials. The new view, going beyond that set forth in Zenger, asserted that if a society was to be considered free it could not suppress criticism under the old rubrics of "seditious libel" or "a licentious press." In fact, the crime of seditious libel, i.e., bringing government into disrepute by attacking its officials was abandoned. The concept that truth was a defense in a libel suit—the central principle in the Zenger case—was established in New York law in the case of Henry Coswell in 1804. . . . The doctrine was reinforced by legislative act in 1805 and inserted, for good measure, in the state constitutions of 1821 and 1846. It was not until 1791, however, with Fox's Act, that English juries were granted the right to determine whether the writing in question was libelous or not, and it was not until 1846 that truth was accepted as a defense in a libel suit under English law.

10.3 CNN Interactive: Speaking Freely

Source 15 Stanley Nider Katz, editor of *A Brief Narrative of the Case and Trial of John Peter Zenger,* 1972

Modern textbooks of American history continue to describe the trial as one of the foundation stones of the freedom of the press, and as an important victory of the popular will over the tyrannical attitudes of aristocratic government.

But recent investigations of the trial and the surrounding circumstances bring all of this into question. Zenger and his associates, it becomes clear, were neither political democrats nor radical legal reformers. They were, in fact, a somewhat narrow-minded political faction seeking immediate political gain rather than long-term governmental or legal reform. Nor was the case a landmark in the history of law or of the freedom of the press in the sense in which it has been discussed. The reformation of the law of libel and the associated un-shackling of the press came about, when they did, as if Peter Zenger had never existed.

⚖ Questioning the Past

1. Defend Governor Cosby's decision to prosecute Zenger. What other course or courses of action might the governor have taken?

2. Why should an individual be permitted to criticize the actions of duly constituted authority? Do not such complaints, whether true or false, undermine the public welfare by weakening government?

3. James Alexander stated that the "freedom of speech is a principal pillar of free government." Defend this position. What are other "pillars" of free government? Are any of them as important as freedom of speech? Why or why not?

4. George Bancroft notes that the Zenger verdict has been hailed as "the morning star" of the American Revolution. What possible impact could this decision have had in either heralding or hastening the Revolution?

5. Was the Zenger case a "landmark in the history of freedom," as Degler asserts? Argue both sides of the question.

Chapter 11

Eleven Days that Never Were

Nothing Happens   *September 3, 1752–September 13, 1752*

11.1 Gregorian
Calendar

Benjamin Franklin, who once observed that "lost time is never found again," must have been particularly upset to retire on the night of September 2, 1752, and wake up the next morning to find it was September 14. He was not the only person who experienced this odd phenomenon; everyone in the American colonies did. In fact, the English Parliament had legislated those 11 days out of existence, which was only one aspect of an unusual calendric adjustment throughout the British Empire in the mid-eighteenth century. As a result, 1751 and 1752 were the shortest years in modern history; 1751 began on March 25 and ended only nine months and six days later, and 1752 lost 11 days. The English and the colonists had always begun the year in March, exactly nine months before Christmas, on Annunciation Day, which marked the conception of Jesus Christ. To them, it seemed extraordinary to begin 1752 in January.

And imagine the implications of these calendric changes. What about people under contract for an annual salary in 1751? Should they receive a year's pay for three-quarters of a year's work? And what of the wages for the month in 1752 that lacked 11 days? Or the rents? What about the birthdays that fell within the missing 11 days? What would it feel like to fall asleep on the evening of September 2 and not wake up until September 14? And imagine the idea of celebrating New Year's Eve on March 24.

∼ *First Impressions*

Parliament Rearranges the Calendar

George Washington's recorded birthdate was February 11, 1732, which became February 22 after the calendric adjustment. If more American retailers were aware of this, consumers might have two Washington's Birthday Sales a year.

Source 1   The *Virginia Gazette,* August 16, 1751

LONDON   Substances of the Bill brought into the House of Peers, for regulating the Commencement of the Year, correcting the Calendar.

It is proposed, that in all his Majesty's Dominions, the **Supputation** of the Year now used, according to which the Year of our Lord beginneth on the 25th of March, shall not be made Use of from and after the last Day of December, 1751, but that the first Day of January next after, shall be reckoned to be the first Day of the Year of our Lord 1752; and every first of January after, shall be reckoned the first Day of the Year . . . and that from and after the said first of January, 1752 the several Days of each Month shall go on, and be reckoned and numbered in the same Order; and the Feast of Easter, and other moveable Feasts thereon depending, shall be ascertained according to the same Method as they now are, until the 2nd Day of September in the said Year of 1752 inclusive; and that the natural Day immediately following the said 2nd Day of September shall be called, reckoned, and accounted, to be the 14th Day of September omitting, for that Time only, the eleven intermediate nominal Days of the common Calendar; and that the several natural Days which shall follow next after the said 14th Day of September shall be called, reckoned, and numbered forwards in numerical Order, from the said 14th Day of September according to the Succession of Days now used in the present Calendar; and that all Acts, Deeds, Writings, Notes, and other Instruments, of what Nature or Kind soever, whether ecclesiastical or civil, publick or private, which shall be made or signed, upon or after the said 1st of January 1752 shall bear date according to the new Supputation. . . .

In order to preserve the Calendar, or Method of Reckoning, and for computing the Days of the Year in the same regular Course in all Times coming, it is proposed, that in the several Years of our Lord 1800, 1900, 2100, 2200, 2300, or any other hundredth Years of our Lord in Time to come, except only every fourth hundredth Year, whereof the Year of our Lord 2000 shall be the first, shall not be taken to be **leap Years,** but shall be common Years, consisting of 365 Days; and that the Year of our Lord 2000, 2400, 2800, and every fourth hundredth Year of our Lord from the Year 2000 inclusive, and also all other Years of our Lord, which by the present Supputation are leap Years, consisting of 366 Days, shall be leap Years as now used. . . .

The Holding and Keeping of all Markets, Fairs, and Marts, for the Sale of Goods or Cattle, or for the Hiring of Servants, which are fix'd to certain nominal Days of the Month, or depending upon the Beginning, or any certain Day of the Month, and all Courts holden or kept with any such Fairs or Marts, fixed to such certain Times, shall not, from and after the said 14th Day of September be continued upon the nominal Days of the Month in the new Calendar, but eleven Days later than the said nominal Days in the new Calendar.

Nothing is proposed to accelerate or anticipate the Days or Times for opening, inclosing, or shutting up any Lands for common Pasture, according to divers Customs, Privileges and Usages in certain Places of this Kingdom; but they shall be opened, inclosed, or shut up, upon the same natural Days and Times, which will be eleven Days later than the same would have happened according to the new Supputation of Time. . . .

Nothing is intended to extend or accelerate or anticipate the Time of Payment of any Rent, Annuity or Sum of Money, . . . or to accelerate the Payment

11.2 The
Calendar Act

of, or increase the Interest of any such Sum of Money which shall become payable aforesaid; or to accelerate the Delivery of Goods, Chattles, &c. or the Time of the Commencement, Expiration, or Determination of any Lease or Demise of Lands, Tenements, or hereditaments, or of any Contract or Agreement whatsoever; . . . or of any Grant for any Term of Years of what Nature or Kind soever, or the Time of attaining the Age of 21 Years, or any other Age requisite by any Law, Usage, Deed, Will, or Writing whatsoever, . . . or the Time of Expiration or Determination of any Apprenticeship or other Service by Indenture . . . ; and that no Person shall be deemed to have attained the Age of 21 Years, or any such other Age as before-mentioned, or to have compleated the Time of any Service . . . until the full Number of Years and Days shall be elapsed, on which such Person or Persons respectively would have attained such Age, or have compleated the Time of such Service, in Case no Alteration of the Style had been proposed or enacted.

📖 *Second Thoughts*

The Cycle of the Seasons

The reason for these adjustments was a belated conversion from the Julian to the Gregorian Calendar. Europe had always used the system introduced by Julius Caesar in 44 B.C., a solar calendar that was 11 minutes and 14 seconds longer than the true solar year. By 1582, the discrepancy had so accumulated that church holidays fell in the wrong seasons. For the vernal equinox to be 10 days late was very disturbing to Roman Catholic prelates. This important event—the one spring day when periods of darkness and daylight are equal—occurs on March 21. To restore the vernal equinox to its rightful place, Pope Gregory redesigned the calendar in 1582, instituting a one-time elimination of 10 days and declaring that century years evenly divisible by 400 would be leap years, while all other century years would not. These changes ensured calendric and seasonal synchronization, and Catholic countries in Europe adopted the Gregorian calendar in 1582 and 1583. Unwilling to appear influenced by the Roman church, England and other Protestant nations refused to make the changes. The Gregorian, or New Style, calendar, did not arrive in the British Empire until almost 200 years later.

Slowly but surely, nations that were neither Catholic nor Protestant also adopted the New Style calendar: Japan in 1873, China in 1912, Russia after the Bolshevik Revolution in 1917, Greece in 1924, and Turkey not until 1927, by which time the discrepancy was 13 days.

11.3 The Gregorian Calendar

Source 2   Astronomer Gail S. Cleere, *Natural History,*
September 1991

The calendar year is supposed to be the same length as the cycle of the seasons, but it never was and never will be. After all, the calendar is an integral number of days, while the cycle of seasons is 365 days plus 5 hours, 48 minutes, and about 45 seconds. That's why Julius Caesar, back in 46 B.C., created the *Julian Calendar* with its Leap Year every fourth year to correct the problem, and things got a little better. On the average, the Julian calendar year was 365 days *and 6 hours* long. This was still roughly 11 minutes longer than the cycle of the seasons. Over the centuries, this discrepancy accumulated, so the calendar was 10 days out of step with the seasons by the 16th century. So along came Pope Gregory XIII in 1582—who instituted *another* calendar reform—making the centennial years that were *not* divisible by 400 *not* Leap Years. We call this the *Gregorian Calendar.*

Now the English (and many other Protestant countries) wouldn't have it. Queen Elizabeth I was on the English throne, and if she conceded to Rome, what would that make her? Of course, there were also a variety of other scientific and social concerns that delayed acceptance of Gregory's calendar in many countries. In the end, the English did not adopt the Gregorian reform for another 200 years or so, and neither did her colonies (that's us).

By the mid-18th century, we were in trouble. The old Julian calendar had gotten 11 days out of step with the seasons. Something had to be done, so the learned men in the English scientific community convinced the king to chop 11 days from September, and he did. The colonials (that's us) followed suit. The dates September 3 to September 13, 1752, were the days that never existed in colonial America and merry-old-England. Think of it . . . in England and her colonies, no one was born, no one died, no events of any kind, great or small, are listed for those dates.

⚖ Questioning the Past

1. So long as all nations agree on a calendar, what difference does it make if the calendar is not aligned properly with the seasons? Why would anyone have considered it necessary to devise, and convert to, the New Style calendar?

2. Why were nations of the non-Catholic world so slow in converting to the New Style calendar?

3. What kinds of disruptions might be expected to follow a conversion in our own time from one calendar to another with a consequent loss of 11 days?

4. What disruptions and what benefits would follow conversion in our own time to a global standard for weights and measures such as the metric system? Or a world currency? Would the benefits outweigh the inconveniences of converting?

5. The need for coordinating railroad schedules led the world to develop during the nineteenth century the present system of time zones. Speculate about the kinds of problems that must have occurred when each community defined noon on the basis of its own determination. And, while you're speculating, what time is it at the North Pole?

Chapter **12**

Eliza Lucas

Eliza Lucas Takes Control of the Family Plantations   *1739*

To be 17 years of age is challenge enough for most. To be 17 and the manager of three plantations seems an extraordinary burden for anyone. Yet one young South Carolinian of the eighteenth century met this challenge in a manner that made an indelible mark on colonial America. Eliza Lucas was born on the island of Antigua in the West Indies and moved with her family to South Carolina in 1738. Shortly after settling near Charleston, her father was called back to Antigua to serve as the royal governor. Since her mother was in poor health and her brother was pursuing his studies in England, the responsibility for managing the family estates fell to Eliza.

Eliza managed her family's business affairs with skill and fervor that guaranteed success. But she went beyond that. She launched a program of agricultural experimentation and research that helped to guarantee the economic success of both South Carolina and neighboring Georgia. The primary product of her experimentation was the introduction of indigo as a cash crop for the southern colonies. Indigo is a weed whose broad leaves yield a rare blue dye. Once the processes of cultivation, fermentation, and drying are completed, the plant leaves are transformed into blue cakes. Rice had been the principal cash crop of South Carolina since its introduction in the 1660s. Indigo was the perfect complement to rice, since it could be cultivated in the upland areas while rice was being grown in the lowlands. Indigo, in its cake form, was relatively lighter and more valuable than cotton, rice, or tobacco, and was therefore attractive to shippers seeking a cargo for the markets of the Old World. However, both indigo and rice required intensive labor. Their cultivation was arduous and unappealing to free laborers. Consequently, rice and indigo farming gave added impetus to the expansion of slavery in the South.

Creative, intelligent, industrious, independent—these were traits of Eliza Lucas. She rejected her father's attempts to arrange marriages for her. In 1744 of her own choice she married Charles Pinckney, a prominent planter. They had two sons: Charles Coatesworth Pinckney and Thomas Pinckney. Both served as generals on the American side during the Revolution. Charles Coatesworth was among the framers of the federal constitution and Thomas served as governor of South Carolina. Both were in the administrations of Washington and Adams, and each was a candidate for vice president of the United States.

Eliza Lucas Pinckney died in May of 1793. So great was her role in the founding of the nation that President George Washington, at his own request, served as a pallbearer at her funeral.

✍ *First Impressions*

"Why Not a Woman?"

The letters of Eliza Lucas Pinckney are a part of the legacy she left to America. These papers offer a glimpse into the life and interests of one of the most prominent Americans of the colonial period.

12.1 Seventeenth- and Eighteenth- Century Women

Source 1 To an acquaintance

May 2, 1740

To Mrs. Boddicott:

Dear Madam,—I flatter myself it will be a satisfaction to you to hear I like this part of the world as my lott has fallen here, which I really do. I prefer England to it 'tis true, but think it preferable to the West Indies, and was my Papa here I should be very happy. . . .

My Papa and Mama's great indulgence to mee leaves it to me to chuse our place of residence either in town or country, but I think it more prudent as well as most agreeable to my Mama and selfe to be in the Country during my father's absence. Wee are 17 mile by land, and 6 by water from Charles Town where wee have about 6 agreeable families around us with whom we live in great harmony. I have a little library well furnished (for my Papa has left mee most of his books) in which I spend part of my time. My Musick and the Garden which I am fond of take up the rest that is not imployed in business, of which my father has left mee a pretty good share, and indeed 'twas unavoidable, as my Mama's bad state of health prevents her from going thro' any fatigue.

I have the business of 3 plantations to transact, which requires much writing and more business and fatigue of other sorts than you can imagine, but least you should imagine it too burdensom to a girl at my early time of life, give mee leave to assure you I think myself happy that I can be useful to so good a father. By rising very early I find I can go through with much business.

Your most affectionet and most obliged humble servant,
Eliza Lucas

Source 2 To her father

1740

To Colonel Lucas

Hond. Sir,—Your letter by way of Philadelphia which I duly received was an additional proof of that paternal tenderness which I have always Experienced from the most Indulgent of Parents from my Cradle to this time, and the subject of it is of the most utmost importance to my peace and happiness.

As you propose Mr. L. to me I am sorry I can't have Sentiments favourable enough of him to take time to think on the Subject, as your Indulgence to me will ever add weight to the duty that obliges me to consult what best pleases you, for so much Generosity on your part claims all my Obedience, but as I know tis my happiness you consult [I] must beg the favour of you to say my thanks to the old gentleman for his Generosity and favourable sentiments of me and let him know my thoughts on the affair in such civil terms as you . . . much better than any I can dictate; and beg leave to say to you that the riches of Peru and Chili if he had them put together could not purchase a sufficient Esteem for him to make him my husband.

As to the other Gentleman you mention, Mr. Walsh, you know, Sir, I have so slight a knowledge of him I can form no judgment of him, and a Case of such consiquence requires the Nicest distinction of humours and Sentiments. But give me leave to assure you, my dear Sir, that a Single life is my only Choice and if it were not, as I am yet but Eighteen, hope you will put aside thoughts of my marrying yet these 2 or 3 years at least.

Your most dutiful and Affecte. Daughter, E. Lucas

Source 3   An entry in the letterbook of Eliza Lucas

July 1740

Wrote my father a long letter on his plantation affairs . . . ; On the pains I had taken to bring the Indigo, Ginger, Cotton and Lucern [alfalfa] and Casada [cassava] to perfection, and had greater hopes from Indigo than from any of the rest of the things I had tryd.

Source 4   Memorandum in her letterbook

Memdam. March 11, 1741.(/2). Wrote a long letter to my father about Indigo and all the plantation affairs, and that Mr. H.B. [Hugh Bryan] had been very much deluded by his own fancys and imagined he was assisted by the divine spirrit to prophesy: Charles Town and the Country as farr as Ponpon Bridge should be destroyed by fire and sword, to be executed by the Negroes before the first day of next month. . . . People in general were very uneasey tho' convinced he was no prophet, but they dreaded the consiquence of such a thing being put in the head of the slaves and the advantage they might take of us. From thence he went on (as it was natural to expect when he gave him self up intirely to his own whims) from one step to another till he came to working mirracles and lived for several days in the woods barefooted and alone and with his pen and Ink to write down his prophesies till at length he went with a wand to divide the waters and predicted he should die that night. But upon finding both fail—the water continued as it was, and himself a living Instance of the falicy of his own predictions—was convinced he was not guided by the infallible spirrit but that of delusion.

Source 5   To her father

June the 4th 1741

To my Father
Hon'd Sir

The Cotton, Guiney corn and most of the Ginger planted here was cutt off by a frost. I wrote you in former letter we had a fine Crop of Indigo Seed upon the ground, and since informed you the frost took it before it was dry. I picked out the best of it and had it planted, but there is not more than a hundred bushes of it come up. . . . I make Tho no doubt Indigo will prove a very valuable Commodity in time. . . . I am sorry we lost this season. We can do nothing towards it now but make the works ready for next year.

> Y. m. obt. and ever D[evoted] D[aughter], E. Lucas

Source 6   To her friend Miss Bartlett

[ca. April 1742]

Dr. Miss B[artlett]

By your enquiry after the Committ I find your curiosity has not been strong enough to raise you out of your bed so much before your usual time as mine has been. But to answer your querie: The Comett had the appearance of a very large Starr with a tail and to my sight about 5 or 6 feet long—its real magnitude must then be prodigious. The tale was much paler than the Commet it self and not unlike the Milky Way. . . .

The brightness of the Committ was too dazleing for me to give you the information you require. I could not see whether it had petticoats on or not, but I am inclined to think by its modest appearance so early in the morning it wont permitt every Idle gazer to behold its splendour, a favour it will grant only to such as take pains for it—from hence I conclude if I could have discovered any clothing it would have been the female garb. Besides if it is any mortal transformed to this glorious luminary, why not a woman.

The light of the Comitt to my unphilosophical Eyes seems to be natural and all its own. How much it may really borrow from the sun I am not astronomer enough to tell.

> Eliza. Lucas

Source 7   To Miss Bartlett

ca. April 1742

Dr. Miss B[artlett]

. . . I assure you the sight of a commit is not the only pleasure you lose if you lie late a bed in a morning. . . . An old lady in our Neighborhood is often querrelin with me for riseing so early as 5 o'Clock in the morning, and is in great pain for me least it should spoil my marriage, for she says it will make me look old long before I am so; in this, however, I believe she is mistaking for what ever contributes to health and pleasure of mind must also contribute to good looks. But admiting what she says, I reason with her thus: If I should look older by this practise I really am so; for the longer time we are awake the longer we live. Sleep is so much the Emblem of death that I think it may be rather called breathing than living. Thus then I have the advantage of the sleepers in point of long life.

> E. Lucas

Source 8   To Miss Bartlett

April 1742

Dr. Miss B[artlett]

. . . Why, my dear Miss B, will you so often repeat your desire to know how I triffle away my time in our retirement in my fathers absence. Could it afford you advantage or pleasure I should not have hesitated, but as you can expect neither from it I would have been excused; however, to show you my readiness in obeying your commands, here it is.

In general then I rise at five o'Clock in the morning, read till Seven, then take a walk in the garden or field, see that the Servants are at their respective business, then go to breakfast. The first hour after breakfast is spent at my musick, the next is constantly employed in recolecting something I have learned least for want of practise it should be quite lost, such as French and short hand. After that I devote the rest of the time till I dress for dinner to our little Polly and two black girls who I teach to read, and if I have my pap's approbation (my Mamas I have got) I intend (them) for school mistres's for the rest of the Negroe children. . . . But to proceed, the first hour after dinner as the first after breakfast at musick, the rest of the afternoon in Needle work till candle light, and from that time to bed time read or write. 'Tis the fashion here to carry our work abroad with us so that having company, without they are great strangers, is no interruption to that affair; but I have particular matters for particular days, which is an interruption to mine. Mondays my musick Master is here. Tuesdays my friend Mrs. Carlson (about 3 mile distant) and I are constantly engaged to each other, she at our house one Tuesday—I at hers the next and this is one of the happiest days I spend. . . . Thursday the whole day except what the necessary affairs of the family take up is spent in writing, either on the business of the plantation, or letters to my friend. Every other Fryday, if no company, we go a vizeting so that I go abroad once a week and no oftener. . . .

O! I had like to forget the last thing I have done a great while. I have planted a large figg orchard with design to dry and export them. I have reckoned my expence and the prophet to arise from these figgs, but was I to tell how great an Estate I am to make this way, and how 'tis to be laid out you would think me far gone in romance. Your good Uncle I know has long thought I have a fertile brain for schemeing. I only confirm him in his opinion; but I own I love the vegitable world extremly.

E. Lucas

Source 9   To an acquaintance, Mrs. R. Evance

[ca. 1780]

To Mrs. R. E[vance]

To find you alive and well, my dear Madam, gave me great pleasure, a Sensation I have been little acquainted with of late as you will perceive when I tell you I have been robbed and deserted by my Slaves; my money of no value, my Children sick and prisoners. . . .

Such is the deplorable state of our Country from two armies being in it for near two years; the plantations have been some quite, some nearly, ruined—and all with very few exceptions great sufferers—their Crops made this year must be very small by the desertion of the Negroes in planting and hoeing time. Besides their losses the Country must be greatly impoverished by the death of slaves as the small pox was in the British camp.

Eliza Lucas Pinckney

Source 10 To her grandson, Daniel

[ca. 1783]

With the most resigned acquiescence in the Divine Will, I submit to the loss of Fortune, when I see my dear children, after being exposed to a variety of suffering, danger and Death, alive and well around me. And when I contemplate with what philosophick firmness and calmness they both of them supported pain, sickness and evils of various sorts, and withstood the utmost efforts of the ennemies' malice, and see with what greatness of mind they now generously conduct themselves to all; my heart overflows with gratitude to their great Preserver for continuing to me such children. Be assured, my dear Daniel, no pleasure can equal that which a mother feels when she knows her children have acted their part well through life. . . .

When I take a retrospective view of our past sufferings, so recent too, and compare them with our present prospects, the change is so great and sudden it appears like a dream, and I can hardly believe the pleasing reality, that peace, with all its train of blessings is returned, and that everyone may find Shelter under his own Vine and his own Fig-tree, and be happy. . . . How much has this unhappy land felt the insolence of power and wanton cruelty; there are but few here but can feelingly tell a tale of woe. . . . But let me forget as soon as I can their cruelties, I wish to forgive and will say no more on this subject, and hope our joy and gratitude for our great deliverance may equal our former anguish, and our contentment in mediocrity, and moderation in prosperity, equal the fortitude with which the greatest number even of our sex sustained the great reverse of fortune they experienced.

Women in Colonial America

While the accomplishments of Eliza Lucas Pinckney were extraordinary, the role she played in the political, economic, and social life of colonial America was not. Because of the labor shortage in the colonies, women of the New World enjoyed status and opportunity greater than that of European women of the time. American women were found among the ranks of many colonial occupations: silversmiths, seamstresses, teachers, butchers, printers, bakers, shopkeepers, jailkeepers. They were able to become physicians, surgeons, pharmacists, midwives, journalists, and attorneys by apprenticing with members of these professions. Nor was it unusual for women to perform the managerial duties on southern plantations. Also, women normally supervised the affairs of the plantation household and its servants, and it was common to find their domain encompassing the management as well as the business affairs of the plantation.

📖 *Second Thoughts*

Eliza Lucas Pinckney and Her Domain

12.2 The Cooper River Bridges

The planter aristocracy of the colonial and pre–Civil War South had over time come to be characterized as lazy and effete, and brutal in its dealings with slaves. The following sources offer spirited comment in defense and attack on the life and times of Eliza Lucas.

Source 11 **Biographer and great-great granddaughter, Harriott Horry Ravenel, *Eliza Pinckney,* 1896**

In ending this account of the life and labors of this southern matron of the old time, I cannot refrain from saying one word in behalf of the bygone civilization and especially of the class which she exemplified. It was, as we are often told, indolent, ignorant, self-indulgent, cruel, overbearing. Does this life (and such were the lives of many) show these faults? Is it not, rather, active, useful, and merciful, accepting without hesitation the conditions it found, and doing its utmost to make those conditions good? . . .

The women of all the colonies had committed to them a great though unsuspected charge to fit themselves and their sons to meet the coming change [self-government] in law and soberness; not in riot and anarchy, as did the women of the French Revolution.

Those of the southern states had more to do. They had to train and teach a race of savages,—a race which had never known even the rudiments of decency, civilization, or religion; a race which, despite the labors of colonists and missionaries, remains in Africa to-day as it was a thousand years ago; but a race, which, influenced by these lives, taught by these southern people for six generations, proved in the day of trial the most faithful, the most' devoted of servants, and was declared in 1863 by the northern people worthy to be its equal in civil and political rights.

Source 12 **Kenneth M. Stampp, *The Peculiar Institution: Slavery in the Ante-Bellum South,* 1956**

The Negroes, declared the preamble to South Carolina's code of 1712, were "of barbarous, wild, savage natures, and . . . wholly unqualified to be governed by the laws, customs, and practices of this province." They had to be governed by such special laws "as may restrain the disorders, rapines, and inhumanity to which they are naturally prone and inclined. . . ."

Whether colonial South Carolinians regarded this as more than an immediate and temporary problem they did not make entirely clear. But it is quite evident that many others since have viewed it as a persistent problem which has perplexed each generation of Southerners. According to this belief, the primitive Negroes who were brought to America could only learn the ways of the civilized white man in the course of many generations of gradual cultural growth. One historian [U. B. Phillips] described the southern plantation as "a school constantly training and controlling pupils who were in a backward state of civilization. . . . On the whole the plantations were the best schools yet invented for the mass training of that sort of inert and backward people which the bulk of the American negroes represented." This belief is implicit in some other historical treatises on southern slavery.

Unquestionably when adult Negroes were imported from Africa they had trouble learning to live in a strange environment and to understand unfamiliar social institutions. But the idea that Negroes needed to be civilized by a slow evolutionary process, during which they would gradually acquire and transmit to their descendants the white man's pattern of social behavior, contains two fallacies. One of them results from a misconception of the problem. Actually, the first generation of Negroes born in America in the seventeenth century was just as well prepared for freedom as the generation that was emancipated in the 1860's. The adaptation to the white man's culture involved a process of education, not one of biological evolution. The only way that Negroes ever learned how to live in America as responsible free men was by experience—by starting to live as free men. The plantation school never accomplished this: its aim was merely to train them to be slaves.

The second fallacy results from a total misapprehension of the Negro's African background. There may be objective standards by which one can designate as "primitive" the cultures of the Ashantis and Fantis of the Gold Coast, the Yorubas and Binis of Nigeria, the Mandingos and Hausas of the western Sudan, the people of Dahomey, and the various tribes of the Congo. But to describe these people as savages who led an animal-like existence is a serious distortion. Long before the seventeenth century they had evolved their own intricate cultures. It is always wise to be cautious about making subjective comparisons of cultures in terms of the superiority of one over the other. It is easy, and perhaps natural, for one people to regard the strange customs of another people as inferior to their own familiar customs. And it is easy to forget that white men were scarcely in a position to judge Africans severely for sanctioning slavery, indulging in inter-tribal warfare, and cherishing superstitions.

The African ancestors of American Negroes had developed an economy based upon agriculture which in some ways approached the complex organization of a plantation. . . . Skilled craftsmen—potters, basketmakers, wood carvers, weavers, and ironworkers—played important roles in African society. Professional traders negotiated exchanges of goods with the aid of monetary systems. Social and political institutions matched the complexity of the economy. . . . Indeed, it was because of the relative complexity of their cultures, their familiarity with a sedentary, agricultural way of life, that white men found it profitable to use native Africans as slaves.

Source 13 George C. Rogers, *Charleston in the Age of the Pinckneys,* 1969

When indigo was first introduced into South Carolina as a crop in the 1740's, the basis for a very important imperial agricultural commodity was laid. Indigo could be grown on the high land behind the rice fields as a supplementary crop to rice. Eliza Lucas solved the problem of preparing the commodity for market on her father's Stono River plantation. . . .

Rice and indigo fitted in well with the British mercantile system. Neither could be grown in England, and not much indigo was grown in the British West Indies. Although rice was not consumed in general quantities in England, it could be shipped to Europe, where it was an important item of diet during times of short crops. Since indigo was needed by the developing British cloth industry, South Carolina was a favored child of England. . . . Indigo was favored by a parliamentary bounty of six pence per pound in 1748, this being reduced to four pence per pound in 1770.

Source 14 Gerda Lerner, *The Woman in American History,* 1971

12.3 Women in
the Workplace

The wives and daughters of southern planters carried considerable responsibilities in the running and management of the plantations. Outstanding among these women was Eliza Lucas Pinckney, who made a major contribution to the economic life of the Carolinas. . . . After long and tedious trials, she finally developed a marketable seed [indigo] and began to introduce it to other planters. Indigo soon became the second biggest export staple of the Carolinas, contributing considerably to the area's economic growth. Eliza also experimented with other agricultural products, planting oaks for sale as lumber, growing and drying figs for export, shipping food to the army in Antigua, and pickling eggs in brine. With all this she managed daily to study some Plutarch and Virgil, to read French, and to practice shorthand. She instructed her little sisters and the Negro children of the plantation in reading, practiced the piano, and did needlework. . . . This remarkable woman was greatly respected in her lifetime. A year before her death President George Washington went out of his way on his trip to South Carolina to greet and honor her publicly.

Source 15 Descendant Elise Pinckney, *The Letterbook of Eliza Lucas Pinckney,* 1972

In 1745, Lucas, after five years of investing in indigo experiments in Carolina, was at last able to realize a considerable income from this crop. . . . Indigo culture spread quickly, for the gold-leafed plant pointed the path to plantation affluence. The blue dye-cakes soon established the kind of credits in London banking houses that supported South Carolina in style during the decades before the Revolution. More than 135,000 pounds were produced for export in 1747, and good seasons were soon to produce more than a million. Thus, in the product that Eliza Lucas had pioneered with vision, industry, and perseverance, she provided at a critical period an export staple invaluable to Carolina's economy.

Source 16 Norman K. Risjord, *Representative Americans: The Colonists,* 1981

Far from the giddy belles of the Cavalier myth, women in the colonial South played a vital role in the plantation economy. They managed the household and its servants, superintended the gardens and slaughtering pens that kept the plantation in daily fare, looked to the health of the labor force, and in some cases kept the business ledgers. The brisk self-confidence with which Eliza Lucas mastered all of these tasks bespoke a woman of uncommon wisdom and maturity. . . .

Crops and profits were not her sole interests, despite her determination to be a success in business. . . . Her spare time in the afternoons was devoted to "little Polly and two black girls, who I teach to read." . . . That project was not an idle pastime. Her purpose in tutoring the three girls was to make them "school mistresses for the rest of the Negro children," a project so daring that she took the trouble to secure the permission of her father. The sheriff, on the other hand, does not seem to have worried her, as well he might have, for the legislature made it illegal to teach slaves to read after the Stono River uprising of 1739. Perhaps she was given a subtle caution, since there is no further mention of the education project in her letters.

Her lack of reaction to the Stono uprising is itself mute testimony to her relations with her slaves. While the rest of South Carolina writhed in fear throughout 1739 and 1740 Eliza Lucas ignored the event. There is not a whisper of it in her correspondence even though it took place a short distance from her plantation. Her one mention of slave insurrection in her letters was in 1741 when a local religious fanatic predicted that slaves would destroy the low country "by fire and sword." Even then she was less alarmed at the prospect than amused by the antics of the enthusiast.

⚖ Questioning the Past

1. What might Eliza Lucas Pinckney claim were her accomplishments in life?

2. What does a study of Eliza Lucas Pinckney say about the status of women of her class during the colonial period? What do her letters reveal of her interests and her lifestyle?

3. Harriott Horry Ravenel asserts that the plantation was an agency to "train and teach" African Americans. Kenneth Stampp makes the opposite point. Discuss these positions. What, if anything, may be concluded about Eliza Lucas Pinckney's feelings on race and slavery matters?

4. What roles were available for women in colonial America? Have these roles changed in our own time?

13

The American Revolution

Blood Is Shed at Lexington and Concord

April 19, 1775

13.1 Core Knowledge in United States History

Tensions had been rising for a decade. So strained was the relationship between colonies and mother country that the colonial assembly of Massachusetts had been dissolved by order of General Thomas Gage. Colonies all along the Atlantic seaboard were disturbed by events unfolding in Massachusetts and apprehensive about future plans of the British authorities. Open rebellion seemed a genuine possibility.

The political leaders of Massachusetts had responded to the dissolution of their legislature by establishing a provincial congress in Concord in defiance of General Gage and the army that was prepared to enforce his decrees. Colonial militiamen had begun drills clearly designed as preparation for resistance to British troops. Arms and munitions were being stockpiled in Concord.

General Gage faced a dilemma. Action against the provincial congress or an attempt to seize the weapons cache at Concord might provoke or preempt bloodshed. Inaction could produce either of these results as well.

Gage chose to seize the colonial weapons stockpile. The colonists chose to resist. The resulting confrontation on the morning of April 19, 1775, was a moment that changed the course of history.

❧ *First Impressions*

The Incidents at Lexington and Concord

The firsthand accounts of Lexington and Concord are noteworthy for their partisanship. Two forces in confrontation, experiencing the same events, cite opposing facts and behaviors.

Source 1 Account of General Thomas Gage, written April 29 and published in the *Virginia Gazette,* May 25, 1775

13.2 Birth of a Nation

The following was this day received by the post, inclosed in a letter from General Gage dated, Boston, April 29, 1775, which we give to the public by authority.

A circumstantial account of an attack, that happened on the 19th of April, 1775, on his Majesty's troops, by a number of the people of the province of Massachusetts Bay.

On Tuesday the 18th of April, about half past ten at night, lieutenant col. Smith of the 10th regiment, embarked from the common at Boston, with the grenadiers and light infantry of the troops there, and landed on the opposite side; from whence he began his march towards [C]oncord, where he was ordered to destroy a magazine of military stores, deposited there for the use of an army, to be assembled in order to act against his Majesty and his government—The colonel called his officers together, and gave orders that the troops should not fire, unless, fired upon; and after marching a few miles, detached six companies of light infantry, under the command of major Pitcairn, to take possession of two bridges on the other side of Concord; soon after, they heard many signal guns and the ringing of alarm bells repeatedly, which convinced them the country was rising to oppose them, and that it was a pre-concerted scheme to oppose the King's troops, whenever there should be a favourable opportunity for it.— About three o'clock the next morning, the troops being advanced within two miles of Lexington, intelligence was received that about 500 men in arms were assembled, and determined to oppose the King's troops; and on major Pitcairn's galloping up to the head of the advanced companies, two officers informed him that a man (advanced from those that were assembled) had presented his musket and attempted to shoot them, but the piece flashed in the pan; on this the Major gave direction to the troops to move forward, but on no account to fire, nor even to attempt it, without orders. When they arrived at the end of the village, they observed about 200 armed men drawn up on a green, and when the troops came within one hundred yards of them, they began to file off towards some stone walls on their right flank; the light infantry observing this, ran after them; and the Major instantly called to the soldiers not to fire, but to surround and disarm them; some of them who had jumped over a wall, then fired 4 or 5 shots at the troops, wounded a man of the 10th regiment, and the Major's horse in two places, and at the same time several shots were fired from a meetinghouse on the left: upon this, without any order or regularity, the light infantry began a scattered fire, and killed several of the country people, but were silenced as soon as the authority of their officers could make them.

After this, colonel Smith marched up with the remainder of the detachment, and the whole body proceeded to Concord, where they arrived about 9 o'clock, without any thing further happening; but vast numbers of armed people were seen assembling on all the heights, while col. Smith, with the grenadiers and part of the light infantry remained at Concord to search for cannon; and there he detached capt. Parsons with six light companies, to secure a bridge at some distance from Concord, and to proceed from thence to certain houses, where it was supposed there was cannon and ammunition: capt. Parsons, in pursuance of these orders, posted three companies at the bridge and some heights near it, under the command of capt. Lawrie of the 43d regiment, and in about an hour near after, a large body of them began to move to the bridge; the light companies of the 4th and 10th then descended and joined capt. Lawrie, the people continued to advance in great numbers, and fired upon the King's troops, killed three men, wounded four officers, one sergeant, and four privates; upon which, after returning the fire, capt. Lawrie and his officers thought it prudent to retreat towards the main body at Concord, and were soon joined by two companies of grenadiers. When capt. Parsons returned with the three companies over the bridge, they observed 3 soldiers on the guard, one of them scalped, his head much mangled and his ears cut, though not quite dead, a sight which struck the soldiers with horror; capt. Parsons marched on and joined the main body, who were only waiting for his coming up to march back to Boston.

Col. Smith had executed his orders without opposition, by destroying all the military stores he could find: Both the colonel and major Pitcairn having taken all possible pains to convince the inhabitants that no injury was intended them, and that if they opened their doors when required to search for the stores, not the slightest mischief should be done, neither had any of the people the least occasion to complain; but they were sulky, and one of them even struck major Pitcairn. Except upon capt. Lawrie at the bridge, no hostilities happened from the affair at Lexington, until the troops began their march back. As soon as the troops had got out of the town of Concord, they received a heavy fire on them from all sides, from walls, fences, houses, trees, barns, [etc.] which continued without intermission, till they met the first brigade with two field pieces near Lexington, ordered out under the command of lord Piercy to support them: upon the firing of the field pieces, the people's fire was for a while silenced, but as they still continued to increase greatly in numbers, they firing again as before from all places where they could find cover, upon the whole body, and continued so doing for the space of 15 miles. Notwithstanding their numbers, they did not attack openly the whole day, but kept under cover on all occasions. The troops were very much fatigued, the greater part of them having been under arms all night, and made a march of upwards of forty miles before they arrived at Charlestown, from whence they were ferried over to Boston.

The troops had above 50 killed, and many more wounded.—Reports are various about the loss sustained by the country people; some make it very considerable, others not so much.

Source 2   Article in the *Spy and Oracle of Liberty,* May 3, 1775.

AMERICANS! LIBERTY OR DEATH! JOIN OR DIE!

AMERICANS! forever bear in mind the BATTLE OF LEXINGTON!—where British troops, unmolested and unprovoked, wantonly and in a most inhuman manner, fired upon and killed a number of our countrymen, then robbed, ransacked and burnt their houses! nor could the tears of defenceless women, some of whom were in the pains of childbirth, the cries of helpless babes nor the prayers of old age, confined to beds of sickness, appease their thirst for blood!—or divert them from their DESIGN of MURDER and ROBBERY! . . .

About 10 o'clock on the night of the 18th of April, the troops in Boston were disclosed to be on the move in a very secret manner, and it was found that they were embarking of boats at the bottom of the Common; expresses set off immediately to alarm the country, that they might be on their guard. . . . The body of troops . . . crossed the river and landed at Phipp's Farm; They immediately, to the number of 1000, proceeded to Lexington, about 6 miles below Concord, with great silence: a company of militia, of about 80 men, mustered near the meeting-house; the troops came in sight of them just before sunrise; the militia upon seeing the troops began to disperse; the troops then set out upon the run, hallooing and huzzaing, and coming within a few rods of them, the commanding officer accosted the militia, in words to this effect, "Disperse, you dam'd rebels!—Damn you disperse!" Upon which the troops again huzzaed and immediately one or two officers discharged their pistols, which were instantaneously followed by the firing of four or five of the soldiers; and then there seemed to be a general discharge from the whole body; It is to be noticed that they fired on our people as they were dispersing, agreeable to their command, and that we did not even return the fire; Eight of our men were killed and nine wounded;—The troops then laughed, and damned the **Yankees**, and said they could not bear the smell of gunpowder.

The Colonists Turn against the Empire

The direct taxing of domestic goods and services under the Stamp Act, the taxing of imports under the Townshend Acts, the tax on tea, the Coercive Acts that followed resistance to British authority by the people of Boston, and the exclusion of colonial representatives from the Parliament that enacted such measures—these were without doubt grievances that stirred the American generation of the 1770s. But were these grievances and others felt by the colonists so unique, oppressive, and unbearable that blood had to be shed to redress them?

Was it the matter of taxation? If a tax on sugar or glass or paint or lead is enough to rouse Americans to rebellion, why are the Americans of today passive? Every single item taxed by Britain in the months before April of 1775 is taxed higher and more pervasively today. Was it the specific tax on tea? The Tea Act of 1773 actually allowed Americans—in spite of the three-pence a pound tax—to buy tea at a lower cost than what they had been paying for the smuggled Dutch tea they had used. And if Americans feel so strongly about the injustice of taxation without representation, why do so few even bother to vote? Rare is the election that draws more than half the electorate to the polls.

If the oppression of British rule was so intolerable, why did the English colonies of Canada and the West Indies continue to tolerate it? The English colonies of Australia and New Zealand were able to grow into mature nations within the "constraints" of the British Empire. Moreover, the "oppressive" British authorities permitted those countries to do so.

Why, then, did Americans think it necessary to rebel?

13.3 The Road to Independence

13.4 Samuel Adams, *The Rights of the Colonists*

📖 *Second Thoughts*

What Led the Americans into Open Rebellion?

Scholar after scholar has sought to explain which grievance or set of grievances provoked the colonists and why such provocation led to the shots exchanged at Lexington and Concord. As yet, no one has come forward with a completely convincing explanation. Great moments in history defy simple explanation; they often defy complex explanations as well.

13.5 The
Declaration
of Arms

Source 3   Observation of George III, king of England, August 23, 1775

[M]any of Our Subjects in divers Parts of Our Colonies and Plantations in North America, misled by dangerous and ill-designing Men, and forgetting the Allegiance which they owe to the Power that has protected and sustained them, after various disorderly Acts committed in Disturbance of the Publick Peace, to the Obstruction of lawful Commerce, and to the Oppression of Our loyal Subjects carrying on the same, have at length proceeded to an open and avowed Rebellion, by arraying themselves in hostile Manner to withstand the Execution of the Law, and traitorously preparing, ordering, and levying War against Us. . . . [T]here is Reason to apprehend that such Rebellion hath been much promoted and encouraged by the traitorous Correspondence, Counsels, and Comfort of divers wicked and desperate Persons within this Realm.

Source 4   Revolutionary pamphleteer Thomas Paine, *The Crisis*,
December 23, 1776

These are the times that try men's souls: The summer soldier and the sunshine patriot will, in this crisis, shrink from the service of his country; but he that stands it NOW, deserves the love and thanks of man and woman. Tyranny, like hell, is not easily conquered; yet we have this consolation with us, that the harder the conflict, the more glorious the triumph. What we obtain too cheap, we esteem too lightly: 'Tis dearness only that gives every thing its value. Heaven knows how to put a proper price upon its goods; and it would be strange indeed, if so celestial an article as FREEDOM should not be highly rated. Britain, with an army to enforce her tyranny, has declared that she has a right (not only to TAX) but "to BIND us in ALL CASES WHATSOEVER" and if being bound in that manner, is not slavery, then is there not such a thing as slavery upon earth.

Source 5   Account of former president John Adams, 1818

[W]hat do we mean by the American Revolution? Do we mean the American war? The Revolution was effected before the war commenced. The Revolution was in the minds and hearts of the people; a change in their religious sentiments of their duties and obligations. While the king, and all in authority under him, were believed to govern in justice and mercy, according to the laws and constitution derived to them from the God of nature and transmitted to them by their ancestors, they thought themselves bound to pray for the king and queen and all the royal family, and all in authority under them, as ministers ordained of God for their good; but when they saw those people renouncing all the principles of authority, and bent upon the destruction of all the securities of their lives, liberties, and properties, they thought it their duty to pray for the continental congress and all the thirteen State congresses. . . .

Another alteration was common to all. The people of America had been educated in an habitual affection for England, as their mother country; and while they thought her a kind and tender parent, (erroneously enough, however, for she never was such a mother,) no affection could be more sincere. But when they found her a cruel beldam, willing like Lady Macbeth, to "dash their brains out," it is no wonder if their filial affections ceased, and were changed into indignation and horror.

This radical change in the principles, opinions, sentiments, and affections of the people, was the real American Revolution.

Source 6   Salma Hale, *History of the United States,* 1841

Great Britain had, by her laws of trade and navigation, confined the commerce of the colonies almost wholly to herself. To encourage her own artisans, she had even, in some cases, prohibited the establishment of manufactories in America. These restrictions, while they increased her revenues and wealth, greatly diminished the profits of the trade of the colonies, and sensibly impeded their internal prosperity. They were most injurious to New England, where the sterility of the soil repelled the people from the pursuits of agriculture; there they were most frequently violated, and there the arbitrary means adopted to enforce them awakened the attention of a proud and jealous people to their natural rights.

Source 7   Richard Hildreth, *The History of the United States of America,* 1849

[T]he American Revolution made no sudden nor violent change in the laws or the political institutions of America beyond casting off the super intending power of the mother country; and even that power, always limited, was replaced to a great extent by the authority of Congress.

The most marked peculiarity of the Revolution was the public recognition of the theory of the equal rights of man. But this principle . . . encountered in existing prejudices and institutions many serious and even formidable obstacles to its general application, giving rise to several striking anomalies . . . the most startling of all was domestic slavery, an institution inconsistent not only with the equal rights of man, but with the law of England . . . but which at the commencement of the struggle with the mother country, existed nevertheless as a matter of fact in every one of the United Colonies. In half the Union it still exists, preventing, more than all other causes, that carrying out of the principles of the Revolution, that assimilation and true social union toward which the states have constantly tended, but which they are still so far from having reached.

Source 8 George Bancroft, *History of the United States,* 1852

From the intelligence that had been slowly ripening in the mind of cultivated humanity, sprung the American Revolution, which was designed to organize social union through the establishment of personal freedom, and thus emancipate the nations from all authority not flowing from themselves. In the old civilization of Europe, power moved from a superior to inferiors and subjects; a priesthood transmitted a common faith, from which it would tolerate no dissent; the government esteemed itself, by compact or by divine right, invested with sovereignty, dispensing protection and demanding allegiance. But a new principle, far mightier than the church and state of the Middle Ages, was forcing itself into power. Successions of increasing culture and heroes in the world of thought had conquered for mankind the idea of the freedom of the individual; the creative but long latent energy that resides in the collective reason was next to be revealed. From this the state was to emerge, like the fabled spirit of beauty and love out of the foam of the ever-troubled ocean. It was the office of America to substitute for hereditary privilege the natural equality of man; for the irresponsible authority of a sovereign, a dependent government emanating from the concord of opinion; and as she moved forward in her high career, the multitudes of every clime gazed towards her example in hopes of untold happiness, and all the nations of the earth sighed to be renewed.

Source 9 Ralph Waldo Emerson's speech at the Centennial Celebration at Concord, April 19, 1875

We had many enemies and many friends in England, but one benefactor was King George III. The time had arrived for that political severance of America that it might play its part in the history of this globe; and the way of divine Providence to do it was to give an insane king to England. On the resistance of the colonies he alone was immovable on the question of force. England was so dear to us that the colonies could only be absolutely united by violence from England and only one man could compel the resort to violence. So the king became insane.

Parliament wavered, all the ministers wavered; but the king had the insanity of one idea. He was immovable; he insisted on the impossible; so the army was sent. America was instantly united and the nation born.

On the 19th of April 800 soldiers with hostile intent were sent hither from Boston. Nature itself put a new face on that day. You see the rude fields of this morning, but on the same day of 1775 a rare forwardness of the spring is recorded. It appears the patriotism of the people was so hot that it melted the snow and the rye waved on the 19th of April. . . .

In all noble action we say 'tis only the first step that costs. Who will carry out the rule of right must take his life in his hand. We have no need to magnify the facts. Only three of our men were killed at this bridge and a few others wounded; here the British army was first fronted and driven back, and if only three men or only one man had been slain, it was the first victory. The thunderbolt falls on an inch of ground, but the light of it fills the horizon. The British instantly retreated. We had no electric telegraph, but the news of the triumph of the farmers over the king's troops sped through the country to New

York, to Philadelphia, to Kentucky, to the Carolinas, with speed unknown before and ripened the colonies to inevitable decision.

Source 10 John Fiske, *The American Revolution,* 1891

The American Revolution, unlike most political revolutions, was essentially conservative in character. It was not caused by actually existing oppression, but by the determination to avoid oppression in the future. Its object was not the acquisition of new liberties, but the preservation of old ones. The principles asserted in the Stamp Act Congress of 1765 differed in no essential respect from those that had been proclaimed five centuries earlier, in Earl Simon's Parliament of 1265. Political liberty was not an invention of the western hemisphere; it was brought to these shores from Great Britain by our forefathers of the seventeenth century, and their children of the eighteenth naturally refused to surrender the treasure which from time immemorial they had enjoyed.

Source 11 Woodrow Wilson, *A History of the American People,* 1902

George III had too small a mind to rule an empire. . . . His stubborn instinct of mastery made him dub the colonists "rebels" upon their first show of resistance; he deemed the repeal of the Stamp Act a fatal step of weak compliance, which had only "increased the pretensions of the Americans to absolute independence." **Chatham** he called a "trumpet of sedition" because he praised the colonists for their spirited assertion of their rights. The nature of the man was not sinister. Neither he nor his ministers had any purpose of making "slaves" of the colonists. Their measures for the regulation of the colonial trade were incontestably conceived upon a model long ago made familiar in practice, and followed precedents long ago accepted in the colonies. Their financial measures were moderate and sensible enough in themselves, and were conceived in the ordinary temper of law-making. What they did not understand or allow for was American opinion. What the Americans, on their part, did not understand or allow for was the spirit in which Parliament had in fact acted. They did not dream with how little comment or reckoning upon consequences, or how absolutely without any conscious theory as to power or authority, such statutes as those which had angered them had been passed; . . . how unaffectedly astonished they were at the rebellious outbreak which followed in the colonies. And, because they were surprised and had intended no tyranny, but simply the proper government of trade and the adequate support of administration throughout the dominions of the crown, as the ministers had represented these things to them, members of course thought the disturbances at Boston a tempest in a teapot, the reiterated protests of the colonial assemblies a pretty piece of much ado about nothing.

Source 12 Andrew C. McLaughlin, *A History of the American Nation,* 1913

Trivial offenses on the part of government cannot justify revolution. Only oppression or serious danger can justify war. It cannot be said that the people of the colonies had actually suffered much. It might even seem that the mother country was not at all tyrannical in taxing the colonies to pay for defending them, and beyond question George III and his pliant ministers had no intention of treating the colonists with cruelty. How, then, can the war that followed be justified? The Revolution was justifiable because the colonists stood for certain fundamental principles that were woven into the very fabric of their lives. They were determined that no one should take money from them without their consent, and that their own local governments should be indeed their own and do their will. They carried to a legitimate conclusion the true political principles for which the English people had fought in the great rebellion of the seventeenth century. . . . It is sometimes said that the American Revolution was conservative or preservative. Such it surely was; but it did more than save the principles of English liberty; it built them up and gave them a logical expression in the institutions of a free people made by themselves and changeable at their own discretion.

Source 13   Claude H. Van Tyne, *The Causes of the War of Independence,* 1921

In the very genesis of English settlement, the leaders of the English colonists were liberal and even radical when they first set foot on the shores of the New World. Their early migrations had in the main been caused by the political and religious conflicts of the age. . . .

In the old civilizations like that of Europe, men of radical or even liberal tendencies are held in check by the enveloping conservative forces, by traditions, by the fear of displeasing those in high social positions, by the nearness of government itself; but on the frontier, three thousand miles away, in the case of these American colonies, these restraining forces did not exist, and men moved forward rapidly, even recklessly, on the path of political and social experiment. . . .

Added to the fact of the remoteness was the novelty of life in the American wilderness. If the chains of tradition were ever to be struck off, it must be in this environment so utterly unlike that of England. . . .

Everything in their new environment tended to make the settlers forget the power or even the need of the British Government. The fundamentals of political organization remained the same, but a thousand laws needed to keep order in the highly complex English society became irrelevant and useless in the sparsely settled forest. New laws of the colonists' own making took the place of those discarded. . . . Having little to fear and often able to dispense with government, the colonist became individualistic; . . . he developed hatred of restraint. . . . As time went on and he conquered the wilderness, he might be pardoned a spirit of independence and of confidence.

Source 14   Charles M. Andrews, "The American Revolution: An Interpretation," 1926

Primarily, the American Revolution was a political and constitutional movement and only secondarily one that was either financial, commercial, or social. At bottom the fundamental issue was the political independence of the colonies, and in the last analysis the conflict lay between the British Parliament and the colonial assemblies. . . .

The colonies had developed a constitutional organization equally complete with Britain's own and one that in principle was far in advance of the British system, and they were qualified to co-operate with the mother country on terms similar to those of a brotherhood of free nations. . . . But England was unable to see this fact or unwilling to recognize it, and consequently America became the scene of a political unrest, which might have been controlled by compromise, but was turned to revolt by coercion.

Source 15 James Truslow Adams, *The Epic of America,* 1931

Opinions will differ regarding Samuel Adams, but there can be no difference of opinion as to his consummate ability as a plotter of revolution. . . . Even when others had no wish to secede from the empire, but merely to be left in peace or to have certain inimical laws repealed, Adams early conceived the belief that the one end to work for was immediate and complete independence. . . .

From about 1761 until independence was declared by the colonies in 1776, Adams worked ceaselessly for the cause to which he had devoted his life, manipulating newspapers and town meetings, organizing committees of correspondence throughout the colonies, even bringing about happenings which would inflame public opinion. . . .

Public opinion is never wholly united, and seldom rises to a pitch of passion without being influenced—in other words, without the use of propaganda. The Great War taught that to those who did not know it already.

Source 16 John C. Miller, *Origins of the American Revolution,* 1943

It was the invasion of Americans' political rights by Parliament after the Peace of Paris which precipitated the struggle between mother country and colonies and inspired the ideals and slogans of the American Revolution. Economic grievances played a secondary part in the patriots' propaganda; from 1765 to 1776, political issues were kept uppermost. . . . Throughout the colonial period, the rights and privileges of the assemblies were regarded as the first line of defense of American liberty, both political and economic. If they were overthrown, the colonists believed themselves destined to become as "errant slaves as any in Turkey." . . .

Englishmen . . . denied the colonists' contention that there were metes and bounds to the authority of Parliament. The authority of Parliament was, in their opinion, unlimited: the supremacy of Parliament had come to mean to Englishmen an uncontrolled and uncontrollable authority. Indeed, the divine right of kings had been succeeded by the divine right of Parliament. . . . It was the refusal of Americans to bow before this new divinity that precipitated the American Revolution.

The absolutism of Parliament admitted of no divisions of authority within the empire: Parliament must have all power or it had none. In Englishmen's eyes, sovereignty was indivisible: it could not be parceled out between the colonies and the mother country. . . .

Viewed in this light, the colonial assemblies were not local parliaments as Americans supposed, but merely corporations subject to the will of Parliament. . . . This doctrine ruled out the American conception of the British Empire as a federation of self-governing commonwealths.

Source 17   Charles and Mary Beard, *A Basic History of the United States,* 1944

Over against colonial maturity in matters political, religious, social, and intellectual on this continent stood, across the sea, the British system of politics, economy, and ecclesiasticism. The system was an oligarchy collected around the monarch—an oligarchy composed of lords and the clerical hierarchy. There was in Great Britain, to be sure, a "popular" legislative body, the House of Commons; but . . . the oligarchy, through personal influence, wealth, and corruption, was generally able to dominate it. In economic terms, the policy of the British system was mercantilism—the permanent subordination of the colonies to the interests of the British governing class. . . .

[T]he ruling classes of Great Britain were fairly united on one thing: they wanted to keep the British Empire intact and to make it contribute to the wealth and power of the mother country. The American colonies furnished many offices and jobs for British lords, their younger sons, and their hangers-on; the American colonies had vast areas of unoccupied land, huge parcels of which royal favorites could obtain for a song if they had the King's approval. British merchants and shippers found American trade highly profitable and naturally sought to keep as much of it as they could. British manufacturers looked upon the American markets as their own and as necessary outlets for their woolen cloth, hardware, and other finished commodities. The arable lands and forests of America were the objects of great desire to British enterprisers. British capitalists, whether landlords, merchants, manufacturers, or bankers, ever hunting more advantageous places for the investment of their capital, regarded the American colonies as offering almost unlimited opportunities for money-making. . . .

For carrying the ideas of mercantilism into effect, certain definite laws and practices were necessary. The bonds of union between the American colonies and Great Britain must be kept firm and made stronger as the colonies matured in wealth and power. Laws favorable to the interests of British merchants, manufacturers, and investors must be enacted; and the American colonists must be stopped from passing laws and doing other things which interfered with the enforcement of British measures. . . .

But in many matters, American interests ran directly counter to British interests. Most Americans were more concerned with developing the lands and resources right at hand than they were in promoting prosperity in Great Britain or upholding the British interests in India and other distant parts of the world. American artisans and manufacturers wanted to develop their own industries and reap the profits accruing from them. American merchants and shippers longed to enlarge their share of international trade. American farmers and planters believed that they could get better prices for their produce if British merchants exercised less control over the export and import trade; if Dutch, French, and other merchants from the continent of Europe could operate more freely in

American markets. . . . American capitalists and enterprisers thought they would have larger opportunities for profitable business if all the lands, forests, and minerals at hand were at the disposal of colonial governments. Farmers and planters on the seaboard looked with hungry eyes toward the vacant lands beyond the near frontier and wanted them thrown open to easy settlement or speculation. Moreover, Americans could scarcely help wanting a larger share of the lucrative offices and jobs filled with appointees of the British King and the colonial governors, whose salaries were paid out of American taxes. . . .

In addition, a highly controversial question arose: Who are to benefit most from the exploitation of Western territories now cleared of the French and opened to development—American or British investors, farmers, land speculators, and fur traders? . . . Both the British and the Americans therefore had logical and legitimate claims regarding all these matters, but there was no high and impartial court above them to which they could appeal for satisfactory adjudication.

Source 18 Winston S. Churchill, *A History of the English-Speaking People,* 1956

Vast territories had fallen to the Crown on the conclusion of the Seven Years' War. From the Canadian border to the Gulf of Mexico the entire hinterland of the American colonies became British soil, and the parcelling out of these new lands led to further trouble with the colonists. Many of them, like George Washington, had formed companies to buy these frontier tracts from the Indians, but a royal proclamation restrained any purchasing and prohibited their settlement. Washington, among others, ignored the ban and wrote his land agent ordering him "to secure some of the most valuable lands in the King's part (on the Ohio), which I think may be accomplished after a while, notwithstanding the proclamation that restrains it at present, and prohibits the settling of them at all; for I can never look upon that proclamation in any other light than as a temporary expedient to quiet the minds of the Indians." This attempt by the British Government to regulate the new lands caused much discontent among the planters, particularly in the Middle and Southern colonies.

Source 19 Lawrence Henry Gipson, *The Triumphant Empire,* 1960

The student of history is fully aware that all great wars in modern times have been followed by great psychological changes—a result equally important to physical modifications of boundaries. When the people of Canada exchanged sovereigns after the Peace of Paris they were forced to modify their outlook. While they bore no love for their new King, neither had they any love for their old King, who, they felt, had turned his back on them in many ways. They would therefore give their blood for neither sovereign. The impact of the outcome of the Great War for the Empire was no less important upon the British colonials—at least those living in North America. Had the British triumph on that continent been less spectacular, less decisive, its effect might have been different. By the same token, had the French dictated the peace—that would surely have enclosed the British colonials firmly within the narrow area between the Atlantic Ocean and the Appalachian Mountains, as seemed likely at the end of the first four years of the struggle for the heart of North America—the effect on the minds of colonials would have been equally profound, but surely of a very different nature. Had the French troops still been occupying such highly strategic military posts as Forts Louisbourg, Beausejour, Ticonderoga, Crown Point, Niagara, Duquesne, and Mobile, while allied with countless hostile Indians ready and eager to raid British settlements to the south and east, there would have been constant insecurity concerning the British North American position, and the need for maintaining a powerful force of regulars at frontier points would have been apparent. Undoubtedly this would not only have led them to implore the King for continued protection, but also to submit without much grumbling to a parliamentary stamp tax levy, as perhaps the fairest way of distributing responsibility among all colonials for helping to share in the common defense.

Source 20   Carl Degler, *Out of Our Past,* 1970

Though the colonists had long been drifting away from their allegiance to the mother country, the chain of events which led to the Revolutionary crisis was set in motion by external events. The shattering victory of the Anglo-American forces over the French in the Great War for Empire ... suddenly revealed how wide the gulf between colonists and mother country had become. The very fact that the feared French were once and for all expelled from the colonial backdoor meant that another cohesive, if negative, force was gone. . . . What actual effect the removal of the French produced upon the thinking of the colonists is hard to weigh, but there can be little doubt that the Great War for Empire opened a new era in the relations between the colonies and the mother country.

Great Britain emerged from the war as the supreme power in European affairs: her armies had swept the once vaunted French authority from two continents; her navy now indisputably commanded the seven seas. A symbol of this new power was that Britain's ambassadors now outranked those of France and Spain in the protocol of Europe's courts. But the cost and continuing responsibilities of that victory were staggering for the little island kingdom.

Before the war, the administration and cost of the Empire were primarily, if not completely, a British affair. . . . Under the pressure of the new responsibilities, the British authorities began to cast about for a new theory and practice of imperial administration. . . . It seemed only simple justice to London officialdom that the colonies should share in the costs as well as the benefits to be derived from the defeat of the ancient enemy. At no time, it should be noticed, were the colonies asked to contribute more than a portion of the price of their own frontier defense. . . . It was not injustice or the economic incidence of the taxes which prompted the colonial protests; it was rather the novelty of the British demands. . . . Too many Americans had grown accustomed to their untrammeled political life to submit now to new English controls. In brief, the colonists suddenly realized that they were no longer wards of Britain, but a separate people, capable of forging their own destiny. . . .

As children enjoying a long history of freedom from interference from their parent, the Americans might well have continued in their loose relationship, even in maturity, for they were conservative as well as precocious. History, however, decreed otherwise. Britain's triumph in the Great War for Empire put a new strain on the family relationship. . . .

Measured against the age of Hitler and Stalin, the British overlords of the eighteenth century appear remarkably benign in their dealings with the colonies in the years after 1763. For it is a fact that the colonies were in revolt against a potential tyrant, not an actual one. Much more fearsome in the eyes of the politically sensitive colonials was the direction in which the British measures tended rather than the explicit content of the acts.

Source 21 Samuel Eliot Morison, *The Oxford History of the American People,* 1971

The Boston Tea Party needled Parliament into passing, and George III into signing, a series of laws that Americans referred to as the Coercive, or Intolerable, Acts. . . . From the day that unhappy law was passed, the question between England and the Thirteen Colonies was one of power; who would rule, or have the last say? All other questions of taxation, customs duties and the like faded into the background. Through all stages of remonstrance, resistance, and outright war, the dominant issue was one of power—should Britain or America dictate the terms of their mutual association, or separation?

Source 22 Howard Zinn, *A People's History of the United States,* 1980

Around 1776, certain important people in the English colonies made a discovery that would prove enormously useful for the next two hundred years. They found that by creating . . . a legal unity called the United States, they could take over land, profits, and political power from favorites of the British Empire. In the process, they could hold back a number of potential rebellions and create a consensus of popular support for the rule of a new, privileged leadership. . . .

We have here a forecast of the long history of American politics, the mobilization of lower-class energy by upper-class politicians, for their own purposes. This was not purely deception; it involved, in part, a genuine recognition of lower-class grievances, which helps to account for its effectiveness as a tactic over the centuries.

⚖ Questioning the Past

1. What happened at Lexington and why was it significant?
2. Present the various theories that attempt to explain the cause or causes of the American Revolution. Why was there an American Revolution? Why did it happen when it did? Was revolution inevitable in America? Why or why not?
3. What were the grievances that led Americans to revolt against British rule? Are any of these grievances present in America today?

4. Was British rule of America benign and well-intentioned? Was it oppressive? Present the case for each position. Which is the more accurate description?

5. George III warned that many colonists were being "misled by dangerous and ill-designing men" into the support of the rebellion in America. Present evidence in support of and in opposition to this assertion.

6. John Adams stated, "The Revolution was effected before the war commenced." Explain his meaning.

7. It has been suggested by some historians that if there had been no Great War for Empire (1754–1763), there would have been no American Revolution. Explain and evaluate this viewpoint.

8. What is a revolution? What is a war for independence? Was the American Revolution one, or both, of these? Explain.

14

The Declaration of Independence

The Declaration Is Adopted   *July 4, 1776*

Three weeks after the first shots of the American Revolution were fired at Lexington and Concord, delegates from 13 of Britain's North American colonies assembled at Philadelphia as the Second Continental Congress, whose purpose was to coordinate the common defense of the colonies and to give them a united voice. For a time the Congress hoped it was possible to reach some sort of reconciliation with Britain. But after a year of open warfare, such hopes were waning.

On May 15, 1776, a convention in Virginia decided the time had come to pursue a new course. Accordingly, instructions were sent from the convention to the Virginia delegates to the Second Continental Congress requesting that they introduce resolutions to forgo further attempts at reconciliation and permanently sever the political ties between colonies and mother country. Richard Henry Lee took the floor of the Congress for this purpose on June 7. The suggestion of such a bold move initially caused a division of opinion among the delegates.

14.1 The
Declaration of
Independence

First Impressions

To Establish a Separate Government

As the following selections show, both the decision to declare independence and the rationale for such a decision, expressed in a declaration, provoked controversy at home and abroad.

Source 1   Proceedings of the Continental Congress, June 7, 1776

Resolution of Independence
Moved by R. H. Lee for the Virginia Delegation

Resolved

That these United Colonies are, and of right ought to be, free and independent States; that they are absolved from all allegiance to the British Crown, and that all political connection between them and the State of Great Britain is, and ought to be, totally dissolved.

That it is expedient forthwith to take the most effectual measures for forming foreign Alliances.

That a plan of confederation be prepared and transmitted to the respective Colonies for their consideration and approbation.

Source 2 Thomas Jefferson's notes of the Continental Congress

Friday June 7, 1776. The Delegates from Virginia moved in obedience to instructions from their constituents that Congress should declare that these United Colonies are & of right ought to be free & independent states. . . . The house being obliged to attend at that time to some other business, the proposition was referred to the next day when the members were ordered to attend punctually at ten o'clock.

Saturday June 8. They proceeded to take it into consideration and referred it to a committee of the whole, into which they immediately resolved themselves, and passed that day & Monday the 10th. in debating the subject.

It was argued by Wilson, Robert R. Livingston, E. Rutlege, Dickinson and others.

That tho' they were friends to the measures themselves, and saw the impossibility that we should ever again be united with Gr. Britain, yet they were against adopting them at this time:

That the conduct we had formerly observed was wise & proper now, of deferring to take any capital step till the voice of the people drove us into it:

That they were our power, & without them our declarations could not be carried into effect:

That the people of the middle colonies were not yet ripe for bidding adieu to British connection but that they were fast ripening & in a short time would join in the general voice of America: . . .

That some of them had expressly forbidden their delegates to consent to such a declaration, and others had given no instructions, & consequently no powers to give such consent:

That if the delegates of any particular colony had no power to declare such colony independent, certain they were the others could not declare it for them . . . :

That if such a declaration should now be agreed to, these delegates must retire & possibly their colonies might secede from the Union:

That such a secession would weaken us more than could be compensated by any foreign alliance:

That in the event of such a division, foreign powers would either refuse to join themselves to our fortunes, or having us so much in their power as that desperate declaration would place us, they would insist on terms proportionably more hard & prejudicial: . . .

That France & Spain had reason to be jealous of that rising power which would one day certainly strip them of all their American possessions:

That it was more likely they should form a connection with the British court, who, if they should find themselves unable otherwise to extricate themselves from their difficulties, would agree to a partition of our territories, restoring Canada to France, & the Floridas to Spain, to accomplish for themselves a recovery of these colonies:

That it would not be long before we should receive certain information of the disposition of the French court, from the agent whom we had sent to Paris for that purpose:

That if this disposition be favourable, by waiting the event of the present campaign, which we all hoped would be successful, we should have reason to expect an alliance on better terms: . . .

That it was prudent to fix among ourselves the terms on which we would form an alliance, before we declared we would form one at all events:

And that if these were agreed on & and our Declaration of Independence ready by the same time our Ambassador should be prepared to sail, it would be as well, as to go into that Declaration at this day.

On the other side it was urged by J. Adams, Lee, Wythe, and others:

That no gentleman had argued against the policy or the right of separation from Britain, nor had supposed it possible we should ever renew our connection: that they had only opposed its being now declared:

That the question was not whether, by a declaration of independence, we should make ourselves what we are not; but whether we should declare a fact which already exists:

That as to the people or parliament of England, we had alwais been independent of them, their restraints on our trade deriving efficacy from our acquiescence only & not from any rights they possessed of imposing them, & that so far our connection had been federal only, & was now dissolved by the commencement of hostilities:

That as to the king, we had been bound to him by allegiance, but that this bond was now dissolved by his assent to the late act of parliament, by which he declares us out of his protection, and by his levying war on us, a fact which had long ago proved us out of his protection; it being a certain position in law that allegiance & protection are reciprocal, the one ceasing when the other is withdrawn: . . .

No delegates then can be denied . . . a power of declaring an existent truth: . . .

That the people wait for us to lead the way:

That they are in favour of the measure, tho' the instructions given by some of their *representatives* are not:

That the voice of the representatives is not alwais consonant with the voice of the people, and that this is remarkably the case in these middle colonies: . . .

That it would be vain to wait either weeks or months for perfect unanimity, since it was impossible that all men should ever become of one sentiment on any question: . . .

That a declaration of Independence alone could render it consistent with European delicacy for European powers to treat with us, or even to receive an Ambassador from us:

That till this they would not receive our vessels into their ports, nor acknowledge the implications of our courts of Admiralty to be legitimate, in cases of capture of British vessels:

That tho' France & Spain may be jealous of our rising power, they must think it will be much more formidable with the addition of Great Britain. . . .

That the present campaign may be unsuccessful, & therefore we had better propose an alliance while our affairs wear a hopeful aspect: ...

And that the only misfortune is that we did not enter into alliance with France six months sooner, as besides opening their ports for the vent of our last year's produce, they might have marched an army into Germany and prevented the petty princes there from selling their unhappy subjects to subdue us.

It appearing in the course of these debates that the colonies of N. York, New Jersey, Pennsylvania, Delaware, Maryland & South Carolina were not yet matured for falling from the parent stem, but that they were fast advancing to that state, it was thought most prudent to wait a while for them, and to postpone the final decision to July 1. but that this might occasion as little delay as possible, a committee was appointed to prepare a declaration of Independence. the Commee. were J. Adams, Dr. Franklin, Roger Sherman, Robert R. Livingston & myself.

The Congress Votes on Independence

14.2 Declaring Independence

The Continental Congress resumed its consideration of Lee's resolution of independence on July 1. The following day, July 2, 1776, it took the historic step of adopting the resolution declaring the colonies independent of Great Britain. The delegates next began consideration of the formal document—prepared by the committee appointed for the purpose—that would announce their decision to the world. On the evening of July 4, this document, the Declaration of Independence, was approved.

The Declaration of Independence, drafted mostly by Thomas Jefferson, was divided into two parts. The first was a preamble offering the theoretical justification for the founding of the United States. The second part consisted of a series of grievances that had led the colonies to take such a bold action.

Source 3 The Declaration of Independence

When in the Course of human events, it becomes necessary for one people to dissolve the political bands which have connected them with another, and to assume among the Powers of the earth, the separate and equal station to which the Laws of Nature and of Nature's God entitle them, a decent respect to the opinions of mankind requires that they should declare the causes which impel them to the separation.

We hold these truths to be self-evident, that all men are created equal, that they are endowed by their creator with certain unalienable Rights, that among these are Life, Liberty and the pursuit of Happiness. That to secure these rights, Governments are instituted among Men, deriving their just powers from the consent of the governed, That whenever any Form of Government becomes destructive of these ends, it is the Right of the People to alter or to abolish it, and institute new Government, laying its foundation on such principles and organizing its powers in such form, as to them shall seem most likely to effect their Safety and Happiness. Prudence, indeed, will dictate that Governments long established should not be changed for light and transient causes; and accordingly all experience hath shown, that mankind are more disposed to suffer, while evils are sufferable, than to right themselves by abolishing the forms to which they are accustomed. But when a long train of abuses and usurpations, pursuing invariably the same Object evinces a design to reduce them under absolute Despotism, it is their right, it is their duty, to throw off such Government, and to provide new Guards for their future security. Such has been the patient sufferance of these Colonies; and such is now the necessity which constrains them to alter their former Systems of Government. The history of the present King of Great Britain is a history of repeated injuries and usurpations, all having in direct object the establishment of an absolute Tyranny over these States. To prove this, let Facts be submitted to a candid world.

He has refused his Assent to Laws, the most wholesome and necessary for the public good.

He has forbidden his Governors to pass Laws of immediate and pressing importance, unless suspended in their operation till his Assent should be obtained; and when so suspended, he has utterly neglected to attend to them.

He has refused to pass other Laws for the accommodation of large districts of people, unless those people would relinquish the right of Representation in the Legislature, a right inestimable to them and formidable to tyrants only.

He has called together legislative bodies at places unusual, uncomfortable, and distant from the depository of their Public Records, for the sole purpose of fatiguing them into compliance with his measures.

He has dissolved Representative Houses repeatedly, for opposing with manly firmness his invasions on the rights of the people.

He has refused for a long time, after such dissolutions, to cause others to be elected; whereby the Legislative Powers, incapable of Annihilation, have returned to the People at large for their exercise; the State remaining in the mean time exposed to all the dangers of invasion from without, and convulsions within.

He has endeavoured to prevent the population of these States; for that purpose obstructing the Laws of Naturalization of Foreigners; refusing to pass others to encourage their migration hither, and raising the conditions of new Appropriations of Lands.

He has obstructed the Administration of Justice, by refusing his Assent to Laws for establishing Judiciary Powers.

He has made Judges dependent on his Will alone, for the tenure of their Offices, and the amount and payment of their salaries.

He has erected a multitude of New Offices, and sent hither swarms of Officers to harass our People, and eat out their substance.

He has kept among us, in times of peace, Standing Armies without the Consent of our legislature.

He has affected to render the Military independent of and superior to the Civil Power.

He has combined with others to subject us to a jurisdiction foreign to our constitution, and unacknowledged by our laws; giving his Assent to their acts of pretended legislation:

For quartering large bodies of armed troops among us:

For protecting them, by a mock Trial, from Punishment for any Murders which they should commit on the Inhabitants of these States:

For cutting off our Trade with all parts of the world:

For imposing taxes on us without our Consent:

For depriving us in many cases, of the benefits of Trial by Jury:

For transporting us beyond Seas to be tried for pretended offences:

For abolishing the free System of English Laws in a neighbouring Province, establishing therein an Arbitrary government, and enlarging its Boundaries so as to render it at once an example and fit instrument for introducing the same absolute rule into these Colonies:

For taking away our Charters, abolishing our most valuable Laws, and altering fundamentally the Forms of our Governments:

For suspending our own Legislature, and declaring themselves invested with Power to legislate for us in all cases whatsoever.

He has abdicated Government here, by declaring us out of his Protection and waging War against us.

He has plundered our seas, ravaged our Coasts, burnt our towns, and destroyed the lives of our people.

He is at this time transporting large armies of foreign mercenaries to compleat the works of death, desolation and tyranny, already begun with circumstances of Cruelty & perfidy scarcely paralleled in the most barbarous ages, and totally unworthy of the Head of a civilized nation.

He has constrained our fellow Citizens taken Captive on the high Seas to bear Arms against their Country, to become the executioners of their friends and Brethren, or to fall themselves by their Hands.

He has excited domestic insurrections amongst us, and has endeavoured to bring on the inhabitants of our frontiers, the merciless Indian Savages, whose known rule of warfare, is an undistinguished destruction of all ages, sexes and conditions.

In every stage of these Oppressions we have Petitioned for Redress in the most humble terms: Our repeated Petitions have been answered only by repeated injury. A Prince, whose character is thus marked by every act which may define a Tyrant, is unfit to be the ruler of a free People.

Nor have We been wanting in attention to our British brethren. We have warned them from time to time of attempts by their legislature to extend an unwarrantable jurisdiction over us. We have reminded them of the circumstances of our emigration and settlement here. We have appealed to their native justice and magnanimity, and we have conjured them by the ties of our common kindred to disavow these usurpations, which, would inevitably interrupt our connections and correspondence. They too have been deaf to the voice of justice and of consanguinity. We must, therefore, acquiesce in the necessity, which denounces our Separation, and hold them, as we hold the rest of mankind, Enemies in War, in Peace Friends.

We, therefore, the Representatives of the United States of America, in General Congress, Assembled, appealing to the Supreme Judge of the world for the rectitude of our intentions, do, in the Name, and by Authority of the good People of these Colonies, solemnly publish and declare, That these United Colonies are, and of Right ought to be Free and Independent States; that they are Absolved from all Allegiance to the British Crown, and that all political connection between them and the State of Great Britain, is and ought to be totally dissolved; and that as Free and Independent States they have full Power to levy War, conclude Peace, contract Alliances, establish Commerce, and to do all other Acts and Things which Independent States may of right do. And for the support of this Declaration, with a firm reliance on the Protection of Divine Providence, we mutually pledge to each other our Lives, our Fortunes and our sacred Honor.

Source 4   John Adams to his wife, Abigail

Philadelphia, July 3, 1776

Yesterday the greatest Question was decided, which was ever debated in America, and a greater perhaps, never was or will be decided among Men. A Resolution was passed without one dissenting Colony, that these united Colonies "are, and of right ought to be free and independent States. . . ." You will see in a few days a Declaration setting forth the Causes, which have impell'd Us to this mighty Revolution, and the Reasons which will justify it, in the Sight of God and Man. . . . Time has been given for the whole People, maturely to consider, the great Question of Independence and to ripen their Judgment, dissipate their Fears and allure their Hopes, by discussing it in News Papers and Pamphletts, by debating it, in Assemblies, Conventions, Committees of Safety and Inspection in Town and County Meetings, as well as in private Conversations, so that the whole People in every Colony of the 13 have now adopted it, as their own Act. This will cement the Union. . . . The second Day of July 1776, will be the most memorable Epoca, in the History of America.—I am apt to believe that it will be celebrated, by succeeding Generations, as the great anniversary Festival. . . . It ought to be solemnized with Pomp and Parade with Shews, Games, Sports, Guns, Bells, Bonfires and Illuminations from one End of this Continent to the other from this Time forward forever more. You will think me transported with Enthusiasm but I am not—I am well aware of the Toil and Blood and Treasure, that it will cost Us to maintain this Declaration, and support and defend these States—Yet through all the Gloom I can see the Rays of ravishing Light and Glory.

Source 5   General George Washington's letter to the Continental Congress

July 10, 1776

Agreeable to the request of Congress I caused the Declaration to be proclaimed before all the Army in my immediate Command, and have the pleasure to inform . . . that the measure seemed to have their hearty assent; The Expressions and behaviour both of Officers and men testifying their warmest approbation of it.

Source 6   King George III's speech to the House of Lords, October 31, 1776

[S]o daring and desperate is the Spirit of those Leaders, whose Object has always been Dominion and Power, that they have now openly renounced all Allegiance to the Crown: They have . . . presumed to set up their rebellious Confederacies for Independent States. If their Treason be suffered to take Root, much Mischief must grow from it, to the Safety of my loyal Colonies, to the Commerce of my Kingdoms, and indeed to the present System of all Europe. One great Advantage, however, will be derived from the Object of the Rebels being openly avowed, and clearly understood; We shall have Unanimity at Home, founded in the general Conviction of the Justice and Necessity of our Measures.

Source 7   English barrister John Lind, *An Answer to the Declaration of the American Congress,* 1776

Of the preamble I have taken little notice. The truth is, little or none does it deserve. The opinions of modern Americans on Government, like those of their good ancestors on witchcraft, would be too ridiculous to deserve any notice, if like them too, contemptible and extravagant as they be, they had not led to the most serious evils.

In this preamble however it is, that they attempt to establish a *theory of Government;* a theory, as absurd and visionary, as the system of conduct in defence of which it is established, is nefarious. Here it is, that maxims are advanced in justification of their enterprises against the British Government. To these maxims, adduced for this purpose, it would be sufficient to say, that they are *repugnant to the British Constitution.* But beyond this they are subversive to every actual or imaginable kind of Government.

They are about "to assume," as they tell us, "among the powers of the earth, that equal and separate station to which"—they have lately discovered—"the laws of Nature, and of Nature's God entitle them." What difference these acute legislators suppose between the laws of *Nature,* and of *Nature's God,* is more than I can take upon me to determine, or even to guess. If to what they now demand they were entitled by any law of God, they had only to produce that law, and all controversy was at an end. Instead of this, what do they produce? What they call self-evident truths. "All men," they tell us, "are created equal." This surely is a new discovery. . . .

The rights of "life, liberty, and the pursuit of happiness"—by which if they mean anything, they must mean the right to *enjoy* life, to *enjoy* liberty, and to *pursue* happiness—they "hold to be unalienable." This they "hold to be among truths self-evident." At the same time, to secure these rights, they are content that Governments should be instituted. They perceive not, or will not seem to perceive, that nothing which can be called Government ever was, or ever could be, in any instance, exercised, but at the expence of one or other of those rights.—That, consequently, in as many instances as Government is ever exercised, some one or other of these rights, pretended to be unalienable, is actually alienated.

That men who are engaged in the design of subverting a lawful Government, should endeavour by a cloud of words, to throw a veil over their design; that they should endeavour to beat down the criteria between tyranny and lawful government, is not at all surprising. But rather surprising it must certainly appear, that they should advance maxims so incompatible with their own present conduct. If the right of enjoying life be unalienable, whence came their invasion of his Majesty's province of Canada? Whence the unprovoked destruction of so many lives of the inhabitants of that province? If the right of enjoying liberty be unalienable, whence came so many of his Majesty's peaceable subjects among them, without any offence, . . . to be held by them under **durance**? If the right of pursuing happiness be unalienable, how is it that so many others of their fellow-citizens are by the same injustice and violence made miserable, their fortunes ruined, their persons banished and driven from their friends and families? Or would they have it believed, that there is in their selves some superior sanctity, some peculiar privilege, by which those things are lawful to them, which are unlawful to all the world besides? . . .

Here then they have put the axe to the root of all Government; and yet, in the same breath, they talk of "Governments," of Governments "long established." To the last, they attribute some kind of respect; they vouchsafe even to go so far as to admit, that "Governments, long established, should not be changed for light or transient reasons."

Yet they are about to change a Government. . . . What causes do they assign? Circumstances which have always subsisted, which must continue to subsist, whenever Government has subsisted, or can subsist.

For what . . . was their original, their *only original grievance*? That they were actually taxed more than they could bear? No; but that they were *liable* to be so taxed. What is the amount of the *subsequent* grievances they allege? That they were actually *oppressed* by Government? That Government had *actually* misused its power? No; but that it was *possible* they might be oppressed; *possible that* Government might misuse its powers. Is there anywhere, can there be imagined any where, that Government, where subjects are not liable to be taxed more than they can bear? where it is not possible that subjects may be oppressed, not possible that Government may misuse its powers?

This, I say, is the amount, the *whole sum and substance of all* their grievances.

Source 8   Thomas Hutchinson, former royal governor of the Massachusetts colony

A Letter to a Noble Lord, &c.

October 15, 1776

They begin . . . with a false hypothesis, That the Colonies are one *distinct people,* and the kingdom another, connected by *political* bands. The Colonies, *politically* considered, never were a *distinct* people from the kingdom. There never has been but one *political* band, and that was just the same before the first Colonists emigrated as it has been ever since. . . . I should therefore be impertinent, if I attempted to shew in what case a *whole people* may be justified in rising up in **oppugnation** to the powers of government, altering or abolishing them, and substituting . . . new powers in their stead; or in what sense all men are created equal; or how far life, liberty, and the *pursuit of happiness* may be said to be unalienable; only I could wish to ask the Delegates of Maryland, Virginia, and the Carolinas, how their Constituents justify the depriving more than an hundred thousand Africans of their rights to liberty, and the *pursuit of happiness,* and in some degree to their lives, if these rights are so absolutely unalienable. . . .

Suffer me . . . to observe, that though the professed reason for publishing the Declaration was a decent respect to the opinions of mankind, yet the real design was to reconcile the people of America to that Independence, which always before, they had been made to believe was not intended. This design has too well succeeded. The people have not observed the fallacy in reasoning from the *whole* to *part*; nor the absurdity of making the *governed* to be *governors*. From a disposition to receive willingly complaints against Rulers, facts misrepresented have passed without examining. Discerning men have concealed their sentiments, because under the present *free* government in America, no man may, by writing or speaking, contradict any part of this Declaration, without being deemed an enemy of his country, and exposed to the rage and fury of the populace.

📖 *Second Thoughts*
"The Genuine Effusion of the Soul of the Country at that Time"

Following Thomas Jefferson's reflections on the 50th anniversary of the Declaration's adoption, evidence was seen as early as 1857 of a debate about his wisdom and motives that is as compelling today as it was then: Did Jefferson and his fellow delegates intend to restrict the unalienable rights they described to white men of European descent? And if they did, must we label them as racist and sexist?

Source 9   Thomas Jefferson's note on the Independence Day celebration, 1826

14.3 The
Unfulfilled
Promise of
the Declaration
of Independence

May [the Declaration] be to the world, what I believe it will be, the signal of arousing men to burst the chains under which monkish ignorance and superstition had persuaded them to bind themselves, and to assume the blessings and security of self-government. That form which we have substituted, restores the free right to the unbounded exercise of reason and freedom of opinion. All eyes are open, or opening, to the rights of man. . . . For ourselves, let the annual return of this day forever refresh our recollection of these rights, and an undiminished devotion to them.

Source 10   Chief Justice Roger B. Taney's opinion in the Supreme Court's 1857 *Dred Scott v. Sandford* decision

The question is simply this: Can a Negro, whose ancestors were imported into this country, and sold as slaves, become a member of the political community formed and brought into existence by the Constitution of the United States, and as such become entitled the rights, and privileges, and immunities guaranteed by that instrument to the citizens? . . .

   In the opinion of the court, the legislation and histories of the times, and the language used in the Declaration of Independence, show, that neither the class of persons who had been imported as slaves, nor their descendents, whether they had become free or not, were then acknowledged as a part of the people, nor intended to be included in the general words used in that memorable instrument. . . .

The general words . . . would seem to embrace the whole human family, and if they were used in a similar instrument at this day would be so understood. But it is too clear for dispute that the enslaved African race were not intended to be included and formed no part of the people who framed and adopted this declaration; for if the language, as understood in that day, would embrace them, the conduct of the distinguished men who framed the Declaration of Independence would have been utterly and flagrantly inconsistent with the principles they asserted; and instead of the sympathy of mankind, to which they so confidently appealed, they would have deserved and received universal rebuke and reprobation.

Yet the men who framed this declaration were great men—high in literary acquirements—high in their sense of honor, and incapable of asserting principles inconsistent with those on which they were acting. They perfectly understood the meaning of the language they used and how it would be understood by others; and they knew that it would not in any part of the civilized world be supposed to embrace the Negro race, which by common consent, had been excluded from civilized governments and the family of nations and doomed to slavery.

Source 11 Illinois senator Stephen A. Douglas, debating Abraham Lincoln, 1858

I believe that the Declaration of Independence, in the words "all men are created equal," was intended to allude only to the people of the United States, to men of European birth or descent, being white men, that they were created equal, and hence that Great Britain had no right to deprive them of their political and religious privileges; but the signers of that paper did not intend to include the Indian or the negro in that declaration. . . . [E]very man who signed that Declaration represented slaveholding constituents. Did those signers mean by that act to charge themselves and all their constituents with having violated the law of God, in holding the negro in an inferior condition to the white man? . . . Did they mean to say that the Indian, on this continent, was created equal to the white man, and that he was endowed by the Almighty with inalienable rights— rights so sacred that they could not be taken away by any constitution or law that man could pass? Why, their whole action towards the Indian showed that they never dreamed that they were bound to put him on an equality. I am not only opposed to negro equality, but I am opposed to Indian equality. I am opposed to putting the coolies, now pouring into this country, on an equality with us, or putting the Chinese or any inferior race on an equality with us. I hold that the white race, the European race, I care not whether Irish, German, French, Scotch, English, or to what nation they belong, so they are the white race, to be our equals, and I am for placing them, as our fathers did, on an equality with us. Emigrants from Europe and their descendants constitute the people of the U.S. The Declaration of Independence only included the white people of the U.S.

Source 12   Abraham Lincoln's rebuttal to Douglas

14.4 "We Hold
These Truths to
Be Self-Evident..."

Wise statesmen as they were, they knew the tendency of prosperity to breed tyrants, and so they established these great self-evident truths, that when in the distant future some man, some faction, some interest, should set up the doctrine that none but the rich men, or none but the white men, were entitled to life, liberty, and the pursuit of happiness, their posterity might look up again to the Declaration of Independence and take courage to renew the battle which their fathers began—so that truth, and justice, and mercy, and all the humane and Christian virtues might not be extinguished from the land; so that no man would hereafter dare to limit and circumscribe the great principles on which the temple of liberty was being built.

Now, my countrymen, if you have been taught doctrines conflicting with the great landmarks of the Declaration of Independence; if you have listened to suggestions which would take away from its grandeur, and mutilate the fair symmetry of its proportions; if you have been inclined to believe that all men are *not* created equal in those inalienable rights enumerated in our chart of liberty, let me entreat you to come back. Return to the fountain whose waters spring close by the blood of the Revolution.

Source 13   George Bancroft, *History of the United States of America,* 1886

This immortal state paper [The Declaration] was "the genuine effusion of the soul of the country at that time," the revelation of its mind, when, in its youth, its enthusiasm, its sublime confronting of danger, it rose to the highest creative powers of which man is capable. The bill of rights which it promulgates is of rights that are older than human institutions, and spring from the eternal justice. Two political theories divided the world: one founded the commonwealth on the advantage of the state, the policy of expediency, the other on the immutable principles of morals; the new republic, as it took its place among the powers of the world, proclaimed its faith in the truth and reality and unchangeableness of freedom, virtue, and right. The heart of Jefferson in writing the declaration, and of congress in adopting it, beat for all humanity; the assertion of right was made for an entire world of mankind and all coming generations, without any exception whatever; for the provision which admits of exceptions can never be self-evident. As it was put forth in the name of the ascendent people of that time, it was sure to make the circuit of the world, passing everywhere through the despotic countries of Europe; and the astonished nations, as they read that all men are created equal, started out of their lethargy, like those who have been exiles from childhood, when they suddenly hear the dimly remembered accents of their mother tongue.

Source 14   Carl Becker, *The Declaration of Independence: A Study in the History of Political Ideas,* 1922

The ostensible purpose of the Declaration was . . . to lay before the world the causes which impelled the colonies to separate from Great Britain. We do, in fact find, in the Declaration, a list or catalogue of acts, attributable to the king of Great Britain, and alleged to have been done by him with the deliberate purpose of establishing "an absolute tyranny." The "causes" which the Declaration sets forth are not quite the same as those which a careful student of history, seeking the antecedents of the Revolution, would set forth. The reason is that the framers of the Declaration were not writing history, but making it. They were seeking to convince the world that they were justified in doing what they had done; and so their statement of "causes" is not the bare record of what the king had done, but rather a presentation of his acts in general terms, and in the form of an indictment intended to clear the colonists of all responsibility and to throw all the blame on the king. From whatever causes, the colonists were in rebellion against established and long recognized political authority. The Declaration was not primarily concerned with the causes of this rebellion; its primary purpose was to present those causes in such a way as to furnish a moral and legal justification for that rebellion. The Declaration was essentially an attempt to prove that rebellion was not the proper word for what they were doing.

Rebellion against established authority is always a serious matter. In that day kings were commonly claiming to rule by divine right, and according to this notion there could be no 'right' of rebellion. The framers of the Declaration knew very well that however long their list of grievances against the king of Great Britain might be, and however oppressive they might make out his acts to have been, something more would be required to prove to the world that in separating from Great Britain they were not really engaged in rebellion against a rightful authority. What they needed, in addition to many specific grievances against their particular king, was a fundamental presupposition against kings in general. What they needed was a theory of government that provided a place for rebellion, that made it respectable, and even meritorious under certain circumstances. . . .

In the Declaration the foundation of the United States is indissolubly associated with a theory of politics, a philosophy of human rights which is valid, if at all, not for Americans only, but for all men. This association gives the Declaration its perennial interest. The verdict of history constrained men to approve of the independence of the United States, or at least to accept it as an accomplished fact; the accomplished fact conferred upon the Declaration a distinction, a fame, which could not be ignored, and gave to its philosophy of human rights the support of a concrete historical example. There they were, and there they remained—stubborn fact married to uncompromising theory; bound for life; jogging along in discord or in harmony as might happen; an inspiration or a scandal to half the world, but in any case impossible to be ignored, with difficulty to be accepted or rejected the one without the other.

Source 15 John C. Miller, *Origins of the American Revolution,* 1943

No one who read the Declaration could fail to see that an experiment in human relations was being made and that the new order which it established was to be chiefly for the benefit of the common man. Equality and liberty—government by the consent of the governed—were the ideals now held up to men. Here, surely, the common man was given something to fight for and, if need be, to die for. The war aims of the Revolution were now complete: the struggle against

Great Britain was to be waged for independence; for the liberty of the individual; and for the creation of a society in which men were free and equal.

Source 16   Samuel Eliot Morison, *Oxford History of the American People,* 1971

If the American Revolution had produced nothing but the Declaration of Independence, it would have been worthwhile. The bill of wrongs against George III and Parliament, naturally, is exaggerated. Facts will not sustain many of the alleged "injuries and usurpations." But the beauty and cogency of the preamble, reaching back to the remotest antiquity and forward to an indefinite future, have lifted the hearts of millions of men and will continue to do so. . . .

These words are more revolutionary than anything written by Robespierre, Marx, or Lenin, more explosive than the atom, a continual challenge to ourselves, as well as an inspiration to the oppressed of all the world.

Source 17   Howard Zinn, *A People's History of the United States,* 1980

The use of the phrase "all men are created equal" was probably not a deliberate attempt to make a statement about women. It was just that women were beyond consideration as worthy of inclusion. They were politically invisible. Though practical needs gave women a certain authority in the home, on the farm, or in occupations like midwifery, they were simply overlooked in any consideration of political rights, any notions of civil equality.

To say that the Declaration of Independence, even by its own language, was limited to life, liberty, and the pursuit of happiness for white males is not to denounce the makers and signers of the Declaration for holding the ideas expected of privileged males of the eighteenth century. Reformers and radicals, looking discontentedly at history, are often accused of expecting too much from a past political epoch—and sometimes they do. But the point of noting those outside the arc of human rights in the Declaration is not, centuries late and pointlessly, to lay impossible moral burdens on that time. It is to try to understand the way in which the Declaration functioned to mobilize certain groups of Americans, ignoring others. Surely, inspirational language to create a secure consensus is still used, in our time, to cover up serious conflicts of interest in that consensus, and to cover up, also, the omission of large parts of the human race.

The philosophy of the Declaration, that government is set up by the people to secure their life, liberty, and happiness, and is to be overthrown when it no longer does that, is often traced to the ideas of John Locke, in his *Second Treatise on Government.* . . . The Declaration, like Locke's *Second Treatise,* talked about government and political rights, but ignored the existing inequalities in property. And how could people truly have equal rights, with stark differences in wealth? . . .

In America, . . . the reality behind the words of the Declaration of Independence (issued in the same year as Adam Smith's capitalist manifesto, *The Wealth of Nations*) was that a rising class of important people needed to enlist on their side enough Americans to defeat England, without disturbing too much the relations of wealth and power that had developed over 150 years of colonial history.

⚖ Questioning the Past

1. From the viewpoint of someone sitting as a delegate in the Continental Congress in June 1776, present and evaluate the arguments for and against proclaiming the colonies independent of Britain. From the vantage point of the late twentieth century, which of the considerations of 1776 were valid concerns?

2. Historian John Hazelton concluded in a 1906 study of the Declaration of Independence that "the Declaration changed a war of principle—a defensive war, a war for the redress of wrongs—into a war for the establishment of a separate government." Is this conclusion valid?

3. What did the writers of the Declaration of Independence mean by the statement, "We hold these truths to be self-evident, that all men are created equal"?

4. The Declaration of Independence asserts that governments derive "their just powers from the consent of the governed." The Constitution, which lists the powers of government, was adopted more than two centuries ago. Is it still legitimate today even though no one presently alive consented to its adoption? Explain.

5. Samuel Eliot Morison asserted that "if the American Revolution had produced nothing but the Declaration of Independence, it would have been worthwhile." Defend this assertion.

Chapter 15

The Constitution

The Founding Fathers Unveil a New Constitution *September 17, 1787*

Throughout the summer of 1787, delegates met to fashion a more effective framework for their union. Though the Articles of Confederation had been strong enough to lead them through war, many felt its structure inadequate to lead them through peace. On September 17, following days of debate and compromise, the delegates prepared to vote on an entirely new constitution.

∞ *First Impressions*

A Rising or a Setting Sun?

The delegates faced two tasks: devise a new constitution, and convince the country to adopt it. The second task would require many more months of debate; but the first was completed on September 17, 1787. As the delegates prepared to approve the new constitution, Benjamin Franklin rose to speak.

Source 1 Remarks of Benjamin Franklin, September 17, 1787, as recorded by James Madison

Mr. President: I confess that there are several parts of this constitution which I do not at present approve, but I am not sure I shall ever approve them. For having lived long, I have experienced many instances of being obliged by better information, or fuller consideration, to change opinions even on important subjects, which I once thought right, but found to be otherwise. It is therefore that the older I grow, the more apt I am to doubt my own judgment, and to pay more respect to the judgment of others. . . .

In these sentiments, Sir, I agree to this Constitution with all its faults, if they are such; because I think a general Government necessary for us. . . . I doubt too whether any other Convention we have obtain, may be able to make a better Constitution. For when you assemble a number of men to have the advantage of their joint wisdom, you inevitably assemble with those men, all their prejudices, their passions, their errors of opinion, their local interests, and their selfish views. From such an assembly can a perfect production be expected? It therefore astonishes me, Sir, to find this system approaching so near to perfection as it does; and I think it will astonish our enemies, who are waiting with confidence to hear that our councils are confounded like those of the Builders of **Babel**; and that our States are on the point of separation, only to meet hereafter for the purpose of cutting one another's throats. Thus I consent, Sir, to this Constitution because I expect no better, and because I am not sure, that it is not the best. The opinions I have had of its errors, I sacrifice to the public good. . . .

On the whole, Sir, I can not help expressing a wish that every member of the convention who may still have objections to it, would with me, on this occasion doubt a little of his infallibility, and to make manifest our unanimity, put his name to this instrument.

Source 2 Convention notes of James Madison, September 17, 1787

He [Franklin] then moved that the Constitution be signed by the members and offered the following as a convenient form viz. "Done in Convention by the unanimous consent of the States present the seventeenth of September etc.—in Witness whereof we have hereunto subscribed our names." . . .

15.1 To Form a More Perfect Union

On the question to agree to the Constitution enrolled in order to be signed. It was agreed to by all the States answering aye.

Mr. Randolph then rose and with an illusion to the observations of Dr. Franklin apologized for his refusing to sign the constitution notwithstanding the vast majority and venerable names that would give sanction to its wisdom and its worth. . . .

Mr. Gerry described the painful feelings of his situation, and the embarrassment under which he rose to offer any further observations on the subject which had been finally decided. . . . Whilst the plan was depending, he had treated it with all the freedom he thought it deserved. He now felt himself bound as he was disposed to treat it with the respect due to the Act of the Convention. He hoped he should not violate that respect in declaring on this occasion his fears that a Civil war may result from the present crisis of the U.S. In Massachusetts, particularly he saw the danger of this calamitous event—In that State there are two parties, one devoted to Democracy, the worst he thought of all political evils, the other as violent in the opposite extreme. From the collision of these in opposing and resisting the Constitution, confusion was greatly to be feared. He had thought it necessary, for this and other reasons that the plan should have been proposed in a more mediating shape, in order to abate the heat and opposition of parties. As it has been passed by the Convention, he was persuaded it would have a contrary effect. . . .

The members then proceeded to sign the instruments.

The Constitution being signed by all the members except Mr. Randolph, Mr. Mason, and Mr. Gerry who declined giving it the sanction of their names, the Convention dissolved itself by an Adjournment sine die.

Whilst the last members were signing it Dr. Franklin looking towards the President's Chair, at the back of which a rising sun happened to be painted, observed to a few members near him, that Painters had found it difficult to distinguish in their art a rising from a setting sun. I have, said he, often and often in the course of the Session, and the vicissitudes of my hopes and fears as to its issue, looked at that behind the President without being able to tell whether it was rising or setting: But now at length I have the happiness to know that it is a rising and not a setting Sun.

Adopting a New Constitution

It was four o'clock on the afternoon of September 17, 1787, and the men who had been working all day in the State House packed up their belongings and adjourned to the City Tavern to relax and discuss the events of the day before heading home. On this day they had finished the job they had been sent to do: write a new constitution for their country. Now their task would be to convince their country that this new constitution was right for America. It was not at all certain they would be able to do so.

Some 75 delegates had been selected from 12 states the previous spring to journey to Philadelphia for what came to be known as the Constitutional Convention. (Rhode Island refused to send a delegation.) Of those selected, 55 had actually made the journey. At least one delegate declined to go for political reasons. Patrick Henry explained he chose not to attend because "I smelt a Rat." As it turned out, Henry and others who suspected the motives of the Convention were justified in their suspicions, for the delegates, once assembled, went beyond their mandate: They were directed to "devise and discuss" alterations to the Articles of Confederation; what they did instead was to propose a completely different form of government.

Following adjournment, the proposed Constitution was transmitted to the Congress of the Confederation on September 20, 1787, where it met initially with a chilly reception. Richard Henry Lee and other members from Virginia, along with representatives of New York, spoke against it. Lee was troubled by the powers to be concentrated in a central government, and he faulted the document for its lack of any guarantee of personal liberty. But outside of the Virginia and New York delegations, no other significant opposition was voiced. After eight days of debate the Constitution was forwarded to the states, where approval by any nine state conventions would bring the new government into existence.

Delaware acted quickly and unanimously to ratify the Constitution. Pennsylvania and New Jersey assented in rapid order. But as time passed and opponents had the opportunity to organize, resistance began to emerge. The struggle in Massachusetts, Virginia, and New York was particularly intense. When George Washington took the oath of office as the nation's first president, he presided over a union of only 11 states. North Carolina withheld its assent pending action on a statement of rights and liberties. Rhode Island remained apart from the new union for almost two years, before its deeply divided convention finally accepted the Constitution.

15.2 Learning Page of the Library of Congress

Source 3   **Argument of Richard Henry Lee, October 16, 1787**

It cannot be denied, with truth, that this new Constitution is, in its first principles, highly and dangerously **oligarchic**; and it is a point agreed, that a government of the few is, of all governments, the worst.

Source 4   Viewpoint of George Washington, December 14, 1787

My decided opinion on the matter is, that there is no alternative between the adoption of it and anarchy. . . . All the opposition to it that I have yet seen is addressed more to the passions than to reason. General government is now suspended by a thread; I might go further, and say it is really at an end. . . .

I saw the imperfections of the constitution I aided in the birth of, before it was handed to the public; but I am fully persuaded it is the best that can be obtained at this time, that it is free from the imperfections with which it is charged, and that it or disunion is before us to choose from. If the first is our election, when the defects of it are experienced, a constitutional door is opened for amendments and may be adopted in a peaceable manner, without tumult or disorder.

Source 5   Opinion of John Adams, December 1787

The public mind cannot be occupied about a nobler object than the proposed plan of government. It appears to be admirably calculated to cement all America in affection and interest as one great nation. A result of compromise cannot perfectly coincide with every one's ideas of perfection; but, as all the great principles necessary to order, liberty, and safety are respected in it, and provision is made for amendments as they be found necessary, I hope to hear of its adoption by all the states.

Source 6   Address of John Jay, 1788, to the people of New York State

The Convention concurred in opinion with the people, that a national government, competent to every national object, was indispensably necessary; and it was as plain to them, as it now is to all America, that the present Confederation does not provide for such a government. These points being agreed, they proceeded to consider how and in what manner such a government could be formed, as, on the one hand, should be sufficiently energetic to raise us from our prostrate and distressed situation, and, on the other, be perfectly consistent with the liberties of the people of every state. . . . Thus far the propriety of their work is easily seen and understood, and it therefore is thus far almost universally approved.

Source 7   Argument of George Mason, June 4, 1788, at the Virginia convention

It is ascertained, by history, that there never was a government over a very extensive country without destroying the liberties of the people: history also, supported by the opinions of the best writers, shows us that monarchy may suit a large territory, and despotic governments ever so extensive a country, but that popular governments can only exist in small territories. Is there a single example, on the face of the earth, to support a contrary opinion? Where is there one exception to this general rule? Was there ever an instance of a general national government extending over so extensive a country, abounding in such a variety of climates, &c., where the people retained their liberty? I solemnly declare that no man is a greater friend to a firm union of the American states than I am. . . . But my principal objection is, that the Confederation is converted into one general consolidated government, which, from my best judgment of it, is one of the worst curses that can possibly befall a nation.

Source 8   **Opinion of Edmund Pendleton, June 5, 1788, at the Virginia convention**

What was the situation of this country before the meeting of the federal Convention? Our general government was totally inadequate to the purpose of its institution; our commerce decayed; our finances deranged; public and private credit destroyed: these and many other national evils rendered necessary the meeting of that Convention. . . . The federal Convention devised the . . . remedy to remove our political diseases.

Source 9   **Arguments of Patrick Henry, June 5 and June 7, 1788, at the Virginia convention**

The question turns, Sir, on that poor little thing—the expression, *We, the People,* instead of the United States of America. I need not take pains to show, that the principles of this system, are extremely pernicious, impolitic, and dangerous. Is this a Monarchy . . . ? Is this a Confederacy . . . ? It is not a democracy, wherein the people retain all their rights securely. Had these principles been adhered to, we should not have been brought to this alarming transition, from a Confederacy to a consolidated Government. . . . Here is a revolution as radical as that which separated us from Great Britain. It is as radical, if in this transition our rights and privileges are endangered, and the sovereignty of the States be relinquished: And cannot we plainly see, that this is actually the case? The rights of conscience, trial by jury, liberty of the press, all your immunities and franchises, all pretensions of human rights and privileges, are rendered insecure, if not lost, by this change so loudly talked of by some, and inconsiderately by others. Is this same relinquishment of rights worthy of freemen? Is it worthy of that manly fortitude that ought to characterize republicans: It is said that eight States have adopted this plan. I declare that if twelve States and an half had adopted it, I would with manly firmness, and in spite of an erring world, reject it. . . .

Guard with jealous attention the public liberty. Suspect everyone who approaches that jewel. . . .

I conceive this new Government to be one of those dangers: It has produced those horrors, which distress many of our best citizens. We are come hither to preserve the poor Commonwealth of Virginia, if it can be possibly done: Something must be done to preserve your liberty and mine: The Confederation; this same despised Government, merits, in my opinion, the highest **encomium**: It carried us through a long and dangerous war: It rendered us victorious in that bloody conflict with a powerful nation: It has secured us a territory greater than any European Monarch possesses: And shall a Government which has been thus strong and vigorous be accused of imbecility and abandoned for want of energy? Consider what you are about to do before you part with this Government. . . .

This Constitution is said to have beautiful features; but when I come to examine these features, Sir, they appear to me horridly frightful: Among other deformities, it has an awful squinting; it squints towards monarchy: And does this not raise indignation in the breast of every American? Your President may easily become King. Your Senate is so imperfectly constructed that your dearest rights may be sacrificed by what may be a small minority; and a very small minority may continue unchangeably this Government, although horridly defective: Where are your checks in this Government? Your strong holds will be in the hands of your enemies: It is on a supposition that our American Governors shall be honest, that all the good qualities of this Government are founded: But its defective, and imperfect construction, puts it in their power to perpetuate the worst of mischiefs, should they be bad men.

Source 10 Viewpoint of James Monroe, June 10, 1788, at the Virginia convention

The Revolution, in having emancipated us from the shackles of Great Britain, has put the entire government in the hands of one order of people only—freemen; not of nobles and freemen. This is a peculiar trait in the character of this revolution. That this sacred deposit may be always retained there, is my most earnest wish and fervent prayer. That union is the first object for the security of our political happiness, in the hands of gracious Providence, is well understood and universally admitted through all the United States. From New Hampshire to Georgia (Rhode Island excepted), the people have uniformly manifested a strong attachment to the Union. . . .

[N]othing can be adduced . . . to warrant a departure from a confederacy to a consolidation, on the principle of inefficacy in the former to secure our happiness. The causes which, with other nations, rendered leagues ineffectual and inadequate to the security and happiness of the people, do not exist here. What is the form of our state governments? They are all similar in their structure—perfectly democratic. The freedom of mankind has found an asylum here which it could find nowhere else. Freedom of conscience is enjoyed here in the fullest degree. . . .

The Confederation has been deservedly reprobated for its inadequacy to promote the public welfare. But this change is, in my opinion, very dangerous. It contemplates objects with which a federal government ought never to interfere. . . . I fear, sir, that it will ultimately end in the establishment of a monarchical government. The people, in order to be delivered from one species of tyranny, may submit to another.

Source 11 Opinion of John Marshall, June 10, 1788, at the Virginia convention

Mr. Chairman, I conceive that the object of the discussion now before us is, whether democracy or despotism be most eligible. I am sure that those who

15.3 The
American
Constitution

framed the system submitted to our investigation, and those who now support it, intend the establishment and security of the former. The supporters of the Constitution claim the title of being firm friends of the liberty and security of mankind. They say that they consider it as the best means of protecting liberty. We sir, idolize democracy. . . . We prefer this system to any monarchy, because we are convinced that it has a greater tendency to secure our liberty and promote our happiness. We admire it, because we think it a well-regulated democracy. It is recommended to the good people of this country: they are, through us, to declare whether it be such a plan of government as will establish and secure their freedom.

Ratification by the State Conventions

		Delegates Voting	
State	Date of Approval	Yes	No
Delaware	December 7, 1787	30	0
Pennsylvania	December 11, 1787	46	23
New Jersey	December 18, 1787	38	0
Georgia	January 2, 1788	26	0
Connecticut	January 9, 1788	128	40
Massachusetts	February 6, 1788	187	168
Maryland	April 26, 1788	63	11
South Carolina	May 23, 1788	149	73
New Hampshire	June 21, 1788	57	47
Virginia	June 25, 1788	89	79
New York	July 26, 1788	30	27
North Carolina	November 21, 1789	194	77
Rhode Island	May 29, 1790	34	32

📖 *Second Thoughts*
"Patriots on Both Sides of the Issue"

15.4 What the
Anti-Federalist
Can Teach Us

Neither those who framed the Constitution nor those who opposed its ratification would have felt confident in predicting what would be the impact of the document or its longevity. Both Federalists and Anti-Federalists would probably have been surprised by the durability of the set of governing rules developed in the summer of 1787.

Only 27 times over a period of more than 200 years has the nation felt it necessary to alter the wording of the Constitution. More than half of these alterations addressed the kinds of concerns that troubled the Anti-Federalists. Ten amendments were added to the Constitution in December 1791—collectively called the Bill of Rights—to protect the rights of the people and states against their usurpation by the federal government. Slavery, sanctioned by the Constitution as ratified, was abolished by an amendment in 1865. A commitment to equality was belatedly written into the Constitution in 1868. The franchise was successively broadened by amendments in 1870, 1920, 1964, and 1971. An amendment in 1913 provided for the selection of senators by popular ballot rather than by legislative appointment. Term limits were placed on the presidency.

Although critics have continued to point out its blemishes, the Constitution has never lost public confidence.

Source 12 Abolitionist William Lloyd Garrison, "The Great Crisis," December 29, 1832

15.5 Today
in History

There is much declamation about the sacredness of the compact which was formed between the free states and slave states on the adoption of the Constitution. A sacred compact, forsooth! We pronounce it the most bloody and heaven-daring arrangement ever made by men for the continuance and protection of a system of the most atrocious villainy ever exhibited on earth. Yes—we recognize the compact, but with feelings of shame and indignation; and it will be held in everlasting infamy by the friends of justice and humanity throughout the world. It was a compact formed at the sacrifice of the bodies and souls of millions of our race, for the sake of achieving a political object—an unblushing and monstrous coalition to do evil that good might come. Such a compact was, in the nature of things and according to the law of God, null and void from the beginning. No body of men ever had the right to guarantee the holding of human beings in bondage. Who or what were the framers of our government, that they should dare confirm and authorise such high-handed villany—such a flagrant robbery of all the inalienable rights of man—such a savage war upon a sixth part of our whole population? They were men like ourselves—as fallible, as sinful, as weak, as ourselves. By the infamous bargain which they made between themselves, they virtually dethroned the Most High God, and trampled beneath their feet their own solemn and heaven-attested Declaration, that all men are created equal, and endowed by their Creator with certain inalienable rights—among which are life, liberty, and the pursuit of happiness. They had no lawful power to bind themselves, or their posterity, for one hour—for one moment—by such an unholy alliance. It is not valid then—it is not valid now. Still they persisted in maintaining it. A sacred compact! a sacred compact! What, then, is wicked and ignominious?

Source 13 French scholar Alexis de Tocqueville, *Democracy in America*, 1835

If America ever approached (for however brief a time) that lofty pinnacle of glory to which the proud imagination of its inhabitants is wont to point, it was at this solemn moment when the national power abdicated, as it were, its authority. All ages have furnished the spectacle of a people struggling with energy to win its independence; and the efforts of the Americans in throwing off the English yoke have been considerably exaggerated. Separated from their enemies by three thousand miles of ocean, and backed by a powerful ally, the United States owed their victory much more to their geography than to the valor of their armies or the patriotism of their citizens. . . . But it is new in the history of society, to see a great people turn a calm and scrutinizing eye upon itself, when apprised by the legislature that the wheels of its government are stopped,— to see it carefully examine the extent of the evil, and patiently wait two whole years while a remedy is discovered, to which it voluntarily submitted without its costing a tear or a drop of blood from mankind.

Source 14 Richard Hildreth, *The History of the United States,* 1849

[T]here existed out of doors, widely diffused among the people, a sentiment, which, in the Convention, except once or twice from Franklin, had hardly found the slightest expression. The members of that Convention, belonging exclusively to what is called the conservative class, had seemed to look upon property not so much as one right, to be secured like the rest, but as the great and chief right, of more importance than all others. The great evils of the times, in their eyes, were the inability of the state governments to collect taxes enough to fulfill the public engagements, and the "leveling spirit of democracy," denounced by Gerry, in his closing speech, as "the worst of all political evils." This very spirit of democracy the new Constitution must now encounter—a spirit which pervaded the mass of the people . . . disposing them rather to throw off old burdens than to submit to new ones, and filling them with apprehensions lest personal freedom should be sacrificed to the interests of property, and the welfare of the many to the convenience of the few. Hence that widespread outcry, so generally raised, the most popular objection to the new Constitution, that it had no Bill of Rights, and was therefore deficient in guarantees for personal liberty.

Source 15 George Bancroft, *History of the United States of America,* 1884

The Constitution establishes nothing that interferes with equality and individuality. It knows nothing of differences by descent, or opinions, of favored classes, or legalized religion, or the political power of property. It leaves the individual alongside of the individual. No nationality of character could take form, except on the principle of individuality, so that the mind might be free, and every faculty have the unlimited opportunity for its development and culture. As the sea is made up of drops, American society is composed of separate, free, and constantly moving atoms, ever in reciprocal action, advancing, receding, crossing, struggling against each other and with each other; so that the institutions and laws of the country rise out of the masses of individual thought, which, like the waters of the ocean, are rolling evermore.

Source 16 J. Allen Smith, *The Spirit of American Government,* 1907

Democracy—government by the people, or directly responsible to them—was not the object which the framers of the American Constitution had in view, but the very thing which they wished to avoid. In the convention which drafted that instrument it was recognized that democratic ideas had made sufficient progress among the masses to put an insurmountable obstacle in the way of any plan of government which did not confer at least the form of political power upon the people. Accordingly the efforts of the Constitutional Convention were directed to the task of devising a system of government which was just popular enough not to excite general opposition and which at the same time gave to the people as little as possible of the substance of political power. . . .

It is difficult to understand how anyone who has read the proceedings of the Federal Convention can believe that it was the intention of that body to establish a democratic government. The evidence is overwhelming that the men who sat in that convention had no faith in the wisdom or political capacity of the people. Their aim and purpose was not to secure a larger measure of democracy, but to eliminate as far as possible the direct influence of the people on legislation and public policy. . . .

The popular notion that this Convention in framing the Constitution was actuated solely by a desire to impart more vigor and efficiency to the general government is but part of the truth. The Convention desired to establish not only a strong and vigorous central government, but one which would at the same time possess great stability or freedom from change. . . . This desired stability the government under the Confederation did not possess, since it was, in the opinion of the members of the Convention, dangerously responsive to public opinion; hence their desire to supplant it with an elaborate system of constitutional checks. The adoption of this system was the triumph of a skillfully directed reactionary movement. . . .

From all the evidence which we have, the conclusion is irresistible that they sought to establish a form of government which would effectively curb and restrain democracy.

Source 17 Charles Beard, *An Economic Interpretation of the Constitution of the United States,* 1913

The movement for the Constitution of the United States was originated and carried through principally by four groups of personalty interests which had been adversely affected under the Articles of Confederation: money, public securities, manufactures, and trade and shipping.

The first firm steps toward the formation of the Constitution were taken by a small and active group of men immediately interested through their personal possessions in the outcome of their labors.

No popular vote was taken directly or indirectly on the proposition to call the Convention which drafted the Constitution.

A large propertyless mass was, under the prevailing suffrage qualifications, excluded at the outset from participating (through representatives) in the work of framing the Constitution.

The members of the Philadelphia Convention which drafted the Constitution were, with a few exceptions, immediately, directly, and personally interested in, and derived economic advantage from, the establishment of the new system.

The Constitution was essentially an economic document based upon the concept that the fundamental private rights of property are anterior to government and morally beyond the reach of popular majorities.

The major portion of the members of the Convention are on record as recognizing the claim of property to a special and defensive position in the Constitution.

In the ratification of the Constitution, about three-fourths of the adult males failed to vote on the question, having abstained from the elections at which delegates to the state conventions were chosen, either on account of their indifference or their disenfranchisement by property qualifications.

The Constitution was ratified by a vote of probably not more than one-sixth of the adult males.

It is questionable whether a majority of the voters participating in the elections for the state conventions in New York, Massachusetts, New Hampshire, Virginia, and South Carolina actually approved the ratification of the Constitution.

The leaders who supported the Constitution in the ratifying conventions represented the same economic groups as the members of the Philadelphia Convention; and in a large number of instances they were also directly and personally interested in the outcome of their efforts.

In the ratification, it became manifest that the line of cleavage for and against the Constitution was between substantial personalty interests on the one hand and the small farming and debtor interests on the other.

The Constitution was not created by "the whole people" as the jurists have said; neither was it created by "the states" as southern nullifiers long contended; but it was the work of a consolidated group whose interests knew no state boundaries and were truly national in their scope.

Source 18 James Truslow Adams, *The Epic of America,* 1932

After more than three months' deliberation the document was complete, the first written Constitution offered to any nation, following in this the precedents set by the several States. It gave no special privileges to any one class or interest, nor did it lodge power in any of them. Unrestricted suffrage, representation based on numbers, and the parity promised to the new States to arise on the frontier, assured as far as any constitution could the growth of economic and political equality. In the course of a century and a half, the Constitution has been greatly developed by interpretation through judicial decisions, but as it stood in 1787 it was considered extremely democratic.

Source 19 Merrill Jensen, *The New Nation,* 1950

The story told . . . and repeated by publicists and scholars who have not worked in the field is based on the assumption that this was the "critical period" of American history during which unselfish patriots rescued the new nation from impending anarchy, if not from chaos itself. . . . The picture is one of stagnation, ineptitude, bankruptcy, corruption, and disintegration. Such a picture is at worst false and at best grossly distorted. . . . We have too long ignored the fact that thoroughly patriotic Americans during the 1780's did not believe there was chaos and emphatically denied that their supposed rescuers were patriotic. The point is that there were patriots on both sides of the issue, but that they differed as to desirable goals for the new nation. At the same time, of course, there were men as narrow and selfish on both sides as their political enemies said they were. . . .

The issue was not, as has been argued from time to time, whether there was a "nation" before the adoption of the Constitution of 1787. There was a new nation, as the men of the time agreed: they disagreed as to whether the new nation should have a federal or a national government. They did so from the outset of the Revolution and men have continued to do so ever since.

Source 20 Eric Goldman, *Rendezvous with Destiny,* 1952

Until the Civil War the country as a whole had been less devoted to the property-conscious Constitution than to the fervidly equalitarian Declaration of Independence. In the later nineteenth century, with the mounting assaults on capital and the growing recognition that the Constitution was the chief bulwark of property, conservatives bestirred themselves to lift the Constitution in public esteem and to dismiss the Declaration as a collection of windy generalities. They succeeded so well that the Constitution reached a position of near sacredness.

Source 21 Robert Brown, *Charles Beard and the Constitution,* 1955

The movement for the Constitution was originated and carried through by men who had long been important in both economic and political affairs in their respective states. Some of them owned personalty, more of them owned realty, and if their property was adversely affected by conditions under the Articles of Confederation, so also was the property of the bulk of the people of the country. . . .

The movement for the Constitution, like most important movements, was undoubtedly started by a small group of men. They were probably interested personally in the outcome of their labors, but the benefits which they expected were not confined to personal property or, for that matter, strictly to things economic. . . .

If the members of the Convention were directly interested in the outcome of their work and expected to derive benefits from the establishment of the new system, so did most of the people of the country. . . .

The Constitution was not just an economic document, although economic factors were undoubtedly important. Since most of the people were middle-class and had private property, practically everybody was interested in the protection of property. A Constitution which did not protect property would have been rejected without any question, for the American people had fought the Revolution for the preservation of life, liberty, and property. . . . [W]e would do a grave injustice to the political sagacity of the Founding Fathers if we assumed that property or personal gain was their only motive. . . .

The Constitution was created about as much by the whole people as any government could be which embraced a large area and depended on representation rather than on direct participation. It was also created by the states, for as the *Records* show, there was strong state sentiment at the time which had to be appeased by compromise. . . .

The Constitution was adopted in a society which was fundamentally democratic, not undemocratic; and it was adopted by a people who were primarily middle-class property owners, especially farmers who owned realty, not just by the owners of personalty.

Source 22   Commentary of Henry Steele Commager, 1961

The generation that brought forth the Revolution and made the Constitution was politically the most inventive, constructive and creative in modern history. Its signal achievement—an achievement whose magnitude grows upon us with the passing of time—was to institutionalize principles and theories that had long been entertained by historians and philosophers, but practiced rarely by statesmen and never by kings. Thus the Americans took the principle that men make government and institutionalized it into the constitutional convention—a mechanism which perfectly satisfied every logical requirement of that philosophical mandate. Thus they took the principle that government is limited by the laws of Nature and Nature's God, and institutionalized it into written constitutions, the separation of powers, and a complex system of checks and balances. They embraced the ancient doctrine of the supremacy of the Law, and institutionalized it in the practice of judicial review. They adopted the notion that sovereignty could in fact be divided and governmental authority distributed, and institutionalized it into federalism. They accepted the theory of equality—a theory that had never been accorded more than philosophical lip-service—and institutionalized it into a series of social and economic and cultural practices designed to create—almost to guarantee—a classless society. And finally they managed to do what had not been done before—they took the principle of nationalism itself, and actually "brought forth a new nation"; they were the first people to do this.

Source 23   Forrest McDonald, *E Pluribus Unum,* 1965

In an ultimate sense, the Constitution confirmed the proposition that original power resided in the people—not, however, in the people as a whole, but in them in their capacity as people of the several states. In 1787 the people were so divided because, having created or acquiesced in the creation of state governments, they were bound by prior contracts. . . .

In short, national or local governments, being the creatures of the states, could exercise only those powers explicitly or implicitly given them by the states; each state government could exercise all powers unless it was forbidden from doing so by the people of the state. But in the Constitution, the states went a step further, and expressly denied to themselves the exercise of certain powers. . . . This is the essence of the American federal system: the division of power along a vertical axis by removing some of it from the central originating point, the states, and shifting some of it up and some of it down the axis. . . .

At the same time, the Constitution . . . provided that the powers so shifted should be further divided on a horizontal axis. That is, the national government's powers would be distributed in accordance with the three traditional aspects of government, legislation, execution, and adjudication.

So far, nothing new. Such a division was but a formalization of the theory and practice of government in England and its adaptation in British North America. . . .

There was, however, one cardinal difference between Britain and America which made a mere copying of the British system unfeasible. England had a hereditary monarchy and a hereditary nobility, each of which, along with the people, prevented the other from an unchecked expression of its will; and the two combined to check the people. In America, which lacked these two hereditary institutions, it was necessary to devise some kind of structural substitute. This did not mean creating an artificial monarch and an aristocracy . . . but dividing the people into various aspects or capacities of themselves.

In other words, "the people" were not, in any part of the multi-level government, allowed to act as the whole people. Instead, for purposes of expressing their will they were separated from themselves both in space and in time, from those they elected.

The national government would have four parts: House of Representatives, Senate, Presidency, and Court. The House was the "democratic" branch, all its members being elected directly by the people every two years—not, however, by the people as a whole, but by the people as citizens of subdivisions of states. The Senate was elected by the legislatures of the several states. . . . Senators were removed further from the people by a time barrier, one-third of them being elected every two years for six-year terms. The chief executive was chosen by electors who were chosen as the state legislatures should direct. . . . The fourth part of the national government, the Court, was chosen by the president, with the approval of the Senate, and for life. . . .

The result of this jerry-built structure was that government in the United States would be of (that is, from), the people; hopefully, it would be for the people; but by no means would it be by the people. The people had no instrumentality through which to exercise "the general will" immediately.

Source 24 Thomas R. Dye and Harmon Zeigler, *The Irony of Democracy,* 1971

The Constitution of the United States was not "ordained and established" by "the people." Only a small fraction of "the people" participated in any way in the adoption of the Constitution. The Constitution was prepared in Philadelphia by a small, educated, talented, wealthy elite, representative of powerful economic interests—bondholders, investors, merchants, real estate owners, and planters. The document itself, and the new government it established, included many provisions for the protection of the elite's political and economic interests from threats by the masses. Ratification was achieved because the elite had skills and political influence disproportionate to its members. The masses of people did not participate in the adoption of the Constitution, and there is some reason to believe that these masses would have opposed the Constitution had they the information, know-how, and resources to do so. The Constitution was not a product of a popular mass movement, but instead the work of a talented, educated, wealthy, and politically skilled elite.

Source 25   Howard Zinn, *A People's History of the United States,* 1980

The Constitution illustrates the complexity of the American system: that it serves the interests of a wealthy elite, but also does enough for small property owners, for middle-income mechanics and farmers, to build a broad base of support. The slightly prosperous people who make up this base of support are buffers against the blacks, the Indians, the very poor whites. They enable the elite to keep control with a minimum of coercion, a maximum of law—all made palatable by the fanfare of patriotism and unity.

∠ Questioning the Past

1. Explain the process that led to the abandonment of the Articles of Confederation and the adoption of the Constitution. By what authority did the Convention draft and present to the American states a new Constitution? The document they drafted proclaimed it would be operative after ratification by the conventions of nine states. By what rationale could such a procedure establish a document proclaiming itself the "supreme law of the land"? What reasons might be offered to explain why the Constitution was not presented to voters themselves for approval?

2. Patrick Henry described the Constitution as a "counter-revolution." What might he have meant by this?

3. Present the arguments for and against the Constitution proposed by the Philadelphia Convention of 1787. Which of the criticisms of the opponents seem valid? Which arguments of the supporters seem particularly convincing?

4. Was the Constitution intended to establish democracy or to retain aristocratic rule? Present arguments in support of both possibilities.

Chapter 16

The Alien and Sedition Acts

Luther Baldwin Utters Seditious Words

July 27, 1798

Americans were preoccupied in 1798 by an undeclared naval war with France. Many feared that a French invasion was imminent and that the French might be joined by Haiti, site of a successful recent slave uprising. Concern that the terror of the French Revolution would spread across the United States was deepened by newspaper predictions of rebellious slaves slitting their masters' throats in the dead of night. Nervous citizens rallied around President John Adams, depending on him to avert disaster.

Political supporters of the Adams administration, known as Federalists, were opposed by Democratic Republicans, under the leadership of Vice President Thomas Jefferson. Jefferson counseled calm, stressing that the French were too busy contending with European monarchies to be interested in war with America. Democratic Republicans argued, in the words of James Madison, that "the censorial power is in the people over the Government, and not in the Government over the people." Federalists countered with statements like that of Congressman John Allen: "The freedom of the press and opinions was never understood to give the right of publishing falsehoods and slanders, nor of exciting sedition, insurrection, and slaughter, with impunity."

❧ *First Impressions*

The Attempt to Silence Domestic Dissent

Fearful that criticism of their diplomatic and defensive measures would undermine Adams's public support and weaken the nation at a critical time, the Federalists took action during the summer. Despite both Democratic Republican objections and the freedoms protected by the First Amendment, they secured the passage of four bills known collectively as the Alien and Sedition Acts. Based on the assumption that the foreign-born were a subversive force in America, the laws also made it illegal for American citizens to criticize their own government.

177

Source 1   Vice President Thomas Jefferson to John Taylor

Philadelphia, June 1, 1798

This [attempt to silence political opposition] is not new; it is the old practice of despots to use part of the people to keep the rest in order; and those who have once got an ascendancy, and possessed themselves of all the resources of the nation, their revenues and offices, have immense means for retaining their advantage. But our present situation is not a natural one. . . .

A little patience, and we shall see the reign of witches pass over, their spells dissolved, and the people recovering their true right and restoring their government to its true principles.

Source 2   Naturalization Act, passed June 18, 1798

16.1 State
Interposition

Be it enacted by the Senate and House of Representatives of the United States of America in Congress assembled, That no alien shall be admitted to become a citizen of the United States . . . unless . . . he shall have declared his intention to become a citizen . . . five years . . . before his admission, and shall . . . declare and prove . . . that he has resided within the United States for fourteen years.

Source 3   Aliens Act, passed June 25, 1798

Be it enacted by the Senate and House of Representatives of the United States of America in Congress assembled, That it shall be lawful for the President . . . to order all such aliens as he shall judge dangerous to the peace and safety of the United States, or shall have grounds to suspect are concerned in any treasonable or secret machinations against the government thereof, to depart out of the territory of the United States.

Source 4   Sedition Act, passed July 14, 1798

Be it enacted by the Senate and House of Representatives of the United States of America in Congress assembled, That if any persons shall unlawfully combine or conspire together, with intent to oppose any measure or measures of the government of the United States . . . he or they shall be deemed guilty of a high misdemeanor, and on conviction . . . shall be punished by a fine not exceeding five thousand dollars, and by imprisonment during a term not less than six months nor exceeding five years. . . .

And be it further enacted, That if any person shall write, print, utter or publish . . . any false, scandalous and malicious writing or writings against the government of the United States, or either house of the Congress of the United States, or the President of the United States, with intent to defame the said government, or . . . the said Congress, or the said President, or bring them . . . into contempt or disrepute; or to excite against them . . . the hatred of the good people of the United States, or stir up sedition within the United States; . . . or to aid, encourage, or abet any hostile designs of any foreign nation against the United States, . . . then such person, being convicted . . . shall be punished by a fine not exceeding two thousand dollars, and by imprisonment not exceeding two years.

Source 5   Alien Enemies Act, passed July 16, 1798

Be it enacted by the Senate and House of Representatives of the United States of America in Congress assembled, That whenever there shall be a declared war between the United States and any foreign nation or government, or any invasion or predatory incursion shall be perpetrated, attempted, or threatened against the territory of the United States, by any foreign nation or government, . . . all natives, citizens, denizens, or subjects of the hostile nation or government, being males of the age of fourteen years and upwards, shall be liable to be apprehended, restrained, secured, or removed, as alien enemies.

Source 6   *The Columbian Mirror & Alexandria Gazette,* August 9, 1798

Benedict Arnold complained bitterly of the *Treason* bill, as *unconstitutional;* and parson Burroughs thought laws against Burglary . . . *an abridgement of natural rights,* yet true patriots, and honest men, feel no alarm at these laws, and would not, were they ten times as severe as they are. [M]ay we not then account for the hue and cry which the **jacobins** have set up against the "Sedition Bill"?

Source 7   John Marshall, candidate for Congress, September 20, 1798

I am not an advocate for the alien and sedition bills; had I been in Congress when they passed, I should . . . certainly have opposed them. Yet I do not think them fraught with all those mischiefs which many gentlemen ascribe to them. I should have opposed them, because I think them useless, and because they are calculated to create, unnecessarily, discontents and jealousies, at a time when our very existence, as a nation, may depend on our union.—I believe that these laws, had they been opposed on these principles by a man not suspected of intending to destroy the government, or of being hostile to it, would never have been enacted.

The Long Arm of the Sedition Law

The new laws were enforced almost immediately against an unfortunate man named Luther Baldwin, of Newark, New Jersey. On July 27, 1798, while most townsfolk were out cheering President John Adams's visit to Newark en route from the temporary Philadelphia capital to his home in Massachusetts, Baldwin was having a few beers in the local tavern. As the departing presidential entourage was given a 16-shot cannon salute, another drinker staggered into the tavern to report, "There goes the president, and they're firing at his ass." To which, the bartender later testified, Baldwin replied, "Hell, I don't care if they're shooting *through* his ass." He was promptly arrested for using seditious words. At a trial presided over by Supreme Court justice Bushrod Washington several weeks later, Baldwin was convicted of "tending to defame the President and Government of the United States," fined $150, and jailed. Nor was his the only case. Some 25 people were tried for sedition, and 10 were convicted, including two of Baldwin's drinking partners; New York assemblyman Jedidiah Peck, who had petitioned for repeal of the Sedition Act; Vermont congressman Matthew Lyon, who opposed the laws in a letter to his constituents; and the editors and publishers of the leading opposition newspapers. Benjamin Franklin Bache, editor of the influential *Philadelphia Aurora,* died in prison following his conviction.

Source 8   Newark *Centinel of Freedom,* 1799

There goes the President and they are firing at his a__. Luther, a little merry, replies, that he did not care if they fired through his a__: Then exclaims the dram seller, that is seditious—a considerable collection gathered—and the pretended federalists, being much disappointed that the president had not stopped that they might have had the honor of kissing his hand, bent their malice on poor Luther and the cry was, that he must be punished.

Source 9   New York *Argus,* October 15, 1799

When we heard that Luther Baldwin was indicted for sedition, we supposed that he had been guilty of something criminal. . . . We must confess that our astonishment has been excessive on hearing the peculiarity of the expressions for which so formal a trial was instituted.

 This prosecution cannot fail of convincing every republican of the extraordinary malignancy of the federal faction, when cognizance is taken of such ridiculous expression, as that uttered by Baldwin in the moment of intoxication. The poor man is consigned, probably, to ruin for what he spoke perhaps as a jest. Can the most enthusiastic federalists or tories suppose that those of us who are opposed to them would feel any gratification in firing at such a disgusting target as the ___ of John Adams . . . ?

 What opinion will the people of Europe form on reading the particulars of this curious trial in our papers? Many royalists will be pleased at the circumstance, as evincing that the cause might yet succeed in this country. Many a Briton will say that he believes that the president of the United States is treated with as much respect as a king, & that persons speaking contemptuously of him are punished in a similar way as such persons so offending against the king would be in England.

Source 10   Newark *Centinel of Freedom,* October 15, 1799

Of what materials must a man be composed, that will become a voluntary informer against another for a mere expression, drawn from him when in liquor, that did not injure anyone's person or property, and by that means ruin a man and distress his family, who has since publicly declared that he (the said Luther) was a good citizen, an honest man, a friend to his country, & meant no harm in what he said? Such inconsistencies we will leave to the public to reconcile, for we confess them dark to us.

Source 11 Letter to the *Argus,* October 15, 1799

COMMUNICATION

As a number of your papers are circulated in this town, and are read with greater avidity, on account of the trouble there is often to procure them at the post office.—I beg leave through your medium to publish a conversation I inadvertently overheard at a tavern between two of the inhabitants, concerning the most eligible person for coroner, as the election is approaching:—

One of the two, who was rather elderly, proposed the dram-seller, the celebrated John Burnet as a man who deserved any office, which the people of that town could bestow on him, and he then pronounced the strongest encomium on that worthy-**wight**, the principal feature of which was that he had the courage to become an informer, and let me tell you, says his eulogist, it requires no little courage to succeed in such a way, as in the first place, he had to overcome all his own feelings, and to turn a deaf ear to all the tender hearted persons, who thought it a pity to punish such an aged man as Luther Baldwin, whose hoary head would perhaps excite compassion in the breasts of those people called philanthropists; but he nobly persevered in prosecuting the old fellow for daring to utter such a contemptuous expression of our beloved president, whom everyone knows is one of the best of men, and thank God, we have shewn the cursed democrats that we will let none of them speak disrespectfully of any part of that dear man.

From a reader in Newark, New Jersey

Source 12 *Guardian: Or New Brunswick Advertiser,* November 13, 1799

Sedition by all the laws of God and man, is, and ever has been criminal; and when it is not, the laws will be crimes and magistrates will swing. Behold France! Government after government has been laid down, till the sword cut off the tip of Sedition's tongue.

Source 13 *Philadelphia Aurora,* Wednesday, November 13, 1799

Sometime since in Jersey, when a pack of people had assembled too late to salute the president with a round of cannon, the great man having gone bye—they fired after him—a rough seafaring man being told of the joke, replied in his rough way, that he did not care a rope yarn value about, or if they had fired the wad at his posteriors—the seafaring man was not indeed turned over to be hanged for this heinous joke—but . . . is now confined under the seditious act in gaol!—and finds that joking may be very dangerous even in a free country.

Reactions to the Alien and Sedition Acts

By the fall of 1798, public hysteria over the quasi-war with France had begun to subside. The Kentucky and Virginia legislatures declared the Alien and Sedition Acts null and void. Matthew Lyon was reelected to Congress from his Vermont prison cell. Jedidiah Peck, awaiting trial for sedition, won another term in the New York Assembly by a landslide.

Further, the public might have been persuaded that powerful politicians and newspaper editors could pose a threat to national security, but it was inconceivable that the remarks of a drunk in a tavern could topple a government. And if Luther Baldwin could be prosecuted, who could be safe?

In the presidential election of 1800, Thomas Jefferson defeated the Federalists. Once in office, he repealed the Naturalization Act, restored the residency requirement for citizenship to five years, and allowed the Alien and Sedition Acts to expire.

Source 14 Kentucky Resolutions, approved November 16, 1798

[P]rovision has been made by one of the amendments to the Constitution which expressly declares, that "Congress shall make no laws respecting an Establishment of religion, or prohibiting the free exercise thereof, or abridging the freedom of speech, or of the press," thereby guarding in the same sentence, and under the same words, the freedom of religion, of speech, and of the press, insomuch, that whatever violates either, throws down the sanctuary which covers the others. . . . That therefore the act of the Congress of the United States passed on the 14th of July, 1798, . . . which does abridge the freedom of the press, is not law, but is altogether void and of no effect. . . .

And that . . . this Commonwealth is determined . . . to submit to undelegated & consequently unlimited powers in no man or body of men on earth: that if the acts . . . should stand, these conclusions would flow from them; that the General Government may place any act they think proper on the list of crimes & punish it themselves, whether enumerated or not enumerated by the Constitution as cognizable by them: that they may transfer its cognizance to the President or any other person, who may himself be the accuser, counsel, judge, and jury, whose suspicions may be the evidence, his order the sentence, his officer the executioner, and his breast the sole record of the transaction: that a very numerous and valuable description of the inhabitants of these states, being by this precedent reduced as outlaws, to the absolute dominion of one man and the barrier of the Constitution thus swept away from us all, no rampart now remains against the passions and powers of a majority of Congress . . . : that the friendless alien has indeed been selected as the safest subject of a first experiment; but the citizen will soon follow, or rather has already followed; for already has a Sedition Act marked him as prey: that these and successive acts of the same character, unless arrested on the threshold, may tend to drive these states into revolution and blood, and will furnish . . . new pretexts for those who wish it believed, that man cannot be governed but by a rod of iron.

Source 15 Virginia Resolutions, adopted December 21, 1798

That the General Assembly doth particularly protest against the palpable and alarming infractions of the constitution, in the two late cases of the "Alien and Sedition Acts," passed in the last session of Congress; the first of which exercises a power nowhere delegated to the Federal Government; and which by uniting legislative and judicial powers, to those of executive, subverts the general principles of free government, as well as the particular organization and positive provisions of the federal constitution: and the other of which acts, exercises in like manner a power not delegated by the constitution, but on the contrary expressly and positively forbidden by one of the amendments thereto; a power which more than any other ought to produce universal alarm, because it is leveled against that right of freely examining public characters and measures, and of free communication among the people thereon, which has ever been justly deemed, the only effectual guardian of every other right.

Source 16 Speech of John Nicholas in the House of Representatives, February 25, 1799

The law has been current by the fair pretense of punishing nothing but false-hood, and by holding out to the accused the liberty of proving the truth of the writing; but it was from the first apprehended . . . that matters of opinion . . . come under the law. . . . Of the trial of facts there is an almost certain test. . . . The trial of the truth of opinions, in the best state of society, would be altogether precarious; and perhaps a jury of twelve men could never be found to agree in any one opinion. At the present moment, when, unfortunately, opinion is almost entirely governed by prejudice and passion, it may be more decided, but nobody will say it is more respectable. Chance must determine whether political opinions are true or false, and it will not unfrequently happen that a man will be punished for publishing opinions which are sincerely his, and are of a nature to be extremely interesting to the public, merely because accident or design has collected a jury of different sentiments.

Source 17 President Thomas Jefferson's first inaugural address, March 4, 1801

During the contest of opinion through which we have passed, the animation of discussions and of exertions has sometimes worn an aspect which might impose on strangers unused to think freely and to speak and write what they think; but this being now decided by the voice of the nation, announced according to the rules of the Constitution, all will, of course, arrange themselves under the will of the law, and unite in common efforts for the common good. All, too will bear in mind this sacred principle, that though the will of the majority is in all cases to prevail, that will to be rightful must be reasonable; that the minority possesses their equal rights, which equal law must protect, and to violate would be oppression. . . . And let us reflect that, having banished from our shores that religious intolerance under which mankind so long bled and suffered, we have yet gained little if we countenance a political intolerance as despotic, as wicked, and capable of as bitter and bloody persecutions. . . . If there be any among us who would wish to dissolve this union or to change its republican form, let them stand undisturbed as monuments of the safety with which error of opinion may be tolerated where reason is left free to combat it. . . . Sometimes it is said that man can not be trusted with the government of himself. Can he, then, be trusted with the government of others? Or have we found angels in the forms of kings to govern him? Let history answer this question.

16.2 Thomas Jefferson on Politics and Government

16.3 *The United States vs. Cooper:* A Violation of the Sedition Law

📖 *Second Thoughts*

Laws that Brought a Reign of Terror

To be arrested for joking about the president in public seems an alien idea to twentieth-century Americans. But in every crisis in American history, some attempt has been made to silence dissent. Historians and scholars looking back at the Alien and Sedition Acts of 1798 have not always agreed about the limits of free expression.

Source 18 Comments of President Thomas Jefferson, July 22, 1804

I discharged every person under punishment or prosecution under the sedition law, because I considered, and now consider, that law to be a nullity, as absolute and as palpable as if Congress had ordered us to fall down and worship a golden image; and that it was as much my duty to arrest its execution at every stage, as would have been to have rescued from the fiery furnace those who should have been cast into it for refusing to worship the image.

Source 19 Richard Hildreth, *The History of the United States of America,* 1851

Whatever might be their defects and deficiencies in other respects, the newspapers of the day had one redeeming feature in able essays communicated to their columns by such men as Hamilton, Madison, Ames, Cabot, and many others, who took that method of operating on the public mind. In the half century from 1765 to 1815, the peculiar literature of America is to be sought and found in these series of newspaper essays, some of them of distinguished ability. . . . Rich jewels now and then glittered on the dung-heap, but the editorial portion of the papers, and no small part of the communications also, consisted, too often, of declamatory calumnies, expressed in a style of vulgar ferocity. The epithets of rogue, liar, scoundrel, and villain were bandied about between the editors without the least ceremony. . . .

Yet the newspapers of that day exercised an individual influence over the minds of their readers very far beyond that of the much abler journals of our times. . . . In those days the *Aurora,* for instance, penetrated to many localities in which no other printed sheet ever made its appearance. There were many who never saw any other newspaper; and its falsehoods and calumnies produced all the effect natural to an uncontradicted statement of fact. . . .

Another circumstance, also, should be taken into consideration before deciding too peremptorily upon the policy of the Sedition Law. That act was not supposed, by those who enacted it, to create any new offenses, or to impose any new punishments. Though the point had not yet come before the full bench of the Supreme Court . . . the opinion had been expressed on circuit . . . that, independently of any authority expressly conferred by statute, the Federal Courts possessed a common law jurisdiction over offenses against the United States. . . .

But it may be asked, why object to criminal prosecutions when the truth may be given as evidence? Because this is a concession in many cases . . . much more showy than substantial. Even when the facts charged are of such nature as to admit of distinct proof, to bring witnesses might often be difficult, and would always be expensive. There is another objection, much more serious. What in political prosecutions for libel is charged as false allegation, very often is but mere statement of opinion, matter of inference . . . ; and often too these charges are made . . . for the very purpose of driving the party accused to confess or deny the allegations.

As all popular governments rest for support, not upon force, but upon opinion, assaults upon them limited to words ought to be repelled by words only. The press is open to the government also. To convict those who assail it of falsehood and malice by a candid exposition of facts, is the most certain means to destroy their influence. To appeal to the law will always expose to the charge of being driven by conscious guilt to silence by force, in default of reason, the complaints and criticisms of the people, part of whose right and liberty is to complain and criticize. . . .

Such are some of the arguments by which the wisdom and expediency . . . of the Sedition Law . . . might have been plausibly, if not, indeed, convincingly assailed. But nothing of this sort proceeded from the mouths of the opposition. They confined themselves very strictly to the constitutional argument. It was a special restriction of the powers of the general government, not the general liberty of the press for which they contended. Not a word was uttered against the exercise of that same power by the states, the exercise of which by the Federal government was denounced as fatal to liberty. The opposition argued, not like liberal statesmen and wise legislators, but only like violent anti-Federal politicians.

Source 20   J. Allen Smith, *The Spirit of American Government*, 1907

It was the purpose of the Constitution . . . to establish the supremacy of the so-called upper class. . . . Criticism, however, was especially irritating to those who accepted the Federalist theory of government. For if the few had a right to rule the many, then the latter, as a matter of course, ought to treat the former with respect; since otherwise the power and influence of the minority might be overthrown.

The Alien and Sedition laws by which the governing class sought to repress criticism were the logical culmination of this movement to limit the power of the majority. This attempt, however, to muzzle the press and overthrow the right of free speech instead of silencing the opposition only strengthened and intensified it. It merely augmented the rising tide of popular disapproval which was soon to overwhelm the Federalist party.

Source 21   James Truslow Adams, *The Epic of America*, 1931

The Alien and Sedition Acts . . . sprang from the Hamiltonian-Federalist distrust of the common man. Even the excesses of the French Revolution had not destroyed Jefferson's implicit faith in him, so long as he remained dependent upon the soil and not upon some capitalist for his living. Whether Jefferson was right or wrong yet remains an open question, for though in political life America's dream and ideal rest on the Jeffersonian faith in the common man, in her economic life she has developed along the lines of Hamiltonian special privilege and moneyed classes. As America grew she tried to serve, so to say, God and Mammon—that is, she insisted upon clinging to the ideal of Jeffersonianism—while gathering in the money profits from Hamiltonianism. By building up a great industrial and financial, instead of an agrarian, State, we have cut the major premise from out the logical structure of Jefferson's faith, and applied that faith to conditions under which he distinctly renounced it. On the other hand, we have erected an economic order according to Hamilton, but on the basis of a political philosophy which he did not believe would work. That is the modern American paradox. In 1800, however, America was still at the parting of the ways, and it yet seemed possible that the nation might choose to follow in the pure doctrine of either one or the other leader.

Source 22 Charles and Mary Beard, *Basic History of the United States,* 1944

These . . . acts, instead of fastening the grip of the Federalists on the government, laid them open to attacks in the name of American liberty. Republicans interpreted the conduct of the Federalists as revealing their true colors—their liking for arbitrary government. [T]he passage of the Sedition Act confirmed Jefferson's suspicion that Federalists were resolved to destroy critics by fine and imprisonment, after the fashion of Old World despots. Adopting underground tactics, Jefferson wrote an indictment of the Alien and Sedition Acts which was sent secretly to a friend in the state of Kentucky. . . . On the basis of this document, the Kentucky legislature formulated and passed, in 1798, a set of resolutions branding the acts as contrary to the Constitution, as null and void. It declared that, when the federal government exceeded its powers, the states had a right to interpose. . . . Receiving little aid and comfort from other states, the Kentucky legislature then passed, in 1799, a second set of resolutions proclaiming the right of states to nullify "unconstitutional" acts of Congress.

Rejecting the doctrine of nullification as likely to endanger the Union, James Madison, now affiliated with the Republican party, induced the legislature of Virginia to pass milder resolutions while joining in the protest against the objectionable acts. In fact Jefferson himself later avowed that he had no intention at the time of encouraging action that might lead to a dissolution of the bonds established by the Constitution. Both he and Madison regarded their tactics as only calculated to fan discontent with the Alien and Sedition Acts and weaken the hold of the sponsors, the Federalists, on the nation.

Source 23 John C. Miller, *Crisis in Freedom: The Alien and Sedition Acts,* 1951

Every administration facing a diplomatic crisis such as that which gripped the country in 1798 must weigh in the balance the imperative necessity of permitting men to search freely for the truth. Without freedom of discussion, without the right of examining the methods and objectives of the party in power and criticizing its acts, democracy becomes an empty name. Unity of purpose, however essential to the existence of the nation, cannot be achieved by suppressing this freedom; but it can be realized in a democracy where common standards are accepted and where the principles of the Bill of Rights are maintained.

Source 24 James Morton Smith, *Freedom's Fetters,* 1956

The criminal law of seditious libel which emerged in England during the seventeenth and eighteenth centuries developed at a time when the accepted view made the rulers the superiors of the people. . . . This view made words punishable, because to find fault with the government tended to undermine the respect of the people for it and to reduce its dignity and authority. . . .

It was to this English common law concept that the Federalists turned for their model. Even so, they attempted to adapt the authoritarian practice to the basic realities of popular government by working out a compromise between the rights of the authorities and the rights of the people. An aristocratic party which deplored political democracy, they based their defense of the right of authorities to freedom from public criticism, paradoxically enough, on the fact that the American government rested on the consent of the governed. They contended that the election of officers by the people demonstrated the confidence which the people had in these officers. Once these officials had been elevated by the people to the highest offices in the land, they became the "constituted authorities" who ran things until the next election. Thus, the Federalists exalted the officeholder above the mass of the citizens. It was a greater offense to criticize one of the rulers than it was to criticize one of the people themselves, because the rulers partook of the majesty of the whole people. . . .

The sharp and lasting defeat administered to the Federalists at the beginning of the nineteenth century made a deep impression on the party leaders of that century. Not until the entry of the United States into World War I did Congress again impose restrictions on utterances and publications and thus encroach on the civil liberties tradition founded on the resentment against the laws of 1798. The Sedition Act of 1918, however, was a wartime measure which was repealed in 1921. The first peacetime sedition statute was not passed until 1940, when Congress enacted the Alien Registration Act, commonly called the Smith Act.

With these two exceptions, the United States has preferred to abide by the principles enunciated by Jefferson in his first inaugural address.

Source 25 Supreme Court justice William O. Douglas, *The Right of the People,* 1957

In 1798, the Alien and Sedition Laws . . . brought a reign of terror to the nation. . . . Those laws would not, of course, pass judicial scrutiny today . . . since they would strike at the very heart of free political comment. . . . Any law forbidding criticism of the government is at war with the First Amendment. . . .

An unconstitutional statute is a lawless act by the legislature. The humblest citizen, confronted by all the forces of the state which insist that he must obey the law, may take matters into his own hands, defy an unconstitutional statute, and risk the outcome on the ultimate decision of the courts. He may forsake the orderly processes of society and proceed as if the law does not exist. That was Jefferson's attitude toward the Alien and Sedition Laws.

⚖ Questioning the Past

1. "What are we to do?" Federalist Fisher Ames asked in the midst of the crisis of 1798. "The devil of sedition is immortal, and we, as saints, have an endless struggle to maintain with him." In the context of 1798, defend his statement. Argue the case against the Alien and Sedition Acts.

2. Describe the features of the four laws collectively known as the Alien and Sedition Acts. Which of these features, if any, contradict the guarantees of civil liberties found in the Bill of Rights? If the French had actually invaded America, would these laws have then been necessary? Is the right of free expression unlimited?

3. What was the significance of the case of Luther Baldwin?

4. What are the implications of the ideas expressed in the Virginia and Kentucky resolves?

5. "If all mankind minus one were of one opinion, and only one person were of the contrary opinion," John Stuart Mill wrote, "mankind would be no more justified in silencing that one person, than he, if he had the power, would be justified in silencing mankind." Is this statement valid or invalid? Present both positions.

Chapter 17

The Monroe Doctrine

Monroe Delivers His Message to Congress

December 2, 1823

The French Revolution sparked revolutions across Europe and beyond. The foundations of monarchical society were set ablaze, and kings were toppled from their thrones. The fires of rebellion spread to colonies beyond Europe, and revolution threatened to leave the old order everywhere in ashes. But with great effort the powers of Europe succeeded in bringing the flames under control. Following the defeat of Napoleon in 1815, there set in a period of conservative backlash. Kings were restored to the thrones of European states, and they moved quickly to suppress the republican movements. They formed a Holy Alliance to extinguish the embers of democratic zeal wherever their glow could be detected. A Quadruple Alliance of the kings of Austria, Prussia, Russia, and Britain within the Holy Alliance constituted a powerful bloc of reactionary force. This coalition, called the Quintuple Alliance after 1818 when joined by France following restoration of its monarchy, attempted to direct the affairs of Europe in the post-Napoleonic period. When new revolutions broke out across southern Europe in 1820 and 1821, the Alliance moved against them swiftly. Austrian troops smothered revolts in Italy and French forces did the same in Spain.

The resurgence of monarchy worried the United States. As a nation whose own revolution had led to a republican form of government, America was uneasy about the ultimate reach of the Alliance. Would the French, America wondered, turn their might toward restoration of Spanish rule over the rebel governments of Latin America? Did the Russian czar have ambitions over larger areas of the Pacific Northwest? American concerns about becoming entangled in European politics had first been raised a generation earlier. President Washington, in his farewell message of 1796, offered that "it is our true policy to steer clear of permanent alliances with any portion of the foreign world." And President James Madison, in 1810, ordered the "temporary occupation" of west Florida, a Spanish possession. Madison feared that Spain was too weak to protect its colonies and might transfer ownership to another European power.

The British began to have second thoughts about involvement with the Alliance. They were concerned that their allies were becoming too powerful and therefore a threat to British independence. The British also worried that a possible restoration of Spanish control over Latin America

17.1 The
American
Presidency:
James Monroe

might block the increasingly lucrative trade that British merchants were developing there. On August 16, 1823, the British foreign secretary, George Canning, approached the American minister in London, Richard Rush, with an unexpected proposition. Canning suggested that the United States and Great Britain issue a joint statement in opposition to any attempt by the French to reassert European control over the former Spanish colonies of Latin America. Minister Rush transmitted details of this proposal to President James Monroe. After consulting with former presidents Jefferson and Madison, Monroe was inclined to accept the British offer. Secretary of State John Quincy Adams, however, dissuaded him. Adams argued that it "would be more candid, as well as more dignified, to avow our principles explicitly to Russa and France, than to come in as a cock-boat in the wake of the British man-of-war."

❧ *First Impressions*

The Monroe Doctrine

With the able advice and assistance of Secretary Adams, James Monroe turned aside the British proposal for a joint manifesto and included instead a unilateral warning to Europe in his State of the Union message. Those American journalists who commented on Monroe's warning generally supported his position. Reaction by the European powers was swift and predictable.

Source 1   Address of President Monroe, December 2, 1823

17.2 James
Monroe
(1758–1831)

[T]he American continents, by the free and independent condition which they have assumed and maintain, are henceforth not to be considered as subjects for future colonization by any European powers. . . .

In the wars of the European powers in matters relating to themselves we have never taken any part, nor does it comport with our policy to do so. It is only when our rights are invaded or seriously menaced that we resent injuries or make preparation for our defense. With the movements in this hemisphere we are of necessity more immediately connected, and by causes which must be obvious to all enlightened and impartial observers. The political system of the allied powers is essentially different in this respect from that of America. . . . We owe it, therefore, to candor and to the amicable relations existing between the United States and those powers to declare that we should consider any attempt on their part to extend their system to any portion of this hemisphere as dangerous to our peace and safety. With the existing colonies or dependencies of any European power we have not interfered and shall not interfere. But with the Governments who have declared their independence and maintained it, and whose independence we have, on great consideration and on just principles, acknowledged, we could not view any interposition for the purpose of oppressing them, or controlling in any other manner their destiny, by any European power in any other light than as the manifestation of an unfriendly disposition toward the United States. In the war between those new Governments and Spain we declared our neutrality at the time of their recognition, and to this we have adhered, and shall continue to adhere, provided no change shall occur which . . . shall make a corresponding change on the part of the United States indispensable to their security.

The late events in Spain and Portugal shew that Europe is still unsettled. Of this important fact no stronger proof can be adduced than that the allied powers should have thought it proper . . . to have interposed by force in the internal concerns of Spain. . . . Our policy in regard to Europe, which was adopted at an early stage of the wars which have so long agitated that quarter of the globe, nevertheless remains the same, which is, not to interfere in the internal concerns of any of its powers. . . . But in regard to those [American] continents circumstances are eminently and conspicuously different. It is impossible that the allied powers should extend their political system to any portion of either continent without endangering our peace and happiness; nor can anyone believe that our southern brethren, if left to themselves, would adopt it of their own accord. It is equally impossible, therefore, that we should behold such interposition in any form with indifference. If we look to the comparative strength and resources of Spain and those new Governments, and their distance from each other, it must be obvious that she can never subdue them. It is still the true policy of the United States to leave the parties to themselves, in the hope that other powers will pursue the same course.

Source 2 *Baltimore Federal Republican,* December 1823

We have the pleasure of laying the President's Message before our readers, in this day's paper. It is a lucid and able public document and will be read with peculiar interest. He delineates the important concerns of the nation with great force and discrimination, and upon the subject of our foreign relations, his language is energetic, bold, and manly; honorable alike to his head and his heart. In regard to the interference of the powers of Europe with the concerns of the people of this hemisphere, he has touched a chord that will vibrate in unison with every honorable feeling in the country.

17.3 Primary Sources: James Monroe

Source 3 *United States Gazette* (Philadelphia), December 1823

The President's Message to Congress . . . has afforded us the highest satisfaction. The noble sentiments of policy it expresses, in the present critical situation of the world, do honor to his discernment, generous feeling, and patriotism, and render us more proud of our country, because they are approved by the whole nation, in the coolest exercise of its judgment, and they throb in the bosom of every man. We allude more particularly to the distinct and candid enunciation of the view he takes of the attempts of the European Alliance to control the world. . . . He says, that "we owe to the candor and to the amicable relations existing between the United States and those Powers, *to declare,* that we should consider any attempt on their part, to extend their system *to any portion* of this hemisphere, as dangerous to *our peace and safety.*" Nothing can be more magnanimously wise and decisive than this.

Source 4   Account of Baron Von Tuyll, Russian minister, in
              Washington, December 1823

The document in question enunciates views and pretensions so exaggerated, it
establishes principles so contrary to the rights of the European powers that it
merits only the most profound contempt.

Source 5   Account of Prince Metternich, chancellor of Austria, January
              1824

The United States of America . . . have cast blame and scorn on the institutions
of Europe. . . . In permitting themselves these unprovoked attacks, in fostering
revolutions wherever they show themselves, in regretting those that have failed,
in extending a helping hand to those which seem to prosper, they lend new
strength to the apostles of sedition and reanimate the courage of every conspirator.

Source 6   *Constitutionnel* (Paris), January 2, 1824

Today for the first time the new continent says to the old, "I am no longer land
for occupation; here men are masters of the soil which they occupy, and the
equals of the people from whom they came, and resolved not to treat with them
except on the basis of the most exact justice." The new continent is right.

Source 7   *L'Etoile* (Paris), January 4, 1824

Mr. Monroe, who is not a sovereign, has assumed in his message the tone of a
powerful monarch, whose armies and fleets are ready to march at the first signal.
. . . Mr. Monroe is the temporary President of a Republic situated on the east
coast of North America. This Republic is bounded on the south by possessions
of the King of Spain, and on the north by those of the King of England. Its
independence was only recognized forty years ago, by what right then would
the two Americas today be under its immediate sway from Hudson's Bay to
Cape Horn?

An Enduring Policy

Following Monroe's bold warning to Europe that the United States would
not tolerate any new colonization of the Western Hemisphere, there was
no attempt for many years by any power of the Old World to gain a new
foothold in the Americas. It is likely, however, that had Monroe never
issued such a warning, European behavior would have been exactly the
same.

It appears that no member of the Quintuple Alliance was seriously
interested in restoring Spanish dominion over Latin America in the 1820s.
Unknown to Monroe or Adams, British foreign secretary Canning and
French ambassador Jules de Polignac had already signed a memorandum
a month prior to the issuance of the Monroe Doctrine in which it was
agreed that no attempt by France would be made to reconquer the former
Spanish colonies of Latin America. Over the years that followed, the

British Navy enforced the principles of the Monroe Doctrine, not because it was in the American interest to do so, but because it satisfied British interests.

📖 *Second Thoughts*

Intervention or Nonintervention?

The Monroe Doctrine received scant notice when issued and was largely ignored until President James K. Polk attempted to apply it in asserting American ambitions in California and Oregon. It was not referred to as a "doctrine" until 1852, and it was more than 70 years before an American president moved to use it to prevent European colonization in the Western Hemisphere.

17.4 Monroe Doctrine

Source 8   **President James Polk, The Polk Corollary to the Monroe Doctrine, December 2, 1845**

We must ever maintain the principle that the people of this continent alone have the right to decide their own destiny. Should any portion of them, constituting an independent state, propose to unite themselves with our Confederacy, this will be a question for them and us to determine without any foreign interposition. We can never consent that European powers shall intervene to prevent such a union.

Source 9   **Address to the U.S. Senate, John C. Calhoun, January 1846**

Mr. Monroe was a wise man, and had no design of burdening the country with a risk which it could not perform. . . . Our own good sense should teach us that we ought not to undertake what we cannot perform. It should be so with individuals and with nations. By the adoption of the principle of the resolution, we would be called on to interfere whenever a European nation, right or wrong, should bring on a conflict of arms between one or another nation on this continent. . . .

[W]ould it not be better to wait for the emergency in which we would have sufficient interest to intervene, and sufficient power to make that interference influential? Why make such a declaration now? What good purpose can it serve? Only to show to the men who come after us that we were wiser and more patriotic than we feared they might be! . . .

Declarations, sir, are easily made. The affairs of nations are not controlled by mere declarations. If a declaration of opinion were sufficient to change the whole course of events, no nation would be more prompt than we. But we must meet interference in our affairs in another way . . . decidedly, boldly, practically. We must meet each particular case by itself, and according to its own merits, always taking care not to assert our rights until we feel ourselves able to sustain our assertions. As to general abstract declarations of that kind, I would not give a farthing for a thousand of them. They do more harm than good, or rather no good at all, but a great deal of harm.

Source 10 **Interpretation of Senator John M. Niles of Connecticut, 1848**

There are two great principles which have been held sacred by this country from its earliest history; and I am not prepared to admit that the declaration of Mr. Monroe, so often referred to, if properly understood, gives any sanction, or recognizes any policy of this Government, which involves a departure from these principles. What are these principles? First, there is the principle of neutrality with regard to belligerents. . . . The second principle we have hitherto held equally sacred, the principle of non-intervention. It is the principle which this Government, above all others, ought to hold sacred, because it strikes at the very foundations of free government. It is the principle which belongs to a free people; which is, that they should take care of their own affairs. Is it consistent with this principle to take possession of a foreign state, and take part in a civil war in which it is engaged? . . .

I wish to say something, Mr. President, in regard to this doctrine which has been said to have been held by President Monroe, and which is gravely spoken of as the settled and established policy of this country: We must look to the circumstances of the nations in this hemisphere and in Europe at the time the declarations of Mr. Monroe were made. These were not abstract declarations of principles to govern the action of this Government, but declarations applied to the then existing state of the countries in Europe and America. I have examined the messages of 1823 and 1824 which contain his doctrines. Some years previous to that, the Spanish colonies in this hemisphere had asserted and declared their independence; but Spain refused to acknowledge them, and still asserted her dominion over them. Mr. Monroe did not deny the right of Spain to reestablish her dominion over them; much less did he assert the right of the United States to interfere between Spain and her colonies, or to set itself up as the arbitrator and guardian of all the nations in this hemisphere. What he declared was, that the political system of Europe must not be extended to America to control the destinies of these Spanish American countries. He did not mean the monarchical system of Europe, as some seem to suppose, but that combination among the great Powers, sometimes called the Holy Alliance, which divided and disposed of the small States of Europe according to their pleasure. . . . After a while, the combination was broken up, and soon after Spain acknowledged the independence of these States on this continent. This is one of the positions of Mr. Monroe, and has no connection whatever with the right of intervention . . . in the concerns of foreign Powers—no connection with the idea which seems to be assumed, that Mr. Monroe claimed for the United States, as the principal and only great nation in this hemisphere, the right to dictate to or to control the destinies of all others, or assume the obligation to protect them. His was not the doctrine of interference, but of resistance to the interference of others.

Source 11 **President Ulysses Grant, The Grant Corollary, May 31, 1870**

The doctrine promulgated by President Monroe has been adhered to by all political parties, and I now deem it proper to assert this equally important principle that hereafter *no territory* on this continent [European or American] shall be regarded as subject to transfer to a European power.

Source 12 Illinois politician Gustave Koerner, the *Nation*, 1882

True statesmen do not rule by doctrines, programmes, or platforms. With them the welfare of the people is the supreme law. They do not commit themselves by generalities. Every conflict that arises is judged by them according to the circumstances of the times. If our interests or our honor be threatened in the particular instance, then they protest, then they arm, then they go to war, independent of sentiments, of traditions, of programmes, of doctrines. The highest commercial interests, the permanency of our republican institutions, would have been seriously threatened had Spain, by the help of the allied powers, reduced her revolted provinces to subjection, or ceded them in part to other more powerful nations. Here was an emergency, and Mr. Monroe met it manfully, but not on philosophical, abstract principles. If allied or single European powers should at this day try to conquer some of our sister republics, and plant monarchical institutions on American soil, so as to endanger our own safety, the American people would calmly weigh the matter, and, without any reference to former action, decide the case for itself, and no President would fail to carry out the decision. It would go to war just as if the Monroe Doctrine had never been made.

Source 13 Secretary of State Richard Olney, The Olney Corollary,
July 20, 1895

[President] Washington, in the solemn admonitions of the Farewell Address, explicitly warned his countrymen against entanglements with the politics or the controversies of European powers. . . .

The Farewell Address, while it took America out of the field of European politics, was silent as to the part Europe might be permitted to play in America. Doubtless it was thought the latest addition to the family of nations should not make haste to prescribe rules for the guidance of its older members. . . .

Twenty years later, however, the situation had changed. The lately born nation had greatly increased in power and resources, had demonstrated its strength on land and sea. The Monroe administration therefore did not hesitate to accept and apply the logic of the Farewell Address by declaring in effect that American non-intervention in European affairs necessarily implied and meant European non-intervention in American affairs. . . .

That America is in no part open to colonization, though the proposition was not universally admitted at the time of its first enunciation, has long been conceded. . . .

Today the United States is practically sovereign on this continent, and its fiat is law upon the subjects to which it confines its interposition. Why? . . . It is because . . . its infinite resources combined with its isolated position render it master of the situation and practically invulnerable as against any or all other powers.

All the advantages of this superiority are at once imperiled if the principle be admitted that European powers may convert American states into colonies or provinces of their own. . . . This is, then, a doctrine of American public law, well founded in principle and abundantly sanctioned by precedent, which entitles and requires the United States to treat as an injury to itself the forcible assumption by any European power of political control over an American state.

Source 14 Repudiation of Olney Corollary, British foreign secretary
Lord Salisbury, November 26, 1895

The contentions set forth by Mr. Olney . . . are well known in American discussion under the name of the Monroe Doctrine. As far as I am aware, this doctrine has never been advanced on behalf of the United States in any communication addressed to the Government of another country; but it has been generally adopted and assumed as true by many eminent writers and politicians in the United States. . . . [I]nternational law is founded on the general consent of nations; and no statesman, however eminent, and no nation, however powerful, are competent to insert into the code of international law a novel principle which was never recognized before, and which has not since been accepted by the Government of any other country. . . .

The Government of the United States is not entitled to affirm as a universal proposition, with reference to a number of independent States for whose conduct it assumes no responsibility, that its interests are necessarily concerned in whatever may befall those States simply because they are situated in the Western Hemisphere.

Source 15 President Theodore Roosevelt, The Roosevelt Corollary, 1903

Chronic wrongdoing, or an impotence which results in a general loosening of the ties of civilized society, may in America, as elsewhere, ultimately require intervention by some civilized nation, and in the Western Hemisphere, the adherence of the United States to the Monroe Doctrine may force the United States, however reluctantly, in flagrant cases of such wrongdoing or impotence, to the exercise of the international police power.

Source 16 Article 21, the Covenant of the League of Nations,
January 10, 1920

Nothing in this Covenant shall be deemed to affect the validity of international engagements, such as treaties of arbitration or regional understandings like the Monroe doctrine, for securing the maintenance of peace.

Source 17 Historian Dexter Perkins, *The Monroe Doctrine,* 1927

In the first place, it is an interesting, if not decisive, episode in the clash of two opposing principles—intervention, on the one hand . . . ; non-intervention, on the other. . . . To Monroe and Adams, . . . believing in the right of peoples to determine their own form of government, nothing could be more odious than the doctrines of the Holy Alliance. . . . In its protean forms, the Monroe Doctrine has not always been a doctrine of liberty, and non-intervention has seemed perilously like intervention in actual practice, but it is, I think, fair to state that it was not so that Monroe and Adams intended it. They made no attempt to force any particular form on the states of the New World, at no time exerted more than a moral influence in favor of republicanism; they were really, in their own day, the champions of principles of liberty. However little this may have meant in practice, it meant something from the standpoint of the history of ideas, and ought so to be regarded.

In the second place, the technique of the message gives it a certain importance. We have heard much, in these latter years, of open diplomacy. One might think that such diplomacy was a novelty. But, as a matter of fact, for more than a century statesmen have known how to make the appeal to public opinion serve the purposes of their policy. And never was that appeal more cleverly and vigorously used than in 1823. . . .

Thirdly, . . . the language of the Monroe Doctrine has had a great effect, in the long run, upon American foreign policy. There are no indications that the President expected this. . . . He was thinking of an immediate danger. . . .

This is the paradox of the message of 1823. From the standpoint of its immediate results, it was close to a futility. It did not even raise American prestige appreciably or for long in South America, and hardly altered the politics of Europe. But as James Monroe could hardly have suspected would be the case, it became in later years an American **shibboleth**, powerful in its appeal, and far-reaching in its influence. It is more important for its ideas than as a piece of practical statesmanship. Nor is this the first or only time in history that words powerless to alter the course of immediate events have lived beyond the moment of their utterance, and played their part in the wide developments of the future.

Source 18 Undersecretary of State J. Reuben Clark, The Clark Memorandum, 1930

The [Monroe] doctrine states a case of United States vs. Europe, not of United States vs. Latin America. . . . Such arrangements as the United States has made, for example, with Cuba, Santo Domingo, Haiti, and Nicaragua, are not within the Doctrine as announced by Monroe.

Source 19 Declaration of Reciprocal Assistance and Cooperation for the Defense of the Nations of the Americas, 1940

Any attempt on the part of a *non-American state* against the integrity or inviolability of the territory, the sovereignty or the political independence of an American state shall be considered an act of aggression against the states which sign this declaration.

Source 20 Samuel Flagg Bemis, *John Quincy Adams and the Foundations of American Foreign Policy,* 1949

Historical scholars have agreed that there was little danger in 1823 of actual Allied intervention by force to restore Spanish America to Spain. Great Britain stopped any conceivable menace there might have been. . . . Because of this fact there has been a tendency to dismiss the Monroe Doctrine as a mere trumpet-blast safely and somewhat imprudently blown behind the protection of the British Navy, and from that to conclude that it did no real good to Latin America. . . .

It is true that the Doctrine had no real force behind it. It was only a pronouncement, but it contained powerful words nevertheless, words that both served the immediate interests of the United States and exalted for the whole Hemisphere the ideals of independence and the sovereignty of the people. The service to the New World of the Monroe Doctrine *at the time of its origin* was not in preventing European intervention against the independence of an American state but rather in galvanizing the preponderant *republican character* of the new states at the outset.

Source 21 George F. Kennan, "Latin America as a Problem in United States Foreign Policy," also called the "Kennan Corollary," memo to the secretary of state, March 29, 1950

We cannot be too dogmatic about the methods by which local Communists can be dealt with. These vary greatly, depending upon the vigor and efficacy of local concepts and traditions of self-government. Where such vigor and efficacy are relatively high, as in our own country, the body politic may be capable of bearing the virus of communism without permitting it to expand to dangerous proportions. This is undoubtedly the best solution to the communist problem, wherever the prerequisites exist, and where the concepts and traditions of popular government are too weak to absorb successfully the intensity of the communist attack, then we must concede that harsh governmental measures of repression may be the only answer; that these measures may have to proceed from regimes whose origins and methods would not stand the test of American concepts of democratic procedures; and that such regimes and such methods may be preferable alternatives, and indeed the only alternatives, to further communist success.

Source 22 Julius W. Pratt, *A History of United States Foreign Policy,* 1955

Of all presidents of the United States from 1789 to 1955, James Monroe alone was honored by having his name attached to a sacred national dogma—the Monroe Doctrine. . . . Rarely, during the last one hundred years, has any American admitted doubt concerning this article of faith. It has been invoked by isolationists on the one hand and internationalists on the other. . . .

It seems safe to say that the Monroe Doctrine owes its long-continued popularity to the circumstance that it was the first official and public pronouncement of a deep-seated American belief—the belief that the Atlantic and Pacific Oceans divide the world so effectively into distinct hemispheres that the nations of the New World should be able to insulate themselves from the quarrels, the interferences, and the colonizing ambitions of the Old World Powers. From this belief stem both the neutrality policy of the United States and the Monroe Doctrine. In so far as the belief meant American abstention from European quarrels, it spelled neutrality. In so far as it meant exclusion from the Americas of the interference and the colonizing activity of Europe, it was set forth in President Monroe's message to Congress of December 2, 1823.

Source 23 Thomas A. Bailey, *A Diplomatic History of the American People*, 1974

What came to be known as the Monroe Doctrine was not law, national or international. . . . It was merely a simple, unilateral, Presidential statement of foreign policy. Adams even spoke of it as a "lecture" to the powers. It did not commit subsequent administrations to any definite course. As Lord Clarendon politely remarked in the 1850's, "The Monroe Doctrine is merely the dictum of its distinguished author." He might have added, no less pointedly, that it was no stronger than the power of the United States to eject the transgressor—no bigger than America's armed forces.

The new dogma did not even need a distinguishing name. It might just as well have been called the Long-Range Self-Defense Doctrine—for that is essentially what it was. Monroe warned the European allies to keep out of Latin America, and Russia to forgo further colonization, primarily because he felt that their presence would be dangerous to the peace and safety of the United States. If, at a later date, the powers should again menace the Americas, all the State Department had to do was to base its protests on self-defense, without having to drag in Monroe's name. Yet Monroe gave definite form, as well as global emphasis, to a fundamental foreign policy. When his successors later had to invoke the Doctrine, it carried greater weight with the American people because it had an "aura of antiquity" and because it was associated with a big name.

Source 24 Gaddis Smith, *The Last Years of the Monroe Doctrine, 1945–1993*, 1994

The American approach to Latin America has always been affected by the larger context of foreign policy. Indeed, had there never been any real or imagined threats to national security from beyond the hemisphere there would never have been a Monroe Doctrine. In late 1949 and early 1950 a dramatic shift in the larger context caused American officials to perceive greater dangers in Latin America than at any time since the high tide of Nazi expansion in 1940–41. The new perceptions led to unprecedented use of the Monroe Doctrine to justify covert intervention against a Latin American government and a general willingness to temper support for democracy in order to stand against Communism.

The shift occurred quickly. During the first part of 1949 the United States seemed to have won the Cold War. The North Atlantic Treaty was signed in April; in May the Soviets lifted the Berlin blockade, a significant retreat, perhaps even recognition that a comprehensive settlement on Western terms might be in the offing. But in August 1949 the Soviet Union detonated its first nuclear explosion, ending the American atomic monopoly. In October the People's Republic of China was formally established in Beijing, signifying the triumph of Communism in the Chinese civil war. The end of the atomic monopoly and the "loss" of China replaced the optimism of mid-1949 in Washington with a growing assumption that the world was now on the eve of war. In the winter and spring of 1950 a group of State and Defense Department officials, headed by Paul Nitze of State, prepared the foundation policy statement for the United States in this seemingly perilous on-the-eve-of-war situation. It was in the form of a 30,000-word report to the National Security Council. Known ever since simply as NSC–68, and widely cited after being declassified and published in 1975, the report used language alarmist in the extreme. A few excerpts will suffice to make the point: "The Soviet Union . . . is animated by a new fanatic faith, antithetical to our own, and seeks to impose its absolute authority over the rest of the world. Conflict has, therefore, become endemic and is waged, on the part of the Soviet Union, by violent or non-violent methods in accordance with the dictates of expediency. . . . The issues that face us are momentous, involving the fulfillment or destruction not only of this Republic but of civilization itself." The Kremlin "design, therefore, calls for the complete subversion or forcible destruction of the machinery of government and structure of society in the countries of the non-Soviet world and their replacement by an apparatus and structure subservient to and controlled from the Kremlin."

The pervading sense of worldwide danger made the highest officials in the American government think about Latin America in terms of global strategy, not in terms of the problems within individual countries or the region or even in terms of the perennial issues between the other American republics and the United States. These men—Secretaries of State, national security advisers, Presidents, directors of the Central Intelligence Agency, and their top advisers throughout the entire period from 1945 to the end of the Cold War—all lacked deep knowledge or experience of Latin America. The foreign policy and national security professionals in the group were experts on Europe, Asia, and relations among the Great Powers. They knew the leaders of Britain, France, Germany, Italy, Japan, Israel, the Soviet Union, and the many other countries of Europe, Asia, and the Middle East—but not leaders of the American republics. None of the members of the high foreign policy establishment in the United States had ever lived in Latin America. None had more than the most rudimentary knowledge of Spanish or Portuguese—if that. And most were condescending and prejudiced toward the people and culture of Latin America. For Harry Truman, Latin Americans were, like Jews and the Irish, "very emotional" and difficult to handle. Secretary of State John Foster Dulles thought he knew how Latin Americans should be handled. "You have to pat them a little bit and make them think you are fond of them." President Eisenhower's attitude was revealed in a remark to President Arturo Frondizi of Argentina, a nation whose population was almost entirely white and European in origin: "Argentines are the same kind of people we are." High officials in their franker moments admitted to feelings of unease, distrust, and racial prejudice toward Latin American politicians. The result was that much of American policy toward Latin America as developed by the highest American officials had little to do with Latin America as such—but everything to do with how those officials saw the United States projecting power around the world and being threatened by the projected power of the Soviet Union. The fear of that projected power led them to the protean principles of the Monroe Doctrine as the foundation of policy toward Latin America.

The above generalizations are nowhere better illustrated than in the case of what we call the Kennan Corollary to the Monroe Doctrine.

⚲ Questioning the Past

1. Explain and evaluate the intent, the meaning, and the significance of the Monroe Doctrine.

2. What common threads run through Washington's Farewell Address, Madison's occupation of west Florida, the Monroe Doctrine, Polk Corollary, Grant Corollary, Olney Corollary, and Roosevelt Corollary? By what right did the United States proclaim such principles?

3. Senator Niles in 1848 asserted that the Monroe's Doctrine "was not the doctrine of interference, but of resistance to the interference of others." Is his analysis correct? Explain.

4. Was the Monroe Doctrine a reaffirmation of United States isolationism or an abrogation of it? Argue the merits of both sides of this question.

Chapter 18

Uniting the States

A Race for the West and the Future Begins

July 4, 1828

By the end of the second decade of the nineteenth century, the United States had expanded from the shores of the Atlantic to the eastern slopes of the Rockies. Few other nations could claim dominion over more territory. But claiming land was not the same as incorporating it. How could a population so widely dispersed ever come to identify itself as American rather than as partisans of regions or states? How could a country so divided by great distance and rugged geographic barriers develop an integrated national economy?

Until 1815, America's river systems had been the primary avenues of travel on both sides of the Appalachians. All cities and towns of any size were located with access to the open sea or on navigable rivers. But the fact that the rivers of the east flowed toward the Atlantic while those of the west emptied into the Mississippi River created a problem. New Orleans was a natural market for western commerce, whereas the eastern ports—Boston, Newport, New York, Philadelphia, Baltimore, Washington, and Charleston—were inaccessible to trade from the west. As the population and commerce beyond the mountains grew, these rival cities began to search for ways to overcome the topographic barriers against western trade, each hoping to become the nation's leading port.

Their efforts were spurred by the War of 1812, which revealed America's dependence on its rivers for commerce and travel as a costly weakness. The British had only to post a few warships at the mouths of the major rivers and the resulting blockade virtually shut down American commerce. Popular support was strong after the war for the development of a more diversified transportation system.

18.1 The Erie Canal: A Brief History

A national endeavor labeled "internal improvements" was launched, encompassing such projects as roads and turnpikes to connect the cities with the countryside, artificial waterways as alternatives to river travel, and the harnessing of steam power and construction of railways. Private development funds were often augmented by financial support from local, state, and even the federal government. In 1817, the state of New York, led by Governor DeWitt Clinton, began an internal improvement that changed the nation—an artificial waterway connecting the Hudson River with the Great Lakes some 363 miles west. Completed in 1825, the Erie Canal established New York City as the first of the Atlantic ports to connect the east and the west with a convenient trade route. New York subsequently became the commercial center of the United States.

✎ *First Impressions*

A Race Begins

The other eastern ports moved quickly to establish their own connections to the west. Alexandria, Georgetown, and Washington, D.C., joined forces to build a canal from the Potomac across the Appalachians to the Ohio River, thereby gaining access to the Mississippi and its tributaries. Baltimore took a bolder course, gambling its future on an untested technology: the railroad.

18.2 America's First Trains

Source 1   **Speech of President John Quincy Adams, groundbreaking for the Chesapeake & Ohio Canal, July 4, 1828**

Friends and Fellow Citizens:

It is nearly a full century since Berkeley, Bishop of Cloyne, turning towards this fair land, which we now inhabit, the eyes of a prophet, closed a few lines of poetical inspiration with this memorable prediction—"Time's noblest empire is the last."

A prediction which, to those of us whose lot has been cast by Divine Providence in these regions, contains not only precious promise but a solemn injunction of duty, since, upon our energies, and upon those of our posterity, its fulfillment will depend. . . .

To the accomplishment of this prophecy, the first necessary step was the acquisition of the right of self-government by the people of the British North American colonies, achieved by the Declaration of Independence, and its acknowledgment by the British nation. The second was the union of all those colonies under our general confederated Government; a task more arduous than that of the preceding separation, but at last effected by the present constitution of the United States.

The third step, more arduous still than either or both the others . . . is the adaptation of the powers, physical, moral, and intellectual, of this whole Union, to the improvement of its own condition—of its moral and political condition, by wise and liberal institutions—by the cultivation of the understanding and the heart—by academies, schools and learned institutes—by the pursuit and patronage of learning and the arts—of its physical condition, by associated labor to improve the bounties, and to supplement the deficiencies of nature—to stem the torrent in its course; to level the mountain with the plain; to disarm and fetter the raging surge of the ocean. Undertakings of which the language I now hold is no exaggerated description, have become happily familiar, not only to the conceptions, but to the enterprise of our countrymen. That for the commencement of which we are here assembled, is eminent among the number. The project contemplates a conquest over physical nature, such as has never yet been achieved by man. The wonders of the ancient world, the pyramids of Egypt, the Colossus of Rhodes, the Temple of Ephesus, the Mausoleum of Artemisia, the Wall of China, sink into insignificance before it. Insignificance in the mass and momentum of human labor required for the execution. Insignificance in the comparison of the purposes to be accomplished by the work when executed. . . .

But while indulging a sentiment of joyous exaltation, at the benefits to be derived from this labor of our friends and neighbors, let us not forget that the spirit of Internal Improvement is catholic and liberal. We hope and believe that its practical advantages will be extended to every individual in our Union. In praying for the blessing of Heaven upon our task, we ask it with equal zeal and sincerity upon every other similar work within this confederation, and particularly upon that which on this same day, and perhaps at this very hour, is commencing from a neighboring city. It is one of the happiest characteristics of the principle of Internal Improvement, that the success of one great enterprise, instead of counteracting, gives assistance, to the execution of another. May they increase and multiply, till, in the sublime language of inspiration, every valley shall be exalted, and every mountain and hill shall be made low—the crooked straight, the rough places plain. Thus shall the prediction of Bishop Cloyne be converted from prophecy into history, and in the virtues and fortunes of our posterity the last shall prove the noblest Empire of Time.

Source 2 *Alexandria Gazette,* July 8, 1828

Breaking Ground upon the Canal

Friday last, the Fourth of July, the anniversary of the Declaration of Independence of the United States, was a proud day for the District of Columbia—for the States interested in an open navigation from the Chesapeake to the Lakes, and to the waters of the Mississippi—for the friends of Internal Improvements everywhere.

On that day which . . . had been fixed upon for breaking ground upon the line of the Canal, this interesting ceremony took place. . . . At an early hour, the members of the several corporations, and those who were invited to accompany them and the President and Directors of the Canal Company on this interesting excursion, began to assemble at Tilley's Hotel. . . . At half past seven o'clock, the President of the United States arrived, escorted by Captain Turner's and Captain Taylor's troops of cavalry, under command of Major Stewart. . . . Amongst the gentlemen composing the company thus assembled . . . were the Secretaries of the Treasury, War, and Navy Departments. . . .

About eight o'clock, the Procession was formed on Bridge-street, and moved on, to the excellent Music of the Full band of the Marine Corps, to High Street Wharf, where they embarked in perfect order . . . and the boats set forward, amidst the cheers of the crowds which lined the wharves.

The Steam Boat *Surprise,* followed by two other Steam Boats and a line of barges & other boats led the Procession up the Potomac, coursing the wild margin of what was once the Virginia Shore—still bordered, as when it came from the hands of its Maker, with primitive rocks, and crowded with the luxuriant and diversified foliage of its natural forest. A kindly sky shed its refreshing influence over the water, whose surface the West wind gently ruffled—The Sun shone now and then from the clear blue Heavens through fleecy clouds. All nature seemed to smile upon the scene. Along the road on the Maryland Shore, crowds of moving spectators attended the voyage of the boats, and met the procession on landing. . . .

Thousands hung upon the overlooking hill . . . and many climbed the umbrageous trees bordering the River and the Canal.

On landing from the boats and reaching the ground the Procession moved around . . . so as to leave a hollow space, in the midst of a mass of people, in the centre of which was the spot marked out . . . for the commencement of the Work. A moment's pause here occurred, while the spade, destined to commence the work, was selected . . . and the spot for breaking ground was precisely denoted.

At that moment the sun shone out from behind a cloud, and amidst a silence so intense as to chasten the animation of hope, and to hallow the enthusiasm of joy, the Mayor of Georgetown handed to Gen. Mercer . . . the consecrated instrument, which having received, he stepped forward . . . and addressed . . . the listening multitude. . . .

As soon as he had ended, the President of the United States, to whom Gen. Mercer had presented the spade, stepped forward, & with an animation of manner and countenance, which showed that his whole heart was in the thing, thus addressed the assembly of his fellow citizens . . . :

Friends and fellow-laborers—we are informed by the Holy Oracles of Truth, that at the creation of man, male and female, the Lord of the Universe, their Maker, blessed and said unto them, be fruitful and multiply, and replenish the earth, and subdue it. To subdue the earth was, therefore, one of the first duties assigned to man at his creation; and now in his fallen condition it remains among the most excellent of his occupations. To subdue the earth is preeminently the purpose of the undertaking, to the accomplishment of which the first stroke of the spade is now struck. That it is to be struck by this hand I invite you to witness—[here the stroke of the blade].

Attending this action was an incident which produced a greater sensation than any other that occurred during the day. The spade which the President held struck a root, which prevented its penetrating the earth. Not deterred by trifling obstacles from doing what he had deliberately resolved to perform, Mr. Adams tried it again, with no better success. Thus foiled, he threw down the spade, hastily stripped off and laid aside his coat, and went seriously to work.— The multitude around, on the hills and trees, who could not hear, because of their distance from the open space, but could see and understand, observing this action, raised a loud and unanimous cheering, which continued for some time after Mr. Adams had mastered the difficulty. . . .

As the President concluded, a national salute was fired by a detachment of United States Artillery posted on the ground.

Source 3 *Baltimore Patriot,* July 8, 1828

CELEBRATION OF THE 4th OF JULY IN BALTIMORE

Between seven and eight o'clock, the procession began to move . . . proceeded by Captain Cox's fine troop of horse. The PIONEERS, with their implements for working on the Rail Road, headed the civic procession. . . . These were followed by the President and Directors of the Rail Road Company, the Engineers, the Cincinnati Society, and the surviving officers and soldiers of the Revolution. Charles Carroll of Carrolton, supported by General Smith, next followed in a most splendid barouche, and was succeeded by two other carriages, in which were Mr. Stevenson, Speaker of the House of Representatives, Governor Coles, of Illinois . . . and several other gentlemen of distinction. These composed the First Division of the Procession.

The Second Division was composed of the different professions, and was the most imposing spectacle we ever saw. . . .

After arriving on the ground, the ceremonies were opened with Prayer by the Rev. Dr. Wyatt. The Declaration of Independence was then read by Col. Heath, with appropriate prefatory remarks. After which, music by an excellent band.

Mr. Morris then delivered an address on behalf of the President and Directors of the Baltimore and Ohio Rail Road. The deputation of Blacksmiths then advanced and presented to the venerable Charles Carroll of Carrolton, the pick, stone hammer and trowell, prepared by them for the commencement of the work. The deputation of Stone Cutters next advanced with the corner stone prepared by them, which was adjusted in its destined place by Mr. Carroll.

(It was a large white marble block, about 3 feet square, and one and a half feet thick, elegantly wrought, and bearing the following inscription, cut on the top of the stone:

THIS STONE,
Presented by the Stone Cutters of Baltimore,
In commemoration of the commencement of the
BALTIMORE AND OHIO RAIL ROAD, was here placed
On the 4th of July, 1828, by the
Grand Lodge of Maryland,
Assisted by CHARLES CARROLL of Carrolton,
The last surviving Signer
OF THE DECLARATION OF AMERICAN INDEPENDENCE,
And under the direction of the President and Directors
OF THE RAIL ROAD COMPANY.)

The deputation of Hatters then presented a hat to Mr. Carroll, and another to General Smith, which were made during the procession; and the Weavers and Tailors presented a coat made during the way to Mr. Carroll. The Book Binders also presented him the Engineer Report, bound in a most splendid manner. After which Mr. Carroll visited the several associations and was received on board the ship Union, commanded by Capt. Gardner, with loud cheers, when a grand National Salute was fired; after which the procession was formed . . . and returned to the city by way of Pratt Street, and was discharged in Baltimore street.

On its return the procession was joined by one hundred and eight females from the Union Factory, in large cars, tastefully decorated, and drawn each by six horses.

Source 4   *Daily National Intelligencer,* 1828

Messrs Editors:

Permit me, through the medium of your valuable paper, to form a calculation shewing the comparative costs for 200 miles on a CANAL and for the same distance on a RAIL ROAD. . . .

Let us take the article of coal . . . and rate the distance for which it is to be transported at 200 miles, either by canal or rail-road. . . .

Then, on a canal 48 feet wide and 5 feet deep, a horse will draw 30 tons at least—as this is known by his performance on much less capacious canals, *independent of the weight of the boat.*

Allow 25 miles per day for his performance in time, and we have 8 days for the journey from Cumberland.

Toll on 30 tons coal at 1 cent per ton
    per mile, the customary toll on a canal $60
Wages of 2 men and 1 boy, for 8 days, at
    $1.75 per day 14
Horse for 8 days at 50 cents per day 4
Cost per Canal $78
At 28 bushels to the ton, is 840 bushels, being about 9½ cents per bushel.

The calculation by the rail-road is extremely simple, because the toll and transportation belong *exclusively* to the Rail Road Company; . . . and the rail-road law gives the company the privilege of charging 4 cents per ton per mile, for toll and transportation, which on 30 tons coal, for 200 miles, as above, is $240.

At 28 bushels to the ton, is 840 bushels, or about 29 cents per bushel for transportation!

A Baltimorean

Source 5   **Report of Jonathon Knight, chief engineer of the Baltimore and Ohio Railroad Company, to the U.S. Congress, 1832**

Seeing . . . that the improvements in railways and cars have been such that, with a velocity of three miles per hour, the effect is greater than on a canal, and that at higher velocities, the effect will be vastly more decided in favor of the railway, . . . and when we also reflect upon the very great improvements which have, in the last few two or three years, been made in the locomotive steam engine, and consider the paramount importance of speed and certainty to a traveling and commercial people, more especially in a country of such extended surface as the United States, and that this avenue of communication will be open throughout the year, in winter as well as summer, shall we hesitate to say that a railroad should be preferred in ninety-nine cases out of a hundred?

18.3 US
History II:
Railroad Links

The Race for Ohio and the Future

It was predicted that the C&O Canal would be completed all the way to the Ohio Valley in three years. This prediction proved a bit too optimistic. After 22 years of construction, the canal was completed as far as Cumberland, Maryland, a distance of 184.5 miles from its origin in the District of Columbia. It rose from sea level to 605 feet above the sea through the use of 74 lift locks. It was a great engineering feat: feeder dams channeled water into the canal, spillways regulated the depth, aquaducts carried the canal over rivers and streams. Barges, pulled by mules walking a towpath parallel to the canal, moved along at rates approaching two miles per hour. Such speed was actually considered remarkable at the time. But the C&O Canal never brought the waters of the Chesapeake to commingle with the waters of the Ohio. It gave up on its race to the west at Cumberland, which had been reached by the railroad some eight years before it.

The B&O Railroad opened its first section, a 13-mile stretch of tracks connecting Baltimore with Ellicott's Mills, in May of 1830. In its first year of operation, the line carried 80,000 passengers. In 1831, the B&O replaced the horses that had powered its trains with steam engines capable of reaching speeds of 30 miles per hour on the straightaways. From that moment on, it became increasingly clear that the future, as well as the race for the west, would be won by the railroad rather than the canal. The railroad was completed to its terminus in Wheeling, Virginia, in 1853. The C&O Canal cost $22 million to construct. The price for the construction of the B&O Railroad was $24.8 million. Each mile of the canal cost an average of $60,000. The railroad averaged $65,500 per mile.

For much of the way to Cumberland, the tracks of the B&O still run parallel to the C&O Canal. The canal continued in operation until 1924, and today is a National Historic Trail under the jurisdiction of the National Park Service. The B&O remains in service.

📖 *Second Thoughts*

The Transportation Revolution

18.4 Transportation Developments in the Early Republic

Before 1815, there were no railroads in the United States and less than a hundred miles of canals. By 1840, there were 3,328 miles of railroad track and 3,326 miles of canal. By 1860, the number of miles of canal had grown only to 3,698, while an explosion of railroad construction had led to completion of some 30,636 miles of track.

Source 6   Thomas P. Kettrell, *Eighty Years' Progress of the United States*, 1860

Of all the marvels that have marked the present century, those which manifest themselves in the development of the means of locomotion and transportation are among the most wonderful. With the emancipation of the states from their colonial condition, and the formation of a federal government, a most extraordinary activity seems to have been imparted to the inventive faculties of the

American people, and to which side soever we direct our attention, we find that all the great and useful creations of genius that date from that auspicious event. The art of transportation has, as it were, been created. Not that our fathers were not possessed of the means of transportation by land or water, but those means were so immeasurably below those now in use, that it may be fairly claimed that a new art has been created. . . .

The condition of affairs in this country before the construction of roads is evident to the hardy pioneers of the western frontier, and has been at times common to every part of the country. . . . The best roads of the day were such as would now nowhere be tolerated; as a general thing, the water-courses, so abundant in this country, were the main arteries, and most roads were directed toward these. . . .

The number of even these roads at the date of the formation of the government was not large, nor was their quality to be admired. The streams and water-courses were well supplied with small craft, that delivered goods and produce between distant points, but where the route left the water, the transportation became difficult and expensive. The war and its success had deeply stirred the public mind, and imparted full activity to the independent genius and enterprise of the people. Those 3,000,000 of souls occupied, as it were, but a foothold of this immense continent, to the ultimate possession of the whole of which they already looked forward. The means of transportation were the first object and desire that presented themselves to thinking men. Steam, as a power of locomotion, was unknown, and the science of road making little developed. Canals, therefore, presented themselves almost simultaneously to leading men in various sections. . . .

The great success of the Erie . . . roused the emulation of other states, and during the five years succeeding the opening of the Erie the air was filled with canal projects. . . . These works were pushed to completion, under various difficulties, inasmuch as they required a large amount of money, but they had an immense influence on traffic, and called into requisition an amount of engineering skill which had never before been demanded in the country, and various success has attained the construction. . . .

These great state works have completed the connection between the Atlantic, the lakes, and the western rivers, and by so doing, have promoted the circulation of the produce of all sections in active competition. The resources of every section have been drawn out in such a manner that the whole people have had the advantages of all. . . .

While yet they were being constructed, however, a new agent of transportation had risen, which was to overshadow their importance, and reduce them to a second rank. The rejoicing for the completion of the Erie had hardly died away, before the locomotive began to throw its shadow over the future. The "astonishing speed" of steamboats and stages was about to dwindle into an intolerable tedium. The capacities of railroads had begun to be discussed, and the discussion rapidly elicited action, which did not cease to extend itself until the whole country has become covered with rails. . . .

While all these rivers, canals, and roads have been busy bringing down produce from swelling numbers of settlers, the traffic of the great outlets has been equally as active. We are to bear in mind that in 1825, when the Erie Canal opened, there was no transportation of produce from west to east of the mountains. Bearing that in mind, we shall inspect the following table with interest. It shows the tonnage and revenues of the five great outlets, for the year 1859, as follows:

Through Tonnage			
Going	*East*	*West*	*Total Tonnage*
New York Canals	2,121,672	317,459	3,781,684
New York Central	234,241	113,833	834,379
New York and Erie	200,000	60,000	869,072
Pennsylvania Railroad	129,767	103,839	1,170,240
Baltimore and Ohio Railroad	135,127	66,470	897,496
Total	3,820,807	667,601	7,552,871

Receipts			
	Freight	*Passengers*	*Total Receipts*
New York Canals (tolls)	$1,723,945	x	x
New York Central	3,337,158	$2,566,369	$6,200,848
New York and Erie	3,108,248	1,154,083	4,394,527
Pennsylvania Railroad	3,419,494	1,412,603	5,362,355
Baltimore and Ohio Railroad	1,928,411	690,207	3,613,618
Total	$14,517,246	$5,823,262	$19,571,348

Thus these five routes collected in 1859 $14,517,246 in tolls and freights, and $5,823,262 from passenger traffic. This has been the sum of the progress across the mountains east and west. The vast lines of railroads now in operation are probably more than the present wants of all parts of the country may require, but the glance we have made at the past shows that the country will very soon outgrow this supply of rails, and call for completion of those projected.

This immense length of continued rail now enables an individual to travel from one extremity of the Union to the other without fatigue; not only are the distances shortened, but every appliance for comfort makes the journey, even to invalids, commodious. For this purpose there have been recently introduced on the long lines, sleeping-cars, wherein the passenger takes his natural rest while the iron horse is whirling him toward his destination at the rate of 30 miles per hour.

***Source* 7**   *Railway World* editor J. L. Ringwalt, *Development of Transportation Systems in the United States,* 1888

[R]oads or other convenient channels of communication are the greatest aids of civilization and progress. The commercial, industrial, social, and in some respects even the moral and political conditions of a country are often controlled by the character of its available roads. There can be no genuine prosperity in large inland districts without good roads, a phrase which, at this day, means railways. Such an extraordinary movement of population from rural districts to towns and cities as has occurred during the last half century would have been impossible if existing facilities for the cheap and rapid movement of persons and property had not been provided. The mining, manufacturing, mechanical, and agricultural developments, which excite wonder and admiration, constantly contribute to the happiness of mankind, and form the vital essence of modern life, could not exist in the absence of the iron highways of the present day.

Source 8   Walter S. Sanderlin, *The Great National Project: A History of the Chesapeake and Ohio Canal,* 1946

In the turnpike and plank-road era water transportation had been less expensive than overland travel. The ratio of costs was estimated to be as high as 8 to 1 in favor of the former as late as 1822. The coming of the railroad, however, and the continual improvements in its services made the iron horse a serious threat to the flesh-and-blood mule. In the wide spaces of the United States, the saving of time in rail transportation often more than made up for the slightly lower overall cost of canal and river transportation. In the case of the Chesapeake and Ohio, the rivalry was most intense with the Baltimore and Ohio Railroad. The canal was an old, established form of transportation. . . . The railroad, on the other hand, was a novelty in America, almost a freak. It faced the necessity of building its road and winning its spurs in competition with a powerful vested interest, with only the political and financial support of Maryland behind it. As it happened, after the end of federal assistance to the canal, the aid of the state became a decisive factor in the immediate welfare of the rival projects.

    The railroad and the canal fought each other constantly and at every point. The struggle over the right of way in the Potomac valley was followed by another for the trade of the Shenandoah and upper Potomac at Harpers Ferry. Later it was the flour trade and, later still, the business of the coal mines over which they clashed. The improvements in railroad transportation and the stronger financial condition of the Baltimore and Ohio placed it in a more favorable position to endure the bitter rate wars of the late 1870's and 1880's. Eventually the canal company was driven into bankruptcy by the combined effects of the rate war which reduced its revenues and the disastrous floods of 1877, 1886, and 1889, which greatly increased its expenses. The railroad company emerged as the victor over the canal, securing control of the waterway in the course of the bankruptcy proceedings in 1890. The victory was complete and the canal was never again a serious competitor of the railroad.

Source 9   Carter Goodrich, "The Revulsion against Internal Improvements," 1950

Why, in the face of financial losses, and in the nation and the century in which the primacy of the laissez-faire philosophy was most nearly unchallenged, was government action so long continued in the important economic field of internal improvements? The financial disappointments were well known. . . . The cases of default and repudiation made the difficulties in programs of internal improvements a matter of public notoriety. "Revulsion" was often sharp, and government action frequently denounced. Why, then, was it revived so often; why did it recur in so many areas; and why did it persist so long?

In some cases the explanation can be found in the success of cynical raids on the public treasury, federal, state, or local. Smooth-tongued promoters often found the smaller communities particularly gullible. Much also must be put to the account of exuberant local optimism. . . .

The case for public action . . . often included arguments based on broader grounds than those of the prospect of return on the stocks and bonds of the enterprise itself. Appeals were made to state and local pride, or to the patriotic national purpose of binding the nation together. . . .

Geography provides a partial clue to the explanation of persistence. Public aid to improvement was often a frontier phenomenon. . . . [T]he most general statement that can be made about the differences from time to time and area to area is that governments continued to participate in the improvement program . . . until private capital and private enterprise were prepared to build the improvements which the communities thought they needed. [Henry V.] Poor's editorials emphasized the point. "No new people can afford to construct their own railroads."

Source 10   George Rogers Taylor, *The Transportation Revolution,* 1951

By 1860 the colonial orientation of the American economy . . . had disappeared, and a national economy had taken its place. No longer were more than nine-tenths of American agriculture and industry concentrated within a narrow strip extending no farther inland than a hundred miles from the Atlantic coast, nor was dependence upon foreign trade and European markets the almost universal characteristic of the economy. . . . [C]hanges, especially those of the transportation revolution, had resulted in the creation of a new and really national orientation. . . .

The great cities of the East no longer faced the sea and gave their chief attention to shipping and foreign trade. Their commerce centered increasingly now at the railroad stations rather than at the docks, and the commercial news from Mobile, Memphis, Louisville, Cleveland, and Chicago was awaited with greater interest than that from Liverpool, Marseilles, or Antwerp. But though the American economy now faced the rapidly developing West, the leadership and organizing genius remained concentrated in the great eastern cities.

Source 11   Carl Degler, *Out of Our Past,* 1970

Even before the Louisiana Purchase in 1803, the United States far exceeded in extent every country in Europe with the exception of the multinational empires of Russia and Austria-Hungary. As a result and in view of the scattered character of the settlements west of the Appalachians, the problems of communication alone were at once enormous and vital if the new nation was to stay together. At the time of the Revolution, Europeans had freely predicted that no country of such dimensions could long remain united. And when one contemplates the travel facilities of the time, the predictions have the ominous ring of truth: one and a half weeks at best to make the trip from New York to Pittsburgh in 1800; four days from New York to Washington; four weeks for the trip from New Orleans to New York. Moreover, it should be remembered that news could travel no faster in those days than a man.

Such great distances carried economic as well as political implications. It meant that surplus goods would have only local, and therefore limited, markets. . . . Politically, the geography of the country was a source of disunity. After the Revolution, thousands of Americans climbed the Appalachians to seek out the untouched territories of the West. With only primitive and tedious communications to connect them with the East, the allegiance of these Westerners was both tested and eroded by the elemental facts of topography. . . .

Though the assorted separatist conspiracies failed, there was nothing inherent in the vastness of the new country to weld it into a nation. Only improved means of communication and transport could do that, for only when a people know one another and their common land do they begin to experience that quickening of emotion and consciousness of kind called national feeling. The material foundation for the growth of a national consciousness, laid down in the first half of the nineteenth century, has come to be called the Transportation Revolution.

⚓ Questioning the Past

1. General John Mason offered the following toast at a banquet of the city fathers of the District of Columbia two days before the ceremonies launching the canal project: *"Allegheny, Mississippi, and Chesapeake*—The Mountain, from her towering cliffs, proclaims the march of science; and beckons to her summit the Father of Waters, and the widely spread estuary; their waters shall commingle." Actually, according to newspaper accounts, his was but one of 54 toasts offered during dinner. Though the papers neglected to mention how many of the city fathers slid out of their chairs and under the table during the course of the evening, they did faithfully record each toast, including this one, which seemed to capture the mood of the occasion: *"The Spirit of Internal Improvements*—its march is irrepressible with blessings; it overwhelms its opponents." What were the "irrepressible blessings" that were expected to follow a linking of the Atlantic seaboard with the Mississippi and Ohio Valleys? Why did some people oppose internal improvements? What geographical, occupational, or philosophical factors might have shaped attitudes about internal improvements?

2. What clues to the importance of internal improvements may be found in the manner in which the C&O Canal and B&O Railroad projects were launched? Why were internal improvements considered so important?

3. John Quincy Adams stated that three steps were necessary for the United States to become "time's noblest empire." Assess the validity of his assertion.

4. A single cloverleaf on an interstate highway today can cost almost as much as the entire construction of the C&O Canal. Are the construction of such highways and their massive cost a worthwhile use of limited public funds?

5. The canal and the railroad were competing systems of transportation. Making the right choice between them allowed Baltimore to emerge as the dominant commercial port of the Chesapeake region. What transportation choices face the American people today, and what implications might result from any decisions among them?

Chapter 19

Nat Turner

Nat Turner Leads a Rebellion in Virginia

August 22, 1831

From the time it was introduced until the time it was abolished, slavery was a powder keg with a short fuse. Few who were subjected to it submitted without coercion and, even then, few submitted completely. The records from America's two-century experiment in tyranny offer ample evidence of an anger seething within the slave population, an anger that often exploded in resistance.

Slaves found a variety of means to resist their bondage. Tens of thousands attempted to run away from their captors, and many of them succeeded in doing so. Those who did not flee frequently feigned illness or injury or incompetence to avoid work. Some resorted to self-mutilation and even suicide to deny their labors to their overlords. In Charleston in 1807, two shiploads of Africans starved themselves to death to escape enslavement. Resistance often took a confrontational form. There are numerous accounts of slaves setting fire to the homes and warehouses of their masters. Sabotage of the workplace was also common. Slaves sometimes murdered their owners and overseers, poison being a favored means. And, on occasion, they rebelled. In fact, scores of rebellions were attempted during the course of slavery.

✒ *First Impressions*

"I Should Commence the Great Work"

19.1 Southampton
Slave Revolt

The most famous of the slave revolts was the Southampton insurrection of Nat Turner. Turner had been born into slavery in 1800. In adulthood, he was a slave on the southeastern Virginia plantation of Joseph Travis. He was literate—an unusual skill for a slave—and a student of the Bible. He was acknowledged by whites and blacks alike as a religious leader in his locality. It was his religious faith that gave him both the inspiration and the courage to rise against his rulers in the summer of 1831.

Source 1　Writings of Nat Turner, 1831

And on the 12th of May, 1828, I heard a loud noise in the heavens, and the Spirit instantly appeared to me and said the Serpent was loosened, and Christ had laid down the yoke he had borne for the sins of man, and that I should take it on and fight against the Serpent, for the time was fast approaching when the first should be last and the last should be first. . . . And by signs in the heavens that it would make known to me when I should commence the great work—and until the first sign appeared, I should conceal it from the knowledge of men—And on the appearance of the sign, (the eclipse of the sun last February) I should arise and prepare myself, and slay my enemies with their own weapons. And immediately on the sign appearing in the heavens, the seal was removed from my lips, and I communicated the great work laid out for me to do, to four in whom I had the greatest confidence. . . . Many were the plans formed and rejected by us . . . and the time passed without our coming to any determination how to commence—Still forming new schemes and rejecting them, when the sign came again, which determined me not to wait longer.

Source 2   *Daily National Intelligencer,* August 17, 1831

The Sun.—For some days past, the sun has had an appearance by no means usual. At times it appeared of a beautiful sea-green—again it had the appearance of a surface handsomely painted, of a light blue color of different degrees of shade, and the streaks running north and south. At other times, again, it bore the appearance of a highly polished plate of silver. We do not profess to be sufficiently versed in astronomy to account for this unusual aspect of the orb of day.

Source 3   Writings of Nat Turner, 1831

On Saturday evening, the 20th of August, it was agreed between Henry, Hark and myself, to prepare a dinner the next day for the men we expected, and then to concert a plan. . . . Hark, on the following morning, brought a pig, and Henry brandy, and being joined by Sam, Nelson, Will and Jack, they prepared in the woods a dinner, where, about three o'clock, I joined them. . . . I . . . asked Will how came he there, he answered, his life was worth no more than others, and his liberty as dear to him. I asked him if he thought to obtain it? He said he would, or lose his life. . . .

[I]t was quickly agreed . . . until we had armed and equipped ourselves and gathered sufficient force, neither age nor sex was to be spared. . . .

It was then observed that I must spill the first blood. On which, armed with a hatchet, and accompanied by Will, I entered my master's chamber, it being dark, I could not give a death blow, the hatchet glanced from his head, he sprang from the bed and called his wife, it was his last word, Will laid him dead, with a blow of his axe, and Mrs. Travis shared the same fate, as she lay in bed. The murder of this family, five in number, was the work of a moment, not one of them awoke.

Source 4   *Petersburg Intelligencer,* August 26, 1831

A great excitement has prevailed in this town for some days past, in consequence of the receipt of information on Monday night last, that an insurrection had broken out among the negroes in Southampton. . . . The number of insurgents has been variously estimated from 150 to 400, acting in detached parties. From twenty-five to thirty families are said to have fallen victims to their ferocity.

Source 5   Writings of Nat Turner, 1831

I ordered them to mount and march instantly, this was about nine or ten o'clock, Monday morning. I proceeded to Mr. Levi Waller's, two or three miles distant. I took my station in the rear, and as it was my object to carry terror and devastation wherever we went, I placed fifteen or twenty of the best armed and most relied on, in front, who generally approached the houses as fast as their horses could run; this was for two purposes, to prevent escape and strike terror to the inhabitants—on this account I never got to the houses, after leaving Mrs. Whitehead's, until the murders were committed, except in one case. I sometimes got in sight in time to see the work of death completed, viewed the mangled bodies as they lay, in silent satisfaction, and immediately started in quest of other victims—having murdered Mr. Waller and ten children, we started for Mr. William Williams'—having killed him and two little boys that were there. . . . I then started for Mr. Jacob Williams, where the family were murdered. . . . Mrs. Vaughn was the next place we visited—and after murdering the family here, I determined on starting for Jerusalem—Our numbers amounted now to fifty or sixty, all mounted and armed with guns, axes, swords and clubs.

Source 6   From a white militiaman to the *Petersburg Intelligencer*

Belfield, Aug. 24, 1831

On Monday night I reached Belfield, (headquarters of the troops) and was given command of a small body, and a piece of artillery, which I stationed so as to command the bridge. I was up the whole night visiting each of my sentinels every ten minutes.

At Jerusalem the blacks made three desperate attempts to cross the bridge but were repulsed with some loss. No whites have been lost in any of the skirmishes which have taken place.

Source 7   From the *Norfolk Herald* editor to Wm. G. Lyford of Baltimore

Norfolk, August 24th, 1831

I have a horrible, a heart rending tale to relate, and lest even its worst features might be distorted by rumor and exaggeration, I have thought it proper to give you all and the worst information that has reached us through the best sources of intelligence which the nature of the case will admit.

A gentleman arrived here yesterday express from Suffolk, with intelligence from the upper part of Southampton county, stating that a band of insurgent slaves (some of them believed to be runaways from the neighboring swamps) had turned out on Sunday night last, and murdered several whole families, amounting to forty or fifty individuals. Some of the families were named, and among them was that of Mrs. Catherine Whitehead, sister of our worthy townsman, Dr. N. C. Whitehead,—who, with her son and five daughters, fell sacrifice to the savage ferocity of these demons in human shape.

The insurrection was represented as one of a most alarming character, though it is believed to have originated only in a design to plunder, and not with a view to a more important object. . . . Unfortunately a large portion of the effective male population was absent at Camp Meeting in Gates county, some miles off, a circumstance which gave a temporary security to the brigands in the perpetration of their butcheries; and the panic which they struck at the moment prevented the assembling of a force sufficient to check their career. . . .

To-day another express arrived from Suffolk, confirming the disastrous news of the preceding one, and adding still more to the number of the slain. The insurgents are believed to have from 100 to 150 mounted men, and about the same number on foot. They are armed with **fowling pieces**, clubs, &c. and have had an encounter with a small number of the militia, who killed six and took eight of them prisoners. They are said to be on their way to South Quay, probably making their way for the **Dismal Swamp**, in which they will be able to remain for a short time in security. For my part I have no fears of their doing further mischief. There is very little disaffection in the slaves generally, and they cannot muster a force sufficient to effect any object of importance. The few who have thus rushed headlong into the arena will be shot down like crows or captured and made examples of. The militia are gathering in all the neighboring counties, and utmost vigilance prevails.

Source 8   *Richmond Whig*, 1831

Thursday Evening, Aug. 25

Jerusalem, Southampton—The Richmond troops arrived here this morning a little after 9 o'clock after a rapid and most fatiguing march from Richmond. On the road we met a thousand different reports no two agreeing, and leaving it impossible to make a plausible guess at the truth. On the route from Petersburg, we found the whole country thoroughly alarmed, every man armed, the dwellings deserted by the white inhabitants, and the farms most generally left in possession of the blacks. . . . Jerusalem was never so crowded from its foundation, for besides the considerable military force assembled here, the ladies from the adjacent county, to the number of 3 or 400, have sought refuge from the appalling dangers by which they were surrounded.

Here for the first time we learnt the extent of the insurrection and the mischief perpetrated. Rumors had infinitely exaggerated the first, swelling the numbers of negroes to a thousand or 1200 men and representing its ramifications as embracing several counties . . . ; but it was hardly in the power of rumor itself, to exaggerate the atrocities which have been perpetrated by the insurgents. Whole families, father, mother, daughters, sons, sucking babes, and school children, butchered, thrown into heaps, and left to be devoured by hogs and dogs or to putrify on the spot. At Mr. Levi Waller's, his wife and ten children were murdered and piled in one bleeding heap on his floor. Waller himself was absent at the moment, but approaching while the dreadful scene was acting, was pursued, and escaped into a swamp with much difficulty. One small child in the house at the time escaped by concealing herself in the fire place, witnessing from the place of her concealment, the slaughter of the family and her elder sisters among them. Another child was cruelly wounded and left for dead, and probably will not survive. All these children was not Mr. Waller's. A school was kept near his house, at which, and between which and his house the ruthless villains murdered several of the helpless children. Many other horrors have been perpetrated. The killing as far as ascertained amount to sixty-two. A large proportion of these were women and children. . . .

The numbers engaged are not supposed to have exceeded 60. One account says a hundred—another not so many as forty. Twelve armed and resolute men were certainly competent to have quelled them at any time. But taken by surprise—with such horrors before their eyes, and trembling for their wives and children, the men, most naturally, only thought in the first place, of providing refuge for those dependent upon them. Since this has been effected, the citizens have acted with vigor. Various parties have scoured the country, and a number of the insurgents have been killed or taken. There are thirteen prisoners now in this place, one or more severely wounded; the principal of them a man about 21 called Marmaduke, who might have been a hero, judging from the magnanimity with which he bears his sufferings. He is said to be an atrocious offender, and the murderer of Miss Vaughan, celebrated for her beauty. The preacher Captain has not been taken. At the Cross Keys, summary justice in the form of decapitation has been executed on one or more prisoners: the people are, naturally enough, wound up to a high pitch of rage.

Jerusalem, Saturday, 27

Since writing the accompanying letter, which was supposed to have been sent off immediately, other prisoners have been taken, and in one or two instances, put to death by the enraged inhabitants. Some of these scenes are hardly inferior in barbarity to the atrocities of the insurgents; and it is to be feared that a spirit of vindictive ferocity has been excited, which may be productive of farther outrage, and prove discreditable to the country. Since Monday the insurgent negroes have committed no aggression, but have been dodged about in the swamps, in parties of three or four. They are hunted by the local militia with great implacability, and will all eventually be slain or made captive. All the mischief was done between Sunday morning and Monday noon. In this time, the rebels traversed a country of near 20 miles in extent, murdering every white indiscriminately and wrecking the furniture. They set fire to no houses, and as far as is known, committed no outrage on any white female. What their ulterior object was is unknown.

Monday, 29th

No murder or any other injury committed or attempted, since Monday last. All the party have been killed or taken, with the exception, as is believed, from the statement of prisoners and other information, of four to five who have retreated into a swamp, and will probably be taken. Nat, the ringleader, who calls himself General, pretends to be a Baptist preacher—a great enthusiast—declares to his comrades, that he is commissioned by Jesus Christ, and proceeds under his inspired direction—that the late singular appearance of the sun was a sign for him, &c., &c.—is among the number not yet taken.

Source 9   *Alexandria Gazette*

Tuesday Morning, August 30, 1831.—Yesterday's mail did not bring us any further intelligence relative to the disturbance in Southampton. We understand that the troops from Norfolk, Richmond, and Petersburg have returned home, their services no longer required. The militia of the adjacent counties are amply sufficient to capture the straggling parties of the broken band of marauding murderers who have so destroyed the peace of society. The *Norfolk Herald* is of our opinion that the insurrection was not the result of concert for any extent, nor rested on any combination to give it the least chance of success. This is evident from the small number of adherents which the ringleaders, with all their threats and persuasion, were able to enlist in their cause. The slaves throughout the country are generally well affected, and even faithful to their employers. A pleasing instance of this is said to have occurred while the black demons of slaughter were executing their horrid work. Before they had received any considerable increase, and in the early stage of their butcheries, they approached the dwelling of Dr. Blout, with the full purpose of murdering him and his family, when they were met by the Doctor's own servants, who resolutely opposed their entrance, declaring that they would lose every drop of blood in defence of their master and his family. The brigands still persisting, a battle ensued in which they were finally routed, leaving one of their party and two horses behind them.

Indeed all accounts now concur in representing the affair as one which [was] organized [by] a few, without any concert or understanding even with the slaves of their own county.... The number that commenced the bloody work was only seven— ... mere marauders bent on plunder; but having steeped their hands in human sacrifice, became infuriated, and, like bloodhounds, pursued the game of murder in mere wanton sport!!! As they followed their desolating career from family to family, they pressed all the men of their own color whom they fell in with to join them on pain of death, and thus accumulated a force of between one and two hundred.

Source 10   *Alexandria Gazette*

Thurs. Sept. 1, 1831

To the Editor:

That a proper discipline should be preserved among, and a reasonable strictness enforced over, a portion of our population, recent events have sufficiently proved. It is an erroneous estimate of true humanity to think otherwise; for lenity to them might be cruelty to us.... Providence has placed us in the position of *Masters,* and we must sustain that position.

Source 11   *Daily National Intelligencer,* September 15, 1831

From Southampton.—The *Richmond Compiler* states that 9 additional convictions have been made by the court of Southampton: four of the convicted have been recommended for reprieve, three of them being boys of 14 or 15 years of age, and it appearing from the evidence that they had been forced to join the banditti. The other 5 were to be hanged on Monday last.

Source 12 *Norfolk Herald*

Norfolk, Sept. 16

Trial of the Insurgents.—The Court of Southampton County have been some time engaged in the trial of the prisoners charged with the atrocious murders lately committed in that county. . . . The Court, we learn, proceeded in the examination with the utmost caution, patiently and carefully sifting the evidence, and cross examining the witnesses, with the humane determination to give the prisoners the entire benefit of a fair and impartial trial. The testimony was chiefly derived from boys 15 or 16 years of age, whom they had pressed into their service, and whose employment was to hold their horse while they perpetrated their butcheries, and who were consequently spectators of the bloody scenes they enacted. As for the prisoners themselves, they protested their innocence to the last, nor could any confession, criminating either himself or his fellows, be obtained from any of them. There were very few of them possessing even ordinary intelligence; the mass of them exhibiting extreme dullness and ignorance.

Source 13 To the *Alexandria Gazette*

Southampton County, October 18, 1831

Negroes in this county are kept under a very rigid discipline, and I fear our jails will never clear again. Capt. *Nat,* (so-called) has not as yet been taken. It is said he is still in the neighborhood and occasionally visits his home. Parties are constantly in search of him, day and night.—The reward offered for his apprehension amounts to a large sum, and would be an object with many.

Source 14 *Maryland Gazette,* October 27, 1831

From Southampton.—We learn by a gentleman from Southampton, that on Saturday last information was brought to Jerusalem by Nelson (a fellow servant of the leader of the late insurrection) that on that day he had seen NAT TURNER in the woods, who had hailed him, but that he, Nelson, seeing Nat armed, was afraid and ran from the villain. This intelligence, as might be expected, caused much sensation among the inhabitants, and in a short time 5 or 6 hundred persons were in pursuit. At the period our informant left, the brigand had not been taken, but his place of concealment (a cave not far from the scene of his atrocities) had been discovered, and some arms, provisions, &c. found. We hope soon to hear of his being in the hands of justice.

Source 15 Writings of Nat Turner, 1831

I scratched a hole under a pile of fence rails in a field, where I concealed myself for six weeks, never leaving my hiding place but for a few minutes in the dead of night to get water which was very near. . . . I know not how long I might have led this life, if accident had not betrayed me, a dog in the neighborhood passing by my hiding place one night while I was out, was attracted by some meat I had in my cave, and crawled in and stole it, and was coming out just as I returned. A few nights after, two negroes having started to go hunting with the same dog, and passed that way, the dog came again to the place, and having just gone out to walk about, discovered me and barked, on which thinking myself discovered, I spoke to them to beg concealment. On making myself known they fled from me. Knowing then they would betray me, I immediately left my hiding place, and was pursued almost incessantly until I was taken a fortnight afterwards.

Source 16 *Norfolk Herald,* November 2, 1831

NAT TURNER

We have now the satisfaction of announcing that we have information which leaves no doubt of the apprehension of this atrocious villain. It is derived from a citizen of Southampton who we saw last evening, and with whom we conversed. He states, that on Thursday last, Nat was started out of a fodder stack by a Mr. Francis, who fired at him with a pistol, but missed him and he escaped. This circumstance being made known in the neighborhood, a number of persons collected together and went in pursuit of him. On Sunday morning last, one of the party, a Mr. Phipps, came upon him in a coverture of brushwood, so suddenly that he had not time to attempt to escape, but at the risk of being shot down, and he surrendered without resistance, and was conducted to Jerusalem, where he was committed to the county jail. . . .

The scene where Nat is said to have been taken, is in the midst of the scene of his massacres, and within a mile or two of Mr. Travis's where they were commenced.

Source 17 *Attorney Thomas R. Gray,* November 1, 1831

The calm, deliberate composure with which he spoke of his late deeds and intentions, the expression of his fiend-like face when excited by enthusiasm, still bearing the stains of the blood of helpless innocence about him; clothed with rags and covered with chains; yet daring to raise his manacled hands to heaven, with a spirit soaring above the attributes of man; I looked on him and my blood curdled in my veins.

19.2 The Confessions of Nat Turner

The Trial of Nat Turner and Its Aftermath

Six days following his capture, Nat Turner stood in chains in the courtroom of the Honorable Jeremiah Cobb, judge for Southampton County. When asked his plea on charges of "conspiring to rebel and making insurrection," Turner replied that he did not feel guilty about anything.

While a heavy guard surrounded the courthouse to ensure that no attempt was made to rescue the accused, witness after witness stepped forward to charge Nat Turner with responsibility for the brutal murders of 57 white residents of the county. Turner remained composed throughout the proceeding and declined an invitation to speak in his own behalf. By the end of the day he had been convicted and condemned to death on the gallows. On November 11, before a large crowd, the sentence was carried out.

What value might be placed on the life and death of Nat Turner? According to the court, the value of Nat Turner's life was $375. Since the court did not consider him to be a human being, this amount was awarded to his owner as compensation for the state's decision to confiscate and destroy private property. The value of Turner's life, however, cannot be measured in dollars alone, for his uprising sent a shock wave across the nation. To African Americans he became a symbol of seething anger and rebellion. White Americans were forced to rethink their convictions about human bondage. As abolitionist William Lloyd Garrison wrote in the *Liberator* of September 3, 1831, "The first drops of blood, which are but the prelude to a deluge from the gathering clouds, have fallen. The first flash of lightning, which is to ignite and consume, has been felt."

In January of 1832, the Virginia House of Delegates opened a historic debate on the future of slavery in the state. Petitions had flooded the legislature in the wake of the Southampton insurrection. Some demanded tighter controls on the free black and slave population of the state. Others called for the emancipation of all slaves. After intense debate between slavery's defenders and its critics, the Virginia Assembly voted down a resolution calling for legislative action against slavery on a vote of 73 to 58.

Following Turner's revolt and the Virginia debate over slavery, southern states turned to more repressive measures to maintain control over the slave population and to ensure the perpetuation of their peculiar institution. And as the southerners grew more and more defensive of their social system, the abolitionists grew louder and louder in their denunciations of it.

Source 18   *Boston Courier*, September 1831

The proposition to establish a College at New Haven, for the education of colored People, seems likely to meet with some opposition. A public meeting of the citizens was called by the Mayor, on Saturday last, "to take into consideration a scheme for the establishment . . . of a 'College for the education of Colored Youth,' and to adopt such measures as may be deemed expedient relative to the same." We are not in the least surprised at the indisposition of the People to have this institution located amongst them. There are a variety of reasons which would make it an unpleasant addition to the public institutions of any city. The Southern States would soon be overrun with graduates preaching emancipation, and the late butcheries in Virginia be renewed under the guidance of fanatics, in every quarter of the Southern States. People who really have the disposition to benefit the blacks, may, perhaps, do something through the Colonization Society; but we know of no other manner in which they can interfere without the risk of injuring both blacks and whites.

Source 19   *New York American*, September 1831

We detest slavery—we have striven, and ever shall strive, against its extension in these United States; but, where it exists . . . we would go to the utmost length to sustain the rights and safety of those whom circumstances have placed in the relation of masters. Such, too, is, we are sure, the feeling of all sound thinking men in the free States; and upon the slightest intimation that they are required, arms, money, men, will be poured forth in profusion for the defense of our Southern brethren.

Source 20 Resolutions adopted in Anne Arundel County, Maryland, October 8, 1831

PUBLIC MEETING

At a public meeting of the citizens of the fourth election district of this county, convened . . . for the purpose of adopting measures of defence against any insurrection among the coloured population . . . , the following resolutions were read and unanimously adopted.

Resolved, That we consider the insurrection of the black population in Southampton county, Virginia, and the diabolical outrages which they committed upon the lives of the helpless and innocent, a most urgent call upon the citizens of every state and county to adopt some measures for preventing the recurrence of similar catastrophe among themselves. That whilst we are actuated by every feeling of humanity towards the coloured population of our country, we cannot, in justice to ourselves and families, refrain from the performance of an act not only necessary for our own security and defence, but which is essential to the well being and good order of the government.

Resolved therefore, That in consideration of the above mentioned melancholy and heartrending event among our Virginia brethren, and the mutinous and rebellious spirit displayed by the coloured population in various parts of the Union, we recommend to every citizen of the district to unite in an association for the purpose of visiting, regularly, the houses of free negroes, and all other places which may be suspected by them, for the prompt correction of all misconduct among them and for restraining them in their nocturnal depredations upon the property of the neighborhood. . . .

Resolved, That every man resident in this district, under the age of forty-five years, be considered as a member of a committee to be called and to act as a committee of vigilance, who are authorized and requested to arrest and retain in custody, any free coloured person found off their premises after dark, under any appearance of suspicion, and to bring them before a magistrate for examination, and when this is not practicable, to punish them at their own discretion according to the nature of the offence. . . .

Resolved, That the Delegates to the General Assembly for Anne Arundel county be requested to use their best efforts for the enactment of a law prohibiting the owners of slaves within this State from manumitting them, except on condition of their emigration to Liberia.

Source 21 *Alexandria Gazette,* 1831

New Orleans, Oct. 18

Another vessel laden with negroes arrived in this port on Sunday last from the state of Virginia. This is an early arrival; and we caution our planters, and the citizens of the state against indiscriminate purchases. The fire brand may too easily be brought among us; we should dread it, bearing in mind, that the majority of the Southampton slaves have been sentenced to transportation. We now suffer under the evil of a bad law.

Source 22 Ordinance enacted by Alexandria, D.C., October 19, 1831

AN ACT concerning Slaves, Free Negroes, and Mulattoes

Section 1. *Be it enacted by the Common Council of Alexandria,* That all meetings or assemblies of slaves, or of free negroes, and mulattoes ... at any meeting or other house, either in the day or night, under the pretense or pretext of attending a religious meeting, or for any amusement, shall be, and the same are, hereby prohibited. ... Every slave who shall be guilty of a violation of this provision of the law, shall be punished by receiving on his or her bare back not less than ten nor more than thirty lashes.

Source 23 *Richmond Enquirer,* February 4, 1832

Our oldest readers will do us justice to say, that we had forborne to touch the subject of colored population, for 27 years. ... But at length the outbreaking in Southampton spreads horror through the Commonwealth. We saw the floodgates of discussion for the first time raised in consequence of this unparalleled event.— We saw meetings of citizens held. Memorials were addressed to the Legislature.—And the Press, too, broke the silence of fifty years.

📖 *Second Thoughts*

The Spirit of Nat Turner Was Never Quelled

19.3 Chronology on the History of Slavery

Nineteenth-century commentaries on the insurrection expressed bewilderment at its motive, since Turner did not accuse his owner of cruelty. Only in later works do historians grapple with the question of whether the uprising hastened or delayed the eventual abolition of slavery.

Source 24 Virginia historian Robert R. Howison, 1846

This insurrection produced a strong movement of the public mind in Virginia. Its progress and total failure had indeed strengthened the conviction that no widespread ruin could ever be brought by her slaves. They were weak and cowardly, killing only the unarmed and feeble, and flying before any determined opposition. Yet the revolt had inflicted painful wounds; many of the young and innocent had fallen, and many had been butchered who had gained a good name for benevolence to their species. The cruelty of the slaves was the more unpardonable, because it was unprovoked. They had never been treated harshly; Nat Turner himself declared that his master was invariably kind to him. Their outrages were prompted by nothing save an inhuman fanaticism. How far they may have been stimulated by the prevalence of abolitionist doctrines, introduced among them by secret agents, has never been determined.

Source 25 Abolitionist Thomas Wentworth Higginson, "Nat Turner's Insurrection," August 1861

During the year 1831, up to the twenty-third of August, the Virginia newspapers were absorbed in the momentous problems which then occupied the minds of intelligent American citizens:—What General Jackson should do with the scolds, and what with the disreputables,—Should South Carolina be allowed to nullify? and would the wives of Cabinet Ministers call on Mrs. Eaton? It is an unfailing opiate, to turn over the drowsy files of the "Richmond Enquirer," until the moment when those dry and dusty pages are suddenly kindled into flame by the torch of Nat Turner. Then the terror flares on increasing, until far-off European colonies, Antigua, Martinique, Caraccas, Tortola, recognize by some secret sympathy the same epidemic alarms.

Source 26 John Esten Cooke, *Virginia: A History of the People,* 1888

Two sinister events of the first half century were the servile insurrections headed by Gabriel and Turner: the one in 1800, and the other in 1831. The immediate cause of these strange affairs has never been ascertained: as far as the record goes they were both the result of a frenzied desire to shed blood, without further aims.... The plausible theory that they were the result of cruelty is not supported by the facts. It is to be presumed that if cruelty had been exercised the fact would have been urged in mitigation of punishment: but the plea was not made, and Turner expressly disclaimed it. The naked fact remains, that the two leaders worked on the passions and superstitions of their people; persuaded them that the time had come to put the white race to death; and that they proceeded to do so.

Source 27 Southern historian Ulrich B. Phillips, *American Negro Slavery,* 1918

This extraordinary event ... set nerves on edge throughout the South.... The only tangible outcome ... was in the form of added legal restrictions on the colored population, slave and free. But when the fright and fervor of the year had passed, conditions normal to the community returned.... [T]he new severities of the law were promptly relegated ... to the limbo of things laid away, like pistols, for emergency use, out of sight and out of mind in the daily routine of peaceful industry.

Source 28 John Cromwell, "The Aftermath of Nat Turner's Insurrection," 1920

Whether Nat Turner hastened or postponed the day of the abolition of slavery ... is a question that admits of little or much discussion in accordance with opinions concerning the law of necessity and free will in national life. Considered in the light of its immediate effect upon its participants, it was a failure, an egregious failure, a wanton crime. Considered in its necessary relation to slavery and as contributory to making it a national issue by the deepening and stirring of the then weak local forces, that finally led to the Emancipation Proclamation and the Thirteenth Amendment, the insurrection was a moral success and Nat Turner deserves to be ranked with the greatest reformers of his day.

This insurrection may be considered an effort of the Negro to help himself rather than depend on other human agencies for the protection which could come through his own strong arm; for the spirit of Nat Turner never was completely quelled. He struck ruthlessly, mercilessly, it may be said, in cold blood, innocent women and children; but the system of which he was the victim had less mercy in subjecting his race to the horrors of the "middle passages" and the endless crimes against justice, humanity and virtue, then perpetrated throughout America. The brutality of his onslaught was a reflex of slavery, the object lesson which he gave brought the question home to every fireside until public conscience, once callous, became quickened and slavery was doomed.

Source 29   Russel B. Nye, *Fettered Freedom: Civil Liberties and the Slavery Controversy*, 1948

[T]he Vesey revolt of 1822 and the Turner revolt of 1831 made the South conscious of the possible effects on slaves of antislavery propaganda. Although it is certain that neither revolt was inspired by antislavery literature, popular opinion tended to connect them. Georgia, for example, shortly after the Turner insurrection, offered a $5000 reward for the trial and conviction "under the laws of this state, [of] the editor or publisher of a certain paper called the Liberator."

Source 30   Kenneth Stampp, *The Peculiar Institution: Slavery in the Ante-Bellum South*, 1955

No ante-bellum Southerner could ever forget Nat Turner. The career of this man made an impact upon the people of his section as great as that of John C. Calhoun or Jefferson Davis. Yet Turner was only a slave in Southampton County, Virginia—and during most of his life a rather unimpressive one at that. He was a pious man, a Baptist exhorter by avocation, apparently as humble and docile as a slave was expected to be. There is no evidence that he was underfed, overworked, or treated with special cruelty. If Nat Turner could not be trusted, what slave could? That was what made his sudden deed so frightening.

Source 31   Actor and civil rights activist Ossie Davis, "Nat Turner: Hero Reclaimed," 1968

In Harriet Beecher Stowe's *Uncle Tom's Cabin* we saw the kind of black the white man loves, and governed ourselves accordingly; in Thomas Dixon's *The Klansman* we saw the kind of black the white man fears, and governed ourselves accordingly. These books defined the limits of acceptable "Negro" behavior, and we ignored them at our peril. Hand-me-down heroes and devils from the white man, his hopes and fears done up in black face and passed along for our instruction.

But we knew all along that even as we tried to live up to their example these were *his* Negroes, not *ours*. We imitated in order to survive, but deep down inside our secret selves—in our stories, our humor, and our music—it was a different story. Deep down inside, even when we didn't know his name,

Nat Turner was always alive. Nat, by whatever name we called him, or dreamed of him, or told stories about him, Nat was our secret weapon, our ace in the hole, our private consciousness of manhood kept strictly between us. Our sacred promise to ourselves that someday . . . somehow . . . we would all rise up, black and beautiful, and throw off our Tomish ways, and stand up against the white man like men, even if it cost us our lives!

Source 32 John Hope Franklin, *From Slavery to Freedom*, 1974

The South was completely dazed by the Southampton uprising. The situation was grossly exaggerated in many communities. Some reports were that whites had been murdered by the hundreds in Virginia. Small wonder that several states felt it necessary to call special sessions of the legislature to consider the emergency. Most states strengthened their Slave Codes, and citizens literally remained awake nights waiting for the Negroes to make another break. But the uprisings continued.

Source 33 Stephen B. Oates, *The Fires of Jubilee: Nat Turner's Fierce Revolt*, 1975

Southern whites in the antebellum period never forgot Nat Turner and the violence he unleashed in southeastern Virginia. . . . In spite of all their precautions and all their resounding propaganda, they could never escape the possibility that somewhere, maybe even in their own slave quarters, another Nat Turner was plotting to rise up and slit their throats. His name became for them a symbol of black terror and violent retribution.

But for antebellum blacks—and for their descendents—the name of Nat Turner took on a profoundly different connotation. He became a legendary black hero—especially in southeastern Virginia, where blacks enshrined his name in an oral tradition that still flourishes today. They regard Nat's rebellion as the "First War" against slavery and the Civil War as the second. So in death Nat achieved a kind of victory denied him in life—he became a martyred soldier of slave liberation who broke his chains and murdered whites because slavery had murdered blacks.

⚔ Questioning the Past

1. What motivated Nat Turner to rise against the planters of Southampton? Was he a man of intellect and vision or a man overwhelmed by superstition and bad judgment? Present evidence to prove each position. Was there any way his rebellion could have won freedom for the rebels? What potential goals could such a rebellion have achieved?

2. What were the short- and long-term impacts of Nat Turner's Rebellion? What lessons might slaves and masters have learned from Nat Turner? What lessons can modern-day America learn from Nat Turner?

3. What was there about Nat Turner's Rebellion that frightened southerners in ways the myriad of previous slave revolts had not?

4. What did Ossie Davis mean when he wrote, "Deep down inside, even when we didn't know his name, Nat Turner was always alive"?

Chapter 20

Prudence Crandall

Prudence Crandall Opens a School for "Young Ladies and Little Misses of Color" *April 1, 1833*

When the aristocratic families of Canterbury, Connecticut, concluded their search for a new teacher for the school where their daughters were boarded, they were pleased to have found a young woman of good character and good credentials. Miss Prudence Crandall, their choice for principal and teacher at the Female Boarding School, was a graduate of the Friends Boarding School of Providence. She had subsequently distinguished herself as a teacher of young women at the neighboring town of Plainfield. And as for her sense of duty, her moral values, and her integrity: these virtues Prudence Crandall possessed in abundance. Indeed, her moral strength was something the townsfolk of Canterbury thought they wanted in their classroom. It ultimately led them to place her in their jail.

For the first 18 months of her tenure at the Female Boarding School of Canterbury, Prudence Crandall won nothing but the praise and admiration of the community for her efforts in instructing their daughters. She was well versed in the arts and sciences and provided her pupils not only a wealth of knowledge but also a model worthy of their emulation. She was popular with her students and respected by the citizens of Canterbury.

Things began to change for Prudence Crandall in January of 1833, however. A young lady 17 years of age approached Prudence Crandall about becoming one of her pupils. This prospective student, Sarah Harris, came from a good family and seemed genuinely interested in learning. Without hesitation, Prudence Crandall admitted Sarah Harris to the school, where she eagerly commenced her studies and quickly won the acceptance and friendship of her fellow students.

Miss Crandall, however, soon found a delegation of Canterbury's most distinguished citizens calling upon her. The delegation voiced its objection to her decision to admit Sarah Harris. They did not object because of any reservation concerning her intelligence or her character, but because Sarah Harris was black. Miss Crandall was warned that she must exclude black children from her school. Prudence Crandall replied with an announcement that henceforth she would accept only black children.

Prudence Crandall temporarily closed her school. She traveled about in New England seeking the assistance of abolitionist organizations for both financial support and recruits for her classroom. She secured financial backing and found 20 "young ladies and little misses of color" who were eager to learn. The Female Boarding School of Canterbury reopened on April 1, 1833, amid a storm of controversy.

❧ *First Impressions*

Controversy at Canterbury

The Canterbury controversy was covered widely by the newspapers of
the day, and caused a national debate of the questions raised by Prudence
Crandall's attempt to offer educational opportunities to African Americans.
The most heated debate occurred within the antislavery movement itself,
between the members of the American Colonization Society, who favored
removal from the United States of all blacks, and the antislavery societies,
which favored abolition and racial equality.

20.1 Women's
Stories

Source 1   Advertisement in *The Liberator,* March 2, 1833

PRUDENCE CRANDALL,
Principal of the Canterbury, (Conn.) Female
Boarding School,

Returns her most sincere thanks to those who have patronized her School, and
would give information that on the first Monday of April next, her school will
be opened for the reception of young Ladies and little Misses of color. The
branches taught are as follows—Reading, Writing, Arithmetic, English Grammar,
Geography, History, Natural and Moral Philosophy, Chemistry, Astronomy, Drawing and Painting, Music on the Piano, together with the French language.

The terms, including *board, washing,* and tuition, are $25 per quarter, one
half paid in advance.

For information respecting the School, reference may be made to the fol-
lowing gentlemen, viz:—Arthur Tappan, Esq., Rev. Peter Williams, Rev. Theodore
Raymond, Rev. Theodore Wright, Rev. Samuel C. Cornish, Rev. George Bourne,
Rev. Mr. Hayborn, New-York city;—Mr. James Forten, Mr. Joseph Cassey, Phila-
delphia, Pa.;—Rev. S.J. May, Brooklyn, Ct.;—Rev. Mr. Beman, Middletown, Ct.;—
Rev. S.S. Jocelyn, New-Haven, Ct.;—Wm. Lloyd Garrison, Arnold Buffum,
Boston, Mass.;—George Benson, Providence, R.I.

Canterbury, (Ct.) Feb. 25, 1833

Source 2   Resolution of Canterbury Town Meeting, March 9, 1833

Whereas it has been publicly announced, that a school is to be opened in this
town, on the 1st Monday of April next, using the language of the advertisement,
"for young ladies and little misses of color," or in other words, for the people
of color, the obvious tendency of which would be, to collect within the town
of Canterbury, large numbers of persons from other States, whose characters and
habits might be various and unknown to us, thereby rendering insecure, the
persons, property, and reputations of our own citizens. Under such circumstances, our silence might be construed as an approval of the project,

Thereupon Resolved, That the localities of a school for the people of color,
at any place within the limits of this town, for the admission of persons from
foreign jurisdictions, meets with our unqualified disapprobation and it is to be

understood that the inhabitants of Canterbury protest against it, in the most earnest manner.

20.2 Debate over School for Colored Girls

Resolved, That a Committee be now appointed, to be composed of the City authority and **Selectmen**, who shall make known to the person contemplating the establishment of said school, the sentiments and objections entertained by this meeting, in reference to said school, pointing out to her the injurious effects, and the incalculable evils, resulting from such an establishment within this town, and persuade her if possible to abandon the project.

Source 3   Henry E. Benson to William Lloyd Garrison, March 12, 1833

Providence, R. I. March 12th 1833

Mr. Wm. Lloyd Garrison,

DEAR FRIEND—You have, ere this, heard of the excitement that prevailed at Canterbury, when the intention of Miss Crandall to open a school for the education of colored females was made known to the inhabitants; and you doubtless wish to hear the result of the Town Meeting. . . .

I arrived at C. from Providence, just at the hour the *freemen* were assembling; and when I entered the meeting-house, found that a moderator had been chosen, and the warrant for the meeting read. . . . [M]y attention was soon called to a protest against the establishment of the school, signed by many of the citizens, which showed precisely the sentiments with which they regarded it. A preamble, with two resolutions annexed, was then handed to the Town Clerk: . . . and read to the people. . . .

Many remarks were offered upon these resolutions by Andrew T. Judson, Esq., Rufus Adams, and others, wholly unworthy of a civilized, much less of an enlightened, Christian community. The injury that would accrue to the town from the introduction of colored children, was represented in an awful light by Mr. Judson. He said that the state of things would be, should such a school go into operation, precisely as they now are in New-Orleans, where there is scarcely, said he, a *happy person*—that their sons and daughters would be forever ruined, and property be no longer safe. For his part, he was not willing, for the *honor* and welfare of the town, that even one corner of it should be appropriated to such a purpose. . . .

Mr. Judson farther stated that they had a law which would prevent that school from going into operation, the law that related to the introduction of foreigners. . . .

Much more was said. Yes, much more was said. Shame, shame, shame to those gentlemen who had no more honor. The character, the motives of Miss Crandall, were basely misrepresented. And you will ask, was there no one to defend her? Yes, there was *one,* one who though he did not seem altogether to approve of the school, had moral courage enough to defend her character against the base insinuations of those who had so much to say about *foreign influence* and oppression. That man was Mr. G. S. White, a tanner. He said the gentlemen were excited, and did not rightly consider what they were about to do—that the resolutions in themselves might be well enough, but he thought it going too far to bring up an old **blue law** to support them—that that law never was intended, and never could be brought to bear upon the school in question. He did not believe that such a state of things would exist as Mr. Judson had represented, if colored children were admitted into the town; for, said he, Miss Crandall is a Christian, and the evening and the morning prayer will daily ascend to the Father of mercies in their behalf, and he will vouchsafe his blessing.

Mr. White was continually interrupted. . . . Indeed, sir, during the whole time that Mr. White was speaking, the house was in the utmost confusion:—and notwithstanding every liberty was allowed Mr. Judson and Mr. Adams, none at all was allowed him. . . .

The votes upon the resolutions were unanimous. . . .

In short, such disgraceful proceedings I never witnessed, before, and little expected to witness in the middle of the nineteenth century. The present generation may hail them as just, but the next will execrate them. The names of those who have been most active in attempting the suppression of this school, may be honored now, but future ages will consign them to ignominy and shame.

I had hoped that, among the enlightened inhabitants of Connecticut, such a school would be hailed with joy. But I was deceived. Let not the voice of remonstrance against Southern tyranny be raised by the people of that State. . . .

You will doubtless ask—How does Miss Crandall bear up under such a mighty opposition? I reply—UNMOVED. Not a purpose of her heart is shaken—not a fear awakened within her bosom. Confident that she is pursuing the path of duty, she is determined to press on to the end. No persecution that can assail her, will alter the steadfast purpose of her soul.

Your friend, Henry E. Benson

Source 4   Letter to the editor, *Norwich Republican*, March 1833

Mr. Editor,—Most of your readers are probably aware that considerable excitement is at present existing in a portion of our community, respecting the location of a school in Canterbury for colored females. And as much pains have been taken to prejudice the public mind, in relation to the opposition made by the citizens of that town to the establishment of such an institution, it has been deemed a duty to all concerned, to lay before the community the real facts of the case as well as the reasons why such opposition has been made.

You are aware, sir, that there are in Boston and Providence a few, at the head of whom stands the editor of the Liberator, who have been engaged for some time past, in bitter and ceaseless hostility to the American Colonization Society. Predicating their notions on the undenied truth that all men are born free and equal, they come out with the fallacious, the unfounded, the inflammable doctrine, that forthwith and at once slavery ought to be abolished—the negroes made free, and received into the bosom of our community on a footing of perfect and entire equality. The Colonization Society they denounce as a combination for the purpose of shipping off the free blacks at the South who are seditious incendiaries and disturbers of the repose of slavery. They have heaped the most opprobrious epithets upon the leaders of the grand, noble scheme of colonizing the liberated blacks upon the coast of Africa—have ascribed the most unworthy motives to them—and at one fell sweep, have denounced the Society, comprising some of the most talented, enlightened and liberal men in the union, as cherishing the basest designs, and wishing to bind upon our country in perpetuity the curse of slavery.

These are the men, sir, who laid the foundation of this Negro School. These are the men who are industriously fanning the flame of Southern hatred toward Northern men and interests: whether or not it be their avowed or secret design, they in fact do much to cherish this sectional hostility and recrimination. These men have founded this School.

And what do they propose to do by means of this institution? Why, to break down the barriers which God has placed between blacks and whites—to manufacture *"Young Ladies of color,"* and to foist upon the community a new species of gentility, in the shape of sable belles. They propose, by softening down the rough features of the African mind, in these wenches, to cook up a palatable morsel for our white bachelors. After this precious concoction is completed, they are then to be taken by the hand, introduced into the best society, and made to aspire to the first matrimonial connections in the country. In a word, they hope to force the two races to amalgamate!

Now, what will be the actual result? Why, sir, the negress, assiduously taught her own dignity and consequence (for this is the express object of the school) comes out flaunting in all the borrowed charms of dress and fashionable demeanour. But she will be [greeted] . . . by a spontaneous, unconquerable aversion of the white toward the black. Educated and accomplished as she may be, she cannot over-leap this deep gulf which nature has dug between the two races. She will then return disappointed and angry to her primitive station and being unfitted, by an injudicious and pernicious education, for usefulness, will sink into degradation and infamy.

The facts in relation to the case are simply these. Miss Crandall was the teacher of a female school in Canterbury. Somebody persuaded her to dismiss her very interesting company of young ladies, and substitute for them, *"young ladies and little misses of color."* Preparations were accordingly made—her house and school room were furnished in a new style—and the purpose avowed, of attempting to instruct a generation of negresses in all the accomplishments and sciences enjoyed by their more favored white sisters. When the astounding news of this change in the condition of Miss C's school was made known to the public, great excitement was produced. In the immediate neighborhood of this proposed institution, such a change was deemed very reprehensible, and the collecting together such a number of blacks in their midst, was thought utterly intolerable.

A Friend of the Colonization Cause

Source 5   Letter of Canterbury Selectmen, March 22, 1833

To the American Colonization Society:

To ameliorate the unfortunate condition of a portion of the human family, in the progress of benevolence, your Society has been devised, embracing many of our worthy, humane and patriotic fellow-citizens. The whole Christian community are united in sentiment and action, to remove as fast as practicable, to their native land, those who are bound in slavery. A Territory has been ceded for their occupancy upon the shores of Africa, and funds are now accumulating to meet all the expenses of their removal, where they may forever enjoy the blessings of education and freedom. It would seem that an institution so benevolent in its character, so well adapted to the condition of its beneficiaries, and our safety, would find none to oppose it. But in this we were mistaken. . . .

A new association has been formed under the specious name of the "Anti-Slavery Society". . . . That Society . . . *oppose* the Colonization Society, on the ground that the blacks ought not to be sent out of the country, but should immediately be made free, and remain within the United States, participating in all the affairs of the Government, and on terms of *entire equality,* admitted within the bosom of our society. And last of all, in their wild career of reform, these gentlemen would justify intermarriages with the white people!!! Sentiments like these are somewhat alarming, and we have been led to an examination of their consequences, by events which have recently transpired in Canterbury, Ct. . . . Miss P. Crandall, in 1831, having received the aid of all our fellow-citizens, engaged to establish a school for *young ladies,* in this place, which was continued down to the last month, when, without consulting a single individual with whom she had made that engagement, took a journey to Providence and Boston, and soon after, unceremoniously dismissed and sent home all the young ladies, and announced her intention to convert her *female seminary* into a *school for blacks.* . . . The citizens of Canterbury assembled, and by a committee requested Miss C. to give up the project, which she declined doing. A still larger meeting . . . urged additional reasons to dissuade her, but to no purpose. A Town meeting was held on the 9th of March, when the unanimous voice of the *town* was expressed. . . .

On the 14th of March these resolutions were communicated to Miss C. by the Civil Authority and Selectmen, who renewedly stated the various objections entertained by the town, and urged the impropriety of placing such an establishment in the town *against all their wishes.* She was informed that the citizens of Canterbury were opposed to this school, which was . . . to become an auxiliary in the work of *immediate abolition,* as well as in opposing colonizing efforts. The *Liberator* was to be the mouth piece of this school, and Miss Crandall herself had declared, that *"colonizing the people of color* was a system of fraud, from beginning to end." . . .

We might here rest our cause in the hands of the public. We might ask the citizens of *any town* in New England, wherever situated, would it be well for *that town* to admit the blacks from slave States, or other States, to an unlimited extent? Once open this door, and New-England will became the **Liberia** of America!!

Source 6   Editorial, *The Abolitionist,* April 1833

We scarcely know how to comment upon the disgraceful proceedings in Canterbury. . . . We never . . . realized in its full measure and extent the blind and frantic prejudice against the people of color, which guides too many of those who style themselves Christians.

The idea entertained by the people of Canterbury that the establishment of a school for the education of twenty or thirty little girls would bring ruin upon their town, would be merely ludicrous if it had not produced such melancholy results. It is perfectly obvious that a flourishing boarding school must tend to enrich the place in which it is situated. Money must be spent there, for the support of the scholars. The resort of their relations and friends to the place to visit them must also bring money to it. Such a school could not be successful without benefiting the town.

We presume that the only serious objection to the proposed institution in Canterbury, was that its pupils were to be of the African race. Is it then to be established as a principle, that every person who has African blood in his veins, is to be denied the common means of education, by the people of New England? If not, how is the course of these misguided villagers to be justified? For no reason can be given why people of color should not be educated, which would not apply to every other place in New England as well as to Canterbury. Do we believe that colored men are to be made better by ignorance? Or that the situation of the whites is to be improved by shutting the light of knowledge from their colored brethren? If we admit that colored people have the same right to be educated as the whites, we must admit that they have a right to be educated in the same place.

Are the people of Canterbury afraid that their village will be ruined, by twenty or thirty young girls coming into it, because they are colored? If these children were to be paupers, we should not think the sensitiveness of the Canterburians so strange. But they will be the daughters of the richest and most intelligent among the colored people. It is absurd to suppose they will impose a burden on the village.

We have endeavored, but in vain, to imagine what specific evil the townsmen of Canterbury could anticipate. We can only ascribe their conduct to the workings of a deep and unrelenting prejudice against the colored people, which views with jealousy every attempt made to improve the African race among us, and wishes to drive the objects of its hatred as far as possible from its sight.

Source 7   Record of Canterbury town meeting, April 1, 1833

At a town meeting legally warned and held at Canterbury, on the 1st of April, 1833, Asahel Bacon, Esq.,

Moderator—

Voted, That a petition in behalf of the town of Canterbury, to the next general assembly, be drawn up in suitable language, deprecating the evil consequences of bringing from other towns, and other states, people of color for any purpose, and more especially for the purpose of disseminating the principles and doctrines opposed to the benevolent colonization system, praying said legislature to pass and enact such laws, as in their wisdom will prevent the evil.

The forgoing is a true copy of Record:
Examined by Andrew T. Judson, Town Clerk.

Source 8   Account of Prudence Crandall, May 7, 1833

I saw that the prejudice of the whites against color was deep and inveterate. In my humble opinion it was the strongest, if not the only chain, that bound these heavy burdens on the wretched slaves, which we ourselves are not willing to touch with one of our fingers. . . . I said in mine heart here are my convictions.

What shall I do? Shall I be inactive and permit prejudice, the mother of abominations, to remain undisturbed? Or shall I venture to enlist into the ranks of those who with the Sword of Truth dare hold combat with prevailing iniquity[?]

The Birth and Death of a Unique Institution

Twenty young African American women began their studies under the direction of Prudence Crandall on April 1, 1833. In the months after, Prudence Crandall and her pupils endured much abuse, becoming targets of a community that sought to deny them the opportunity of learning. The young women were subjected to taunts and insults by the citizens of Canterbury. They were followed by angry whites whenever they left the school grounds. Young men jeered and tooted horns at them. On occasion, they were pelted with rocks and rotten eggs. The town physician refused to answer their calls for medical care. The town pharmacist refused to sell them medicines. The shopkeepers would not sell food or other supplies for use at the school. The stage company would not transport them to or from their homes. These rebukes might have been overwhelming had not Quakers from neighboring communities, Prudence Crandall's father, Pardon Crandall, and an African American farmer with a wagon stepped forward to assure the school a continuing supply of goods and services.

In April and May of 1833, the town of Canterbury attempted to prosecute two of the students, Eliza Ann Hammond and Ann Peterson, under Connecticut's Pauper and Vagrancy Law. An obscure law, this act made it illegal for nonresidents who had no visible means of support to stay in a town for longer than ten days without the written consent of the town selectmen. The fine for violating the Pauper and Vagrancy Law was $1.67 per week; and, after ten days, those who lacked the permission of the selectmen were subject to ten lashes with a whip on the naked body. Before any penalties might be enforced upon the students, the Rev. Samuel May of Brooklyn, Connecticut, posted a $10,000 bond to cover the costs of any and all vagrancy fines. So little intimidated was Eliza Ann Hammond that she volunteered to submit to the whip. It was the townsfolk who then backed down.

The school facilities were the target of frequent vandalism. A load of manure was dumped into the school's well. Refuse from a local slaughter house was piled upon the school's front porch. Rocks were hurled through school windows at all hours of day and night. Two attempts were made to burn the school building down.

On May 24, 1833, the Connecticut legislature enacted what came to be called the Connecticut "Black Law." This act made it a crime punishable by fine for any person "to set up or establish in this State any school, academy, or literary institution for the instruction or education of colored persons, who are not inhabitants of this State . . . without the consent in writing first obtained of a majority of the civil authority, and also of the Selectmen of the town in which such school . . . is situated." It was also made a crime to teach, harbor, or board "any colored person who is not an inhabitant of any town" of Connecticut. On June 27, 1833, Prudence Crandall was arrested for violation of the Connecticut Black Law and spent that night in the county jail at Brooklyn, Connecticut. The next morning, Samuel May and other abolitionists posted her bail.

On August 23, 1833, Prudence Crandall was tried in county court. The prosecuting attorney, Andrew T. Judson, argued that the Black Law must be enforced or Connecticut would become a haven for freed slaves from the South. The judge instructed the jury that the Black Law must be considered constitutional and that the jurors had only to decide whether or not Prudence Crandall had violated it. Still, the jury was unable to reach a unanimous decision. Seven jurors voted for conviction, five favored acquittal. The judge dismissed the jury and set Prudence Crandall free.

In October, Prudence Crandall found herself again in court facing the same charges. This time she was tried before Judge David Daggett, Chief Justice of the Connecticut Supreme Court. Daggett not only was opposed to civil liberties for free blacks, he was a supporter of slavery. His charge to the jury left little room for a verdict other than guilty. Accordingly, Prudence Crandall was convicted of violating the Black Law.

Prudence Crandall meanwhile continued to operate her school while awaiting appeal of her conviction. The Supreme Court of Errors set aside her conviction in July of 1834, on grounds of insufficient information, but declined the opportunity to reverse it. On September 9, 1834, a mob attacked the Female Boarding School under the cover of darkness. Wielding iron bars and clubs, the mob members smashed windows, destroyed furniture, and left two school rooms uninhabitable. The local authorities declined either to investigate the offense or to provide protection against similar events in the future. The next morning, Prudence Crandall, with the aid of her friend Samuel May, told the children that the costs and the risks of maintaining the school were too high and they must return to their families. The school was then permanently closed.

📖 *Second Thoughts*

The Significance of Crandall and Her School

Across America in the 1830s there was a popular fear of racial equality and, especially, racial "amalgamation." In the sources that follow, commentators probe the inflamed racial feelings that the Prudence Crandall case ignited.

Source 9   Judge William Jay, *Inquiry into the Character and Tendency of the American Colonization and American Anti-Slavery Societies,* 1834

That *black* girls should presume to learn reading, and writing, and music, and geography, was past all bearing. Committee after committee waited on Miss Crandall, to remonstrate against the intended school but to no purpose. More efficient means were found necessary to avert the impending calamity, and a legal town meeting was summoned to consider the awful crisis. At this meeting resolutions were passed, expressing the strongest disapprobation of the proposed school, and the preamble declared that "the obvious tendency of this school would be to collect within the town of Canterbury, large numbers of persons from other States, whose characters and habits might be various and unknown to us, thereby rendering insecure the *persons, property, and reputations* of our citizens." Had this extreme nervous apprehension of danger, been excited in the good people of Canterbury, by the introduction of some hundreds of Irish laborers into their village to construct a rail road or canal, we should still have thought their temperament very peculiar; but when we find them thus affecting to tremble not merely for their property, but for their persons and reputations, at the approach of fifteen or twenty "young ladies and misses of color," we confess we are astonished that the collected wisdom of these people was not able to frame an argument against the school, less disgraceful to themselves.

Source 10   Interview of Prudence Crandall, age 82, by journalist George B. Thayer, 1886

My whole life has been one of opposition. I never could find anyone near me to agree with me. Even my husband opposed me, more than anyone. He would not let me read the books that he himself read, but I did read them. I read all sides, and searched for the truth whether it was in science, religion, or humanity. I sometimes think I would like to live somewhere else. Here, in Elk Falls [Kansas], there is nothing for my soul to feed upon. Nothing, unless it comes from abroad in the shape of books, newspapers, and so on. There is no public library, and there are but one or two persons in the place that I can converse with profitably for any length of time. No one visits me, and I begin to think they are afraid of me. I think the ministers are afraid I shall upset their religious beliefs, and advise the members of their congregation not to call on me, but I don't care. I speak on spiritualism sometimes, but more on temperance, and I am a self-appointed member of the International Arbitration League. I don't want to die yet. I want to live long enough to see some of these reforms consummated.

Source 11   James Schouler, *History of the United States*, 1894

In our free States all the while, the negro, though usually unmolested and permitted to earn his own livelihood, was the victim of caste from the color of his skin, and seldom encouraged to better his condition. He might brush boots, sweep a store, ply the razor, wear a livery, and perform menial work of all sorts for a living, but he was rarely a mechanic, and the idea of having him educated up to the standard of a merchant or professional man was not to be thought of. One Prudence Crandall undertook to open a school for colored girls in the town of Canterbury, Connecticut; but so furious an opposition did she stir up that the legislature reached out a hand to suppress, and after suffering brutal annoyances from her neighbors she was forced to close her establishment. And again in this proud State of the common schools, when private benefactors proposed to set up a manual-labor college for blacks in the same city as Yale, New Haven was so alarmed that at a public indignation meeting the mayor and respectable citizens joined in voting down the project and threatening resistance by all means lawful. No such sedition eggs could be laid in alert New England that the good society of the place did not sit down with its whole weight upon the nest and crush them under the rustling folds of its **bombazine** before the brood could be hatched. The utmost that private munificence could do at the North was to teach young children of the despised race apart the bare rudiments of learning, such a school thriving in New York city under Quaker auspices, through the inattention of a great populace. Negroes and mulattoes were kept humble, even in States where they were on a nominal equality with the whites; to aspire was forbidden; and while one of superior intelligence among them might direct a band of barbers or waiters of his own complexion, a white man would rather starve than work under a jet supervision in any capacity.

Source 12 Edwin and Miriam Small, "Prudence Crandall: Champion of Negro Education," 1944

Some of the irritation against the school arose from the fact that members of the community regarded themselves as the true friends of the Negro in their capacity as members of the Friends of Colonization in Africa. The insistence upon maintaining separation from people of color even in worship reflects the arguments against the amalgamation of the races voiced in letters continually printed in newspapers of the day, written usually by friends of the Cause of Colonization. This seemed the most hopeful solution to many persons, since it pointed toward a future when this country would be entirely free of the race problem. The Friends of Colonization, including many religious leaders, actively opposed any education for Negroes beyond training them to be leaders of their race in Africa, since any other efforts pointed to eventual equality, and the much-feared "amalgamation."

Source 13 Dwight Lowell Dumond, *Antislavery: The Crusade for Freedom in America,* 1961

People always have found it easy to crucify those who differ with them. They never succeed in suppressing ideas in this way, but they never fail to try, and they seem to get a sadistic pleasure from the effort. Such was the public attitude toward the slaves and the free Negroes and their antislavery friends. Great souls must always bear a certain amount of rudeness and disrespect. The liberals, the humanitarians, the intellectuals, the philanthropists, and practitioners of Christian benevolence of the 1830's were no exception. The American people in 1830, certainly, were an ill-mannered lot, and when slaveholders, men in high public office, and political newspapers chanted a hymn of hate, ill manners turned to brutality. The shame of what happened then will always be with us. It could not have happened if public officials had performed the most elementary duty of protecting persons and property. They did not do so. The caprice of public opinion in a given community at a given time took from the law control of the affairs of men. The result was either mob violence or legal persecution, or both.

The first outburst of public hostility toward Negroes and their antislavery friends to attract national attention was the Prudence Crandall case.... Sentiment in the town against Miss Crandall was whipped into a frenzy by Andrew T. Judson, ambitious local politician and guiding genius of the local colonization society.

Andrew T. Judson realized his ambition of going to Congress, but was defeated for re-election. The tide of public opinion was already running heavily against such men.

Source 14 Russel B. Nye, *Fettered Freedom: Civil Liberties and the Slave Controversy, 1830–1860,* 1963

Since both abolitionists and antiabolitionists considered the Canterbury affair as a test case, it furnished the clearest examination of the issues involved in the question of Negro education in the North. Samuel J. May, who was projected into national prominence by his part in the proceedings, believed that the importance of Prudence Crandall's right to maintain her school transcended Connecticut, that it was a question of "whether the people in any part of our land will recognize and generously protect the inalienable rights of man without distinction of color." The abolitionist lawyers based their defense on the principle that the Negro possessed an inalienable right, as well as a constitutional one, to education. [Andrew T.] Judson's prosecution rested on the thesis that the Negroes were not citizens and as such had no rights at all, that the Declaration and the Constitution had never meant them to be citizens or to have rights, and that Prudence Crandall's actions were in defiance of public policy. Quite clearly defined in the case was the popular fear of racial equality and racial amalgamation; though the school was originally intended to be biracial and was then changed to a Negro school, neither policy was acceptable to Canterbury citizens. . . . Judson informed the jury during the course of the first trial that "the professed object is to educate the blacks, but the real object is, to make the people yield their assent by degrees, to this amalgamation of the two races, and have the African race placed on the footing of perfect equality with Americans." Out of court, he spread the story that Miss Crandall's aim really was to train Negro girls as brides for New England bachelors. In addition, the antagonism of the American Colonization Society to the school served to define the divergent educational aims of the abolitionists and the colonizationists, the latter desiring to educate the Negro for life in a far-removed colony of his own race, the former wishing to prepare him for a place in American society.

Source 15 Alma Lutz, *Crusade for Freedom: Women of the Antislavery Movement,* 1968

Neither persecution, nor disappointment, nor a conservative husband, nor the traditional role of a clergyman's wife were able to close Prudence Crandall's active mind nor curb her liberal ideals. . . . This courageous woman, who faced mob violence before Garrison or any of the antislavery lecturers, blazed the trail for women in the antislavery movement.

Source 16 Eleanor Flexner, *Century of Struggle,* 1975

Prudence Crandall's struggle is all the more memorable when viewed in the context of her day. In 1833, Mount Holyoke was still a dream in Mary Lyon's mind. The voices of the first women to speak against slavery in public had not yet been raised. Yet Prudence Crandall traveled widely ("unladylike," Miss Lyon's friends called *her* fund-raising travels!), disregarded not only threats but flying stones, and carried on her school in a virtual state of siege for eighteen months. Here was a struggle to give many a woman not only food for thought but heart as well. Prudence Crandall belongs not only to the anti-slavery movement, but also to that for women's rights.

⟍ Questioning the Past

1. Why did the city leaders of Canterbury oppose a school in their community that would educate African American children? What arguments could be made to counter their concerns? Why would Prudence Crandall persist in opening a school against the wishes of the community?

2. Compare the premises of colonization and abolition. Why would these two movements come to such bitter opposition on the school question?

3. Education is the greatest of equalizers. The Virginia Assembly in the years before the Civil War stated its philosophy regarding education for African Americans, whether free or slave: "We have, as far as possible, closed every avenue by which light can enter [their] minds. If we could extinguish their capacity to see the light, our work would be completed; they would then be on a level with the beasts of the field, and we should be safe." American states, north and south, attempted to ensure that blacks would not receive the same educational opportunities as whites, not only before the Civil War, but after it. It was not until 1954 that the Supreme Court decreed that all must be given equal opportunities for learning. Nevertheless, the gap in education that is the legacy of generations of inferior schooling for blacks has yet to be closed. What would have been the short- and long-term consequences in 1833 if Connecticut and every other American state had been committed to providing for African Americans the same quality of education as was offered to whites?

Chapter 21

The Cherokee Removal

The Government Begins the Roundup of the Cherokee Nation *May 12, 1838*

When the Spanish adventurer Hernando de Soto passed through **Cherokee** country in 1540, his scribe recorded that the natives were "a very gentle people." The Cherokees lived, as they had for centuries, in villages throughout much of what is now northern Georgia and Alabama, eastern Tennessee, the western Carolinas, and southwestern Virginia. Their hunting ranges stretched across present-day Kentucky to the Ohio Valley and westward almost to the Mississippi. When European settlers began to encroach on their eastern frontiers in 1684, the Cherokees signed a treaty with the English authorities of the Colony of South Carolina. It was the first of 29 such agreements negotiated through 1835. Most often the impetus was the illegal settlement of whites on Cherokee lands, and all but the last treaty contained a common theme: The Cherokees would cede the land already occupied by squatters in exchange for an understanding that white authorities would prevent future encroachments. In each treaty the English, and later the American, authorities acknowledged Cherokee sovereignty and territorial integrity.

At the time of de Soto's visit, the Cherokee Nation had no central political authority. At the center of every village stood a council house whose interior was divided into seven sections, one for each of the Cherokee clans. Faced with an important decision, a village leader, who might be either male or female, convened the entire population in the council house for a general discussion, assisted by the Beloved Men, the clan elders. Decisions required the unanimous agreement of every man, woman, and child in the village. The earliest treaties signed by the Cherokees, probably negotiated by individual villages, ceded only their most distant hunting grounds to the white settlers. But as their borders tightened around their principal villages in Georgia and eastern Tennessee, the Cherokees were forced to add a new layer of government atop their village assemblies—a national council of representatives of each clan, who spoke for the entire nation. Following land cessions in 1819, the nation strengthened its resolve. Approached in 1823 to cede more territory, the Cherokees replied, "It is the fixed and unalterable determination of this nation never again to cede one foot more of our land." A delegation of Cherokee leaders visited Washington and informed Secretary of War John C. Calhoun that "the Cherokee are not foreigners, but original

21.1 North Georgia's Cherokee Indians

241

inhabitants of America, and that they now inhabit and stand on the soil of their own Territory, and that the limits of their Territory are defined by the Treaties which they have made with the Government of the United States, and that the States by which they are now surrounded have been created out of land which was once theirs, and that they cannot recognize the Sovereignty of any State, within the limits of their Territory."

✎ *First Impressions*

We Appeal to the Good People of the United States

But the states surrounding the Cherokees, led by Georgia, became more insistent. In 1828 Georgia extended the jurisdiction of its state laws over Cherokee lands, declared the nation's laws and customs null and void, and made provisions to survey their territory and divide it into 160 plots for distribution to white Georgians through a public lottery. The Cherokee Nation protested, but President Andrew Jackson ignored them. With his support, Congress passed the Indian Removal Act of 1830, which declared the exile of Indian nations located in the East to new lands west of the Mississippi to be in the interest of the United States. The president was given authority to choose between voluntary and forced evictions.

Once more, the Cherokees protested.

Source 1   The Cherokee National Committee and Council, July 17, 1830

To the people of the United States:

We have been called a poor, ignorant, and degraded people. We certainly are not rich; nor have we ever boasted of our knowledge, or our moral or intellectual elevation. But there is not a man within our limits so ignorant as not to know that he has a right to live on the land of his fathers, in the possession of his immemorial privileges, and that this right has been acknowledged and guaranteed by the United States; nor is there a man so degraded as not to feel a keen sense of injury, on being deprived of this right and driven into exile.

It is under a sense of the most pungent feelings that we make this, perhaps our last appeal to the good people of the United States. It cannot be that the community we are addressing, remarkable for its intelligence and religious sensibilities, and pro-eminent for its devotion to the rights of man, will lay aside this appeal, without considering that we stand in need of its sympathy and commiseration. We know that to the Christian and the philanthropist, the voice of our multiplied sorrows and fiery trials will not appear as an idle tale. In our own land, our own soil, and in our own dwellings, which we reared for our wives and for our little ones, when there was peace on our mountains and in our valleys, we are encountering troubles which cannot but try our very souls. But shall we, on account of these troubles, forsake our beloved country? Shall we be compelled by a civilized and Christian people, with whom we have lived in perfect peace for the last forty years, and for whom we have willingly bled in war, to bid a final adieu to our homes, our farms, our streams, and our beautiful forests? No. We are still firm. We intend still to cling, with our wonted affection, to the land which gave us birth, and which, every day of our lives, brings to us new and stronger ties of attachment. We appeal to the Judge of all the earth, who will finally award us justice, and to the good sense of the American people, whether we are intruders upon the land of others. Our consciences bear us witness that we are the invaders of no man's rights—we have robbed no man of his territory—we have usurped no man's authority, nor have we deprived any one of his unalienable privileges. How then shall we indirectly confess the right of another people to our land by leaving it forever? On the soil which contains the ashes of our beloved men, we wish to live, on this soil we wish to die.

We entreat those to whom the foregoing paragraphs are addressed, to remember the great law of love, "do to others as ye would that others should do to you." Let them remember that of all nations on the earth, they are under the greatest obligation to obey this law. We pray them to remember that, for the sake of principle, their forefathers were *compelled* to leave, therefore *driven* from the old world, and that the winds of persecution wafted them over the great waters, and landed them on the shores of the new world, when the Indian was the sole lord and proprietor of these extensive domains. Let them remember in what way they were greeted by the savage of America, when power was in his hand, and his ferocity could not be restrained by any human arm. We urge them to bear in mind, that those who would now ask of them a cup of cold water, and a spot of earth, a portion of their own patrimonial possessions, on which to live and die in peace, are the descendents of those whose origin, as inhabitants of North America, history and tradition are alike insufficient to reveal. Let them bring to remembrance all these facts, and they *cannot,* and we are sure, they *will* not fail to remember, and sympathize with us in these our trials and sufferings.

Source 2   **Georgia governor George Gilmer's statement to the state legislature, 1830**

Treaties were expedients by which ignorant, intractable, and savage people were induced without bloodshed to yield up what civilized people had a right to possess by virtue of that command of the Creator delivered to man upon his formation—be fruitful, multiply, and replenish the earth, and subdue it.

The Cherokee Nation

In 1827 the Cherokees had strengthened their national council with a new constitution that created a bicameral national legislature and divided the nation into eight districts. Twice annually the population of each district met at regional council houses to discuss common concerns, elect district officials, and choose representatives to the national legislature.

The central government of the Cherokee Nation undertook the task of elevating the condition of its people. It worked to improve roads and encourage commerce between the Cherokees and the outside world. It levied and collected taxes and operated a system of courts to administer justice under Cherokee law. It presided over a nation whose population not only tilled the earth but operated sawmills, gristmills, blacksmith shops, stores, ferries, and turnpikes.

21.2 History of the Cherokee

The Cherokee government ignited an intellectual explosion among the Cherokees through its promotion of a syllabary invented by a Cherokee genius named Sequoya. By encouraging the Cherokees to read and write in their own language, the Cherokee government helped its people to attain one of the highest literacy rates in the world. By purchasing printing presses in the Cherokee syllabary, the Cherokee government assured that its people would make use of this literacy. Newspapers, printed in both Cherokee and English, gave the Cherokees local and international news. Almanacs, laws, and books were printed in the 85 characters of the syllabary, and great works of the Western world were translated into Cherokee. After the Bible was translated into Cherokee, an elder member of the nation, Yonaguska, commented that "it seems to be a good book—strange that the white people are not better, having had it so long."

Though the Cherokee government labored hard to promote the prosperity of those inside its nation, it worked harder to protect its nation from the external threat. Following the Indian Removal Act of 1830 and the pressures from Georgia, the Cherokees appealed their case to public opinion in the United States and to the American judicial process. In *Worchester v. Georgia* (1832), the United States Supreme Court gave support to the Cherokee cause. Chief Justice John Marshall, speaking for the Court, ruled that "the Cherokee Nation . . . is a distinct community, occupying its own territory, with boundaries accurately described, in which the laws of Georgia can have no force. . . ."

Though it appeared to the Cherokees that they had finally found justice, their elation was short-lived. Andrew Jackson is alleged to have commented following the ruling in *Worchester v. Georgia,* "John Marshall has made his decision, now let him enforce it." Whether he uttered those words or not, Jackson's conduct betrayed his adherence to their sentiment. He refused to enforce treaty obligations toward the Cherokees and continued to press the Cherokee government to sign a treaty of removal. The Cherokees persistently refused to surrender their lands.

Finding the leaders of the Cherokee Nation steadfast in their determination not to cede any additional land to the United States, a negotiator appointed by Jackson bypassed the Cherokee government and in December of 1835 signed a treaty with 20 Cherokees who had no legal authority to speak for their people. The treaty called for the removal of the Cherokee Nation within two years and offered $5 million and some additional compensation in return. When this treaty was revealed, the Cherokee chiefs denounced it. The Cherokee legislature refused to ratify it. The Cherokee people rejected it by a petition containing the signatures of 96 percent of their entire population. But the United States Senate ratified the treaty on May 26, 1836, by a margin of a single vote.

21.3 Agreement with the Cherokee, 1835

The Cherokees were ordered to vacate their ancestral lands and move to a new homeland west of the Mississippi. Two years were allowed for preparations. On May 10, 1838, General Scott gave orders to begin the removal. The roundup of the Cherokees began on May 12.

Source 3   Proclamation of General Scott, May 10, 1838

Cherokees:—The President of the United States has sent me with a powerful army to cause you, in obedience to the treaty of 1835, to join that part of your people who are already established in prosperity on the other side of the Mississippi. Unhappily the two years allowed for that purpose you have suffered to pass without making any preparations to follow, and now the emigration must be commenced in haste, but, I hope, without disorder. I have no power, by granting a further delay, to correct the error you have committed. The full moon of May is already on the wane, and before another shall have passed away every Cherokee man, woman, and child, in these States, must be in motion to join their brethren in the far West. . . .

My troops already occupy many positions in the country you are to abandon, and thousands and thousands more are approaching from every quarter to render resistance and escape alike hopeless. . . . Will you, then, by resistance compel us to resort to arms? God forbid!

Source 4 **Statement of John Ross, principal chief of the Cherokee Nation**

Washington City, May 14th 1838

Gentlemen:
. . . I am still in the midst of efforts to prevail on the United States Government to turn aside . . . the ruin they are bringing upon my native Country; yes, Gentlemen, the ruin—and for what? Have we done any wrong? We are not charged with any. We have a Country which others covet. This is the only offense we have ever yet been charged with.

It has been said, Gentlemen, that we are obstinate and will not depart from our present possessions. We have told the United States that we are ready to go. We will not acknowledge the forgery palmed off upon the world by a knot of unauthorized individuals as a treaty, nor stir one step with reference to that false paper, and yet we are now ready, under the necessity of circumstances, to go. It is our wish to stay where we are; but to prevent strife, we are at length ready to go. We will go unforced, if the United States will pay us far less for our public lands than they demand for the wildest of their own; if they will indemnify us fairly for private claims, and for the expenses of removal; and if they will discharge the debts they owe us under former treaties. Are these conditions unreasonable?

Source 5 **General Charles Floyd, Georgia militia commander, to Georgia governor Gilmer**

18th June [1838]

Sir:
I have the pleasure to inform your excellency that I am now fully convinced there is not an Indian within the limits of my command, except a few in my possession. . . . My scouting parties have scoured the whole country without seeing an Indian, or late Indian signs. . . . Georgia is ultimately in possession of her rights in the Cherokee country.

Source 6 Message of John Ross to the Cherokee Nation

Camp Aquohee
July 21, 1838

My Friends & Fellow Citizens
From the extraordinary position in which we are placed . . . it is useless that
your patience and time should be wasted by a detailed report of the proceedings
of your Delegation who have just returned from their Mission to Washington
City. . . . Suffice, to say, that . . . your Delegation have . . . most scrupulously
observed to the best of their full abilities the known wishes and sentiments of
the whole Nation, in the support of our common rights and interests. But, when
the strong arm of power is raised against the weak and defenseless, the force of
argument must fail. Our Nation has been besieged by a powerful Army and you
have been captured in peace from your various domestic pursuits. And your
wives and children placed in forts under a military guard for the purpose of
being immediately transported to the West of the Mississippi—and a portion of
them have actually been sent off!! Your leading men feeling for your distress,
respectfully appealed to the magnanimity of the gallant and generous Commanding General for a suspension of your removal until autumn, a season more
propitious for a healthful and comfortable removal from a salubrious clime to
a sickly one. As you all well know, this petition has been favorably received and
kindly granted.

Source 7 John Benge, George C. Loury, and George Lowrey,
detachment leaders, to John Ross

Wills Valley (Cherokee Nation)
Sept. 29th 1838

Sir
We find on examination of the conditions of the detachment of Cherokees collected at this place for Emigration that many of them, say at least Two thirds
are in destitute condition and in want of shoes Clothing and Blankets. . . . The
Detachment consists of One Thousand and Ninety Persons and three families
yet to come in. We have only Eighty three Tents. You will see the necessity of
providing an additional supply as many families are compelled to start without
a Tent.

Source 8 Detachment leader Elijah Hicks, to John Ross

Port Royal near Kentucky line
Octo. 24th 1838

Dear Sir
We have progressed to this point on our journey west and shall proceed in the
morning. . . . The detachment of the people are very loth to go on, and unusually
slow in preparing for starting each morning. I am not surprised at this because

they are moving not from choice to an unknown region not desired by them, I am disposed to make full allowance for their unhappy movement.

Source 9   Detachment leader George Hicks, to John Ross

Mouse Creek
Nov. 4th 1838

Dear Sir

We are now about to take our final leave and kind farewell to our native land, the country that the Great Spirit gave our Fathers, we are on the eve of leaving that Country that gave us birth.... [W]e are forced by the authority of the white man to quit the scenes of our childhood, but stern necessity says we must go.... [W]e know that it is a laborious undertaking, but with firm resolutions we think we will be able to accomplish it, if the white citizens will permit us, but since we have been on our march many of us have been stoped and our horses taken from our Teams for the payment of unjust & just Demands, yet the Government says we must go, and its citizens say you must pay me, and if the Debtor has not the means, the property of his next friend is levied on and yet the Government has not given us our spoilations as promised. Our property has been stolen and Robed from us by white men and no means given to us to pay our Debts, when application is made to ... the agents of government, and the commanding offices of the military ... says we have no jurisdiction over any thing, only such as happens in their own sight.... They can give us no assistance, yet they have the power to force us off....

They may not think it necessary to delay any time to try to recover our property robed of us in open Day light and in open view of Hundreds. And why are they so bold. They know we are in a defenseless situation, dependent on the Government for protection who they know have denied us that protection and have made their Brags that General Scott would not intervene in our behalf. Therefore we will have to leave our property in the hands of whosoever may have the conscience to rob us of it. And those appear to be plenty since protection have been denied.

Source 10   President Martin Van Buren's second annual message to Congress, December 3, 1838

It affords me sincere pleasure to be able to apprise you of the entire removal of the Cherokee Nation of Indians to their new homes west of the Mississippi. The measures authorized by Congress at its last session, with view to the long-standing controversy with them, have had the happiest effects. By an agreement concluded with them by the commanding general in that country, who has performed the duties assigned to him on the occasion with commendable energy and humanity, their removal has been principally under the conduct of their own chiefs, and they have emigrated without any apparent reluctance.

The successful accomplishment of this important object, the removal also of the entire Creek Nation with the exception of a small number of fugitives amongst the Seminoles in Florida, the progress already made toward a speedy completion of the removal of the Chickasaws, the Choctaws, the Pottawatamies, the Ottawas, and the Chippewas, with the extensive purchases of Indian lands during the present year, have rendered the speedy and successful result of the long-established policy of the Government upon the subject of Indian affairs entirely certain. The occasion is therefore deemed a proper one to place this policy in such a point of view as will exonerate the Government of the United States from the undeserved reproach which has been cast upon it through several successive Administrations. That a mixed occupancy of the same territory by the white and red man is incompatible with the safety or happiness of either is a position in respect to which there has long since ceased to be room for a difference of opinion. Reason and experience have alike demonstrated its impracticability. The bitter fruits of every attempt heretofore to overcome the barriers interposed by nature have only been destruction, both physical and moral, to the Indian, dangerous conflicts of authority between the Federal and State Governments, and detriment to the individual prosperity of the citizen as well as to the general improvement of the country. The remedial policy, the principles of which were settled more than thirty years ago under the Administration of Mr. Jefferson, consists in an extinction, for a fair consideration, of the title to all the lands still occupied by the Indians within the States and Territories of the United States; their removal to a country west of the Mississippi much more extensive and better adapted to their condition than that on which they then resided; the guarantee to them by the United States of their exclusive possession of that country forever, exempt from all intrusions by white men, with ample provisions for their security against external violence and internal dissensions, and the extension to them of suitable facilities for their advancement in civilization. . . . The manner of its execution has, it is true, from time to time given rise to conflicts of opinion and unjust imputations; but in respect to the wisdom and necessity of the policy itself there has not from the beginning existed a doubt in the mind of every calm judicious, disinterested friend of the Indian race accustomed to reflection and enlightened by experience.

Source 11 Editorial, *Daily National Intelligencer,* December 8, 1838

We differ from the Message, in the first place, in the history of the "remedial policy," as the President terms it, which includes the removal of the Indians to a country west of the Mississippi, the principles of which he says were settled more than thirty years ago, under the Administration of Mr. Jefferson. This policy is, we apprehend, of much more recent date, and is the fruit of a different era in our national history. So far from thinking that "a mixed occupancy of the same territory by the white and red man is incompatible with the safety or happiness of either," the uniform tenor of Mr. Jefferson's communications to Congress during his Presidency was directly to the opposite effect. In his first Message to Congress, in his last, and in all the intermediate Messages, he held the same language, of which the following, from his Message of Dec. 5, 1805, affords a sample:

> Our Indian neighbors are advancing, many of them with spirit, and others beginning to engage, in the pursuits of agriculture and household manufactures. They are becoming sensible that the earth yields subsistence with less

labor and more certainty than the forest, and find it their interest, from time to time, to dispose of parts of their surplus and waste lands for the means of improving those they occupy, and of subsisting their families while they are preparing their farms.

This passage shows that Mr. Jefferson had never entertained the thought of removing these Indians beyond the reach of white men, or of any such thing as the extinction of the title of the Indians to all the lands within the States and Territories of the United States. He was bent upon domesticating the red man, and not upon expelling him from the bounds of civilization.

This difference from the statement of the Message on a mere point of history is, however, of much less interest to us than the dissent we feel ourselves bound to avow, from the opinion expressed in the Message, that the "dealings of this Government with the Indians have been *just* and friendly throughout." Would that we *could* conscientiously affirm or tacitly admit this claim of credit for justice towards the Indians throughout! But we cannot. We have, it is true, paid and stipulated for the payment of vast sums of money in exchange for Indian titles; and if the Indians received all this money, instead of being fleeced out of a great proportion of their claims by cunning and grasping white men, they have had it squandered upon them, even to extravagance. But this, unhappily, does not constitute justice; and we should be just, in all things, before we are generous. Before we can claim for our Government the credit for having dealt *justly* with the Indians, we must sponge from the tablet of memory the enforcement of a treaty with the Seminoles which the Seminoles never made; the removal of the Creeks from their lands in the face of a solemn covenant; the refusal to fulfill our treaty stipulations with the Cherokees for ten years; and the final enforcement of a treaty to which they never assented, and which never could have been carried into execution but by an armed force which it was in vain for them to contend against.

Source 12 "A Native of Maine Traveling in the Western Country," *New York Observer*, December 1838

We met several detachments in the southern part of Kentucky on the 4th, 5th and 6th of December. . . . The last detachment which we passed on the 7th embraced . . . two thousand Indians. . . . The sick and feeble were carried in waggons—about as comfortable for travel as a New England ox cart with a covering over it—a great many ride on horseback and multitudes go on foot— even aged females, apparently nearly ready to drop into the grave, were traveling with heavy burdens attached to the back—on the sometimes frozen ground, and sometimes muddy streets, with no covering for the feet except what nature had given them. . . . We learned from the inhabitants on the road where the Indians passed, that they buried fourteen or fifteen at every stopping place, and they made a journey of ten miles per day only on an average. . . .

The Indians as a whole carry in their countenances every thing but the appearance of happiness. Some carry a downcast dejected look bordering upon the appearance of despair; others a wild frantic appearance as if about to burst the chains of nature and pounce like a tiger upon their enemies. . . . Most of them seemed intelligent and refined. . . . Some of the Cherokee are wealthy and travel in style. One lady passed on in her **hack** in company with her husband, apparently with as much refinement and equipage as any of the mothers of New England; and she was a mother too and her youngest child about three years old was sick in her arms, and all she could do was to make it comfortable as circumstances would permit. . . . [S]he could only carry her dying child in her arms a few miles farther, and then she must stop in a stranger land and consign her much loved babe to the cold ground, and that too without pomp or ceremony, and pass on with the multitude. . . .

When I past the last detachment of those suffering exiles and thought that my native countrymen had thus expelled them from their native soil and their much loved homes, and that too in this inclement season of the year in all their suffering, I turned from the sight with feelings which language cannot express and 'wept like childhood then.' . . .

When I read in the President's Message that he was happy to inform the Senate that the Cherokees were peaceably and without reluctance removed—and remember that it was on the third day of December when not one of the detachments had reached their destination; and that a large majority had not made even half their journey when he made that declaration, I thought I wished the President could have been there that very day in Kentucky with myself, and have seen the comfort and the willingness with which the Cherokees were making their journey.

Source 13   Account of the Reverend Evan Jones, December 30, 1838

Travelling along the Trail of Tears

We have now been on our road to Arkansas seventy-five days, and have traveled five hundred and twenty-nine miles. We are still nearly three hundred miles short of our destination. It has been exceedingly cold. . . . At the Mississippi River, we were stopped from crossing, by the ice . . . for several days. . . . I am afraid that with all the care that can be exercised . . . , there will be an immense amount of suffering, and loss of life attending the removal. Great numbers of the old, the young, and the infirm will inevitably be sacrificed. . . . And the fact that the removal is effected by coercion makes it the more galling to the feelings of the survivors.

Source 14   Report of the Commissioner of Indian Affairs, 1839

The case of the Cherokees is a striking example of the liberality of the Government in all its branches. . . . A retrospect of the last eight months in reference to this numerous and more than ordinarily enlightened tribe cannot fail to be refreshing to well constituted minds. . . . If our acts have been generous, they have not been less wise and politic. . . . Good feeling has been preserved, and we have quietly and gently transported 18,000 friends to the west bank of the Mississippi.

📖 *Second Thoughts*
A Weight of Grief and Pathos

After their resettlement west of the Mississippi, the Cherokees set about reconstructing their civilization. By the 1870s, they had reestablished their government, purchased new printing presses for their syllabary, resumed publication of a national newspaper, and founded a school system that included two institutions of higher learning. Their population had begun to grow, and their nation was again achieving a measure of prosperity. However, by the 1890s, the advance of the white frontier again engulfed their lands. Several cessions were forced upon them in the two decades before Oklahoma was admitted to statehood. With Oklahoma statehood in 1907, the Cherokees finally lost the right of self-government that they had exercised from the days before recorded history.

Source 15 Wilson Lumpkin, governor of Georgia from 1831 through 1835, *The Removal of the Cherokee Indians from Georgia*, 1852

I entered upon the duties of the Executive office resolved, as far as my duties were involved on questions connected with the constitutional rights of Georgia, to yield nothing to Federal usurpation in any of its departments. Moreover, I knew that my views in regard to the management of our then existing Indian affairs would at once bring me into conflict with the Supreme Court of the United States. . . . Northern fanatics and an assuming State and Federal Judiciary [had] combined to sustain the pretensions of Indian sovereignty. Therefore, regardless of the opinions of religious fanaticism, of selfish and corrupt lawyers, State Judiciary, or Supreme Courts, I studied well the rights of the State, natural law, the policy and history of the past, the present condition of things, and marched forward, as the record of the country will prove, to triumph and success, against an opposition unparalleled in our history. I suffered no court to determine for me, as the Executive of Georgia, what were my constitutional duties. I felt bound by my oath of office to judge for myself in regard to my duty. And this policy, and this alone, brought our Indian troubles to a speedy and successful close—a termination so advantageous to Georgia, in the speedy development of all her great national resources, the great increase of her population, wealth and prosperity. And the Cherokees themselves derived even greater benefits from this policy. They escaped from a certain destruction which was rapidly consuming them. They changed a land of affliction, trouble and deep distress for a country far better suited to all their capacities and necessities.

Source 16 Novelist Helen Hunt Jackson, *Century of Dishonor*, 1881

In the whole history of our Government's dealings with the Indian tribes, there is no record so black as the record of its perfidy to this nation. There will come a time in the remote future when, to the student of American history, it will seem well-nigh incredible. From the beginning of the century they had been steadily advancing in civilization. As far back as 1800 they had begun the manufacturing of cotton cloth, and in 1820 there was scarcely a family in that part of the nation living east of the Mississippi but what understood the use of the **card** and the spinning-wheel. Every family had its farm under cultivation. The territory was laid off into districts, with a council-house, a judge, and a marshal in each district. A national committee and council were the supreme authority in the nation. Schools were flourishing in all the villages. Printing-presses were at work. Their territory was larger than the three States of Massachusetts, Rhode Island, and Connecticut combined. . . . There is no instance in all history of a race of people passing in so short a span of time from the barbarous stage to the agricultural and civilized. And it was such a community as this that the State of Georgia, by one high-handed outrage, made outlaws!—passing on the 19th of December, 1829, a law "to annul all laws and ordinances made by the Cherokee nation of Indians"; declaring "all laws, ordinances, orders, and regulations of any kind whatever, made, passed, or enacted by the Cherokee Indians, either in general council or in any way whatever, or by any authority whatever, null and void, and of no effect, as if the same had never existed; also, that no Indian, or descendent of any Indian residing within the Creek or Cherokee nations of Indians, shall be deemed a competent witness in any court of this State to which a white man may be a party."

What had so changed the attitude of Georgia to the Indians within her borders? Simply the fact that the Indians, finding themselves hemmed in on all sides by fast-thickening white settlements, had taken a firm stand that they would give up no more land. So long as they would cede and cede, and grant and grant tract after tract, and had millions of acres still left to cede and grant, the selfishness of white men took no alarm; but once consolidated into an empire, with fixed and inalienable boundaries, powerful, recognized, and determined, the Cherokee nation would be a thorn in the flesh to her white neighbors. The doom of the Cherokees was sealed on the day when they declared, once and for all, officially as a nation, that they would not sell another foot of land. This they did in an interesting and pathetic message to the United States Senate in 1822.

Source 17 James Schouler, *History of the United States,* 1894

Northern philanthropists, always sentimental, leaned to the side of these Indians, too far off for disagreeable neighbors, who were yielding to Christian influences and the arts of civilized life; but white men of the South in their immediate vicinity could ill brook the equality of a race of different complexion from their own. . . . Our Indian policy of wardship had led to miserable makeshifts, and this nursing of a red nation within the precincts of a State was one of them. It was like suckling a tiger's whelps in the lion's den. . . . Disheartened in their hopeless struggle for equal rights with the white man, the Cherokees joined the dusky herd of children that was being half coaxed, half driven, in these years across the Mississippi, and in the land of the setting sun they relapsed into happier barbarism.

Source 18 Anthropologist James Mooney, *Historical Sketch of the Cherokee,* 1900

The history of this Cherokee removal of 1838, as gleaned from the lips of actors in the tragedy, may well exceed in weight of grief and pathos any other passage in American history. . . . Under Scott's orders the troops were disposed at various points throughout the Cherokee country, where stockade forts were erected for gathering in and holding the Indians preparatory to removal. From these, squads of troops were sent to search out with rifle and bayonet every small cabin hidden away in the coves or by the sides of mountain streams, to seize and bring in as prisoners all the occupants, however and wherever they might be found. Families at dinner were startled by the sudden gleam of bayonets in the doorway and rose up to be driven with blows and oaths along the weary miles of trail that led to the stockade. Men were seized in their fields or going along the road, women were taken from their wheels and children from their play. In many cases, on turning for one last look as they crossed the ridge, they saw their homes in flames, fired by the lawless rabble that followed on the heels of the soldiers to loot and pillage. So keen were these outlaws on the scent that in some instances they were driving off the cattle and other stock of the Indians almost before the soldiers had fairly started their owners in the other direction. Systematic hunts were made by the same men for Indian graves, to rob them of the silver pendants and other valuables deposited with the dead. A Georgia volunteer, afterward a colonel in the Confederate service, said, "I fought through the civil war and have seen men shot to pieces and slaughtered by the thousands, but the Cherokee removal was the cruelest work I ever knew." . . .

To prevent escape the soldiers had been ordered to approach and surround each house, so far as possible, so as to come upon the occupants without warning. One old patriarch, when thus surprised, calmly called his children and grandchildren around him, and, kneeling down, bid them pray with him in their own language, while the astonished soldiers looked on in silence. Then rising he led the way into exile. A woman, on finding the house surrounded, went to the door and called up the chickens to be fed for the last time, after which, taking her infant on her back and her two other children by the hand, she followed her husband with the soldiers. . . .

When nearly seventeen thousand Cherokee had thus been gathered into the various stockades the work of removal began. . . . Hundreds died in the stockades and the waiting camps, chiefly by reason of the rations furnished. . . . Hundreds of others died soon after their arrival in Indian territory, from sickness and exposure on the journey. Altogether it is asserted, probably with reason, that over 4,000 Cherokee died as the direct result of the removal.

Source 19 Ulrich B. Phillips, *Georgia and States Rights,* 1902

After 1795 no considerable portion of the Cherokee Nation was at any time seriously inclined to war. . . . The chief complaint which Georgia could make of them in later years was that they kept possession of the soil, while white men wanted to secure it for themselves. . . .

As a matter of fact, the average member of the tribe, while not savage, was heavy and stupid; but the nation was under the complete control of its chiefs, who were usually half-breeds, or white men married into the nation. Many of these chiefs were intelligent and wealthy, but their followers continued to live from hand to mouth, with little ambition to better themselves. . . .

The Cherokee national constitution was adopted in a convention of representatives on July 26, 1827. It asserted that the Cherokee Indians constituted one of the sovereign and independent nations of the earth, having complete jurisdiction over its territory, to the exclusion of the authority of any State, and it provided for a representative system of government, modeled upon that of the United States.

Of course Georgia could not countenance such a procedure.

Source 20   Grant Foreman, *Indian Removal*, 1932

More than white people they cherished a passionate attachment for the earth that held the bones of their ancestors and relatives. The trees that shaded their homes, the cooling spring that ministered to every family, friendly watercourses, familiar trails and prospects, **busk** grounds, and council houses were their property and their friends; these simple possessions filled their lives; their loss was cataclysmic. It is doubtful if white people with their readier adaptability can understand the sense of grief and desolation that overwhelmed the Indians when they were compelled to leave all these behind forever and begin the long sad journey toward the setting sun which they called the Trail of Tears.

Source 21   Albert K. Weinberg, *Manifest Destiny*, 1935

It is generally believed that the motives of Indian policy were, if not profoundly villainous, at least not illustrative of the role of moral ideology in politics.

But an expansionist society "never admits that it is doing violence to its moral instincts" and is least disposed to do so when this violence is condemned by others. Thus in a congressional debate of 1830 an advocate of Indian removal contended with apparent sincerity that he had "advanced no principle inconsistent with the most rigid morality." So little, indeed, had the principles advanced appeared immoral to their exponents that the ultimate authority for them was ascribed to God. The principles centered in a philosophy of the use of the soil. The white race seemed to Senator Benton to have a superior right to land because they "used it according to the intentions of the Creator." The theory that a use of the soil was ordained by God or morality figured not only in the entire history of Indian relations but also in all issues in which Americans found themselves desiring soil occupied by an "inferior" race. . . .

This argument for dispossession developed as jurists of the natural law school based the criteria of sovereignty over new lands upon the utilitarian values suggested by the crowded conditions of the Old World. . . . Pasturage and hunting . . . required too much soil and did not develop civilization; therefore property claims based upon a nomadic mode of life were not justified by natural law. . . .

The moral philosophy of dispossession had been founded and developed in a time when the Indians were huntsmen. . . . But one of the tribes, the very tribe upon which the controversy of the twenties centered, had turned to agriculture as though with a perverse intention of confounding the race desirous of their removal! This was the Cherokee nation of Georgia.

The whole difficulty with the Cherokees, Calhoun observed in a cabinet meeting, arose from their progress in civilization.... In Governor Troup's exposition of the "destiny which is fixed and unchangeable" it was made clear that, though the Georgian soil was destined to be tilled, it was destined to be tilled by the white man and not by the Indian.... It is (therefore) because of the possessive instinct and not the plough that the soil is destined for the race using the cannon rather than the bow and arrow.

Source 22   E. Merton Coulter, *Georgia: A Short History,* 1947

This threat of being deprived of a great part of her domain by an alien and semi-barbarous people appeared intolerable and unthinkable to Georgia; she would resist it to the utmost limits.... John Forsyth, former minister to Spain and now governor, put a swift end to this new nation trying to erect itself in the state of Georgia. He recommended to the legislature that it extend the laws of the state over the Cherokee country, since it was as much a part of Georgia as was the remainder of the state, and that body proceeded to do so on December 20, 1828. Two years later it forbade the Indians to play longer with their make-believe government. Now, there was no Cherokee nation nor were there treaty rights....

Georgia's long struggle with the Indians was of widespread interest.... It upset Congress frequently and brought into play the oratory of Clay, Webster, and Calhoun as well as the heated clashes of others. It became a subject of angry conversation among abolitionist groups and Northern sewing circles, and led to the widening of the ugly rift of sectionalism, which slavery had already created. Georgia heard enough to make her resent Northerners coming south to exploit these troubles....

Though Georgia was not the only state to have Indians, she had greater difficulty than any other in getting rid of them or settling their status.... It had happened that more through natural developments than design, the United States had cleared out most of the Indians from the states north of the Mason and Dixon Line and of the Ohio River, while they remained in great strength in the South. This led Georgia to charge sectional partiality.

With the Indians finally out of the way, Georgia was for the first time in her existence master of her own territorial destiny. Now she was unshackled; with exuberance and enthusiasm she could now move forward.

Source 23   Russell Thornton, "The Demography of the Trail of Tears Period: A New Estimate of Cherokee Population Losses," 1991

[T]he demographic devastation of Cherokee removal was far more severe than has yet been realized. Over 10,000 additional Cherokees would have been alive sometime during the period 1835 to 1840 had Cherokee removal not occurred. Not all of this population represents deaths, to be sure; a number of nonbirths (those that would be expected statistically that did not occur) were involved undoubtedly, as were some number of lost migrants. One must remember, too, that many Cherokees, perhaps a few thousand, would have died anyway during the time period had removal not occurred. Nevertheless, the five-year mortality

21.4 The Cherokee Trail of Tears

estimate of 10,362 suggests that Cherokee deaths directly due to removal far exceeded the number of 4,000 generally accepted by contemporary scholars. A total mortality figure of 8,000 for the Trail of Tears period, twice the supposed 4,000, may not be at all unreasonable.

Source 24   Theda Perdue and Michael Green, *The Cherokee Removal,* 1995

To focus solely on the tragedies of Cherokee history, even the tragedy of the removal, is to tell only part of the Cherokee's story. The adaptability, resilience, creativity, and persistence of the Cherokee People also characterize their past. Following removal the Cherokees reestablished their republican political institutions and elected John Ross principal chief, a position he held until his death in 1866. Missionaries built churches and schools, and the Nation developed a system of public instruction including the Cherokee Male and Female Seminaries, institutions of higher education, which opened in the 1850s. The Nation replaced the press that had been lost in removal, and the *Cherokee Advocate* began publication. The Cherokee's struggle, however, was not over. The American Civil War reopened old wounds, and the Cherokee Nation divided its allegiance between Union and Confederacy. Invading troops as well as Native partisans on both sides destroyed property, neighbor killed neighbor, and at war's end the Cherokee Nation had twelve hundred orphans. Once again, the Cherokees rebuilt. The former Confederates failed in their attempt to divide the Nation, and reconstruction brought a realignment of factions that resulted in a period of peace and unity. New challenges appeared when railroads, granted rights-of-way in the Reconstruction treaties, laid their tracks and encouraged further economic development. Some Cherokees profited, but many looked on in dismay as whites poured into the Nation to take advantage of new economic opportunities. By the end of the century, a policy was in place to allot Cherokee lands to individuals, open excess land to white settlement, dissolve the government of the Cherokee Nation, and create the state of Oklahoma, which gained admission to the Union in 1907. Even then, the Cherokees did not disappear. From traditionalists who found solace performing ancient rituals at ceremonial grounds to highly acculturated individuals who proudly held on to their Indian identity, the Oklahoma Cherokees endured without a land base or a tribe that had governing powers. In North Carolina, a much smaller group that had avoided removal maintained both their ethnicity and their land base. Today the Cherokee Nation in Oklahoma numbers a quarter of a million while the Eastern band of Cherokee Indians in North Carolina has ten thousand members. They form separate tribes that have distinct treaties and agreements with the federal government. But each year these groups commemorate their common history and the tragedy that separated them at two major events—the Trail of Tears Singing, a gospel music festival in the Snow Bird community in western North Carolina, and a joint council meeting at Red Clay in Tennessee, the site of the last council before removal. Removal is still the central event in their lives as Cherokees. By rising above that terrible tragedy and refusing to be merely victims, however, the Cherokees force us to confront the removal policy and acknowledge the viability of cultural pluralism in modern America.

Questioning the Past

1. John Marshall, writing the opinion of the Supreme Court, stated that "the Cherokee Nation . . . is a distinct community, occupying its own territory, with boundaries accurately described, in which the laws of Georgia can have no force. . . ." Defend this statement. Argue the other side of the question. Which argument is the more persuasive?

2. What motivated United States policy toward the Cherokee people? Why did the United States remove the Cherokees from Cherokee lands? Why did the Cherokees respond to U.S. policy in the manner they did? What alternatives were available to both parties?

3. "The progress of the Cherokees was especially rapid," Angie Debo wrote in 1940 in *And Still the Waters Run.* "But this advancement in civilization only provoked the frontiersmen to increased hostility." Explain this paradox.

4. For untold centuries the Cherokee people made their own laws in a democratic manner. For the last century and a half they have been forced to accept the sovereignty of the United States over their lives and their lands. There are examples in Europe—Andorra, San Marino, Monaco—of small countries within large countries, and there are member-states of the United Nations with less population and land than those of the Navajo and some other Native American nations. Argue the case for and against the reestablishment within the United States of independent Native American countries.

Chapter 22

The Texas Question

A Tragic Accident Changes the Course of Annexation   *February 28, 1844*

By the 1830s, the slavery question had infected the national debate on almost every issue, especially the fate of Texas, then a part of Mexico. After the Louisiana Purchase in 1803, many in the United States, particularly those in the South, sought the addition of Texas to the Union. Following Mexico's independence from Spain in 1821, Americans settled in Texas at the invitation of the new Mexican government. By 1830, more than 20,000 white Americans had immigrated, attracted to the fertile farm lands, bringing with them some 2,000 slaves. Settlers from the United States soon outnumbered the Mexicans in the territory. In October of 1835, the Texans rose in revolt, angered by political, cultural, and economic grievances with Mexico, as well as by the decision of Mexico to abolish slavery. In December, the rebel forces in Texas captured San Antonio, the territory's largest city, but were unable to hold it. A Mexican army overwhelmed the rebel defenders of San Antonio at the Alamo on March 6, 1836. Six weeks later, however, the decisive battle was fought at San Jacinto, near present-day Houston, and this engagement resulted in a decisive victory for the Texans.

With the treaties signed on the San Jacinto battlefield, Texas became an independent country. Leaders of the Republic of Texas petitioned for admission to statehood in the United States, but the request was not well received. President Jackson, and President Van Buren after him, feared that annexation of Texas would not only provoke war with Mexico but add fuel to the burning debate over slavery. The southern states, led by John C. Calhoun of South Carolina, wanted to expand the number of slave states, while northern leaders did not. The issue of annexation dogged the administration of President John Tyler, who as vice president had succeeded to the presidency upon the death, one month into his term, of President William Henry Harrison.

22.1 Lone Star Junction

✐ *First Impressions*

The Question of Slavery in Texas

The Republic of Texas led a difficult early life. Financing proved difficult and its efforts to obtain loans from foreign governments failed. Great Britain, too, was in the forefront of an international crusade against slavery, and fears that the British would work to undermine slavery in the Republic of Texas caused great anxiety among southerners. President Tyler and his

secretary of state, Abel Upshur, in the early months of 1844, were negotiating with Texas over an annexation treaty when a tragic accident altered
the course of the Texas acquisition.

Source 1　Duff Green, special American envoy to England, to John C.
Calhoun

London, Aug 2nd [1843]

My Dear Sir,

I have been a close observer of events here and have had access to the most
accurate sources of intelligence. There are a few facts which deserve your most
serious consideration. . . .

The Abolitionists of Texas have deputed a Mr. Andrews as an agent, with
a proposition to this Government for a loan to be applied to the purchase &
emancipation of the slaves of Texas and Lord Aberdeen told Mr. Smith the Texian
Chargé that the British Govt deem it so important to prevent the annexation of
Texas to the United States, that they were disposed to support the loan if it
should be required to prevent annexation.

Source 2　John C. Calhoun to Secretary of State Abel P. Upshur

[August 27, 1843]

You do not, in my opinion, attach too much importance to the designs of Great
Britain in Texas. That she is using all her diplomatic arts and influence to abolish
slavery there, with the intention of abolishing it in the United States, there can
no longer be a doubt. . . .

That her object is power and monopoly, and abolition but the pretext, I
hold to be not less clear. . . .

If she can carry out her schemes in Texas, & through them her designs
against the Southern States, it would prove the profoundest & most successful
stroke of policy she ever made; and would go far towards giving her the exclusive
control of the cotton trade, the greatest trade, by far, of modern Commerce.
This she sees and is prepared to exert every nerve to accomplish it.

The danger is great & menacing, involving in its consequences the safety
of the Union and the very existence of the South.

Source 3　William S. Murphy, U.S. minister to Texas, to Abel Upshur

September 24, 1843

I learn here that the plan proposed . . . to Lord Aberdeen . . . was this: that the
abolition society of London should raise a fund sufficient for the purchase of all
the slaves in Texas, and place it under the control of the Government of Texas.

The Government of Texas would grant land to the abolition society, fully
and amply sufficient to secure the society against all loss, and be to the society
a vast fund, in addition to their advances, for their future operations (in the
United States of course).

The British Government entered warmly into the plan, and offered to secure the payment of the money to Texas. . . . And if there was the least delay in the payment of the money, after the regular transfer of the lands, England would pay the interest during the delay.

Source 4   Public letter of Senator Richard J. Walker of Mississippi

Washington City, Jan. 8, 1844

Does . . . humanity require that we should render the blacks more debased and miserable, by this process of abolition, with greater temptations to crime, with more of real guilt, and less of actual comforts? As the free blacks are thrown more and more upon the cities of the North, and compete more there with the white laborer, the condition of the blacks becomes worse and more perilous every day, until we have already seen, the masses of Cincinnati and Philadelphia rise to expel the negro race beyond their limits. Immediate abolition, whilst it deprived the South of the means to purchase the products and manufactures of the North and West, would fill those States with an inundation of free black population, that would be absolutely intolerable. . . .

It was in view, no doubt, of these facts that Mr. Davis, of New York, declared, upon the floor of Congress, on the 29th December, 1843 that "the abolition of slavery in the Southern States must be followed by a *deluge of black population to the North,* filling our *jails* and *poor houses,* and bringing *destruction* upon the *laboring portion of our people."* . . . If such be the case . . . , what will be the result when, by abolition, . . . the number of these free negroes shall be doubled and quadrupled, and decupled, in the more northern of the slaveholding States, before slavery had receded from their limits, and nearly the whole of which free black population would be thrown on the adjacent non-slaveholding States. Much, if not all of this great evil, will be prevented by the reannexation of Texas.

Since the purchase of Louisiana and Florida, and the settlement of Alabama and Mississippi, there have been carried into this region, as the census demonstrates, from the States of Delaware, Maryland, Virginia, and Kentucky, half a million slaves, including their descendents, that otherwise would now be within the limits of those four States. Such has been the result as to have diminished, in two of these States nearest to the North, the number of their slaves far below what they were at the census of 1790. . . . Now, if we double the rate of diminution, as we certainly will by the reannexation of Texas, slavery will disappear from Delaware in ten years, and from Maryland in twenty, and have greatly diminished in Virginia and Kentucky.

As, then, by reannexation, slavery advances into Texas, it must recede to the *same extent* from the more northern of the slaveholding States; and consequently, the evil to the northern States, from the expulsion into them of free blacks, by abolition, . . . would thereby be greatly mitigated, if not entirely prevented. . . .

Nor can it be disguised that, by the reannexation, as the number of free blacks augmented in the slaveholding States, they would be diffused gradually through Texas into Mexico, and Central and Southern America, where ninetenths of their present population are already of the colored races, and where, from their vast preponderance in number, they are not a degraded caste, but upon a footing . . . of actual equality with the rest of the population. Here, then, if Texas is reannexed throughout the vast region and salubrious and delicious climate of Mexico, and of Central and Southern America, a large and rapidly increasing portion of the African race will disappear from the limits of the Union.

The process will be gradual and progressive, without a shock, and without a convulsion; whereas, by the loss of Texas, and the imprisonment of the slave population of the Union within its present limits, slavery would *increase* in nearly all the slaveholding States, and a change in their condition would become impossible; or if it did take place by sudden or gradual abolition, the result would . . . be the . . . introduction of hundreds of thousands of free blacks into the States of the North. . . . Then, . . . from the competition for employment of the free black with the white laborer of the North,—his wages would be reduced until they would fall to ten or twenty cents a day, and starvation and misery would be introduced among the white laboring population.

There is but one way in which the North can escape these evils; and that is the reannexation of Texas, which is the only safety-valve for the whole Union, and the only practicable outlet for the African population through Texas, into Mexico and Central and Southern America. . . .

Thus, the same overruling Providence that watched over the landing of the emigrants and pilgrims at Jamestown and Plymouth; that gave us the victory in our struggle for independence; that guided by His inspiration the framers of our wonderful constitution; that has thus far preserved this great Union from dangers so many and imminent, and is now shielding it from abolition, its most dangerous and internal foe—will open Texas as a safety-valve, into and through which slavery will slowly and gradually disappear into the boundless regions of Mexico, and Central and southern America.

Source 5   *Alexandria Gazette and Virginia Advertiser,* 1844

[February 17]

[To the Editor:]
There are now 14 square-rigged vessels in this harbor [Galveston] loading with cotton, and but one of the fourteen belongs to the United States; the others are English, Bremen, French and Belgian. Almost all of our cotton goes to Europe, and all for the want of a proper treaty between the two countries, and the absurd duty which the United States imposes upon our cotton.

A "Dreadful Disaster" Occurs on Board the *Princeton*

In the early afternoon hours of February 28, 1844, it must have seemed to John Tyler as though he had finally escaped for the moment from the pressures of his presidency. He had embarked on a festive excursion down the Potomac aboard America's greatest warship. He was surrounded by the elite of Washington society: Senators, congressmen, Cabinet members, diplomats, and military officers were to be found in abundance among the 300 guests on board the *Princeton*.

John Tyler, for a moment rare in his presidency, was the center of celebration. His days as the occupant of the White House had not been easy. Following the death of William Henry Harrison, Tyler had become the first vice president to be elevated to the nation's highest office, and, as such,

22.2 President John Tyler

"His Accidency" had never seemed to enjoy the respect accorded to previous chief executives. He had become a man without a party; and though he still entertained the hope of winning the presidency in his own right, the prospects were growing dimmer by the day. His best chance to redeem his presidency was through securing admission of Texas into the Union. Already, he had, through his secretary of state, Abel P. Upshur, almost completed negotiation of a treaty of annexation and was assured that at least 40 of the 52 members of the Senate would support it. Unfortunately for John Tyler, however, the support for the treaty, not unlike the jubilation of the moment, was to be adversely affected by events of this day.

Source 6   *Alexandria Gazette and Virginia Advertiser,* **February 29, 1844**

Alexandria, D.C. Thursday Morning, February 29. STEAMSHIP PRINCETON.— Yesterday this fine ship made an excursion down the river with a large party of ladies and gentlemen from the District and elsewhere. The President and Heads of Department were among the guests, and were received on board under a national salute. The ship left her anchorage opposite this town about one o'clock P.M. and proceeded on her excursion, gaily decorated with flags, and with a lively and joyous company on board.

POSTSCRIPT

AWFUL DISASTER!

Yesterday the U.S. Steamship Princeton, Captain Stockton, which had left this place about noon, on a pleasure excursion down the river, returned at 5 o'clock P.M., with colors at half mast, indicating some disaster. About three or four miles below town, she fired one of her large guns at the bow, which BURSTED AT THE BREECH, scattering death and destruction on every side. The intelligence blew like wild fire through town, and in a few minutes the wharves were crowded, numbers, including our physicians, going out to the ship to offer assistance. It shortly became known that among those standing near the gun and KILLED by the explosion were

The Hon. A. P. Upshur, Secretary of State.
The Hon. T. W. Gilmer, Secretary of Navy.
Com. B. Kennon, U.S. Navy.
Virgil Maxcy, Esq. of Md.
Mr. Gard[i]ner, of New York.

Capt. Stockton, and the first officer of the Princeton, Lieut. Hunt were both wounded, Mr. Benton of the Senate, and some of the other visitors, together with several of the sailors were slightly wounded. . . .

The gun was discharged with the ordinary load—about twenty-five pounds of powder, and there was no blundering in the firing.

Thus awfully has ended this day, commenced in joy. Whilst pleasure sparkled in every eye, the messenger of death came in its most dreadful form and turned the whole scene to woe!

The whole nation will be stricken with grief. Two of the highest officials of the Government have been suddenly hurried to eternity. . . .

The ship will stop here, until this morning, whence she will proceed with the remains of the dead to Washington. . . .

The President returned to Washington, last night, deeply affected at the melancholy occurrences of the day.

Source 7   Letter of President John Tyler to Congress, February 29, 1844

To the Senate and House of Representatives of the United States:

I have to perform the melancholy duty of announcing to the two Houses of Congress the death of the Hon. Abel P. Upshur, late Secretary of State, and the Hon. Thomas W. Gilmer, late Secretary of the Navy.

This most lamentable occurrence transpired on board the United States ship of war Princeton, on yesterday, at about half past four in the evening, and proceeded from the explosion of one of the large guns of the ship. . . .

I shall be permitted to express my great grief at an occurrence which has thus so suddenly stricken from my side two gentlemen upon whose advice I so confidently relied in the discharge of my arduous task of administering the office of the Executive department, and whose services at this interesting period were of such vast importance.

Source 8   *National Intelligencer,* February 29, 1844

The scene upon the deck may more easily be imagined than described. Nor can the imagination picture to itself the half of its horrors. Wives, widowed in an instant by the murderous blast! Daughters smitten with the heart-rending sight of their father's lifeless corpse! The wailings of agonized females! The piteous grief of the unhurt but heart-stricken spectators! The wounded seamen borne down below! The silent tears and quivering lips of their brave and honest comrades, who tried in vain to subdue or to conceal their feelings! What words can adequately depict a scene like this?

Source 9   The *Globe,* February 29, 1844

The only circumstance calculated to relieve the all pervading distress, is, that of the multitude of ladies who were on board the ship, not one was injured. The happy exemption of such a multitude of the tender sex, who witnessed the havoc made in the midst of them of the most distinguished and beloved of their countrymen, while it brings some solace to the circle of their immediate friends, cannot but deepen the sympathies which they, and the whole community, feel for the bereaved families of those who have fallen. Mr. Upshur and Mr. Gilmer were idols in the happy family by which each was surrounded. . . . We understand that Mrs. Gilmer was upon the deck when her husband fell. It was the third discharge of the gun (and fired at the request of Mr. Gilmer) that burst it. The daughter of Mr. Upshur, several of the family of Com. Kennon, and the daughters of Mr. Gard[i]ner, were on board the steamer. Almost all the ladies were below, at dinner when the catastrophe occurred. There were two hundred ladies on board, and during the two discharges of the gun, were on the deck; and many of them approached very near to observe the course of the ball after it struck the water. President Tyler was there also, but had attended the ladies to dinner before the third discharge.

Source 10 *Alexandria Gazette and Virginia Advertiser,* **March 1, 1844**

We copy the following graphic account of the excursion of the Princeton, on Tuesday the 20th ultimo, from the Boston Times. Its joyousness and hilarity, are sadly contrasted by the deplorable catastrophe which has occurred.

VISIT TO THE PRINCETON

Washington, Feb. 20, 1844—The party were invited to be on board at 11 o'clock in the morning, but as all great bodies move slowly, and none more so than Congress, it was near 1 o'clock before the Captain was enabled to get his ship under way. The party embarked from the pier at the foot of the Arsenal; the Princeton lay in the stream near a mile from the shore. The moment the last boat load had reached the main deck, the anchor was weighed, and a grand salute was fired from the cannonades. The party consisted of between three and four hundred persons.

The ship proceeded down the river, and when a short distance below Alexandria, the Captain gave orders to load the "peace maker" with powder and ball. This nice little gun is stationed on the bow of the ship, on a revolving carriage, so that it may be fired from either side. An ordinary charge of powder for it is thirty pounds. It carries a ball weighing two hundred and twenty-five pounds; and such is the precision with which it may be fired, as ascertained from actual experiments, that the Captain will guaranty to hit an object the size of a **hogshead**, in the water, nine times in ten, at a distance of half a mile. . . .

All the preparations for firing, with the exception simply of putting the powder and ball into the gun, was made by Captain Stockton personally. . . . The ball in this case travelled about two miles before it hit the water, and then bounded several times. The Princeton went down the river as far as Mount Vernon. In going down, the "peace maker" was discharged three times, and in returning twice.

On the fourth fire the ball struck on the land, and its effect was lost sight of by those on board—so the party demanded another fire, and respectfully requested the Captain to put a little more powder this time. Before firing for the fifth and last time, the Captain said he should take the sense of the company. "All those in favor of another fire will say, Aye." The air resounded with "Aye!" "All those opposed to another fire say, No." Not a solitary voice.—"The Ayes have it," said the Captain. "I have the assent of Congress, and I'll go ahead."—Probably fifty pounds of powder went into the "peace maker" this time. As before the gun was fired by the Captain himself. The ball went, probably, four miles before it struck. It bounded fifteen times on the ice, in the course of which it performed a half circle.

Source 11 **Senator George McDuffie to John C. Calhoun**

Washington, 1st March, 1844

My dear Sir;
You will have received, before this reaches you, the astounding intelligence of the sudden death of Mr. Upshur, the Sec of State, Mr. Gilmer, Sec of the Navy & other distinguished men, by the bursting of one of the large guns on the Steamer Princeton. By this melancholy event a great calamity has fallen upon the country & especially upon the South. At a moment when one important & delicate negociation was coming . . . to a close . . . poor Upshur, the main pillar

of the executive government & poor Gilmer the only member of the cabinet who could be depended upon to aid him, were stricken down. The first question asked by every one—after the overwhelming shock produced by this disaster had in some sort ceased—was what is Mr. Tyler to do? . . .

Mr. Wise called upon me today to say that he believed you are the only man in the country who could meet all the exigencies of the crisis, & to request that I would immediately write to you to know whether if the office of Secretary of State should be tendered to you unsolicited . . . you would not put aside all personal considerations, & accept the appointment. He expressed in the strongest terms his deep conviction that your services were imperiously demanded by the country & especially by the Southern interests now so deeply involved in the questions to be decided. . . . In expressing my concurrence to Mr. Wise as I now do to you, I added that it must be distinctly understood that this is a proceeding, in which your personal friends had no agency. He replied that he would take care that there should be no misapprehension on that point.

As I write in haste I will only say in conclusion that if the office is tendered, I think you ought to accept it and come on immediately.

Source 12 *Alexandria Gazette and Virginia Advertiser,* March 2, 1844

By order of the Committee of Arrangements, the Volunteer Soldiers and Citizens of the District of Columbia and the neighboring cities, are invited to participate in the solemnities of the burial of those who were recently killed on board the steamship Princeton. The funeral will take place at the President's House, on this, Saturday morning, at 11 o'clock, and from thence the procession will proceed to the Congressional Burial Ground.

Source 13 *National Intelligencer,* March 4, 1844

NARROW ESCAPE OF THE PRESIDENT.—Although, we have already remarked, and are happy on inquiry to find, that no accident occurred at the Funeral of last Saturday, or, indeed, in the course of the day, a narrow escape was experienced by the President of the United States, who in returning from the Congress Burial Ground in a carriage, with his son, Mr. John Tyler, had his life jeopardized and saved in a manner almost providential. It seems the horses attached to the carriage took fright, or started at the foot of the Capitol, and galloped off at a most furious rate along Pennsylvania avenue, which at the time was crowded with hacks and vehicles of every description, and persons on foot returning from the Funeral. When we saw the carriage, as with the utmost rapidity it passed Seventh street, the danger of its coming in collision with other carriages seemed imminent; but the horses, although galloping at the top of their speed, fortunately were kept in a pretty straight course along our broad avenue, where there was room enough for other horses and carriages to get out of the way. The horses of the President's carriage continued their course at full speed notwithstanding every effort of the driver . . . to stop them. When the carriage reached a point opposite Gallabrun's European Hotel, a colored man fortunately succeeded in stopping the horses, and thus the President, Mr. John Tyler, Jr., and the driver were most seasonably and happily rescued from their perilous situation.

Source 14   *Alexandria Gazette and Virginia Advertiser,* **March 8, 1844**

THE NEW CABINET, AND OTHER APPOINTMENTS.—The report relative to the appointment of Mr. Calhoun as Secretary of State, mentioned yesterday, was correct. The Hon. John C. Calhoun, of South Carolina, was on Wednesday nominated to the Senate by the President of the United States to fill the office of Secretary of State, and before the Senate adjourned for the day, the nomination was unanimously confirmed. . . .

The Globe says: "Mr. Calhoun, if he accepts the office, will have it in his power to do much good for his country, and for his own fame. He has not sought the office, directly or indirectly. No friend of his, we understand, has approached the President on the subject. Not one of them, we believe, can answer to the probability of his accepting it. For the most part, they are in favor of his taking the office."

The Issues in the Texas Question

Of the 300 guests aboard the *Princeton,* the one who seemed most to catch the eye of the president was Miss Julia Gardiner, the daughter of a prominent state senator from New York. The president invited Miss Gardiner to join him in the salon below deck for a light meal and champagne. The president, seated next to Miss Gardiner, began to offer a series of toasts. When Tyler clamored for another display of the *Princeton*'s big bow gun, Captain Stockton assented to the request and the crowd surged toward the ladder to be on deck for the firing. At the foot of the ladder, Tyler paused to hear out a song by one of the passengers. The pause may have saved his life. In an instant there were screams coming from the deck. The president and his lady friend rushed to discover the tragedy. Julia Gardiner's father lay dead and the sight caused her to faint. The president later carried her in his arms down the gangplank to a rescue vessel.

In the days and weeks following the explosion on the *Princeton,* Tyler's initiative on the Texas matter began to unravel. John C. Calhoun entered the cabinet as the new secretary of state and further emotionalized the question of Texas by injecting a stronger emphasis on the need for annexation as a means of protecting slavery. John Quincy Adams, who had declined his invitation to be aboard the *Princeton* on that fateful day, railed about a slave power conspiracy to expand the peculiar institution through a series of land grabs, Texas being only the first. Both of the leading candidates for the major party presidential nominations, Henry Clay and Martin Van Buren, came out against the annexation treaty. Senate support for the treaty dissolved, and the annexation agreement failed to win ratification when it came to a vote on June 10, 1844.

All was not yet lost, however. The expansionists in the Democratic Party blocked Van Buren's nomination because of his stand on Texas, and a lesser-known leader within the party, James K. Polk, was chosen the Democratic standard-bearer in the 1844 election. Polk campaigned as an advocate of expansion and defeated Clay. Tyler and Calhoun, sensing a national mandate to push forward again on the Texas matter, won approval following the election for a joint resolution of Congress offering statehood to Texas.

And, to show that even a dark cloud like the *Princeton* disaster can have a silver lining, John Tyler and Julia Gardiner were married following a short courtship.

Source 15 **Representative Dixon H. Lewis to publicist Richard Cralle**

House of Reps, March 19th, 1844

My Dear Sir,
[T]he Texas Question . . . is the greatest of the Age, & I predict will agitate the country more than all the other public questions ever have. Public opinion will boil & effervesce & eructate more like a volcano tha[n] a cider barrel—but at last it will settle down with *unanimity* for annexation in the South & West & a large majority in the North. It will in the meantime *unite* the *hitherto divided South,* while it will make Abolition and Treason synonimous & thus destroy it in the North.

The beauty of the thing is, that Providence rather than Tyler has put Calhoun at the head of this great question, to direct its force and control its fury.

22.3 Texas History and Culture

Source 16 **Henry Clay to the *National Intelligencer***

[April 17, 1844]

[To The Editor:]
I consider the annexation of Texas, at this time, without the assent of Mexico, as a measure compromising the national character, involving us certainly in war with Mexico, probably with other foreign powers, dangerous to the integrity of the Union, inexpedient to the present financial condition of the country, and not called for by any general expression of public opinion.

Source 17 **Public letter from Martin Van Buren, *Alexandria Gazette and Virginia Advertiser,* April 20, 1844**

It is said . . . that if Texas is not acquired now, the opportunity will be forever lost—that some other power will acquire it; and indeed, some of the rumors of the day have gone so far as to say that the Texan minister is already instructed, in case of failure here, to proceed forthwith to Europe, with full authority for the accomplishment of that object. We must not forget that besides great public considerations, there are extensive private interests involved in this matter; and we may therefore well be distrustful of the thousand rumors which are from day to day afloat upon this subject. What a comparatively few individuals, acting under the influence of personal interest, may not desire to have done, I will not undertake to say. . . . But the people of Texas—so many of whom carry in their veins the blood of our revolutionary ancestors—thousands of whom are thoroughly imbued with democratic principles—who achieved by their own gallantry that independence which we were the first to acknowledge—who have established and subsequently maintained institutions similar to our own;—that such a people and such a government would be found capable of sending a minister to the crowned heads of Europe, to barter away their young and enterprising republic, and all that they have purchased with their blood, to the highest bidder, is what I cannot believe.

Source 18   Message of President John Tyler to the Senate

Washington, April 22, 1844

To the Senate of the United States:

I transmit herewith, for your approval and ratification, a treaty which I have caused to be negotiated between the United States and Texas, whereby the latter, on the conditions therein set forth, has transferred and conveyed all its right of separate and independent sovereignty and jurisdiction to the United States. . . .

The country thus proposed to be annexed has been settled principally by persons from the United States, who emigrated on the invitation of both Spain and Mexico, and who carried with them into the wilderness which they have partially reclaimed the laws, customs, and political and domestic institutions of their native land. . . . The country itself thus obtained is of incalculable value in an agricultural and commercial point of view. To a soil of inexhaustible fertility it unites a genial and healthy climate, and is destined at a day not distant to make a large contribution to the commerce of the world. Its territory is separated from the United States . . . by an imaginary line. . . .

[I]f the boon now tendered be rejected Texas will seek for the friendship of others. In contemplating such a contingency it can not be overlooked that the United States are already surrounded by the possessions of European powers. The Canadas, New Brunswick, and Nova Scotia, the islands in the American seas, with Texas trammeled by treaties of alliance . . . differing in policy from that of the United States would complete the circle. . . .

Nor was (the Executive) ignorant of the anxiety of other powers to induce Mexico to enter into terms of reconciliation with Texas, which, affecting the domestic institutions of Texas, would operate most injuriously upon the United States and might most seriously threaten the existence of this happy Union. Nor could it be unacquainted with the fact that although foreign governments might disavow all design to disturb the relations which exist under the Constitution between these States, yet that one, the most powerful amongst them, had not failed to declare its marked and decided hostility to the chief feature in those relations and its purpose on all suitable occasions to urge . . . in negotiating with Texas . . . the obliteration of that feature of her domestic policy.

Source 19   John Quincy Adams, *Diary of John Quincy Adams*, 1844

June 10.—The vote in the United States Senate on the question of advising and consenting to the Texan Treaty was, yeas, 16; nays, 35. I record this vote as a deliverance, I trust, by the special interposition of Almighty God, of my country and of human liberty from a conspiracy. . . . The annexation of Texas to the Union is the first-step to the conquest of all Mexico, of the West India islands, of a maritime, colonizing, slave-tainted monarchy, and of extinguished freedom.

Source 20   *Diary of John Quincy Adams*, 1845

February 27, 1845.—The Senate this evening, by a vote of 27 to 25, adopted the resolutions of the House of Representatives for admitting Texas as a state into this Union. . . . It is a signal triumph of the slave representation in the Constitution of the United States.

Feb. 28.—The day passes, and leaves scarcely a distinct trace upon the memory of anything, and precisely because, among numerous other objects of comparative insignificance, the heaviest calamity that ever befell myself or my country was this day consummated. . . . [T]he joint resolutions of the House for the admission of Texas as a State into this Union were returned from the Senate . . . and forced through without the allowance of any debate. . . .

I took in this transaction no part save that of silent voting. I regard it as the apoplexy of the Constitution. The final vote . . . was 132 to 76.

Second Thoughts

The Issues in Hindsight

The appointment of Calhoun, former vice president under both John Quincy Adams and Andrew Jackson, and an ardent supporter of states' rights and slavery, inextricably linked slavery to the annexation of Texas. Historian John Hope Franklin, in his book, *From Slavery to Freedom: A History of Negro Americans,* wrote, "Nothing more clearly demonstrates the insatiable appetite of plantation slavery for new lands than the generation-long struggle for the acquisition of Texas. It was, perhaps, the high-water mark in the effort of the South to absorb all the lands into which the cotton kingdom could be extended." Scholars and historians offer varying interpretations of the Texas question in the sources that follow.

Source 21 Former Virginia governor Henry A. Wise, *Seven Decades of the Union,* 1881

To return to the catastrophe of the Princeton . . . there was one man left who was necessary above all others to the South in settling and obtaining the annexation of Texas. We need hardly say that man was John C. Calhoun, of South Carolina. But we knew that, for some reason of which we were never informed, the President was opposed to calling him to his Cabinet. It is vain to conjecture the reason, . . . but the fact was known, and that caused us to be guilty of assuming an authority and taking a liberty with the President which few men would have excused and few would have taken.

We thought of Mr. McDuffie, then in the Senate, and determined to act through him. . . . We determined, through him, to act on Mr. Calhoun, whilst we took unprecedented license with Mr. Tyler. Before breakfast, by sunrise the next morning, the 29th of February, 1844, we visited Mr. McDuffie's parlor. . . . We . . . urged him to write to Mr. Calhoun immediately, saying to him that his name would, in all probability, be sent to the Senate at once, and begging him not to decline the office if his nomination should be made and confirmed. Mr. McDuffie's delicacy towards us doubtless prevented him from inquiring whether we spoke by Mr. Tyler's authority or not, and we made no statement to him pro or con on that point, but presume he must have, supposed that we were authorized to make the request, for he promised to write to Mr. Calhoun at once.

On parting from him we went directly to the presidential mansion to break-fast. . . . Mr. Tyler was standing with his right elbow resting on the mantel of the fireplace, and held a morning paper in his left hand, containing an account of the awful catastrophe of the day before. As soon as he saw us he accosted us with tremulous emotion, saying how humbled he was by his providential escape whilst such valuable friends had fallen from around him, and he turned his face to the wall in a flood of tears. We came to his relief at once by saying that it was no time for mourning. . . . He must subdue his grief and find relief . . . in turning to his tasks. He asked at once, "What is to be done?" The answer was ready: "Your most important work is the annexation of Texas, and the man for that work is Mr. Calhoun. Send for him at once."

His air changed at once, and he quickly and firmly said, "No: Texas is important, but Mr. Calhoun is not the man of my choice." . . .

During the whole breakfast we were exceedingly uneasy, thinking how we should prevail upon him to nominate Mr. Calhoun and justify us to Mr. McDuf-fie. . . . As soon as breakfast was over, we rose, hat in hand, to depart, went with some impressiveness of manner to Mr. Tyler, and said, "Sir, in saying good-morning to you now, I may be taking a lasting farewell. . . . I fear I have done that which will forfeit your confidence and cause us to be friends no longer. You say that you will not nominate Mr. Calhoun as your Secretary of State. If so, then I have done both you and him a great wrong, and must go immediately to Mr. McDuffie to apologize for causing him to commit himself, and you too, by an unauthorized act of mine."

"What do you mean?" exclaimed the President, evidently disturbed.

"I mean that this morning, before coming here, . . . I went to Mr. McDuffie and prevailed upon him to write to Mr. Calhoun and ask him to accept the place of Secretary of State at your hands."

"Did you say you went at my instance to make that request?"

"No, I did not in words, but my act, as your known friend, implied as much. . . . I went to him without your authority, for the very reason that I knew I could not obtain it; and I did not tell Mr. McDuffie that I had not your authority, for I knew he would not in that case have written to Mr. Calhoun as I requested. And now, if you do not sanction what I have done, you will place me where you would loath to place a foe, much less a friend. . . ."

He looked at us in utter surprise for some minutes, and then, lifting both hands, said, "Well, you are the most extraordinary man I ever saw!—the most willful and wayward, the most incorrigible! . . . No one else would have done it in this way but you, and you are the only man who could have done it with me. Take the office and tender it to Mr. Calhoun; I doubtless am wrong in refusing the services of such a man."

Source 22   Mary M. Brown, *A School History of Texas,* 1894

Great Britain and France both interested themselves in bringing about an armi-stice between the belligerent powers, Texas and Mexico. The passage of British war vessels between Vera Cruz and Galveston, bearing secret dispatches, in-terviews between the ministers of those countries, and a known diplomatic correspondence with Texas officials, aroused the jealousy of the United States—imperiling the Monroe Doctrine and the possession of the Gulf of Mexico.

Source 23 Ephraim Douglass Adams, *British Interests and Activities in Texas, 1838–1846,* 1910

In the summer of 1843 occurred the abolition convention in England and Aberdeen's conference with the committee which urged upon him the necessity for the effort to bring about abolition in Texas. Up to this point, . . . Aberdeen had taken no official notice of the institution in Texas, but with the revival of anti-slavery agitation in England he was induced to press for abolition. . . . Aberdeen . . . [was] wholly ignorant of annexation plans maturing under Tyler and Upshur in the United States. It was Aberdeen's misfortune, as it was Tyler's good luck, that these measures were undertaken at about the same time. The opportunity to publish British intentions in regard to Texas and to interpret these to mean interference with a national institution was precisely what was needed in America to solidify American support of annexation.

Source 24 Charles M. Wiltse, *John C. Calhoun,* 1951

It makes a good story, but it is most unlikely that Wise consulted McDuffie without Tyler's knowledge, or that he found at the White House any such reluctance as he depicts. The contemporary record seems to indicate that the great Nullifier was the immediate choice of the President, whose only problem was whether a man who had twice refused the same office at his hand would accept it now. Wise brought him a promise that McDuffie's influence would be used to that end, but Tyler did not stop there. He sounded out the whole South Carolina Congressional delegation and as many of Calhoun's friends from other states as he could reach. . . . If the circumstances had actually been as Wise relates them, there would have been no necessity for the lapse of a week, during which these various consultations were going on, before Calhoun's name was sent to the Senate. . . .

Far from being fixed against Calhoun to the first office in the cabinet, Tyler appears to have been singularly eager to bring that event to pass. . . . The mere presence of the Carolinian in the official family would give prestige and power to the President.

Source 25 Frederick Merk, *The Mississippi Valley Historical Review,* December 1962

In 1844 a nation-wide debate took place in the United States. It was on the issue of the annexation of Texas to the Union. It turned on three theses relating to slavery, each of which was sponsored by an individual well known to American history. One was the conspiracy thesis, sponsored by John Quincy Adams. Another was the safety valve thesis, sponsored by Robert J. Walker, the "king maker" of that era. The third was the protection of slavery thesis, sponsored by John C. Calhoun. . . .

In an opinion poll neither [Calhoun nor Adams] would have commanded the vote Walker would have commanded for his thesis.

Source 26 Robert Seager II, *And Tyler Too*, 1963

Upshur's death brought John C. Calhoun into the State Department. This disastrous change, cunningly foisted on Tyler by Henry A. Wise, introduced the extraneous slavery issue more forcefully into the Texas debate and ultimately destroyed any hope Tyler had of obtaining a two-thirds majority for the Texas treaty in the Senate in 1844. . . . Unhappily for Tyler, the arrival of Calhoun in the Cabinet stamped the word *slavery* all over the controversial annexation issue.

Source 27 Frederick and Lois Merk, *Fruits of Propaganda in the Tyler Administration*, 1971

The Walker *Letter* had an enormous distribution; . . . It was the most cited of the writings on annexation in Congress and in the nation.

In the [presidential] campaign the Walker *Letter* was spread before a wider audience and, if contemporary opinion is correct, tipped the balance in the closely-divided Northern states in favor of Polk—the annexation candidate—by holding wavering antislavery Democrats to party loyalty, while the Whig vote was split. Its ultimate effect appeared several months later when the Joint Resolution of annexation was passed by a lame-duck Congress in March 1845.

Source 28 Norma Lois Peterson, *The Presidencies of William Henry Harrison and John Tyler*, 1989

Perhaps the most significant indication of Tyler's probable reluctance to name Calhoun secretary of state in 1844 was the President's desire to have annexation considered a national issue, not as acquisition of territory solely in the interest of the South. Tyler, who was as concerned as Calhoun was about the deteriorating position of the South in the Union, believed this was not the time to focus on the problem. Annexation required the support of the entire nation. Calhoun tended to emphasize the sectional and slavery aspect; Tyler tried to minimize it, while stressing the economic and strategic values.

✒ Questioning the Past

1. What were the arguments for and against the annexation of the Republic of Texas by the United States?
2. What were the British interests in the Texas question? What might have been the short- and long-range consequences of a British commitment to militarily and financially support the independence of Texas in exchange for a Texas commitment to abolish slavery?
3. Explain and evaluate the rationale for the annexation of Texas offered by Senator Richard J. Walker.
4. What was John C. Calhoun's strategy for achieving the annexation of Texas? Was Calhoun's approach to this objective helpful or detrimental to the cause?
5. Random events can upset the best of plans. What impact, if any, did the explosion on board the *Princeton* have upon the Texas question?

Chapter 23

War with Mexico

American Blood Is Shed on American Soil

April 24, 1846

Relations between Mexico and the United States had been strained for some years before 1846. After winning its independence from Spain, Mexico had at first encouraged Americans to settle in its northern provinces, but later attempted, unsuccessfully, to close its frontiers to the flood of immigrants. After only 15 years of independence, Mexico lost Texas to a revolution led in large measure by settlers from the United States, a turn of events that Mexico deeply resented. It also resented the unabashed American ambition to possess more of Mexico's northern provinces, and had rejected repeated United States' efforts to purchase California and New Mexico. Its government had refused to meet with American envoy James Slidell when he was sent in 1845 with new offers to purchase Mexican territory. Further, the country was weakened by domestic troubles, including frequent coups and rebellions, political disagreements over whether Mexico should be a republic or a monarchy, and an economy so unstable that American business investors often lost their investments. In fact, a commission of representatives from both countries had determined in 1840 that Mexico should pay $8.5 million in compensation, of which it paid $5.25 million before exhausting its treasury and defaulting.

By July 1845, General Zachary Taylor had established an American military outpost on the left bank of the Nueces River near Corpus Christi. Both Mexico and the United States claimed the land between the Nueces and the **Rio Grande Del Norte**; the United States claimed it had been ceded in a treaty following the battle of San Jacinto, but the only Mexican signatory had been President-General Santa Anna, a prisoner of war at the time. Mexico felt the terms had been negotiated under duress but made no military move to reoccupy Texas. Mexican forces remained south of the Rio Grande, and, for a time, the United States also respected the sensitive nature of the disputed zone. But on January 13, 1846, after learning of the Mexican government's refusal to negotiate with Slidell, President Polk ordered General Taylor to advance into the contested territory. Taylor's troops began to form along the Rio Grande on March 23, training their guns across the river toward the Mexican city of Matamoras. When the Mexican commander at Matamoras demanded that American forces withdraw beyond the Nueces, Taylor imposed a blockade at the mouth of the Rio Grande, severing Mexican supply lines to Matamoras. On April 24, General Arista of the Mexican Army sent a scouting party some 30 miles up the river from Matamoras, which crossed to the north bank of the Rio Grande. Taylor promptly dispatched a reconnaissance

23.1 The U.S.–
Mexican War

party of 63 **dragoons** to monitor Mexican troop movements. The American detachment was challenged by the Mexican cavalry unit. Shots were exchanged, and 16 American soldiers were killed or wounded. As a member of Taylor's forces wrote in his journal that night, "War has commenced." In battles on May 8 and 9 at Palo Alto and Resaca de la Palma, American troops pushed much larger Mexican forces back across the Rio Grande.

First Impressions
"By Act of the Republic of Mexico, War Exists"

Before learning of the incident at the Rio Grande, President Polk and his Cabinet had decided to go to war. Despite Polk's initial success in winning congressional approval of his plans, the debate over whether or not American actions were justified was far from over.

Source 1   President James K. Polk's diary

Saturday, 9th May, 1846.—The Cabinet held a regular meeting today; all the members were present. I brought up the Mexican question, and the question of what was the duty of the administration in the present state of our relations with that country. The subject was very fully discussed. All agreed that if the Mexican forces at Matamoras committed any act of hostility on General Taylor's forces I should immediately send a message to Congress recommending an immediate declaration of war. I stated to the Cabinet that up to this time, as we knew, we had heard of no open act of aggression by the Mexican army, but that the danger was imminent that such acts would be committed. I said that in my opinion we had ample cause of war, and that it was impossible that we could stand in *statu quo,* or that I thought I could remain silent much longer; that I thought it was my duty to send a message to Congress very soon and recommend definite measures. I told them that I thought I ought to make such a message by Tuesday next, that the country was excited and impatient on the subject, and if I failed to do so I would not be doing my duty. I then propounded the distinct question to the Cabinet, and took their opinions individually, whether I should make a message to Congress on Tuesday, and whether in that message I should recommend a declaration of war against Mexico. All except the Secretary of the Navy gave their advice in the affirmative. Mr. Bancroft dissented but said if any act of hostility should be committed by the Mexican forces he was then in favour of immediate war. Mr. Buchanan said he would feel better satisfied in his course if the Mexican forces had or should commit any act of hostility, but that as matters stood we had ample cause of war against Mexico, and gave his assent to the measure. . . .

About 6 O'Clock p.m. Gen. R. Jones, the Adjutant-General of the army, called and handed to me dispatches received from General Taylor by the Southern mail which had just arrived, giving information that a part of the Mexican army had crossed the Del Norte and attacked and killed and captured two companies of dragoons of General Taylor's army consisting of 63 officers and men. . . . I immediately summoned the Cabinet to meet at 7½ O'Clock this evening. The Cabinet accordingly assembled at that hour; all the members present. The subject of the dispatch received this evening from General Taylor, as well as the state of our relations with Mexico, were fully considered. The Cabinet were unanimously of opinion, and it was so agreed, that a message should be sent to Congress on Monday . . . recommending vigorous & prompt measures to enable the Executive to prosecute the war.

Source 2 President Polk's diary

23.2 PBS
Online: The
U.S.–Mexican
War

Monday, 11th May, 1846.—I refused to see company generally this morning. I carefully revised my message on the Mexican question. . . .

I addressed [notes] to Senators Cass and Benton this morning requesting them to call. Gen. Cass called first. The message was read to him and he highly approved it. Col. Benton called before Gen. Cass left, and I gave him the copy of the message and he retired to an adjoining room and read it. After he had read it I had a conversation with him alone. I found he did not approve it in all its parts. He was willing to vote men and money for defense of our territory, but was not prepared to make aggressive war on Mexico. He disapproved the marching of the army from Corpus Christi to the left bank of the Del Norte, but said he had never said so to the public. I had a full conversation with him, and he left without satisfying me that I could rely on his support . . . further than the mere defence of our territory. I inferred, too, from his conversation that he did not think the territory of the United States extended West of the Nueces River.

At 12 O'Clock I sent my message to Congress. It was a day of great anxiety with me. Between 5 & 6 O'Clock p.m. Mr. Slidell, United States Minister to Mexico, called and informed me that the House of Representatives had passed a bill carrying out the recommendations of the message by a vote of 173 ayes to 14 noes, and that the Senate had adjourned after a debate without coming to a decision.

My private secretary brought me a note from Col. Benton desiring information as to the number of men and amount of money required to defend the country. . . . The Secretaries of War and State called a few minutes before 8 O'Clock but before I had consulted the former in relation to Col. Benton's note, Col. Benton came in . . . I told him if the war [was] recognized by Congress, that with a large force on land and sea I thought it could be speedily terminated. Col. Benton said that the Ho. Repts. [House of Representatives] had passed a bill today declaring war in only two hours, and that one and a half hours of that time had been occupied in reading the documents which accompanied my message, and that in his opinion in the nineteenth century war should not be declared without full discussion and much more consideration than had been given to it in the Ho. Repts. Mr. Buchanan then remarked that war already existed by the act of Mexico herself and therefore did not require much deliberation to satisfy all that we ought promptly and vigorously to meet it. Mr. Marcy and Mr. Buchanan discussed the subject for some time with Mr. Benton, but without any change of opinion. . . .

The Whigs in the Senate will oppose it [the war declaration] on party grounds probably, if they can get Mr. Calhoun, Mr. Benton, and two or three other Senators professing to belong to the Democratic party to join them so as to make a majority against the bill. . . . I am fully satisfied that all that can save the bill in the Senate is the fear of the people by the few Democratic Senators who wish it defeated.

Source 3   President Polk's message to Congress, May 11, 1846

The grievous wrongs perpetrated by Mexico upon our citizens throughout a long period of years remain unredressed, and solemn treaties pledging her public faith for this redress have been disregarded. A government unable or unwilling to enforce execution of such treaties fails one of its plainest duties.

Our commerce with Mexico has been almost annihilated. It was formerly highly beneficial to both nations, but our merchants have been deterred from prosecuting it by the system of outrage and extortion which the Mexican authorities have pursued against them, whilst their appeals through their own Government for indemnity have been made in vain. Our forbearance has gone to such an extreme as to be mistaken in its character. Had we acted with vigor in repelling the insults and redressing the injuries inflicted by Mexico at the commencement, we should doubtless have escaped all the difficulties in which we are now involved.

Instead of this, however, we have been exerting our best efforts to propitiate her good will. Upon the pretext that Texas, a nation as independent as herself, thought proper to unite its destinies with our own, she has affected to believe that we have severed her rightful territory, and in official proclamations and manifestoes has repeatedly threatened to make war on us for the purpose of reconquering Texas. In the meantime we have tried every effort at reconciliation. The cup of forbearance had been exhausted even before the recent information from the frontier of the Del Norte. But now, after reiterated menaces, Mexico has passed the boundary of the United States, has invaded our territory, and shed American blood upon the American soil. She has proclaimed that hostilities have commenced, and that the two nations are now at war.

As war exists, and, notwithstanding all our efforts to avoid it, exists by the act of Mexico herself, we are called upon by every consideration of duty and patriotism to vindicate with decision the honor, the rights, and the interests of our country.

Source 4   Editor Horace Greeley, *New York Tribune*, May 12, 1846

Our Country, Right or Wrong!

This is the spirit in which a portion of the Press, which admits that our treatment of Mexico has been ruffianly and piratical, and that the invasion of her territory by Gen. Taylor is a flagrant outrage, now exhorts our People to rally in all their strength, to lavish their blood and treasure in the vindictive prosecution of War on Mexico. We protest against such counsel. . . .

We can easily defeat the armies of Mexico, slaughter them by the thousands, and pursue them perhaps to their capital; we can conquer and 'annex' their territory; but what then? Have the histories of the ruin of Greek and Roman liberty consequent on such extensions of empire by sword no lesson for us? Who believes that a score of victories over Mexico, the 'annexation' of half her provinces, will give us more Liberty, a purer morality, a more prosperous Industry, than we now have? . . . Is not Life miserable enough, comes not Death soon enough, without resort to the hideous enginery of War?

People of the United States! Your Rulers are precipitating you into a fathomless abyss of crime and calamity! Why sleep you thoughtless on its verge, as though this was not your business, or Murder could be hid from the sight of God by a few flimsy rags called banners? Awake and arrest the work of butchery ere it shall be too late to preserve your souls from the guilt of wholesale slaughter!

Source 5   President Polk's diary

Tuesday, 12th May, 1846.—The Cabinet held a regular meeting today. . . . The Mexican question was the subject of conversation, and all had doubts whether the Bill which passed the House on yesterday would pass the Senate to-day. . . .

At 7 O'Clock p.m. my private secretary returned from the Capitol and announced that the Bill which passed the Ho. Repts. on yesterday, making a formal declaration of war against Mexico had passed the Senate by a vote of 42 ayes to 2 noes, with some immaterial amendment in its details. He represented to me that the debate in the Senate today was most animating and thrilling.

Source 6   By the President of the United States of America: A Proclamation

Whereas the Congress of the United States, by virtue of the constitutional authority vested in them, have declared by their act bearing date this day that "by the act of the Republic of Mexico a state of war exists between that Government and the United States."

Now, therefore, I, James K. Polk, President of the United States of America, do hereby proclaim the same to all whom it may concern. . . .

Done at the city of Washington, the 13th day of May, A.D. 1846, and of the Independence of the United States the seventieth.

Source 7   President Polk's diary

Saturday, 30th May, 1846.—A plan of the campaign against Mexico and the manner of prosecuting the war was fully considered. I brought directly to the consideration of the Cabinet the question of ordering an expedition of mounted men to California. I stated that if the war should be protracted for any considerable time, it would in my judgment be very important that the U.S. should hold military possession of California at the time peace was made, and I declared my purpose to be to acquire for the U.S., California, New Mexico, and perhaps some others of the Northern Provinces of Mexico whenever a peace was made. In Mr. Slidell's secret instructions last autumn these objects were included. Now that we were at war the prospect of acquiring them was much better. . . . In these views the Cabinet concurred.

Source 8   Senator Lewis Cass of Michigan's speech supporting
appropriations for the war with Mexico, February 10, 1847

We do not want the people of Mexico, either as citizens or subjects. All we
want is a portion of territory which they nominally hold, generally uninhabited,
or, where inhabited at all, sparsely so, and with a population which would soon
recede, or identify itself with ours.

Source 9   Senator Thomas Corwin of Ohio's speech opposing
appropriations for the war, February 11, 1847

What is the territory, Mr. President, which you propose to wrest from Mexico?
It is consecrated to the heart of the Mexican by many a well-fought battle, with
his old Castilian master. His Bunker Hills, and Saratogas, and Yorktowns are
there. The Mexican can say, "There I bled for liberty! and shall I surrender that
consecrated home of my affections to the Anglo-Saxon invaders! What do they
want with it? They have Texas already. . . . What else do they want? To what
shall I point my children as memorials of that independence which I bequeath
to them, when those battle-fields shall have passed from my possession?"

Sir, had one come and demanded Bunker Hill of the people of Massachusetts, had England's lion ever showed himself there, is there a man over thirteen,
and under ninety who would not have been ready to meet him—is there a field
but would have been piled high with the unburied bones of slaughtered Americans before these consecrated battle-fields of liberty should have been wrested
from us? But this same American goes into a sister republic, and says to poor,
weak Mexico, "Give up your territory—you are unworthy to possess it—I have
got a one-half already—all I ask of you is to give up the other!" England might
as well, in the circumstances I have described, have come and demanded of us,
"Give up the Atlantic slope—give up this trifling territory from the Alleghany
mountains to the sea; it is only . . . about one-third of your Republic, and the
least interesting portion of it." What would be the response? They would say, we
must give this up to John Bull. Why? "He wants room." The Senator from Michigan [Lewis Cass] says he 'must' have this. Why, my Christian brother, on what
principle of justice? "I want room!"

Sir, look at this pretense of want of room. With twenty millions of people,
you have about one thousand millions of acres of land, inviting settlement by every
conceivable argument . . . and allowing every man to squat where he pleases. But
the Senator from Michigan says we will be two hundred millions in a few years,
and we want room. If I were a Mexican I would tell you, "Have you not room in
your own country to bury your dead men? If you come into mine we will greet
you with bloody hands, and welcome you to hospitable graves."

Why, says the Chairman of this Committee of Foreign Relations, it is the
most reasonable thing in the world! We ought to have the Bay of San Francisco.
Why? Because it is the best harbor on the Pacific! It has been my fortune, Mr.
President, to have practiced a good deal in criminal courts in the course of my
life, but I never yet heard a thief, arraigned for stealing a horse, plead that it
was the best that he could find in the country! . . .

Let us abandon all idea of acquiring further territory, and by consequence
cease at once to prosecute this war. Let us call home our armies, and bring

them at once within our own acknowledged limits. Show Mexico that you are sincere when you say you desire nothing by conquest. She has learned that she cannot encounter you in war, and if she had not, she is too weak to disturb you here. Tender her peace, and my life on it, she will then accept it. But whether she shall or not, you will have peace without her consent. It is your invasion that has made war, your retreat will restore peace.

Source 10 Resolution of the Massachusetts legislature, April 26, 1847

Resolved, that the present war with Mexico . . . was unconstitutionally commenced by the order of the President to General Taylor to take possession of territory in dispute . . . and that it is now waged by a powerful nation against a weak neighbor . . . for the dismemberment of Mexico, and for the conquest of . . . territory from which slavery has been . . . excluded, with the triple object of extending slavery, of strengthening the slave power, and of obtaining the control of the Free States.

    Resolved, that such a war of conquest, so hateful in its objects, so wanton, unjust and unconstitutional in its origin and character, must be regarded as a war against freedom, against humanity, against justice, against the Union . . . and against the free states.

Source 11 Democratic Party Platform of 1848

Resolved, That the war with Mexico, provoked on her part by years of insult and injury, was commenced by her army crossing the Rio Grande, attacking the American troops, and invading our sister State of Texas; and that, upon all the principles of patriotism and laws of nations, it is a just and necessary war on our part, in which every American citizen should have shown himself on the side of his country, and neither morally nor physically, by word or by deed, have "given aid and comfort to the enemy."

Source 12 Congressman Abraham Lincoln's speech in the House of Representatives, January 12, 1848

[I]f any one should declare the President sent the army into the midst of a settlement of Mexican people, who had never submitted, by consent or by force, to the authority of Texas or of the United States, and that *there,* and *thereby* the first blood of the war was shed, there is not one word in all the President has said, which would either admit or deny the declaration. This strange omission . . . could not have occurred but by design. . . .

    I introduced a preamble, resolution, and interrogatories, intended to draw the President out, if possible, on this hitherto untrodden ground. To show their relevancy, I propose to state my understanding of the true rule for ascertaining the boundary between Texas and Mexico. It is, that *wherever* Texas was *exercising* jurisdiction, was hers; and *wherever* Mexico was exercising jurisdiction, was hers; and that *whatever* separated the actual exercise of jurisdiction of the one, from that of the other, was the true boundary between them. If, as is probably true, Texas was exercising jurisdiction along the western bank of the Nueces, and

Mexico was exercising it along the eastern bank of the Rio Grande, then *neither* river was the boundary; but the uninhabited country between the two, was. . . .

[A]ll Mexico, including Texas revolutionized against Spain; and still later, Texas revolutionized against Mexico. In my view, just so far as she carried her revolution, by obtaining the *actual,* willing or unwilling submission of the people, *so far,* the country was hers, and no farther. Now, sir, for the purpose of obtaining the very best evidence, as to whether Texas had actually carried her revolution, to the place where the hostilities of the present war commenced, let the President answer the interrogatories I proposed. . . . Let him answer fully, fairly, and candidly. Let him answer with *facts,* and not with arguments. Let him remember he sits where Washington sat, and so remembering, let him answer, as Washington would answer. . . . And if, so answering, he can show that the soil was ours, where the first blood of the war was shed—that it was not within an inhabited country, or, if within such, that the inhabitants had submitted themselves to the civil authority of Texas, or of the United States, . . . then I am with him for his justification. . . . But if he *can* not, or *will* not do this . . . , then I shall be fully convinced, of what I more than suspect already, that he is deeply conscious of being in the wrong—that he feels the blood of this war, like the blood of Abel, is crying to Heaven against him; that he ordered General Taylor into the midst of a peaceful Mexican settlement, purposely to bring on a war.

The Outcome of the War

The conflict that began on the banks of the Rio Grande in April 1846 ended two years later with the triumphal entry of an American army into Mexico City, an action that ultimately provided the opening phrase of the Marine Hymn, "From the halls of Montezuma (to the shores of Tripoli)." Nor were United States triumphs confined to Texas. On June 7, 1846, American settlers in California proclaimed the territory's independence of Mexico; Commodore John Sloat soon landed at Monterey to claim California for the United States, which annexed it in August. The war inspired great acts of courage and heroism on both sides. The Treaty of Guadelupe Hidalgo that restored peace granted the United States possession of New Mexico and California and acknowledged the Rio Grande as the Texas border. The United States paid Mexico $15 million for these land cessions and agreed to reimburse its own citizens the $3.25 million owed them by Mexico.

Source 13   President Polk's message to Congress, July 6, 1848

I lay before the Congress copies of a treaty of peace, friendship, limits, and settlement between the United States and the Mexican Republic. . . .

The war in which our country was reluctantly involved, in the necessary vindication of the national rights and honor, has been thus terminated. . . .

The extensive and valuable territories ceded by Mexico to the United States constitute indemnity for the past, and the brilliant achievements and signal successes of our arms will be a guaranty of security for the future, by convincing all nations that our rights must be respected. The results of the war with Mexico have given to the United States a national character abroad which our country never before enjoyed. Our power and our resources have become known and are respected throughout the world, and we shall probably be saved from the necessity of engaging in another foreign war for a long series of years. . . .

New Mexico and Upper California have been ceded by Mexico to the United States, and now constitute a part of our country. Embracing nearly ten degrees of latitude, lying adjacent to the Oregon Territory, and extending from the Pacific Ocean to the Rio Grande, . . . it would be difficult to estimate the value of these possessions to the United States. . . . Rich in mineral and agricultural resources, with a climate of great salubrity, they embrace the most important ports on the whole Pacific coast of the continent of North America. The possession of the ports of San Diego and Monterey and the Bay of San Francisco will enable the United States to command the already valuable and rapidly increasing commerce of the Pacific. . . .

While the war has been conducted with great humanity and forbearance and with complete success on our part, the peace has been concluded on terms the most liberal and magnanimous to Mexico. In her hands the territories now ceded had remained, and, it is believed, would have continued to remain, almost unoccupied, and of little value to her or to any other nation, whilst as part of our Union they will be productive of vast benefits to the United States, to the commercial world, and the general interests of mankind.

Source 14 *Daily National Intelligencer,* July 7, 1848

The reader's attention will be strongly arrested by the message which the President sent to Congress yesterday touching our Mexican relations; and there are few, we presume, who will not be amused at the claims to credit set up by his Excellency on account of the war into which he unnecessarily and unrighteously plunged the country, and which, after costing us some thousands of valuable lives and some hundred or two millions of money, we are extricated from by agreeing to pay our Mexican claims ourselves (which we went to war to make Mexico pay) and giving her many millions more to make peace; for it cannot be seriously urged that the distant deserts which Mexico grants us are any equivalent for the money she receives; indeed, we might well afford to give her five times as much to take them back again.

23.3 California
History:
Mexican Period

📖 *Second Thoughts*
A Determination to Secure California

The debate over the fairness of waging war with Mexico became less passionate as time passed, but historians on both sides of the Rio Grande have continued their efforts to understand the politics and the facets of American character that led to the conflict.

Source 15 Abiel A. Livermore, *The War with Mexico Reviewed,* 1849

To specify a leading cause [of the war], we would avert to what Sir Robert Peel has called, in the British Parliament, "a development of military ambition in the United States"; in one sense, both cause and effect of the war with Mexico. The attentive student of history will be at no loss to trace the origin and growth of this fearful passion. For the time we have existed as a people, we have been no sluggards in the use of the sword.... The martial spirit is always a tiger, and we have given the tiger too much room and freedom.... Though most of our wars have been small ones, that circumstance has not prevented their imbuing a large portion of our citizens with the ambition of arms. It is one of our maxims, that "in time of peace we should prepare for war." The whole population are armed; there is not, probably, a house in the country, unless it belong to a Quaker or Non-resistant, without its sword, pistol, musket, or rifle. The expenses of our army and navy, even in time of peace, have always exceeded, by many millions, the maximum of the civil list. Hence there is always existing a large profession of men, whose seeming interest it is to have their country engaged in war; for then every expenditure in this direction is enormously increased; active service creates vacancies and accelerates promotions; and the prize money of war is better than the earnings of industry....

It has been openly avowed on the floor of Congress, by the most distinguished men of the country, that the time had arrived for us to do "some great thing," to let the Old World know we were not the cowards or sluggards they might otherwise suppose us to be. As if it were not well known in every land ... that the United States was rising to be a leading power in the earth ... without seeking a quarrel with a rent and distracted nation to show our republican manhood.

Source 16   Mexican historian Ramon Alcaraz, *The Other Side: Notes for the History of the War between Mexico and the United States,* 1850

The real and effective cause of this war ... was the spirit of aggrandizement of the United States of the North, availing itself of its power to conquer us.

Source 17   James Ford Rhodes, *History of the United States from the Compromise of 1850,* 1892

The story of the annexation and the conquest of New Mexico and California is not a fair page in our history. The extension of our boundary to the Rio Grande, and the rounding of our Pacific possessions by the acquisition of California, gave symmetrical proportions to our territory, and this consideration has induced many writers to justify the winning of this domain. But in pondering the plain narrative of these events, more reason for humiliation than pride will be found....

Although that unfortunate country [Mexico] had officially notified the United States that the annexation of Texas would be treated as a cause of war, so constant were the internal quarrels in Mexico that open hostilities would have been avoided had the conduct of the administration been honorable.... But as the satirist [James Russell Lowell] expressed it, the Southerners were after "bigger pens to cram with slaves." Having acquired Texas, they longed for New Mexico and California. A dispute arose whether the southwestern boundary was the river Nueces or the Rio Grande. Negotiation ... would undoubtedly have settled the difficulty, but the President arrogated the right of deciding the question. Mexico was actually goaded on to the war. The principle of the **manifest**

destiny of this country was invoked as a reason for the attempt to add to our territory at the expense of Mexico. . . .

An incident in the negotiation of the treaty displayed whither was our drift in obedience to the behest of the slave power. The reader will remember that slavery did not exist under Mexican law, and that New Mexico and California were free territory. During the progress of the negotiations, Mexico begged for the insertion of an article providing that slavery should not be permitted in any of the territories ceded. Our commissioner replied that the bare mention of the subject in a treaty was an utter impossibility; that if the territory should be increased tenfold in value, and, besides, covered all over a foot thick with pure gold, on the single condition that slavery should be excluded therefrom, he could not then even entertain the proposition, nor think for a moment of communicating it to the President.

Source 18 Albert K. Weinberg, *Manifest Destiny*, 1935

In the "roaring 'forties," a decade thus designated because the spirit of American life rose into high and turbulent flame, there was welded an association of two ideals which gave a new integration to the Americans' consciousness of national destiny. One of the two ideals was territorial expansion. After several decades of relative quiescence, expansionism was rekindled by the issues of Texas and Oregon and was fanned to white heat by the oratory of Democrats in the presidential election of 1844. For the first time the wish of numerous Americans fathered the thought that their eventual possession of no less a domain than the entire North American continent was "manifest destiny.". . .

The central implication of "manifest destiny" in the 'forties, however, was less a matter of the scope of expansion than of its purpose. The conception of expansion as a destiny meant primarily that it was a means to the fulfillment of a certain social ideal the preservation and perfection of which was America's providential mission or destiny. This ideal, conceived as "the last best revelation of human thought," was democracy—a theory of mass sovereignty but in a more important aspect a complex of individualistic values which . . . Americans most frequently summarized by the inspiring word "freedom." It was because of the association of expansion and freedom in a means-end relationship that expansion now came to seem most manifestly a destiny. . . .

It was because of its infusion with this ideal that American expansionism of the middle 'forties became possessed . . . of a "spiritual exaltation" in contemplation of the assumed superiority of American institutions. A recognition of the role played by idealistic American nationalism in this expansion movement has led to an explanation which is very different from that of most early American historians. Writers close to the passions of the Civil War attributed expansionism to "the glut of our slaveholders," the desire of the Southern States to extend the system of slavery. More objective contemporary historians believe that the intensity and extensity of expansionism, while due partly to sectional interests, were caused primarily by nationalistic attitudes resting not merely upon practical interests but also upon the "emotion" of "manifest destiny" and its correlate, the "idealism" of the spirit of democracy.

Source 19   Norman Graebner, *Empire on the Pacific,* 1955

Some suggested that American laws be extended to include the downtrodden peons of South America. . . . This was a magnificent vision for a democratic purpose, but it hardly explains the sweep of the United States across the continent.

For American expansion to the Pacific was always a precise and calculated movement. It was never limited in its objectives. American diplomatic and military policy that secured the acquisition of both Oregon and California was in the possession of men who never defined their expansionist purpose in terms of a democratic ideal. The vistas of all from Jackson to Polk were maritime and they were always anchored to specific waterways along the Pacific Coast. Land was necessary to them merely as a right of way to ocean ports—a barrier to be spanned by improved avenues of commerce. Any interpretation of westward expansion beyond Texas is meaningless unless defined in terms of commerce and harbors. . . .

The threat of European encroachment convinced them that the grandeur of the Pacific Coast must accrue to the wealth, prosperity, and commercial eminence of the United States. By 1845, . . . American expansionism had lost its broad nationalism and had become anchored to the mercantile interests of the United States. . . .

Polk alone could fulfill the expansionist goals of the 'forties. Although he was an advocate of agrarian democracy, his expansionist outlook as President was . . . narrowly mercantile. . . . His wartime expansionist policy was aimed primarily at San Francisco and San Diego, and as the war neared completion Polk acknowledged no other objectives to Congress. In his message of December, 1847, he declared that the bay of San Francisco and other harbors on the California coast "would afford shelter for our navy, for our numerous whale ships, and other merchant vessels employed in the Pacific ocean, (and) would in a short period become the marts of an extensive and profitable commerce with China, and other countries of the East." . . .

Indeed, manifest destiny is an inadequate description of American expansionism in the 'forties. The mere urge to expand or even the acceptance of a destiny to occupy new areas on the continent does not create specific geographical objectives.

Source 20   Julius W. Pratt, *A History of United States Foreign Policy,* 1955

The complicated factors that gave rise to the war with Mexico may be thus summarized: (1) Mexican resentment over the annexation of Texas by the United States, (2) a dispute as to what in reality constituted the southwestern boundary of Texas, (3) the failure of Mexico to pay certain damage claims of citizens of the United States, (4) President Polk's anxiety to obtain California for the United States. These factors interacted upon one another in a manner adverse to a maintenance of peaceful relations. Mexico's resentment over the annexation of Texas proved an insuperable obstacle to amicable negotiation over claims and boundary, and the glitter of California in the eyes of James K. Polk (though its golden treasure was unknown to him) probably made him less forbearing toward Mexico on other points than he might otherwise have been.

Source 21   Ray Allen Billington, *The Far Western Frontier,* 1956

War with Mexico followed America's expansionist spree as inevitably as night follows day. The annexation of Texas and President Polk's blatant demands for California left a legacy of hatred that the best will in the world could not have resolved—and that will was lacking. To the Mexicans the United States was a ruthless colossus bent on dismembering its southern neighbor step by step. To the Americans Mexico was an irresponsible troublemaker, indifferent to its obligations and hopelessly sunk in anarchy. . . .

By nature Polk was no aggressive dictator. . . . Yet he was a stubborn man, and he was unmovable in his determination to secure California for the United States. If legal steps could succeed, he vastly preferred them, but if Mexico refused to negotiate, he was willing to resort to war. He reached this conclusion only after every effort to purchase California had failed, after commercial and diplomatic intercourse between the two nations had been broken off at Mexico's insistence, after foreign intervention seemed imminent, and after his own diplomats assured him that a peaceful settlement was impossible.

Nor does the picture of the United States as a land-grabbing colossus take into account the desire of the Mexican people for war. There was not a red-blooded man among them but felt the national honor could be redeemed and the nation saved from future aggression only by challenging America at once.

Questioning the Past

1. List and evaluate the various causes of the war between the United States and Mexico. Which cause or causes seem to best explain the war? Which side, the United States or Mexico, was responsible for the commencement of the fighting? Explain.

2. Was the United States justified in going to war with Mexico? Why or why not?

3. What were the consequences of the Mexican War for the United States?

4. How can the United States, or any other nation, justify the extension of its borders through war?

Chapter 24

The Seneca Falls Convention

The Women's Rights Movement Is Born

July 19, 1848

Delegates from around the globe responded in 1840 to the call for a World's Anti-Slavery Convention in London, England. The agenda for the convention was the important question of obtaining the liberty and equality of all men held in human bondage. When the planners and organizers of the convention had issued the invitation to antislavery societies around the world, they had not even imagined that the delegates who might respond to their call would be other than male. They stood aghast when the delegation from the United States arrived. It included eight women.

Women had been active in the campaign to abolish slavery in the United States, and it was only natural that they should represent their antislavery societies at the London gathering. At least that had been the thinking of most of the antislavery associations in America. Most of the male delegates assembled in London thought otherwise.

A heated debate ensued at the World's Anti-Slavery Convention, as male delegates argued whether female delegates should be seated. The women themselves were not permitted to participate in the discussion. Finally, the delegates who had come from around the world to discuss the urgency and justice of human freedom voted to exclude women from their meeting.

Since the women had expended the time, effort, and resources to cross the Atlantic, however, the male delegates decided to permit the women to stay inside Freemasons' Hall, where the convention would take place. But the women would be required to sit in the balcony, separate and apart from the men. The women must sit in silence. And to ensure that their presence would not distract the men from the difficult questions they would debate, the women must sit silently in the balcony behind a curtain.

Lucretia Mott, one of the female delegates, and Elizabeth Cady Stanton, the wife of one of the male delegates, decided as they sat behind that curtain that the time had come to worry about the freedom of women as well as the freedom of blacks. They determined to hold a meeting with other women upon their return to America to consider the status of their gender.

🕶 *First Impressions*

To Be Free as Man Is Free

24.1 Seneca Falls Conference: The Beginning of Women's Rights

Eight years passed before they followed through on their decision by organizing a local event that, though they could hardly have known it at the time, would launch a national women's rights movement in America.

Source 1   Advertisement, *Seneca County Courier,* July 14, 1848

WOMAN'S RIGHTS CONVENTION—A convention to discuss the social, civil, and religious rights of women, will be held in the Wesleyan Chapel, at Seneca Falls, N.Y., on Wednesday and Thursday, the nineteenth and twentieth of July, current; commencing at 10 o'clock A.M. During the first day the meeting will be exclusively for women, who are earnestly invited to attend. The public generally are invited to be present on the second day, when Lucretia Mott, of Philadelphia, and other ladies and gentlemen, will address the convention.

Source 2   Elizabeth Cady Stanton's address to the convention, July 19, 1848

I should feel exceedingly diffident to appear before you at this time, having never before spoken in public, were I not nerved by a sense of right and duty, did I not feel the time had fully come for the question of women's wrongs to be laid before the public, did I not believe that woman herself must do this work; for woman alone can understand the height, the depth, the length, and the breadth of her own degradation. . . .

Among the many important questions which have been brought before the public, there is none that more vitally affects the whole human family than that which is technically called Women's Rights. Every allusion to the degraded and inferior position occupied by women all over the world has been met by scorn and abuse. From the man of highest mental cultivation to the most degraded wretch who staggers in the streets do we meet ridicule, and coarse jests, freely bestowed upon those who dare assert that woman stands by the side of man, his equal, placed here by her God, to enjoy with him the beautiful earth, which is her home as it is his, having the same sense of right and wrong, and looking to the same Being for guidance and support. So long has man exercised tyranny over her, injurious to himself and benumbing to her faculties, that few can nerve themselves to meet the storm; and so long has the chain been about her that she knows not there is a remedy. . . .

Let us consider . . . man's superiority, intellectually, morally, physically.

Man's intellectual superiority cannot be a question until woman has had a fair trial. When we shall have had our freedom to find out our own sphere, when we shall have had our colleges, our professions, our trades, for a century, a comparison then may be justly instituted. . . .

In consideration of man's claim to moral superiority, . . . [i]n my opinion, he is infinitely woman's inferior in every moral quality, not by nature, but made so by a false education. In carrying out his own selfishness, man has greatly improved woman's moral nature, but by an almost total shipwreck of his own.

Woman has now the noble virtues of a martyr. She is early schooled to self-denial and suffering. But man is not so wholly buried in selfishness that he does not sometimes get a glimpse of the narrowness of his soul, as compared with woman. Then he says, by way of an excuse for his degradation, "God has made woman more self-denying than man. It is her nature. It does not cost her as much to give up her wishes, her will, her life, even, as it does him. He is naturally selfish. God made him so."

No, I think not.... God's commands rest upon man as well as woman. It is as much his duty to be kind, self-denying and full of good works, as it is hers. As much his duty to absent himself from scenes of violence as it is hers. A place or position that would require the sacrifice of the delicacy and refinement of woman's nature is unfit for man, for these virtues should be as carefully guarded in him as in her. The false ideas that prevail with regard to the purity necessary to constitute the perfect character in woman, and that requisite for man, has done an infinite deal of mischief in the world. I would not have woman less pure, but I would have man more so. I would have the same code of morals for both....

Let us consider man's claim to physical superiority. Methinks I hear some say, surely, you will not contend for equality here. Yes, we must not give an inch, lest you take an **ell**.... We cannot say what the woman might be physically, if the girl were allowed the freedom of the boy in romping, climbing, swimming, playing whoop and ball.... Physically, as well as intellectually, it is use that produces growth and development....

We have met here to-day to discuss our rights and wrongs, civil and political, and not, as some have supposed, to go into the detail of social life alone. We do not propose to petition the legislature to make our husbands just, generous and courteous, to seat every man at the head of a cradle, and to clothe every woman in male attire. None of these points, however important they may be considered by leading men, will be touched in this Convention.

We are assembled to protest against a form of government, existing without the consent of the governed—to declare our right to be free as man is free, to be represented in the government which we are taxed to support.... And, strange as it may seem to many, we now demand our right to vote.

The Business of the Convention

"Husband and-wife are one in the law, and the husband is that one." So wrote seventeenth-century British jurist Sir Edward Coke, and so thought most Americans of the eighteenth century. With rare exceptions, American women were under the control of men from cradle to grave. A father had sole responsibility for the guardianship of his children, and, as his sons reached their majority, each became his own master. But as each of his daughters matured, the father gave her hand in marriage to a man who then assumed responsibility for her. Upon divorce, the wife had no legal right to her children. Though in some states women were permitted to own property, and required to pay taxes on what they owned, in no state were they allowed to spend their earnings without their husbands' consent or to vote in any election. Women could not sit on juries. They were denied admission to most colleges. They were not permitted membership in most professions. It was thought improper for women to hold opinions on political matters, and it was a serious breach of etiquette for a woman to discuss politics in public.

It was the desire to remove the social, religious, and political restraints that kept women from rising to their full potential as human beings that brought 300 people together at the Wesleyan Chapel at Seneca Falls, New York. For the two days of the convention, the 260 women and 40 men discussed the rights of women as members of the human family and the wrongs done to them as citizens of the United States. A list of 12 resolutions denouncing discrimination against women, asserting their equality with men, and calling upon society to allow women to take part in the religious and public life of the nation were discussed. All but one of these resolutions were adopted without a dissenting vote.

The exception was a resolution that declared "that it is the duty of the women of this country to secure to themselves the sacred right to the elective franchise." Many of the convention participants were worried that demanding the right for women to vote was much too controversial and would only serve to subject their entire proceedings to ridicule. Following eloquent pleas from Elizabeth Cady Stanton and Frederick Douglass, the resolution on women's suffrage was approved by a thin majority. Ironically, this most controversial demand was the one that would most captivate the attention and consume the energies of the women's rights movement for the next 70 years. And only one of the Seneca Falls participants would live long enough to see the ratification of the constitutional amendment granting women the franchise.

In addition to the resolutions, the convention participants considered and approved a Declaration of Sentiments drafted by Cady Stanton, with considerable inspiration from Thomas Jefferson. This document has served as a blueprint for the women's movement from that day to this. Some of its objectives have been realized; others remain unfulfilled.

After the two days of deliberations, the convention participants still had much to discuss, and a second convention was held two weeks later at Rochester. In fact, conventions patterned after the one at Seneca Falls were held throughout the remainder of the nineteenth century and through the twentieth, as the movement that began at Seneca Falls on July 19, 1848, proceeded generation after generation toward the realization of its goals: the liberty and equality of women.

Source 3   The Declaration of Sentiments, July 20, 1848

When, in the course of human events, it becomes necessary for one portion of the family of man to assume among the people of the earth a position different from that which they have hitherto occupied, but one to which the laws of nature and of nature's God entitle them, a decent respect to the opinions of mankind requires that they should declare the causes that impel them to such a course.

We hold these truths to be self-evident: that all men and all women are created equal; that they are endowed by their Creator with certain inalienable rights; that among these are life, liberty, and the pursuit of happiness; that to secure these rights governments are instituted, deriving their just powers from the consent of the governed. Whenever any form of government becomes destructive of these ends, it is the right of those who suffer from it to refuse allegiance to it, and insist upon the institution of a new government, laying its foundation on such principles, and organizing its powers in such form, as to them shall seem most likely to effect their safety and happiness. Prudence, indeed, will dictate that governments long established should not be changed for light and transient causes; and accordingly all experience hath shown that mankind are more disposed to suffer, while evils are sufferable, than to right themselves by abolishing the forms to which they are accustomed. But when a long train of abuses and usurpations pursuing invariably the same object evinces a design to reduce them under absolute despotism, it is their duty to throw off such government, and to provide new guards for their future security. Such has been the patient sufferance of the women under this government, and such is now the necessity which constrains them to demand the equal station to which they are entitled.

The history of mankind is a history of repeated injuries and usurpations on the part of man toward woman, having in direct object the establishment of an absolute tyranny over her. To prove this, let facts be submitted to a candid world.

He has never permitted her to exercise her inalienable right to the elective franchise.

He has compelled her to submit to laws, in the formation of which she had no voice.

He has withheld from her rights which are given to the most ignorant and degraded men—both natives and foreigners.

Having deprived her of this first right of a citizen, the elective franchise, thereby leaving her without representation in the halls of legislation, he has oppressed her on all sides.

He has made her, if married, in the eyes of the law, civilly dead.

He has taken from her all right in property, even to the wages she earns.

He has made her, morally, an irresponsible being, as she can commit many crimes with impunity, provided they be done in the presence of her husband. In the covenant of marriage, she is compelled to promise obedience to her husband, he becoming, to all intents and purposes, her master—the law giving him power to deprive her of her liberty, and to administer chastisement.

He has so framed the laws of divorce, as to what shall be the proper causes, and in case of separation, to whom the guardianship of the children shall be given, as to be totally regardless of the happiness of woman—the law, in all cases, going upon a false supposition of the supremacy of man, and giving all power into his hands.

After depriving her of all rights as a married woman, if single, and the owner of property, he has taxed her to support a government which recognizes her only when her property can be made profitable to it.

He has monopolized nearly all the profitable employments, and from those she is permitted to follow, she receives but a scanty remuneration. He closes against her all the avenues to wealth and distinction which he considers most honorable to himself. As a teacher of theology, medicine, or law, she is not known.

He has denied her the facilities for obtaining a thorough education, all colleges being closed against her.

He allows her in Church, as well as State, but a subordinate position, claiming Apostolic authority for her exclusion from the ministry, and, with some exceptions, from any public participation in the affairs of the Church.

He has created a false public sentiment by giving to the world a different code of morals for men and women, by which moral delinquencies which exclude women from society, are not only tolerated, but deemed of little account in man.

He has usurped the prerogative of Jehovah himself, claiming it as his right to assign for her a sphere of action, when that belongs to her conscience and to her God.

He has endeavored, in every way that he could, to destroy her confidence in her own powers, to lessen her self-respect, and to make her willing to lead a dependent and abject life.

Now, in view of this entire disfranchisement of one-half of the people in this country, their social and religious degradation,—in view of the unjust laws above mentioned, and because women do feel themselves aggrieved, oppressed, and fraudulently deprived of their most sacred rights, we insist that they have immediate admission to all the rights and privileges which belong to them as citizens of the United States.

In entering upon the great work before us, we anticipate no small amount of misconception, misrepresentation, and ridicule; but we shall use every instrumentality within our power to effect our object. We shall employ agents, circulate tracts, petition the State and National legislatures, and endeavor to enlist the pulpit and the press in our behalf. We hope this Convention will be followed by a series of Conventions embracing every part of the country.

Source 4   *Public Ledger and Daily Transcript,* July–August 1848

Our Philadelphia ladies not only possess beauty, but they are celebrated for discretion, modesty, and unfeigned diffidence, as well as wit, vivacity, and good nature. Whoever heard of a Philadelphia lady setting up for a reformer, or standing out for women's rights, or assisting to *man* the election grounds, raise a regiment, command a legion, or address a jury? . . . But all women are not as reasonable as ours of Philadelphia. . . . The New York girls aspire to mount the rostrum, to do all the voting, and we suppose, all the fighting too. . . . Women have enough influence over human affairs without being politicians. Is not everything managed by female influence? Mothers, grandmothers, aunts, sweethearts manage everything. Men have nothing to do but to listen and obey to the "of course, my dear, you will, and of course, my dear, you won't." Their rule is absolute; their power unbounded. Under such a system men have no claim to rights, especially "equal rights."

A woman is nothing. A wife is everything. A pretty girl is equal to ten thousand men, and a mother is, next to God, all powerful.

Source 5   *Lowell Courier* (Massachusetts), July 1848

The women folks have just held a Convention up in New York State, and passed a sort of "bill of rights," affirming it their right to vote, to become teachers, legislators, lawyers, divines, and do all and sundries the "lords" may, and of right now do. They should have resolved at the same time, that it was obligatory also upon the "lords" aforesaid, to wash dishes, scour up, be put to the tub, handle the broom, darn stockings, patch britches, scold the servants, dress in the latest fashion, wear trinkets, look beautiful, and be as fascinating as those blessed morsels of humanity whom God gave to preserve that rough animal man, in something like a reasonable civilization.

Source 6   Frederick Douglass, former slave, abolitionist, and editor, *The North Star,* July 28, 1848

One of the most interesting events of the past week, was the holding of what was technically styled a Woman's Rights Convention at Seneca Falls. The speaking, addresses, and resolutions of this extraordinary meeting was almost wholly conducted by women; and although they evidently felt themselves in a novel position, it is but simple justice to say that their whole proceedings were characterized by marked ability and dignity. . . .

Several interesting documents setting forth the rights as well as the grievances of women were read. Among these was a Declaration of Sentiments, to be regarded as the basis of a grand movement for attaining the civil, social, political, and religious rights of women. . . .

[W]e are not insensible that the bare mention of this truly important subject in any other than terms of contemptuous ridicule and scornful disfavor, is likely to excite against us the fury of bigotry and the folly of prejudice. A discussion of the rights of animals would be regarded with far more complacency by many of what are called the *wise* and the *good* of our land, than would a discussion of the rights of women. It is, in their estimation, to be guilty of evil thoughts, to think that woman is entitled to equal rights with man. Many who have at last made the discovery that the Negroes have some rights as well as other members of the human family, have yet to be convinced that women are entitled to any. . . .

Standing as we do upon the watch-tower of human freedom, we cannot be deterred from an expression of our approbation of any movement, however humble, to improve and elevate the character of any member of the human family. . . . [W]e hold woman to be justly entitled to all we claim for man. . . . All that distinguishes man as an intelligent and accountable being, is equally true of woman, and if that government only is just which governs by the free consent of the governed, there can be no reason in the world for denying to woman the exercise of the elective franchise.

Source 7   *Mechanic's Advocate* (Albany), July–August 1848

We are sorry to see that the women in several parts of this State are holding what they call "Women's Rights Conventions," and setting forth a formidable list of those Rights in a parody upon the Declaration of Independence. . . .

The women who attend these meetings, no doubt at the expense of their more appropriate duties, . . . affirm, as among their rights, that of unrestricted franchise. . . . Now, it requires no argument to prove that this is all wrong. Every true hearted female will instantly feel this is unwomanly, and that to be practically carried out, the males must change their position in society to the same extent in the opposite direction. . . . Society would have to be radically remodelled in order to accommodate itself to so great a change in the most vital part of the compact of the social relations of life; and the order of things established at the creation of mankind, and continued *six thousand years,* would be completely broken up.

Source 8   *Rochester Democrat* (New York), July 1848

The women in various parts of the State have taken the field in favor of a petticoat empire, with a zeal and energy which show that their hearts are in the cause, and that they are resolved no longer to submit to the tyrannical rule of the *heartless* "lords of creation," but have solemnly determined to demand their "natural and inalienable right" to attend the polls, and assist in electing our Presidents, and Governors, and Members of Congress, and State Representatives, and Sheriffs, and County Clerks, and Supervisors, and Constables, etc, etc., and to unite in the general scramble for office. This is right and proper. It is but just that they should participate in the beautiful and feminine business of politics, and enjoy their proportion of the "spoils of victory." Nature never designed that they should be confined exclusively to the drudgery of raising children, and superintending the kitchens, and to the performance of various other household duties which the cruelty of men and the customs of society have so long assigned to them. This is emphatically the age of "democratic progression," of *equality and fraternization*—the age when all colors and sexes, the bond and free, black and white, male and female, are, as they by right ought to be, all tending downward and upward toward the common level of equality.

The harmony of this great movement in the cause of freedom would not be perfect if women were still to be confined to petticoats, and men to breeches. There must be an "interchange" of these "commodities" to complete the system. Why should it not be so? Can not women fill an office, or cast a vote, or conduct a campaign, as judiciously and vigorously as men? And, on the other hand, can not men "nurse" the babies, or preside at the wash-tub, or boil a pot as safely and as well as women? It they can not, the evil is in that arbitrary organization of society which has excluded them from the practice of these pursuits. It is time these false notions and practices were changed, or, rather, removed, and for the political millennium foreshadowed by this petticoat movement to be ushered in.

Source 9   Elizabeth Cady Stanton, (Rochester) *National Reformer*

September 14, 1848

[To the Editor:]
There is no danger of the Woman Question dying for want of notice. Every paper you take up has something to say about it, and in proportion to the refinement and intelligence of the editor has this movement been favorably noticed. But one might suppose from the articles that you find in some papers, that there are editors so ignorant as to believe that the chief object of these recent conventions was to seat every lord at the foot of the cradle, and to clothe every woman in her lord's attire. Now neither of these points, however important they be considered by humble minds, was touched upon in the conventions. We did not meet to discuss fashions, customs, or dress, the rights of men or the propriety of the sexes changing positions, but simply our own inalienable rights, our duties, our true sphere.

📖 *Second Thoughts*

Seneca Falls Gave Them Hope

24.2 "All Men and Women Are Created Equal"

Although American women as far back as Abigail Adams had pressed for the right to vote, the greater employment of women in the nineteenth century gave added impetus to the effort. Nevertheless, though there were signs of increased equality after Seneca Falls, women were granted suffrage only slowly, state by state, in the early twentieth century.

Source 10   Sojourner Truth, a former slave, Akron (Ohio) women's convention, May 29, 1851

Dat man ober dar say dat womin needs to be helped in carriages, and lifted ober ditches, and to hab the best place everywhar. Nobody eber helps me into carriages, or ober mud-puddles, or gibs me any best place! And a'n't I a woman? Look at me!

I have ploughed, and planted, and gathered into barns, and no man could head me! And a'n't I a woman? I could work as much and eat as much as a man—when I could get it—and bear de lash as well! And a'n't I a woman?

I have borne thirteen chilern, and seen 'em mos' all sold off into slavery, and when I cried out with my mother's grief, none but Jesus heard me! And a'n't I a woman?

Den dey talks 'bout dis ting in de head; what dis dey call it? ("Intellect," whispered some one near.) Dat's it, honey. What's dat got to do wid womin's rights or niggers' rights? If my cup won't hold but a pint, and yourn holds a quart, wouldn't ye be mean not to let me have my half-measure full?

Den dat little man in black dar, he say women can't have as much rights as men, 'cause Christ wan't a woman! Whar did your Christ come from? Whar did your Christ come from? From God and a woman! Man had nothin' to do wid Him.

If de fust woman God ever made was strong enough to turn de world upside down all alone, dese women togedder ought to be able to turn it back, and get it right side up again! And now dey is asking to do it, de men better let 'em.

Source 11   Elizabeth Cady Stanton's convention lecture, March 25, 1888

We are assembled here to-day to celebrate the fortieth anniversary of the first organized demand made by women for the right of suffrage. . . .

Half a century ago the women of America were bond slaves, under the old common law of England. Their rights of person and property were under the absolute control of fathers and husbands. They were shut out of the schools and colleges, the trades and professions, and all offices under government; paid the most meager wages in the ordinary industries of life, and denied everywhere the necessary opportunities for their best development. Worse still, women had no proper appreciation of themselves as factors in civilization. Believing self-denial a higher virtue than self-development, they ignorantly made ladders of themselves by which fathers, husbands, brothers, and sons reached their highest ambitions, creating an impassable gulf between them and those they loved that no magnetic chords of affection or gratitude could span. Nothing was more common forty years ago than to see the sons of a family educated, while the daughters remained in ignorance; husbands at ease in the higher circles, in which their wives were unprepared to move. . . .

The active interest women are taking in all the questions of the day is in strong contrast with the apathy and indifference in which we found them a half-century ago, and the contrast in their condition between then and now is equally marked. Those who inaugurated the movement for woman's franchise, who for long years endured the merciless storm of ridicule and persecution, mourned over by friends, ostracized in social life, scandalized and caricatured by the press, may well congratulate themselves. . . .

Now even married women enjoy, in measure, their rights of person and property. They can make contracts, sue and be sued, testify in courts of justice, and with honor dissolve the marriage relation when it becomes intolerable. . . . Their political status is so far advanced that they enjoy all the rights of citizens in two Territories, municipal suffrage in one State, and school suffrage in half of the States of the Union. Here is a good record of the work achieved in the past half-century; but we do not intend to rest our case until all our rights are secured. . . .

Thus far women have been the mere echoes of men. Our laws and constitutions, our creeds and codes, and the customs of social life are all of masculine origin. The true woman is as yet a dream of the future. A just government, a humane religion, a pure social life await her coming.

Source 12 Elizabeth Cady Stanton's reflections on the Seneca Falls Convention, *Eighty Years and More,* 1898

I received an invitation to spend the day with Lucretia Mott . . . in Waterloo . [New York]. There I met several members of different families of Friends, earnest, thoughtful women. I poured out, that day, the torrent of my long-accumulating discontent, with such vehemence and indignation that I stirred myself, as well as the rest of the party, to do and dare anything. . . . We wrote the call that evening and published it in the *Seneca County Courier* the next day, the 14th of July, 1848, giving only five days' notice, as the convention was to be held on the 19th and 20th. . . .

These were the hasty initiative steps of "the most momentous reform that had yet been launched on the world—the first organized protest against the injustice which had brooded for ages over the character and destiny of one-half the race." No words could express our astonishment, on finding, a few days afterward, that what seemed to us so timely, so rational, and so sacred, should be a subject for sarcasm and ridicule to the entire press of the nation. With our Declaration of Rights and Resolutions for a text, it seemed as if every man who could wield a pen prepared a homily on "woman's sphere." All the journals from Maine to Texas seemed to strive with each other to see which could make our movement appear the most ridiculous. The anti-slavery papers stood by us manfully and so did Frederick Douglass, . . . but so pronounced was the popular voice against us, in the parlor, press, and pulpit, that most of the ladies who had attended the convention and signed the declaration, one by one, withdrew their names and influence and joined our persecutors. Our friends gave us the cold shoulder and felt themselves disgraced by the whole proceeding.

Source 13 James Schouler, *History of the United States under the Constitution*, 1904

A new agitation took its rise in these [ante-bellum] years which made decided progress in spite of ridicule. "Women's rights" was its subject, or the enlargement of that sphere of worldly activity to which custom and masculine opinion had long confined the gentler sex. It was kindled by the spirit of individual freedom, whose spread characterized . . . American society. Our first women's rights convention met . . . in the autumn of 1848, under the auspices of Lucretia Mott and Elizabeth Cady Stanton, both married women of American birth, who had already espoused the philanthropic cause of the negro. . . . This movement . . . took some hue from the crusade for negro emancipation, a cause in which woman saw or fancied a parallel to her own condition; and like our Northern abolitionists, with whom the self-chosen preachers of the fair inclined to fraternize, they threw down the gauntlet to society and the Christian church, and preferred conspicuousness to positive influence. "Bloomerism" realized, in 1852, the exaggeration of this feminine tendency to make both sexes alike, when some young reformers—and those neither the youngest nor the most comely—walked the streets with short kilts and Turkish trousers, in token of the solemn mission they were bound to fulfil. . . . [W]oman's good taste and abundant prudery soon banished the grotesque spectacle. . . . But the sexual agitation, confining its scope more closely to marriage equality, produced greater laxity in the divorce laws of our several States; and more than this, after New York in 1849 had set a strong example, wholly revolutionized in the course of twenty years the common law which merged the wife for the time being in her husband, by statutes, which at length prevail in every State, recognizing in a greater or less degree her separate existence and independent rights of contract and property. Whatever woman herself truly asks, male legislators have shown themselves quite ready to grant her. But the grant of co-equality in public affairs will be the last to accord; so contrary is it to human experience, and to woman's own instinct to make the home and social life her sphere of influence. Nature, perhaps, will prove stronger than all laws to solve the permanent relations of the sexes who were created for mutual comfort and not rivalry.

Source 14 Carrie Chapman Catt, former president of the National American Woman Suffrage Association, and Nettie Rogers Shuler, *Woman Suffrage and Politics*, 1926

These two conventions [the Seneca Falls and Rochester Conventions of 1848] had in no sense been national in scope but newspapers throughout the country regarded them as an innovation worthy of comment and full press accounts were carried far and wide. . . . [A] widespread discussion for and against the long list of liberties claimed was inaugurated by the two conventions.

Never in all history did so small a beginning produce so great an effect in so short a time.

Source 15   Barbara Welter, "The Cult of True Womanhood: 1820–1860,"
1966

The nineteenth-century American man was a busy builder of bridges and rail-roads, at work long hours in a materialistic society. The religious values of his forbears were neglected in practice if not intent, and he occasionally felt some guilt that he had turned this new land, this temple of the chosen people, into one vast countinghouse. But he could salve his conscience by reflecting that he had left behind a hostage, not only to fortune, but to all the values which he held so dear and treated so lightly. Woman, in the cult of True Womanhood presented by the women's magazines, gift annuals and religious literature of the nineteenth century, was the hostage in the home. In a society where values changed frequently, where fortunes rose and fell with frightening rapidity, where social and economic mobility provided instability as well as hope, one thing at least remained the same—a true woman was a true woman, wherever she was found. If anyone, male or female, dared to tamper with the complex of virtues which made up True Womanhood, he was damned immediately as an enemy of God, of civilization, and of the Republic. It was a fearful obligation, a solemn responsibility, which the nineteenth-century American woman had—to uphold the pillars of the temple with her frail white hand.

The attributes of True Womanhood, by which a woman judged herself and was judged by her husband, her neighbors and society, could be divided into four cardinal virtues—piety, purity, submissiveness and domesticity. Put them altogether and they spelled mother, daughter, sister, wife—woman. Without them, . . . all was ashes. With them she was promised happiness and power. . . .

But even while the women's magazines and related literature encouraged this ideal of the perfect woman, forces were at work in the nineteenth century which impelled woman herself to change, to play a more creative role in society. The movements for social reform, westward migration, missionary activity, uto-pian communities, industrialism, the Civil War—all called forth responses from women which differed from those she was trained to believe were hers by nature and divine decree. The very perfection of True Womanhood, moreover, carried within itself the seeds of its own destruction. For if woman was so very little less than the angels, she should surely take a more active part in running the world, especially since men were making such a mess of things.

Real women often felt they did not live up to the ideals of True Woman-hood: some of them blamed themselves, some challenged the standard, some tried to keep the virtues and enlarge the scope of womanhood. Somehow through this mixture of challenge and acceptance, of change and conformity, the True Woman evolved into the New Woman—a transformation as startling in its way as the abolition of slavery or the coming of the machine age.

Source 16 Miriam Gurko, *The Ladies of Seneca Falls,* 1976

[T]his first small venture in Seneca Falls had some surprisingly large and tangible results. It gave shape to a dissatisfaction that some women hadn't been able to take hold of or express in concrete terms. The Declaration of Sentiments clearly outlined their dependent legal and vocational handicaps. Women realized that they were not alone in their frustrations; this lessened the awful self-doubts of many, and gave them courage to look closely at their lives. The convention gave them hope: it was a form of action, however vague.

Source 17 Gerda Lerner, *The Majority Finds Its Past,* 1979

The women . . . at the first woman's rights convention . . . did not speak for the truly exploited and abused working woman. . . . Like most revolutionaries, they were not the most down-trodden but rather the most status-deprived group. Their frustrations and traditional isolation from political power funneled their discontent into fairly utopian declarations. . . .

The four decades preceding the Seneca Falls Convention were decisive in the history of American women. They brought an actual deterioration in their political status, and a rising level of expectation and subsequent frustration in a privileged elite group of educated women. . . .

American women were the largest disenfranchised group in the nation's history, and they retained this position longer than any other group. Although they found ways of making their influence felt continuously, not only as individuals but as organized groups, power eluded them. The mill girl and the lady, both born in the age of Jackson, would not gain access to power until they learned to cooperate, each for her own separate interests. It would take almost six decades before they would find common ground. The issue around which they finally would unite and push their movement to victory was the "impractical and utopian" demand raised at Seneca Falls—the means to power in American society—female suffrage.

Source 18 Lois W. Banner, *Elizabeth Cady Stanton,* 1980

24.3 150th Anniversary of Seneca Falls Convention

Cady Stanton's appropriation of the Declaration of Independence was a brilliant stroke. She thereby connected her cause to a powerful American symbol of liberty. . . . As did many radicals after her, using the 1776 declaration as the basis of their creeds and manifestoes, she astutely placed her movement within the mainstream of the American tradition and iterated her own loyalty to the revolutionary generation, whom she often identified as "fathers" of the feminists, at least in revolutionary temper. . . .

Despite the boldness of their action in calling the convention, Cady Stanton and her confederates were seized by insecurity when the convention opened in a local Methodist chapel. On the spot, none of them had sufficient self-possession to chair the meeting. They pressed James Mott, Lucretia Mott's husband, into service, even though the women had previously agreed that men should not take part in the event. But their audience of 300 was much larger than they had expected, and it included forty men. The Waterloo Quakers were there in full force, as were representatives from the Rochester reform community, including black abolitionist Frederick Douglass. In Seneca Falls the meeting was a major event, and it attracted many townspeople, including aggrieved women factory workers, committed reformers, and the curious.

Questioning the Past

1. What conditions produced the Seneca Falls Convention of 1848?

2. Read and explain the grievances listed in the Declaration of Sentiments. Which of these grievances have been redressed and which have not? What additional grievances, if any, might be added to the list today?

3. The Declaration of Principles asserts that "the history of mankind is a history of repeated injuries and usurpations on the part of man toward woman, having in direct object the establishment of an absolute tyranny over her." Debate this point.

4. Is it possible to see in the selections any changing attitudes toward the rights of women over the decades?

Chapter 25

Oil

Edwin L. Drake Strikes Oil

August 28, 1859

Ships began sailing from the ports of New England in the seventeenth century to search the seas for whales. By the 1850s there were more than 650 whaling ships from America, and hundreds more from Britain and other countries, engaged in the hunt. The primary reason for this effort was to produce whale oil, an illuminant that was used to fire lamps. These whalers, however, did their work too well, and by the middle of the nineteenth century, the whales had been hunted to the edge of extinction.

Meanwhile, another potential illuminant, a thick, dark, oily substance, was seeping uncontrollably into the springs and streams of western Pennsylvania. Native Americans had used this substance as a liniment, and hence whites had christened it "Seneca Oil," after the Seneca Nation. Were it not for the profit it provided to patent medicine salesmen who played upon the gullibility of nineteenth-century Americans, this substance would have been only a nuisance.

In 1854, George Bissell, a journalist, visited a lab at his alma mater, Dartmouth, and found a chemist there toying with a bottle of Seneca Oil. The chemist noted that the oil was flammable, and that if it were possible to gather enough of the annoying substance that seeped into the waterways of Pennsylvania, it might find a market as an illuminant. This idea found a receptive ear on Bissell.

By the end of the year, Bissell and his partner, J.G. Eveleth, had leased land along Oil Creek near Titusville, Pennsylvania, formed a company to gather the oily substance, and hired the services of Professor Benjamin Silliman of Yale to research and report on the commercial potential of oil. Bissell and Eveleth were hopeful that Silliman would confirm the conclusions of the Dartmouth chemist, and if not, they were certain they could still profit from their investment. How hard could it be to convince the American people to drink and rub over their bodies a substance as luscious as petroleum?

The report issued by Professor Silliman in 1855 vindicated Bissell's efforts. Silliman concluded that petroleum would yield illuminants, lubricants, paraffin, gas, and, most importantly, profits for its producers. "In short, your company have in their possession a raw material from which, by a simple and not expensive process, they may manufacture very valuable products," Silliman wrote. "It is worthy of note that my experiments prove that nearly the whole of the raw product may be manufactured without waste, and this solely by a well-directed process which is in practice one of the most simple of all chemical processes."

In 1858, the Seneca Oil Company—the venture organized by Bissell and Eveleth and financed by investors from New Haven—sent Colonel Edwin L. Drake to its property near Titusville to gather oil through whatever means he could develop. Drake had few work experiences that related to his new task. He had labored on farms. He had been a clerk in a hotel and a dry goods store. He had been a conductor on the New York & New Haven Railroad. None of which gave him any foundation for the petroleum industry. And the title of "colonel" was an invention of his employers hoping to lend him some measure of credibility. But he was a dedicated worker and tenacious in seeing a project through to completion. Moreover, he was available and, because of his connections with the railroad, could obtain a pass for free passage to Titusville. It is not clear which of these attributes was most important in his selection.

Drake spent months getting organized and assembling laborers and materials. He tried several methods of extracting oil but to no avail. It is not clear whether the idea to drill a well to reach petroleum lying in wait in underground reservoirs originated with Drake, Bissell, or someone else. Both Bissell and Drake later accepted credit for the proposal, as did many other people. But when Drake first began to talk of drilling, it was an idea whose authorship no one seemed eager to claim. The local population around Titusville did not take the notion of drilling for oil very seriously, and many thought Drake mentally unbalanced for pursuing the idea. His work earned him the nickname, "Drake's Folly," and many refused to supply him with their materials or their labor. Still, Drake persevered.

25.1 Oil History

Finally, Drake procured the services of a professional well driller, William "Uncle Billy" Smith, and his sons. Smith took an operation floundering for months and devised the means to see it through.

❧ *First Impressions*
"An Excitement Unparalled"

On the 29th of August, 1859, the *New York Times* ran a front page article on French action during the Battle of Solferino in the distant Austro-Sardinian War. The Washington *Evening Star* of that date devoted the lead section of its front page to a report on a "tall, sharp-eyed, dark-featured and angular" fortune-teller named Madame B. whose accuracy had been called into question. The *Savannah Daily News* offered "news of an alarming nature concerning recent attacks by Indians upon settlers of the Whitewater and Walnut Rivers" in Kansas Territory. These newspapers, and all the other publications of their day, missed the big story. They did not report on the one event of the previous day that would most alter the course of history. In fact, a whole week passed before any newspaper took note of the event on Oil Creek, and even then, it was impossible for anyone of that time to comprehend the full significance of what had happened.

Source 1 "Discovery of a Subterranean Fountain of Oil," *New York Tribune*

Titusville, Penn., September 8, 1859.—Perhaps you will recollect that in 1854, there was organized a company, under the name of the Pennsylvania Rock Oil

25.2 The
Drake Well
Museum

Company, which for some good reason, passed into the hands of New Haven capitalists, and was by them removed to New Haven. In 1858, the directors leased the grounds to E. L. Drake, well known on the New Haven railroad. He came out here and in May last commenced to bore for salt, or to find the source of the oil, which is common along the banks of Oil Creek. Last week, at the depth of seventy-one feet, he struck a fissure in the rock through which he was boring, when to the surprise and joy of everyone he found he had tapped a vein of water and oil, yielding four hundred gallons of pure oil to every twenty-four hours.

The pump now in use throws only five gallons per minute of water and oil into a large vat, where the oil rises to the top and the water runs out at the bottom. In a few days he will have a pump of three times the capacity of the one now in use, and then from ten to twelve hundred gallons will be the daily yield. . . .

The excitement attendant on the discovery of this vast source of oil was fully equal to what I ever saw in California, when the large lump of gold was accidentally turned up.

Source 2   George Bissell, letter to his wife, November 4, 1859

We find here an excitement unparalleled. The whole population are crazy almost. Farms that could have been bought for a trifle 4 months ago, now readily command $200 and $300 an acre, and that too when not a drop of oil has ever been discovered on them. . . . Judge of the value assigned by the people to *our lands* where from one well only they are now raising 1200 gallons of pure oil a day. Brewer has just left us and says that Pittsburgh men consider our property worth millions. Last week Ives, Townsend, and all the New Haven men were here. Did I tell you that about ten days ago, one of the workmen went into the store house with a lighted candle and the oil took fire and during the night burnt over $12,000 worth of oil. That loss, however, is a trifle—they can make it up in a week.

Source 3   Statement of driller William A. Smith, *Titusville Weekly Herald,* January 15, 1880

I came to Titusville first in 1859. Drake was here then and I came from Sauna, twenty miles this side of Pittsburgh. The place is now called Hite Station. . . . I carried on blacksmithing, working most of the time for the salt wells and salt works.

Mr. Drake had . . . been to Sauna several times and when he went into the "Seneca Oil Company" with his New Haven, Conn., friends, he came to me. He had hired men three times before, but they didn't keep their promise to drill the well for him. I was about to quit blacksmithing at the time to go on a farm, when a man named Lewis Peterson told Drake of me. Drake was on his way to Pittsburgh and Peterson was to see me before he came back. When he got back, Peterson brought him to me and we made a bargain. I asked Drake if he had any tools. He told me I had better make some and bring them with me, so I made them and he sent a team to haul them up.

The first night I came to Titusville, I took lodgings in the Eagle House, and the next morning went to see Mr. Drake. He was sick and I told him to get the man, that brought the tools, to come down to the oil spring. We called it an oil spring then. This man, Cord Redfield, took me around and showed me everything about the spring; that was on the 19th of May, '59, and on Saturday, the next day, I went to work. Mr. Drake wanted my opinion by Monday on the oil prospects. About 10 o'clock that day he came to the well or spring. There was a saw mill about seven or eight rods off and the hands all stopped work to hear what I had to say. Mr. Drake asked me what I thought his prospects were. I said very good. I told him I would not be afraid to insure him ten barrels a day. He said, Stop! half that will satisfy me. I said no, I would sooner say twenty barrels, but he said again that half of ten would do him and I told him he was sure of not less than ten.

We went to work and I wanted some driving pipe right away, but Mr. Drake thought we could get down without it.

Before I came there had been eight men at work six weeks and only got the cribbing down eight feet. I told them we couldn't possibly get down without drive pipe to keep the water out. We rigged up a plank pump with a sucker eight inches square, and the next morning I commenced to put my curb down. I got a six foot piece down and eighteen inches of the second one when the water came in so fast that we had to work knee deep in it. It was so cold that we couldn't work more than ten minutes at a time. Well, it still kept rising on us, although the pump was throwing a big stream of water. I got an iron rod and run it down the hole, but touched no rock. When I drew the rod the water gushed out at a big rate, and we had to get out with our tools. The crib was about sixteen feet deep and there was water enough in it to drown us all. I saw it was no use trying to get down without drive pipe.

There was a lot of five-eighth inch rods lying around and I welded two together and run them down but they wouldn't reach any rock. I put a third one and struck what I thought was rock at twenty-six feet. Next I commenced drilling in this rock and got into the gravel again. Our pipe was small, about two and three-quarter inches and the tools wouldn't go into it further than two feet, so we got a new set of tools. I told Drake if he didn't get me what I wanted I would go back home. He said you go and move your family here and give me a list of what you want and I'll get it. He got fifty feet of driving pipe, but there were no bands on pipes then and I made some myself. On the 9th of July I got ready for driving and drove 49 feet 8 inches of the pipe and came to the rock.

I then commenced drilling, and on the 12th day of August, at 4 o'clock, I struck the oil. Mr. Drake was there with a lot of others. I found my tools drop and kept watching the pipe, which had water in about four feet from the top. In about five minutes I saw the oil come up. I says to Mr. Drake, "Look there! What do you think of this?" He looked down in the pipe and said, "What is that?" I said, "That is your fortune." . . .

Mr. Drake called for Jonathon Locke at the saw mill to stop the mill and bring his hands. They all came, sixteen or eighteen of 'em. Drake said just look there what Smith has done, and Locke said, "Good! Why, we all thought Smith was crazy, and look what he has got now."

On the next Monday, Mr. Drake got a tin pump, here in Titusville, about twenty-five feet long. We got a little pump, too, like a water well pump used in houses, run our pipe down and worked the pump by hand. For a tank we got an old oil cask and in this way we pumped from eight to nine barrels a day. We kept dipping the oil out of the cask with pails and putting it in barrels. At that time my oldest son was pumping.

One day I thought the tank was not filling up fast enough and I went to see if the oil had stopped. I had a lighted lamp in my left hand. A little streak of light, like the flash of lightning, went to the oil, set everything in a blaze and in a few minutes the well rig and the house near by, in which I lived, were all burned up. This was on a Friday and on Saturday following it rained very hard, so that the best I could do was to hunt up what things I could save from the wreck of my house.

While I was thus engaged Mr. R. D. Fletcher came down from Titusville. He had a kind sort o' look about him and seemed sorry for our misfortune. After walking around a little while, he noticed a cook stove all burned and broken up. "Smith, what can I help you to?" I felt very downhearted and I told him he was very kind, but I hardly knew what he could do for me. He knew, though, and without saying a great deal more rode up home. Pretty soon there came a team stacked up as full as it could hold. There was a cook stove, flour, meat, dishes of all kinds, furniture, bedding, and a whole house full of goods, sent by Mr. Fletcher for the use of me and my family. I shan't forget Mr. Fletcher very soon for his kindness to me then, for, if it hadn't been for him I should ha' been in hard shape, though I must say, the mill hands and others around there were all very good.

When the fire happened, Mr. Drake was away in Erie and knew nothing about what had occurred. He was coming home on the day after the fire when two men met him. They asked him if he knew about the big oil spring being burned up. He said, "No." They told him it was all burned up. Mr. Drake looked astonished and said, "Is anybody hurt?" They said, "No." He replied, "That's all right then. I'm glad of that."

On Monday Mr. Drake came down to the well. I was still gathering up the things and he called out, "Helloa Smith, I think you have a black frost here."

I said it was too black for me. He said, "Oh! that's all right Smith." So we went to work and started again.

We got started up on the 7th of November, and singular as it might be the well did thirty-two barrels a day right-away from that time. It kept on averaging that for a year, too, although it never pumped on Sunday.

Source 4   *New York Times,* November 10, 1880

The death of Col. E. L. Drake, the first man to sink a well in Pennsylvania in search of oil, and the pioneer in the petroleum business of that State, is announced as having occurred in New Bethlehem, Penn., on Monday last. Like the majority of the early operatives, in oil, he made a fortune, lost it, and in his declining years found himself in poverty. Unlike many of the same class, however, he was not reduced to abject want, for the State of Pennsylvania, recognizing the benefits which she had derived from his ingenuity and enterprise, granted him a pension, which has been the support of himself and his family now for several years.

It was by the merest accident that Col. Drake's attention was first directed to the value of petroleum in 1858. Half a century before that date, old Nat Carey had peddled the peculiar oil which was skimmed in small quantities from the waters of Oil Creek, and had paraded its virtues as a purgative and liniment. He called it Seneca Oil, from the fact that Red Jacket, the Seneca Chief, had imparted to the whites the secret of its powers. Its fame as a medicinal agent was purely local, when Carey, with vials of the stuff, plodded from hamlet to hamlet and established a demand for it that brought him no small profit. An attempt by Gen. Franklin to introduce this "great natural medicine" to a Southern market later on ended disastrously, the Baltimore merchant to whom a wagon load of it was consigned dumping it into the Chesapeake Bay, unable to endure the odor which it set forth, and unwilling to believe that his Southern customers could accustom themselves to the remedy, no matter what the nature of their ailments. Northern patients, however, took more kindly to it, but among them even it was known more as a liniment than as a medicine.

For several years, until 1858, a firm in this City, Evelith & Bissell, had received from Titusville, Penn., about a gallon of this oil a day, which, mixed with other ingredients they sold as the then celebrated "Mustang Liniment." Their supply of oil was gathered in the very primitive method of dipping blankets in a spring permeated with the article and wringing them into pans. This spring was owned by the firm, and when they were unable to meet their indebtedness to persons in New Haven, Conn., the latter took the Titusville property in payment. This was 1858. Col. Drake was then a conductor on the New York and New Haven Railroad, whose shrewdness had already attracted the attention of the owners of the newly acquired property. They sent him to Pennsylvania to perfect their title to it. He became satisfied from his observations that Seneca oil was possessed of more properties than had ever been credited to it, and that a fortune was in store for the man who could secure it in any quantity. He suggested the idea that the oil could be obtained in paying quantities by sinking a well. He was laughed at as a lunatic by the Pennsylvanians. Returning to New Haven he succeeded in interesting some capitalists in the novel theory, and in organizing the Seneca Oil Company, of which he was appointed manager. In the Spring of 1859 he commenced sinking a well on Watson's Flat, at a spot about a mile below Titusville. The move was considered so ridiculous that it was only with the greatest difficulty that he could hire assistance in the work. He finally secured the services of an old salt borer named William A. Smith and his two sons. The boring of the first petroleum well was begun on the first of July, 1859. When the three men quit work at sunset on the 29th of August they had drilled to a depth of 69 feet 6 inches. The elder Smith was first at the hole the following morning, and to his astonishment it was filled with oil. A barrel of it was dipped out in a few minutes, and the news of Col. Drake's sanity ran like wildfire up Oil Creek Valley. The discovery was flashed over the country, and then began the ever memorable oil excitement, which made and beggared men before it subsided. To-day the oil region is honeycombed with wells, the supply of petroleum far exceeds the demand, and farmers who own no oil stock are skimming from the waters of the same creeks over which old Nat Carey labored hundreds of gallons of the stuff which is running to waste.

Col. Drake continued his operations in petroleum until 1864, when, broken in health and ruined in pocket, although at one time he had amassed a princely fortune, he abandoned the oil fields. In 1873, the State granted him a pension of $1,500 a year, payable to his wife in the event of her surviving him. He settled in New Bethlehem, where he spent the last years of his life a confirmed invalid. His co-pioneer, Smith, still lives in Butler, County, Penn., destitute, and with a large family on his hands. A statue to Col. Drake's memory is to be erected on the new Oil Exchange now being built in Titusville.

An Industry Is Born

A few days before Drake struck oil, his employers in New Haven reached the conclusion that the venture on Oil Creek was not leading to a profitable end. A letter was sent to Drake ordering him to close down the operation, settle his financial obligations, and return to New Haven. Owing to the slow movement of the mails, this message arrived too late to prevent his monumental discovery.

Within weeks of the success of "Drake's Folly," thousands of prospectors were leasing lands and drilling for oil. The price of oil by January of 1860 had reached $20 a barrel. By the end of 1861, so much oil was being produced that the price of petroleum dropped to ten cents a barrel. It was the first phase of a long cycle of glut and shortage in the oil business.

By 1872, oil wells were bringing up petroleum all over a 2000-square mile area of western Pennsylvania, eastern Ohio and West Virginia. Already, though, a trend was emerging that would come to characterize the industry: Though there were many companies competing for trade in oil, one company alone, Standard Oil, accounted for one-fifth of the petroleum refined that year.

The share of the business controlled by Standard Oil increased every year thereafter. By 1880, Standard had consumed or driven into insolvency almost all of its competitors and gained control of the industry from the extraction of the oil through its transportation, refinement, distribution, and sale. The means by which Standard Oil founder John D. Rockefeller accomplished this consolidation of the oil industry have been a source of criticism. Rockefeller used the weight of his economic fortune to pressure the railroads into giving him rebates on the transportation of his product and to give him drawbacks on the shipping costs of his competitors. His company intimidated merchants into using only the petroleum products produced by Standard Oil. Competitors were eliminated by cutthroat tactics. Standard Oil underpriced its product in local markets to force local businesses into joining Standard Oil or into bankruptcy. The company developed a management structure that bypassed the intentions of the laws of the land. Influence was bought with public officials from courthouse to White House. In 1911, however, federal courts found Standard Oil in violation of antitrust laws and broke the company into 38 pieces.

By the time the Standard Oil Trust was dissolved, Pennsylvania had ceased to be the sole source of oil. In 1901, the massive Spindletop field in east Texas was tapped. Soon, oil was also discovered in California, west Texas, Oklahoma, Louisiana, off the Gulf Coast, the Middle East, the East Indies, Russia, North Africa, Nigeria, Angola, Venezuela, and the North Sea. Global corporations, each mightier than Standard Oil at its peak, moved quickly to organize the world's energy production and distribution. By midcentury, seven giant companies controlled most of the

25.3 History of the Standard Oil Company

global petroleum industry: Exxon, Mobil, Socal, Texaco, Gulf, British Petroleum, and Royal Dutch Shell. The first three were remnants of Standard Oil.

As the twentieth century progressed, the United States, along with the rest of the world's population, grew increasingly dependent upon petroleum products. In 1973, a decision by several oil-producing countries, supported by the major oil companies, to embargo the supply of oil destined for the United States produced a severe energy crisis while illustrating clearly the American dependence on foreign sources of oil.

Second Thoughts
"Save the Wells"

When Drake and his neighbors began to ship oil, they placed it in barrels that held 42 gallons each. The 42-gallon barrel remains the standard of measurement for oil today. In 1859, Edwin Drake felt himself fortunate to produce 32 barrels of oil per day. At the turn of the twentieth century, the world was producing 410,959 barrels per day. At the turn of the twenty-first century, the world is producing 66,301,369 barrels per day.

From Drake's well came a substance that made the twentieth century unlike any preceding one. From this same well has come a global industry whose economic strength and pervasion of society are without precedent in history.

Source 5   J. H. A. Bone, *Petroleum and Petroleum Wells*, 1865

From Maine to California it lights our dwellings, lubricates our machinery, and is indispensable in numerous departments of arts, manufactures, and domestic life. To be deprived of it now would be setting us back a whole cycle of civilization. To doubt the increased sphere of its usefulness would be to lack faith in the progress of the world.

Source 6   Henry D. Lloyd, *Wealth against Commonwealth*, 1894

It was an American idea to "strike oil." Those who knew it as the "slime" of Genesis, or used it to stick together the bricks of the Tower of Babel, or knelt to it in the fire temples, were content to take it as it rose, the easy gift of nature, oozing forth on brook or spring. But the American struck it.

The world, going into partial eclipse on account of the failing supply of whale oil, had its lamps all ready for the new light, and industries beyond number needed only an expansion of the supply. . . .

With Drake's success in "striking oil" came an end to the period, lasting thousands of years, of fire temples, sweep and bucket, Seneca oil; and came to an end, also, the Arcadian simplicity of the old times—old though so recent—in which Professor Silliman could say, "it is not monopolized by any one, but is carried away freely by all who care to collect it."

The oil age begins characteristically. As soon as Drake's well had made known its precious contents, horses began running, and telegrams flying, and money passing to get possession of the oil lands for the few who knew from those who did not. The primitive days when "it was not monopolized by any one" were over.

Source 7   Ida M. Tarbell, *The History of the Standard Oil Company,* 1904

[T]o-day, as at the start, the purpose of the Standard Oil Company is . . . the regulation of the price of crude and refined oil by the control of the output; and the chief means for sustaining this purpose is still that of the original scheme—a control of oil transportation giving special privileges in rates. . . .

[T]he Standard Oil Company is probably in the strongest financial position of any aggregation in the world. And every year its position grows stronger. . . .

In 1898 the Standard Oil Company reported to the Industrial Commission that it produced 35.58 per cent. of Eastern crude—the production that year was about 52,009,000 barrels. . . . But while Mr. Rockefeller produces only about a third of the entire production, he controls all but about ten per cent of it; that is, all but about ten per cent. goes immediately into his custody on coming from the wells. It passes entirely out of the hands of the producers when the Standard pipe-line takes it. The oil is in Mr. Rockefeller's hands, and he, not the producer, can decide who is to have it. The greater portion of it he takes himself, of course, for he is the chief refiner of the country. In 1898 there were about twenty-four million barrels of petroleum produced in this country. Of this amount about twenty million barrels were made by the Standard Oil Company; fully a third of the balance was produced by the Tidewater Company, of which the Standard holds a large minority stock, and which for twenty years has had a running arrangement with the Standard. Reckoning out of the Tidewater's probable output, and we have an independent output of about 2,500,000 in twenty-four million. It is obvious that this great percentage of the business gives the Standard the control of prices. . . .

From the beginning the Standard Oil Company has studied thoroughly everything connected with the oil business. It has known, not guessed at conditions. It has had a keen authoritative sight. It has applied itself to its tasks with indefatigable zeal. It has been as courageous as it has been cautious. Nothing has been too big to undertake, as nothing has been too small to neglect. . . .

These qualities alone would have made a great business, and unquestionably it would have been along the line of combination, for when Rockefeller undertook to work out the good of the oil business the tendency to combination was marked throughout the industry, but it would not have been the combination whose history we have traced. To the help of these qualities Mr. Rockefeller . . . secured an alliance with the railroads to drive out rivals. For fifteen years he received rebates of varying amounts on at least the greater part of his shipments, and for at least a portion of that time he collected drawbacks of the oil other people shipped; at the same time he worked with the railroads to prevent other people getting oil to manufacture, or if they got it he worked with the railroads to prevent the shipment of the product. If it reached a dealer, he did his utmost to bully or wheedle him to countermand his order. If he failed in that, he undersold until the dealer, losing on his purchase, was glad enough to buy thereafter of Mr. Rockefeller. . . .

Very often people who admit the facts, who are willing to see that Mr. Rockefeller has employed force and fraud to secure his ends, justify him by declaring, "It's business." That is, "it's business" has come to be a legitimate excuse for hard dealing, sly tricks, special privileges. It is a common enough thing to hear men arguing that the ordinary laws of morality do not apply in business. Now, if the Standard Oil Company were the only concern in the country guilty of the practices which have given it monopolistic power, this story never would have been written. Were it alone in these methods, public scorn would long ago have made short work of the Standard Oil Company. But it is simply the most conspicuous type of what can be done by these practices. The methods it employs with such acumen, persistency, and secrecy are employed by all sorts of business men, from corner grocers up to bankers. If exposed, they are excused on the ground that this is business. If the point is pushed, frequently the defender of the practice falls back on the Christian doctrine of charity, and points that we are erring mortals and must allow for each other's weaknesses!—an excuse, which, if carried to its legitimate conclusion, would leave our business men weeping on one another's shoulders over human frailty, while they picked one another's pockets.

One of the most depressing features of the ethical side of the matter is that instead of such methods arousing contempt they are more or less openly admired. And this is logical. Canonise "business success," and men who make a success like that of the Standard Oil Trust become national heroes!

Source 8   Petroleum administrator for war during World War II, and secretary of interior, Harold L. Ickes, *Fightin' Oil*, 1943

It becomes more evident, as distances are annihilated, that this organized human slaughter in which the world is now engaged, is moving to a tempo that petroleum may, in a sense, have set. Had there been no such thing as oil, I doubt if there would have been a global war. Without oil, I don't see how we could now be fighting on all sides of the earth. It is possible that nature would have given us something else to fight with. Hitler, naturally, expected to "blitz" his way to world power from the sky. He was thinking of himself as the "reincarnation" of the great god Wotan. But without petroleum the idea would scarcely have presented itself even to a mad Austrian paperhanger.

We may at least be sure that, without oil, this war would not have been fought on its present grand scale. The spectacular hit-and-run attacks which our fliers are staging every day over many wide fronts . . . would have been impossible but for petroleum. An oilless war, had there been a war, would have been pretty dull business compared with the well-lubricated maneuverings of millions of men, not only on the ground, but on the surface of the waters, in the air, and under the seas. If, therefore, oil has set the pace of this war, oil must see it through, and the side that can throw the most oil into the fray over the longest period of time will win.

Source 9　Political scientist Hans J. Morgenthau, *Politics among Nations: The Struggle for Power and Peace,* First Edition, 1948

As the absolute importance of the control of raw materials for national power has increased in proportion to the mechanization of warfare, so certain raw materials have gained in importance over others. This has happened whenever fundamental changes in technology have called for the use of new materials or the increased use of old ones. In 1936, a statistician rated the share of a number of basic minerals in industrial production for military purposes and assigned them the following values: coal, 40; oil, 20; iron, 15; copper, lead, manganese, sulphur, 4 each; zinc, aluminum, nickel, 2 each. Half a century before, the share of coal would certainly have been considerably greater, since as a source of energy it had then only small competition from water and wood and none from oil. The same would have been true of iron, which then had no competition from light metals and substitutes, such as plastics. Thus it is not by accident that Great Britain, which was self-sufficient in coal and iron, was the one great world power of the nineteenth century.

　　Since the First World War, oil as a source of energy has become more and more important for industry and war. Most mechanized weapons and vehicles are driven by oil, and, consequently, countries which possess considerable deposits of oil have acquired an influence in international affairs which in some cases can be attributed primarily, if not exclusively, to that possession. "One drop of oil," said Clemenceau during the First World War, "is worth one drop of blood of our soldiers." The emergence of oil as an indispensable raw material has brought a shift in the relative power of the politically leading nations. The United States and the Soviet Union have become more powerful since they are self-sufficient in this respect, while Great Britain has grown considerably weaker, the British Isles being completely lacking in oil deposits.

Source 10　J. Stanley Clark, *The Oil Century from the Drake Well to the Conservation Era,* 1958

The development of the internal-combustion engine in the 1890's, the advent of the automobile, and its rapid ascendancy in transportation set off the phenomenal growth of the petroleum industry during the first half of the twentieth century. Commonplace instances come to mind: the development of the automobile for family and business use; buses, vans, and trucks that revolutionized the transportation industry; tractors and motor-driven farm equipment; the conversion of locomotives and seagoing vessels to the use of petroleum fuels for power; factory and industrial uses of residual and fuel oils; the rapid expansion of aviation; and the dominant role played by petroleum in two global wars.

　　There are many ways of stating the remarkable rise of the petroleum industry during this period. For example, in 1955, there were twelve industrial corporations in the United States with a net worth of more than one billion dollars: Standard Oil (New Jersey), the General Motors Corporation, United States Steel, the Du Pont Company, the Ford Motor Company, Socony, Mobil Oil, Standard Oil of Indiana, the Texas Company, Gulf, Standard Oil of California, Bethlehem Steel, and the General Electric Company. It is significant that among the first ten, six are oil companies and two of the remainder represent the automobile industry. Also, in 1955, twenty-six companies of the country had net sales in excess of one billion dollars; eight of the twenty-six are oil companies.

In 1900, less than 8 percent of the power and heat requirements in the United States were furnished by oil and gas; by 1918, 14 percent; by 1940, 44 percent; and it is now estimated that over 65 percent of the national supply of energy is furnished by natural gas, gasoline, and other petroleum products.

Source 11 Harold F. Williamson and Arnold R. Daum, *The American Petroleum Industry: The Age of Illumination, 1859–1899*, 1959

It is doubtful whether Drake gauged the significance of his accomplishment any better than the initial output of his well. There was little implicit or explicit in his attitude and actions suggestive of a man with an entrepreneurial vision. He was a man doggedly, almost stolidly, carrying out the specific project he had been employed to undertake. As a driller, Drake was a rank amateur. At a time when it usually took only six to eight months to bore 1,000 feet or more through solid rock in the great salt fields along the Kanawha River, it took him two years to drill 69 feet. When Drake finally reached his peak of three feet a day in August, 1859, he was boring at only about one-half of the Kanawha rate of a decade earlier.

But whatever Drake's shortcomings as driller, businessman, or entrepreneur, he was the first to demonstrate that petroleum could be drilled for and obtained in substantial quantities. By this demonstration he removed the major barrier to the rise of a new industry.

Source 12 Historian John B. Rae, *The American Automobile,* 1965

As more and more vehicles poured onto American highways, their effect on the American economy became increasingly pronounced. In the first ten years of the twentieth century, automobile manufacturing climbed from 150th to 21st in value of products among American industries, and in this phenomenal climb it had a marked influence on the growth and direction of other industries. . . .

The effects were naturally greatest in the industries that contributed most directly to the motor vehicle. . . . The petroleum industry was literally revolutionized. Before 1900 only about one-tenth of the petroleum refined was converted into gasoline. Gasoline, in fact, was frequently regarded as an undesirable waste product and thrown away. It was known to have high illuminating qualities, but its volatility made it dangerous. As a fuel for internal-combustion engines, however, gasoline was clearly to be preferred.

The advent of the gasoline automobile was materially aided by a spectacular increase in the supply of crude oil through the opening of new fields, beginning with the Spindletop field in East Texas in 1901. The presence of oil there was dramatically demonstrated on January 10 of that year when the first gusher in the United States shot 160 feet into the air, carrying with it the drilling rig and the derrick. Other new fields followed in quick succession, with the result that by 1914 crude-oil production rose from the 60 million barrels of 1900 to about 250 million. Without the motor car the petroleum industry would have been in trouble, since the kerosene lamp was retreating before gas and electric illumination; but this great increase in the supply of petroleum occurred fortuitously just as the automobile began to create a limitless demand for gasoline.

Source 13   Anthony Sampson, *The Seven Sisters: The Great Oil Companies and the World They Shaped,* 1975

These seven companies—[Exxon, Mobil, Gulf, Texaco, Socal, B.P. and Shell] five American, one British, one Anglo-Dutch—had all become major players in the oil industry before the twenties. There were many others, including the other offspring of Rockefeller's Standard Oil, that were to play important roles. But it was the seven "majors" who were to dominate the world oil business in the following decades, and to become new kinds of industrial organization—in some respects the forerunners of the modern multinational corporation. Each of them soon developed into an "integrated oil company" controlling not only its own production, but also transportation, distribution and marketing. With their own fleets of tankers, they could soon operate across the world in every sector of the industry, from the "upstream" business of drilling and producing at the oilfields, to the "downstream" activity of distributing and selling at the pumps or the factories. And each company strove, with varying success, to be self-sufficient at both ends, so that their oil could flow into their tankers through their refineries to their filling stations. It was this worldwide integration, together with their size, which was the common characteristic of these seven.

There were plenty of signs that the seven companies were competing, often ferociously, to sell their precious fuel: and nowhere was the competition more evident than in the promotion of the new product gasoline for the new automobiles. The names Standard, Gulf or Texaco, first on cans, then on filling stations, then on the bright signs sticking up from the landscape, were visible symbols of the choice facing the consumer. Yet the competition also had striking limitations. It was not just that the product, as far as any consumer could detect, was identical—much more identical than cars or soaps. Nor that the new garages and filling stations seemed to huddle in clusters on the roadside as if they dreaded to stick their tall necks out alone. More seriously disturbing for the advocates of free enterprise was the tendency of the giant companies, as they ventured further abroad, to cling together in consortia and to reach hidden understandings with each other in their attempts to bring order to the volatile market. The name the Seven Sisters, that came to be applied to them and which they so much resented, was not altogether inappropriate. Like the classical sisters, who were translated by Zeus into stars, they seemed to have acquired immortality. But also like mortal sisters, they fought and competed with each other, while still preserving a family likeness and closing ranks when challenged by outsiders. . . .

The failure of the western governments to keep track of the companies and control them has marked their history since Rockefeller. It was never clear who was using who. As the business became more global in the forties and fifties, so governments thought they were using their companies by encouraging them abroad, with anti-trust clearances, tax advantages and diplomatic support, while the companies were in fact far better at using them, in ways that were often against their governments' interest. Thus Harold Ickes, having safeguarded Socal and Texaco in wartime, soon found them overcharging the U.S. Navy for oil. Thus the tax concession given to Aramco in 1951 became the instrument of the companies' growing dependence on the Middle East producers. Thus BP, having been set up by Churchill as a more patriotic alternative to Shell, soon became uncontrollable, and landed the British government in the Abadan fiasco of 1951.

Source 14 President Jimmy Carter, televised speech from the White House, April 18, 1977

Tonight I want to have an unpleasant talk with you about a problem unprecedented in our history. With the exception of preventing war, this is the greatest challenge our country will face during our lifetimes. The energy crisis has not yet overwhelmed us, but it will if we do not act quickly.

It's a problem we will not solve in the next few years, and it is likely to get progressively worse through the rest of this century. . . .

I know that some of you may doubt that we face real energy shortages. The 1973 gas lines are gone, and with the springtime weather our homes are warm again.

But our energy problem is worse tonight than it was in 1973 or a few weeks ago in the dead of winter. It is worse because more waste has occurred, and more time has passed by without our planning for the future. And it will get worse every day until we act.

The oil and natural gas we rely on for 75 percent of our energy are simply running out. In spite of increased effort, domestic production has been dropping steadily at about 6 percent a year. Imports have doubled in the last five years. And our nation's independence of economic and political action is becoming increasingly constrained. Unless profound changes are made to lower oil consumption, we now believe that early in the 1980s the world will be demanding more oil than it can produce.

The world now uses about 60 million barrels of oil a day, and demand increases each year about 5 percent. This means that just to stay even we need the production of a new Texas every year, an Alaskan North Slope every nine months, or a new Saudi Arabia every three years. Obviously this cannot continue.

We must look back into history to understand our energy problem. Twice in the last several hundred years there has been a transition in the way people use energy. The first was about 200 years ago, when we changed away from wood—which had provided about 90 percent of all fuel—to coal, which was more efficient. This change became the basis of the Industrial Revolution.

The second change took place in this century, with the growing use of oil and natural gas. They were more convenient and cheaper than coal, and the supply seemed to be almost without limit. They made possible the age of automobile and airplane travel. Nearly everyone who is alive today grew up during this age and we have never known anything different.

Because we are now running out of gas and oil, we must prepare quickly for a third change, to strict conservation and to renewed use of coal and permanent renewable energy sources, like solar power.

The world has not prepared for the future. During the 1950s, people used twice as much oil as during the 1940s. During the 1960s, we used twice as much as during the 1950s. And in each of those decades, more oil was consumed than in all of mankind's previous history combined.

World consumption of oil is still going up. . . . Demand will overtake production. We have no choice about that. But we do have a choice about how we will spend the next few years. Each American uses the energy equivalent of 60 barrels of oil per person each year. Ours is the most wasteful nation on earth. We waste more energy than we import. With about the same standard of living, we use twice as much energy per person as do other countries like Germany, Japan and Sweden.

Our choice is to continue doing what we have been doing. We can drift for a few more years. Our consumption of oil would keep going up every year. Our cars would continue to be too large and inefficient. Three-quarters of them would continue to carry only one person—the driver—while our public transportation system continues to decline. We can delay insulating our houses, and they will continue to lose about 50 percent of their heat in waste. . . .

. . . [W]e will live in fear of embargoes. We could endanger our freedom as a sovereign nation to act in foreign affairs. . . . We will feel mounting pressure to plunder the environment. . . . Intense competition for oil will build up among nations, and among the different regions within our country. If we fail to act soon, we will face an economic, social, political crisis that will threaten our free institutions.

But we still have another choice. We can begin to prepare now. We can decide to act while there is still time.

Source 15 Jimmy Carter, The Carter Doctrine, January 23, 1980

The Soviet Union must realize that its decision to use military force in Afghanistan will be costly to every political and economic relationship it values.

The region now threatened by Soviet troops in Afghanistan is of great strategic importance. It contains more than two-thirds of the world's exportable oil. The Soviet effort to dominate Afghanistan has brought Soviet military forces to within 300 miles of the Indian Ocean and close to the Strait of Hormuz—a waterway through which much of the free world's oil must flow. The Soviet Union is now attempting to consolidate a strategic position that poses a threat to the free movement of Middle Eastern oil. . . .

Let our position be absolutely clear: An attempt by any outside force to gain control of the Persian Gulf region will be regarded as an assault on the vital interests of the United States. It will be repelled by use of any means necessary, including military force.

Source 16 Political scientists Hans J. Morgenthau and Kenneth W. Thompson, *Politics among Nations: The Struggle for Power and Peace*, Sixth Edition, 1985

Aside from its location as the land bridge of three continents, the Near East is strategically important because of the oil deposits of the Arabian peninsula.

Control over them traditionally has been an important factor in the distribution of power, in the sense that whoever is able to add them to his other sources of raw materials adds that much strength to his own resources and deprives his competitors proportionately. It is for this reason that Great Britain, the United States, and, for a time, France embarked in the Near East on what has aptly been called "oil diplomacy"; that is, the establishment of spheres of influence giving them exclusive access to the oil deposits in certain regions.

Yet oil is no longer one of many raw materials important in the measurement of a nation's power. It is now a material factor whose very possession threatens to overturn centuries—old patterns of international politics. The embargo on oil by the oil-producing states in the winter of 1973–1974, together with the drastic rise in the price of oil, suddenly clarified certain basic aspects of world politics which we might have understood theoretically, but which were brought home in earnest by the drastic change in power relations brought on by the new politics of oil.

Traditionally a functional relationship has existed between political, military, and economic power. That is to say, political power has been throughout history a function of military and—in recent times more particularly—of economic power. Take for instance the expansion of Europe into what later became the colonial areas of the Western Hemisphere, Africa, and Asia. That expansion was primarily due to a technological gap between the colonial powers and the colonized nations. In other words, the conquest of India by Great Britain (much inferior in manpower and in many other aspects of national power) was largely made possible by Great Britain's possession of a higher technology which, when transformed into military power, the Indian states could not resist.

Those relationships of a functional nature between technology and economic power, on the one hand, and political and military power, on the other, have been disturbed—one might even say destroyed—by the recent use of oil as a political weapon. Many of those oil producing states are states only by way of what might be called semantic courtesy. Measured in terms of natural resources, they have nothing but sand and oil. But it is the oil which seemingly overnight has made these small plots on the map which we call states important and even powerful factors in world politics. In other words, a state which has nothing to go on by way of power, which is lacking in all the elements which traditionally have gone into the making of national power, suddenly becomes a powerful factor in world politics because it has one important asset—oil. This is indeed of revolutionary importance for world politics. . . .

The power which oil bestows is, first of all, the result of the technological development of modern industrial nations. Twenty or fifty years ago oil did not bestow such power upon producing nations—because the use of oil as the lifeblood of modern industry was limited. When nations which have large deposits of oil are able to co-operate and co-ordinate policies, as the oil-exporting states were during the fall of 1973, they can apply a stranglehold to the consuming nations; they can impose political conditions which the consuming nations can refuse to meet only at the risk of enormous political, economic, and social dislocations.

A state which is powerless in all other respects, which is not a major force in terms of traditional power, can exert enormous—and under certain conditions even decisive—power over nations which have all the implements of power at their disposal except one—deposits of oil. Thus a nation like Japan, one of the foremost industrial nations of the world and potentially a great power, is completely dependent upon the supply of oil from abroad. If for some reason the oil-producing nations were to impose a total embargo upon Japan, they could destroy her political, economic, and social fabric, and if they were to connect that threat of a total embargo with political conditions, they could reduce Japan to the status of satellite, a dependence of the oil-producing nations. To a certain extent those nations have already tasted that power. During the Middle Eastern war of October, 1973, they forced Japan and the nations of Western Europe (which are only partially dependent on the import of oil) to take certain political steps which they would not have taken on their own initiative, but, which they had to take under the circumstances because otherwise they would have risked political, social, and economic ruin.

Source 17 Jim Wallis, "The Forgotten Moral Issues [of the Persian Gulf War]," *The Progressive*, March 1991

The moral issues of this war, with which the American people wrestled in the months leading up to it, seem to have been forgotten. In the churches, we continue to condemn the aggression and brutality of Saddam Hussein and call for Iraq's immediate withdrawal from Kuwait. But as people of faith, we cannot applaud the violence that the United States has unleashed—violence that will reverberate around the region and the world in the days and weeks ahead, likely even for generations to come. . . .

It is crucial to separate our support for the troops from support for the war. We must return to the fundamental moral questions that underlie this conflict. We must not let media fascination with the illuminated skies over Baghdad block out the illumination of our conscience at home. . . .

To unleash the demons of war in the Middle East and thereby risk inflaming the whole region with the unpredictability, bitterness, and destructiveness is a moral issue.

To undertake one of the greatest aerial bombardments in history is a moral issue of yet undetermined proportions. We are just beginning to hear reports of civilian casualties from refugees who have been eyewitnesses to the destruction, and from religious sources in the region. Cutoffs of water and electricity to people in Iraqi cities as well as damage to schools, hospitals, and places of worship are an ominous harbinger of human suffering yet to come.

To subject Iraqi soldiers in the desert to carpet bombing is a moral issue. Whether or not they wear a uniform, the massacre of young Iraqi draftees cannot be justified.

To send hundreds of thousands of young Americans into battle is an issue of great moral consequence. That U.S. troops are disproportionately people of color reflects the injustice of this nation's continued racial polarization.

To attract young people to military service through offers of education and career advancement only to send them off to fight and die is a moral issue. To promise young people an open door to the future through the military, while the door to a better life is closed in their home communities, is a moral issue.

To suffer the ravages of poverty and neglect here at home while the military consumes billions of dollars in the Middle East is a moral issue. In the first hour of the U.S attack, the firing of 100 cruise missiles cost more than $139 million, a small fraction of what is being poured into the desert sand.

To control and manipulate the Arab world for so long just to feed the West's insatiable thirst for oil is a moral issue. To maintain an American way of life in which 6 percent of the world's population consumes 25 percent of the world's oil is a moral issue that undergirds the whole conflict. The West's lack of an energy policy that honors our responsibilities both to human justice and to the environment is a moral failure.

Questioning the Past

1. How should history remember George Bissell, Edwin Drake, and William Smith? How should history remember John D. Rockefeller? Were they men of vision? Were they men of luck? Are they role models who epitomize ethical business practices?

2. Behind every Rockefeller there is a Drake and behind every Drake, a Smith. Which of the three do we, and which should we, most admire and why?

3. Is there a resource more vital to the American way of life than oil? In what ways has oil, a commodity relatively unknown to generations of Americans before the Civil War, become the essential ingredient of the twentieth and twenty-first centuries? And if it is essential, what are the implications of it being also finite?

4. "There is something alarming," wrote Ida M. Tarbell (Source 7), "to those who believe that commerce should be a peaceful pursuit, and who believe that the moral law holds good throughout the entire range of human relations, in knowing that so large a body of young men in this country are consciously or unconsciously growing up with the idea that business is war and that morals have nothing to do with its practice." Does Tarbell's observation have any relevance to the business world today?

5. Present the arguments for and against the Carter Doctrine. Which arguments are the more persuasive? Defend your answer.

6. There was a time in American history when the defense of the nation meant protecting its borders from invasion. Does national defense mean also the protection of resources thousands of miles beyond America's borders?

7. If petroleum is essential to modern society, who should control it and to what ends should it be controlled? Should it be rationed? Should it be distributed equitably or to the highest bidder as it becomes increasingly more scarce? Should it be produced and distributed by global corporations, whose motives are primarily company profits, by the worlds governments, by an international organization, or by producers' cartels, such as the Organization of Petroleum Exporting Countries (OPEC)?

26

Harper's Ferry

John Brown Raids Harper's Ferry   *October 16, 1859*

At eight o'clock on the night of October 16, 1859, John Brown, a man who had gained a wide reputation as a skilled guerrilla fighter in Kansas and an uncompromising abolitionist, climbed onto the seat of a wagon loaded with weapons and tools. "Men, get on your arms," he told his Army of Liberation. "We will proceed to the Ferry." The time had come to forcibly bring down the institution of slavery.

The Army—consisting of 17 white men and 5 blacks, some of whom were former slaves—moved quietly into the night away from the Maryland farmhouse where they had been in hiding for several months, down the country road five miles to Harper's Ferry, Virginia.

Many of these men had been with John Brown the year before when he led a successful raid into Missouri, liberated some slaves, and escorted them safely to freedom in Canada. The raid they were embarking on in Virginia, however, was much more ambitious.

26.1 John Brown and the Valley of Shadows

The plan was to attack the city of Harper's Ferry under the cover of darkness and capture the federal armory and rifle works located there. The arms and ammunition would be needed in the coming guerrilla war that Brown envisioned, and the news that the city was under abolitionist control would draw dissident whites and rebellious blacks as recruits. The raid would be carried off with such lightning-quick precision that the slaveholders would be caught off guard and unable to organize a retaliation. Once the town had been held long enough for the recruits to begin pouring in, Brown planned to move his growing army rapidly to the South, striking at slave owners, freeing their slaves, taking hostages, and confiscating provisions. Freed slaves who wished to join their liberators would be issued weapons. Those who did not wish to fight would be sent north through the Alleghenies and into Canada. The mountains would also serve as a base to strike from while out-maneuvering federal troops.

As his Army of Liberation moved southward, slave uprisings would ripple from it across the entire South. "If I could conquer Virginia," Brown later explained, "the balance of the Southern states would nearly conquer themselves, there being such a large number of slaves in them."

Many people in the North knew of Brown's plans. Some had provided financial aid, though not nearly in the amounts promised. The anticipated influx of volunteers to the Maryland hideaway also had not materialized. Brown would have preferred to postpone the raid until his army was larger, but his followers had been growing restless, and with each passing day the chance that the authorities would uncover his plot became greater.

✏ *First Impressions*
Serious Disturbance at Harper's Ferry

The midnight hour had passed when gunshots broke the silence of the night at Harper's Ferry. Quickly the word spread outward through the telegraph wires, causing hysteria across the region and anxiety around the country. No one knew what exactly was happening in the Virginia mountains, but everyone understood it was momentous.

Source 1 *Alexandria Gazette and Virginia Advertiser,* October 18, 1859

Baltimore, Oct. 17—The following dispatch has just been received from Frederick; but, as it seems very improbable, it should be received with great caution until confirmed:

Frederick, Oct. 17th a.m.—There is an insurrection at Harper's Ferry. A band of armed Abolitionists have full possession of the United States Arsenal. The express train was fired into twice, and one of the railroad hands—a negro—killed while trying to get the train through the town. The insurgents arrested two men who came into town with a load of wheat, took the wagon, loaded it with rifles, and sent them into Maryland. The band is composed of a gang of about 250 whites, followed by a band of negroes, who are now fighting.

Baltimore, Oct. 17, 10 a.m.—It is apprehended that the affair at Harper's Ferry is more serious than people here are willing to believe. The telegraph wires are cut from Harper's Ferry, consequently we have no communication beyond Monocacy.

The reported stampede of negroes is from Maryland.

The train due here early this morning has not yet arrived.

There are many wild rumors here, but nothing authentic yet.

TUESDAY MORNING, OCTOBER 18, 1859

—It will be seen by reference to a telegraphic dispatch, in another column of this morning's Gazette, that a serious disturbance is reported to have occurred at Harper's Ferry yesterday. The War Department on receipt of information of the disturbance, ordered three companies of troops from Fort Monroe to Harper's Ferry, Col. Robert Lee U.S.A. in command; also, 80 marines from headquarters at Washington.

Source 2 *Alexandria Gazette and Virginia Advertiser,* October 19, 1859

October 17th

Balt. and Ohio R. Road Office
11½ o'clock A.M.

The Wheeling express train in charge of Conductor Phelps, reached the Camden station at 12 M. yesterday. The train was detained by rioters at Harper's Ferry until 7 o'clock in the morning. From Mr. Jacob Cromwell, the baggage master of the train, we gather the following particulars:

"The train reached Harper's Ferry about 12 o'clock midnight. Knew nothing of the disturbance or the plot going on in the town until the train was stopped on the bridge by a band of armed men. At the request of Conductor Phelps, I went ahead with a lantern, and was immediately confronted by two men who, with rifles at my head, told me to stand. At this moment one of the watchman on the bridge, a colored man named Haywood Sheppard, was confronted in the same way, and being told to stand, became frightened and ran, and was shot through the back.

Thinking the moment was my best chance, I then started and dodged behind the bridge, but was fired after before I could gain shelter. The other watchman at the bridge was subsequently taken by the insurgents, and confined in the office at the bridge. When this condition of things was made plain to Conductor Phelps, he ordered William Wollery, the engineer to back the train, and went forward himself and had a conference with the rioters. He was introduced to the reputed captain of the insurgents, an old man. . . .

Conductor Phelps told them he was in charge of the train, and carried the United States mail, and desired to go through. This was granted, and he was given five minutes to pass. Phelps was then conducted to his train, with a man before and behind, with a rifle pointed to his head. He was told not, on pain of death, to look either way. The train immediately left, and that is all I know."

From a gentleman well known in Baltimore, who came passenger in the Western Express Train . . . we have the following account. Our informant was an eye witness to the violent scene there enacting . . . :

The express train in which our informant was passenger, reached Harper's Ferry about one o'clock this morning. On arriving, the clerk of the Wager House informed Captain Phelps, conductor of the train, that serious trouble was existing in the town, and there was great apprehensions of danger.

He stated that a large body of men had mysteriously come into town during the evening and night from the surrounding country, and were about to take possession of the place. . . . The bridge across the Potomac, was filled with the insurgents, all of whom were armed. The conductor deemed it most prudent to remain, as he feared some terrible accident, in attempting to cross the bridge, supposing its arches or timbers might have been cut.

Every light in the town had been previously extinguished by the lawless mob. The train therefore remained stationary and the passengers, terribly affrighted, remained in the cars all night. . . .

All the streets were in possession of the mob, and every road, lane, and avenue leading to the town guarded, or barricaded by them. . . . The men were seen in every quarter with muskets and bayonets. It was thought that there were not less than from 250 to 300 of the insurgents. They had arrested every citizen they could find. . . .

The captain of the outlaw band or a person who seemed to be prime mover was a middle-aged man with gray hair, beard, and moustache. . . . He . . . was heard to say in addressing the conductor, that "if you knew me and understood my motives as well as I and others understand them, you would not blame me so much." . . .

Our informant states that the consternation was intense. It was difficult to divine the cause of this outbreak or attack. Some are of the opinion that it was a bold, concerted scheme to rob the government pay-house. . . . Others imagined it might have been a demonstration of abolitionists connected with some negro affair.

About five or half-past five o'clock this morning the deputation of armed insurgents approached the conductor, and gave him five minutes to start his train and cross the bridge. . . .

When our informant left, the whole town, government works and everything else, were in the hands of the insurgents, who seemed to be gradually receiving reinforcements, composed of negroes and white men from the surrounding country.

Source 3   *Alexandria Gazette and Virginia Advertiser*

WEDNESDAY MORNING, OCTOBER 19, 1859

The news of the outbreak at Harper's Ferry, whatever may be the true history and causes of the disturbance, has come upon us as suddenly and unexpectedly as would a peal of thunder fall on the ear, on a clear and cloudless day. When the first telegraphic dispatches reached here on Monday afternoon, they were universally believed to be exaggerations of some difficulties among the workmen at the Armory, which would be speedily settled. As the hours, however, wore on, and further news was received, it was perceived that there was fearful reality in the reports of riot, insurrection, and murder, and public interest and concern were raised to the highest pitch. Scarcely any thing else is talked about—or much thought of. Imperfect as the intelligence is, the account remains strange and wonderful—the whole affair mysterious—We shall, doubtless, be soon put in possession of all the facts, which will enable us to know the ramifications of the plot. . . . We are in hopes that prompt and energetic steps taken by the President and the Secretary of War, and the Governor of Virginia . . . will have the effect of quelling this insurrection without loss of time and with as little effusion of blood as possible. But after it is quelled, and the guilty parties are fairly before the civil tribunals, we expect to see *stern justice* meted out to all concerned in bringing about, or acting in, this outrage upon law, this rebellion and treason, this *great crime* against the laws of the country, and the rights of our peaceable citizens.

Source 4   Account of Elijah Avey, eyewitness to the Harper's Ferry raid

[A]s time wore on, further advices, with particulars and circumstances, left no room to doubt the substantial truth of the original report. An attempt had actually been made to excite a slave insurrection in Northern Virginia, and the one man in America to whom such an enterprise would not seem utter insanity and suicide, was at the head of it.

Source 5   Wire service report, October 18, 1859

Harper's Ferry, 6 a.m.—Preparations are making to storm the Armory. The soldiers are all around the ground, and for the last hour everything has been quiet. . . . Three rioters are lying dead in the street, and three more lying dead in the river. Several are said to be lying dead within the Armory enclosure. . . .

Another rioter named Lewis Leary, has just died, and confessed to the particulars of the plot which he says was concocted by Brown. . . . The rioters have just sent out a flag of truce. If they are not protected by the soldiers present here, every one captured will be hung.

[Later]

The Armory has just been stormed and taken after determined resistance. Colonel Shutt approached with a flag of truce, and demanded their surrender; after expostulating some time, they refused to surrender. The marines advanced, charged, and endeavored to break down the doors with sledge hammers, which resisted all efforts.

A large ladder was then used as a battering ram, and the door gave way. The rioters fired briskly, and shot three marines. . . . Marines then forced through the breach, and in a few minutes resistance was at an end, and the rioters brought out amidst most intense excitement. Many of the armed militia are trying to get an opportunity to shoot them. Capt. Brown, . . . dying, now lies in the Armory enclosure talking freely; says he is old Ossawatomie Brown, whose feats in Kansas have had such wide notoriety; says the whole object was to free slaves, and justified his action; that he had the entire possession of the town, and could have murdered all the people, but did not.

John Brown's Raid at Harper's Ferry

Brown's men entered Harper's Ferry by way of the covered railroad and wagon bridge that led across the Potomac. With clock-like precision and without firing a shot, the band cut the telegraph lines and seized their objectives. Hostages were rounded up and brought to the engine house near the gate of the Armory.

Shortly after midnight a relief watchman was shot by one of Brown's guards. A few minutes later an express train from Wheeling pulled slowly into Harper's Ferry and stopped short of the now-barricaded bridge. Brown subsequently allowed the train to pass through because, as he later explained, "I wanted to allay the fears of those who believed we came here to burn and kill." Allowing the train to pass proved to be a mistake.

The shots at the approach of the train had aroused the town. Word spread quickly through the city and surrounding area that the event Southern whites had most feared for generations was beginning at Harper's Ferry: a slave insurrection. Hysteria reigned supreme. Reports of slaves raping and butchering whites in the streets spread like wildfire. Church bells in Charlestown, Martinsburg, and Chepherdstown tolled the warning and white militiamen grabbed their rifles and headed for Harper's Ferry. The express train carried the news of the insurrection to Monocacy and in minutes the telegraph had informed Baltimore, Washington, and Richmond. Newspaper headlines in the East and South quickly proclaimed the news, "Fire and Rapine on the Virginia Border," "Negro Insurrection at Harper's Ferry!"

As militiamen poured into town, the battle with Brown's forces grew intense. Federal troops under the command of Robert E. Lee and J. E. B. Stuart arrived on the night of October 17. Brown's retreat was cut off and his war of liberation doomed. Still, he remained poised and determined. As one of his hostages, Col. Lewis W. Washington, a grand-nephew of George Washington, commented, "Brown was the coolest and firmest man I ever saw. With one dead son by his side and another shot through, he felt the pulse of his dying son with one hand and held his rifle with the other, and commanded his men with the utmost composure, encouraging them to sell their lives as dearly as they could." On the morning of October 18, marines stormed and captured the engine house where Brown and his surviving liberators were holed up. This assault succeeded in overwhelming the raiders.

John Brown was severely wounded during his capture at Harper's Ferry. In addition to several bayonet wounds, Brown had also been struck across his head with the blade of a sabre. Assuming Brown's death to be imminent, his captors pressed him for an interview. Despite his injuries, Brown consented and engaged in a heated exchange with a number of prominent figures of the day, including Virginia's governor Henry A. Wise, Senator James M. Mason of Virginia, Congressmen Faulkner of Virginia and Vallandigham of Ohio, Robert E. Lee, J. E. B. Stuart, and several reporters and militiamen.

Surprising almost everyone, John Brown survived the wounds he sustained at Harper's Ferry. He was therefore quickly tried and sentenced to hang. His strength as he awaited death won him the respect of even slave-holding Southerners. He was hanged in Charlestown on December 2, 1859. His raid had aroused the South. His martyrdom aroused the North.

26.2 Toward
Secession

Source 6   Interview at Harper's Ferry, October 18, 1859

Militiaman: Ain't the ole turkey buzzard dead yet?

(Laughter)

Militiaman: (Pointing a rifle at Brown): Why listen to him, gentlemen? He is nothing but a common robber and outlaw.

Brown: You call me a robber, standing there with a valuable gun you have filched from a dying man. You militiamen are worse than robbers . . . [Y]ou steal men. . . .

Gov. Wise: Mr. Brown, the silver of your hair is reddened by the blood of crime, and . . . you should eschew these hard allusions and think upon eternity.

Brown: Governor, I have from all appearances not more than fifteen or twenty years the start of you to that eternity of which you kindly warn me. And whether my tenure here shall be fifteen months, or fifteen days, or fifteen hours, I am equally prepared to go. There is an eternity behind, and an eternity before, and the little speck in the center, however long, is but comparatively a minute. The difference between your tenure and mine is trifling, and I want, therefore, to tell *you* to be prepared. I *am* prepared. You slaveholders have a heavy responsibility, and it behooves *you* to prepare more than it does me.

Sen. Mason: Can you tell us, at least, who furnished money for your expedition?

Brown: I furnished most of it myself. I cannot implicate others. It is by my own folly that I have been taken. . . . I allowed myself to be surrounded by a force by being too tardy.

Mason: If you would tell us who sent you here—who provided the means—that would be information of some value.

Brown: I will answer freely and faithfully about what concerns myself. I will answer anything I can with honor, but not about others.

Vallandigham: Mr. Brown, who sent you here?

Brown: No man sent me here; it was my own prompting and that of my Maker, or that of the devil, whichever you please to ascribe it to. I acknowledge no man in human form. . . .

Mason: What was your object in coming?

Brown: We came to free the slaves, and only that. . . .

Mason: How do you justify your acts?

Brown: I think, my friend, you are guilty of a great wrong against God and humanity—I say it without wishing to be offensive—and it would be perfectly right in anyone to interfere with you so far as to free those you willfully and wickedly hold in bondage. I do not say this insultingly.

Mason: I understand that.

Brown: I think I did right, and that others will do right who interfere with you at any time and at all times. "Do unto others as you would that others should do unto you," applies to all who would help others to gain their liberty.

Stuart: But you don't believe in the Bible.

Brown: Certainly I do.

A Bystander: Do you consider this a religious movement?

Brown: It is, in my opinion, the greatest service a man can render to God.

Bystander: Do you consider yourself an instrument in the hands of Providence?

Brown: I do.

Bystander: Under what principle do you justify your acts?

Brown: Upon the golden rule. I pity the poor in bondage that have none to help them; that is why I am here. . . . It is my sympathy with the oppressed and the wronged, that one as good as you and as precious in the sight of God.

An Officer: Brown, suppose you had every nigger in the United States, what would you do with them?

Brown: Set them free.

Officer: Your intention was to carry them off and free them?

Brown: Not at all. Free them here. The slaves should have this land, everything on it, the fruits of their labors.

📖 *Second Thoughts*

A Madman or a Martyr?

Both contemporary chroniclers and later historians point to the raid at Harper's Ferry as an event that dramatically escalated tensions between North and South. It might be said to have set spark to the fuse that exploded some months later at Fort Sumter. Observers, then and now, also debate the mental and emotional stability of John Brown. Whatever his motivations or capacity, Brown's last statement prior to being hanged accurately predicted the coming strife and bloodshed: "I . . . am now quite certain that the crimes of this guilty land will never be purged away but with blood. I had . . . vainly flattered myself that without very much blood it might be done."

26.3 The Life of John Brown

Source 7   *Chicago Press and Tribune,* October 21, 1859

A squad of fanatics whose zeal is wonderfully disproportioned to their senses, and a double-handful of slaves whose ignorance is equalled only by their desire for the freedom of which they have been robbed, . . . all commanded by a man who has, for years been mad as a March hare, unite in making an insurrection at Harper's Ferry. . . . They are guilty of the most incomprehensible stupidity and folly as well as unpardonable criminality in all these acts. . . . [T]here is not a public journal of any party . . . found to approve their means or justify their ends.

Source 8   Speech of abolitionist Wendell Phillips, November 1, 1859

I said that the lesson of the hour was insurrection. I ought not to apply that word to John Brown of Osawatomie, for there was no insurrection in his case. It is a great mistake to call him an insurgent. This principle that I have endeavored so briefly to open to you, of absolute right and wrong, states what? Just this: "Commonwealth of Virginia!" There is no such thing. Lawless, brutal force is no basis of a government. . . . No civil society, no government, can exist except on the basis of the willing submission of all its citizens, and by the performance of the duty of rendering equal justice between man and man.

Whatever calls itself a government, and refuses that duty, or has not that assent, is no government. It is only a pirate ship. Virginia, the Commonwealth of Virginia! She is only a chronic insurrection. I mean exactly what I say. I am weighing my words now. She is a pirate ship, and John Brown sails the sea as Lord High Admiral of the admiralty, with his commission to sink every pirate he meets on God's ocean of the nineteenth century. (Cheers and hisses.). . . .

John Brown has twice as much right to hang Governor Wise as Governor Wise has to hang him. (Cheers and hisses.)

Source 9   E. N. Sill, November 14, 1859

I have had some acquaintance with John Brown, . . . a most excellent but very peculiar man . . . I admire Mr. Brown's courage and devotion to his beliefs. But I have no confidence in the sanity of his judgments in matters appertaining to slavery. I have no doubt that, upon this subject, . . . he is surely a monomaniac as any inmate of any insane asylum in the country.

Source 10   Writings of Brown's wife, Mary, November 18, 1859

I never knew of his insanity until I read it in the newspapers. He is a clear-headed man. He has always been cool, deliberate, and never over-hasty; but he has always considered that his first perceptions of duty, and his first impulses to action, were the best, and the safest to be followed. He has almost always acted on his first suggestions. No, he is not insane. His reason is clear. His last act was the result, as all others have been, of his truest and strongest conscientious convictions.

Source 11   Observation of abolitionist Wendell Phillips, 1859

Hard to tell who's mad. The world says one man is mad. John Brown said the same of the Governor. You remember the madman in Edinburgh. A friend asked him what he was there for. "Well," cried he, "they said at home that I was mad and I said I was not; but they had the majority." Just so it is in regard to John Brown. The nation says he is mad. . . . I appeal from the American people, drunk with cotton . . . to the American people fifty years hence, when the light of civilization has had more time to penetrate . . . when it is not a small band of abolitionists, but the civilization of the twentieth century . . . which undertakes to . . . discuss this last great reform.

Source 12   Remarks of Governor Henry Wise to the Virginia Assembly, 1859

As well as I know the state of mind of anyone, I know that he was sane, if quick and clear perception, if assumed rational premises and consecutive reasoning from them, if cautious tact in avoiding disclosures and in covering conclusions and inferences, if memory and conception and practical common sense, and if composure and self-possession are evidence of a sound state of mind. He was more sane than his prompters and promoters, and concealed well the secret which made him seem to do an act of mad impulse . . . ; but he did not conceal his contempt for the cowardice which did not back him better than with a plea of insanity, which he spurned to put in at his trial at Charlestown.

Source 13   Notes of Henry David Thoreau, December 2, 1859

Some eighteen hundred years ago, Christ was crucified; this morning, perchance, Captain Brown was hung. These were two ends of a chain which is not without its links. He is not Old Brown any longer; he is an angel of light.

I see now that it was necessary that the bravest and humanest man in all the country should be hung.

Source 14 *Alexandria Gazette and Virginia Advertiser*

SATURDAY MORNING, DECEMBER 3, 1859
Execution of John Brown

John Brown, convicted of conspiracy, murder, and treason, was, according to sentence, executed at Charleston yesterday, at 11 o'clock by being hung by the neck until he was dead. He maintained his calmness, according to the accounts, to the last, and addressed those who could hear him, at length. The military and police maintained order—there was no attempt at a rescue—and the majesty and authority of the law were fully asserted. His crimes were great, but as he knowingly perilled his life when he embarked in them, and knew exactly what would be his fate, if unsuccessful, there can be no regret for the result, or for the end of his career. He will live in history, not as a martyr, but as branded with the just sentence of the law which consigned him to an ignominious end. He struck at the peace of society, the supremacy of the law, the safety of our institutions, the harmony of the states, and the lives of our citizens, and he richly merited the punishment he has received.

Source 15 Editor Horace Greeley, *New York Tribune*, December 3, 1859

We are not those who say, "If slavery is wrong, then John Brown was wholly right." There are fit and unfit modes of combating a great evil; we think Brown at Harper's Ferry pursued the latter. . . . But his are the errors of a fanatic, not the crimes of a felon. . . . Unwise, the world will pronounce him. . . . [B]ut his very errors were heroic—the faults of a brave, impulsive, truthful nature, impatient of wrong, and only too conscious that "Resistance to tyrants is obedience to God." Let whoever would cast a stone ask himself whether his noblest act was equal in grandeur and nobility to that for which John Brown pays the penalty of a death on the gallows.

Source 16 Editor William Lloyd Garrison, *The Liberator*, December 16, 1859

Was John Brown justified in his attempt? Yes, if Washington was in his. . . . If men are justified in striking a blow for freedom when the question is one of a three-penny tax on tea, then, I say, they are a thousand times more justified, when it is to save fathers, mothers, wives and children from the slave-coffle and the auction-block.

Source 17 Southern writer George Fitzhugh, January 1860

The Harper's Ferry affair, with its extensive Northern ramifications, gives new interest to the question of disunion. The most conservative must see, and if honest will admit, that the settlement of Northerners among us is fraught with danger. Not one in twenty of such settlers might tamper with our slaves and incite them to insurrection, but one man can fire a magazine, and no one can foresee where the match will be applied, or what will be the consequences of the explosion. Our wives and our daughters will see in every new Yankee face an abolition missionary.

Source 18 Account of Ralph Waldo Emerson, January 6, 1860

Who makes the Abolitionist? The Slaveholder. The sentiment of mercy is the natural recoil which the laws of the universe provide to protect mankind from destruction by savage passions. And our blind statesmen go up and down with committees of vigilance and safety, hunting for the origin of this new heresy. They will need a vigilant committee indeed to find its birthplace, and a very strong force to root it out. For the arch-abolitionist, older than Brown, and older than the Shenandoah Mountains, is Love, whose other name is Justice, which was before slavery, and will be after it.

Source 19 Writings of Edmund Ruffin, advocate of Southern secession, March 1860

[T]he indirect results of this Northern Virginia conspiracy, and attempted deadly assault and warfare on Virginia are all important for the consideration and instruction of the Southern people, and especially in these respects, to wit: 1st, As proving to the world the actual condition of entire submission, obedience, and general loyalty of our negro slaves, in the fact that all the previous and scarcely impeded efforts of Northern abolitionists . . . aided by all that falsehood and deception could effect, did not operate to seduce a single negro in Virginia to rebel, or even to evince the least spirit of insubordination. 2d, As showing, in the general expression of opinion in the . . . North, that the majority, or at least the far greater number of all whose opinions have yet been expressed, either excuse, or desire to have pardoned, or sympathise with, or openly and heartily applaud the actors in this conspiracy and attack, which could have been made successful only by the means of laying waste the South and extinguishing its institutions and their defenders by fire and sword.

Source 20 Platform of the Republican Party, 1860

[T]he maintenance inviolate of the rights of the states, and especially the right of each state to order and control its own domestic institutions according to its own judgment exclusively, is essential to that balance of powers on which the perfection and endurance of our political fabric depends; and we denounce the lawless invasion by armed force of the soil of any state or territory, no matter under what pretext, as among the gravest of crimes.

Source 21 Observation of James Buchanan, president 1857–1861, 1866

In the present state of civilization, we are free to admit that slavery is a great political and social evil. . . . But even admitting slavery to be a sin, have the adherents of John Brown never reflected that the attempt by one people to pass beyond their own jurisdiction, and to extirpate by force of arms whatever they may deem sinful among other people, would involve the nations of the earth in perpetual hostilities?

Source 22 James Schouler, *The United States under the Constitution,* 1891

Had this sporadic and nonsensical movement been calmly and considerately viewed by those against whom it was directed, had the pitiful and deluded assailants been treated with the decent magnanimity for which so good an opportunity was afforded, John Brown's raid would have passed out of the public mind, like any other nine-days' wonder, and been forgotten. . . . But the slave master showed on this occasion his innate tyranny and cruelty towards an adversary, by something of that gloating vengeance which our English code once inflicted when it quartered and disembowelled political traitors. . . . John Brown . . . became a martyr, and consequently an inspiration and a figure in history. . . .

Though of decided character, his mind had been strangely unstrung by the murderous scenes in Kansas in which he had borne a part. . . . Yet mono-maniacs may plot most cunningly; their folly develops more properly at the stage of action. . . . [W]hat quintessence of nonsense is curtained in that night descent of scarcely twenty confederates upon Harper's Ferry[?] . . . Any town of five thousand inhabitants ought, one would think, to have disarmed this amateur array; and any United States arsenal, in which were usually stored a hundred thousand stand of arms, should not . . . have been left so utterly unguarded. John Brown makes the property his own without firing a gun, and with subli-mated zeal posts guards on the railroad bridge near by, and makes a night arrest of two slave-owning farmers. So far does the . . . strategy sustain him; but when he stops the midnight train, and then suffers it, with chivalrous expressions, to go on its way towards Baltimore, why does he not scud like the fox to the mountain covert, instead of returning complacently with his pike-bearers into the premises of which he has robbed thirty millions of people? . . . [I]t is not strange that morning overwhelms the whole crazy exploit. . . . John Brown was no Caesar, no Cromwell, but a plain citizen of a free republic, whom distressing events drove into a fanaticism to execute purposes to which he was incompetent.

Source 23 W. E. B. Du Bois, *John Brown,* 1909

When a prophet like John Brown appears, how must we of the world receive him? . . . Shall we hesitate and waver before his clear white logic, now helping, now fearing to help, now believing, now doubting? Yes, this we must do so long as the doubt and hesitation are genuine; but we must not lie. If we are human, we must thus hesitate until we know the right. How shall we know it?

That is the Riddle of the Sphinx. We are but darkened groping souls, that know not light often because of its blinding radiance. Only in time is truth revealed. To-day at last we know: John Brown was right.

Source 24   Oswald Garrison Villard, *John Brown,* 1910

Governor Wise was correct in his estimate of John Brown's mentality; the final proof is the extraordinary series of letters written by him in jail after his doom was pronounced. No lunatic ever penned such elevated and high-minded, and such consistent epistles. If to be devoted to one idea, or to a single cause, is to be a monomaniac, then the world owes much of its progress toward individual and racial freedom to lunacy of this variety.

Source 25   C. Vann Woodward, *The Burden of Southern History,* 1952

It seems best to deal with the insanity question promptly. . . . In dealing with the problem it is important not to blink, as many of his biographers have done, at the evidence of John Brown's close association with insanity in both his heredity and his environment. In the Brown Papers at the Library of Congress are nineteen affidavits signed by relatives and friends attesting the record of insanity in the Brown family. John Brown's maternal grandmother and his mother both died insane. His three aunts and two uncles, sisters and brothers of his mother, were intermittently insane, and so was his only sister, her daughter, and one of his brothers. Of six first cousins, all more or less mad, two were deranged from time to time, two had been repeatedly committed to the state insane asylum, and two were still confined at the time [of the raid]. Of John Brown's immediate family, his first wife and one of his sons died insane, and a second son was insane at intervals. . . .

The insurrectionist himself, of course, stoutly maintained that he was perfectly sane, and he was certainly able to convince many intelligent people, both friend and foe, that he was sane. . . .

What seems sane to some people at some times seems insane to other people at other times. In our own time we have witnessed what we consider psychopathic personalities rise to power over millions of people and plunge the world into war. Yet to the millions who followed them these leaders appeared sublime in their wisdom.

Source 26   Louis Ruchames, *The Making of a Revolutionary,* 1959

Among recent historians, . . . C. Vann Woodward . . . [has] emphasized the case for Brown's insanity. Prof. Vann Woodward had made much of the nineteen affidavits testifying to insanity in Brown's family, especially on his mother's side and to Brown's own insanity or "monomania" on the question of slavery. Putting aside the basic question of whether one's insanity may be established by the presence or absence of insanity in one's family, it may be noted that the affidavits are highly suspect as valid evidence. Their primary purpose was to save Brown from execution by showing him to be insane. . . . By accepting the affidavits at their face value, Prof. Vann Woodward, though a very careful historian, is led into committing . . . errors. . . .

The lesson to be learned . . . is simply that to be deeply sensitive to injustice, to be willing to devote one's own life to an unpopular cause, to give up the pursuit of one's own gain to alleviate the suffering of others, involves running the risk of being called fanatic and even insane by the smug, the callous and the well-placed members of society. "The prophet is a fool, the man of spirit is mad!" has echoed through the ages, from the days of **Hosea** to our own.

Source 27 The *Chicago Defender*, an African American newspaper, November 7, 1959

The centennial of John Brown's raid on the federal arsenal at Harper's Ferry, Va., passed almost without notice. . . . Yet the raid and Brown's execution set off the powder keg of emotion which rendered the moral dispute over the status of the Negro and the political conflict over states' rights insoluble by anything short of civil war.

The paradox of Brown's idealistic goals and his fearless methods are still being argued in college seminars a century later. Some would exonerate him on grounds of congenital insanity; others see him as a fanatic whose passions knew no bounds. Only a conspicuous few see him in the true perspective of history, as a martyr to a cause—human freedom.

History books are not replete with instances in which men have mounted the scaffold and placed their necks in the hangman's noose, forfeiting their lives for impersonal principles, for freedom, freedom of black men at that.

Source 28 Stephen B. Oates, *To Purge This Land with Blood,* 1970

Since many writers have accepted these affidavits at face value and have used them as proof that Brown was a "madman" out of touch with "reality," the documents—the whole insanity question—merit careful examination. To begin with, the word "insanity" is a vague, emotion-charged, and clinically meaningless term. Modern psychology has abandoned it in describing mental and emotional disorders. And historians should abandon it as well. . . .

Modern psychologists themselves do not agree on how much of the human personality is inherited (if any of it is) and how much is the result of environment. Any biographer or historian who argues that "insanity" is hereditary intrudes upon his craft the controversies and disagreements of what is still an imprecise science. . . .

All this is not to argue that Brown was a "normal," "well-adjusted," "sane" individual. These terms are meaningless too. That he was a revolutionary who believed himself called by God to a special destiny (a notion that stemmed from his Calvinist beliefs), that he had an excitable temperament and could get carried away with one idea, that he was inept, egotistical, hard on his sons, . . . and enraged enough at his "slave-cursed" country to contemplate destroying it, . . . and that he wanted to become either an American **Spartacus** at the head of a slave army or a martyred soldier who was the first to die in a sectional war over slavery—all this is true. Yet to dismiss Brown as an "insane" man is to ignore the tremendous sympathy he felt for the suffering of the black man in the United States; it is to disregard the fact that at a time when most Northerners and almost all Southerners were racists who wanted to keep the Negro at the bottom of society, John Brown was able to treat America's "poor despised Africans" as fellow human beings. And to label him a "maniac" out of touch with "reality" is to ignore the piercing insight he had into what his raid—whether it succeeded or whether it failed—would do to sectional tensions which already existed between North and South.

Source 29   John Hope Franklin, *From Slavery to Freedom,* 1974

He terrified the South and captivated the North. Many had died fighting for freedom, but none had done it so heroically or at such a propitious moment. The crusade against slavery now had a martyr. Literally thousands of people who had been indifferent were now persuaded that slavery must be abolished. There can be no doubt that many voted the Republican ticket in 1860 because of this conviction.

Source 30   David Brion Davis, *The Great Republic,* 1977

Brown claimed to have acted under the "higher law" of the New Testament, and insisted, "If I had done what I have for the white men, or the rich, no man would have blamed me." For Brown the higher law was not a philosophical abstraction but a moral command to shed blood and die in the cause of freedom. In the eyes of sedentary reformers and Transcendentalists, this courage to act on principle made Brown not only a revered martyr but a symbol of what America lacked. In the eyes of Democratic editors and politicians however, Brown's criminal violence was the direct result of the irresponsible preaching of William H. Seward and other "Black Republicans."

Source 31   John Garraty, *The American Nation,* 1991

No incident so well illustrates the role of emotion and irrationality in the sectional crisis as John Brown's raid. Over the years before his Kansas escapade, Brown had been a drifter, horse thief, and swindler—a failure in everything he attempted. . . . [I]t should have been obvious to anyone that he was both fanatical and mentally unstable. . . . Even execution would probably not have made a martyr of Brown had he behaved like a madman after his capture. Instead, an enormous dignity descended on him as he lay in his Virginia jail awaiting death. Whatever his faults, he truly believed in racial equality. . . . This conviction served him well in his last days. . . . This John Brown, with his patriarchal beard and sad eyes, so apparently incompatible with the bloody terrorist of Pottawatomie and Harper's Ferry, led thousands in the North to ignore his past and treat him almost as a saint. And so Brown became to the North a hero and to the South a symbol of Northern ruthlessness.

Questioning the Past

1. Discuss John Brown's strategy at Harper's Ferry. How would history have been changed if his plan had succeeded? Would America today be different if slavery had fallen, not to the Union Army, but to an insurrection of the slaves themselves?

2. John Brown fought a guerrilla war against a society that declared slavery to be an acceptable institution. Do citizens have an obligation to support laws and institutions they feel are unjust and immoral? Are citizens justified in disobeying such laws and resisting such institutions?

3. "Old John Brown has just been executed for treason against a state," wrote Abraham Lincoln on December 3, 1859. "We cannot object, even though he agreed with us in thinking slavery wrong. That cannot excuse violence, bloodshed, and treason." Recently, historian Howard Zinn wrote, "In 1859, John Brown was hanged, with federal complicity, for attempting to do by small-scale violence what Lincoln would do by large-scale violence several years later—end slavery." Compare and contrast these two statements and discuss their message.

4. Historians John M. Blum and Bruce Catton wrote in 1963 that if Brown, "was not himself mad, he was at least a monomaniac about religion and slavery, a psychopathic individual . . . who revealed the symptoms of paranoia and, by his deeds, provoked it in others." Was John Brown a patriot or a lunatic? Explain.

Chapter 27

Civil War

Fort Sumter Is Fired Upon *April 12, 1861*

Never before had the White House been captured by a candidate whose electoral majority had been won without the vote of even a single southern elector. The significance of Abraham Lincoln's victory was clear to southerners: The days when they could direct the course of the country were now a part of the past. South Carolina seceded from the United States on December 20, 1860. Mississippi, Alabama, Florida, Georgia, and Louisiana declared in January of 1861 that they, too, were no longer members of the American Union. Texas joined the new confederation created by these seceding states in February.

Following their secession from the Union, the states of the South assumed control of all federal property within their borders. This assumption was accomplished without resistance in most instances. Two federal outposts, however, refused to submit to the imposition of Confederate control: Fort Pickens in Pensacola, Florida, and Fort Sumter, a military installation situated on an island in Charleston Harbor, South Carolina. The continuing federal control of these outposts was an irritant to the South and a potentially volatile burden for the North.

ᕗᕊᕉ *First Impressions*

The Move toward Confrontation

27.1 The American Civil War Homepage

As Lincoln formed his new Republican administration, there were important questions awaiting answer. Should his government abandon Forts Pickens and Sumter, or reinforce and attempt to hold them? This question was inseparable from a far more fundamental policy issue. Would the dissolution of the United States occur peaceably? Would it be allowed to occur at all? The answers to these questions did not come until the morning of April 12, 1861.

Source 1 *Diary of Gideon Welles,* Secretary of the Navy

On the 6th of March, 1861, two days after the inauguration of President Lincoln, Secretary Holt, who continued to discharge the duties of Secretary of War, . . . called at the Navy Department with the compliments of General Scott and requested my attendance at the War Department on matters of special importance. I went immediately with him to the office of the Secretary of War, where were

Generals Scott and Totten, and I think Secretary Cameron, and perhaps one or two others.

General Scott commenced with a statement of the perilous condition of the country and of the difficulties and embarrassments he had experienced for months past; related the measures and precautions he had taken for the public safety, the advice and admonitions he had given President Buchanan, which, however, had been disregarded, and, finally, his apprehensions, perhaps convictions, that hostilities were imminent and, he feared, inevitable. He had . . . taken the responsibility of ordering a small military force to Washington for the protection of the government and the public property and archives. . . . His statement was full, clear in its details, and of absorbing interest. . . . Among other matters, and that for which he had especially requested our attendance that morning, was certain intelligence of a distressing character from Major Anderson at Fort Sumter, stating that his supplies were almost exhausted, that he could get no provisions in Charleston, and that he with his small command would be totally destitute in about six weeks. Under these circumstances it became a question what action should be taken, and for that purpose, as well as to advise us of the condition of affairs, he had convened the gentlemen present.

The information was to most of us unexpected and astounding, and there was, on the part of such of us as had no previous intimation of the condition of things at Sumter, an earnest determination to take immediate and efficient measures to relieve and reinforce the garrison. But General Scott, without opposing this spontaneous resolution, related the difficulties which had already taken place, and stated the formidable obstacles which were to be encountered from the numerous and well-manned batteries that were erected in Charleston Harbor. Any successful attempt to reinforce or relieve the garrison by sea he supposed impracticable. An attempt had already been made and failed. The question was, however, one for naval authorities to decide, for the army could do nothing.

(Confidential)

Navy Department, April 5, 1861

Captain Samuel Mercer, commanding U.S. Steamer Powhatan . . .

The United States Steamers Powhatan, Pawnee, Pocahontas, and Harriet Lane will compose a naval force under your command, to be sent to the vicinity of Charleston, S.C., for the purpose of aiding in carrying out the objects of an expedition of which the War Department has charge.

The primary object of the expedition is to provision Fort Sumter. . . . Should the authorities at Charleston permit the fort to be supplied, no further particular service will be required of the force under your command. . . .

Should the authorities at Charleston, however, refuse to permit, or attempt to prevent the vessel or vessels having supplies on board from entering the harbor, or from peaceably proceeding to Fort Sumter, you will protect the transports or boats of the expedition in the object of their mission, disposing your force in such manner as to open the way for their ingress, and afford as far as practicable security to the men and boats, and repelling by force if necessary all obstructions toward provisioning the fort and reinforcing it; for in case of a

27.2 Fort Pickens and Fort Sumter

resistance to the peaceable primary object of the expedition, a reinforcement of the garrison will also be attempted. . . .

I am, respectfully,
Your Obd't Serv't,
Gideon Welles, Secretary of the Navy

Source 2   *Alexandria Gazette and Virginia Advertiser*

FROM CHARLESTON

Charleston, April 9.—At last the ball has opened.

The state authorities last night received official notification that supplies would be furnished to Anderson at any hazard—peaceably if possible, by force if necessary.

Immense preparations immediately were commenced suitable to the emergency.

Orders were issued to the entire military force of the city, held in reserve, to proceed to their station without delay.

Four regiments of a thousand men each have been telegraphed for from the country. . . .

The community has been thrown into a fever of excitement by the discharge of seven guns from Citadel square, the signal for the assembling of all the reserves ten minutes afterward.

Hundreds of men left their beds, hurrying to and fro toward their respective destinations. In the absence of sufficient armories, [at] the corners of the streets, public squares, and other convenient points companies were formed, for all night the long roll of the drum, and the steady tramp of the military, and the gallop of the cavalry, resounding through the city, betokened the close proximity of the long anticipated hostilities. . . .

South Carolinians are anxious to meet the enemy at the point of the bayonet rather than . . . an exchange of iron compliments. The latter is a too deliberate style of fighting to suit the impetuous nature of the most desperate set of men ever brought together. . . .

No attempt is likely to be made upon the city. Officers acquainted with the caliber of Major Anderson's guns say the longest shot will fall short three-eighths of a mile.

FROM WASHINGTON

THE GAZETTE'S SPECIAL DISPATCH.
Washington, April 10.—I am authorized to say by a member of the Cabinet that the steamers for Charleston carried no arms and no men, but a supply of provisions for the garrison at Fort Sumter, and also that Gov. Pickens was notified that that was the object of the steamers' visit.

FROM CHARLESTON

Charleston, April 10, 1 P.M.—All is still quiet up to this hour. . . . It is believed that no order for attack on Fort Sumter has as yet been received from Montgomery. Nothing outside the bar.

The floating **battery** having been finished, mounted, and manned, was taken out of the dock last evening and anchored in a cove near Sullivan's Island, ready for service.

Our people are not excited, but there is a fixed determination to meet the issue.

An additional regiment of one thousand men is hourly expected from the interior.

Governor Pickens was in secret session with the State Convention to-day before their final adjournment, which took place at 1 o'clock.

About 1,000 troops were sent to the fortifications to-day, and 1,800 more will go down to-morrow. . . .

Large numbers of the members of the convention, after adjournment, volunteered as privates.

About 7,000 troops are now at the fortifications, the "beginning of the end" is coming to a final closing.

Washington, April 11.—The general excitement occasioned here yesterday by the calling out [of] the volunteer militia of the District to be mustered into the federal service has abated, and to-day four or five more companies marched to the War Department and took the army oath, namely; "to bear true allegiance to the United States and serve them honestly and faithfully against all their enemies and opposers, whomsoever, and observe and obey the orders of the President of the United States and the orders of the officers appointed over them, according to the rules and articles for the government of the United States."

Previous to taking the oath, the volunteers were informed that the obligation was for three months, unless they were sooner discharged.

Montgomery, April 11.—The War Department is overwhelmed with applications from Regiments, battalions, and companies to enter the service. Over 7000 men from the Border States offer their services besides two thousand Indian warriors, who have signified a desire to co-operate with the Confederate forces. Numbers of companies are daily arriving at Charleston, Savannah, and Pensacola.

Charleston, April 11, P.M.—A collision is hourly expected.

Northern dispatches state that attempts will be made to-day to reinforce Sumter in small boats protected by schooners lined with sand bags, the war vessels in the meantime to protect the landing party on Morris Island.

It is reported that Gen. Beauregard has demanded the immediate surrender of Fort Sumter.

EDITORIAL

What is Sumter . . . worth, in comparison with the preservation of the public peace, and the avoidance of civil war? Why hinge upon the question of a formal *recognition* of the Confederate States—when the Confederate States have a government, an army, a civil, political, and military organization? Why have the public been left under the impression for weeks past, that Sumter was to be relinquished, without disturbance? Has not the reported "military necessity" for its evacuation been acquiesced in by reasonable people everywhere, North and

South? We believe, not only in the "military necessity," but, under the circumstances, in the propriety of its evacuation. Patriots and statesmen have to look at things as they find them, and to deal with them accordingly. Will holding on to Sumter, or reinforcing the garrison, make *Secession* less a reality than it is— alter the condition of South Carolina—or, in any degree, injure the Confederate States—supposing injury to be intended? Will it strengthen the United States, or any position of the States yet in the Union? Will it strengthen the Union feeling in any of the Southern States which have not yet seceded? Will it not irritate and heighten angry feelings? Will it not, finally, and most of all, . . . tend to, and probably produce, a *civil war*?

Charleston, April 11, 8 o'clock P.M.—It has now been ascertained that a demand for the surrender of the fort was made to-day at 2 o'clock. . . . Thousands of people are assembled on the Battery this evening anticipating the commencement of the fight. . . .

The steamer Harriet Lane is reported off the bar, and signals are being displayed by the guard boats and answered by the batteries, but what is indicated cannot be more than guessed at.

Source 3   Diary of Mary Boykin Chesnut, wife of General Beauregard's aide-de-camp, James Chesnut

April 12— . . . I do not pretend to go to sleep. How can I? If Anderson does not accept terms at 4 o'clock, the orders are he shall be fired upon.

I count four by St. Michael's chimes, and I begin to hope. At half past four, the heavy booming of a cannon! I sprang out of bed and on my knees, prostrate, I prayed as I never prayed before.

There was a sound of stir all over the house, a pattering of feet in the corridor. All seemed hurrying one way. I put on my double-gown and a shawl and went to the house top. The shells were bursting. In the dark I heard a man say: "Waste of ammunition!" I knew my husband was rowing about in a boat somewhere in that dark bay, and that the shells were roofing it over, bursting toward the Fort. If Anderson was obstinate, Mr. Chesnut was to order the Forts on our side to open fire. Certainly fire had begun. The regular roar of the cannon, there it was! And who could tell what each **volley** accomplished in death and destruction.

The women were wild, there on the house top. Prayers from the women and imprecations from the men; and then a shell would light up the scene.

Source 4   *Alexandria Gazette and Virginia Advertiser*

SURRENDER OF FORT SUMTER

Charleston, April 13, 10½ A.M.—At intervals of fifteen minutes the firing was kept up all night on Sumter. Anderson ceased fire at six in the morning. All night he was engaged in repairing damages, and protecting the **barbette** guns on the top of Sumter. He commenced to return the fire this morning at seven o'clock.

An explosion has occurred at Sumter, as a dense volume of smoke was seen suddenly to rise. Anderson has ceased to fire for above an hour. His flag is still up. . . .

April 13—Forenoon—Fort Sumter is undoubtedly on fire. Major Anderson has thrown out a raft, and men are passing up buckets of water from it to extinguish the flames. The fort is scarcely discernible in the smoke. The men on the raft are now subjected to the fire from the Cummings Point batteries. With good glasses, balls can be seen skipping along the surface of the water and occasionally striking near the raft, creating great consternation among the men thereon.

The flames can now be seen issuing from all the portholes, and the destruction of all combustible matter in the fort appears to be inevitable. . . .

A reliable source states that up to 10 a.m. no one at Fort Moultrie had been killed. Eleven shots had penetrated the famous floating battery below her water line. The few shots fired by Anderson, early in the morning, knocked the bricks and chimneys of the officers quarters in Moultrie like a whirlwind.

It seems to be Anderson's only hope to hold out for aid from the fleet.

Two ships are making in towards Morris Island, apparently with a view to land troops to silence the destructive battery. . . .

April 13, 1 p.m.—Anderson's flag and mast are down. Supposed to have been shot away.

The federal flag has again been hoisted. Wm. Porcher Miles, under a white flag, has gone to Sumter.

Anderson has hauled down the federal flag, and hoisted a white one.

The batteries have all stopped firing, and two boats with Confederate flags are on their way to the fort.

Fort Sumter has surrendered. The Confederate flag has been hoisted.

Source 5 Jefferson Davis's message to the Confederate Congress

April 29, 1861

The declaration of war made against this Confederacy, by Abraham Lincoln, President of the United States, . . . renders it necessary . . . to devise the measures necessary for the defence of the country. . . .

The war of the Revolution was successfully waged, and resulted in the treaty of peace with Great Britain in 1783, by the terms of which the several States were each by name recognized to be independent. . . .

It was by the delegates chosen by the several States . . . that the Constitution of the United States was formed in 1787, and submitted to the several States for ratification.

Strange, indeed, must it appear to the impartial observer, that . . . an organization created by the States, to secure the blessings of liberty and independence against foreign aggression, has been gradually perverted into a machine for their control in their domestic affairs.

The creature has been exalted above its Creator—the principals have been made subordinate to the agent appointed by themselves.

The people of the Southern States, whose almost exclusive occupation was agriculture, early perceived a tendency in the Northern States to render a common government subservient to their own purposes by imposing burthens on commerce as protection to their manufacturing and shipping interests.

Long and angry controversies grew out of these attempts . . . to benefit one section of the country at the expense of the other. . . .

When the several States delegated certain powers to the United States Congress, a large portion of the laboring population were imported into the colonies by the mother country. In twelve out of the fifteen States, negro slavery existed, and the right of property existing in slaves was protected by law; this property was recognized in the Constitution, and provision was made against its loss by the escape of the slave. . . .

The climate of the Northern States soon proved unpropitious to the continuance of slave labor, while the reverse being the case at the South, made unrestricted free intercourse between the two sections unfriendly.

The Northern States consulted their own interests by selling their slaves to the South and prohibiting slavery between their limits. . . .

As soon, however, as the Northern States, that had prohibited slavery within their limits, had reached a number sufficient to give their representation a controlling vote in Congress, a persistent and organized system of hostile measures against the rights of the owners of slaves in the Southern States was inaugurated and gradually extended. A series of measures was devised and prosecuted for the purpose of rendering insecure the tenure of property in slaves.

Fanatical organizations . . . were assiduously engaged in exciting amongst the slaves a spirit of discontent and revolt. Means were furnished for their escape from their owners, and agents secretly employed to entice them to abscond.

The constitutional provision for their rendition to their owners was first evaded, then openly denounced. . . . Often owners of slaves were mobbed and even murdered in open day solely for applying to a magistrate for the arrest of a fugitive slave. . . .

Finally, a great party was organized for the purpose of obtaining the administration of the Government, with the avowed object of using its power for the total exclusion of the slave States from all participation in the benefits of the public domain. . . . This party, thus organized, succeeded in the month of November last in the election of its candidate for the Presidency of the United States. . . .

Early in April the attention of the whole country was attracted to extraordinary preparations for an extensive military and naval expedition in New York and other Northern ports. These preparations commenced in secrecy, for an expedition whose destination was concealed, and only became known when nearly completed, and on the 5th, 6th, and 7th of April, transports and vessels of war with troops, munitions and military supplies, sailed from Northern ports bound southward. . . .

According to the usual course of navigation, the vessels composing the expedition, and designed for the relief of Fort Sumter, might be looked for in Charleston harbor on the 9th of April. . . . [O]ur flag did not wave over the battered walls until after the appearance of the hostile fleet off Charleston. . . .

The people of Charleston for months had been irritated by the spectacle of a fortress held within their principal harbor as a standing menace against their peace and independence—built in part with their own money— . . . intended to be used . . . for their own protection against foreign attack. How it was held out with persistent tenacity as a means of offence against them by the very Government which they had established for their own protection, is well known. . . .

Scarcely had the President of the United States received intelligence of the failure of the scheme which he had devised for the reinforcement of Fort Sumter, when he issued a declaration of war against the Confederacy.

Source 6   President Abraham Lincoln's Special Session message

July 4, 1861

Fellow-Citizens of the Senate and House of Representatives:

27.3 The History Place: A Nation Divided

Having been convened on an extraordinary occasion, your attention is not called to any ordinary subject of legislation.

At the beginning of the present Presidential term, four months ago, the functions of the Federal Government were found to be generally suspended within the several States of South Carolina, Georgia, Alabama, Mississippi, Louisiana, and Florida, excepting those of the Post Office Department.

Within these States all the forts, arsenals, dockyards, custom-houses, and the like . . . had been seized and were held in open hostility to this Government, excepting only Forts Pickens, Taylor, and Jefferson, on or near the Florida coast, and Fort Sumter, in Charleston Harbor, South Carolina. . . .

The forts remaining in the possession of the Federal Government in and near these States were either besieged or menaced by warlike preparations, and especially Fort Sumter was nearly surrounded by well-protected hostile batteries. . . .

On the 5th of March, the present incumbent's first full day in office, a letter of Major Anderson, commanding at Fort Sumter, . . . received at the War Department on the 4th of March, was by that Department placed in his hands. This letter expressed the professional opinion of the writer that reenforcements could not be thrown into the fort within the time for his relief rendered necessary by the limited supply of provisions. . . . The whole was immediately laid before Lieutenant-General Scott, who at once concurred with Major Anderson in opinion. . . . In a purely military point of view this reduced the duty of the Administration in the case to the mere matter of getting the garrison safely out of the fort.

It was believed, however, that to so abandon that position under the circumstances would be utterly ruinous; that the *necessity* under which it was done would not be fully understood; that by many it would be construed as a part of a *voluntary* policy; that at home it would discourage the friends of the Union, embolden its adversaries, and go far to insure to the latter a recognition abroad; that, in fact, it would be our national destruction consummated. This could not be allowed. . . . [I]t was resolved . . . to notify the governor of South Carolina that he might expect an attempt would be made to provision the fort, and that if the attempt should not be resisted there would be no effort to throw in men, arms, or ammunition without further notice, or in case of attack upon the fort. This notice was accordingly given, whereupon the fort was attacked and bombarded to its fall, without even awaiting the arrival of the provisioning expedition.

It was thus seen that the assault upon and reduction of Fort Sumter was in no sense a matter of self-defense on the part of the assailants. . . . They knew that this Government desired to keep the garrison in the fort, not to assail them, but merely to maintain visible possession, and thus to preserve the Union from actual and immediate dissolution, trusting, . . . to time, discussion, and the ballot box for final adjustment; and they assailed and reduced the fort for precisely the reverse object. . . .

It might seem at first thought to be of little difference whether the present movement at the South be called "secession" or "rebellion." The movers, however, well understand the difference. At the beginning they knew they could never raise their treason to any respectable magnitude by any name which implies *violation* of the law. . . . They invented an ingenious sophism, which, if conceded, was followed by perfectly logical steps through all the incidents to the complete destruction of the Union. The sophism itself is that any State may *consistently* with the National Constitution, and therefore, *lawfully* and *peacefully*, withdraw from the Union without the consent of the Union or of any other State. . . .

This sophism derives much . . . of its currency from the assumption that there is some omnipotent and sacred supremacy pertaining to a *State*—to each State of our Federal Union. Our States have neither more nor less power than that reserved to them in the Union by the Constitution, no one of them ever having been a State *out* of the Union. The original ones passed into the Union even before they cast off their British colonial dependence, and the new ones each came into the Union directly from a condition of dependence, excepting Texas. . . . Having never been States, either in substance or in name, *outside* of the Union, whence this magical omnipotence of "State rights," or asserting a claim of power to lawfully destroy the Union itself? Much is said about the "sovereignty" of the States. . . . What is a "sovereignty" in the political sense of the term? Would it be far wrong to define it "a political community without a political superior?" Tested by this, no one of our States, except Texas, ever was a sovereignty; and even Texas gave up the character on coming into the Union, by which act she acknowledged the Constitution of the United States . . . to be for her the supreme law of the land. The States have their status in the Union, and they have no other legal status. If they break from this, they can do so only against law and by revolution. The Union, and not themselves separately, procured their independence and their liberty. By conquest or purchase the Union gave each of them whatever of independence and liberty it has. The Union is older than any of the States, and, in fact, it created them as States. . . .

Our popular Government has often been called an experiment. Two points in it our people have already settled—the successful *establishing* and the successful *administering* of it. One still remains—its successful *maintenance* against a formidable internal attempt to overthrow it. It is now for them to demonstrate to the world that those who can fairly carry an election can also suppress a rebellion; that ballots are the rightful and peaceful successors of bullets, and that when ballots have fairly and constitutionally decided there can be no successful appeal back to bullets; that there can be no successful appeal except to ballots themselves at succeeding elections. Such will be a great lesson of peace, teaching men that what they cannot take by an election neither can they take it by a war. . . .

The Constitution provides, and all the States have accepted the provision, that "the United States shall guarantee to every State in this Union a republican form of government." But if a State may lawfully go out of the Union, having done so it may also discard the republican form of government; so that to prevent its going out is an indispensable *means* to the end of maintaining the guaranty mentioned. . . .

It was with the deepest regret that the Executive found the duty of employing the war power in defense of the Government forced upon him. He could but perform this duty or surrender the existence of the Government.

Second Thoughts
Why Did North and South Go to War?

Great events in history seldom admit of easy explanation. So it is with the American Civil War. While all agree that the war started at Fort Sumter, few agree on why. Theories cite Northern aggression or Southern secession, slavery and racism, abolitionist agitation and Southern paranoia, capitalism vanquishing feudalism, the inevitable tension between incompatible cultures locked into an artificial union, bumbling political leadership, the assumption of power by a regional rather than a national party, and even an excess of democratic zeal. Some find the origin of the war in the tensions resulting from the expansion of the nation's borders. Samuel Eliot Morison viewed the struggle between North and South for control of the west as key, declaring that "with no Mexican War there would have been no Civil War, at least not in 1861." Though the Civil War remains one of the most momentous events in the history of the United States, neither those who waged it nor those who have since studied it have ever reached agreement on its causes.

27.4 Civil War

Source 7   Henry Wilson, radical Republican, speech to the United States Senate, May 1, 1862

How can any man looking over this broad land today and seeing flashing from every quarter of the heavens the crimes of human slavery against this country, labor to uphold, strengthen, and support human slavery in America? It is the cause and the whole cause of this rebellion. We talk about "Jeff" Davis, Slidell, Mason, and Toombs, and their treasonable confederates; but they are not the cause of this rebellion; they are simply the hands, the tools, the heart, the brain, the soul is slavery; the motive power is slavery. Slavery is the great rebel; Davis and his compeers are but its humble tools and instruments.

Slavery for thirty years has been hostile to and aggressive upon the free institutions of America. There is not a principle embodied in our free institutions, there is not an element of our government that elevates or blesses mankind, there is not anything in our government or our institutions worth preserving, that slavery for a generation has not warred against and upon.

It smote down thirty years ago the right of petition in these halls. It destroyed in large sections of the country the constitutional freedom of the press. It suppressed freedom of speech. It corrupted presses, churches, and political organizations. It plunged the nation into a war for the acquisition of slave-holding territory. It enacted a fugitive-slave law, inhuman, unchristian, disgraceful to the country and to the age. It repealed the prohibition of slavery over a half a million square miles in the central regions of the continent. It seized the ballot boxes in Kansas; it usurped the government of the Territory; it enacted inhuman and unchristian laws; it made a slave constitution and attempted to force it upon a free people; it bathed the virgin sods of that magnificent Territory with the blood of civil war. It mobbed, flogged, expelled, and sometimes murdered Christian men and women in the slave-holding States for no offence against law, humanity, or religion. It turned the hearts of large masses of men against their brethren, against the institutions of their country, against the glorious old flag, and the constitution of their fathers. It has now plunged this nation into this unholy rebellion, into this gigantic civil war that rends the country, and stains our waters and reddens our fields with fraternal blood.

Sir, I never see a loyal soldier upon a cot of sickness, sorrow, or death, without feeling that slavery has laid him there. I never gaze upon the wounds of a loyal soldier fallen in support of the flag of the republic without feeling that slavery inflicted those wounds upon him. I never see a loyal soldier wounded and maimed hobbling through your streets without feeling he was wounded and maimed by slavery. I never gaze upon the lowly grave of a loyal soldier dying for the cause of his country without feeling he was murdered by slavery. I never see a mourning wife or sorrowing children without realizing that slavery has made that mourning wife a widow and those children orphans.

Sir, all these sacrifices of property, of health, of life, all this sorrow, agony, and death, now upon us, are born of slavery. Slavery is the prolific mother of all those woes that blight our land and fill the heart of our people with sorrows.

Slavery pronounced long ago against the free elements of our popular institutions; it scoffed at the Declaration of Independence; it pronounced free society a failure; it jeered and sneered at the laboring masses as mudsills and white slaves. Scoffing at everything which tended to secure the rights and enlarge the privileges of mankind, it has pronounced against the existence of democratic institutions in America. Proud, domineering, defiant, it has pronounced against the supremacy of the government, the unity and life of the nation.

Sir, slavery is the enemy, the clearly pronounced enemy of the country. Slavery is the only enemy our country has on God's earth. There it stands. Hate is in its heart, scorn in its eye, defiance in its mien. It hates our cherished institutions, despises our people, defies our government. Slavery is the great rebel, the giant criminal, the murderer striving with dirty hands to throttle our government and destroy our country.

Source 8   Clement L. Vallandigham, Democratic congressman for Ohio, "Speech on the War and Its Conduct," January 14, 1863

Sir, I am one of that number who have opposed abolitionism, or the political development of the anti-slavery sentiment of the North and West, from the beginning. . . . Sir, it is but the development of the spirit of intermeddling, whose children are strife and murder. Cain troubled himself about the sacrifices of Abel and slew his brother. Most of the wars, contentions, litigations, and bloodshed, from the beginning of time have been its fruits. The spirit of non-intervention is the very spirit of peace and concord.

I do not believe that if slavery had never existed here we would have had no sectional controversies. This very civil war might have happened fifty, perhaps a hundred, years later. Other and stronger causes of discontent and of disunion, it may be, have existed between other states and sections, and are now being developed into maturity. The spirit of intervention assumed the form of abolitionism because slavery was odious in name and by association to the Northern mind, and because it was that which most obviously marks the different civilizations of the two sections.

The South herself, in her early and later efforts to rid herself of it, had exposed the weak and offensive parts of slavery to the world. Abolition intermeddling taught her at last to search for and defend the assumed social, economic, and political merits and values of the institution. But there never was an hour from the beginning when it did not seem to me as clear as the sun at broad noon that the agitation in any form, in the North and West, of the slavery question must sooner or later end in disunion and civil war.

Source 9 Edward Pollard, editor of the *Richmond Examiner, The Lost Cause: A New Southern History of the War of the Confederates,* 1866

No one can read aright the history of America, unless in the light of a North and a South; two political aliens existing in a Union imperfectly defined as a confederation of states. . . .

The slavery question is not to be taken as an independent controversy in American politics. It was not a moral dispute. It was the mere incident of a sectional animosity, the causes of which lay far beyond the domain of morals. Slavery furnished a convenient line of battle between the disputants; it was the most prominent ground of distinction between the two sections; it was, therefore, naturally seized upon as a subject of controversy, became the dominant theatre of hostilities, and was at last so conspicuous and violent, that occasion was mistaken for cause, and what was merely an incident came to be regarded as the main subject of controversy. . . .

The North naturally found or imagined in slavery the leading cause of the distinctive civilization of the South, its higher sentimentalism, and its superior refinements of scholarship and manners. It revenged itself on the cause, diverted its envy in an attack on slavery. . . . [T]he slavery question was not a moral one in the North, unless, perhaps, with a few thousand persons of disordered conscience. It was significant only of a contest for political power, and afforded nothing more than a convenient ground of dispute between two . . . opposite civilizations.

In the ante-revolutionary period, the differences between the populations of the Northern and Southern colonies had already been strongly developed. The early colonists did not bear with them from the mother-country to the shores of the New World any greater degree of congeniality than existed among them at home. They had come not only from different stocks of population, but from different feuds in religion and politics. There could be no congeniality between the Puritan exiles who established themselves upon the cold and rugged and cheerless soil of New England, and the Cavaliers who sought the brighter climate of the South. . . .

[T]he intolerance of the Puritans, the painful thrift of the Northern colonists, their external forms of piety, their jaundiced legislation, their convenient morals, their lack of sentimentalism . . . , and their unremitting hunt after selfish aggrandizement are traits of character which are yet visible in their descendents. On the other hand, the colonists of Virginia and the Carolinas were from the first distinguished by their polite manners, their fine sentiments, their attachment to a sort of feudal life, their landed gentry, their love of field-sports and dangerous adventure, and the prodigal and improvident aristocracy that dispensed its stores in constant rounds of hospitality and gaiety.

Slavery established in the South a peculiar and noble type of civilization. . . . The South had an element in its society—a landed gentry—which the North envied, and for which its substitute was a coarse ostentatious aristocracy that smelt of trade, and that, however it cleansed itself and aped the elegance of the South, and packed its houses with fine furniture, could never entirely subdue a sneaking sense of its inferiority. There is a singular bitter hate which is inseparable from a sense of inferiority.

Source 10   Alexander H. Stephens, former vice president of the Confederacy, *A Constitutional View of the Late War between the States*, 1868

It is a postulate, with many writers of this day, that the late war was the result of two opposing ideas, or principles, upon the subject of African Slavery. Between these, according to their theory, sprung the "irrepressible conflict," in principle, which ended in the terrible conflict of arms. Those who assume this postulate, and so theorize upon it, are but superficial observers.

That the War had its origin in *opposing principles* . . . may be assumed as an unquestionable fact. But the opposing principles which produced these results in physical action were of a very different character from those assumed in the postulate. They lay in the organic Structure of the Government of the States. The conflict in principle arose from different and opposing ideas as to the nature of what is known as the General Government. The contest was between those who held it to be strictly Federal in its character, and those who maintained that it was thoroughly National. It was a strife between the principles of Federalism, on the one hand, and Centralism, or Consolidation, on the other.

Source 11   Vice President Henry Wilson, *The History of the Rise and Fall of Slavepower in America*, 1877

By means illegitimate and indefensible, reckless of principle and of consequences, a comparatively few men succeeded in dragooning whole States into the support of a policy the majority condemned, to following leaders the majority distrusted and most cordially disliked. . . . [A] class of men who despised the colored man because he was colored, and the poor whites because they were poor, inspire[d] the latter with a willingness, an enthusiasm even, to take up arms, subject themselves to all the hardships and hazards of war, for the express purpose of perpetuating and making more despotic a system which had already despoiled them of so much, and was designed to make still more abject their degradation.

Source 12 James Ford Rhodes, *Lectures on the American Civil War,* 1913

[O]f the American Civil War it may be safely asserted that there was but a single cause, slavery. . . . The question may be isolated by the incontrovertible statement that if the Negro had never been brought to America, our Civil War would never have occurred.

Source 13 Charles and Mary Beard, *The Rise of American Civilization,* 1933

The Civil War . . . , called in these pages the "Second American Revolution," was merely the culmination of the deep-running transformation that shifted the center of gravity in American society between the inauguration of Jackson and the election of Lincoln. . . .

[T]he so-called Civil War, or the War between the States, . . . was a social war, ending in the unquestioned establishment of a new power in the government, making vast changes in the arrangement of classes, in the accumulation and distribution of wealth, in the course of industrial development, and in the Constitution inherited from the Fathers. Merely by the accidents of climate, soil, and geography was it a sectional struggle. If the planting interest had been scattered evenly throughout the industrial region, had there been a horizontal rather than a perpendicular cleavage, the irrepressible conflict would have been resolved by other methods. . . .

In any event neither accident nor rhetoric should be allowed to obscure the intrinsic character of the struggle. If the operations by which the middle classes of England broke the power of the king and the aristocracy are to be known collectively as the Puritan Revolution, if the series of acts by which the bourgeois and peasants of France overthrew the king, nobility, and clergy is to be called the French Revolution, then accuracy compels us to characterize by the same term the social cataclysm in which the capitalists, laborers, and farmers of the North and West drove from power in the national government the planting aristocracy of the South. Viewed in the light of universal history, the fighting was a fleeting incident; the social revolution was the essential, portentous outcome.

Source 14 Allan Nevins, *The Emergence of Lincoln,* 1950

The main root of the conflict (and there were minor roots) was the problem of slavery with *its complementary problem of race-adjustment;* the main source of the tragedy was the refusal of either section to face these conjoined problems squarely and pay the heavy costs of a peaceful settlement. Had it not been for the difference in race, the slavery issue would have presented no great difficulties. But as the racial gulf existed, the South inarticulately but clearly perceived that elimination of this issue would still leave it the terrible problem of the Negro.

Those historians who write that if slavery had simply been left alone it would soon have withered overlook this heavy impediment.

Source 15   David Donald, *Lincoln Reconsidered*, 1961

The Civil War, I believe, can best be understood neither as the result of accident nor as the product of conflicting sectional interests, but as the outgrowth of social processes which affected the entire United States during the first half of the nineteenth century. . . .

In the early nineteenth century all sections of the United States were being transformed with such rapidity that stability and security were everywhere vanishing values; nowhere could a father predict what kind of world his son would grow up in. . . .

In a nation so new that, as President James K. Polk observed, its history was in the future, in a land of such abundance, men felt under no obligation to respect the lessons of the past. . . . Every aspect of American life witnessed this desire to throw off precedent and to rebel from authority. Every institution which laid claim to prescriptive right was challenged and overthrown. The Church . . . was first disestablished . . . and then strange new sects . . . appeared to fragment the Christian community. The squirearchy, once a powerful conservative influence in the Middle States and the South, was undermined by the abolition of primogeniture and entails. . . . All centralizing economic institutions came under attack. The Second Bank of the United States, which exercised a healthy restraint upon financial chaos, was abolished during the Jackson period. . . .

Nowhere was the American rejection of authority more complete than in the political sphere. . . . By the 1850's the authority of all government in America was at a low point; government to the American was, at most, merely an institution with a negative role, a guardian of fair play.

Declining power of government was paralleled by increased popular participation in it. The extension of the franchise in America has rarely been the result of a concerted reform drive, . . . rather it has been part of the gradual erosion of all authority, of the feeling that restraints and differentials are necessarily anti-democratic, and of the practical fact that such restrictions are difficult to enforce. . . .

Possibly in time this disorganized society might have evolved a genuinely conservative solution for its problems, but time ran against it. At a stage when the United States was least capable of enduring shock, the nation was obliged to undergo a series of crises, largely triggered by the physical expansion of the country. . . .

These crises . . . were not in themselves calamitous experiences. Revisionist historians have correctly pointed out how little was actually at stake: slavery did not go into New Mexico or Arizona; Kansas, after having been opened to the peculiar institution for six years, had only two Negro slaves; the Dred Scott decision declared an already repealed law unconstitutional; John Brown's raid had no significant support in the North and certainly aroused no visible enthusiasm among Southern Negroes. When compared to crises which other nations have resolved without great discomfort, the true proportions of these exaggerated disturbances appear.

But American society in the 1850's was singularly ill-equipped to meet any shocks, however weak. It was a society so new and so disorganized that its nerves were rawly exposed. It was . . . a land which had . . . no resistance to strain. The very similarity of the social processes which affected all sections of the country—the expansion of the frontier, the rise of the city, the exploitation of great natural wealth—produced not cohesion but individualism. The structure of the American political system impeded the appearance of conservative states-manship, and the rapidity of the crises in the 1850's prevented conservatism from crystallizing. The crises themselves were not world-shaking, nor did they inevitably produce war. They were, however, the chisel strokes which revealed the fundamental flaws in the block of marble, flaws which stemmed from an excess of democracy.

Source 16 Eugene Genovese, *The Political Economy of Slavery,* 1967

I do say that the struggle between North and South was irrepressible. From the moment that slavery passed from being one of several labor systems into being the basis of the Southern social order, material and ideological conflict with the North came into being and had to grow worse. If this much is granted, the question of inevitability becomes a question of whether or not the slaveholders would give up their world, which they identified properly with slavery itself, without armed resistance. The slaveholders' pride, sense of honor, and commit-ment to their way of life made a final struggle so probable that we may safely call it inevitable without implying a mechanistic determinism against which man cannot avail.

Source 17 Howard Zinn, *A People's History of the United States,* 1980

Behind the secession of the South from the Union . . . was a long series of policy clashes between South and North. The clash was not over slavery as a moral institution—most northerners did not care enough about slavery to make sacrifices for it, certainly not the sacrifice of war. It was not a clash of peoples (most northern whites were not economically favored, not politi-cally powerful; most southern whites were poor farmers, not decisionmakers) but of elites. The northern elite wanted economic expansion—free land, free labor, a free market, a high protective tariff for manufacturers, a bank of the United States. The slave interests opposed all that; they saw Lincoln and the Republicans as making continuation of their pleasant and prosperous way of life impossible in the future.

So, when Lincoln was elected, seven states seceded from the Union. Lin-coln initiated hostilities by trying to repossess the federal base at Fort Sumter, South Carolina, and four more states seceded. The Confederacy was formed; the Civil War was on.

Questioning the Past

1. Did Lincoln intentionally provoke the incident at Fort Sumter? Was South Carolina at fault for firing on the fort? Which side was responsible for the firing on Fort Sumter? With the benefit of hindsight, should either Lincoln or South Carolina have handled the incident any differently?

2. Present the various theories offered to explain why North and South went to war. What theory, or theories, seem most valid?

3. What role did slavery play in producing the tensions that led to war?

4. Historian Samuel Eliot Morison wrote that "with no Mexican War there would have been no Civil War, at least not in 1861." What rationale could be offered in support of this thesis?

5. Suppose Lincoln had not resisted the effort of the southern states to secede, and the Confederacy had been allowed to establish itself as a sovereign nation. In what ways might the history of America since 1860 have been different? What would North America be like today?

Chapter **28**

The Emancipation Proclamation

Lincoln Signs an Executive Order *January 1, 1863*

Abraham Lincoln convened a meeting of his Cabinet on Tuesday, July 22, 1862, and surprised his advisers with a bold proposal. He announced that he had drafted a document proclaiming the liberation of all slaves held in states that were then in rebellion against the United States. He said he intended to release this document immediately and welcomed the Cabinet's comments on the proposal.

The Cabinet members were taken aback by Lincoln's announcement. Always in the past when the idea of emancipation had been raised in the Cabinet room, it had been the president himself who had quashed the suggestion, on grounds that slavery was a matter beyond the reach of the federal government. Now, one by one, it was his advisers who urged caution. Such a pronouncement might incite slaves to rebel and lead to a bloody massacre of slaves and slave masters alike, one warned. Another speculated about the effects of the proclamation on the congressional elections of the coming fall. Lincoln was not dissuaded. Then Secretary of State Seward raised a question that Lincoln had not considered: Seward argued that the issuance of the document at a time when Union forces were faring so poorly on the battlefield would be interpreted as a sign of desperation. Lincoln accepted the validity of Seward's point and laid the proclamation aside.

In early September of 1862, Robert E. Lee brought his Army of Northern Virginia across the Potomac into Maryland. It was Lee's first attempt to take the war into a state loyal to the Union. Lee's forces were met at Antietam Creek by General McClellan and the Union Army, and battle raged throughout the day of September 17, 1862. Both armies suffered staggering losses in what was to be the bloodiest single day of combat in the entire Civil War. Neither side, however, was able to deliver a decisive blow against the other, and the following evening Lee withdrew his forces back across the Potomac into Virginia.

The Battle of Antietam was not a tactical victory for the Union, but, with the retreat of the Confederate forces, it could at least be claimed as a strategic victory. Lincoln seized the moment to unveil his proclamation.

🐚 *First Impressions*
An Attempt to Save the Union

28.1 The
Emancipation
Proclamation

On September 22, 1862, President Lincoln signed and released a pre-
liminary proclamation concerning the emancipation of the slaves. This
document was a warning. If the armies in rebellion against the Union
did not lay down their weapons before the first of the coming year, the
president advised, he would proclaim all slaves in the territories controlled
by these rebellious forces to be free.

During the remaining days of 1862, there was much speculation
in both the North and the South as to whether the president would actually carry through with this threat. The prospect of such a proclamation,
however, did not move any of the seceding states to return to the Union.

On the afternoon of January 1, 1863, President Lincoln signed the
Emancipation Proclamation.

Source 1   President Lincoln's "Address on Colonization to a Deputation
of Negroes," August 14, 1862

Your race are suffering, in my judgment, the greatest wrong inflicted on any
people. But even when you cease to be slaves, you are yet far removed from
being placed on an equality with the white race. You are cut off from many of
the advantages which the other race enjoy. The aspiration of men is to enjoy
equality with the best when free, but on this broad continent, not a single man
of your race is made the equal of a single man of ours. Go where you are treated
the best and the ban is still upon you.

I do not propose to discuss this, but to present it as a fact with which we
have to deal. I cannot alter it if I would. It is a fact, about which we all think
and feel alike, I and you. We look to our condition, owing to the existence of
the two races on this continent. I need not recount to you the effects upon
white men, growing out of the institution of Slavery. I believe in its general evil
effects on the white race. See our present condition—the country engaged in
war!—our white men cutting each other's throats, none knowing how far it will
extend; and then consider what we know to be the truth. But for your race
among us there could not be war, although many men engaged in either side
do not care for you one way or the other. Nevertheless, I repeat, without the
institution of Slavery and the colored race as a basis, the war could not have
an existence.

It is better for us both, therefore, to be separated. I know that there are
free men among you, who even if they could better their condition are not as
much inclined to go out of the country as those, who being slaves, could obtain
their freedom on this condition. You may believe you can live in Washington
or elsewhere in the United States the remainder of your life . . . and hence you
may come to the conclusion that you have nothing to do with the idea of going
to a foreign country. This is an extremely selfish view of the case.

But you ought to do something to help those who are not so fortunate as
yourselves. There is an unwillingness on the part of our people, harsh as it may
be, for you free colored people to remain with us. . . .

The place I am thinking about for a colony is in Central America. . . . The political affairs in Central America are not in quite as satisfactory condition as I wish. There are contending factions in that quarter; but it is true all the factions are agreed alike on the subject of colonization, and want it, and are more generous than we are here. To your colored race they have no objection. Besides, I would endeavor to have you made equals, and have the best assurance that you would be the equals of the best.

Source 2   President Lincoln to Horace Greeley

August 22, 1862

My paramount object in this struggle *is* to save the Union, and is not either to save or to destroy slavery. If I could save the Union without freeing *any* slave I would do it, and if I could save it by freeing *all* the slaves I would do it; and if I could save it by freeing some and leaving others alone I would also do that. What I do about slavery, and the colored race, I do because I believe it helps to save the Union; and what I forbear, I forbear because I do not believe it would help to save the Union. I shall do less whenever I shall believe what I am doing hurts the cause, and I shall do *more* whenever I shall believe doing more will help the cause. I shall try to correct errors when shown to be errors; and I shall adopt new views so fast as they shall appear to be true views.

I have here stated my purpose according to my view of *official* duty; and I intend no modification of my oft-expressed *personal* wish that all men every where could be free.

Source 3   President Lincoln's reply to petition for emancipation, September 13, 1862

What good would a proclamation of emancipation from me do, especially as we are now situated? I do not want to issue a document that the whole world will see must necessarily be inoperative, like the Pope's bull against the comet! Would *my word* free the slaves, when I cannot even enforce the Constitution in the rebel States? Is there a single court, or magistrate, or individual that would be influenced by it there?

Source 4   The Emancipation Proclamation

Whereas, on the twenty-second day of September, in the year of our Lord one thousand eight hundred and sixty-two, a proclamation was issued by the President of the United States, containing, among other things, the following, to wit:

"That on the first day of January, in the year of our Lord one thousand eight hundred and sixty-three, all persons held as slaves within any State or designated part of a State, the people whereof shall then be in rebellion against the United States, shall be then, thenceforth, and forever free; and the Executive Government of the United States, including the military and naval authority thereof, will recognize and maintain the freedom of such persons, and will do no act or acts to repress such persons, or any of them, in any efforts they may make for their actual freedom.

"That the Executive will, on the first day of January aforesaid, by proclamation, designate the States and parts of States, if any, in which the people thereof, respectively, shall then be in rebellion against the United States; and the fact that any State, or the people thereof, shall on that day be, in good faith, represented in the Congress of the United States by members chosen thereto at elections wherein a majority of the qualified voters of such State shall have participated, shall, in the absence of strong countervailing testimony, be deemed conclusive evidence that such State, and the people thereof, are not then in rebellion against the United States."

Now, therefore I, Abraham Lincoln, President of the United States, by virtue of the power in me vested as Commander-in-Chief, of the Army and Navy of the United States in time of actual armed rebellion against the authority and government of the United States, and as a fit and necessary war measure for suppressing said rebellion, do, on this first day of January, in the year of our Lord one thousand eight hundred and sixty-three, and in accordance with my purpose so to do publicly proclaimed for the full period of one hundred days, from the day first above mentioned, order and designate as the States and parts of States wherein the people thereof respectively, are this day in rebellion against the United States, the following, to wit:

Arkansas, Texas, Louisiana, (except the Parishes of St. Bernard, Plaquemines, Jefferson, St. John, St. Charles, St. James Ascension, Assumption, Terrbonne, Lafourche, St. Mary, St. Martin, and Orleans, including the City of New Orleans) Mississippi, Alabama, Florida, Georgia, South Carolina, North Carolina, and Virginia, (except the forty-eight counties designated as West Virginia, and also the counties of Berkley, Accomac, Northampton, Elizabeth City, York, Princess Ann, and Norfolk, including the cities of Norfolk and Portsmouth), and which excepted parts, are for the present, left precisely as if this proclamation were not issued.

And by virtue of the power, and for the purpose aforesaid, I do order and declare that all persons held as slaves within said designated States, and parts of States, are, and henceforward shall be free; and that the Executive government of the United States, including the military and naval authorities thereof, will recognize and maintain the freedom of said persons.

And I hereby enjoin upon the people so declared to be free to abstain from all violence, unless in necessary self-defense; and I recommend to them that, in all cases when allowed, they labor faithfully for reasonable wages.

And I further declare and make known, that such persons of suitable condition, will be received into the armed service of the United States to garrison forts, positions, stations, and other places, and to man vessels of all sorts in said service.

And upon this act, sincerely believed to be an act of justice, warranted by the Constitution, upon military necessity, I invoke the considerate judgment of mankind, and the gracious favor of Almighty God.

In witness thereof, I have hereunto set my hand and caused the seal of the United States to be affixed.

Done at the City of Washington, this first day of January, in the year of our Lord one thousand eight hundred and sixty three, and of the Independence of the United States of America the eighty-seventh.

Abraham Lincoln

A Document Whose Meaning Transcends Its Intent

A reading of the Emancipation Proclamation neither inspires nor excites. It is a document that seems unaware that it addresses a fundamental issue of human liberty. It lacks the moral bearing and persuasive force of Jefferson's earlier expression of American ideals, the Declaration of Independence. It lacks even the moving eloquence of other messages delivered by Lincoln.

The Emancipation Proclamation freed not a single slave. It left in chains the slaves of Delaware, Maryland, Kentucky, Missouri, and West Virginia because their masters had remained loyal to the Union. It left shackled the slaves of Tennessee even though their masters had been disloyal. It exempted areas of the Confederate states, already in Union hands, where **manumission** could actually have been enforced.

The Emancipation Proclamation protected slavery in areas controlled by the United States, while declaring the slaves free in areas the Union did not control. A document decreeing perpetual fair weather or good health would have had the same legal impact.

Nor did the proclamation even pretend to abolish the institution of slavery in the states in rebellion. It merely asserted the freedom of those who, at the moment the document was signed, were enslaved there. The freeing of southern slaves would no more affect the right of southerners to own human beings than would the confiscation of southern cattle destroy the right to own livestock.

Lincoln believed that those removed from slavery should likewise be removed from the country. He did not share the view of many members of his own party who sought the full incorporation of the freed slaves into American society. He sought instead the exile of the former slaves abroad. Colonization, not citizenship, was the consequence he expected for the beneficiaries of his proclamation. "I have sometimes doubted," Lincoln's secretary of the navy wrote, "whether he would not have hesitated longer in issuing the decree of emancipation had he been aware that colonization would not be accepted as an accompaniment."

Nonetheless, the Emancipation Proclamation stands as one of the most important documents in American history.

28.2 "Free At Last"

Source 5   Washington *Evening Star*, January 1, 1863

JUBILEE AMONG THE CONTRABANDS

Last evening the contrabands in camp at the corner of Twelfth and Q Streets determined to celebrate the incoming of the new year and at the same time hold a jubilee in view of the President's proclamation of to-day. About 8 o'clock the school room and vicinity was crowded, many not able to get in the door way, to the number of about three hundred.

The exercises were commenced by Mr. Morgan, of the Quartermaster's Department, who sang a song relating to the proclamation. Dr. D. B. Nichols, the

Superintendent, then addressed the contrabands on the rebellion . . . and closed by giving his audience some advice as to their conduct in future.

Dr. Nichols then called on them to give their experience, when an old man named Thornton got up and spoke as follows:—"I cried all night. What de matter, Thornton?

To-morrow my child is to be sold, neber more see till judgment—no more dat! no more dat! no more dat! With my hans on my breast, goin' to work, I feel bad, overseer behind me. No more dat! no more dat! no more dat! Can't sell your wife and children any more!"

EDITORIAL

If it answers the purpose of the Executive—aids in restoring the Union—all loyal men will surely rejoice that he issued it. . . . We care little about the means necessary to those ends: being willing to sacrifice slavery to their attainment, as we are certainly willing to sacrifice anti-slavery to it. . . .

If, on the contrary, it shall really militate against the grand purpose of the Executive, as many sincerely believe it will do, great good to the country will still result, in inclining the Executive hereafter to listen to conservative counsels, from which, alone, we apprehend ultimate success in the persecution of the war will come.

Source 6   *Alexandria Gazette,* January 3, 1863

FROM NORFOLK

Fortress Monroe, Jan. 1.—There was some excitement at Norfolk, yesterday, caused by the contrabands, to the number of some four thousand, making a procession through the town in honor of emancipation. They had a band of music and carried several Union flags, and cheered most lustily for the downfall of Southern slavery.

Source 7   *New York Times,* January 3, 1863

President Lincoln's proclamation . . . marks a new era in the history, not only of this war, but of this country and the world. It is not necessary to assume that it will set free instantly the enslaved blacks of the South, in order to ascribe to it the greatest and most permanent importance. Whatever may be its immediate results, it changes entirely the relations of the National Government to the institution of Slavery. Hitherto Slavery has been under the protection of the Government, henceforth it is under its ban. . . . This change of attitude is itself a revolution. . . .

What effect the Proclamation will have remains to be seen. We do not think that it will at once set free any considerable number of slaves beyond the actual and effective jurisdiction of our armies. It will lead to no immediate insurrections, and involve no massacres, except such as the rebels in the blindness of their wrath may themselves set on foot. The slaves have no arms, are without organization, and in dread of the armed and watchful whites. Besides, they evince no disposition to fight for themselves so long as they see we are fighting for them. They understand . . . that the tendency of this war is to give them freedom, and that the Union armies, whatever may be their motive, are actually and practically fighting for their liberty. If the war should suddenly end,—if they should see the fighting stop, and the Constitution which protects Slavery restored to full vigor in the Slave States, their disappointment would vent itself in the wrathful explosion of insurrection and violence. But so long as the war continues, we look for nothing of that kind.

Source 8 Confederate president Jefferson Davis's speech to the Confederate Congress, January 12, 1863

The public journals of the North have been received, containing a proclamation, dated on the 1st day of the present month, signed by the President of the United States, in which he orders and declares all slaves within ten of the States of the Confederacy to be free, except such as are found within certain districts now occupied in part by the armed forces of the enemy. We may well leave it to the instincts of that common humanity which a beneficent Creator has implanted in the breasts of our fellowmen of all countries to pass judgment on a measure by which several millions of human beings of an inferior race, peaceful and contented laborers in their sphere, . . . are encouraged to a general assassination of their masters by the insidious recommendation "to abstain from violence unless in necessary self-defense." Our own detestation of those who have attempted the most execrable measure recorded in the history of guilty man is tempered by profound contempt for the impotent rage which it discloses. . . . This proclamation is . . . an authentic statement by the Government of the United States of its inability to subjugate the South by force of arms.

Source 9 Abolitionist and author, Lydia Child, 1863

However we may inflate the emancipation balloon, it will never ascend among the constellations. The ugly fact cannot be concealed that it was done reluctantly and stintedly, and that even the degree that was accomplished was done selfishly; was merely a war measure, to which we were forced by our own perils and necessities; and that no recognition of principles of justice or humanity surrounded the political act with a halo of moral glory.

Source 10 John Greenleaf Whittier, "The Proclamation," February 1863

> O dark, sad millions, patiently and dumb
> Waiting for God, your hour, at last has come,
>   And freedom's song
> Breaks the long silence of your night of wrong!

Source 11 President Lincoln to James C. Conkling

August 26, 1863

[Y]ou are dissatisfied with me about the negro. Quite likely there is a difference of opinion between you and myself upon that subject. I certainly wish that all men could be free, while I suppose you do not. Yet I have never adopted, nor proposed any measure, which is not consistent with even your view, provided you are for the Union. . . .

You dislike the emancipation proclamation; and, perhaps, would have it retracted. You say it is unconstitutional—I think differently. I think the Constitution invests its commander-in-chief, with the law of war, in time of war. The most that can be said . . . is, that slaves are property. Is there . . . any question that by the law of war, property, both of enemy and friends, may be taken when needed? And is it not needed whenever taking it, helps us, or hurts the enemy? . . .

But the proclamation, as law, either is valid, or is not valid. If it is not valid, it needs no retraction. If it is valid, it can not be retracted, any more than the dead can be brought to life.

Second Thoughts
A Mortal Wound to Slavery

28.3 Pride over Prejudice

Historian Richard Hofstadter wrote that the Emancipation Proclamation "had all the moral grandeur of a bill of lading," while Samuel Eliot Morison said of its effect: "This proclamation, more revolutionary in human relationships than any event in American history since 1776, lifted the Civil War to the dignity of a crusade." Other interpreters discuss the historical paradox in the following selections.

Source 12 Lincoln's law partner William Herndon, *Life of Lincoln,* 1888

As the bloody drama of war moves along we . . . come to the crowning act in Mr. Lincoln's career—that sublime stroke with which his name will be forever and indissolubly united—the emancipation of the slaves. In the minds of many people there had been a crying need for the liberation of the slaves. Laborious efforts had been made to hasten the issuance by the President of the Emancipation Proclamation, but he was determined not to be forced into premature and inoperative measures. . . . All his life Mr. Lincoln had been a believer in the doctrine of gradual emancipation. He advocated it while in Congress in 1848; yet even now, as a military necessity, he could not believe the time was ripe for the general liberation of the slaves. All the coercion from without, and all the blandishments from within, his political household failed to move him. An heroic figure, indifferent alike to praise and blame, he stood at the helm and waited. In the shadow of his lofty form the smaller men could keep up their petty conflicts. Towering thus, he overlooked them all, and fearlessly bided his time. At last the great moment came. He called his Cabinet together and read the decree. The deed was done, unalterably, unhesitatingly, irrevocably, and triumphantly. The people, at first profoundly impressed, stood aloof, but seeing the builder beside the great structure he had so long been rearing, their confidence was abundantly renewed. It was a glorious work. . . .

I believe Mr. Lincoln wished to go down in history as the liberator of the black man. He realized to its fullest extent the responsibility and magnitude of the act, and declared it was "the central act of his administration and the great event of the nineteenth century." . . . As the years roll slowly by, and the participants in the late war drop gradually out of the ranks of men, let us pray that we may never forget their deeds of patriotic valor; but even if the details of that bloody struggle grow dim, as they will with the lapse of time, let us hope that so long as a friend of free man and free labor lives the dust of forgetfulness may never settle on the historic form of Abraham Lincoln.

Source 13 Lincoln's secretary John Nicolay and statesman John Hay, *Abraham Lincoln: A History*, 1890

Grand as was the historical act of signing his decree of liberation, it was but an incident in the grander contest he was commissioned and resolved to maintain. That was an issue, not alone of the bondage of a race, but of the life of a nation, a principle of government, a question of primary right.

Was this act, this step, this incident in the contest wise or unwise? Did it bring success or failure? Would it fill the army, weaken the enemy, inspirit the country, unite public opinion? These, we may assume, and not a lawyer's criticisms of phrase or text, dictum or precedent, were the queries which filled his mind when he wrote his name at the bottom of the famous document. If the rebellion should triumph, establishing a government founded on slavery as its corner-stone, manifestly his proclamation would be but waste paper. . . . If, on the other hand, the Union arms were victorious, every step of that victory would become clothed with the mantle of law. But if, in addition, it should turn out that the Union arms had been rendered victorious through the help of the negro soldiers, called to the field by the promise of freedom contained in the proclamation, then the decree and its promise might rest secure in the certainty of legal execution and fulfillment. To restore the Union by the help of black soldiers under pledge of liberty, and then for the Union, under whatever legal doctrine or construction, to attempt to reenslave them, would be a wrong at which morality would revolt. . . .

The problem of statesmanship therefore was not one of theory, but of practice. Fame is due Mr. Lincoln, not alone because he decreed emancipation, but because events so shaped themselves under his guidance as to render the conception practical and the decree successful. Among the agencies he employed none proved more admirable or more powerful than this double-edged sword of the final proclamation, blending sentiment with force, leaguing liberty with Union, filling the voting armies at home and the fighting armies in the field. In the light of history we can see that by this edict Mr. Lincoln gave slavery its vital thrust, its mortal wound. It was the word of decision, the judgment without appeal, the sentence of doom.

Source 14 James Ford Rhodes, *History of the United States from the Compromise of 1850*, 1900

The proclamation . . . completed the process which the war had commenced, of making every slave in the South the friend of the North. Every negro knew that if he got within the lines of the Federal armies, the aspiration of his life would be realized; he would become a free man. Before the close of the year there were in the United States military service 100,000 former slaves. . . . Without the policy of emancipation, these negroes would probably have remained at the South raising food for the able-bodied white men, all of whom were forced into the Confederate army by the rigorous conscription. The proclamation, making clear as it did the real issue of the war, was of incontestable value in turning England into the right channel.

Source 15 David Donald, *Lincoln Reconsidered,* 1956

Repeatedly, throughout the war, Lincoln's passive policy worked politically. Because any action would offend somebody, he took as few actions as possible. Outright abolitionists demanded that he use his wartime powers to emancipate the Negroes. Border-state politicians insisted that he protect their peculiar institutions. Lincoln needed the support of both groups; therefore, he did nothing— or, rather, he proposed to colonize the Negroes in Central America, which was as near to nothing as he could come—and awaited events. After two years of hostilities, many even in the South came to see that slavery was doomed, and all the important segments of Northern opinion were brought to support emancipation as a wartime necessity. Only then did Lincoln issue the Emancipation Proclamation.

Source 16 Benjamin Quarles, *Lincoln and the Negro,* 1962

Entering into Lincoln's deliberation and fixing his determination about issuing an emancipation proclamation were considerations of a varied nature—military, political, and diplomatic. To Lincoln the first of these was pre-eminent: military necessity required that the enemy be deprived of his slaves. Lincoln knew that the black population of the South was one of its greatest assets. . . . To weaken this black arm of the Confederacy had become the first order of military business, a blunt fact from which Lincoln could not flinch.

In the late summer of 1863, Lincoln told Secretary Chase that the Emancipation Proclamation had been issued solely as a military necessity and not because it was politically expedient or morally right. Nonetheless, political considerations had influenced the issuing of the edict. Himself a Republican, Lincoln was obliged to make concessions to the point of view of his party, including its Radical wing. . . .

A third important factor in bringing about and supporting the proclamation was European, particularly English, opinion. In England the governing and aristocratic classes were anti-North and would have been glad to extend diplomatic recognition to the Confederacy. . . . Lincoln knew that reformist groups and workingmen's associations in England would hail an edict of emancipation. He was aware, too, that such a proclamation would be a heavy blow to the foreign policy of the Confederacy, striking "King Cotton diplomacy" in a most vulnerable spot. After the Emancipation Proclamation was issued, the Confederate agents stationed in European capitals were no longer able to play down the slavery issue by asserting that the North had no intention of changing the status of the black man. . . .

True enough, Lincoln had originally conceived of the proclamation as a measure for the self-preservation, rather than for the regeneration, of America.

But the proclamation, almost in spite of its creator, changed the whole tone and character of the war.

Questioning the Past

1. Lincoln is known to history as the "Great Emancipator." Is he deserving of such adulation? Explain Lincoln's position on the question of slavery.

2. What purposes did Lincoln have in mind when he issued the Emancipation Proclamation? What purposes did the proclamation actually serve?

3. "The principle is not that a human being cannot own another," the London *Spectator* noted in its editorial response to the proclamation, "but that he cannot own him unless he is loyal to the United States." Explain and defend this statement.

4. A southern critic of the Emancipation Proclamation, Edward Pollard, wrote in his 1866 book, *The Lost Cause,* "A candid world found no difficulty in interpreting it as an act of malice towards the master rather than one of mercy to the slave." Is this a valid conclusion? Would Lincoln have shown greater mercy toward the slaves had he never issued the proclamation?

Chapter 29

Pickett's Charge

General George E. Pickett Leads the Assault against Cemetery Ridge *July 3, 1863*

29.1 Civil War:
General Interest

Sunrise on July 3, 1863, revealed two great armies facing each other across a Pennsylvania valley. Atop Seminary Ridge, formed in a battle line stretching for several miles, was the Army of Northern Virginia, the heart of the Confederate Army, under General Robert E. Lee. On Cemetery Ridge opposite the Confederate forces was the Army of the Potomac, commanded by General George G. Meade. For the past two years these armies had been colliding in a series of battles extending across Virginia and into Maryland. For the past two days they had been engaged in their first confrontation north of the Mason-Dixon Line. Before the sun set again, they would meet in the decisive engagement of this battle and of this war.

Following the Confederate success at Chancellorsville, Lee had decided to take the war to the North. An invasion of Pennsylvania would relieve Virginia from some of the pressures of the Union campaign to capture Richmond by forcing the North to pull back in defense of its own cities. The presence of the Army of Northern Virginia in Pennsylvania might also strike a decisive blow at northern morale, which already was crumbling under the strains of war-weariness, anger over conscription, and the paucity of Union victories on the battlefield. Furthermore, it could be expected that a Southern victory on Northern soil would bring the long-anticipated and long-delayed British and French diplomatic recognition of the Confederacy. The first two days of battle at Gettysburg saw heavy but inconclusive fighting. On the afternoon of the third day, Lee massed his artillery and 15,000 troops under command of General George Pickett for an attack on the center of the Union line. Following a fierce **cannonade**, Pickett's troops set off on a daring advance over three-quarters of a mile of open terrain leading across the valley and up the slope to the federal positions along Cemetery Ridge. The Rebels moved steadily forward against a virtual wall of lead fired down on them from the Union positions, making a final desperate charge that carried the Confederate banners over the top of Union defenses. At that moment, the prospect of Confederate or Union victory—and the future course of American history itself—teetered in a tenuous balance.

🐚 *First Impressions*
The Panorama of Death and Wounds

As contemporary newspaper accounts described, both sides displayed tremendous bravery, and both sides sustained tremendous casualties. When the Associated Press reported on July 3, "The decisive battle has been fought to-day, the enemy have been repulsed with terrific loss," the characterization could have applied to both Union and Confederate forces.

Source 1   *Richmond Enquirer,* correspondent's report, July 3, 1863

29.2 The Insiders' Guide: The Civil War

Now the storming party was moved up: Pickett's division in advance, supported on the right by Wilcox's brigade and on the left by Heth's division, commanded by Pettigrew. . . . I stood upon an eminence and watched this advance with great interest; I had seen brave men pass over that fated valley the day before; I had witnessed their death-struggle with the foe on the opposite heights; I had observed their return with shattered ranks, a bleeding mass, but with unstained banners. Now I saw their valiant comrades prepare for the same bloody trial, and already felt that their efforts would be vain unless their supports should be as true as steel and brave as lions. Now they moved forward; with steady, measured tread, they advance upon the foe. Their banners float defiantly in the breeze, as onward in beautiful order they press across the plain. I have never seen since the war began troops enter a fight in such splendid order as did this splendid division of Pickett's. Now Pettigrew's command emerge from the woods upon Pickett's left, and sweep down the slope of the hill to the valley beneath, and some two or three hundred yards in rear of Pickett.

Just as Pickett was getting well under the enemy's fire, our batteries ceased firing. This was a fearful moment for Pickett and his brave command. Why do not our guns reopen their fire? is the inquiry that rises from every lip. Still, our batteries are silent as death! But on press Pickett's brave Virginians; and now the enemy open upon them, from more than fifty guns, a terrible fire of **grape**, shell, and **canister**. On, on they move in unbroken line, delivering a deadly fire as they advance. Now they have reached the Emmitsburg road; and here they meet a severe fire from the masses of the enemy's infantry, posted behind the stone fence; while their artillery, now free from the annoyance of our artillery, turn their whole fire upon this devoted band. Still, they remain firm. Now again they advance; they storm the stone fence; the Yankees fly. The enemy's batteries are, one by one, silenced in quick succession as Pickett's men deliver their fire at the gunners and drive them from their pieces. I see Kemper and Armistead plant their banner in the enemy's works. I hear the shout of victory!

Let us look after Pettigrew's division. Where are they now? While the victorious shout of the gallant Virginians is still ringing in my ears, I turn my eyes to the left, and there, all over the plain, in utmost confusion, is scattered this strong division. Their line is broken; they are flying, apparently panic-stricken, to the rear. The gallant Pettigrew is wounded; but he still retains command, and is vainly striving to rally his men. . . . Pickett is left alone to contend with the hordes of the enemy now pouring in upon him on every side. Garnett falls . . . and Kemper, the brave and chivalrous, reels under a mortal wound, and is taken to the rear. The order is given to fall back, and our men commence the movement, doggedly contending for every inch of ground. The enemy press heavily our retreating line, and many noble spirits who had passed safely through the fiery ordeal of the advance and charge now fall on the right and on the left. Armistead is wounded and left in the enemy's hands. At this critical moment, the shattered remnant of Wright's Georgia brigade is moved forward to cover their retreat, and the fight closes here. Our loss in this charge was very severe; and the Yankee prisoners taken acknowledge that theirs was immense.

Source 2   Correspondent S. Wilkeson, *New York Times*

GREAT BATTLE OF FRIDAY

Gettysburg, Friday, July 3

The experience of all the tried and veteran officers of the Army of the Potomac tells of no such desperate conflict as has been in progress during this day. The cannonading of Chancellorsville, Malvern, and Manassas were pastimes compared to this. . . .

While I write the ground around me is covered thick with rebel dead, mingled with our own. . . . The losses are heavy on both sides.

It is near sunset. Our troops hold the field, with many rebel prisoners in their hands. The enemy has been magnificently repulsed for three days—repulsed on all sides—most magnificently to-day. Every effort made by him since Wednesday morning to penetrate Meade's lines has been foiled. The final results of this action, I hope to be able to give you at a later hour this evening.

Source 3   *New York World*, special correspondence

HEADQUARTERS, ARMY OF THE POTOMAC

Friday, July 3–7¼ P.M.

The sun of **Austerlitz** is not more memorable than that which is just flinging its dying rays over the field of this the third day of successful battle. The victory won by Gen. Meade is now so decisive that no one in this army pretends to question the rout and demoralization of the rebel army under Gen. Lee. The battles of Wednesday and yesterday were sufficiently terrible, but in that which has raged to-day the fighting done, not only by our troops, but by those of Lee's army, will rank in heroism, in perseverance, and in savage energy with that of Waterloo.

The position of Lee at the close of last evening was such that he was forced to-day to reduce all his energies into one grand, desperate, and centralized attempt to break through our army. His divisions were so much cut up as to render a pitched battle from wing to wing one of awful hazard. The dilemma was a terrible one, and that the rebel commander fully appreciated all its risks is evinced by the desperation of his onset to-day. . . .

The engagement began by an assault of our troops upon some rifle-pits on the extreme right, which were left in the possession of the enemy last evening. Their fire was returned by the rebels, and the fight immediately became general. Until nearly noon the battle raged without intermission, but with no loss to us, when we finally obtained possession of the rifle-pits—the rebel force which had previously held them retreating. The firing then slackened, but at one o'clock was renewed at different points along the line with a fierceness premonitory of the terrific engagement that ensued.

Several charges were made by the rebels as feints, their troops falling back after the first rush in every part of the field, except that held by their troops under Gen. Ewell, who was seen to concentrate the infantry and artillery together, and who soon opened a murderous fire of cannon on our left centre. Then the engagement began in earnest. The firing became a continuous roar; battery after battery was discharged with a swiftness amazing; yell on yell from the rebels succeeded each gust of shot and shell, until the valley, overhung with smoke from whence these horrible sounds issued, seemed alive with demons. It appeared at times as though not a foot of air was free from the hail of missiles that tore over and through our ranks, thinned but not shaken. Our men stood the shock with a courage sublime—an endurance so wonderful as to dim even the heroic record of the band that fell upon the acre of Tourney [**Tournai**]. The corps against which this deadly fire was mainly directed was the Second, the position being commanded by Gen. Hayes.

The artillery fire continued without intermission for three hours, when suddenly, having been formed under cover of the smoke of their own guns, the rebel troops were hurled against our lines by their officers in masses the very tread of whose feet shook the declivity up which they came, with cries that might have caused less dauntless troops than those who waited the onset to break with terror. Not a man in the Federal ranks flinched from his position. Not an eye turned to the right or left in search of security, not a hand trembled as the long array of our heroes grasped their muskets at a charge, and waited the order to fire.

On and up came the enemy, hooting, crowding, and showing their very teeth in the venom of their rage until within thirty yards of our cannon. As the turbulent mass of gray uniforms, of flashing bayonets and gleaming eyes, lifted itself in a last leap forward almost to the very mouths of guns, a volley of shot, shell, shrapnel, and bullets went crashing through it, leveling it as a scythe. Its overwhelming onward rush was the next instant turned to the hesitating leap forward of a few soldiers more daredevil than the rest, the wild bounding upwards of more than a few mortally wounded heroes, and the succeeding backward surge of the disjointed remainder, which culminated in a scamper down the slope that was in some instances retarded by the pursuing bullets of our men.

The carnage of this assault among the rebels was so fearful that even Federal soldiers who rested on their arms triumphant, after the foe had retreated beyond their fire, as they cast their eyes downward upon the panorama of death and wounds illuminated by the sun that shown upon the slope before them, were seen to shudder and turn sickening away. . . .

The musketry firing slowly ceased, and the discharge of artillery continued for a brief period, but even these reverberations finally died away. . . .

The victory was secure.

Source 4   Correspondent L. L. Crounse, *New York Times*

OUR SPECIAL TELEGRAMS FROM THE BATTLE-FIELD

Near Gettysburg, Saturday, July 4

Another great battle was fought yesterday afternoon, resulting in a magnificent success to the National arms.

At 2 o'clock P.M., Longstreet's whole corps advanced from the rebel centre against our centre. The enemy's forces were hurled upon our position by columns in mass, and also in lines of battle. Our centre was held by Gen. Hancock, with the noble old Second army corps, aided by Gen. Doubleday's division of the First Corps. . . .

The battle was a most magnificent spectacle.

Source 5   S. Wilkeson, *New York Times*, July 4, 1863

DETAILS FROM OUR SPECIAL CORRESPONDENT

Headquarters, Army of Potomac

A silence as of deep sleep fell upon the field of battle. Our army cooked, ate and slumbered. The rebel army moved 120 guns to the west, and massed there Longstreet's corps and Hill's corps, to hurl them upon the really weakest point of our entire position. . . .

In the shadow cast by the tiny farm house 16 by 20, which Gen. Meade had made his headquarters, lay wearied Staff officers and tired reporters. There was not wanting to the peacefulness of the scene the singing of a bird, which had a nest in a peach tree within the tiny yard of the whitewashed cottage. In the midst of its warbling, a shell screamed over the house, instantly followed by another, and another, and in a moment the air was full of the most complete artillery prelude to an infantry battle that was ever exhibited. Every size and form of shell known to British and to American gunnery shrieked, whirled, moaned, whistled and wrathfully fluttered over our ground. As many as six in a second, constantly two in a second, bursting and screaming over and around the headquarters, made a very hell of fire that amazed the oldest officers. They burst in the yard—burst next to the fence on both sides, garnished as usual with the hitched horses of aid[e]s and orderlies. The fastened animals reared and plunged with terror. Then one fell, then another—sixteen laid dead and mangled before the fire ceased, still fastened by their halters, which gave the expression of being wickedly tied up to die painfully. Those brute victims of a cruel war touched all hearts. Through the midst of the storm of screaming and exploding shells, an ambulance, driven by its frenzied conductor, at full speed, presented to all of us the marvelous spectacle of a horse going rapidly on three legs. A hinder one had been shot off at the hock. A shell tore up the little step of the Headquarters Cottage, and ripped bags of oats as with a knife. Another soon carried off one of its two pillars. Soon a spherical case burst opposite the open door—another ripped through the low garret. The remaining pillar went almost immediately to the howl of a fixed shot that a Whitworth must have made. During this fire the houses at twenty and thirty feet distant, were receiving their death, and soldiers in Federal blue were torn to pieces in the road and died with the peculiar yells that blend the extorted cry of pain with horror and despair. Not an orderly—not an ambulance—not a straggler was to be seen upon the plain swept by this tempest of orchestral death thirty minutes after it commenced. Were not one hundred and twenty pieces of artillery, trying to cut from the field every battery we had in position to resist their proposed infantry attack, and to sweep away the slight defences behind which our Infantry were waiting? Forty minutes—fifty minutes— counted on watches that ran oh so languidly. Shells through the two lower rooms. A shell into the chimney that daringly did not explode. Shells in the yard. The air thicker and fuller and more deafening with the howling and whirring of these infernal missiles. The chief of Staff struck. . . . An Aid[e] bored with a fragment of iron through the bone of the arm. Another, cut with an exploded piece. And the time measured on the sluggish watches was one hour and forty minutes.

Then there was a lull, and we knew that the rebel infantry was charging. And splendidly they did this work—the highest and severest test of the stuff that soldiers are made of. Hill's division, in the line of battle, came first on the double-quick. Their muskets at the "right-shoulder-shift." Longstreet's came as the support, at the usual distance, with war cries and a savage insolence as yet untutored by defeat. They rushed in perfect order across the open field up to the very muzzles of the guns, which tore lanes through them as they came. But they met men who were their equals in spirit, and their superiors in tenacity: There never was better fighting since **Thermopylae** than was done yesterday by our infantry and artillery. The rebels were over our defences. They had cleaned cannoniers and horses from one of our guns, and were whirling it around to use upon us. The bayonet drove them back.

Source 6   Correspondent Whitelaw Reid, pen name Agate, *Cincinnati Gazette,* July 4, 1863

The great, desperate, final charge came at 4. The Rebels seemed to have gathered up all their strength and desperation for one fierce, convulsive effort that should sweep over and wash out our obstinate resistance. They swept up as before: the flower of their army to the front, victory staked upon the issue. . . .

The Rebels—three lines deep—came steadily up. They were in point-blank range.

At last the order came! From thrice six thousand guns, there came a sheet of smoky flame, a crash, a rush of leaded death. The line literally melted away; but there came the second, resistless still. It had been our supreme effort—on the instant, we were not equal to another.

Up to the rifle-pits, across them, over the barricades, the mere machine strength of their combined action—swept them on. Our thin line could fight, but it had not weight enough to oppose to this momentum. It was pushed behind the guns. Right on came the Rebels. They were upon the guns—were bayoneting the gunners—were waving their flags above our pieces.

But they had penetrated to the fatal point. A storm of grape and canister tore its way from man to man, and marked its track with corpses straight down their line! They had exposed themselves to the **enfilading** fire of the guns on the western slope of Cemetery Hill; that exposure sealed their fate.

The line reeled back—disjointed already—in an instant in fragments. . . .

It was a fruitless sacrifice. They gathered up their broken fragments, formed their lines, and slowly marched away. It was not a rout, it *was* a bitter, crushing defeat. For once, the Army of the Potomac had won a clean, honest, acknowledged victory.

Source 7   Major General Meade's statement

HEADQUARTERS, ARMY OF THE POTOMAC

July 4.—The following order has been issued, viz:

General Order, No. 68.—The Commanding General, in behalf of the country, thanks the Army of the Potomac for the glorious result of the recent operations.

Our enemy, superior in numbers, and flushed with the pride of successful invasion, attempted to overcome or destroy this army. Utterly baffled and defeated, he has now withdrawn from the contest. The privations and fatigues the army has endured, and the heroic courage and gallantry it has displayed, will be matters of history to be ever remembered.

Our task is not yet accomplished; and the Commanding General looks to the army for greater efforts to drive from our soil every vestige of the presence of the invader.

It is right and proper that we should on suitable occasions return our grateful thanks to the Almighty Disposer of Events, that, in the goodness of His Providence, he has thought fit to give victory to the cause of the just.

Source 8   War correspondent Thomas W. Knox, *Daily National Intelligencer,* July 6, 1863

To-day I have passed from end to end of the whole ground where the lines of battle were drawn. The place bears evidence of having been the scene of a fierce struggle. The shocks of those two masses of humanity, surging and resurging the one against the other, could hardly pass without leaving their traces in fearful characters. . . . The fields of Gettysburg . . . hereafter shall more bountifully reward the farmer as he tills the soil which has been made richer by the outpoured blood of thousands of America's sons.

Passing out of Gettysburg by the Baltimore turnpike, we come to the entrance of the cemetery. . . . The hill on which this cemetery is located was the centre of our line of battle and the key to the whole position. Had the rebels been able to carry this point they would have forced us into retreat, and the whole battle would have been lost. To pierce our line here was Lee's great endeavor, and he threw his best brigades against it. Wave after wave of living valor rolled up that slope, only to roll back again under the deadly fire of our artillery and infantry. . . .

From the summit of this hill a large portion of the battleground is spread out before the spectator. In front and at his feet lies the town of Gettysburg, containing in quiet times a population of four or five thousand souls. . . . To the left of the town stretches a long valley, bounded on each side by a gently sloping ridge. The crest of each ridge is distant a good three-fourths of a mile or more from the other. It was on these ridges that the lines of battle on the second and third days were formed, the rebel line being on the ridge to the westward. . . . Halfway between the ridges are the ruins of a large brick building burnt during the engagement, and dotted about here and there are various brick and frame structures. Two miles at our left hand rises a sharp pointed elevation, known to the inhabitants of the region as Round Hill. . . .

The battle is over. The enemy is in full retreat toward Virginia with our victorious army in pursuit. Ere this reaches you the two hosts may again measure their strength. Flushed with its present victory and increased by the thousands now marching to join it, who can doubt that our army will achieve success. As great or greater than those of Waterloo are the results of this battle of Gettysburg. Lee victorious, Baltimore, Washington, and Philadelphia would have fallen before him. The rebel flag would have floated over the National Capital. The nations of Europe would no longer withhold the recognition that the rebel leaders have for so many months been asking. The way would have been opened for a peace which should embrace the downfall of our Government. Lee defeated, and driven again to Virginia, with our Army in pursuit, the nation breathes in safety. A terrible blow is struck at the hopes of the rebellion.

Source 9   Commanding general Robert E. Lee's statement

HEADQUARTERS, ARMY OF NORTHERN VIRGINIA
JULY 11

General Order No. 16.—After the long and trying marches, endured with the fortitude that has ever characterized the soldiers of the army of Northern Virginia, you have penetrated the country of our enemies, and recalled to the defenses of their own soil those who were engaged in the invasion of ours. You have fought a fierce and sanguinary battle which if not attended with the success that has hitherto crowned your efforts, was marked by the same heroic spirit that has commanded the respect of your enemies, the gratitude of your country, and the admiration of mankind.

Once more you are called upon to meet the enemy, from whom you have torn, on so many fields, a name that will never die.—Once more the eyes of your countrymen are turned upon you, and again do wives and sisters, fathers and mothers, and helpless children lean for defence on your strong arms and brave hearts. Let every soldier remember that on his courage and fidelity depends all that makes life worth having, the freedom of his country, the honor of his people and the security of his home. Let each heart grow strong in the remembrance of our glorious past, and in the thought of the inestimable blessings for which we contend; and, invoking the assistance of that Power which has so signally blessed our former efforts, let us go forth in confidence to secure the peace and safety of our country. Soldiers, your old enemy is before you. Win from him honor worthy of your righteous cause, worthy of your comrades, dead on so many illustrious fields.

R. E. Lee, Gen. Commanding

📖 *Second Thoughts*

A Gallant Disaster

29.3 Gettysburg
Revisited

Lee brought 75,000 men with him on his invasion of the North. Meade confronted him at Gettysburg with a force of 90,000 federal troops. After the three days at Gettysburg, Lee's Army of Northern Virginia and Meade's Army of the Potomac had suffered between them 51,000 casualties. The South sustained losses of 3,903 killed, 18,735 wounded, and 5,425 missing and or imprisoned. Of the northern forces, 3,155 were killed, 14,529 wounded, and 5,365 missing or imprisoned.

On the battlefield itself, the contest might be called a draw. In terms of its impact beyond the battlefield, it was a devastating defeat for the Confederacy. But Americans have remained in awe of the soldiers who fought at Cemetery Ridge ever since. In the words of historian James Ford Rhodes, "Who would not thrill with emotion to claim for his countrymen the men who made that charge and the men who met it?"

Source 10   President Lincoln's address, Gettysburg cemetery dedication,
            November 19, 1863

Four score and seven years ago our fathers brought forth on this continent a new nation, conceived in liberty, and dedicated to the proposition that all men are created equal.

Now we are engaged in a great civil war, testing whether that nation, or any nation so conceived and so dedicated, can long endure. We are met on a great battlefield of that war. We have come to dedicate a portion of that field as a final resting-place for those who here gave their lives that the nation might live. It is altogether fitting and proper that we should do this.

But, in a larger sense, we cannot dedicate—we cannot consecrate—we cannot hallow—this ground. The brave men, living and dead, who struggled here consecrated it far above our poor power to add or detract. The world will take little note nor long remember what we say here, but it can never forget what they did here. It is for us, the living, rather, to be dedicated here to the unfinished work which they who fought here have thus far so nobly advanced. It is rather for us to be here dedicated to the great task remaining before us—that from these honored dead we take increased devotion to that cause for which they gave the last full measure of devotion; that we here highly resolve that these dead shall not have died in vain; that this nation, under God, shall have a new birth of freedom; and that government of the people, by the people, for the people, shall not perish from the earth.

Source 11   Edward A. Pollard, wartime editor of the *Richmond Examiner,*
            The Lost Cause: A New Southern History of the War of the
            Confederates, 1867

About noon there was a deep calm in the warm air. Gen. Lee determined to mass his artillery in front of Hill's corps, and under the cover of this tremendous fire to direct the assault on the enemy's centre. To this end more than one hundred pieces of artillery were placed in position. On the opposite side of the valley might be perceived the gradual concentration of the enemy in the woods, the preparations for the mighty contest that was at last to break the ominous silence with a sound of conflict such as was scarcely ever before heard on earth. It was a death-like silence. At 12:30, p.m., the shrill sound of a Whitworth gun pierced the air. Instantly more than two hundred cannon belched forth their thunder at one time. It was absolutely appalling. An officer writes: "The air was hideous with most discordant noise. The very earth shook beneath our feet, and the hills and rocks seemed to reel like a drunken man. For one hour and a half this most terrific fire was continued, during which time the shrieking of shell, the crash of falling timber, the fragments of rocks flying through the air, shattered from the cliffs by solid shot, the heavy mutterings from the valley between the two opposing armies, the splash of bursting shrapnell, and the fierce neighing of wounded artillery horses, made a picture terribly grand and sublime."

Into this scene of death moved out the Confederate column of assault. Pickett's division proceeded to descend the slope of hills and to move across the open ground. The front was thickly covered with skirmishers; then followed Kemper's and Garnett's brigades, forming the first line, with Armistead in support. On the flanks were—Heth's division, commanded by Pettigrew, of Hill's corps, and Wilcox's brigade of McLaw's corps, the former on the left, the latter on the right of the Virginians. Pickett led the attack. The five thousand Virginians descended the hill with the precision and regularity of a parade. As they reached the Emmittsburg road, the Confederate guns, which had fired over their heads to cover the movement, ceased, and there stood exposed these devoted troops to the uninterrupted fire of the enemy's batteries, while the fringe of musketry fire along a stone wall marked the further boundary of death to which they marched. No halt, no wave. Through half a mile of shot and shell pressed on the devoted column. It was no sudden impetus of excitement that carried them through this terrible ordeal; it was no thin storm of fire which a dash might penetrate and divide. In every inch of air was the wing of death. Against the breadth of each man's body reared the red crest of Destruction.

Steadily the Virginians press on. The name of Virginia was that day baptized in fire, and illuminated forever in the temples of History. There had been no such example of devotion in the war. Presently wild cries ring out; the smoke-masked troops are in the enemy's works; there is a hand-to-hand contest, and again and again the Confederate flag is lifted through the smoke over the shrinking columns of the enemy. Garnett is dead, Armistead is mortally wounded. Kemper is shot down. Every brigadier of the division is killed or wounded. But Pickett is unscathed in the storm; his flashing sword has taken the key of the enemy's position, and points the path of the conflict through his broken columns; the glad shout of victory is already heard; and on the distant hill of observation, where a little group of breathless spectators had watched the scene, Longstreet turns to Gen. Lee to congratulate him that the day is won.

Vain! vain! Overlooking the field, Gen. Lee saw that the troops of Pettigrew's division had wavered. Another moment, and they had fallen back in confusion, exposing Pickett's division to attack both from front and flank. The courage of Virginians could do no more. Overwhelmed, almost destitute of officers, and nearly surrounded, the magnificent troops of Pickett gave way. Slowly and steadily they yielded ground, and, under the heavy fire which the artillery poured into their broken ranks, they retraced their steps across the fatal valley.

Gen. Lee was never known to betray on any battle-field a sign, either of exultation or disappointment. As he witnessed the last grand effort of his men, and saw it fail, he was seen for a moment to place his finger thoughtfully between his lips. Presently he rode quietly in front of the woods, rallying and encouraging the broken troops, uttering words of cheer and encouragement. To a foreign military officer of rank, who had come to witness the battle, he said very simply: "This has been a sad day for us, Colonel—a sad day; but we can't expect always to gain victories." . . .

Gettysburg may be taken as the grand climacteric of the Southern Confederacy. It was the customary phrase of John M. Daniel, editor of the *Richmond Examiner*, that on the 3rd July, on the heights of Gettysburg, the Confederates were "within a stone's throw of peace." The expression is not extravagant, when we reflect what would have been the moral effect of defeating Meade's army, and uncovering New York, Philadelphia, and Washington.

29.4 Civil War Resources on the Internet

Source 12 George R. Stewart, *Pickett's Charge: A Microhistory of the Final Attack at Gettysburg, July 3, 1863,* 1959

If we grant—as many would be ready to do—that the Civil War furnishes the great dramatic episode of the history of the United States, and that Gettysburg provides the climax of the war, then the climax of the climax, the central moment of our history, must be Pickett's Charge.

Thus to hold, indeed, is not to maintain that a different result, there by the clump of trees and the angle in the stone wall, would of itself have reversed the course of the war and decisively altered history. The moment is, rather, a symbolic one, not even recognized at the time, but gaining significance in retrospect. This significance, moreover, is a part of world history, since the existence of two rival republics would probably have prevented the United States from turning the balance of two World Wars and becoming a global power.

Source 13 Allan Nevins, *The War for the Union,* 1971

Pickett's charge, as Longstreet and other Confederate officers saw at the time, was a blunder founded on two miscalculations; first that it was possible for the Confederate guns to silence a greater number of Union cannon, and second, that a charge over a mile of ground against well-entrenched troops, superior in number, could ever succeed. . . . The Southern army was defeated because, distant from its bases, outnumbered, and limited in ammunition, it had accepted battle where it must not only attack, but attack under a grave disadvantage. . . . Lee might have even striven more vigorously to compel Meade to deliver the attack. He might even have endeavored to accomplish this, as Longstreet proposed, by a final flank movement that placed his army between Meade and Baltimore, for Meade would never have dared to let Lee hold for long an inner position, with roads open even to Washington.

It was a glorious charge, but it was not war. Some thought it glorious that color-bearers of thirty-five regiments were shot down, and that seven Confederate colonels were buried on the battleground after Pickett fell back; glorious that a Union general could write, "I tried to ride over the field, but could not, for the dead and wounded lay too thick to guide a horse through them." Yet futile carnage is never glorious. From any humanitarian point of view such losses were as horrible as they were calamitous from the Confederate standpoint.

Source 14 Emory M. Thomas, *The Confederate Nation: 1861–1865*, 1979

By mid-1863 white Southerners had already adopted some reforms toward liberalizing the institution of slavery. This process would continue and almost reach the logical extreme of emancipation. . . . Ironically, as Confederate nationality ripened and defined itself, prospects for the continued existence of the southern nation suffered severe setbacks on three fronts. Even while Southerners were realizing their identity as Confederates, reordering their world view, and adjusting their social and racial mores, their nation trembled on two continents.

At Vicksburg, . . . [t]he garrison surrendered on July 4; Pemberton's entire army were prisoners, and the Mississippi was open to the enemy all the way to its mouth.

In Pennsylvania, Lee's campaign came to grief at Gettysburg. The battle . . . began on July 1 as the two armies concentrated. . . . When Lee reached the field, he found his troops held the town of Gettysburg, but that Meade's Federals were fortifying Cemetery Hill and the ridge extending round to two domelike hills known as Big Round Top and Little Round Top. Next day Lee ordered Longstreet's corps to attack the Round Tops and Richard S. Ewell's corps to extend the Southern line around Cemetery Hill. Neither attack enabled the Confederates to dislodge their enemies from the heights. Finally on July 3, Lee determined to have a showdown. Meade's reinforcements kept arriving to strengthen his position, but Lee believed his men could breach Meade's center and felt that victory was worth the risk involved in a frontal assault. "Pickett's Charge," the attack on the Union center, was a gallant disaster. In a way it was the entire Confederate war in microcosm—a gathering of clans instead of military organizations led by an officer corps distinguished by its individual eccentricities, marching forth with bands playing and flags flying to take a gamble justified largely by the size of the stakes. Lee risked all and lost all.

The third Confederate disaster of summer 1863 occurred in Europe. On June 30, [Member of Parliament John A.] Roebuck introduced his resolution to recognize the Southern nation in concert with France in the House of Commons. Amid debate on the resolution, he revealed the substance of his conversations with the French Emperor. Commons was incensed at Roebuck's . . . free-lance diplomacy, and Roebuck withdrew his resolution. Roebuck's faux pas deepened the English chill, and Napoleon III, after learning of Vicksburg and Gettysburg, resisted the notion of recognizing the Confederacy unilaterally. France needed a strong New World ally.

Vicksburg's defenders had numbered 30,000. Gettysburg had cost nearly as many in killed, wounded, and missing. The Confederacy had lost France as well, and in the aftermath of debacle, the Confederates suffered a severe loss of confidence in themselves.

Source 15   Bruce Catton, *Bruce Catton's Civil War,* 1988

The smoke lifted like a rising curtain, and all of the great amphitheater lay open at last, and the Yankee soldiers could look west all the way to the belt of trees on Seminary Ridge. They were old soldiers and had been in many battles, but what they saw then took their breath away, and whether they had ten minutes or seventy-five years yet to live, they remembered it until they died. There it was, for the last time in this war, perhaps for the last time anywhere, the grand pageantry and color of war in the old style, beautiful and majestic and terrible: fighting men lined up for a mile and a half from flank to flank, slashed red flags overhead, soldiers marching forward elbow to elbow, officers with drawn swords, sunlight gleaming from thousands of musket barrels, lines dressed as if for parade.

Questioning the Past

1. Why did Lee bring his Army of Northern Virginia across the Mason-Dixon line? What was the significance of the Battle of Gettysburg? What was the significance of Pickett's charge? Why did Pickett's charge fail?

2. John Daniel of the *Richmond Examiner* is quoted as having said that on July 3, 1863, at Gettysburg, the Confederates were "within a stone's throw of peace." What did he mean by this? Suppose Pickett's charge had prevailed, and victory at Gettysburg had been won by Lee, what might have been the short- and long-term implications? What might North America be like today?

3. "It was a glorious charge," Allan Nevins said of Pickett's attempt to overrun the Union center at Cemetery Ridge, "but it was not war." Explain and evaluate this observation.

Chapter 30

A Surprise Ally

A Foreign Fleet Is Welcomed at Northern Ports

October 2, 1863

There was little support for the Northern cause among the more powerful nations of Europe. The two greatest world powers of the mid-nineteenth century were England and France. Neither had much reason to wish for a Union victory in the American Civil War. Both saw the United States as a rising threat to their preeminent position in world affairs. Each saw advantages in a war that might result in the permanent dissolution of the United States. Indeed, England and France harbored sympathy for the Confederate cause, seeing economic advantages in a successful Southern secession from the Union. England, France, and the North had long been rivals in the pursuit of Southern raw materials and markets. All three were industrialized, and all three wanted the produce of the South to supply their factories and to feed their factory workers. All three wanted to sell their manufactured goods to Southern buyers. As long as the United States existed with the Southern states a part of the Union, the North had an advantage over England and France in the competition for Southern trade. The federal government maintained a heavy tariff on imports from England and France while goods flowed between North and South without being subject to interstate taxation.

There was even reason to believe that England and France might intervene in the American Civil War on the Southern side. The English had been angered by the boarding of one of their ships on the high seas by a Union warship. Moreover, the Union blockade of the ports of the South was a double-edged sword: The choking of Southern commerce hurt not only the South but its European trading partners as well. England and France began to help the South acquire blockade runners and warships to ease the stranglehold on Southern trade. The British reinforced their troops in Canada and France gained a foothold in Mexico.

While England and France were positioning themselves for a possible intervention, the morale of the North was slowly sinking. Fully two years into what had been expected to be a short conflict, an end to the war was nowhere in sight. Union armies had fared poorly on the battlefield. The Lincoln administration and its war policies seemed to grow more unpopular with each passing day. Violent antidraft riots broke out in New York and other cities in the east while Peace Democrats sowed disaffection with the war effort among voters in the west.

Northern morale was boosted by the important Union victories at Vicksburg and Gettysburg in July of 1863. But even with these successes it was clear to most in the North that many more battles lay ahead. The

375

costs in lives and resources were mounting daily. With the threat of intervention by Europeans still hanging overhead and war-weariness settling in among the populace, the Lincoln administration was in need of something to bolster the sagging public morale.

It was during this difficult time that a surprise ally arrived. The Russian Baltic Fleet sailed into New York Harbor. The Russian Far Eastern Fleet sailed into San Francisco Bay.

ᴥ *First Impressions*

An Ally Is Welcomed

The warships of the Russian Baltic Fleet began to arrive in New York Harbor around the middle of September of 1863. By October 1, all had made port. The Russian Far Eastern Fleet dropped anchor in San Francisco Bay on October 12. That the arrival of the Russian navy in American waters gave a great boost to Union morale there is no question. Speculation about the motive of the visit, however, has been a source of ongoing debate.

Source 1   New York Times, October 2, 1863

30.1 National
Civil War
Association

Yesterday was a memorable one in the history of the City, as having been set apart for the formal reception of the Russian Admiral Lisovsky and the Officers of his Fleet, and as being the occasion of a welcome exceeding in warmth and earnestness any that busy and big-hearted New York has yet extended. The day was beautiful, and the feeling of the people hospitable and exuberant. There was evidently a desire among all to extend to our distinguished guests an unmistakably hearty and cordial welcome. The desire was more than fulfilled, for, from the landing of the Officers until their departure from the City Hall, the ovation was one of the most brilliant, hearty and gratifying nature. Of course, it was not to the individuals so much as to the Sovereign and People of the great empire they represented, whose consistent and sincere friendship has been appreciated by the public heart.

Source 2   Editorial, New York Times, October 2, 1863

HONORS TO THE RUSSIAN NAVAL OFFICERS

[T]he ovation to the Russians yesterday may justly claim the highest importance as a manifestation of national feeling. The emotions it had its origin in . . . are founded in the memories of long-standing friendship with Russia in time of peace, but also in the equity with which she has treated us, and the international sympathy she has shown for us, while we were suffering the pangs of a dreadful war. . . .

The day was golden Autumn and beamed with mild, unbroken lustre from morning till night. The arrangements of the occasion were perfect, and from the moment when the Russian squadron, near noon, trembled under the crashing broadsides with which it announced the departure of its officers, down to the tumultuous cheering with which the citizen-multitude hailed the City's guests on their departure from City Hall, nothing occurred to break the continuity, harmony and gladness of the occasion. Cannons boomed at intervals all through the day; flags streamed from every house-top, drooped gracefully from windows, and fluttered gaily over the streets. The broad cross of St. Andrew was caressed by the dancing "Stars and Stripes." The miles of grand avenue through which the procession moved, were literally jammed with the thick, unmoving masses, who, with waving hats, fluttering handkerchiefs and resounding cheers, gave our Russian guests a welcome that the fewest of living men have received. . . . Would that every American could have been here to see the spectacle!

Source 3   *New York Times,* October 11, 1863

THE RUSSIANS INVITED TO THE MONUMENTAL CITY

The Harbor was especially enlivened, yesterday, by the formal visit of the Committees from Baltimore to Admiral Lisovsky, for the purpose of tendering to him and the officers of his squadron the hospitalities of the commercial metropolis of Maryland. On the 5th inst. the Common Councils of Baltimore, in both branches, passed resolutions and appointed delegations of their members to convey to the Russian commanding officer of the fleet now at anchor in the Hudson, a formal and special invitation to visit the Monumental City and receive the attentions of its authorities and people. . . .

30.2 New York State and the Civil War

Between 1 and 2 o'clock P.M., the entire party proceeded to the Barge Office at Pier No. 1. . . . The steam revenue-cutter *Addison T. Andrews* was placed at their disposal. . . . [T]he cutter made directly for the Russian flagship, the *Alexander Nevsky,* where she was received with much apparent satisfaction, the Admiral's band striking up "Yankee Doodle" with immense vigor as she came in earshot. The full-manned barges of the *Nevsky* quickly came alongside to transfer the party to the frigate, and for a few minutes the neighborhood of the latter vessel was alive with the dancing boats and their white-capped, blue-shirted oarsmen, the gay flags of the *Andrews,* and the white **pennon** of the Russians at the stern of every barge, fluttering wildly in the fresh breeze.

As the visitors ascended the sides of the Russian [ship], they were received by the Admiral, and his officers, in full uniform, and most cordially welcomed. They then were escorted along the clean white decks, past groups of seamen and marines, all in their places near the guns, and shown into the Admiral's cabin, where the main saloon was neatly arranged for their reception. After a few moments of conversation, . . . S. F. Strebter, Esq., Chairman of the Committee of the Baltimore Councils, rose, and addressing Admiral Lisovsky, who took his place at the table in the centre of the saloon, surrounded by his officers, proceeded to trace in warm and eloquent terms, the friendship manifested to us even during our struggle for independence by the Empress Catherine, who refused to hire to England any of her victorious troops returning from their successful Turkish campaign. From that day down to the present, the Empire had been our friend. At this moment, when we are battling for the nation's existence, we had anticipated the sympathies of a kindred race (Britain) . . . and of a neighboring powerful nation (France) that had once been the friend of America. But the one stands timidly aloof, its government hesitating and its aristocracy hostile. . . . The other avails itself of our trouble to build up an Austro-Mexican Empire on our borders and prepares the way for a clandestine back-door recognition of the rebels. Still Russia—great, Imperial Russia—from first to last, holds out the hand of fellowship and sympathy . . .

The speaker then . . . read aloud . . . the following resolution . . . :

Resolved, by the Mayor and City Council of Baltimore, that a Committee . . . proceed to New York and extend an invitation to the officers of the Russian ships-of-war . . . to visit the city of Baltimore . . . and accept of its hospitalities, as a testimonial of the high respect of the authorities and citizens of Baltimore for the sovereign and people of Russia, who, when other Powers and people, more strongly bound to us by the ties of interest or common descent, have lent material and moral aid to the rebels of the South, have honorably abstained from all attempts to assist the rebellion, and have given our Government reliable assurances of their sympathy and good will.

Approved, October 5, 1863

John Lee Shipman, Mayor.

During the delivery of his remarks Mr. Strebter was frequently applauded, the Admiral repeatedly evincing the most marked satisfaction. As he handed to Admiral Lisovsky a copy of the above resolution . . . , that officer warmly expressed his acknowledgements, and promised to visit Baltimore. . . .

Conversation was here renewed for a few minutes, the Committee partaking of the abundant collation of fruit and wine displayed on the table in the centre of the saloon. This agreeable part of the entertainment was further signalized by the Admiral, who summoning his guests to fill their glasses proposed:

The health of the President of the United States—may God give him health in these troubled times.

As the last word was spoken, the band outside burst into the grand air of "The Star Spangled Banner," and mingling with it, in notes of thunder crashed, gun after gun, a royal salute, from a whole deck of 60 pound Dahlgrens [cannons], their roar and smoke filling the vast reaches of the upper bay. . . .

Mr. Wilmot gave—

Russia and America—in time of peace, friends, in time of war, allies.

America's One True Friend?

30.3 The Diplomats and Diplomacy of the American Civil War

There was little doubt in 1863 in the minds of Northerners about the motivation of the Russian czar in sending his navy to America. The Russians had long been considered America's only true friend among the powers of Europe. Russian friendship had begun with sympathy for the colonies in their struggle for independence, and it had matured into a cordial relationship and a mutually beneficial commerce between the two nations. Northerners easily convinced themselves that the Russian fleets had been sent to shield America from British and French military might at a time when internal division had left the United States exposed to European adventurism. The governments of Britain and France, likewise, perceived the visit to be a manifestation of a Russian-American alliance.

The Russian fleets remained in American waters through April of 1864. During that time, the officers and crews of the Russian warships were feted by expressions of friendship and appreciation from the Northern officialdom and public. Parades, parties, and banquets honored the Russian guests. Delegations from Northern cities called upon the Russian officers to express gratitude. The finale of the Russian visit was a gala reception in Washington attended by congressmen and Cabinet officers. Never did the Russians deny that they had come to stand beside their American friends in America's time of distress, nor, on the other hand, did they ever lift a hand to defend the Union against its enemies.

Only once did the Russians reveal any intent to take arms on behalf of the Union. During the winter of 1863–64, San Francisco was without a Union warship to defend it. When rumors that Confederate warships were en route to bombard the city, the commander of the Russian Far Eastern Fleet, Rear Admiral Popov, issued orders for his squadron to protect San Francisco through whatever means necessary, including force. When the Russian minister in Washington was apprised of these orders, he wrote to Admiral Popov asserting that while the Russian government chose not to interfere in the internal affairs of the United States, the Russian fleet did indeed have "the right, in the name of humanity," to protect a defenseless city from attack. But no Confederate vessels appeared in San Francisco Bay, and, other than the valuable aid the Russians provided when a huge fire swept the city in November of 1863, the Russian navy was never called upon to protect San Francisco.

The friendly bond between the United States and Russia remained strong until the latter years of the nineteenth century. As emigrants from Eastern Europe began to pour into American ports, they told tales of despotism that altered American impressions of Russia and its rulers. This negative image grew more pronounced after the turn of the twentieth century and became indelibly etched in the public mind with the Bolshevik takeover of Russia in 1917. With this shift in attitude toward Russia came a shift in the explanation for the arrival of the Russian fleet. Where before Americans had seen the dispatching of the Russian navy as a generous act of friendship, they came in time to view it as a cold and calculated act of Russian selfishness.

Second Thoughts

Why Did the Russians Send Their Fleet?

While most discussions of the motivation for the presence of the Russian fleet in American waters centered around the question of Russian friendship versus Russian self-interest, another view cited the importance of diplomacy.

The Union representative to St. Petersburg was perhaps the most extraordinary diplomat America has ever produced. His name was Cassius Marcellus Clay, and he was an abolitionist from Kentucky. Clay thrived on adversity. He enjoyed single-handedly disrupting proslavery rallies armed only with a bowie knife. He carved up a string of Southern politicians and slaveholders, and no authority seemed able to subdue him.

Cassius Clay found the serf-owning aristocracy of Russia to be not unlike the slaveholding Southern planters he had left behind, and he engaged in ongoing and widely publicized knife fights with a series of rapier-bearing Russian noblemen. As was befitting for a man of his station, he carried what he called "a dress-up" bowie knife with a pearl handle for formal occasions. This unorthodox diplomacy actually made him immensely popular with the Russian people and the Russian royal family, and there is some reason to believe his popularity was a factor in the Russian czar's decision to send his navy to America. Reflecting on his diplomatic mission in 1869, Clay observed, "As to my diplomacy, I leave that to history. What reason was there why Russia should stand by us, when other monarchies desired to destroy us? . . . Who shall say then how much all this is owing to myself?"

Source 4   Diary of Secretary of the Navy Gideon Welles, September 25, 1863

Things look a little threatening from France. . . . Should we meet with defeat at Chattanooga, it is by no means certain England will not again assume unfriendly airs. . . .

The Russian fleet has come out of the Baltic and are now in New York, or a large number of the vessels have arrived. . . . In sending them to this country at this time there is something significant. What will be its effect on France and the French policy we shall learn in due time. It may moderate; it may exasperate. God bless the Russians.

Source 5   Poem of Oliver Wendell Holmes, 1871

Shadowed so long by the storm-cloud of danger,
Thou whom the prayers of an empire defend,
Welcome, thrice welcome! but not as a stranger,
Come to the nation that calls thee its friend.

Bleak are our shores with the blasts of December,
Fettered and chilled is the rivulet's flow;
Throbbing and warm are the hearts that remember
Who was our friend when the world was our foe.

Look on the lips that are smiling to greet thee,
See the fresh flowers that a people has strewn.
Count them thy sisters and brothers that meet thee;
Guest of the Nation, her heart is thine own!

Fires of the North, in eternal communion,
Blend your broad flashes with evening's bright star!
God bless the Empire that loves the Great Union;
Strength to her people! Long life to the Czar!

Source 6   Statement of Secretary of State James G. Blaine, 1881

The Emperor sent a large and powerful fleet of war vessels [in 1863] as a proclamation to the world of his sympathy in our struggle and of his readiness to strike a blow on the side of the Union if any foreign power should strike a blow in aid of the insurrection.

Source 7   James Ford Rhodes, *History of the United States*, 1899

The friendly welcome of a Russian fleet of war vessels, which arrived in New York City in September; the enthusiastic reception by the people of the admiral and officers when offered the hospitalities of the city; the banquet given at the Astor House by the merchants and business men in their honor; the marked attention shown them . . . on their visit to Washington, "to reflect the cordiality and friendship which the nation cherishes towards Russia": all these manifestations of gratitude to the one great power of Europe which had openly and persistently been our friend, added another element to the cheerfulness which prevailed in the closing months of 1863.

Source 8   F. A. Golder, *American Historical Review*, 1915

The coming of the Russian fleet to our shores in 1863 has been a topic of discussion for many years. A great deal of importance has been attached to this event both in the United States and in Russia. Curiously enough, in neither of the two countries is it generally recognized that this official visit was of any consequence to the other. In Russia it is regarded from the point of view of European politics, while in America many people associate it with the Civil War. Through the kindness of the Russian Minister of the Marine in permitting the writer to examine the official documents . . . it is now possible to learn the real motives of the expedition.

It will be remembered that during the period of our Civil War Russia was having difficulties in Poland. . . . France, England, Austria, and the other powers stood out against Russia and her treatment of the Poles. . . . Russia expected to be called on to defend her cause by arms. . . . Russia's fleet was too weak to make an effective fight against the combined naval strength of England and France, but it was strong enough to prey upon their commerce. . . . If the fleet remained at home it would be blocked in; it was therefore necessary that it be sent away to some place more conveniently suited for the purpose. . . .

Since the cruise had nothing whatever to do with American affairs it is interesting to know why United States ports were selected for a base of operation. Aside from the friendly relations that had always existed between the two nations there were special reasons why they should draw close to each other at this critical period. [Czar] Alexander had freed the serfs; Lincoln was emancipating the slaves. The United States had been invited by France to join the powers in dictating to Russia upon the Polish problem and had declined; Russia had been asked by France to intervene in the Civil War and had refused. Russia was fighting against insurrection; the United States to put down rebellion. The two governments had similar problems and the same European enemies and that was reason enough why they should feel kindly towards each other.

There were, however, other reasons why the fleet should come to America. [T]he ships could not remain in Russia, and there was no other place in Europe where they would be received in friendliness. On the other hand, if anchored in one of the Atlantic ports of the United States, it would be possible to dash out quickly and in a short time be on the trade routes. This condition held true in the Pacific as well as in the Atlantic. . . .

During the winter months the European war clouds passed away. Russia held fast and won. England was willing to call names but not to fight, and France was helpless without England. Gradually the insurrection was put down and the excitement subsided. Officers of the Russian navy assert that the coming of the fleet to America was, if not altogether, at least in a very great measure, responsible for England's change of front and consequently for the prevention of war. . . .

No one can question for a moment that this visit gave much moral support to the cause of the Union. At a time when European powers were plotting against us, when conditions at home were most discouraging, we felt we had a friend in Russia. It put life and strength into the people of the North. Everyone took the visit as a special mark of friendship and it was highly appreciated. . . .

It is, of course, true that the fleet was not ordered to America for our benefit, but this should not blind us to the fact that we did profit by the event as if this had been the case. If, as the Russians maintain, the presence of their ships in our waters saved them from a struggle in which they were not in a position to engage, we should be very proud that it was in our power to do so. It was a most extraordinary situation: Russia had not in mind to help us but did render us distinct service; the United States was not conscious that it was contributing in any way to Russia's welfare and yet seems to have saved her from humiliation and perhaps war. There is probably nothing to compare with it in diplomatic history.

Source 9   Journalist Walter Lippmann, *U.S. Foreign Policy: Shield of the Republic*, 1943

The enduring element in Russian-American relations is that in critical times each nation has always been "for the other a potential friend in the rear of potential enemies." In the War of Independence the Continental Congress sought the assistance of Russia, and Russia practised, entirely in her own interest, an armed neutrality which favored the colonies. In 1863, at the darkest moment of the Civil War, there occurred the Polish insurrection against Russia. Both Britain and France were considering giving support to the Confederacy in America and to the Polish rebellion. In spite of American ideological sympathy with the Polish national rebellion, Lincoln and Seward refused to intervene diplomatically against Russia. In spite of Russian antipathy to the American democracy, the Czar's government stated, in the official journal of the Foreign Office, that the preservation of the United States was an imperative necessity for Russia, and backed up this declaration by dispatching a squadron of warships from its Baltic fleet to New York and from the Pacific squadron to San Francisco. This gesture had its effect in London and in Paris, warning them not to recognize the Confederacy or support the Polish insurrection.

Source 10   Thomas A. Bailey, *Mississippi Valley Historical Review*, 1951

The traditional tale is that Czar Alexander II sent his two fleets to the United States in the autumn of 1863 primarily as a gesture of friendship, with the tacit understanding that they would fight for the Union should France and Britain attempt armed intervention on behalf of the South. This legend received a heavy blow in 1915 when Dr. Frank A. Golder published an article, based on documents in the Russian archives, which proved the fleets had come primarily because of the Polish crisis. The Russian government, faced with the strong probability of war with both Britain and France, wanted to get its ships out of icebound and British dominated seas and base them in neutral ports, whence they could sally forth and ravage the commerce of the enemy. The Golder version has been accepted by scholars, but the legend lives merrily on in the world of journalism and popular fancy. . . .

The story of Russian friendship in connection with the fleets has endured partly because there is some measure of truth in it. The Czar dispatched his ships primarily to confound his enemies, but he probably would not have sent them to the United States if there had not been the tradition of friendliness and the prospect of securing bases from the well-disposed Americans in the event of hostilities between Russia and her enemies. It had long been a cardinal policy of the St. Petersburg Foreign Office to build up the United States as a makeweight against the might of Great Britain. If a general war had broken out in 1863, with America and Russia on the same side, the Czar presumably would have derived satisfaction by secondarily subserving the interests of the United States while primarily serving his own.

Source 11 Robert H. Ferrell, *American Diplomacy,* 1969

[P]erhaps the first minister whom Lincoln sent to St. Petersburg, the Kentucky statesman Cassius Marcellus Clay, so scared the Russians that he made them friendly to the northern cause. They could hardly have been otherwise with Clay in the vicinity. . . . In Russia, . . . he made a considerable impression. . . .

By the mid-point of the American Civil War, 1863, the Russians were unquestionably friendly toward the United States, perhaps because of Clay. That year a rebellion broke out in Poland, and for a short time it seemed to the St. Petersburg government that the European powers might intervene. The Russians sent their Baltic fleet to New York and their Far Eastern squadron to San Francisco, supposedly for goodwill visits, actually for protection and replenishment in event of hostilities.

Source 12 David L. Smiley, *The Lion of Whitehall: The Life of Cassius M. Clay,* 1969

Realizing that their fleet would be bottled up if hostilities broke out [in Europe], they sent it to the comparative safety of American ports, ostensibly upon a good-will tour. As no other European power made so tangible a show of friendship during the Civil War, Americans readily interpreted the visit as evidence of Russian sympathy for the Union cause. Thus, the existence of two widely separated rebellions, which had only one factor in common—the fear of British intervention—made Clay's diplomatic task simpler. Through no unusual action of his own, but because a common enemy confronted the United States and Russia, his ministry to the Court of the Czars was a success from the beginning.

Source 13 John G. Stoessinger, *Nations in Darkness*, 1978

History, in psychological terms, is the memory of nations. It is the repository not only of objective events, but also of illusions and misunderstandings that filter down to our own time. . . .

[T]he stage of world politics lends itself all too easily to the development of wide gaps between what reality is and the way it is perceived. Because of this fact, perception probably plays almost as important a role in international relations as does objective reality. . . .

There is a strange sense of paradox about the relations between Russia and the United States during the eighteenth and nineteenth centuries. The two peoples saw little of one another and their systems of government were radically different; yet the two nations almost always encountered each other with intensity. Relations between them at different times ranged from affection through ambivalence all the way to hostility and hatred . . . Most of the time, these intense emotional reactions rested on images, fictions, and legends rather than on facts. Policy decisions with the most serious consequences often flowed from these legends, particularly on the American side. . . .

Perhaps the most remarkable conclusion to be drawn about American perceptions of Russia . . . is how violently they swung from one extreme to the other, while Russia, the object of these perceptions, changed relatively little. For an entire century, Russia was America's trusted friend. Catherine's refusal to lend troops to King George, Alexander's dispatch of the Russian fleet to American ports, and Alexander's sale of Alaska, all were perceived as selfless and generous acts and uncritically accepted as such. The legend of Russia, the "trusted ally," was born in these events, and policy decisions of far-reaching importance were based upon the assumption that all the legends were true.

Russia, under both Catherine and Alexander, had acted purely in accord with the dictates of her national interest. Though somewhat surprised by the effusive gratitude of the Americans, the czars did little to dispel it. When the pendulum of American perceptions swung to the other extreme, Nicholas II was bewildered and shocked. . . . Americans saw prisons and **pogroms** in Russia where before they had seen only good will and benevolence. This perception, equally one-sided as its predecessor, led to policies that helped to estrange America from Russia.

One cannot help but note the unevenness of the American attitudes. Russian views of America were fairly accurate, and Russian policy was cold and selfish, but steady and fairly predictable. The young American republic tended to see the Russians either as angels or as monsters. . . .

The truth was that the fate of the United States was a matter of complete indifference to Czarist Russia. . . . Actually, in all . . . cases, the Czars followed the dictates of their national interest. The fact that these interests happened to converge with those of the Americans was purely coincidental. . . . When, under Czar Nicholas II, American and Russian interests began to diverge and ultimately to collide, the Americans went to the other extreme. Even though Nicholas' policies had as little to do with the United States as those of his predecessors, the Americans—once again relating these policies to themselves alone—overreacted in the opposite direction. Affection now turned to suspicion, and romanticism gave way to hatred. Thus, the consequence of basing policy on legends rather than on facts was naivete and lack of balance.

Questioning the Past

1. Discuss the foreign relations of the United States during the Civil War. Why were many of Europe's great powers sympathetic to the Confederacy?
2. In what ways, if any, did the arrival of the Russian fleets in America affect the war between North and South? In what ways did it affect the relations of the United States and the great powers of Europe?
3. Why did the Russians send their navy to America?
4. Why has the American view of the Russian motivation in sending the Baltic and Far Eastern fleets to American waters varied over time?

Chapter 31

The Assassination

Lincoln Is Shot at Ford's Theatre *April 14, 1865*

31.1 Abraham
Lincoln:
Sixteenth
President

Ford's Theatre was packed for the final performance of *Our American Cousin*, and the mood of the audience was a relaxed and merry one. Not only were people out to enjoy a fine play, they were out to enjoy the first Friday night in four years when the omnipresence of war did not weigh heavily on their minds. General Lee had surrendered the Army of Northern Virginia to General Grant five days earlier, and the end of the terrible conflict was at last in sight. Even the president had come to Ford's for an evening at ease.

But while the audience was being seated at Ford's Theatre, a band of conspirators was gathering a few blocks away at the Surratt Boarding House. For months this band had plotted against the leadership of the United States. At first they plotted to kidnap the president and take him to Richmond as a hostage. An attempt to carry out such a venture had failed in March. Now, their plans took a more drastic turn: They would on this evening attempt to assassinate the three highest-ranking officials of the federal government. Lewis Payne would target the secretary of state, William Henry Seward. George Atzerodt would attempt to kill the vice president of the United States, Andrew Johnson. The organizer of the conspiracy, John Wilkes Booth, would proceed to Ford's Theater, where he expected to find the president with his guard down.

The play was well into its second act when a man in riding boots and spurs stepped through the front door of Ford's. He did not appear dressed for the theater, but he ascended the stairs to the balcony without meeting any challenge. He then walked down the aisle along the wall to a door that led to an anteroom, beyond which was the presidential box. The door was not guarded. Booth entered the anteroom and braced the door shut behind him with a board. Only one door now separated Booth from the president of the United States.

Through a small hole in the door he could see the back of the president's head. Quietly, Booth opened the door, pointed a small, 44-caliber single-shot derringer at Lincoln's head, and pulled the trigger.

Many in the audience thought the noise of the gunshot to be a part of the performance. But Major Rathbone, the guest of President and Mrs. Lincoln for the evening, leaped to his feet and rushed at the assassin. Booth stopped Rathbone's advance with the point of a dagger. The wounded Rathbone reeled backwards, and Booth jumped over the railing at the front of the box. As he did, one of his boots became entangled in the banner that draped the box, and his spur caught the edge of a portrait hanging on the box front. Consequently, he landed off balance on the stage 12 feet beneath the box and fractured his leg.

The injury slowed him only slightly, however; and after dramatically brandishing his dagger at the audience and shouting in Latin, "Thus be it ever to Tyrants!" Booth dashed out through the stage door into the alley behind Ford's Theatre, mounted his horse, and made good his escape.

▄ *First Impressions*

A Nation Will Weep for Him

Abraham Lincoln had spent a lifetime in public service. He had led his country through its most tragic era. And for that, Abraham Lincoln earned a place in our history books. John Wilkes Booth, by firing one shot taking less than a second, had caused his own name to be placed on the same page as that of Abraham Lincoln. Such is the irony of history.

31.2 The History Place Presents Abraham Lincoln

Source 1   Statement of Secretary of War Edwin M. Stanton

War Department,
Washington, D.C.,
April 15—1:30 A.M.

Last evening, at 10:30 p.m., at Ford's Theatre, the President, while sitting in his private box with Mrs. Lincoln, Miss Harris, and Major Rathbone, was shot by an assassin who suddenly entered the box. He approached behind the President. The assassin then leaped upon the stage, brandishing a dagger or knife, and made his escape by the rear of the theatre. The pistol ball entered the back of the President's head. The wound is mortal. The President has been insensible ever since it was inflicted, and is now dying.

About the same hour an assassin, either the same or another, entered Mr. Seward's house, and under pretense of having a prescription, was shown to the Secretary's sick chamber. The Secretary was in bed, a nurse and Miss Seward with him. The assassin immediately rushed to the bed, inflicting two or three stabs on the throat, and two in the face. It is hoped the wounds may not be mortal. My apprehension is that they will prove fatal. The nurse alarmed Mr. Frederick Seward, who was in an adjoining room, and hastened to the door of his father's room, where he met the assassin, who inflicted upon him one or more dangerous wounds. The recovery of Frederick Seward is doubtful.

It is not probable that the President will live through the night.

Source 2   Washington *Evening Star,* April 15, 1865

From the Associated Press:
President Lincoln and wife, together with other friends, last evening visited Ford's Theater for the purpose of witnessing the performance of the American Cousin. It was announced in the newspapers that General Grant would also be present, but that gentleman, instead, took the late train of cars for New Jersey. The theater was densely crowded, and everybody seemed delighted with the scene before them.

During the third act, and while there was a temporary pause for one of the actors to enter, a sharp report of a pistol was heard, which merely attracted attention, but suggesting nothing serious, until a man rushed to the front of the President's box, waving a long dagger in his right hand, and exclaiming "Sic Semper Tyrannis," and immediately leaped from the box, which was of the second tier, to the stage beneath, and ran across to the opposite side, thus making his escape, amid the bewilderment of the audience, from the rear of the theater, and mounting a horse, fled.

The screams of Mrs. Lincoln first disclosed the fact to the audience that the President had been shot, when all present rose to their feet, rushing toward the stage, exclaiming, "Hang him!" "Hang him!"

The excitement was of the wildest possible character; and, of course there was an abrupt termination of the theatrical performance. . . .

On hasty examination it was found that the President had been shot through the head, above and back of the temporal bone, and that some of the brain was oozing out. He was removed to the private residence of Mr. Peterson, opposite to the theater, and the Surgeon General of the army and other surgeons sent for to attend to his condition.

On examination of the private box blood was discovered on the back of the cushioned rocking chair in which the President had been sitting, also on the partition and on the floor.

A common single barrelled pocket pistol was found on the carpet.

A military guard was placed in front of the private residence to which the President had been conveyed.

An immense crowd was in front of it, all deeply anxious to learn the condition of the President. . . .

The shock to the community was terrible. . . .

When the excitement at the theater was at its wildest height, reports were circulated that Secretary Seward had also been assassinated.

On reaching this gentleman's residence a crowd and a military guard were found at the door, and on entering, it was ascertained that the reports were based upon truth.

Everybody was so much excited that scarcely an intelligible account could be gathered. . . .

The entire city last night presented a scene of wild excitement, accompanied by violent expressions of indignation, and the profoundest sorrow. Many persons shed tears.

The military authorities have dispatched mounted troops in every direction, in order, if possible to arrest the assassins. . . .

Vice President Johnson is in the city, and his hotel quarters are guarded by troops.

31.3 Abraham Lincoln's Assassination

Source 3   *National Intelligencer,* April 15, 1865

THE TRAGEDY OF LAST NIGHT

Our heart stands almost still as we take our pen to speak of the tragedy of last night. We have no words at command by which to express anything that we feel. Before this paper shall go to press, the fact may reach us that the President has been assassinated! We already know enough to be compelled to record the fact that he was shot in the Theatre, and that the ball entered his head. God Almighty grant that his life may be preserved! Still we have hope. . . .

And, horror upon horrors! It seems that the house of Mr. Seward was entered on a pretext by a murderer or murderers, who, it is represented to us on authority which we cannot doubt, beat and stabbed his son, the Hon. F. Seward, wounded others of his household, and who finally succeeded in stabbing the Secretary of State. The fact seems to be that his throat is cut. Up to this hour—2 A.M.—we have no assurance that the perpetrators of this terrible crime have been arrested. Nor are we advised as to the condition of the Secretary or of his son.

Rumors are so thick and contradictory, the excitement at this hour is so intense, that we rely entirely upon our reporters to advise the public of the details and result of this night of horrors.

Evidently conspirators are among us! To what extent does the conspiracy exist? This is a terrible question! When a spirit so horrible as this is abroad, what man is safe? We can only advise the utmost vigilance and the most prompt measures by the authorities. We can only pray God to shield us, His unworthy people, from further calamities like these.

If the President is dead, a noble and good man has fallen at his post, and the only one among us who had the power and the will to do as much as he could have done, and as humanely, and liberally, for the whole country. A nation will weep for him. The loss of the Secretary of State would be irreparable. But our heart is too full to say more.

Saturday Morning, 2½ O'Clock.—The President is still alive, but is growing weaker. The ball is lodged in his brain, three inches from where it entered the skull. He remains insensible, and his condition is utterly hopeless.

The Vice President has been to see him, but all company, except the Cabinet, his family, and a few friends, are rigidly excluded.

Large crowds still continue in the street, as near to the house as the line of guards allow.

Source 4   Secretary of War Edwin M. Stanton's communiqués to Lieutenant General Grant

War Department,
Washington, D.C., 3 A.M.,
April 15, 1865.

Lieutenant General Grant:
The President still breathes, but is quite insensible, as he has been ever since he was shot. He evidently did not see the person who shot him, but was looking on the stage, as he was approached behind.

Mr. Seward has rallied, and it is hoped he may live. Frederick Seward's condition is very critical. The attendant who was present was stabbed through the lungs, and is not expected to live. . . .

Investigation strongly indicates J. Wilkes Booth as the assassin of the President.

War Department,
Washington, D.C.
April 15,—4:10 A.M.

The President continues insensible, and is sinking. Secretary Seward remains without change. Frederick Seward's skull is fractured in two places, besides a severe cut upon the head. The attendant is still alive, but hopeless. . . .

It is now ascertained with reasonable certainty that two assassins were engaged in the horrible crime—Wilkes Booth being the one that shot the President; the other, a companion of his, whose name is not known, but whose description is so clear that he can hardly escape.

Source 5   Washington *Evening Star,* afternoon of April 15, 1865

EXTRA
THE DEATH OF THE PRESIDENT

At 22 minutes past seven o'clock the President breathed his last, closing his eyes as if falling to sleep, and his countenance assuming an expression of perfect serenity. There were no indications of pain, and it was not known that he was dead until the gradually decreasing respiration ceased altogether.

Rev. Dr. Gurley, (of the New York Avenue Presbyterian Church) immediately on its being ascertained that life was extinct, knelt at the bedside and offered an impressive prayer, which was responded to by all present.

Dr. Gurley then proceeded to the front parlor, where Mrs. Lincoln, Capt. Robert Lincoln, Mr. John Hay, the Private Secretary, and others were waiting, when he again offered prayer for the consolation of the family. . . .

Immediately after the President's death a Cabinet meeting was called by Secretary Stanton, and held in the room in which the corpse lay. Secretaries Stanton, Welles, and Usher, Postmaster General Dennison, and Attorney General Speed present. The results of the Conference are as yet unknown.

Shortly after nine o'clock this morning the remains were placed in a temporary coffin and removed to the White House, six young men of the Quartermaster's Department carrying the body to the house.

Source 6   *Richmond Whig,* April 17, 1865

The heaviest blow which has ever fallen upon the people of the South has descended. Abraham Lincoln, the President of the United States, has been assassinated. . . . The thoughtless and the vicious may affect to derive satisfaction from the sudden and tragic close of the President's career, but every reflecting person will deplore the awful event. Just as everything was happily conspiring to a restoration of tranquility, under the benignant and magnanimous policy of Mr. Lincoln, comes this terrible blow. God grant that it may not rekindle excitement or inflame passion again.

That a state of war, almost fratricidal, should give rise to bitter feelings and bloody deeds in the field was to be expected, but that the assassin's knife and bullet should follow the great and best loved of the nation in their daily walks, and reach them when surrounded by their friends, is an atrocity which will shock and appall every honorable man and woman.

Source 7   Washington *Evening Star,* April 18, 1865

EXTRA
THE ASSAILANT OF SECRETARY SEWARD ARRESTED!!

About three o'clock this morning a man clad in laboring clothes, covered with mud and bearing a pick-axe on his shoulder, was arrested entering a house occupied by members of the Surratt family on H street, between 9th and 10th. On removing the mud from his person he turned out to be of much more genteel appearance than his disguise indicated.

He has since his arrest been confronted with those at Secretary Seward's, who saw the Secretary's assailant on Friday night, and he was at once identified as the man.

It is reported that his name is Paine, but the full particulars have not yet transpired.

Surratt, it is now believed, was not a direct actor in the assassination, but seems to have been in some way implicated in the plot.

Upon the prisoner being brought to General Augur's headquarters this morning, Mr. Seward's colored servant, who was at the door at the time the assassin applied for admission, was sent for. The servant had no knowledge of the arrest of the prisoner, but upon entering the room in which the prisoner and a number of persons were, instantly exclaimed, "Why, here is the man that cut Mr. Seward."

Source 8   Washington *Evening Star,* April 21, 1865

THE REMAINS OF PRESIDENT LINCOLN

Yesterday the throng of persons visiting the remains of the late President, as they laid in state in the Capitol, continued until dark, at which time the doors were closed and the guard for the night . . . set. The number of visitors is estimated at about forty thousand, and but for the inclement weather the number would have been probably twice as many.

Source 9   Washington *Evening Star,* April 22, 1865

ARREST OF THE SURRATT FAMILY

Colonel Wells, Provost Marshall General of this Department, was pursuing investigation into the recent assassinations. He had decided to arrest Mrs. Surratt, who resides in this city at 541 H street, but subsequently decided to arrest the whole family, including her daughter Kate, two young ladies, whom she calls her nieces, and two colored servants. . . . Major Smith, Assistant Adjutant on General Augur's staff, proceeded to the house about 11 o'clock.

Major Smith proceeded up the steps alone, the house being a three story brick, with high stoop, and rapped. A woman raised a window, and asked, who is there? The reply was, "I'm an officer; let me in." The door was opened and the Major entered. Immediately after, the rest of the party entered one by one, until all were in. The purpose of the visit was announced and the inmates seemed somewhat surprised, the daughter especially being frightened, but the mother took it calmly as though she had been expecting it.

They were all assembled in the parlor, and not allowed to communicate with each other while the officers hunted up the bonnets, shawls, and shoes of the ladies, preparatory to conveying them to Colonel Ingraham's office. This took some little time, during which Miss Kate Surratt broke out into sobs, while her mother chided her for such an exhibition of her feelings.

Source 10 Washington *Evening Star*

PRESIDENT LINCOLN'S REMAINS IN NEW YORK

New York, April 24.—Business is generally suspended.

On the arrival of the funeral cortege Broadway was crowded to the utmost by people anxious to witness the funeral car and accompanying escort. The utmost quiet prevailed on the route, and the dense masses remained uncovered as the procession slowly wended its way to City Hall. The coffin was conveyed by eight soldiers to the Governor's room, and one thousand singers sang a mournful dirge as it was borne to its temporary resting place. . . . Immense crowds, numbering thousands, are in the streets, awaiting an opportunity to view for the last time the face of Abraham Lincoln.

New York, April 25.—The action of the Common Council against the colored citizens appearing in the procession to morrow is overruled by the Police Commissioner. The Secretary of War to-day telegraphed General Dix, expressing a desire that there should be no discrimination respecting color.

CEREMONIES AT ALBANY

Albany, April 26.—From the time the remains of the President were deposited in the Capitol until now, persons have been pressing thither. This morning the line of people extends at least a mile and a half. The place presents a solemn scene. There in the presence of death, hearts are bowed with grief, which often finds relief in tears.

OFFICIAL BULLETIN

War Department,
Washington, D.C.,
April 27, 1865.

J. Wilkes Booth and Harrold were chased from the swamp in St. Mary's county, Md., pursued yesterday morning to Garrett's farm, near Port Royal, on the Rappahannock, by Col. Baker's force.

The barn in which they took refuge was fired.

Booth in making his escape was shot through the head and killed, lingering about three hours, and Harrold taken alive.

Booth's body and Harrold are now here.

Edwin M. Stanton, Secretary of War

PRESIDENT LINCOLN'S REMAINS AT CLEVELAND

Cleveland, April 28.—All along the route from Buffalo to this city, which was reached this morning, the usual demonstrations of sorrow were witnessed.

The remains were escorted by a large military and civic procession to a beautiful constructed temple prepared to receive them, and soon thereafter the face of the honored dead was open to thousands of spectators, who in admirable order entered and retired from the enclosure.

EDITORIAL
"The End of the Assassin"

The manner of death of J. Wilkes Booth though at first a disappointment to the public has in some respects a peculiar fitness. For sympathy with his deed he received the fiercest execration; instead of a brilliant escape to a refuge of safety the officers of justice hunted the crippled fugitive like a starved beast from swamp to swamp, and at last, exhausted by hunger and pain, the wretch died the death of a cur. What may have been the anguish of his craven soul as the tolls closed around him no man may ever know. Whatever torture a frenzied people might have inflicted upon his carcass had he fallen into their hands alive has been exceeded by the misery of his flight. . . .

It is best that he should have passed beyond human passion as he did. The wretch whom a righteous trial might have invested with some degree of respectful detestation, is now only the despised malefactor, dying the death of a mad dog in an out house.

THE PRESIDENT'S REMAINS

Springfield, Ill., May 3.—The funeral train arrived at 8 o'clock this morning. All the way from Chicago, on the road, funeral arches were erected and mourning emblems displayed. An immense crowd assembled at the principal depot here. The remains were conveyed to the Capitol, where the apartments were decorated in the most elaborate manner. Deep solemnity prevailed, bells tolled, and minute guns were fired. Thousands of persons were here from adjoining States, contributing to swell the proportions of the vast multitude which assembled to honor the illustrious dead.

THE OBSEQUIES IN SPRINGFIELD—THE CLOSING EXERCISES

Springfield, May 4.—About noon the remains of President Lincoln were brought from the State-house and placed in the hearse. . . .

The procession consisting of the governors of seven States, members of Congress, State and municipal authorities, delegations from adjoining States, Free Masons, Odd Fellows, and citizens, including the colored procession, arrived at Oak Ridge Cemetery at 1 o'clock. . . .

There was a platform on which singers and an instrumental band were engaged in singing and playing appropriate music. On the right was the speakers' stand. The vault is at the foot of a knoll in a beautiful part of the ground which contains forest trees and all other varieties. It has a Doric gable, resting on pilasters; the main wall being rustic. The vault is fifteen feet high, and about the same in width, with semicircular wings projecting from its hillsides. The material is limestone. . . .

After a hymn by the choir, Rev. Mr. Hubbard read the last inaugural of President Lincoln. Next a dirge was sung by the choir, when Bishop Simpson delivered the funeral address, which was in the highest degree solemn and patriotic; portions were applauded. Then followed another dirge and another hymn, when the benediction was pronounced by Rev. Dr. Gurley. The procession then reformed and returned.

Our mournful duty of escorting the mortal remains of Abraham Lincoln hither is performed. We have seen them deposited in the tomb. Bereaved friends, with saddened faces and grief-stricken hearts have taken their adieu and turned their faces homeward, ever to remember the affecting and impressive scene they have witnessed.

The injunction so often repeated on the way, "Bear him gently to his rest," has been obeyed, and "the great heart of the nation throbs heavily at the portals of the tomb."

Second Thoughts

Avenging a Martyr's Death

The assassination of Abraham Lincoln traumatized a nation that thought itself inured to violence following years of internecine bloodshed. Millions mourned Lincoln's passing. The timing of his death at the concluding moments of the Civil War and the coincidence of his being taken on Good Friday made him a martyr. He attained after death a popularity greater than he had ever enjoyed while alive. As Samuel Eliot Morison wrote in 1972, John Wilkes Booth "gave fresh life to the very forces of hate and vengeance which Lincoln himself was trying to kill."

Eight people were arrested in the days immediately following the assassination and brought before a military court. Four—Lewis Payne, George Atzerodt, David E. Herold, and Mary Surratt—were found guilty and met death on the gallows. Three others—including the physician who set Booth's broken leg—were sentenced to life imprisonment. Another of the conspirators was condemned to a prison term of six years. John Surratt, yet another of the conspirators, managed to flee the country but was brought back to stand trial in 1867. His trial ended in a hung jury.

Source 11 Walt Whitman, "O Captain, My Captain," 1865

O Captain! My Captain! our fearful trip is done,
The ship has weathered every rack, the prize we sought is won,
The port is near, the bells I hear, the people all exulting,
While follow eyes the steady keel, the vessel grim and daring,
    But O heart! heart! heart!
      O the bleeding drops of red.
        Where on the deck my Captain lies,
          Fallen cold and dead.

O Captain! My Captain! rise up and hear the bells;
Rise up—for you the flag is flung—For you the bugle trills,

For you bouquets and ribboned wreaths—For you the shores
    a-crowdeing,
For you they call, the swaying mass, their eager faces turning;
    Here Captain! dear father!
        This arm beneath your head!
           It is some dream that on the deck,
              You've fallen cold and dead.

My Captain does not answer, his lips are pale and still,
My father does not feel my arm, he has no pulse nor will,
The ship is anchor'd safe and sound, its voyage closed and done,
From fearful trip the victor ship comes in with object won;
    Exult O shores and ring, O bells!
        But I with mournful tread,
           Walk the deck my Captain lies,
              Fallen cold and dead.

Source 12   Presidential Proclamation, May 2, 1865

Whereas it appears from evidence in the Bureau of Military Justice that the atrocious murder of the late President, Abraham Lincoln, and the attempted assassination of the Hon. William H. Seward, Secretary of State, were incited, concerted, and procured by and between Jefferson Davis, late of Richmond, Va., and Jacob Thompson, Clement C. Clay, Beverley Tucker, George N. Sanders, William C. Cleary, and other Rebels and traitors against the Government of the United States harbored in Canada:

Now, therefore, to the end that justice may be done, I, Andrew Johnson, President of the United States, do offer and promise for the arrest of said persons, or either of them, within the limits of the United States, so that they can be brought to trial, the following rewards:

One hundred thousand dollars for the arrest of Jefferson Davis.

Twenty-five thousand dollars for the arrest of Clement Clay.

Twenty-five thousand dollars for the arrest of Jacob Thompson, late of
    Mississippi.

Twenty-five thousand dollars for the arrest of George N. Sanders.

Twenty-five thousand dollars for the arrest of Beverly Tucker.

Ten thousand dollars for the arrest of William C. Cleary, late clerk of Clement C. Clay.

The Provost-Marshal-General of the United States is directed to cause a description of said persons, with notice of the above rewards, to be published.

In testimony whereof I have hereunto set my hand and caused the seal of the United States to be affixed.

Source 13   Editorial, "The Trial of Jeff. Davis," *New York Times,* May 5, 1865

It is extremely desirable that the charges which have been solemnly made against Jefferson Davis, Jacob Thompson & Co., in the President's Proclamation, should be fully borne out on the trial.

If they are, and we have no doubt they will be, it will fix very accurately the place which the rebellion will occupy in history. The course which it has run has been simple and consistent from the commencement. It began with an attempt to found an empire upon wholesale robbery of servants' wages, and if its last act was really the murder of the President, Mr. Davis has the satisfaction of knowing that he has run through the whole gamut of crime in the short space of four years. There is a completeness and unity in the movement of which he has been the chief, which, whatever its moral complexion may be, must always entitle it to the highest place as an attempt to apply the rules of war to the commission of villainy.

Source 14   Horace Greeley, *The American Conflict: A History of the Great Rebellion,* 1867

That President Lincoln was the victim of a conspiracy of partisans of the Rebellion is established by undeniable proof; not so the charge that the chiefs and master-spirits of the Confederacy were implicated in the crime. Booth himself was, so far as had been shown, the projector and animating soul of the monstrous plot. . . . Booth was simply one of the many badly educated, loose-living young men infesting the purlieus of our great cities, who, regarding Slavery as the chief bulwark of their own claim to birthright in a superior caste, and the Federal Constitution as established expressly and mainly to sustain and buttress Slavery, could never comprehend that any political action adverse to whatever exactions and pretensions of the Slave Power could possibly be other than unjustly aggressive and treasonable. Few of this class were radically Disunionists; they sympathized with the Rebellion, not because it aimed at a division of the Republic, but because it was impelled by devotion to Slavery; and was thus hallowed, in their view, as a laudable effort, however irregular, to achieve and firmly secure the chief end of both the Constitution and the Union. There is no particle of evidence that Booth, or any of his fellow conspirators, had been in any-wise offended by, or that they cherished any feeling of aversion to, the President, save as the 'head center' of resistance to the Slaveholders' Rebellion. . . .

The quiet accession to the Presidency of Vice-President Johnson—the funeral honors to the good, beloved President, so suddenly snatched away at the moment when long years of trial and disaster had at length been crowned by a fullness of triumph and gladness rarely paralleled—the flight, pursuit, and capture of Booth, so severely wounded by his captors that he died a few hours afterward—the arraignment, trial, and conviction before a military court of Payne and several of their fellow-conspirators or accomplices—may here be hurriedly passed over, as non-essential to this history. Not so the burst of unmeasured, indignant wrath, the passionate grief, the fierce cry for vengeance, which the crime of the assassins very generally incited. Mr. Lincoln was widely known as radically, immovably averse to aught that savored of severity in dealing with the defeated insurgents. No 'railing accusations,' no incitements to severity or bitterness on the part of the loyal, had ever found utterance through his lips. Inflexibly resolved that the Rebellion should be put down, he was equally determined that its upholders, having submitted to the Nation's authority, should experience to the utmost the Nation's magnanimity. . . . And now, the butchery of this gentle, forbearing spirit, by the hand, hardly less blundering than bloody, of a pro-Rebel assassin, incited a fierce, agonized, frantic yell for retaliation . . . ; and the appearance of an official proclamation, signed by the new President . . . charging that the appalling crime of Booth and his associates had been "incited, concerted, and procured by and between Jefferson Davis . . . and other Rebels and traitors against the Government of the United States" was widely hailed as justifying the suspicions already current, and rendering the Confederates as a body morally guilty of the murder of Mr. Lincoln, and justly liable therefor to **condign** punishment.

Source 15   Remarks of John H. Surratt, son of hanged conspirator Mary Surratt, Rockville, Maryland, December 6, 1870

In the fall of 1864 I was introduced to John Wilkes Booth, who, I was given to understand, wished to know something about the main avenues leading from Washington to the Potomac. We met several times, . . . as he seemed to be very reticent with regard to his purposes, . . . but finally said he would make known his views to me provided I would promise secrecy. . . . He then said, "I will confide my plans to you; but before doing so I will make known to you the motives that actuate me. In the Northern prisons are many thousands of our men whom the United States Government refuses to exchange. You know as well as I the efforts that have been made to bring about that much desired exchange. Aside from the great suffering they are compelled to undergo, we are sadly in want of them as soldiers. We cannot spare one man, whereas the United States Government is willing to let their own soldiers remain in our prisons because she has no need of the men. I have a proposition to submit to you, which I think if we can carry out will bring about the desired exchange." There was a long and ominous silence which I at last was compelled to break by asking, "Well, Sir, what is your proposition?" He sat quiet for an instant, and then . . . in a whisper said, "it is to kidnap President Lincoln, and carry him off to Richmond!" "Kidnap President Lincoln!" I said. . . . I was amazed—thunderstruck—and in fact, I might also say, frightened at the unparalleled audacity of his scheme. After two day's reflection I told him I was willing to try it. I believed it practicable at that time, though I now regard it as a foolhardy undertaking. I hope you will not blame me for going thus far. I honestly thought an exchange of prisoners could be brought about could we have once obtained possession of Mr. Lincoln's person. And now reverse the case. Where is there a young man in the North with one spark of patriotism in his heart who would not have with enthusiastic ardor joined in any undertaking for the capture of Jefferson Davis and brought him to Washington? There is not one who would not have done so. And so I was led on by a sincere desire to assist the South in gaining her independence. I had no hesitation in taking part in anything honorable that might tend towards the accomplishment of that object. Such a thing as the assassination of Mr. Lincoln, I never heard spoken of by any member of the party. Never! . . .

It may be well to remark here that this scheme of abduction was concocted without the knowledge or assistance of the Confederate government in any shape or form. Booth and I often consulted together as to whether it would not be well to acquaint the authorities in Richmond with our plan, as we were sadly in want of money, our expenses being very heavy. In fact the question arose among us as to whether, after getting Mr. Lincoln, if we succeeded in our plan, the Confederate authorities would not surrender us to the United States again, because of doing this thing without their consent or knowledge. But we never acquainted them with the plan, and they never had anything in the wide world to do with it. In fact, we were jealous of our undertaking and wanted no outside help. I have not made this statement to defend the officers of the Confederate government. They are perfectly able to defend themselves. What I have done myself I am not ashamed to let the world know.

Source 16   Abraham Lincoln's former law partner, William H. Herndon, *The Life of Lincoln,* 1888

In the death of Lincoln the South, prostrate and bleeding, lost a friend; and his unholy taking-off at the very hour of the assured supremacy of the Union cause ran the iron into the heart of the North. His sun went down suddenly, and whelmed the country in a darkness which was felt by every heart; but far up the clouds sprang apart, and soon the golden light, flooding the heavens with radiance, illuminated every uncovered brow with the hope of a fair tomorrow. His name will ever be the watchword of liberty. His work is finished, and sealed forever with the veneration given to the blood of martyrs. Yesterday a man reviled and abused, a target for the shafts of malice and hatred: today an apostle. Yesterday a power: today a prestige, sacred, irresistible. The life and the tragic death of Mr. Lincoln mark an epoch in history from which dates the unqualified annunciation by the American people of the greatest truth in the bible of republicanism—the very keystone of that arch of human rights which is destined to overshadow and remodel every government upon the earth. The glorious brightness of that upper world, as it welcomed his faint and bleeding spirit, broke through upon the earth at his exit—it was drawn of a day growing brighter as the grand army of freedom follows in the march of time. . . .

This is the true lesson of Lincoln's life: real and enduring greatness, that will survive the corrosion and abrasion of time, of change, and of progress, must rest upon character. . . . Not eloquence, nor logic, nor grasp of thought; not statesmanship, nor power of command, nor courage; not any nor all of these have made him what he is, but these, in the degree in which he possessed them, conjoined to those qualities comprised in the term character, have given him his fame—have made him for all time to come the great American, the grand, central figure in American—perhaps in the world's—history.

Source 17   Lincoln's secretary John Nicolay and statesman John Hay, *Abraham Lincoln: A History,* 1890

The death of Lincoln awoke all over the world a quick and deep emotion of grief and admiration. If he had died in the days of doubt and gloom which preceded his reelection, he would have been sincerely mourned and praised by the friends of the Union, but its enemies would have curtly dismissed him as one of the necessary and misguided victims of sectional hate. They would have used his death to justify their malevolent forebodings, to point the moral of new lectures on the instability of democracies. But as he had fallen in the moment of a stupendous victory, the halo of a radiant success enveloped his memory and dazzled the eyes even of his most hostile critics.

Source 18 William A. Dunning, *Reconstruction: Political and Economic,* 1907

The first six weeks of Johnson's administration were dominated by the emotions which the assassination of his predecessor excited in all parts of the land. At Washington affairs fell largely under the direction of the secretary of war, whose total loss of self-control in the crisis contributed to intensify the panicky and vindictive feeling that prevailed. The idea that leading Confederates were concerned in Booth's plot . . . strengthened the hands of those who were demanding that the conquered people as a whole should receive harsh treatment. . . .

When, however, the excitement caused by the assassination of Lincoln subsided, and the suspicions that Davis and his associates had been concerned in the deed were seen by sane minds to be unfounded, conservative northern sentiment began to show alarm at the vindictive course to which the president seemed tending.

Source 19 W. E. B. Du Bois, *Black Reconstruction in America,* 1934

The tragic death of Lincoln has given currency to the theory that the Lincoln policy of Reconstruction would have been far better and more successful than the policy afterward pursued. If it is meant by this that Lincoln would have more carefully followed public opinion and worked to adjust differences, this is true. But Abraham Lincoln himself could not have settled the question of Emancipation, Negro citizenship and the vote, without tremendous difficulty.

Source 20 Kenneth M. Stampp, *The Era of Reconstruction,* 1965

To Lincoln, restoring the old relationship between the southern states and the Union was the essence of reconstruction. . . . For him, reconstruction was to be essentially a work of restoration, not of innovation; it was the old Union—the Union as it was—that he hoped to rebuild. . . .

Lincoln's plan of reconstruction, then, was designed to restore the southern states to the Union with maximum speed and with a minimum of federal intervention in their internal affairs. The great majority of white southerners would receive amnesty and full power to re-establish loyal state governments; Confederate leaders, with few exceptions, would receive special pardons when they applied for them. . . . The Negroes, if they remained, would be governed by the white men among whom they lived, subject only to certain minimum requirements of fair play. Such a program, in Lincoln's mind, was at once humane, politically practical, and constitutionally sound.

For a few years after Lincoln's death, a combination of northern humanitarians and radical Republicans overturned this conservative plan of reconstruction and came near to imposing upon the South a far-reaching social revolution, particularly in the relations of the two races. During the 1870's, however, conservative men regained control of the southern state governments, and the struggle to give political and legal equality to Negroes was virtually abandoned. . . .

This being the case, there would seem to be cause to revise somewhat the traditional images we have of the radical Republicans and of Lincoln. In some respects the radical leaders, rather than Lincoln, proved to be the sentimental idealists.

✍ Questioning the Past

1. What immediate and long-term effects did the assassination of Lincoln have on the development of America? Had Lincoln lived, would the restoration of the South to the Union and the reconstruction of the relations between the races have progressed any differently?

2. Though General Lee surrendered the Army of Northern Virginia on April 9, 1865, other Confederate armies continued to fight for several more weeks. The last land battle of the Civil War, a Confederate victory, was waged on May 12–13, 1865, along the Rio Grande at Palmetto. Confederate forces west of the Mississippi under General Kirby-Smith negotiated a surrender on May 26, 1865. Tens of thousands of Northern and Southern lives were lost before Lincoln's murder. Many lives, Northern and Southern, were lost following Lincoln's death. Why is the reaction of history more horrified by the wartime murder of a governmental leader than by the wartime deaths of 600,000 soldiers? Should a commander-in-chief be considered any less legitimate a target than the forces he commands?

3. A majority of the voters of the Union elected Lincoln to a second term in the White House. One man vetoed the decision of this majority. Since Lincoln's murder, other assassins have made attempts upon the lives of other presidents, three of which were successful. Can a democratic people have access to their public servants and protect them too? Can elected officials whose contact with their constituents must be filtered through a wall of security maintain an accurate feel for the public mood?

Glossary

ambuscaded went into the woods 11

animadvert literally, turn the mind to; notice or observe 107

Antinomian one who rejects religious or moral law in the belief that salvation is achieved by faith alone 87

Arawaks an Indian people native to South America and the West Indies, now living chiefly along the coast of Guyana 14

Austerlitz Czechoslovakian town where Napoleon's army of 65,000 defeated a Russian/Austrian force of 83,000; Napoleon lost only 10 percent of his soldiers 364

Babel biblical city where the building of a tower, according to the account in the Book of Genesis, was halted by the confusion of languages 163

bagatelle a game in which balls are rolled into scoring areas 69

barbette an armored structure protecting a gun turret on a warship 338

bark a small boat propelled by sails or oars 69

Barrowist follower of Isaac Barrow (1630–1677), a mathematician, theologian, priest in the Church of England, and author of *Treatise on the Pope's Supremacy* 87

battery group of warship guns 337

blue law in colonial New England, one of numerous very rigorous laws designed to regulate morals and conduct; later any statute regulating work, commerce, or amusement on Sundays 230

bombazine a twilled fabric of silk and worsted 237

bottoms boats or ships 108

Brownist follower of Robert Browne (1550?–1633?), an English Separatist clergyman who wrote several controversial works on religion and eventually emigrated with his followers to the Netherlands 87

Burgesses English term for borough representatives to Parliament; the colonists used the term for representatives to their legislature 38

busk obsolete word that probably meant undeveloped ear of corn; green corn was used in Cherokee dance rituals 254

cacique a native Indian chief in areas of predominantly Spanish culture 2

Camus, Albert (1913–1960) French writer of novels, essays, and plays 22

canaille rabble, riffraff 109

canister encased shot for close-range artillery fire 363

cannonade heavy artillery fire; bombardment 362

card implement used to clean and disentangle fibers; originally thistles or chard; later bent-wire teeth attached to a piece of leather 252

Cathay old name for China 16

Chatham English statesman William Pitt, first Earl of Chatham (1708–1778), who urged conciliation with the American colonies and called for the repeal of the Stamp Act 139

Cherokee name adopted by white settlers from the Creek/Muskogean word *tciloki*, meaning people of a different language; the Cherokees' own language was related to those of Iroquoian tribes 241

circumvallation surrounding an area, as with a rampart 10

City on the Hill from the Gospel of Matthew, the challenge of leading a life of virtue and religious faith when all eyes are upon one; image also used by John Winthrop in a sermon on board the ship bringing settlers to New England in 1630 63

condign deserved, appropriate 397

cosmographers scientists of the general nature of the world 18

Dismal Swamp now called the Great Dismal Swamp, a 750-square-mile region of southern Virginia and North Carolina; portions are heavily timbered and rich in game; the area includes the 22-mile-long Dismal Swamp Canal connecting Chesapeake Bay with the Albemarle (NC) Sound, as well as the 7-mile-long Lake Drummond 217

dragoons units of heavily armed mounted troops 274

ductile capable of being drawn out or hammered thin 11

durance restraint, such as by physical force 155

ell a former English unit of length, often used for cloth, and equal to about 45 inches 288

encomium warmly enthusiastic praise 166

enfilading gunfire from a flanking position along the length of an enemy battle line 367

equinoctial circle the Equator 18

fictile made of clay 11

fire and faggot to be burned at the stake with a bundle of flaming sticks 33

fowling pieces shotguns used for small game 217

glebe land cultivated fields belonging to the parish church 37

grape grapeshot; cluster of small iron balls shot from a cannon 363

hack saddle horse 250

Hector hero of the Trojans in their war with the Greeks, who slew Patroclus, friend of Achilles 101

hogshead a large cask or barrel holding up to 63 gallons 264

Hosea Hebrew prophet of the eighth century B.C. who urged Israel to return to the Lord; his name means salvation 331

idolaters idol worshipers 31

Jacobins members of a radical terrorist group in France in 1789 who advocated egalitarian democracy 179

Kronshtadt Russian city on an island near St. Petersburg, site of an anti-Bolshevik uprising on March 17, 1921, that was brutally crushed by Red Army troops 221

leap years feature of the calendar first used by Ptolemy III in 238 B.C. to keep the solar year from becoming increasingly out of synchronization with the changing seasons; called leap years because the dates in months after February "leap" two weekdays ahead of those in the prior year 119

letterbook a bound journal where the writer keeps copies of correspondence 124

Liberia small republic in West Africa established by the National Colonization Society, an American group founded in 1816 to repatriate freed slaves to Africa 233

Manifest Destiny a tenet holding that American expansion was not only inevitable but divinely ordained; the phrase was first used by journalist and diplomat John L. O'Sullivan in 1845 in support of the annexation of Texas 282

manumission emancipation of slaves 355

Massachusett an Algonquian tribe, people of the great hill country 48

mastic aromatic resin used in varnish 17

Mris abbreviation for Mistress, feminine form of Mister or Master, all of which indicated ownership or supervision rather than marital relationship 40

Narragansett an Algonquian tribe, people of the point; all Native American tribes of the East Coast were Algonquins, with similar languages 49

oligarchic describing a government in which a small group exercises control, especially for corrupt and selfish purposes 164

oppugnation fighting against 155

Pawtuxet an Algonquian place name, little falls, and tribe 51

Peare of England peer, or member of one of the five ranks (duke, marchess, earl, viscount, or baron) of the British peerage 96

pennon a long, usually triangular streamer 377

Penobscot Algonquian term for rocky slope 49

Pentelicus a mountain in the region of Athens, Greece, celebrated for its marble 7

Pequot an Algonquian tribal name meaning "the destroyers" 53

pikes heavy spears with very long shafts 2

pogroms organized massacres of groups of helpless people 384

poulder colonial spelling of (gun) powder; combination of Latin *pulver* and French *poudre* 40

recusant term for an English Catholic who refused to attend Anglican services, which was a statutory offense 88

right bank the side on the right of someone facing downstream; in this case, the eastern bank 85

Rio Grande Del Norte Spanish name for the river that forms the Texas-Mexico border; often shortened by Americans in the 1840s to Del Norte 273

Roundhead derogatory term for a Puritan, taken from their style of short-cropped hair, as distinguished from a Cavalier, or member of the parliamentary party of Charles I 87

sachem an Algonquian word for chief, or "he has the mastery" 47

selectmen members of official boards elected in all New England towns except those in Rhode Island to serve as the chief administrative authorities of the towns 230

shibboleth originally a Hebrew word for stream, different pronunciations of which betrayed people's regional origins; now a word or saying used by adherents of a party or cause, which opponents usually regard as empty of real meaning 197

Spartacus Thracian bandit captured and sold to a trainer of gladiators; he persuaded some 70 of his fellow prisoners to join him in escaping; with other runaway slaves, they formed a force that defeated several Roman armies over a two-year period 331

supputation obsolete word, originally from Latin, meaning to count up; similar to compute, to reckon or number 119

Thermopylae the pass where Leonidas's 300 Spartan soldiers defeated a very much larger Persian force under King Xerxes in 400 B.C. 367

Tilly and Wallenstein commanders of the Catholic League armies in the Thirty Years' War, begun in 1618, against European Protestants 60

Tournai city in Belgium that was a frequent battle site during the Napoleonic Wars 365

tumuli artificial hillocks or mounds 10

villinage a peasant who is tenured to his or her lord but remains legally free in respect of others 66

volley simultaneous discharge of a battery of weapons 338

Wampanoag an Algonquian tribe, people of the east 50

Western Antipodes lands on the opposite side of the world from Europe 18

wight a human being; from the Middle English word for creature 181

Yankees natives or residents of New England; said to be the Native American pronunciation of English, or Yenguese 135

Sources

Chapter 1: Mysterious Mounds

Source 1: James Mooney, *Myths of the Cherokee and Sacred Formulas of the Cherokee* (Nashville, TN: Charles Elder, 1972), pp. 336–337.

Source 2: Cyrus Thomas, "Report on the Mound Explorations of the Bureau of Ethnology," *Twelfth Annual Report of the Bureau of Ethnology, 1890–91* (Washington, D.C.: Government Printing Office, 1894), p. 647.

Source 3: Robert Silverberg, *Mound Builders of Ancient America: The Archeology of a Myth* (Greenwich, CT: New York Graphic Society, 1968), pp. 44–45. Copyright © 1968 by Robert Silverberg.

Source 4: Benjamin Smith Barton, "Observations on Some Parts of Natural History: An Account of Several Remarkable Vestiges of an Ancient Date, which Have Been Discovered in Different Parts of North America" (London: Benjamin Smith Barton, 1787), pp.18–27.

Source 5: Caleb Atwater, *Description of Antiquities Discovered in the State of Ohio and Other Western States* (New York: AMS Press, 1973), pp. 171–172.

Source 6: Ibid., pp 120–121, 209–210.

Source 7: Silverberg, p. 87.

Source 8: Silverberg, p. 83.

Source 9: George Bancroft, *History of the Colonization of the United States*, vol. III (London: John Murray, Albemarle Street, 1842), pp. 307–308.

Source 10: John D. Baldwin, "Ancient America," in *Notes on American Archaeology* (New York: Harper & Brothers, 1872) pp. 33–34, 58–61.

Source 11: Thomas, pp. 601, 615; Silverberg, p. 157.

Source 12: Thomas, pp. 631–632.

Source 13: J. W. Powell, "Report of the Director," *Twelfth Annual Report of the Bureau of Ethnology, 1890–91* (Washington, DC: U.S. Government Printing Office, 1894), pp. xxxix, xli–xlii, xliii–xliv.

Source 14: Silverberg, pp. 57–58. Reprinted by permission of Little, Brown.

Source 15: George E. Stuart, "Who Were the Mound Builders?" *National Geographic,* December 1972, pp. 786–787.

Source 16: Heather Pringle, "Oldest Mound Complex Found at Louisiana Site," *Science,* vol. 277, no. 5333, September 19, 1997, p. 1761.

Source 17: Colin Calloway, *First Peoples: A Documentary Survey of American Indian History* (Boston: Bedford/St. Martin's, 1999), pp. 22–24.

Chapter 2: Columbus

Source 1: Christopher Columbus, *The Diario of Christopher Columbus's First Voyage to America, 1492–1493,* abstracted by Fray Bartolomé de las Casas, trans. Oliver Dunn and James E. Kelley, Jr. (Norman, OK: University of Oklahoma Press, 1989), pp. 57–69. Copyright © 1989 by Oliver Dunn and James E. Kelley, Jr.

Source 2: Christopher Columbus, *The Journal of Christopher Columbus,* trans. Cecil Jane (New York: Clarkson N. Potter, 1960), pp. 191–201.

Source 3: John Boyd Thacher, *Christopher Columbus: His Life, His Work, His Remains* (New York: AMS Press, 1967), p. 59.

Source 4: Ibid., p. 536.

Source 5: William Robertson, *The History of the Discovery and Settlement of North America* (New York: Harper & Brothers, 1843), pp. 63–64.

Source 6: Richard Hildreth, *The History of the United States of America,* vol. 1 (New York: Harper & Brothers, 1880), p. 33.

Source 7: Woodrow Wilson, *A History of the American People,* vol. 1 (New York: Harper & Brothers, 1902), p. 6–7.

Source 8: John Fiske, *The Discovery of America,* vol. 2 (New York: Houghton Mifflin, 1902), pp. 131–132.

Source 9: Henry Bamford Parkes, *The American Experience* (New York: Vintage Books, a division of Random House, Inc., 1959), p. 15.

Source 10: Samuel Eliot Morison, *The Oxford History of the American People* (New York: Mentor Books, 1972), p. 55.

Source 11: Alfred W. Crosby, Jr., *The Columbian Exchange: Biological and Cultural Consequences of 1492*

(Westport, CT: Greenwood Publishing, 1972), pp. xiv, 3, 218–219. Reprinted by permission of Greenwood Publishing Group, Inc., Westport, CT.

Source 12: Howard Zinn, *A People's History of the United States* (New York: Harper & Row, 1980), pp. 7–11, 17. Copyright © 1980 by Howard Zinn. Reprinted by permission of HarperCollins Publishers, Inc.

Source 13: Stuart B. Schwartz, *The Iberian Mediterranean and the Atlantic Traditions in the Formation of Columbus as a Colonizer* (Minneapolis: University of Minnesota, the Associates of the James Ford Bell Library, 1986), p. 15.

Source 14: J. M. Roberts, *The Pelican History of the World* (London: Penguin Books, 1987), p. 496.

Source 15: Kirkpatrick Sale, *The Conquest of Paradise: Christopher Columbus and the Columbian Legacy* (New York: Alfred A. Knopf, 1990), p. 3. Copyright © 1990 by Kirkpatrick Sale. Reprinted by permission of Alfred A. Knopf, Inc.

Source 16: Paolo Emilio Taviani, *Columbus, the Great Adventure*, trans. Luciano F. Farina and Marc A. Beckweth (New York: Orion Books, 1991), pp. 260–261. Copyright © 1991 by ERI. Reprinted by permission of Crown Publishers, Inc.

Source 17: Edwin M. Yoder, "Columbus Discovers Pasadena," *Washington Post,* November 24, 1991, pp. C1–2. Copyright © 1991 by The Washington Post Writers Group. Reprinted by permission.

Source 18: Boris Biancheri, "Good Guy Columbus: For Europe, the Explorer's Voyage Hastened the Renaissance," *Washington Post,* October 4, 1992.

Source 19: Peter H. Gibbon, "Apologize for Columbus?," *Washington Post,* October 12, 1998, A21. Copyright © by The Washington Post.

Chapter 3: The Requirement

Source 1: William Robertson, *The History of the Discovery and Settlement of America* (New York: Harper & Brothers, 1843), pp. 459–460.

Source 2: Lewis Hanke, *The Spanish Struggle for Justice in the Conquest of America* (Philadelphia: University of Pennsylvania Press, 1949), pp. 27–28. Copyright © 1949 by American Historical Association. Reprinted by permission of University of Pennsylvania Press.

Source 3: Ibid., p. 32.

Source 4: Arthur Helps, *The Spanish Conquest in America* (London and New York: John Lane, 1900), p. 277.

Source 5: William H. Prescott, *History of the Conquest of Mexico and the History of the Conquest of Peru* (New York: Modern Library, 1979), p. 940.

Source 6: Hanke, pp. 122–123.

Source 7: Ibid., p. 7.

Source 8: Robertson, p. 99.

Source 9: Prescott, pp. 275–276.

Source 10: Helps, pp. 269, 271.

Source 11: Hanke, pp. 34–35.

Source 12: Gerhard von Glahn, *Law Among Nations* (New York: Macmillan Publishing, 1986), pp. 311–312. Copyright © 1986 by Macmillan College Publishing Company, Inc. Reprinted by permission of Macmillan College Publishing Company

Chapter 4: Jamestown

Source 1: Lyon Gardiner Tyler, ed., *Narratives of Early Virginia: 1606–1625* (New York: Charles Scribner's Sons, 1907), p. 285.

Source 2: Philip L. Barbour, ed., *The Complete Works of Captain John Smith,* vol. 2 (Chapel Hill: University of North Carolina Press, 1986), pp. 267–269. Published for the Institute of Early American History and Culture, Williamsburg, VA. Copyright © 1986 by University of North Carolina Press. Used by permission of the publisher. (It is probable that John Smith edited the words of John Rolfe in this selection.)

Source 3: Ibid., p. 269.

Source 4: Susan Myra Kingsbury, *The Records of the Virginia Company of London,* vol. III (Washington, DC: U.S. Government Printing Office, 1933), pp. 153–177.

Source 5: Susan Myra Kingsbury, *The Records of the Virginia Company of London,* vol. I (Washington, DC: U.S. Government Printing Office, 1906), pp. 256–257.

Source 6: Ibid., p. 566.

Source 7: William Robertson, *The History of the Discovery and Settlement of America* (New York: Harper & Brothers, 1843), p. 412.

Source 8: George Bancroft, *History of the United States of America, from the Discovery of the Continent* (New York: D. Appleton, 1888), pp. 112, 113, 119, 126.

Source 9: John Fiske, *Old Virginia and Her Neighbors,* vol. 1 (Boston: Houghton Mifflin, 1897). pp. 188–189.

Source 10: Ernest R. Groves, *The American Woman: The Feminine Side of a Masculine Civilization* (New York: Arno Press, 1972), pp. 43–44. Reprinted by permission of Ayer Company Publishers, Inc.

Source 11: Abbot Emerson Smith, *Colonists in Bondage: White Servitude and Convict Labor in America, 1607–1776* (Chapel Hill: University of North Carolina Press, 1971), pp. 226–227. Published for the Institute of Early American History and Culture, Williamsburg, VA. Copyright © 1947 renewed 1975 by the University of North Carolina Press. Used by permission of the author and publisher.

Source 12: John Hope Franklin, *From Slavery to Freedom: A History of Negro Americans* (New York: Alfred A. Knopf, 1974), pp. 56–57. Copyright © 1947, 1956, 1967, 1974, 1980 by Alfred A. Knopf, Inc. Reprinted by permission of the publisher.

Source 13: Eleanor Flexner, *Century of Struggle: The Women's Rights Movement in the United States* (Cambridge, MA: Belknap Press of Harvard University Press, 1975), pp. 3–4.

Source 14: Carl Bridenbaugh, *Jamestown, 1544–1699* (New York: Oxford University Press, 1980), p. 53.

Chapter 5: Samoset and Squanto

Source 1: William Bradford, *Bradford's History "Of Plimoth Plantation"* (Boston: Wright & Potter Printing, State Printers, 1898), pp. 94–95.

Source 2: Ibid., pp. 114–116.

Source 3: J. Franklin Jameson, ed., *Johnson's Wonder-Working Providence, 1628–1651* (New York: Charles Scribner's Sons, 1910), pp. 41–43.

Source 4: William Robertson, *The History of the Discovery and Settlement of America* (New York: Harper & Brothers, 1843), p. 432.

Source 5: Richard Hildreth, *The History of the United States of America*, vol. 1 (New York: Harper & Brothers, 1880), p. 161.

Source 6: John Fiske, *The Beginnings of New England* (Boston: Houghton Mifflin, 1902), pp. 101–103.

Source 7: Andrew C. McLaughlin, *A History of the American Nation* (New York: D. Appleton, 1913), pp. 52–54.

Source 8: James Truslow Adams, *The Epic of America* (Boston: Little, Brown, 1931), pp. 28–29.

Source 9: Henry Bamford Parkes, *The American Experience* (New York: Vintage Books, 1959), pp. 29–30.

Source 10: Amelia G. Bingham, *Mashpee: Land of the Wampanoags* (Mashpee, MA: Mashpee Historical Commission, 1970), p. 29.

Source 11: T. J. Brasser, "Early Indian-European Contacts," *Handbook of North American Indians*, vol. 15, Bruce G. Trigger, ed. (Washington, DC: Smithsonian Institution, 1978), p. 78.

Source 12: Robert F. Berkhofer, Jr., "White Conceptions of Indians," *Handbook of North American Indians*, vol. 4 (Washington, DC: Smithsonian Institution, 1988), p. 535.

Chapter 6: Fort Mystic

Source 1: Charles M. Segal and David C. Stineback, *Puritans, Indians, and Manifest Destiny* (New York: G. P. Putnam's Sons, 1977), 132–133. Used by permission of the authors.

Source 2: William Bradford, *Bradford's History "Of Plimoth Plantation"* (Boston: Wright & Potter Printing, State Printers, 1898), pp. 419, 423–426.

Source 3: Segal and Stineback, pp. 110, 135–37.

Source 4: Bradford, pp. 419, 423–426.

Source 5: James Kendell Hosmer, ed., *Winthrop's Journal* (New York: Charles Scribner's Sons, 1908), p. 220.

Source 6: Bradford, pp. 427, 429–430.

Source 7: J. Franklin Jameson, *Johnson's Wonder-Working Providence, 1628–1651* (New York: Charles Scribner's Sons, 1910), p. 170.

Source 8: John Oldmixon, *The British Empire in America*, vol. 1 (New York: Augustus M. Kelley Publishers, 1969), pp. 72–73.

Source 9: Thomas Hutchinson, *The History of the Colony and Province of Massachusetts Bay*, vol. 1, Lawrence Shaw Mayo, ed. (Cambridge, MA: Harvard University Press, 1936), pp. 69–70.

Source 10: William Robertson, *The History of the Discovery and Settlement of America* (New York: Harper & Brothers, 1843), pp. 442–444.

Source 11: George Bancroft, *History of the United States of America, from the Discovery of the Continent*, vol. 1 (New York: D. Appleton, 1888), pp. 267–268.

Source 12: John Fiske, *The Beginnings of New England, or the Puritan Theocracy in its Relations to Civil and Religious Liberty* (Boston: Houghton Mifflin, 1902), pp. 162–163.

Source 13: Woodrow Wilson, *A History of the American People*, vol. 1 (New York: Harper & Brothers, 1902), pp. 153–154.

Source 14: Segal and Stineback, pp. 108–109.

Source 15: James Axtell, *The European and the Indian* (New York: Oxford University Press, 1981), pp. 138–139.

Source 16: Gary B. Nash, *Red, White, and Black: The Peoples of Early America* (Englewood Cliffs, New Jersey: Prentice Hall, 1982), pp. 84–86. Adapted by permission of Prentice Hall, Inc.

Source 17: Yasuhide Kawashima, "Indian Servitude in the Northeast," *Handbook of North American Indians*, vol. 4 (Washington, DC: Smithsonian Press, 1988), p. 404.

Source 18: "Mashantucket Pequot Tribal Nation-History," 1998. Reprinted by courtesy of the Mashantucket Pequot Tribal Nation.

Chapter 7: Slavery

Source 1: Albert P. Blaustein and Robert L. Zangrando, *Civil Rights and the American Negro: A Documentary History* (New York: Washington Square Press, 1968), p. 8.

Source 2: Leslie H. Fishel, Jr., and Benjamin Quarles, *The Black American: A Documentary History* (Glenview, Illinois: Scott, Foresman & Company, 1976), pp. 20–21. The spelling and punctuation have been modernized.

Source 3: Blaustein and Zangrando, pp. 20–21.

Source 4: Fishel and Quarles, pp. 21–22.

Source 5: Blaustein and Zangrando p. 69.

Source 6: Paul Leicester Ford, *The Works of Thomas Jefferson*, vol. XII, (New York: G.P. Putnam's Sons, 1905), pp. 158–160.

Source 7: Fishel and Quarles, pp. 150–151.

Source 8: Robet Young Hayne, "On Foot's Resolution," Mayo W. Hazeltine, ed., *Masterpieces of Eloquence: Famous Orations of Great World Leaders from Early Greece to the Present Time*, vol. XII (New York: P.F. Collier & Son, 1905), pp. 4984–4986.

Source 9: Daniel Webster, "The Reply to Hayne," Mayo W. Hazeltine, ed., *Masterpieces of Floquence: Famous Orations of Great World Leaders from Early Greece to the Present Time*, vol. X (New York: P.F. Collier & Son, 1905), pp. 4314–4315.

Source 10: Herbert Aptheker, *And Why Not Every Man? Documentary Story of the Fight against Slavery in the U.S.* (New York: International Publishers, 1970), pp. 132–133.

Source 11: Horace Mann, "The Institution of Slavery," Mayo W. Hazeltine, ed., *Masterpieces of Eloquence: Famous Orations of Great World Leaders from Early Greece to the Present Time*, vol. XIII (New York: P.F. Collier & Son, 1905), pp. 5342–5344.

Source 12: Orestes Augustus Brownson, "Oration on Liberal Studies," Mayo W. Hazeltine, ed., *Masterpieces of Eloquence: Famous Orations of Great World Leaders from Early Greece to the Present Time*, vol. XIV (New York: P.F. Collier & Son, 1905), pp. 5893–5894.

Source 13: Victor Cousin, "The True, the Beautiful, and the Good" Mayo W. Hazeltine, ed., *Masterpieces of Eloquence: Famous Orations of Great World Leaders from Early Greece to the Present Time,* vol. XII (New York: P.F. Collier & Son, 1905), pp. 5015–5016.

Source 14: Richard Hildreth, *Despotism in America: An Inquiry into the Nature, Results, and Legal Basis of the Slave-holding System in the United States* (Boston: John P. Jewett & Company, 1854), pp. 35–36.

Source 15: James Henry Hammond, *Congressional Globe,* 35th Congress, 1st Session, pp. 961–962.

Source 16: William Henry Seward, "On the Irrepressible Conflict," Mayo W. Hazeltine, ed., *Masterpieces of Eloquence: Famous Orations of Great World Leaders from Early Greece to the Present Time*, vol. XIV (New York: P.F. Collier & Son, 1905), pp. 5710–5714.

Source 17: "Another Step of Slavery," *New York Times,* September 29, 1859, p. 3.

Source 18: Charles L. Flint, C.F. McCay, J.C. Merriam, and Thomas Kettrell, *Eighty Years' Progress of the United States: A Family Record of American Industry, Energy, and Enterprise* (Hartford, CT: L. Stebbins, 1868), pp. 199–221.

Source 19: John Fiske, *Old Virginia and Her Neighbors,* vol. II (Boston: Houghton Mifflin Company, 1897), pp. 325–327.

Source 20: Ulrich Bonnell Phillips, *Life and Labor in the Old South* (Boston: Little, Brown, 1929), p. 3.

Source 21: Charles A. and Mary R. Beard, *The Beards' Basic History of the United States* (New York: Doubleday, Doran, 1944), pp. 34–35.

Source 22: Kenneth M. Stampp, *The Peculiar Institution: Slavery in the Ante-Bellum South* (New York: Vintage Books, 1956), pp. 3–5. Copyright © by Kenneth M. Stampp. Reprinted by permission of Alfred A. Knopf, Inc., a division of Random House, Inc.

Source 23: Eugene D. Genovese, *The Political Economy of Slavery: Studies in the Economy of the Slave South* (New York: Vintage Books, 1967), pp. 7–8.

Source 24: Richard Claxton Gregory, *No More Lies: The Myth and the Reality of American History* (New York: Perennial Library, Harper & Row, 1972), p. 44.

Source 25: John Hope Franklin, *From Slavery to Freedom: A History of Negro Americans* (New York: Alfred A. Knopf, 1974), pp. 56–57.

Source 26: David Brion Davis, *The Problem of Slavery in Western Culture* (New York: Oxford University Press, 1988), pp. 9–10.

Chapter 8: An Act of Toleration

Source 1: Woodrow Wilson, *A History of the American People*, vol. 1 (New York: Harper & Brothers, 1902), p. 130a.

Source 2: William Hand Browne, *George Calvert and Cecilius Calvert, Barons Baltimore* (New York: Dodd Mead, 1890), pp. 147–148.

Source 3: Ibid., p. 149.

Source 4: William Stevens Perry, ed., *Historical Collections Relating to the American Colonial Church*, vol. 4 ([Printed for Subscribers] Hartford, CT: 1878), pp. 24–25.

Source 5: Ibid., pp. 41–42.

Source 6: John Oldmixon, *The British Empire in America,* vol. 1 (New York: Augustus M. Kelley Publishers, 1969), p. 330.

Source 7: E. Milton Altfield, *The Jew's Struggle for Religious and Civil Liberty in Maryland,* (Baltimore, MD: M. Curlander, 1924), pp. 70–75.

Source 8: Ibid., pp. 77–78.

Source 9: John Leeds Bozman, *The History of Maryland, from Its First Settlement to the Restoration in 1660,* vol. 2 (Bowie, MD: Heritage Books, 1990), pp. 351–352.

Source 10: Francis Newton Thorpe, *The Federal and State Constitutions, Colonial Charters, and Other Organic Laws of the States, Territories, and Colonies Now or Hereafter Forming the United States of America,* vol. 3 (Washington, DC: U.S. Government Printing Office, 1909), pp. 1715–1716.

Source 11: Ibid., p. 1782.

Source 12: George Bancroft, *History of the United States of America, from the Discovery of the Continent,* vol. 1 (New York: D. Appleton, 1888), p. 169.

Source 13: Wilson, pp. 126, 127, 129.

Source 14: Herbert L. Osgood, *The American Colonies in the Seventeenth Century,* vol. 2 (New York: Macmillan, 1904), pp. 319–320.

Source 15: William O. Douglas, *The Right of the People* (New York: Arena Books, 1972), p. 90.

Source 16: Charles M. Andrews, *The Colonial Period of American History,* vol. 2 (New Haven: Yale University Press, 1936), pp. 310–311.

Source 17: Douglas, p. 90.

Chapter 9: Bacon's Rebellion

Source 1: Warren M. Billings, *The Old Dominion in the Seventeenth Century: A Documentary History of Virginia, 1607–1689* (Chapel Hill: University of North Carolina Press, 1975), p. 267. Published for the Institute of Early American History and Culture, Williamsburg, VA. Copyright © 1975 by University of North Carolina Press. Used by permission of the publisher.

Source 2: Ibid., 267–269.

Source 3: Ibid., pp. 271–272.

Source 4: Ibid., pp. 272–273.

Source 5: Ibid., pp. 273–274.

Source 6: William Sherwood, "Virginia's Deploured Condition," in the Massachusetts Historical Society, *Collections* series 4, vol. 9, 1871, pp. 170–172.

Source 7: Virginius Dabney, *Virginia: The New Dominion* (Charlottesville: University Press of Virginia, 1971), pp. 62–63.

Source 8: Wilcomb E. Washburn, *The Governor and the Rebel: A History of Bacon's Rebellion in Virginia* (Chapel Hill: University of North Carolina Press, 1957), p. 59. Published for the Institute of Early American History and Culture, Williamsburg, VA. Copyright © 1957 by University of North Carolina Press. Used by permission of the publisher.

Source 9: Sherwood, pp. 170–172.

Source 10: Thomas Jefferson Wertenbaker, *Virginia under the Stuarts, 1607–1688* (New York: Russell & Russell, 1959), p. 171.

Source 11: *Virginia Magazine of History and Biography,* vol. 1 (Richmond, VA: Richmond Historical Society, 1893) pp. 53–58.

Source 12: Howard Zinn, *A People's History of the United States* (New York: Harper & Row, 1980), p. 39. Copyright © 1980 by Howard Zinn. Reprinted by permission of HarperCollins Publishers, Inc.

Source 13: Robert Beverley, *The History and Present State of Virginia,* Louis B. Wright, ed. (Chapel Hill: University of North Carolina Press, 1947), pp. 74–75. Published for the Institute of Early American History and Culture, Williamsburg, VA. Copyright © 1947 by University of North Carolina Press. Used by permission of the publisher.

Source 14: Jane Carson, *Bacon's Rebellion, 1676–1976* (Jamestown, VA: The Jamestown Foundation, 1976), p. 65

Source 15: John Oldmixon, *The British Empire in America,* vol. 1 (New York: Augustus M. Kelley Publishers, 1969), pp. 382, 387.

Source 16: Edmund Randolph, *History of Virginia,* ed. Arthur H. Shaffer (Charlottesville: University of Virginia Press, for the Virginia Historical Society, 1970), pp. 155–156.

Source 17: George Bancroft, *History of the United States,* vol. 2. (Boston: Little, Brown, 1855), pp. 228–229, 232–233.

Source 18: Wertenbaker, p. v.

Source 19: Frederick Jackson Turner, *Frontier and Section* (Englewood Cliffs, New Jersey: Prentice Hall, Inc., 1961), p. 80.

Source 20: Wertenbaker, pp. 151, 164, 194, 223.

Source 21: Louis B. Wright, *The First Gentlemen of Virginia: Intellectual Qualities of the Early Colonial Ruling Class* (Charlottesville: University of Virginia Press, 1964), pp. 76–77.

Source 22: Washburn, pp. 1–2, 162–163, 166.

Source 23: Dabney, pp. 67–68.

Source 24: Wilcomb E. Washburn, "Seventeenth Century Indian Wars," in *Handbook of North American Indians,* vol. 15, Bruce G. Trigger, ed. (Washington, DC: Smithsonian Institution,

1978), p. 97. Reprinted by permission of Smithsonian Institution Press.

Chapter 10: The Zenger Trial

Source 1: James Alexander, *A Brief Narrative of the Case and Trial of John Peter Zenger,* Stanley Nider Katz, ed. (Cambridge, MA: Belknap Press of Harvard University Press, 1972), p. 100. Copyright © 1963, 1972 by the President and Fellows of Harvard College.

Source 2: Ibid., pp. 41–42.

Source 3: *New York Weekly Journal,* November 12, 1733.

Source 4: *New York Weekly Journal,* January 28, 1734.

Source 5: *New York Weekly Journal,* April 8, 1734.

Source 6: Alexander, pp. 58–101.

Source 7: Ibid., p. 100.

Source 8: Ibid., p. 98.

Source 9: Ibid., pp. 175, 176, 178, 179.

Source 10: Ibid., p. 181.

Source 11: John Oldmixon, *The British Empire In America,* vol. 1 (New York: Augustus M. Kelley Publishers, 1969), pp. 266–267.

Source 12: Salma Hale, *History of the United States,* (New York: Harper & Brothers, 1841), pp. 137–138.

Source 13: George Bancroft, *History of the Colonization of the United States,* vol. 3 (Boston: Little, Brown, 1842), pp. 393–394.

Source 14: Carl Degler, *Out of Our Past: The Forces that Shaped Modern America* (New York: Harper Colophon Books, 1970), pp. 65–66. Copyright © 1959, 1970 by Carl Degler. Reprinted by permission of HarperCollins Publishers, Inc.

Source 15: Alexander, pp. 1–2.

Chapter 11: Eleven Days that Never Were

Source 1: *Virginia Gazette,* August 16, 1751. The draft of the statute as published left blank the dates; they have been added.

Source 2: Gail S. Cleere, "Eleven Lost Days," *Natural History,* September 1991, p. 78. Copyright © 1991 by the American Museum of Natural History. Reprinted by permission of *Natural History.*

Chapter 12: Eliza Lucas

Source 1: Harriott Horry Ravenel, *Eliza Pinckney* (New York: Charles Scribner's Sons, 1896), pp. 5–6.

Source 2: Elise Pinckney, ed., *The Letterbook of Eliza Lucas Pinckney* (Chapel Hill: University of North Carolina Press, 1972), pp. 5–6. Courtesy of the South Carolina Historial Society.

Source 3: Ibid., p. 8.

Source 4: Ibid., p. 16.

Source 5: Ibid., p. 30.

Source 6: Ibid., p. 31.

Source 7: Ibid., pp. 32–33.

Source 8: Ibid., pp. 34–35.

Source 9: Ibid., pp. xxiii–xiv.

Source 10: Ravenel, pp. 307–310.

Source 11: Ibid., pp. 322–323.

Source 12: Kenneth M. Stampp, *The Peculiar Institution: Slavery in the Ante-Bellum South* (New York: Vintage Books, 1956), pp. 11–13. Copyright © 1956 by Kenneth M. Stampp. Reprinted by permission of Alfred A. Knopf, Inc.

Source 13: George C. Rogers, *Charleston in the Age of the Pinckneys* (Norman: University of Oklahoma Press, 1969), pp. 10–11.

Source 14: Gerda Lerner, *The Woman in American History* (Menlo Park, CA: Addison-Wesley Publishing, 1971), pp. 17–19.

Source 15: Pinckney, pp. xix–xx.

Source 16: Norman K. Risjord, *Representative Americans: The Colonists* (Lexington, MA: D.C. Heath, 1981), pp. 217, 222–223.

Chapter 13: The American Revolution

Source 1: "General Gage's Account of the Late Battle at Boston," *Virginia Gazette of the Norfolk Intelligencer,* May 25, 1775.

Source 2: *Spy & Oracle of Liberty,* (Worcester, MA: May 3, 1775).

Source 3: Woodrow Wilson, *A History of the American People,* vol. 2 (New York: Harper & Brothers, 1902), p. 218.

Source 4: Thomas Paine, *Common Sense and the Crisis* (Garden City, NY: Anchor Books, 1973), p. 69.

Source 5: Charles Francis Adams, ed., *The Works of John Adams,* vol. 10 (Boston: Little, Brown, 1856), pp. 282–283.

Source 6: Salma Hale, *History of the United States, from their First Settlement as Colonies to the Close of the Administration of Mr. Madison,* vol. 1 (New York: Harper & Brothers, 1841), p. 220.

Source 7: Richard Hildreth, *The History of the United States of America,* vol. 3 (New York: Harper & Brothers, 1880), pp. 390–391.

Source 8: George Bancroft, *History of the United States,* vol. 4 (Boston: Little, Brown, 1855), p. 12.

Source 9: Ralph Waldo Emerson, "The Minute-Man," in Mayo W. Hazeltine, ed., *Masterpieces of Eloquence: Famous Orations of Great World Leaders from Early Greece to the Present Time* (New York: P.F. Collier & Son, 1905), pp. 6001–6002.

Source 10: John Fiske, *The American Revolution*, vol. 2 (Boston: Houghton Mifflin, 1902), pp. 350–351.

Source 11: Wilson, pp. 215–217.

Source 12: Andrew C. McLaughlin, *A History of the American Nation* (New York: D. Appleton, 1913), pp. 152–153.

Source 13: Claude H. Van Tyne, *The Causes of the War of Independence*, vol. 1 (Boston: Houghton Mifflin, 1922), pp. 7, 9, 17–18.

Source 14: Charles M. Andrews, "The American Revolution: An Interpretation," *American Historical Review*, XXXI (January, 1926), pp. 218–232.

Source 15: James Truslow Adams, *The Epic of America* (Boston: Little, Brown, 1932), pp. 81–82.

Source 16: John C. Miller, *Origins of the American Revolution* (Boston: Little, Brown, 1943), pp. 25, 216–217. Copyright © 1943, 1959 by John C. Miller. Excerpted by permission of the publishers.

Source 17: Charles A. and Mary R. Beard, *The Beards' Basic History of the United States* (New York: Doubleday, Doran, 1944), pp. 87–90, 92. Copyright © 1944, 1960, 1968, by Doubleday, a division of Bantam Doubleday Dell Publishing Group, Inc. Used by permission of Doubleday, a division of Random House, Inc.

Source 18: Winston S. Churchill, *A History of the English-Speaking People* (New York: Bantam Books, 1963), p. 141.

Source 19: Lawrence Henry Gipson, *The Triumphant Empire: Thunder-Clouds in the West, 1763–1766*, vol. 10 of *The British Empire before the American Revolution* (New York: Alfred A. Knopf, 1961), pp. 282–283. Copyright © 1961 by Alfred A. Knopf, Inc. Reprinted by permission of the publisher.

Source 20: Carl Degler, *Out of Our Past: The Forces That Shaped Modern America* (New York: Harper Colophon, 1970), pp. 73–74, 75, 76, 77, 81. Copyright © 1959, 1970 by Carl N. Degler. Reprinted by permission of HarperCollins Publishers, Inc.

Source 21: Samuel Eliot Morison, *The Oxford History of the American People*, vol. 1 (New York: Mentor Books, 1971), p. 275.

Source 22: Howard Zinn, *A People's History of the United States* (New York: Harper & Row, 1980), pp. 59, 60–61. Copyright © 1980 by Howard Zinn. Reprinted by permission of HarperCollins Publishers, Inc.

Chapter 14: The Declaration of Independence

Source 1: Julian P. Boyd, ed., *The Papers of Thomas Jefferson* vol. 1, 1770–1776 (Princeton: Princeton University Press, 1950), p. 298.

Source 2: Ibid., pp. 309–313. (According to Boyd, Jefferson wrote these notes on the proceedings sometime between August 1, 1776, and June 1, 1783.)

Source 3: The Declaration of Independence.

Source 4: John H. Hazelton, *The Declaration of Independence: Its History* (New York: Dodd, Mead, 1906), pp. 166–168.

Source 5: Ibid., p. 253.

Source 6: Ibid., pp. 234–235.

Source 7: Robert Ginsberg, ed., *A Casebook on the Declaration of Independence* (New York: Thomas Y. Crowell, 1967), pp. 9–11.

Source 8: Malcolm Freiberg, ed., *Thomas Hutchinson's Strictures upon the Declaration of the Congress at Philadelphia; In a Letter to a Noble Lord, &c. (London 1776)* (Boston: The Old South Association, Old South Meeting-House), pp. 10–11, 30.

Source 9: Hazelton, p. 586.

Source 10: Richard B. Heffner, ed., *A Documentary History of the United States* (New York: Mentor Books, 1965), pp. 133, 135, 136–137.

Source 11: Ginsberg, pp. 61–62.

Source 12: Ibid., pp. 64–65. (Both this statement and the preceding remarks of Douglas were made on July 17, 1858, at Springfield, Illinois.)

Source 13: George Bancroft, *History of the United States of America*, vol. 4 (New York: D. Appleton, 1886), p. 450.

Source 14: Carl Becker, *The Declaration of Independence: A Study in the History of Political Ideas* (New York: Harcourt, 1922), pp. 5–8, 225–226.

Source 15: John C. Miller, *Origins of the American Revolution* (Boston: Little, Brown, 1943), p. 493.

Source 16: Samuel Eliot Morison, *The Oxford History of the American People,* vol. 1 (New York: Mentor Books, 1971), p. 296.

Source 17: Howard Zinn, *A People's History of the United States* (New York: Harper & Row, 1980), pp. 73–75. Copyright © 1980 by Howard Zinn. Reprinted by permission of HarperCollins Publishers, Inc.

Chapter 15: The Constitution

Source 1: James Madison, *Journal of the Federal Convention* (Chicago: Scott Foresman, 1898), pp. 741–743, 744, 746–747.

Source 2: Ibid. pp. 748, 763.

Source 3: Jonathon Elliot, *The Debates of the Several State Conventions, on the Adoption of the Federal Constitution*, vol. 1 (Philadelphia: J. B. Lippincott, 1859), p. 503.

Source 4: George Bancroft, *History of the United States of America*, vol. 6 (New York: D. Appleton, 1912), p. 380.

Source 5: Ibid., p. 408.

Source 6: Elliot, pp. 496–497.

Source 7: Elliot, vol. 3, p. 30.

Source 8: Ibid., p. 36.

Source 9: Ibid., pp. 44–46, 58–59.

Source 10: Ibid., pp. 208–209, 211, 217.

Source 11: Ibid., p. 222.

Source 12: Truman Nelson, Documents of Upheaval: Selections from William Lloyd Garrison's The Liberator, 1831–1865 (New York: Hill & Wang, 1966), pp. 55–56.

Source 13: Alexis de Tocqueville, *Democracy in America,* Richard D. Heffner, ed. (New York: Mentor Books, 1961), pp. 78–79.

Source 14: Richard Hildreth, *The History of the United States of America,* vol. 3 (New York: Harper & Brothers, 1880), p. 534.

Source 15: Bancroft, pp. 442–443.

Source 16: J. Allen Smith, *The Spirit of American Government,* Cushing Strout, ed. (Cambridge, MA: Belknap Press of Harvard University Press, 1965), pp. 29–32, 36–39. Copyright © 1965 by the President and Fellows of Harvard College. Reprinted by permission of the Belknap Press of Harvard University Press.

Source 17: Charles A. Beard, *An Economic Interpretation of the Constitution of the United States* (New York: Macmillan, 1929), pp. 325–326. Copyright © 1935 by Macmillan Publishing Company, renewed 1963 by William Beard and Miriam Beard Vagts. Excerpted by permission of Scribner, a division of Simon & Schuster, Inc.

Source 18: James Truslow Adams, *The Epic of America* (Boston: Little, Brown, 1932), pp. 108–109.

Source 19: Merrill Jensen, *The New Nation: A History of the United States during the Confederation, 1781–1789* (New York: Alfred A. Knopf, 1950), pp. xiii–xiv.

Source 20: Eric F. Goldman, *Rendezvous with Destiny* (New York: Alfred A. Knopf, 1952), p. 87.

Source 21: Robert E. Brown, *Charles Beard and the Constitution: A Critical Analysis of "An Economic Interpretation of the Constitution"* (Princeton, NJ: Princeton University Press, 1956), pp. 196–200. Copyright © 1956, renewed 1984 by the publisher.

Source 22: Henry Steele Commager, "Introduction," in Andrew C. McLaughlin, *The Foundations of American Constitutionalism* (New York: Fawcett Publications, 1966), pp. vii–viii.

Source 23: Forrest McDonald, *E Pluribus Unum: The Formation of the American Republic, 1776–1790* (Boston: Houghton Mifflin, 1965), pp. 191–194. Copyright © 1965 by Forrest McDonald. Reprinted by permission of Sterling Lord Literistics, Inc.

Source 24: Thomas R. Dye and L. Harmon Zeigler, *The Irony of Democracy: An Uncommon Introduction to American Politics* (Belmont, CA: Duxbury Press, 1971), p. 54.

Source 25: Howard Zinn, *A People's History of the United States* (New York: Harper & Row, 1980), pp. 98–99. Copyright © 1980 by Howard Zinn. Reprinted by permission of HarperCollins Publishers, Inc.

Chapter 16: The Alien and Sedition Acts

Source 1: Richard Hildreth, *The History of the United States of America,* vol. 5 (New York: Harper & Brothers, 1880), pp. 233, 235.

Source 2: James Morton Smith, *Freedom's Fetters: The Alien and Sedition Laws and American Civil Liberties* (Ithaca, New York: Cornell University Press, 1966), p. 435.

Source 3: Ibid., p. 438.

Source 4: Ibid., p. 440.

Source 5: Ibid., p. 441–442.

Source 6: The *Columbian Mirror & Alexandria Gazette,* August 9, 1798.

Source 7: John Marshall, letter, *Providence Gazette,* October 27, 1798.

Source 8: *Philadelphia Aurora,* October 12, 1799.

Source 9: *The Argus, Greenleaf's New Daily Advertiser,* New York, October 15, 1799.

Source 10: Ibid.

Source 11: Ibid.

Source 12: John C. Miller, *Crisis in Freedom: The Alien and Sedition Acts* (Boston: Little, Brown, 1951), p. 113.

Source 13: *Philadelphia Aurora,* November 13, 1799.

Source 14: Woodrow Wilson, *A History of the American People,* vol. 3 (New York: Harper & Brothers, 1902), pp. 336, 339–340.

Source 15: Ibid., p. 344.

Source 16: John Nicholas, "On the Proposed Repeal of the Sedition Law," in Alexander Johnston, *American Eloquence: Studies in American Political History* (New York: G. P. Putnam's Sons, 1896), pp. 135–136.

Source 17: James D. Richardson, ed., *Messages and Papers of the Presidents,* vol. 1 (Washington, DC: U.S. Government Printing Office, 1896), p. 322.

Source 18: William O. Douglas, *The Right of the People* (New York: Arena Books, 1972), p. 106.

Source 19: Hildreth, pp. 229–230, 301–302.

Source 20: J. Allen Smith, *The Spirit of American Government* (Cambridge, MA: Belknap Press of Harvard University Press, 1965), pp. 165–66.

Copyright © 1965 by the President and Fellows of Harvard College. Reprinted by permission of the Belknap Press of Harvard University Press.

Source 21: James Truslow Adams, *The Epic of America* (Boston: Little, Brown, 1931), pp. 134–135.

Source 22: Charles A. and Mary R. Beard, *The Beards' Basic History of the United States* (New York: Doubleday, Doran, 1944), pp. 168–169. Copyright © 1944, 1960, 1968, by Doubleday, a division of Bantam Doubleday Dell Publishing Group, Inc. Used by permission of Doubleday.

Source 23: Miller, pp. 232–233.

Source 24: James Marton Smith, *Freedom's Fetters: The Alien and Sedition Laws and American Civil Liberties* (Ithaca, New York: Cornell University Press, 1966), pp. 419–420, 432. Copyright © 1956 by Cornell University. Used by permission of the publisher.

Source 25: Douglas, pp. 28–29, 106.

Chapter 17: The Monroe Doctrine

Source 1: James D. Richardson, ed., *Messages and Papers of the Presidents* (Washington, DC: U.S. Government Printing Office, 1896) vol. 2, pp. 209, 217–219.

Source 2: *National Intelligencer* (Washington, DC), December 8, 1823.

Source 3: Norman A. Graebner, *Ideas and Diplomacy: Readings in the Intellectual Tradition of American Foreign Policy* (New York: Oxford University Press, 1964), p. 214.

Source 4: Ibid.

Source 5: *National Intelligencer* (Washington, DC), December 8, 1823.

Source 6: Dexter Perkins, *The Monroe Doctrine, 1823–1826* (Cambridge, MA: Harvard University Press, 1927), pp. 30–31. Reprinted by permission.

Source 7: Ibid., p. 30.

Source 8: Richardson, vol. 4, pp. 398–399.

Source 9: *Congressional Globe*, 29th Cong., 1st sess., pp. 245–246.

Source 10: *Congressional Globe*, 30th Cong., 1st sess., pp. 609–610, 613.

Source 11: J. Lloyd Mecham, *A Survey of United States-Latin American Relations* (Boston: Houghton Mifflin, 1965), p. 62.

Source 12: Gustave Koerner, "The True Monroe Doctrine," *The Nation* (January 5, 1882), pp. 9–11.

Source 13: U.S. Department of State, *Papers Relating to the Foreign Relations of the United States*, Part 1, (Washington, DC: U.S. Government Printing Office), pp. 553–562.

Source 14: Ibid., pp. 563–567.

Source 15: Thomas Brockway, *Basic Documents in United States Foreign Policy* (Princeton, NJ: Van Nostrand, 1957), p. 73.

Source 16: Covenant of the League of Nations, Article 21.

Source 17: Dexter Perkins, *The Monroe Doctrine, 1823–1826; Harvard Historical Studies, # 29* (Cambridge, MA: Harvard University Press, 1927), pp. 159–160. Copyright © 1927 by the President and Fellows of Harvard College. Reprinted by permission of Harvard University Press.

Source 18: Julius W. Pratt, *The History of United States Foreign Policy*, 3rd ed. (Englewood Cliffs, NJ: Prentice Hall, 1955), p. 608. Copyright © 1972 by Prentice Hall.

Source 19: Mecham, p. 80.

Source 20: Samuel Flagg Bemis, *John Quincy Adams and the Foundations of American Foreign Policy* (New York: Alfred A. Knopf, 1969), pp. 406–407.

Source 21: Gaddis Smith, *The Last Years of the Monroe Doctrine, 1945–1993* (New York: Hill & Wang, 1994), pp. 70–71. Copyright © 1994 by Gaddis Smith. Reprinted by permission of Hill & Wang, a division of Farrar, Straus & Giroux, LLC.

Source 22: Pratt, pp. 167–168.

Source 23: Thomas A. Bailey, *A Diplomatic History of the American People*, 10th ed. (Englewood Cliffs, NJ: Prentice Hall, 1974), p. 189. Copyright © 1980 by Prentice Hall.

Source 24: Smith, pp. 65–71.

Chapter 18: Uniting the States

Source 1: *Alexandria Gazette,* July 8, 1828.

Source 2: Ibid.

Source 3: Ibid. (The paragraph in parenthesis was moved from a different part of the article.)

Source 4: *Daily National Intelligencer,* July 4, 1828.

Source 5: J. L. Ringwalt, *Development of Transportation Systems in the United States* (Philadelphia: Ringwalt, Railway World Office, 1888), p. 49.

Source 6: Charles Fling, C. F. Mackay, J. C. Merriam, and Thomas P. Kettrell, *Eighty Years' Progress of the United States: A Family Record of American Industry, Energy, and Enterprise* (Hartford, CT: L. Stebbins, 1868), pp. 172–173, 185, 190, 221.

Source 7: Ringwalt, p. 384.

Source 8: Walter S. Sanderlin, *The Great National Project: A History of the Chesapeake and Ohio Canal* (Baltimore: The Johns Hopkins University Press, 1946), pp. 288–289. Reprinted by permission of the Johns Hopkins University Press.

Source 9: Carter Goodrich, "The Revulsion against Internal Improvements," *Journal of Economic His-*

tory, vol. 10, no. 2 (November 1950), pp. 165–168. Reprinted by permission of Cambridge University Press.

Source 10: George Rogers Taylor, *The Transportation Revolution, 1815–1860* (New York: Harper & Row, 1968), pp. 396, 398.

Source 11: Carl Degler, *Out of Our Past: The Forces That Shaped Modern America* (New York: Harper & Row, 1970), pp. 110–111. Copyright © 1959, 1970 by Carl N. Degler. Reprinted by permission of HarperCollins Publishers, Inc.

Chapter 19: Nat Turner

Source 1: Nat Turner: *The Confessions of Nat Turner,* 1831, pp. 3–8.

Source 2: *Daily National Intelligencer* (Washington, DC), September 20, 1831. The account is reprinted from an Arkansas paper.

Source 3: Turner, pp. 3–8.

Source 4: "The Insurrection," *Daily National Intelligencer,* August 29, 1831; and in Henry Irving Tragle, *The Southampton Slave Revolt of 1831: A Compilation of Source Material* (New York: Vintage Books, 1973), p. 38.

Source 5: Turner, pp. 3–8.

Source 6: *Daily National Intelligencer* (Washington, DC), August 29, 1831.

Source 7: Ibid., August 27, 1831.

Source 8: *Alexandria Gazette,* September 1, 1831.

Source 9: Ibid., August 30, 1831.

Source 10: Ibid., September 1, 1831.

Source 11: *Daily National Intelligencer* (Washington, DC), September 15, 1831.

Source 12: Ibid., September 20, 1831.

Source 13: *Alexandria Gazette,* October 18, 1831.

Source 14: *Maryland Gazette,* October 27, 1831.

Source 15: Turner, pp. 3–8.

Source 16: *Maryland Gazette,* November 10, 1831.

Source 17: Eric Foner, ed., *Nat Turner (Great Lives Observed)* (Englewood Cliffs, NJ: Prentice Hall, 1971), p. 51.

Source 18: *Daily National Intelligencer* (Washington, DC), September 20, 1831.

Source 19: Ibid., September 22, 1831.

Source 20: *Maryland Gazette,* October 20, 1831.

Source 21: *Alexandria Gazette,* November 14, 1831.

Source 22: *Alexandria Gazette,* October 26, 1831.

Source 23: Tragle, p. 153.

Source 24: Ibid., p. 324.

Source 25: Thomas Wentworth Higginson, "Nat Turner's Insurrection," *Atlantic Monthly* (August 1861), p. 173.

Source 26: John Esten Cooke, *Virginia: A History of the People* (Boston: Houghton Mifflin, 1888), pp. 485–487.

Source 27: Ulrich B. Phillips, *American Negro Slavery,* (New York: D. Appleton, 1918), pp. 482, 484.

Source 28: John W. Cromwell, "The Aftermath of Nat Turner's Insurrection," *The Journal of Negro History,* vol. 5 (1920), pp. 233–234.

Source 29: Russel B. Nye, *Fettered Freedom: Civil Liberties and the Slavery Controversy, 1830–1860* (East Lansing: Michigan State University Press, 1972), p. 67.

Source 30: Kenneth M. Stampp, *The Peculiar Institution: Slavery in the Ante-Bellum South* (New York: Vintage Books, 1956), pp. 132–33. Copyright © 1956 by Kenneth M. Stampp. Reprinted by permission of Alfred A. Knopf, Inc.

Source 31: Ossie Davis, "Nat Turner: Hero Reclaimed," *Freedomways,* vol. 8, no. 3 (Summer 1968), p. 231.

Source 32: John Hope Franklin, *From Slavery to Freedom: A History of Negro Americans* (New York: Alfred A. Knopf, 1974), p. 162. Copyright © 1947, 1956, 1967, 1974, 1980 by Alfred A. Knopf, Inc. Reprinted by permission of the publisher.

Source 33: Stephen B. Oates, *The Fires of Jubilee: Nat Turner's Fierce Revolt* (New York: Mentor Books, 1976), pp. 164–166.

Chapter 20: Prudence Crandall

Source 1: *The Liberator,* April 13, 1833. (This ad appeared beginning in the issue of March 2, 1833, and was carried in subsequent editions over the following eighteen months.)

Source 2: Ibid., April 6, 1833

Source 3: *The Abolitionist,* vol. 1, no. 4, pp. 62–63.

Source 4: *The Liberator,* April 6, 1833.

Source 5: *The Liberator,* April 6, 1833.

Source 6: *The Abolitionist,* vol. 1, no. 4, p. 61.

Source 7: *The Liberator,* May 18, 1833.

Source 8: Ibid., May 25, 1833.

Source 9: William Jay, *An Inquiry into the Character & Tendency of the American Colonization and American Anti-Slavery Societies* (New York: Leavitt, Lord, 1835; Boston: Crocker & Brewster, 1835).

Source 10: Edwin W. Small and Miriam R. Small, "Prudence Crandall: Champion of Negro Education," *New England Quarterly,* vol. 17, no. 4, December 1944, pp. 528–529.

Source 11: James Schouler, *History of the United States under the Constitution,* vol. 4 (New York: Dodd, Mead, 1894), pp. 209–210.

Source 12: Small and Small, p. 513.

Source 13: Dwight Lowell Dumond, *Antislavery: The Crusade for Freedom in America* (Ann Arbor: University of Michigan Press, 1961), pp. 211, 212. Copyright 1961 © by the University of Michigan.

Source 14: Russel B. Nye, *Fettered Freedom: Civil Liberties and the Slavery Controversy, 1830–1860* (East Lansing: Michigan State University Press, 1972), pp. 106–107.

Source 15: Alma Lutz, *Crusade for Freedom: Women of the Antislavery Movement* (Boston: Beacon Press, 1968), pp. 44–45.

Source 16: Eleanor Flexner, *Century of Struggle: The Woman's Rights Movement in the United States* (Cambridge, MA: Belknap Press of Harvard University Press, 1975), pp. 39–40.

Chapter 21: The Cherokee Removal

Source 1: Jeremiah Evarts, *Cherokee Removal*, ed. Francis Paul Prucha (Knoxville: University of Tennessee Press, 1981), pp. 261–262.

Source 2: Albert Weinberg, *Manifest Destiny: A Study of Nationalist Expansionism in American History* (Chicago: Quadrangle Books, 1963), p. 83.

Source 3: Glen Fleischmann, *The Cherokee Removal, 1838: An Entire Indian Nation Is Forced Out of Its Homeland* (New York: Franklin Watts, 1971), pp. 49, 50; and John P. Brown, *Old Frontiers* (New York: Arno Press, 1971), p. 506.

Source 4: Gary E. Moulton, ed., *The Papers of Chief John Ross*, vol. 1 (Norman: University of Oklahoma Press, 1985), p. 636, Norman. Copyright © 1985 by University of Oklahoma Press, Norman.

Source 5: Grant Foreman, *Indian Removal: The Emigration of the Five Civilized Tribes of Indians* (Norman: University of Oklahoma Press, 1966), p. 296. Copyright © 1932, 1953, and 1972 by University of Oklahoma Press, Norman.

Source 6: Moulton, p. 649.

Source 7: Ibid., p. 673.

Source 8: Ibid., p. 684.

Source 9: Ibid., pp. 687–688.

Source 10: James D. Richardson, ed., *Messages and Papers of the Presidents, 1789–1897*, vol. 3 (Washington, DC: Bureau of National Literature and Art, 1901), pp. 497–498.

Source 11: *Daily National Intelligencer* (Washington, DC), December 8, 1838.

Source 12: Foreman, pp. 306–307.

Source 13: Ibid., p. 309.

Source 14: Fleischmann, p. 73.

Source 15: Wilson Lumpkin, *The Removal of the Cherokee Indians from Georgia* (New York: Dodd, Mead, 1907), pp. 181–182.

Source 16: Helen Hunt Jackson, *A Century of Dishonor: The Early Crusade for Indian Reform* (New York: Harper Torchbooks, 1962), pp. 270–272.

Source 17: James Schouler, *History of the United States under the Constitution*, vol. 4 (New York: Dodd, Mead, 1894), pp. 236–238.

Source 18: James Mooney, *Historical Sketch of the Cherokee* (Chicago: Aldine Publishing, 1975), pp. 124–125, 127.

Source 19: Ulrich B. Phillips, *Georgia and States Rights* (Washington, DC: U.S. Government Printing Office, 1902), pp. 68, 70, 71.

Source 20: Foreman, pp. 306–307.

Source 21: Weinberg, pp. 73, 77, 87, 99.

Source 22: E. Merton Coulter, *Georgia: A Short History* (Chapel Hill: University of North Carolina Press, 1947), pp. 232, 236–237. Copyright © 1933, renewed 1961 by University of North Carolina Press. Used by permission of the publisher.

Source 23: William L. Anderson, ed., *Cherokee Removal: Before and After* (Athens: University of Georgia Press, 1991), p.93.

Source 24: Theda Purdue and Michael Green, *The Cherokee Removal: A Brief History with Documents* (Boston: St. Martins, 1995), pp. 174–175. Copyright © 1993, 1995 by St. Martin's Press. Reprinted by permission of Bedford/St. Martin's Press, Inc.

Chapter 22: The Texas Question

Source 1: Clyde Wilson, ed., *The Papers of John C. Calhoun*, vol. 17 (Columbia: University of South Carolina Press), p. 329.

Source 2: St. George Leakin Sioussat, "John Caldwell Calhoun," in *The American Secretaries of State and Their Diplomacy*, vol. 5, Samuel Flagg Bemis, ed. (New York: Cooper Square Publishers, 1963), pp. 141–142.

Source 3: *Alexandria Gazette and Virginia Advertiser*, May 1, 1844.

Source 4: Richard J. Walker, "Letter of Mr. Walker, of Mississippi, Relative to the Annexation of Texas," in Frederick and Lois Merk, *Fruits of Propaganda in the Tyler Administration* (Cambridge, MA: Harvard University Press, 1971), pp. 233–235.

Source 5: *Alexandria Gazette and Virginia Advertiser*, March 8, 1844.

Source 6: Ibid., February 29, 1844.

Source 7: Ibid., March 2, 1844.

Source 8: Ibid., March 1, 1844.

Source 9: Ibid.

Source 10: Ibid.

Source 11: Wilson, pp. 809–810. Reprinted by permission of the University of South Carolina Press.

Source 12: *Alexandria Gazette and Virginia Advertiser,* March 2, 1844.

Source 13: Ibid., March 5, 1844.

Source 14: Ibid., March 8, 1844.

Source 15: Wilson, p. 879.

Source 16: Henry Clay, "Mr. Clay on the Texas Question," *Alexandria Gazette and Virginia Advertiser,* April 29, 1844.

Source 17: Martin Van Buren, letter of April 20, 1844, in *Alexandria Gazette and Virginia Advertiser,* April 30, 1844.

Source 18: James D. Richardson, ed., *Messages and Papers of the Presidents* (Washington, DC: U.S. Government Bureau of National Literature and Art, 1909), pp. 307–313.

Source 19: John Quincy Adams, *The Diary of John Quincy Adams, 1794–1845,* Allan Nevins, ed. (New York: Longmans, Green, 1928), p. 570.

Source 20: Ibid., pp. 573–574.

Source 21: Henry A. Wise, *Seven Decades of the Union* (Philadelphia: J. B. Lippincott, 1881), pp. 220–225.

Source 22: Mary M. Brown, *A School History of Texas* (Dallas, TX: Mary M. Brown, 1894), p. 219.

Source 23: Ephraim Douglass Adams, *British Interests and Activities in Texas, 1838–1846* (Baltimore: Johns Hopkins University Press, 1910), pp. 229–230.

Source 24: Charles M. Wiltse, *John C. Calhoun,* vol. 3 (New York: Russell & Russell, 1968), pp. 161–162.

Source 25: Frederick Merk, "A Safety Valve Thesis and Texan Annexation," *The Mississippi Valley Historical Review,* vol. 49 (December 1962), pp. 413, 423.

Source 26: Robert Seager II, *And Tyler Too* (New York: McGraw-Hill, 1963), p. 214–215, 217.

Source 27: Merk & Merk, pp. 26–27.

Source 28: Norma Lois Peterson, *The Presidencies of William Henry Harrison and John Tyler* (Lawrence: University of Kansas Press, 1989), p. 205.

Chapter 23: War with Mexico

Source 1: James K. Polk, *Polk: The Diary of a President, 1845–1849,* Milo Milton Quaife, ed. (Chicago: A. C. Clung, 1910), pp. 384–386.

Source 2: Ibid., pp. 390–393.

Source 3: James D. Richardson, ed., *Messages and Papers of the Presidents,* vol. 4 (Washington, DC: U.S. Government Bureau of National Literature and Art, 1901), pp. 441–442.

Source 4: *New York Tribune,* May 12, 1846.

Source 5: Polk, pp. 393–394.

Source 6: Richardson, p. 470.

Source 7: Polk, pp. 437, 438.

Source 8: Frederick Merk, *Manifest Destiny and Mission in American History: A Reinterpretation* (New York: Alfred A. Knopf, 1963), p. 159.

Source 9: Louis Filler, ed., *Abolition and Social Justice in the Era of Reform* (New York: Harper & Row, 1972), pp. 278–280.

Source 10: Samuel Eliot Morison, Frederick Merk, Frank Freidel, *Dissent in Three Wars,* (Cambridge, MA: Harvard University Press, 1970), p. 44.

Source 11: David Bruce Johnson and Kirk H. Porter, *National Party Platforms, 1840–1972* (Urbana: University of Illinois Press, 1975), p. 11.

Source 12: Roy P. Basler, ed., *The Collected Works of Abraham Lincoln,* vol. 1 (New Brunswick, NJ: Rutgers University Press, 1953), pp. 437–439. Copyright © 1953 by Abraham Lincoln Association. Reprinted by courtesy of the Abraham Lincoln Association.

Source 13: Richardson, pp. 587–589.

Source 14: *Daily National Intelligencer* (Washington, DC), July 7, 1848.

Source 15: Abiel Abbot Livermore, *The War with Mexico Reviewed* (Boston: Wm. Crosby and H. P. Nichols, 1850), pp. 6–8.

Source 16: Ray Allen Billington, *The Far Western Frontier, 1830–1860* (New York: Harper & Row, 1956), p. 172. Copyright © 1956 by Harper & Row, Publishers, Inc. Reprinted by permission of HarperCollins Publishers, Inc.

Source 17: James Ford Rhodes, *History of the United States from the Compromise of 1850* (New York: Macmillan, 1904), pp. 75–76, 87, 93.

Source 18: Albert K. Weinberg, *Manifest Destiny: A Study of Nationalist Expansionism in American History* (Chicago: Quadrangle Books, 1963), pp. 100–101.

Source 19: Norman Graebner, *Empire on the Pacific: A Study in American Continental Expansion* (New York: John Wiley & Sons, 1955), pp. 218, 220, 224–225, 228. Reprinted by permission of John Wiley & Sons, Inc.

Source 20: Julius W. Pratt, *A History of United States Foreign Policy,* 3rd ed. (Englewood Cliffs, NJ: Prentice Hall, 1955), pp. 237–238. Copyright © 1972 by Prentice Hall.

Source 21: Billington, p. 172.

Chapter 24: The Seneca Falls Convention

Source 1: Eleanor Flexner, *Century of Struggle* (Cambridge, MA: Belknap Press of Harvard University Press, 1975), p. 74.

Source 2: Ellen Carol DuBois, ed., *Elizabeth Cady Stanton, Susan B. Anthony Correspondence, Writings, Speeches* (New York: Schocken Books, 1981), pp. 28–31.

Source 3: *Women's Rights Conventions: Seneca Falls & Rochester, 1848* (New York: Arno & The New York Times), pp. 5–7. Ayer Company Publishers, Inc., Salem, NH.

Source 4: Elizabeth Frost and Kathryn Cullen-DuPont, *Women's Suffrage in America: An Eyewitness Account* (New York: Facts on File, 1992), pp. 85–86. Copyright © 1992 by Elizabeth Frost and Kathryn Cullen-DuPont.

Source 5: Ibid., p. 87.

Source 6: Philip S. Foner, *The Life and Writings of Frederick Douglass: Early Years, 1817–1849* (New York: International Publishers, 1950), pp. 320–321.

Source 7: Frost and Cullen-DuPont, pp. 87–88.

Source 8: Ibid., pp. 88–89.

Source 9: Ibid., p. 89.

Source 10: Mari Jo Buhle and Paul Buhle, *The Concise History of Woman Suffrage: Selections from the Classic Work of Stanton, Anthony, Gage, and Harper* (Urbana: University of Illinois Press, 1978), p. 104.

Source 11: DuBois, pp. 209–212.

Source 12: Elizabeth Cady Stanton, *Eighty Years and More (1815–1897): Reminiscences of Elizabeth Cady Stanton* (New York: European Publishing Company, 1898), pp. 148–149.

Source 13: James Schouler, *History of the United States under the Constitution*, vol. 5 (New York: Dodd, Mead, 1904), pp. 263–265.

Source 14: Carrie Chapman Catt and Nettie Rogers Shuler, *Woman Suffrage and Politics: The Inner Story of the Suffrage Movement* (New York: Charles Scribner's Sons, 1926), p. 20.

Source 15: Barbara Welter, "The Cult of True Womanhood: 1820–1860," *American Quarterly* (Summer 1966). Reprinted by permission of the author and the Johns Hopkins University Press.

Source 16: Miriam Gurko, *The Ladies of Seneca Falls: The Birth of the Woman's Rights Movement* (New York: Schocken Books, 1976), pp. 102–3.

Source 17: Gerda Lerner, *The Majority Finds Its Past: Placing Women In History* (New York: Oxford University Press, 1979), pp. 27, 28, 29–30. Copyright © 1967 by Gerda Lerner.

Source 18: Lois Banner, *Elizabeth Cady Stanton: A Radical for Woman's Rights* (Boston: Little, Brown, 1980), p. 41.

Chapter 25: Oil

Source 1: Edwin C. Bell, *History of Petroleum: Life of Col. Edwin L Drake* (Titusville: The Bugle Print, 1900), pp. 38–40.

Source 2: J. Stanley Clark, *The Oil Century: From the Drake Well to the Conservation Era* (Norman, Oklahoma: University of Oklahoma Press, 1958), pp. 30–31.

Source 3: Bell, pp. 94–102.

Source 4: "Col. Drake, Who Sank the First Oil Well in Pennsylvania," *New York Times,* November 10, 1880.

Source 5: Anthony Sampson, *The Seven Sisters: The Great Oil Companies and the World They Shaped,* (New York: The Viking Press, 1975), p. 24. Copyright © 1985 by Anthony Sampson. Reprinted by permission of Sterling Lord Literistic, Inc.

Source 6: Henry D. Lloyd, *Wealth against Commonwealth* (Washington, DC: National Home Library Foundation, 1936), pp. 36–38.

Source 7: IDA M. Tarbell, *The History of the Standard Oil Company,* David M. Chambers, ed., (New York: W.W. Norton 1966), pp. 209, 213–214,216–217, 223–224.

Source 8: Harold L. Ickes, *Fightin' Oil* (New York: Alfred A. Knopf, 1943), pp. 6–7.

Source 9: Hans J. Morgenthau, *Politics among Nations: The Struggle for Power and Peace* 1st ed. (New York: Alfred A. Knopf, 1948), p. 84.

Source 10: Clark, pp. 3124–3125.

Source 11: Harold F. Williamson and Arnold R. Daum, *The American Petroleum Industry: The Age of Illumination,* 1859–1899 (Evanston: Northwestern University Press, 1959), p. 81.

Source 12: John B. Rae, *The American Automobile: A Brief History* (Chicago: University of Chicago Press, 1965), pp 48–49. Reprinted by permission of the publisher.

Source 13: Sampson, pp. 70–71, 373–374.

Source 14: U.S. Government, *Public Papers of the Presidents of the United States, Containing the Public Messages, Speeches, and Statements of the President: Jimmy Carter,* 1977, Book 1 (Washington, DC: Government Printing Office, 1977), pp. 656–662.

Source 15: James Earl Carter, "State of the Union Address," *Department of State Bulletin* vol. 80, no. 2035, February, 1980, pp. A–D.

Source 16: Hans J. Morgenthau and Kenneth W. Thompson, , *Politics among Nations: The Struggle for Power and Peace,* 6th ed. (New York: Alfred

A. Knopf, 1985), pp. 133–135. Copyright © 1985 by Alfred A. Knopf, Inc. Reprinted by permission of Alfred A. Knopf, Inc., a division of Random House, Inc.

Source 17: Jim Wallis, "The Forgotten Moral Issues," *The Progressive,* March 1991, pp. 30-31.

Chapter 26: Harper's Ferry

Source 1: *Alexandria Gazette and Virginia Advertiser,* October 18, 1859.

Source 2: Ibid., October 19, 1859.

Source 3: Ibid.

Source 4: Elijah Avey, *The Capture and Execution of John Brown: An Eyewitness Account* (New York: Apollo Editions, 1971), p. 72.

Source 5: *Alexandria Gazette and Virginia Advertiser,* October 19, 1859.

Source 6: Truman Nelson, *The Old Man: John Brown at Harper's Ferry* (New York: Holt, Rinehart & Winston, 1973), pp. 187–97. Copyright © 1973 by Truman Nelson.

Source 7: Richard Warch and Jonathon Fanton, eds., *John Brown* (Englewood Cliffs, NJ: Spectrum Books, 1973), pp. 119–120.

Source 8: Louis Filler, ed., *Wendell Phillips on Civil Rights and Freedom* (New York: Hill & Wang, 1965), pp. 101–102. Copyright © by Louis Filler.

Source 9: Warch and Fanton, p. 86.

Source 10: Ibid., p. 87.

Source 11: Filler, pp. 106–107.

Source 12: Oswald Garrison Villard, *John Brown, 1800–1859: A Biography Fifty Years After* (Gloucester, MA: Peter Smith, 1965), p. 509.

Source 13: Ibid.

Source 14: *Alexandria Gazette and Virginia Advertiser,* December 3, 1959.

Source 15: *New York Tribune,* December 3, 1859.

Source 16: *The Liberator,* December 16, 1859.

Source 17: Warch and Fanton, p. 113.

Source 18: Ibid., p. 112.

Source 19: Ibid., pp. 115–116.

Source 20: Donald Bruce Johnson and Kirk H. Porter, *National Party Platforms, 1840–1972* (Chicago: University of Chicago Press, 1975), p. 32.

Source 21: Kenneth M. Stampp, ed., *The Causes of the Civil War* (Englewood Cliffs, NJ: Prentice Hall, 1974), pp. 84–85.

Source 22: James Schouler, *History of the United States under the Constitution,* vol. 5 (New York: Dodd, Mead, 1904), pp. 433–434, 435–38.

Source 23: W. E. B. Du Bois, *John Brown* (Northbrook, IL: Metro Books, 1972) pp. 338–339.

Source 24: Villard, p. 509.

Source 25: C. Vann Woodward, *The Burden of Southern History* (New York: Mentor Books, 1968), pp. 43–44

Source 26: Louis Ruchames, *The Making of a Revolutionary* (New York: Grosset & Dunlap, 1969), p. 38, n. 38. Copyright © 1969 by Louis Ruchames.

Source 27: Benjamin Quarles, ed., *Blacks on John Brown* (Urbana: University of Illinois Press, 1972), pp. 124–25.

Source 28: Stephen B. Oates, *To Purge This Land with Blood: A Biography of John Brown* (New York: Harper & Row, 1970), pp. 331–333. Copyright © 1969 by Stephen B. Oates. Reprinted by permission of HarperCollins Publishers, Inc.

Source 29: John Hope Franklin, *From Slavery to Freedom: A History of Negro Americans* (New York: Alfred A. Knopf, 1974), pp. 211–212.

Source 30: Bernard Bailyn, et al., *The Great Republic* (Lexington, MA: D. C. Heath, 1977), pp. 636–637.

Source 31: John A. Garraty and Robert A. McCaughey, *The American Nation: A History of the United States* (New York: Harper & Row, 1991), pp. 406–407.

Chapter 27: Civil War

Source 1: Gideon Welles, *Diary of Gideon Welles* (Boston: Houghton Mifflin, 1911), pp. 3–4.

Source 2: *Alexandria Gazette and Virginia Advertiser.*

Source 3: Mary Boykin Chesnut, *A Diary From Dixie* (Boston: Houghton Mifflin, 1949), p. 36.

Source 4: *Alexandria Gazette and Virginia Advertiser,* April 15, 1861.

Source 5: Frank Moore, ed., *The Rebellion Record,* vol. 1 (New York: G. P. Putnam, 1861), pp. 166–75.

Source 6: James D. Richardson, ed., *Messages and Papers of the Presidents,* vol. 6 (Washington, DC: U.S. Government Printing Office, 1897), pp. 20–31.

Source 7: Henry Wilson, "Speech on Bill to Confiscate the Property and Free the Slaves of Rebels," Mayo W. Hazeltine, ed., *Masterpieces of Eloquence: Famous Orations of Great World Leaders from Early Greece to the Present Time,* vol. XVII, (New York: P. F. Collier & Son, 1905), pp. 7224–7226.

Source 8: Clement L. Vallandigham, "Speech on the War and Its Conduct," Mayo W. Hazeltine, ed., *Masterpieces of Eloquence: Famous Orations of Great World Leaders from Early Greect to the Present Time,"* vol. XIX, (New York; P. F. Collier & Son, 1905), pp. 8138–8139.

Source 9: Edward Pollard, *The Lost Cause: A New Southern History of the War of the Confederates* (New York: E. B. Treat, 1866), pp. 46–51.

Source 10: Alexander H. Stephens, *A Constitutional View of the Late War between the States,* vol. 1, (Philadelphia: National Publishing Company, 1868), pp. 9–10.

Source 11: Henry Wilson, *The History of the Rise and Fall of Slavepower in America* (Boston: Osgood & Company, 1877), pp. 127–128.

Source 12: James Ford Rhodes, *Lectures on the American Civil War* (New York: The Macmillan Company, 1913), pp. 2, 6.

Source 13: Charles and Mary Beard, *The Rise of American Civilization* (New York: Macmillan Company, 1933), vol. 1, pp. 632–633, vol. 2, pp. 53–54. Copyright © 1933 by Macmillan Publishing Company, Inc. Renewed 1961 by William Beard and Miriam B. Vagts. Reprinted by permission of Simon & Schuster, Inc.

Source 14: Allan Nevins, *The Emergence of Lincoln*, vol. 2, (New York: Charles Scribner's Sons, 1950), p. 468.

Source 15: David Donald, *Lincoln Reconsidered: Essays on the Civil War Era* (New York: Vintage Books, 1961), pp. 215, 217, 226–228, 233–235. Copyright © 1947, 1950, 1951, 1956 by David Donald. Reprinted by permission of Alfred A. Knopf, Inc.

Source 16: Eugene Genovese, *The Political Economy of Slavery: Studies in the Economy and Society of the Slave South* (New York: Vintage Books, 1967), p. 8.

Source 17: Howard Zinn, *A People's History of the United States* (New York: Harper & Row, 1980), p. 184. Copyright © 1980 by Howard Zinn. Reprinted by permission of HarperCollins Publishers, Inc.

Chapter 28: The Emancipation Proclamation

Source 1: Roy P. Basler, ed., *The Collected Works of Abraham Lincoln*, vol. 5 (New Brunswick, NJ: Rutgers University Press, 1953), pp. 371–374. Copyright © 1953 by Abraham Lincoln Association. Reprinted by courtesy of the Abraham Lincoln Association.

Source 2: Ibid., pp. 388–389.

Source 3: Ibid., p. 420.

Source 4: Benjamin Quarles, *Lincoln and the Negro* (New York: Oxford University Press, 1962), p. 132. Copyright © 1962 by Oxford University Press, Inc. Reprinted by permission of Oxford University Press, Inc.

Source 5: *Evening Star*, Washington, DC, January 1, 1863.

Source 6: *Alexandria Gazette,* January 3, 1863.

Source 7: *New York Times,* January 3, 1863.

Source 8: Albert P. Blaustein and Robert L. Zangrabdo, *Civil Rights and the American Negro: A Documentary History* (New York: Washington Square Press, 1968), pp. 203, 205.

Source 9: George M. Fredrickson, *The Inner Civil War: Northern Intellectuals and the Crisis of the Union* (New York: Harper & Row, 1968), p. 119.

Source 10: John Greenleaf Whittier, "The Proclamation," *Atlantic Monthly*, (February 1863), p. 241.

Source 11: Basler, pp. 407–408.

Source 12: Paul M. Angle, ed., *Herndon's Life of Lincoln* (New York: Albert & Charles Boni, 1936), pp. 442–443.

Source 13: John Nicolay and John Hay, *Abraham Lincoln: A History* (New York: Century, 1914), pp. 436–437.

Source 14: James Ford Rhodes, *History of the United States from the Compromise of 1850* (New York: Macmillan, 1900), pp. 214–215.

Source 15: David Donald, *Lincoln Reconsidered: Essays on the Civil War* (New York: Vintage Books: 1961), pp. 69–70. Copyright 1947, 1950, 1951, © 1956 by David Donald. Reprinted by permission of Alfred A. Knopf, Inc.

Source 16: Quarles, pp. 134–37, 150.

Chapter 29: Pickett's Charge

Source 1: Horace Greeley, *The American Conflict: A History of the Great Rebellion in the United States of America, 1860–65*, vol. 2 (New York: O. D. Case, 1867), p. 385.

Source 2: S. Wilkeson, "From Another Correspondent," *New York Times,* July 6, 1863.

Source 3: *Daily National Intelligencer* (Washington, DC), July 7, 1863.

Source 4: L. L. Crounse, *New York Times,* July 6, 1863.

Source 5: S. Wilkeson, "Details From Our Special Correspondent," *New York Times,* July 6, 1863.

Source 6: Greeley, p. 386.

Source 7: *Daily National Intelligencer,* July 15, 1863.

Source 8: Washington *Evening Star,* July 6, 1863.

Source 9: *Alexandria* (Virginia) *Gazette,* July 15, 1863.

Source 10: Richard D. Heffner, *A Documentary History of the United States* (New York: Mentor Books, 1965), p. 157.

Source 11: Edward A. Pollard, *The Lost Cause: A New Southern History of the War of the Confederates* (New York: E. B. Treat, 1867), pp. 408–410, 412.

Source 12: George R. Stewart, *Pickett's Charge: A Microhistory of the Final Attack at Gettysburg, July 3, 1863* (Boston: Houghton Mifflin, 1959), p. ix.

Source 13: Allan Nevins, *The War for the Union, vol. III: The Organized War, 1863–1864* (New

York; Charles Scribner's Sons, 1971), pp. 110–111. Copyright © 1971 by Mary R. Nevins. Excerpted by permission of Scribner, a division of Simon & Schuster, Inc.

Source 14: Emory M. Thomas, *The Confederate Nation: 1861–1863* (New York: Harper & Row, 1979), pp. 242–243. Copyright © 1979 by Emory M. Thomas. Reprinted by permission of HarperCollins Publishers, Inc.

Source 15: Bruce Catton, *Bruce Catton's Civil War* (New York: The Fairfax Press, 1988), pp. 410–411.

Chapter 30: A Surprise Ally

Source 1: *New York Times,* October 2, 1863, p. 1.
Source 2: Ibid., p. 4.
Source 3: Ibid., October 11, 1863, p. 5.
Source 4: Gideon Welles, *Diary of Gideon Welles,* vol. 1 (Boston: Houghton Mifflin, 1911), pp. 442–443.
Source 5: Horace E. Scudder, ed., *The Complete Poetical Works of Oliver Wendell Holmes* (Boston: Houghton Mifflin, 1923), p. 199. Copyright © 1923 by Houghton Mifflin. (This composition was sung to the Russian national air by public school children for the Grand Duke Alexis.)
Source 6: U.S. Department of State, *Papers Relating to the Foreign Relations of the United States, 1881* (Washington, DC, 1882), p. 1014.
Source 7: James Ford Rhodes, *History of the United States from the Compromise of 1850* (New York: Macmillan, 1900), p. 418.
Source 8: F. A. Golder, "The Russian Fleet and the Civil War," *American Historical Review* (July 1915), pp. 801–803, 805, 810–812.
Source 9: Walter Lippmann, *U.S. Foreign Policy: Shield of the Republic* (Boston: Little, Brown, 1943), pp. 141–142.
Source 10: Thomas A. Bailey, "The Russian Fleet Myth Re-Examined," *Mississippi Valley Historical Review,* vol. 38 (1951), pp. 81, 88–89.
Source 11: Robert H. Ferrell, *American Diplomacy: A History* (New York: W. W. Norton, 1969), pp. 291–292.
Source 12: David L. Smiley, *The Lion of Whitehall: The Life of Cassius M. Clay* (Gloucester, MA: Peter Smith, 1969), p. 199.

Source 13: John G. Stoessinger, *Nations in Darkness: China, Russia, and America* (New York: Random House, 1978), pp. 9, 4, 103, 116, 234–35. Copyright © 1971 by Random House, Inc. Reprinted by permission of Random House, Inc.

Chapter 31: The Assassination

Source 1: Washington *Evening Star,* April 15, 1865; (Washington) *National Intelligencer,* April 15, 1865.
Source 2: *Evening Star,* April 15, 1865.
Source 3: *National Intelligencer,* April 15, 1865.
Source 4: *Evening Star,* April 15, 1865.
Source 5: Ibid.
Source 6: Ibid., April 18, 1865.
Source 7: Ibid.
Source 8: Ibid., April 21, 1865.
Source 9: Ibid., April 22, 1865.
Source 10: Ibid., April 25, 1865; April 27, 1865; April 28, 1865.
Source 11: Louis Untermeyer, ed., *A Treasury of Great Poems English and American* (New York: Simon & Schuster, 1955), pp. 904–905.
Source 12: James D. Richardson, ed., *Messages and Papers of the Presidents, 1787–1897,* vol. 6 (Washington, DC: U.S. Government Bureau of National Art and Literature, 1900), pp. 307–308.
Source 13: *New York Times,*. May 5, 1865.
Source 14: Horace Greeley, *The American Conflict: A History of the Great Rebellion in the United States, 1860–65,* vol. 2 (Hartford: O. D. Case, 1976), pp. 748–750.
Source 15: *Evening Star,* December 7, 1870.
Source 16: Paul M. Angle, ed. *Herndon's Life of Lincoln* (New York: Albert & Charles Boni, 1936), p. 460.
Source 17: John G. Nicolay and John Hay, *Abraham Lincoln: A History* (New York: Century, 1909), p. 431.
Source 18: William Archibald Dunning, *Reconstruction: Political & Economic* (New York: Harper Torchbook, 1962), pp. 20–21.
Source 19: W. E. B. Du Bois, *Black Reconstruction in America* (New York: Russell & Russell, 1963), p. 165.
Source 20: Kenneth M. Stampp, *The Era of Reconstruction, 1865–1877* (New York: Alfred A. Knopf, 1965), pp. 27, 36, 48–49.